Lecture Notes in Computer Science 14263

The series Lecture Notes in Computer Science (LNCS), including its subseries Lecture Notes in Artificial Intelligence (LNAI) and Lecture Notes in Bioinformatics (LNBI), has established itself as a medium for the publication of new developments in computer science and information technology research, teaching, and education.

LNCS enjoys close cooperation with the computer science R & D community, the series counts many renowned academics among its volume editors and paper authors, and collaborates with prestigious societies. Its mission is to serve this international community by providing an invaluable service, mainly focused on the publication of conference and workshop proceedings and postproceedings. LNCS commenced publication in 1973.

Lazaros Iliadis · Antonios Papaleonidas ·
Plamen Angelov · Chrisina Jayne
Editors

Artificial Neural Networks and Machine Learning – ICANN 2023

32nd International Conference on Artificial Neural Networks
Heraklion, Crete, Greece, September 26–29, 2023
Proceedings, Part X

Editors
Lazaros Iliadis
Democritus University of Thrace
Xanthi, Greece

Antonios Papaleonidas
Democritus University of Thrace
Xanthi, Greece

Plamen Angelov
Lancaster University
Lancaster, UK

Chrisina Jayne
Teesside University
Middlesbrough, UK

ISSN 0302-9743 ISSN 1611-3349 (electronic)
Lecture Notes in Computer Science
ISBN 978-3-031-44203-2 ISBN 978-3-031-44204-9 (eBook)
https://doi.org/10.1007/978-3-031-44204-9

This Springer imprint is published by the registered company Springer Nature Switzerland AG
The registered company address is: Gewerbestrasse 11, 6330 Cham, Switzerland

Paper in this product is recyclable.

Preface

The European Neural Network Society (ENNS) is an association of scientists, engineers and students, conducting research on the modelling of behavioral and brain processes, and on the development of neural algorithms. The core of these efforts is the application of neural modelling to several diverse domains. According to its mission statement ENNS is the European non-profit federation of professionals that aims at achieving a worldwide professional and socially responsible development and application of artificial neural technologies.

The flagship event of ENNS is ICANN (the International Conference on Artificial Neural Networks) at which contributed research papers are presented after passing through a rigorous review process. ICANN is a dual-track conference, featuring tracks in brain-inspired computing on the one hand, and machine learning on the other, with strong crossdisciplinary interactions and applications.

The response of the international scientific community to the ICANN 2023 call for papers was more than satisfactory. In total, 947 research papers on the aforementioned research areas were submitted and 426 (45%) of them were finally accepted as full papers after a peer review process. Additionally, 19 extended abstracts were submitted and 9 of them were selected to be included in the front matter of ICANN 2023 proceedings. Due to their high academic and scientific importance, 22 short papers were also accepted.

All papers were peer reviewed by at least two independent academic referees. Where needed, a third or a fourth referee was consulted to resolve any potential conflicts. Three workshops focusing on specific research areas, namely Advances in Spiking Neural Networks (ASNN), Neurorobotics (NRR), and the challenge of Errors, Stability, Robustness, and Accuracy in Deep Neural Networks (ESRA in DNN), were organized.

The 10-volume set of LNCS 14254, 14255, 14256, 14257, 14258, 14259, 14260, 14261, 14262 and 14263 constitutes the proceedings of the 32nd International Conference on Artificial Neural Networks, ICANN 2023, held in Heraklion city, Crete, Greece, on September 26–29, 2023.

The accepted papers are related to the following topics:

Machine Learning: Deep Learning; Neural Network Theory; Neural Network Models; Graphical Models; Bayesian Networks; Kernel Methods; Generative Models; Information Theoretic Learning; Reinforcement Learning; Relational Learning; Dynamical Models; Recurrent Networks; and Ethics of AI.

Brain-Inspired Computing: Cognitive Models; Computational Neuroscience; Self-Organization; Neural Control and Planning; Hybrid Neural-Symbolic Architectures; Neural Dynamics; Cognitive Neuroscience; Brain Informatics; Perception and Action; and Spiking Neural Networks.

Neural applications in Bioinformatics; Biomedicine; Intelligent Robotics; Neurorobotics; Language Processing; Speech Processing; Image Processing; Sensor Fusion; Pattern Recognition; Data Mining; Neural Agents; Brain-Computer Interaction; Neuromorphic Computing and Edge AI; and Evolutionary Neural Networks.

September 2023

Lazaros Iliadis
Antonios Papaleonidas
Plamen Angelov
Chrisina Jayne

Organization

General Chairs

Iliadis Lazaros	Democritus University of Thrace, Greece
Plamen Angelov	Lancaster University, UK

Program Chairs

Antonios Papaleonidas	Democritus University of Thrace, Greece
Elias Pimenidis	UWE Bristol, UK
Chrisina Jayne	Teesside University, UK

Honorary Chairs

Stefan Wermter	University of Hamburg, Germany
Vera Kurkova	Czech Academy of Sciences, Czech Republic
Nikola Kasabov	Auckland University of Technology, New Zealand

Organizing Chairs

Antonios Papaleonidas	Democritus University of Thrace, Greece
Anastasios Panagiotis Psathas	Democritus University of Thrace, Greece
George Magoulas	University of London, Birkbeck College, UK
Haralambos Mouratidis	University of Essex, UK

Award Chairs

Stefan Wermter	University of Hamburg, Germany
Chukiong Loo	University of Malaysia, Malaysia

Communication Chairs

Sebastian Otte	University of Tübingen, Germany
Anastasios Panagiotis Psathas	Democritus University of Thrace, Greece

Steering Committee

Stefan Wermter	University of Hamburg, Germany
Angelo Cangelosi	University of Manchester, UK
Igor Farkaš	Comenius University in Bratislava, Slovakia
Chrisina Jayne	Teesside University, UK
Matthias Kerzel	University of Hamburg, Germany
Alessandra Lintas	University of Lausanne, Switzerland
Kristína Malinovská (Rebrová)	Comenius University in Bratislava, Slovakia
Alessio Micheli	University of Pisa, Italy
Jaakko Peltonen	Tampere University, Finland
Brigitte Quenet	ESPCI Paris, France
Ausra Saudargiene	Lithuanian University of Health Sciences, Lithuania
Roseli Wedemann	Rio de Janeiro State University, Brazil

Local Organizing/Hybrid Facilitation Committee

Aggeliki Tsouka	Democritus University of Thrace, Greece
Anastasios Panagiotis Psathas	Democritus University of Thrace, Greece
Anna Karagianni	Democritus University of Thrace, Greece
Christina Gkizioti	Democritus University of Thrace, Greece
Ioanna-Maria Erentzi	Democritus University of Thrace, Greece
Ioannis Skopelitis	Democritus University of Thrace, Greece
Lambros Kazelis	Democritus University of Thrace, Greece
Leandros Tsatsaronis	Democritus University of Thrace, Greece
Nikiforos Mpotzoris	Democritus University of Thrace, Greece
Nikos Zervis	Democritus University of Thrace, Greece
Panagiotis Restos	Democritus University of Thrace, Greece
Tassos Giannakopoulos	Democritus University of Thrace, Greece

Program Committee

Abraham Yosipof	CLB, Israel
Adane Tarekegn	NTNU, Norway
Aditya Gilra	Centrum Wiskunde & Informatica, Netherlands
Adrien Durand-Petiteville	Federal University of Pernambuco, Brazil
Adrien Fois	LORIA, France
Alaa Marouf	Hosei University, Japan
Alessandra Sciutti	Istituto Italiano di Tecnologia, Italy
Alessandro Sperduti	University of Padua, Italy
Alessio Micheli	University of Pisa, Italy
Alex Shenfield	Sheffield Hallam University, UK
Alexander Kovalenko	Czech Technical University in Prague, Czech Republic
Alexander Krawczyk	Fulda University of Applied Sciences, Germany
Ali Minai	University of Cincinnati, USA
Aluizio Araujo	Universidade Federal de Pernambuco, Brazil
Amarda Shehu	George Mason University, USA
Amit Kumar Kundu	University of Maryland, USA
Anand Rangarajan	University of Florida, USA
Anastasios Panagiotis Psathas	Democritus University of Thrace, Greece
Andre de Carvalho	Universidade de São Paulo, Brazil
Andrej Lucny	Comenius University, Slovakia
Angel Villar-Corrales	University of Bonn, Germany
Angelo Cangelosi	University of Manchester, UK
Anna Jenul	Norwegian University of Life Sciences, Norway
Antonios Papaleonidas	Democritus University of Thrace, Greece
Arnaud Lewandowski	LISIC, ULCO, France
Arul Selvam Periyasamy	Universität Bonn, Germany
Asma Mekki	University of Sfax, Tunisia
Banafsheh Rekabdar	Portland State University, USA
Barbara Hammer	Universität Bielefeld, Germany
Baris Serhan	University of Manchester, UK
Benedikt Bagus	University of Applied Sciences Fulda, Germany
Benjamin Paaßen	Bielefeld University, Germany
Bernhard Pfahringer	University of Waikato, New Zealand
Bharath Sudharsan	NUI Galway, Ireland
Binyi Wu	Dresden University of Technology, Germany
Binyu Zhao	Harbin Institute of Technology, China
Björn Plüster	University of Hamburg, Germany
Bo Mei	Texas Christian University, USA

Brian Moser	Deutsches Forschungszentrum für künstliche Intelligenz, Germany
Carlo Mazzola	Istituto Italiano di Tecnologia, Italy
Carlos Moreno-Garcia	Robert Gordon University, UK
Chandresh Pravin	Reading University, UK
Chao Ma	Wuhan University, China
Chathura Wanigasekara	German Aerospace Centre, Germany
Cheng Shang	Shanghai Jiaotong University, China
Chengqiang Huang	Huawei Technologies, China
Chenhan Zhang	University of Technology, Sydney, Australia
Chenyang Lyu	Dublin City University, Ireland
Chihuang Liu	Meta, USA
Chrisina Jayne	Teesside University, UK
Christian Balkenius	Lund University, Sweden
Chrysoula Kosma	Ecole Polytechnique, Greece
Claudio Bellei	Elliptic, UK
Claudio Gallicchio	University of Pisa, Italy
Claudio Giorgio Giancaterino	Intesa SanPaolo Vita, Italy
Constantine Dovrolis	Cyprus Institute, USA
Coşku Horuz	University of Tübingen, Germany
Cunjian Chen	Monash, Australia
Cunyi Yin	Fuzhou University, Singapore
Damien Lolive	Université Rennes, CNRS, IRISA, France
Daniel Stamate	Goldsmiths, University of London, UK
Daniel Vašata	Czech Technical University in Prague, Czech Republic
Dario Pasquali	Istituto Italiano di Tecnologia, Italy
David Dembinsky	German Research Center for Artificial Intelligence, Germany
David Rotermund	University of Bremen, Germany
Davide Liberato Manna	University of Strathclyde, UK
Dehao Yuan	University of Maryland, USA
Denise Gorse	University College London, UK
Dennis Wong	Macao Polytechnic University, China
Des Higham	University of Edinburgh, UK
Devesh Jawla	TU Dublin, Ireland
Dimitrios Michail	Harokopio University of Athens, Greece
Dino Ienco	INRAE, France
Diptangshu Pandit	Teesside University, UK
Diyuan Lu	Helmholtz Center Munich, Germany
Domenico Tortorella	University of Pisa, Italy
Dominik Geissler	American Family Insurance, USA

DongNyeong Heo	Handong Global University, South Korea
Dongyang Zhang	University of Electronic Science and Technology of China, China
Doreen Jirak	Istituto Italiano di Tecnologia, Italy
Douglas McLelland	BrainChip, France
Douglas Nyabuga	Mount Kenya University, Rwanda
Dulani Meedeniya	University of Moratuwa, Sri Lanka
Dumitru-Clementin Cercel	University Politehnica of Bucharest, Romania
Dylan Muir	SynSense, Switzerland
Efe Bozkir	Uni Tübingen, Germany
Eleftherios Kouloumpris	Aristotle University of Thessaloniki, Greece
Elias Pimenidis	University of the West of England, UK
Eliska Kloberdanz	Iowa State University, USA
Emre Neftci	Foschungszentrum Juelich, Germany
Enzo Tartaglione	Telecom Paris, France
Erwin Lopez	University of Manchester, UK
Evgeny Mirkes	University of Leicester, UK
F. Boray Tek	Istanbul Technical University, Turkey
Federico Corradi	Eindhoven University of Technology, Netherlands
Federico Errica	NEC Labs Europe, Germany
Federico Manzi	Università Cattolica del Sacro Cuore, Italy
Federico Vozzi	CNR, Italy
Fedor Scholz	University of Tuebingen, Germany
Feifei Dai	Chinese Academy of Sciences, China
Feifei Xu	Shanghai University of Electric Power, China
Feixiang Zhou	University of Leicester, UK
Felipe Moreno	FGV, Peru
Feng Wei	York University, Canada
Fengying Li	Guilin University of Electronic Technology, China
Flora Ferreira	University of Minho, Portugal
Florian Mirus	Intel Labs, Germany
Francesco Semeraro	University of Manchester, UK
Franco Scarselli	University of Siena, Italy
François Blayo	IPSEITE, Switzerland
Frank Röder	Hamburg University of Technology, Germany
Frederic Alexandre	Inria, France
Fuchang Han	Central South University, China
Fuli Wang	University of Essex, UK
Gabriela Sejnova	Czech Technical University in Prague, Czech Republic
Gaetano Di Caterina	University of Strathclyde, UK
George Bebis	University of Nevada, USA

Gerrit Ecke	Mercedes-Benz, Germany
Giannis Nikolentzos	Ecole Polytechnique, France
Gilles Marcou	University of Strasbourg, France
Giorgio Gnecco	IMT School for Advanced Studies, Italy
Glauco Amigo	Baylor University, USA
Greg Lee	Acadia University, Canada
Grégory Bourguin	LISIC/ULCO, France
Guillermo Martín-Sánchez	Champalimaud Foundation, Portugal
Gulustan Dogan	UNCW, USA
Habib Khan	Islamia College University Peshawar, Pakistan
Haizhou Du	Shanghai University of Electric Power, China
Hanli Wang	Tongji University, China
Hanno Gottschalk	TU Berlin, Germany
Hao Tong	University of Birmingham, UK
Haobo Jiang	NJUST, China
Haopeng Chen	Shanghai Jiao Tong University, China
Hazrat Ali	Hamad Bin Khalifa University, Qatar
Hina Afridi	NTNU, Gjøvik, Norway
Hiroaki Aizawa	Hiroshima University, Japan
Hiromichi Suetani	Oita University, Japan
Hiroshi Kawaguchi	Kobe University, Japan
Hiroyasu Ando	Tohoku University, Japan
Hiroyoshi Ito	University of Tsukuba, Japan
Honggang Zhang	University of Massachusetts, Boston, USA
Hongqing Yu	Open University, UK
Hongye Cao	Northwestern Polytechnical University, China
Hugo Carneiro	University of Hamburg, Germany
Hugo Eduardo Camacho Cruz	Universidad Autónoma de Tamaulipas, Mexico
Huifang Ma	Northwest Normal University, China
Hyeyoung Park	Kyungpook National University, South Korea
Ian Nabney	University of Bristol, UK
Igor Farkas	Comenius University Bratislava, Slovakia
Ikuko Nishikawa	Ritsumeikan University, Japan
Ioannis Pierros	Aristotle University of Thessaloniki, Greece
Iraklis Varlamis	Harokopio University of Athens, Greece
Ivan Tyukin	King's College London, UK
Iveta Bečková	Comenius University in Bratislava, Slovakia
Jae Hee Lee	University of Hamburg, Germany
James Yu	Southern University of Science and Technology, China
Jan Faigl	Czech Technical University in Prague, Czech Republic

Jan Feber	Czech Technical University in Prague, Czech Republic
Jan-Gerrit Habekost	University of Hamburg, Germany
Jannik Thuemmel	University of Tübingen, Germany
Jeremie Cabessa	University Paris 2, France
Jérémie Sublime	ISEP, France
Jia Cai	Guangdong University of Finance & Economics, China
Jiaan Wang	Soochow University, China
Jialiang Tang	Nanjing University of Science and Technology, China
Jian Hu	YiduCloud, Cyprus
Jianhua Xu	Nanjing Normal University, China
Jianyong Chen	Shenzhen University, China
Jichao Bi	Zhejiang Institute of Industry and Information Technology, China
Jie Shao	University of Electronic Science and Technology of China, China
Jim Smith	University of the West of England, UK
Jing Yang	Hefei University of Technology, China
Jingyi Yuan	Arizona State University, USA
Jingyun Jia	Baidu, USA
Jinling Wang	Ulster University, UK
Jiri Sima	Czech Academy of Sciences, Czech Republic
Jitesh Dundas	Independent Researcher, USA
Joost Vennekens	KU Leuven, Belgium
Jordi Cosp	Universitat Politècnica de Catalunya, Spain
Josua Spisak	University of Hamburg, Germany
Jozef Kubík	Comenius University, Slovakia
Junpei Zhong	Hong Kong Polytechnic University, China
Jurgita Kapočiūtė-Dzikienė	Vytautas Magnus University, Lithuania
K. L. Eddie Law	Macao Polytechnic University, China
Kai Tang	Independent Researcher, China
Kamil Dedecius	Czech Academy of Sciences, Czech Republic
Kang Zhang	Kyushu University, Japan
Kantaro Fujiwara	University of Tokyo, Japan
Karlis Freivalds	Institute of Electronics and Computer Science, Latvia
Khoa Phung	University of the West of England, UK
Kiran Lekkala	University of Southern California, USA
Kleanthis Malialis	University of Cyprus, Cyprus
Kohulan Rajan	Friedrich Schiller University, Germany

Koichiro Yamauchi	Chubu University, Japan
Koloud Alkhamaiseh	Western Michigan University, USA
Konstantinos Demertzis	Democritus University of Thrace, Greece
Kostadin Cvejoski	Fraunhofer IAIS, Germany
Kristína Malinovská	Comenius University in Bratislava, Slovakia
Kun Zhang	Inria and École Polytechnique, France
Laurent Mertens	KU Leuven, Belgium
Laurent Perrinet	AMU CNRS, France
Lazaros Iliadis	Democritus University of Thrace, Greece
Leandro dos Santos Coelho	Pontifical Catholic University of Parana, Brazil
Leiping Jie	Hong Kong Baptist University, China
Lenka Tětková	Technical University of Denmark, Denmark
Lia Morra	Politecnico di Torino, Italy
Liang Ge	Chongqing University, China
Liang Zhao	Dalian University of Technology, China
Limengzi Yuan	Shihezi University, China
Ling Guo	Northwest University, China
Linlin Shen	Shenzhen University, China
Lixin Zou	Wuhan University, China
Lorenzo Vorabbi	University of Bologna, Italy
Lu Wang	Macao Polytechnic University, China
Luca Pasa	University of Padova, Italy
Ľudovít Malinovský	Independent Researcher, Slovakia
Luis Alexandre	Universidade da Beira Interior, Portugal
Luis Lago	Universidad Autonoma de Madrid, Spain
Lukáš Gajdošech Gajdošech	Comenius University Bratislava, Slovakia
Lyra Puspa	Vanaya NeuroLab, Indonesia
Madalina Erascu	West University of Timisoara, Romania
Magda Friedjungová	Czech Technical University in Prague, Czech Republic
Manuel Traub	University of Tübingen, Germany
Marcello Trovati	Edge Hill University, UK
Marcin Pietron	AGH-UST, Poland
Marco Bertolini	Pfizer, Germany
Marco Podda	University of Pisa, Italy
Markus Bayer	Technical University of Darmstadt, Germany
Markus Eisenbach	Ilmenau University of Technology, Germany
Martin Ferianc	University College London, Slovakia
Martin Holena	Czech Technical University, Czech Republic
Masanari Kimura	ZOZO Research, Japan
Masato Uchida	Waseda University, Japan
Masoud Daneshtalab	Mälardalen University, Sweden

Oleg Bakhteev	EPFL, Switzerland
Olga Grebenkova	Moscow Institute of Physics and Technology, Russia
Oliver Sutton	King's College London, UK
Olivier Teste	Université de Toulouse, France
Or Elroy	CLB, Israel
Oscar Fontenla-Romero	University of A Coruña, Spain
Ozan Özdenizci	Graz University of Technology, Austria
Pablo Lanillos	Spanish National Research Council, Spain
Pascal Rost	Universität Hamburg, Germany
Paul Kainen	Georgetown, USA
Paulo Cortez	University of Minho, Portugal
Pavel Petrovic	Comenius University, Slovakia
Peipei Liu	School of Cyber Security, University of Chinese Academy of Sciences, China
Peng Qiao	NUDT, China
Peter Andras	Edinburgh Napier University, UK
Peter Steiner	Technische Universität Dresden, Germany
Peter Sutor	University of Maryland, USA
Petia Georgieva	University of Aveiro/IEETA, Portugal
Petia Koprinkova-Hristova	Bulgarian Academy of Sciences, Bulgaria
Petra Vidnerová	Czech Academy of Sciences, Czech Republic
Philipp Allgeuer	University of Hamburg, Germany
Pragathi Priyadharsini Balasubramani	Indian Institute of Technology Kanpur, India
Qian Wang	Durham University, UK
Qinghua Zhou	King's College London, UK
Qingquan Zhang	Southern University of Science and Technology, China
Quentin Jodelet	Tokyo Institute of Technology, Japan
Radoslav Škoviera	Czech Technical University in Prague, Czech Republic
Raoul Heese	Fraunhofer ITWM, Germany
Ricardo Marcacini	University of São Paulo, Brazil
Riccardo Renzulli	University of Turin, Italy
Richard Duro	Universidade da Coruña, Spain
Robert Legenstein	Graz University of Technology, Austria
Rodrigo Clemente Thom de Souza	Federal University of Parana, Brazil
Rohit Dwivedula	Independent Researcher, India
Romain Ferrand	IGI TU Graz, Austria
Roman Mouček	University of West Bohemia, Czech Republic
Roseli Wedemann	Universidade do Estado do Rio de Janeiro, Brazil

Rufin VanRullen	CNRS, France
Ruijun Feng	China Telecom Beijing Research Institute, China
Ruxandra Stoean	University of Craiova, Romania
Sanchit Hira	JHU, USA
Sander Bohte	CWI, Netherlands
Sandrine Mouysset	University of Toulouse/IRIT, France
Sanka Rasnayaka	National University of Singapore, Singapore
Sašo Karakatič	University of Maribor, Slovenia
Sebastian Nowak	University Bonn, Germany
Seiya Satoh	Tokyo Denki University, Japan
Senwei Liang	LBNL, USA
Shaolin Zhu	Tianjin University, China
Shayan Gharib	University of Helsinki, Finland
Sherif Eissa	Eindhoven University of Technology, Afghanistan
Shiyong Lan	Independent Researcher, China
Shoumeng Qiu	Fudan, China
Shu Eguchi	Aomori University, Japan
Shubai Chen	Southwest University, China
Shweta Singh	International Institute of Information Technology, Hyderabad, India
Simon Hakenes	Ruhr University Bochum, Germany
Simona Doboli	Hofstra University, USA
Song Guo	Xi'an University of Architecture and Technology, China
Stanislav Frolov	Deutsches Forschungszentrum für künstliche Intelligenz (DFKI), Germany
Štefan Pócoš	Comenius University in Bratislava, Slovakia
Steven (Zvi) Lapp	Bar Ilan University, Israel
Sujala Shetty	BITS Pilani Dubai Campus, United Arab Emirates
Sumio Watanabe	Tokyo Institute of Technology, Japan
Surabhi Sinha	Adobe, USA
Takafumi Amaba	Fukuoka University, Japan
Takaharu Yaguchi	Kobe University, Japan
Takeshi Abe	Yamaguchi University, Japan
Takuya Kitamura	National Institute of Technology, Toyama College, Japan
Tatiana Tyukina	University of Leicester, UK
Teng-Sheng Moh	San Jose State University, USA
Tetsuya Hoya	Independent Researcher, Japan
Thierry Viéville	Domicile, France
Thomas Nowotny	University of Sussex, UK
Tianlin Zhang	University of Manchester, UK

Tianyi Wang	University of Hong Kong, China
Tieke He	Nanjing University, China
Tiyu Fang	Shandong University, China
Tobias Uelwer	Technical University Dortmund, Germany
Tomasz Kapuscinski	Rzeszow University of Technology, Poland
Tomasz Szandala	Wroclaw University of Technology, Poland
Toshiharu Sugawara	Waseda University, Japan
Trond Arild Tjostheim	Lund University, Sweden
Umer Mushtaq	Université Paris-Panthéon-Assas, France
Uwe Handmann	Ruhr West University, Germany
V. Ramasubramanian	International Institute of Information Technology, Bangalore, India
Valeri Mladenov	Technical University of Sofia, Bulgaria
Valerie Vaquet	Bielefeld University, Germany
Vandana Ladwani	International Institute of Information Technology, Bangalore, India
Vangelis Metsis	Texas State University, USA
Vera Kurkova	Czech Academy of Sciences, Czech Republic
Verner Ferreira	Universidade do Estado da Bahia, Brazil
Viktor Kocur	Comenius University, Slovakia
Ville Tanskanen	University of Helsinki, Finland
Viviana Cocco Mariani	PUCPR, Brazil
Vladimír Boža	Comenius University, Slovakia
Vojtech Mrazek	Brno University of Technology, Czech Republic
Weifeng Liu	China University of Petroleum (East China), China
Wenxin Yu	Southwest University of Science and Technology, China
Wenxuan Liu	Wuhan University of Technology, China
Wu Ancheng	Pingan, China
Wuliang Huang	ICT, China
Xi Cheng	NUPT, Hong Kong, China
Xia Feng	Civil Aviation University of China, China
Xian Zhong	Wuhan University of Technology, China
Xiang Zhang	National University of Defense Technology, China
Xiaochen Yuan	Macao Polytechnic University, China
Xiaodong Gu	Fudan University, China
Xiaoqing Liu	Kyushu University, Japan
Xiaowei Zhou	Macquarie University, Australia
Xiaozhuang Song	Chinese University of Hong Kong, Shenzhen, China

Xingpeng Zhang	Southwest Petroleum University, China
Xuemei Jia	Wuhan University, China
Xuewen Wang	China University of Geosciences, China
Yahong Lian	Nankai University, China
Yan Zheng	China University of Political Science and Law, China
Yang Liu	Fudan University, China
Yang Shao	Hitachi, Japan
Yangguang Cui	East China Normal University, China
Yansong Chua	China Nanhu Academy of Electronics and Information Technology, Singapore
Yapeng Gao	Taiyuan University of Technology, China
Yasufumi Sakai	Fujitsu, Japan
Ye Wang	National University of Defense Technology, China
Yeh-Ching Chung	Chinese University of Hong Kong, Shenzhen, China
Yihao Luo	Yichang Testing Technique R&D Institute, China
Yikemaiti Sataer	Southeast University, China
Yipeng Yu	Tencent, China
Yongchao Ye	Southern University of Science and Technology, China
Yoshihiko Horio	Tohoku University, Japan
Youcef Djenouri	NORCE, Norway
Yuan Li	Military Academy of Sciences, China
Yuan Panli	Shihezi University, China
Yuan Yao	Tsinghua University, China
Yuanlun Xie	University of Electronic Science and Technology of China, China
Yuanshao Zhu	Southern University of Science and Technology, China
Yucan Zhou	Institute of Information Engineering, Chinese Academy of Sciences, China
Yuchen Zheng	Shihezi University, China
Yuchun Fang	Shanghai University, China
Yue Zhao	Minzu University of China, China
Yuesong Nan	National University of Singapore, Singapore
Zaneta Swiderska-Chadaj	Warsaw University of Technology, Poland
Zdenek Straka	Czech Technical University in Prague, Czech Republic
Zhao Yang	Leiden University, Netherlands
Zhaoyun Ding	NUDT, China
Zhengwei Yang	Wuhan University, China

Zhenjie Yao	Chinese Academy of Sciences, Singapore
Zhichao Lian	Nanjing University of Science and Technology, China
Zhiqiang Zhang	Hosei University, Japan
Zhixin Li	Guangxi Normal University, China
Zhongnan Zhang	Xiamen University, China
Zhongzhan Huang	Sun Yat-sen University, China
Zi Long	Shenzhen Technology University, China
Zilong Lin	Indiana University Bloomington, USA
Zuobin Xiong	Georgia State University, USA
Zuzana Cernekova	FMFI Comenius University, Slovakia

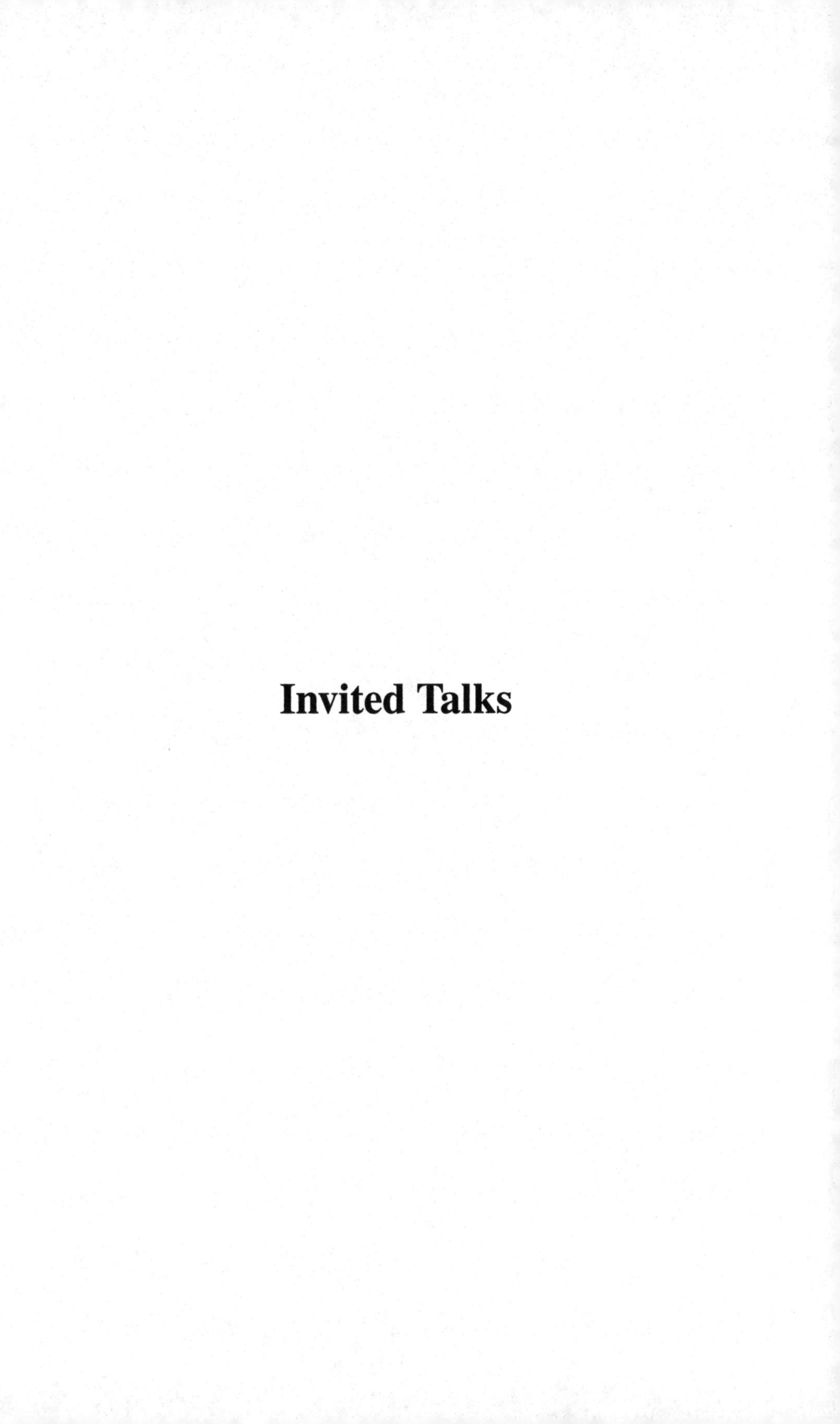

Invited Talks

Developmental Robotics for Language Learning, Trust and Theory of Mind

Angelo Cangelosi

University of Manchester and Alan Turing Institute, UK

Growing theoretical and experimental research on action and language processing and on number learning and gestures clearly demonstrates the role of embodiment in cognition and language processing. In psychology and neuroscience, this evidence constitutes the basis of embodied cognition, also known as grounded cognition (Pezzulo et al. 2012). In robotics and AI, these studies have important implications for the design of linguistic capabilities in cognitive agents and robots for human-robot collaboration, and have led to the new interdisciplinary approach of Developmental Robotics, as part of the wider Cognitive Robotics field (Cangelosi and Schlesinger 2015; Cangelosi and Asada 2022). During the talk we presented examples of developmental robotics models and experimental results from iCub experiments on the embodiment biases in early word acquisition and grammar learning (Morse et al. 2015; Morse and Cangelosi 2017) and experiments on pointing gestures and finger counting for number learning (De La Cruz et al. 2014). We then presented a novel developmental robotics model, and experiments, on Theory of Mind and its use for autonomous trust behavior in robots (Vinanzi et al. 2019, 2021). The implications for the use of such embodied approaches for embodied cognition in AI and cognitive sciences, and for robot companion applications, was also discussed.

Challenges of Incremental Learning

Barbara Hammer

CITEC Centre of Excellence, Bielefeld University, Germany

Smart products and AI components are increasingly available in industrial applications and everyday life. This offers great opportunities for cognitive automation and intelligent human-machine cooperation; yet it also poses significant challenges since a fundamental assumption of classical machine learning, an underlying stationary data distribution, might be easily violated. Unexpected events or outliers, sensor drift, or individual user behavior might cause changes of an underlying data distribution, typically referred to as concept drift or covariate shift. Concept drift requires a continuous adaptation of the underlying model and efficient incremental learning strategies. Within the presentation, I looked at recent developments in the context of incremental learning schemes for streaming data, putting a particular focus on the challenge of learning with drift and detecting and disentangling drift in possibly unsupervised setups and for unknown type and strength of drift. More precisely, I dealt with the following aspects: learning schemes for incremental model adaptation from streaming data in the presence of concept drift; various mathematical formalizations of concept drift and detection/quantification of drift based thereon; and decomposition and explanation of drift. I presented a couple of experimental results using benchmarks from the literature, and I offered a glimpse into mathematical guarantees which can be provided for some of the algorithms.

Reliable AI: From Mathematical Foundations to Quantum Computing

Gitta Kutyniok[1,2]

[1]Bavarian AI Chair for Mathematical Foundations of Artificial Intelligence, LMU Munich, Germany
[2]Adjunct Professor for Machine Learning, University of Tromsø, Norway

Artificial intelligence is currently leading to one breakthrough after the other, both in public life with, for instance, autonomous driving and speech recognition, and in the sciences in areas such as medical diagnostics or molecular dynamics. However, one current major drawback is the lack of reliability of such methodologies.

In this lecture we took a mathematical viewpoint towards this problem, showing the power of such approaches to reliability. We first provided an introduction into this vibrant research area, focussing specifically on deep neural networks. We then surveyed recent advances, in particular concerning generalization guarantees and explainability methods. Finally, we discussed fundamental limitations of deep neural networks and related approaches in terms of computability, which seriously affects their reliability, and we revealed a connection with quantum computing.

Intelligent Pervasive Applications for Holistic Health Management

Ilias Maglogiannis

University of Piraeus, Greece

The advancements in telemonitoring platforms, biosensors, and medical devices have paved the way for pervasive health management, allowing patients to be monitored remotely in real-time. The visual domain has become increasingly important for patient monitoring, with activity recognition and fall detection being key components. Computer vision techniques, such as deep learning, have been used to develop robust activity recognition and fall detection algorithms. These algorithms can analyze video streams from cameras, detecting and classifying various activities, and detecting falls in real time. Furthermore, wearable devices, such as smartwatches and fitness trackers, can also monitor a patient's daily activities, providing insights into their overall health and wellness, allowing for a comprehensive analysis of a patient's health. In this talk we discussed the state of the art in pervasive health management and biomedical data analytics and we presented the work done in the Computational Biomedicine Laboratory of the University of Piraeus in this domain. The talk also included Future Trends and Challenges.

Contents – Part X

A Comparative Study of Sentence Embedding Models for Assessing Semantic Variation

Deven M. Mistry and Ali A. Minai(✉)

University of Cincinnati, Cincinnati, OH 45221-0030, USA
mistryds@mail.uc.edu, ali.minai@uc.edu

Abstract. Analyzing the pattern of semantic variation in long real-world texts such as books or transcripts is interesting from the stylistic, cognitive, and linguistic perspectives. It is also useful for applications such as text segmentation, document summarization, and detection of semantic novelty. The recent emergence of several vector-space methods for sentence embedding has made such analysis feasible. However, this raises the issue of how consistent and meaningful the semantic representations produced by various methods are in themselves. In this paper, we compare several recent sentence embedding methods via time-series of semantic similarity between successive sentences and matrices of pairwise sentence similarity for multiple books of literature. In contrast to previous work using target tasks and curated datasets to compare sentence embedding methods, our approach provides an evaluation of the methods "in the wild". We find that most of the sentence embedding methods considered do infer highly correlated patterns of semantic similarity in a given document, but show interesting differences.

Keywords: Semantic Variation · Sentence Embedding Models · Novelty Detection

1 Introduction

The semantic structure of natural real-world texts – especially long documents such as books – is interesting for several reasons. Since the text is the result of a compositional cognitive process, the pattern of sequential semantic variation in it gives clues about that process. The global pattern of semantic relationships can also characterize the style, type, and content of the document (e.g., the plot of a novel). Semantic structure is also useful as the basis of semantic segmentation [1–3], and for identifying unusual or novel statements in texts based on semantic difference, which is the motivating application for our work. In all these cases, it is important to use a semantic embedding method that captures

This work was partially supported by Army Research Office Grant No. W911NF-20-1-0213.

L. Iliadis et al. (Eds.): ICANN 2023, LNCS 14263, pp. 1–12, 2023.
https://doi.org/10.1007/978-3-031-44204-9_1

meaning correctly, but this is difficult to determine objectively. In this study, we use a novel *semantic cross-validation* approach to compare eight recent sentence representation methods on several literary texts, using the *mutual consistency* of their inferred semantic representations to assess the validity of these representations. This is not a hypothesis-driven investigation but a comparison study to look at the similarities and differences of several representation models that all claim to capture the actual meaning of text.

2 Motivation

The success of recently developed deep learning-based models for sentence representation [4–7] on systematic tests reveals their utility, but does not demonstrate whether they detect the *same* semantic relationships in a text, or how semantically accurate they are per se. Typically, the tests – including those directly inferring semantic similarity between labeled sentence pairs [5,7] – use carefully curated benchmark datasets. Alternatively, performance on downstream benchmark tasks is used to evaluate the quality of sentence representations. These controlled evaluation methods are very valuable but limited by their constraints – as is the case with most laboratory studies. The present study takes a complementary approach by looking directly at the structure of semantic variation inferred by various methods on several large real-world documents with a complex semantic structure, i.e., literary books.

Since the texts are not specially constructed or selected to fit the evaluative task (e.g., sets of labeled sentence pairs or items from different newsgroups), but are real-world documents used *as found*, we term this approach as evaluation "in the wild" (as opposed to evaluation in the lab.) While this complicates the process of evaluation, it provides a more realistic and explicit assessment of how the various computational models fare when they encounter truly natural texts.

3 Conceptual Framework

Foregoing the use of curated benchmarks, labeled data, and downstream tasks necessitates the adoption of a new evaluative method based on some *intrinsic* aspect of the results obtained. In this study, we propose and use a framework based on the following sequence of postulates:

1. Every document has a specific (but latent) *intrinsic meaning* and any effective semantic representation method must capture this.
2. A specific intrinsic meaning implies a specific *semantic structure* in a document, and all effective semantic representation methods must infer the *same* semantic structure for a given document
3. The semantic structure of a document can be represented as the *pattern of semantic similarity* between the sentences of the document.
4. If two sufficiently different semantic representation methods infer mutually consistent semantic structures for a document, they are both likely to be inferring its true semantic structure.

5. If two semantic representation methods infer very different semantic representations for the same document, one or both must have failed to capture its intrinsic semantic structure.

Essentially, this proposes that, while it is difficult to determine whether a given vector representation captures the intrinsic meaning of any individual sentence, the overall semantic structure of an entire document, as represented in its sentence similarity pattern, can be used as an *observable surrogate representation* for its meaning, and if very different semantic representation methods infer consistent structure for a document, they must be capturing the ground truth, even though the ground truth is not explicitly known. Thus, the *mutual consistency* of the inferred semantic structure can be used as an implicit *semantic cross-validation* to evaluate a group of semantic representation methods. From a practical viewpoint, if multiple methods indicate that a particular sentence or passage in the text is dissimilar to the bulk of the document, it would provide a more reliable identification of novel statements, which is our motivating application.

4 Methods

4.1 Datasets

We use a dataset comprising the following eighteen texts:

1. *A Christmas Carol* by Charles Dickens (1,942 sentences, 29,112 word tokens).
2. *Heart of Darkness* by Joseph Conrad (2,430 sentences, 39,061 word tokens).
3. *Metamorphosis* by Franz Kafka (translated by David Wyllie, 2002 - used under Project Gutenberg License) (795 sentences, 22,373 word tokens).
4. *The Prophet* by Khalil Gibran (647 sentences, 12,360 word tokens).
5. *A Modest Proposal* by Jonathan Swift (68 sentences, 3431 word tokens)
6. *A Study in the Scarlet* by Arthur Conan Doyle (2,689 sentences, 43,919 word tokens)
7. *Adventures of Huckleberry Finn* by Mark Twain (5,789 sentences, 116,313 word tokens)
8. *Dragons and Cherry Blossoms* by Mrs. Robert C. Morris (1,174 sentences, 29,157 word tokens)
9. *Laughter: An essay on the Meaning of the Comic* by Henri Bergson (1,794 sentences, 42,947 word tokens)
10. *Little Women* by Louisa May Alcott (9,438 sentences, 190,752 word tokens)
11. *The Picture of Dorian Gray* by Oscar Wilde (6,479 sentences, 79,978 word tokens)
12. *Ruth of the U.S.A* by Edwin Balmer (5,093 sentences, 98,880 word tokens)
13. *Siddarhtha* by Hermann Hesse (1,850 sentences, 39,719 word tokens)
14. *The Catspaw* by George O. Smith (1,555 sentences, 19,271 word tokens)
15. *The Hound Of The Baskervilles* by Arthur Conan Doyle (3,876 sentences, 59,802 word tokens)
16. *The Scarlet Letter* by Nathaniel Hawthorne (3,500 sentences, 84,709 word tokens)

17. *The Sons Of Japheth* by Richard Wilson (203 sentences, 2327 word tokens)
18. *Treasure Island* by Robert Louis Stevenson (3,732 sentences, 70,077 word tokens)

The main considerations in choosing these were: a) moderate length - which makes it possible to inspect the results visually; b) diversity of type; and c)literary value, so that the texts are semantically complex and the results are of general interest; and d) Availability without violation of copyright. All documents were downloaded from the Project Gutenberg website (https://www.gutenberg.org/).

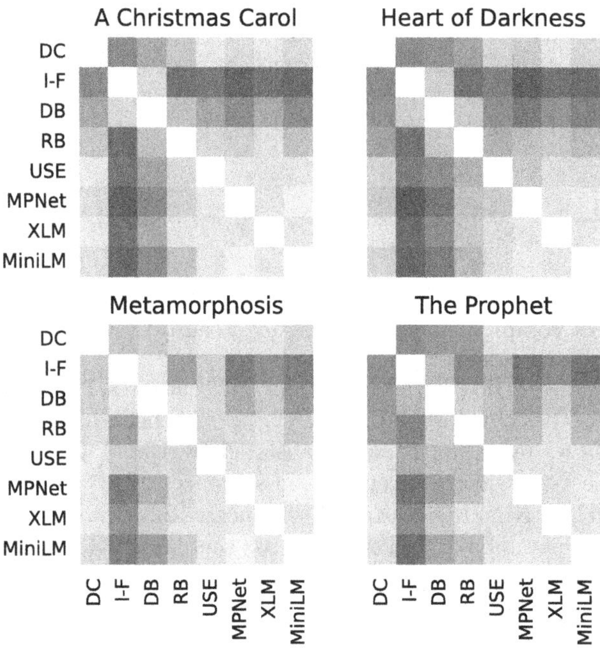

Fig. 1. Correlation maps showing pairwise similarity between all methods for four books. Lighter color indicates a higher correlation.

4.2 Sentence Representation Models

It is impractical to include all the currently available sentence representation methods in our analysis, and we have tried to include a broad selection of different approaches. Specifically, the following methods are included:

1. DeCLUTR Base (DC) [8]
2. InferSent with FastText (I-F) [9]
3. DistilBERT (DB) [10]

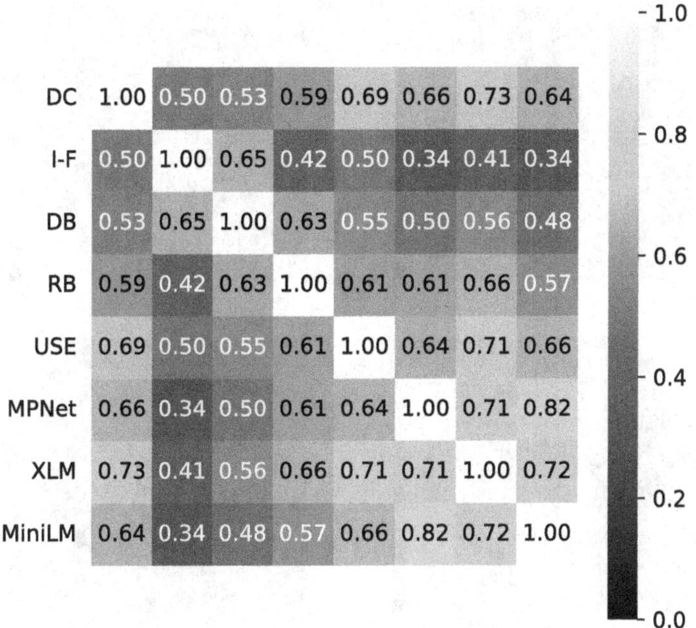

Fig. 2. Mean Correlation map showing pairwise similarity between all methods for all eighteen books.

4. RoBERTa (RB) [11]
5. Universal Sentence Encoder (USE) [12]
6. MPNet (MPNet) [13]
7. XLM - R (XLM) [14]
8. MiniLM (MiniLM) [15]

The labels in parentheses are used to denote the methods in the figures.

DeCLUTR is an unsupervised learning method that explicitly uses neighboring sentences as a proxy for semantic similarity to train sentence representations. The InferSent model [9], like DeCLUTR, is trained explicitly to represent sentence semantics, but using recurrent neural networks and supervised learning on a variety of tasks. There are versions that differ in their underlying method of representing words – based either on FastText word embeddings [16,17] or GloVe embeddings [18]. The FastText version is used here. DistilBERT and RoBERTa are based on the BERT language model [19]. Thus, their sentence representations are tuned to the task of text-generation rather than capturing semantic similarity. The Universal Sentence Encoder (USE) model [12] is also trained explicitly for representing sentences by training a feed-forward deep averaging network (DAN) (or a transformer) simultaneously on multiple tasks. We use the DAN version of USE, which is computationally more efficient. MiniLM [15] proposes an effective way to compress a large transformer using deep self-distillation, where a student learns to mimic the last self-attention module of the transformer layer

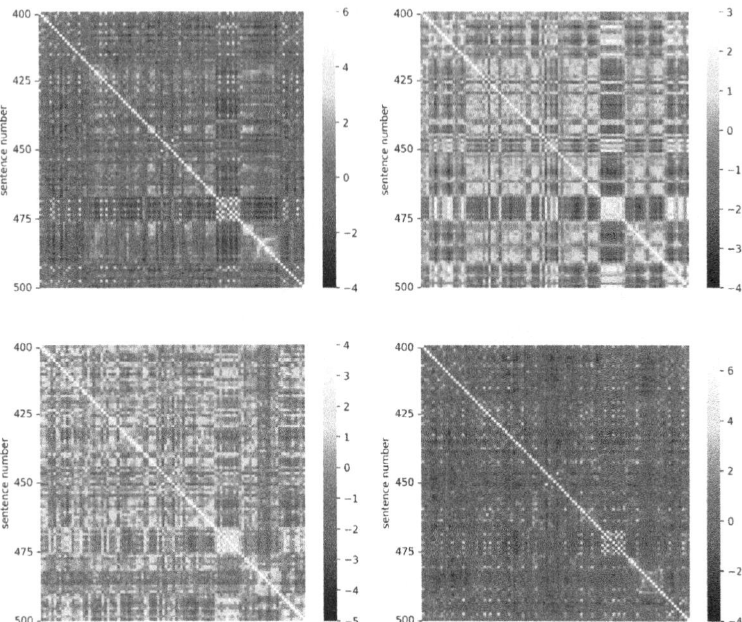

Fig. 3. Sentence similarity maps for *A Christmas Carol*, using DeCLUTR-Base (top left); InferSent-FasText (top right); DistilBERT (bottom left); and MPNet (bottom right).

of the teacher. Using this approach, the trained model outperforms state-of-the-art baselines in SQuAD [20,21] and GLUE [22]. XLM-R [14] is a transformer trained using masked language modeling on one hundred languages using over two terabytes of filtered CommonCrawl data. The trained model shows significant performance improvement over multilingual BERT (mBERT). MPNet [13] adopts MLM (masked language modelling) from the original BERT model and PLM (permuted language modeling) from XLNet. The model is trained on over 160 gigabytes of data and then fine-tuned on a variety of downstream tasks to achieve better results than the existing state-of-the-art models. Given the very different architectures and training regimes of the models, it would not be surprising if they captured meaning in different ways and focused on different aspects. Demonstrating the degree and manner of this difference is a goal of this study.

4.3 Calculating Sentence Similarity

For each document in the corpus, the eight models listed above are used without fine-tuning to generate embeddings for each sentence. The similarity between every pair of sentences in the document is calculated using the cosine similarity between their embeddings, thus generating an $N \times N$ *semantic similarity matrix* (SSM), where N is the number of sentences in the document. The values in

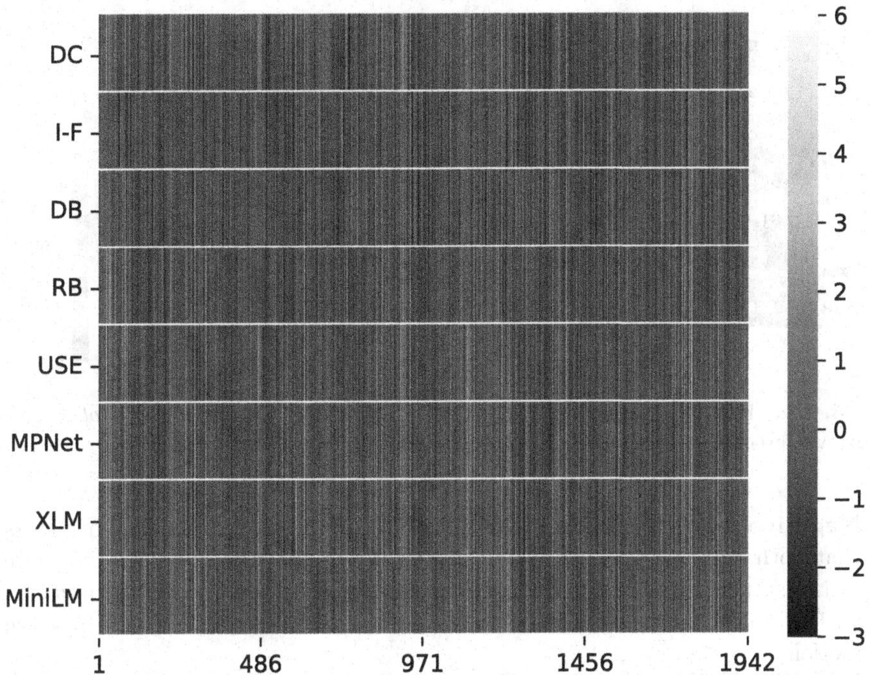

Fig. 4. Time series of successive sentence similarities for *A Christmas Carol.*

each matrix are standardized to zero-mean, unit variance values corresponding to z-scores. Thus, a negative value in cell (i, j) indicates a below average similarity inferred for sentences i and j, and a positive value indicates above average similarity within the document.

4.4 Analysis Methods

We use the global pattern of semantic similarity across the entire document as captured in the SSM to evaluate and visualize the relationships between the sentence similarity patterns inferred by all the models on each given document. In addition to the SSMs, it is also interesting (and computationally simpler) to look at the time-series of similarity between successive sentences, which reflects the rhythm of meaning in the document and in the underlying generative cognitive process.

To get a more detailed comparison, we also calculate three other metrics for each pair of models, A and B:

1. **Positive Agreement Fraction (PAF):** The fraction of all sentence pairs that both model A and model B consider more similar than average (positive in the standardized SSMs for both models.) This matrix is symmetric, with the diagonal showing the fraction of positive sentence pairs for each model.

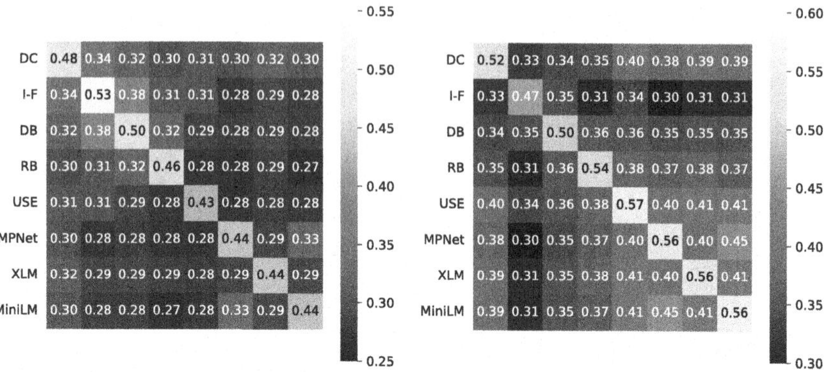

Fig. 5. Left: Positive agreement fraction (PAF) map for *A Christmas Carol.* Right: Negative agreement fraction (NSF) map for *A Christmas Carol.*

2. **Negative Agreement Fraction (NAF):** The fraction of all sentence pairs that both model A and model B consider less similar than average (negative in the standardized SSMs for both models.) This matrix is also symmetric, with the diagonal showing the fraction of negative sentence pairs for each model.
3. **Directional Disagreement Fraction (DDAF):** The fraction of all sentence pairs that model A considers more similar than average (positive in the standardized SSMs for A) and model B considers less similar than average (negative in the standardized SSMs for B.) This matrix is asymmetric, with the upper triangle showing the fraction of sentence pairs that are positive in A and negative in B, and the lower triangle showing the converse.

5 Results and Discussion

5.1 Semantic Structure Comparison

To quantify the correspondences between the SSMs generated by all the methods, we calculate the pairwise Pearson correlation coefficients between the time-series for each pair of models on each book, producing an 8×8 *correlation map* for each book. These are shown as heatmaps in Fig. 1 for four of the books. To get a more global view, these maps are averaged over all 18 documents to give the *mean correlation map* shown in Fig. 2. Several observations can be noted from these:

1. Overall, a fairly similar pattern of pairwise correlation is seen in the semantic structures inferred for the four books, but the absolute level of correlation varies significantly. In general, correlations are highest for *Metamorphosis* and lowest for *The Prophet.*
2. In general, six of the methods are quite strongly correlated, with correlation coefficients well above 0.6. However, two methods – InferSent and DistilBERT – are less correlated with the others.

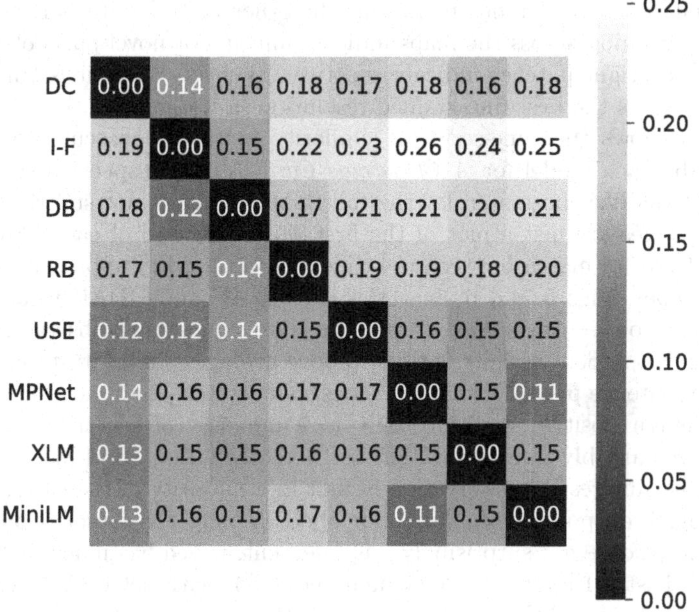

Fig. 6. Directed disagreement fraction (DDAF) map for *A Christmas Carol.*

3. Structures inferred by InferSent have significantly lower correlation with those inferred by the other methods except DistilBERT. The lower correlation probably reflects the fact that InferSent uses a model that is significantly different than the other methods.
4. Somewhat surprisingly, DistilBERT has high correlation with both InferSent and RoBERTa. The latter is understandable, since both are BERT-based methods, but similarity with InferSent is intriguing since RoBERTa has much lower correlation with InferSent. In a sense, DistilBERT seems to bridge between InferSent and RoBERTa, agreeing with the former on some sentence pairs and agreeing with the latter on a different (though probably overlapping) set of sentence pairs.
5. Interestingly, DeCLUTR has very substantial correlation with methods other than InferSent and DistilBERT even though it uses a very different approach.
6. The highest correlation of any pair of methods is between MPNet and MiniLM.
7. Leaving aside InferSent and DistilBERT, XLM appears to have the most correlation on average with the other four methods, which is interesting given its very different approach compared to other methods. This suggests the training on multiple languages might provide some advantage in generalization.

Figure 3 shows partial SSMs obtained for *A Christmas Carol* using four methods. They show that these four – and the other – models all infer a broadly similar pattern of semantic variation in the document, though InferSent tends to assign higher similarities to sentence pairs that the other methods. In particular, the dark bands running across the maps indicate unusual or novel parts of the document, while bright patches indicate repetitive themes. While it is hard to see here, MPNet has the best fine-grained resolution in the map.

Figure 4 shows the time-series of similarity between consecutive sentences generated by each model for *A Christmas Carol*. Visual inspection shows similarity patterns like those seen for the full SSMs, which is not surprising, since these time-series are just a plot of the first super-diagonal of each SSM. However, the degree of match between the time series is hard to appreciate visually. To look deeper, Figs. 5 and 6 show the PAF, NAF and DDAF values for all method pairs on *A Christmas Carol*. The most interesting observation from Fig. 5 is that InferSent assigns positive (above average) similarity to more than half of the sentence pairs, DistilBERT does so for exactly half, and all the other methods assign positive similarity only to a minority of sentence pairs. This fraction is remarkably similar for USE, MPNet, XLM, and MiniLM – all around 0.44. Another interesting observation is that in a majority of the cases, pairs of methods agree on positive similarity for about 30% of the sentence pairs. The clearest exception – not surprisingly – is InferSent. which has much higher PAF (0.38) with DistilBERT and a fairly high one (0.34) with deCLUTR. The other slight exception is a PAF of 0.33 between MPNet and MiniLM. On the NAF, InferSent has notably lower values relative to almost all other methods, reflecting its bias towards assigning positive similarities. This is also the main reason why, in Fig. 6, Infersent has much higher positive-to-negative disagreements with other methods than vice-versa.

The patterns shown here for *A Christmas Carol* are qualitatively similar for the other 17 books as well (not shown for lack of space).

6 Conclusion

This comparative study arrived at the following conclusions: 1) The semantic structure inferred for all 18 books by all the evaluated methods shows some consistency, indicating that they all partially capture the actual semantics of the document; 2) Significant differences in the semantic structure inferred by different methods indicates that each provides a distinctive take on the same document; and 3) Of the methods considered, InferSent had the lowest match with the other methods except DistilBERT, but DistilBERT also had good agreement with RoBERTa – perhaps because both use BERT.

Based on these observations and the postulates that motivated this study, our main conclusion is that, of the 8 methods evaluated, four – USE, MPNet, XLM, and MiniLM - provide sufficiently reliable agreement on semantic variation to be used for novelty detection. InferSent is the outlier, and its use would require much more detailed study of its biases. DeCLUTR, RoBERTa and DistilBERT fall somewhere in the middle. An interesting follow-up would to use ensembles of these methods for novelty detection.

References

1. Choi, F.Y.Y.: Advances in domain independent linear text segmentation. In: 1st Meeting of the North American Chapter of the Association for Computational Linguistics (2000)
2. Riedl, M., Bieman, C.: Text segmentation with topic models. J. Lang. Technol. Comput. Linguist. **27**(1), 47–69 (2012)
3. Alemi, A.A., Ginsparg, P.H.: Text segmentation based on semantic word embeddings. ArXiv arxiv.org1503.05543 (2015)
4. Hill, F., Cho, K., Korhonen, A.: Learning distributed representations of sentences from unlabelled data. In: Proceedings of the 2016 Conference of the North American Chapter of the Association for Computational Linguistics: Human Language Technologies, San Diego, California, June 2016, pp. 1367–1377. Association for Computational Linguistics (2016)
5. Cer, D., Diab, M., Agirre, E., Lopez-Gazpio, I., Specia, L.: SemEval-2017 task 1: semantic textual similarity multilingual and crosslingual focused evaluation. In: Proceedings of the 11th International Workshop on Semantic Evaluation (SemEval-2017), Vancouver, Canada, August 2017, pp. 1–14. Association for Computational Linguistics (2017)
6. Arora, S., Liang, Y., Ma, T.: A simple but tough-to-beat baseline for sentence embeddings. In: Proceedings of the International Conference on Learning Representations (2017)
7. Conneau, A., Kiela, D.: SentEval: an evaluation toolkit for universal sentence representations. In: Proceedings of the Eleventh International Conference on Language Resources and Evaluation (LREC 2018), Miyazaki, Japan, May 2018. European Language Resources Association (ELRA) (2018)
8. Giorgi, J., Nitski, O., Wang, B., Bader, G.: DeCLUTR: deep contrastive learning for unsupervised textual representations. In: Proceedings of the 59th Annual Meeting of the Association for Computational Linguistics and the 11th International Joint Conference on Natural Language Processing, vol. 1: Long Papers, August 2021, Online, pp. 879–895. Association for Computational Linguistics (2021)
9. Conneau, A., Kiela, D., Schwenk, H., Barrault, L., Bordes, A.: Supervised learning of universal sentence representations from natural language inference data. In: Proceedings of the 2017 Conference on Empirical Methods in Natural Language Processing, Copenhagen, Denmark, September 2017, pp. 670–680. Association for Computational Linguistics (2017)
10. Sanh, V., Debut, L., Chaumond, J., Wolf, T.: DistilBERT, a distilled version of bert: smaller, faster, cheaper and lighter. ArXiv arXiv:1910.01108 (2019)
11. Liu, Y., et al.: RoBERTa: a robustly optimized BERT pretraining approach. arXiv preprint arXiv:1907.11692 (2019)
12. Cer, D., et al.: Universal sentence encoder for English. In: Proceedings of the 2018 Conference on Empirical Methods in Natural Language Processing: System Demonstrations, Brussels, Belgium, November 2018, pp. 169–174. Association for Computational Linguistics (2018)
13. Song, K., Tan, X., Qin,T., Lu, J., Liu, T.Y.: MPNet: masked and permuted pre-training for language understanding. arXiv preprint arXiv:2004.09297 (2020)
14. Conneau, A., et al.: Unsupervised cross-lingual representation learning at scale. arxiv:1911.02116 (2019)
15. Wang, W., Wei, F., Dong, L., Bao, H., Yang, N., Zhou, M.: MiniLM: deep self-attention distillation for task-agnostic compression of pre-trained transformers. arXiv preprint arXiv:2002.10957 (2020)

16. Joulin, A., Grave, E., Bojanowski, P., Mikolov, T.: Bag of tricks for efficient text classification. In: Proceedings of the 15th Conference of the European Chapter of the Association for Computational Linguistics, Valencia, Spain, April 2017, vol. 2, Short Papers, pp. 427–431. Association for Computational Linguistics (2017)
17. Bojanowski, P., Grave, E., Joulin, A., Mikolov, T.: Enriching word vectors with subword information. Trans. Assoc. Comput. Linguist. **5**, 135–146 (2017)
18. Pennington, J., Socher, R., Manning, C.D.: GLoVe: global vectors for word representation. In: Empirical Methods in Natural Language Processing (EMNLP), pp. 1532–1543 (2014)
19. Devlin, J., Chang, M.W., Lee, K., Toutanova, K.: BERT: pre-training of deep bidirectional transformers for language understanding. In: Proceedings of the 2019 Conference of the North American Chapter of the Association for Computational Linguistics: Human Language Technologies, Minneapolis, Minnesota, June 2019, vol. 1 (Long and Short Papers), pp. 4171–4186. Association for Computational Linguistics (2019)
20. Rajpurkar, P., Zhang, J., Lopyrev, K., Liang, P.: SQuAD: 100,000+ questions for machine comprehension of text. In: Proceedings of the 2016 Conference on Empirical Methods in Natural Language Processing, Austin, Texas, November 2016, pp. 2383–2392. Association for Computational Linguistics (2016)
21. Rajpurkar, P., Jia, R., Liang, P.: Know what you don't know: unanswerable questions for SQuAD. In: Proceedings of the 56th Annual Meeting of the Association for Computational Linguistics, Melbourne, Australia, July 2018, vol. 2: Short Papers, pp. 784–789. Association for Computational Linguistics (2018)
22. Wang, A., Singh, A., Michael, J., Hill, F., Levy, O., Bowman, S.R.: GLUE: a multi-task benchmark and analysis platform for natural language understanding. In: International Conference on Learning Representations (2019)

A Deep Learning Based Method for Generating Holographic Acoustic Fields from Phased Transducer Arrays

Shuai Wang, Xuewei Wang(✉), Fucheng You, and Han Xiao

College of Information Engineering, Beijing Institute of Graphic Communication, Beijing, China
{wangxuewei,youfucheng}@bigc.edu.cn

Abstract. The phased transducer array can control the phase of the ultrasonic waves to produce a holographic acoustic field, and this forward propagation system can be described as a straightforward linear system of equations. However, obtaining the phase of the corresponding phased transducer array from the holographic acoustic field is an inverse propagation problem, which leads to an unsolvable non-linear system. To address this problem, we develop a physical model of the holographic acoustic field generated by a phased transducer array using a piston source theory model, and use a deep learning method incorporating an attention mechanism to obtain the array phase information required to reconstruct the holographic acoustic field. The results show that the array phases obtained by the proposed neural network fully supports the generation of the corresponding holographic acoustic field, and that both the sound pressure intensity and the sound pressure phase of the holographic acoustic field can be reconstructed with high quality and accuracy.

Keywords: Holographic acoustic fields · Machine learning · Phased transducer arrays · Ultrasonic waves · Attention mechanisms

1 Introduction

The Phased Transducer Array (PTA) is a device that uses an acoustic transducer as an ultrasonic waves generating unit. The PTA generally takes the form of several transducers arranged in a two-dimensional array, where each transducer is an independently existing sound source. During operation each transducer emits acoustic waves of uniform amplitude, the phase of the acoustic signal is adjusted independently using electrical signals, and multiple groups of acoustic waves are dynamically superimposed to produce a specific shape of acoustic radiation potential field. The holographic acoustic field is an acoustic field that records both sound pressure intensity and phase information. The PTA generates the expected holographic acoustic field by using the principle of superimposed interference of sound waves. During the generation of holographic acoustic fields, each transducer emits sound waves at a constant frequency, and the signal delay is used to change the phase difference between the individual transducers. The ultrasonic

L. Iliadis et al. (Eds.): ICANN 2023, LNCS 14263, pp. 13–24, 2023.
https://doi.org/10.1007/978-3-031-44204-9_2

waves emitted by the PTA can superimpose interference in the target space to achieve the focus, deflection, and deflected focus of the acoustic waves [1]. PTA generates holographic acoustic fields that can be used for some specific operations, such as traveling wave tweezers based on acoustic radiation force can drive particles toward acoustic pressure nodes or anti-node positions [2], which allows us to create one or more focal points to non-contact rotate or move particles [3].

The process of generating the holographic acoustic field from the PTA is straightforward and forward, however, solving the phase of each transducer in the PTA backwards from the holographic acoustic field is difficult, and it is a mathematically unsolvable nonlinear problem. Accurately calculating the phase of each transducer in the PTA for a given target holographic acoustic field is still a challenge, and low quality holographic acoustic fields may lead to inaccurate focal points and affect the accuracy. Various methods exist to solve this problem, such as traditional methods are iterative angular spectrum method [4] and iterative methods such as projection iterative method [5], and emerging methods are AcousNet [6] method based on machine learning by Chengxi Zhong et al. However, all these methods have certain drawbacks, the iterative methods are very time consuming and cannot be applied in real time, and are not applicable to complex holographic acoustic field generation. AcousNet method has the problem of low accuracy. To address these problems, this paper proposes a deep learning (DL) network framework with higher prediction accuracy to solve this nonlinear inverse mapping problem quickly and efficiently by using the feature extraction capability of deep learning.

2 Build Physical Models

In this section, a physical model of the holographic acoustic field generated by the PTA is constructed. The physical model in which $\mathbf{H} \in R_{n\times n\times n}$ describes the complex acoustic field in space and $\mathbf{I} \in R_{n\times n}$ describes the transducer distribution on the PTA. According to the piston source theory model [7], the forward propagation can be solved directly by considering each transducer as a point source or a square source by the cumulative method [8]. Therefore, the forward propagation of ultrasonic waves from the PTA generates a holographic acoustic field which is described by the forward mapping **F** as:

$$\boldsymbol{F}{:}I(a,b)\text{-}>H(x,y,z) \tag{1}$$

To produce some highly controllable expected holographic acoustic field in practical applications, it is necessary to solve the inverse propagation problem, i.e., to determine the phases of the acoustic waves emitted by different transducers. Therefore, this inverse mapping $\overline{\boldsymbol{F}}$ of the PTA phase distribution from the holographic acoustic field is described as.

$$\overline{\boldsymbol{F}} : H(x,y,z)\text{-}>I(a,b) \tag{2}$$

where *(a,b)* are the position coordinates of the transducer and *(x, y, z)* are the position coordinates of the physical points in space. Eq. (1) is the forward propagation process can be solved directly with the acoustic theory model, while Eq. (2) is the inverse propagation process, which is difficult to solve due to its nonlinearity.

To visually describe the two propagation processes through the model and accurately simulate the holographic acoustic field **H**, a three-dimensional Cartesian coordinate system with the origin O at the center of the PTA is established, and there are N*N transducers in the PTA, all of which are located in the XOY plane, with the target holographic acoustic field region above the XOY plane. The shape of the input tensor of the neural network depends on the discretization of the holographic acoustic field. To ensure that the input structure of the neural network remains constant, the target region always generates a determined number of samples $L \times W \times K$, regardless of the spatial size and location of the target acoustic field. This experiment sets $W = K = L = 20$ to effectively quantize the acoustic field **H**. This allows 8000 discrete sample points to be obtained from a given holographic acoustic field **H** so that it can be used as the input to the neural network for training processing. Based on these sample points, 8000 sets of forward propagation equations can be established, as shown in Fig. 1 for the holographic acoustic field generated by the PTA:

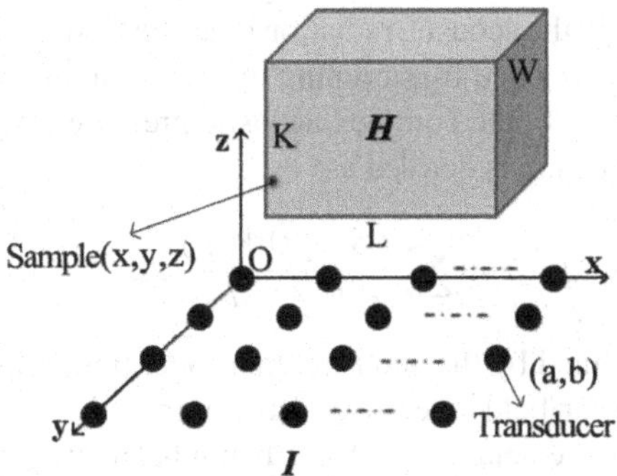

Fig. 1. Schematic diagram of the holographic acoustic field generated by PTA

3 Dataset Preparation and Pre-Processing

This section will elaborate on the data set preparation and preprocessing in a deep learning scheme. The input to the neural network is composed of information from sampled physical points in the holographic acoustic field and the phase of the PTA as the ground truth values label, and the two are composed into data pairs and then normalized to form the complete dataset.

3.1 Dataset Preparation

This study is devoted to the problem of "backward propagation" of the holographic acoustic field, while the forward propagation is known and easy to calculate, so the dataset used for the experiments is generated using a simulation method [9]. In the previous section, a geometric model relationship has been established for the PTA to generate a holographic acoustic field, and the next step is to describe the numerical

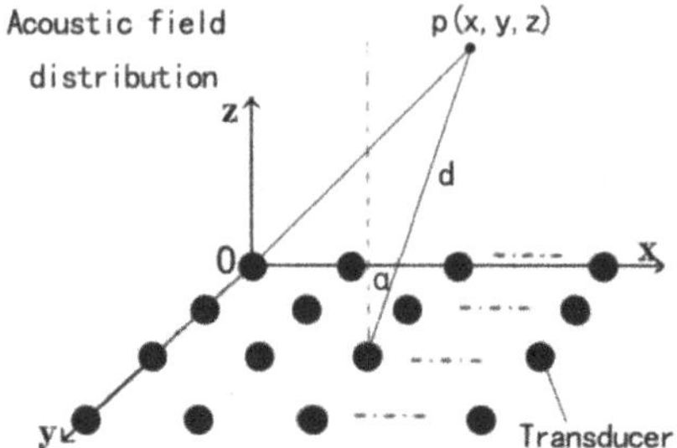

Fig. 2. Model relationship diagram of the pressure generated by PTA at a spatial control point

relationship between the parameters. Figure 2 is a schematic diagram of a control point *p(x,y,z)* generated in space by the PTA.

The square piston source [7] far-field model is used in this experiment. For arrays with multiple transducers, the total acoustic radiation pressure to which the object is subjected is linearly superimposed by the acoustic radiation pressure from each transducer, the total acoustic pressure field is obtained by summing the contributions from each source. By this theoretical approach [10], the complex acoustic pressure *p(x,y,z)* generated by the PTA at a sampling point *(x,y,z)* is derived as:

$$p(x, y, z) = \sum\nolimits_{a,b=0}^{M,N} A\frac{D(\theta, \beta)}{d} e^{j(\varphi_{a,b}+kd)} \tag{3}$$

where A is a constant defined by the acoustic transducer power, $M*N$ is the number of transducers, $D(\theta,\beta)$ is a far-field directivity function based on a square piston source model, which depends on the polar angle θ and azimuthal angle β between the sampling point and the transducer normal in the holographic acoustic field, d is the Euclidean distance between the transducer and the sampling point, and $\varphi_{a,b}$ is the initial emission phase of the transducer. $k = 2\pi/\lambda$ is the wave number, λ is the wavelength of the acoustic wave ($\lambda = c/f$, wave speed $c = 346$ m/s in air at 25 °C, ultrasonic frequency $f = 40$ kHz).

The known information of the sampling points in the holographic acoustic field includes coordinates and sound pressure intensity, and the known information in the PTA includes transducer coordinates and transducer emitted acoustic wave amplitude. Based on this information the iterative back propagation (IBP) algorithm [3] can be used to iteratively optimize the phase of the PTA, and the calculation results are used as the ground truth values labels of the data set. To clearly describe the computational process of IBP, let **S** denote the set of information about the control points (focus or trap) in the holographic acoustic field, and let **T** denote the set of phases of the transducers in the PTA. The unique feature of the IBP algorithm is that the phase values of the transducers in the PTA are considered as the sum of the contributions of each sample point in the holographic acoustic field. The calculation process first sets the initial sound pressure phase of each sampling point in **S** to zero, and then back propagates the solution to obtain the phase in **T**. Then the phase information in **T** is substituted into Eq. (3) and forward propagates the solution to obtain the sound pressure phase of the sampling points in **S**. By iterating through the loop continuously, the algorithm stops if the phase change in **T** in two consecutive iterations is below a certain threshold. In this way, the phase of the transducer in the PTA corresponding to the target sound field can be found.

In order to perform supervised learning, the data set needs to be composed of the same data pairs as **(S, T)**. The sampled point information **S** in the holographic acoustic field is used as the network input, and the phase **T** of the transducer in the PTA is used as the network ground truth values. The structure of the input data is shown as **S** in Eq. (4), which has an input dimension of $5 \times 8000 \times 1$. The number of columns $(L \times W \times K)$ of **S** represents the number of sampled points in the acoustic field, and each row in **S** from top to bottom is the polar coordinates (ρ, θ, β), sound pressure intensity (A) and sound pressure phase (φ) information of the sampled points. The phase **T** of the transducer in the PTA can be regarded as an image with pixel value $R_{n \times n}$. The size of the dataset selected for this experiment is 20,000 groups, which are divided into training, validation and test sets in the ratio of 17:2:1.

$$S = \begin{bmatrix} \rho_1\ \rho_2 & & \rho_{L\times W\times K-1}\ \rho_{L\times W\times K} \\ \theta_1\ \theta_2 & & \theta_{L\times W\times K-1}\ \theta_{L\times W\times K} \\ \beta_1\ \beta_2 & \cdots\cdots & \beta_{L\times W\times K-1}\ \beta_{L\times W\times K} \\ A_1\ A_2 & & A_{L\times W\times K-1}\ A_{L\times W\times K} \\ \varphi_1\ \varphi_2 & & \varphi_{L\times W\times K-1}\ \varphi_{L\times W\times K} \end{bmatrix} \tag{4}$$

3.2 Data Pre-processing

To improve the stability of the training process and to speed up the network learning, the input data set of a deep neural network needs to be normalized. In this paper, we use a special normalization method that takes into account the physical background. Each horizontal cross-section of the holographic acoustic field is treated separately, and the sound pressure intensity greater than a certain threshold (α) and less than a certain threshold (β) will be reassigned. As shown in Eqs. (5) and (6), the energy extremes of the sound pressure intensity are bounded in a reasonable interval. Finally, all data sets are saved using the same format and size.

$$\begin{cases} \alpha = 2^{-0.25} max(\mathrm{A_{x,y,z}})_i + (1 - 2^{-0.25}) min(\mathrm{A_{x,y,z}})_i \\ \beta = 2^{-0.25} min(\mathrm{A_{x,y,z}})_i + (1 - 2^{-0.25}) max(\mathrm{A_{x,y,z}})_i \end{cases} \tag{5}$$

$$\mathrm{A_{x,y,z}} = \begin{cases} \alpha, & \mathrm{A_{x,y,z}} > \alpha \\ \beta, & \mathrm{A_{x,y,z}} < \beta \\ \mathrm{A_{x,y,z}}, & \mathrm{A_{x,y,z}} \end{cases} \tag{6}$$

where $A_{x,y,z}$ is the sound pressure intensity, $max(A_{x,y,z})_i$ is the maximum value of sound pressure intensity in cross-section i, $min(\mathrm{A_{x,y,z}})_i$ is the minimum value of sound pressure intensity in cross-section i.

4 Neural Network Architecture

This section proposes a network framework to learn the inverse mapping process from the holographic acoustic field **H** to the transducer array **I**, and introduces the loss function design. The implementation process is as follows: the information of the sampled points in the holographic acoustic field **S** is input to the network to predict the phase **T** of the transducer in the PTA, and the loss function is calculated by comparing the difference between the ground truth phase mean and the predicted phase mean, and then optimized using the gradient descent algorithm. Finally, the transducer phase satisfying the error requirement is obtained.

4.1 Construction of Network Architecture

In this paper, a multiple regression model incorporating attention mechanism is built, and the backbone network of the model is divided into three parts. The first part expands the channels after four feature extraction operations, and each time feature map passes through a convolutional layer followed by a batch normalization (BN) layer and an activation function. Considering the small scale of focal information in the sound field, the kernel size of the convolutional layer is 1×1, which can extract features quickly and efficiently while reducing the computational effort. After that, the feature map is passed through a maximum pooling layer, which helps to reduce the feature dimension and expand the perceptual field. The second part deepens the channel again after 4 feature extraction operations, each time the feature map passes through a residual layer [11] or Inception layer [12]. Considering the randomness and imbalance of intensity information distribution in the sound field, the feature map passes through a channel attention mechanism layer [13] with an adaptive convolution kernel size, which can enhance the network's ability to focus on detailed information in the feature map. The first two parts of the model need to be reasonably choreographed to optimize the structure and widen the hierarchy to enhance performance. The second part of the model uses the residual, Inception, and inverse residual layers alone as the three network model architectures for the experimental comparison. In the third part of the model, the feature map is processed by the spreading layer and two fully connected layers with output dimensions of 3072 and 2500, and finally generates a feature vector with output dimension of 1×2500 representing the transducer phase in the PTA. The overall structure of the model is shown in Fig. 3.

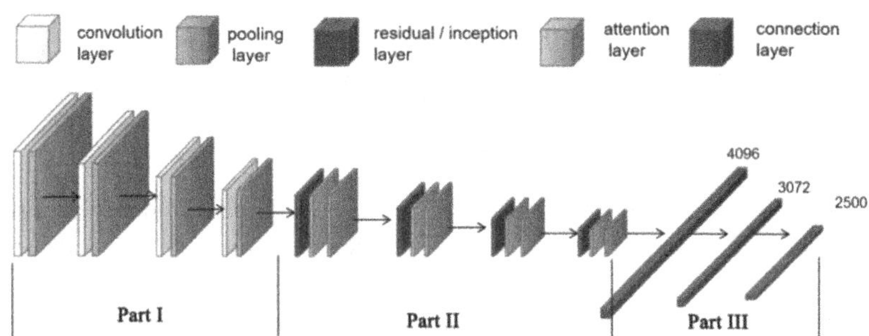

Fig. 3. Residual/inception network model architecture incorporating attention mechanisms

4.2 Loss Function Design

Acoustic waves are periodic in nature, and the *L1/L2* loss in the traditional regression problem [14] cannot be used directly in this physical context. In order to be able to penalize the difference between the predicted phase value (φ_{pred}) and the ground truth values (φ_{truth}), we solves it by calculating the cosine of the difference between φ_{pred} and φ_{truth}, as shown in Eq. (7), which is a loss function characterized by the cosine operation that fully takes into account the periodicity of acoustic waves.

$$L = \frac{1}{N^2}\sum_{(u,v)}^{(N,N)} (1 - cos(2\pi((\varphi_{u,v})_{pred} - (\varphi_{u,v})_{truth}))) \tag{7}$$

where $(\varphi_{u,v})_{pred}$ is the predicted phase value, $(\varphi_{u,v})_{truth})$ is the ground truth phase value, and N^2 is the number of transducers.

5 Experiments and Results

This section provides some implementation details and results that visualize the predicted PTA phase in images, evaluating the test results of the network model and the performance of solving the inverse mapping problem.

5.1 Implementation Details

The initial learning rate of the network model was 0.002 for optimal parameter estimation, and the learning rate was adjusted autonomously during training. The optimizer uses RAdam [15], and the model reaches full convergence after 120 rounds of training. To effectively quantify the difference between the predicted phase and the ground truth values, the prediction accuracy of the model is measured using the loss function proposed in the previous section. Figure 4 shows the error mean results of the three network models proposed in this paper and the AcousNet model [6] on the test dataset. The test comparison reveals that the network model proposed in this paper can achieve the lowest error mean in the second step using the Inverted-Residuals structure, and its error mean on the test dataset is stable at about 0.03, and the R^2 of fit can reach 0.97.

5.2 Analysis of Results

The best-performing model structure in the experiment was used as the final test model (EIR-Net, ECA-Inverted-Residuals-Net). Five samples from the test set were randomly selected to evaluate the prediction performance of the proposed network model by comparing the difference between the predicted phase and the ground truth values. Figure 5 shows the prediction performance of the neural network as an image (size 50 × 50), where the phase differences of 0 and 2π are the same as each other due to the periodicity of the ultrasonic waves. Figure 5(a) shows the ground truth phase of the transducer in the PTA and Fig. 5(b) shows the phase of the transducer in the PTA predicted by the neural network, whose high contrast illustrates the good performance of the neural network

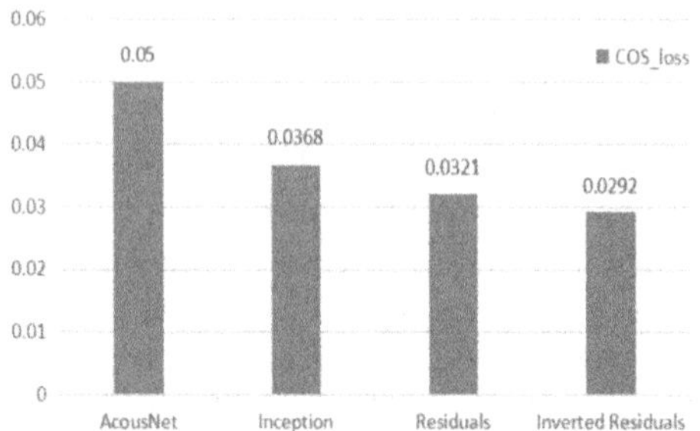

Fig. 4. Mean values of errors in predicting transducer phase for four network models AcousNet [6], inception, Residuals and Inverted Residuals on the test dataset

proposed in this paper. Figure 5(c) shows the direct difference between the predicted phase and the ground truth, and the comparison can directly show the small difference between them. Using the powerful information extraction capability of the neural network, the phase information required to reconstruct the target holographic acoustic field can be extracted, eliminating the time-consuming mathematical iteration [16] process. This forward propagation of the holographic acoustic field generated by the PTA is directly calculable by Eq. (3), so it is completely feasible to achieve the reconstruction of the holographic acoustic field with the accurate prediction of the transducer phase in the PTA by the neural network.

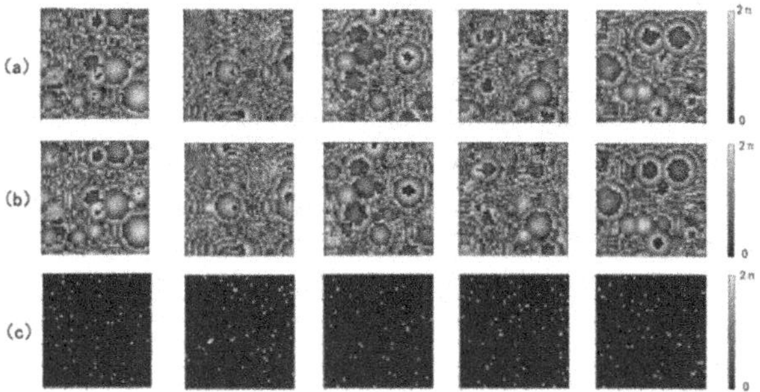

Fig. 5. Prediction results of the neural network for five random samples (a) Plot of the ground truth phase distribution of PTA. (b) Predicted phase distribution of PTA. (c) The difference between the predicted phase distribution and the ground truth phase distribution of PTA.

To further illustrate the accuracy of the EIR-Net neural network prediction results, the average prediction error ($2\pi\,|\varphi_{pred} - \varphi_{truth}|$) of the neural network over the transducers (50×50) was experimentally tested. Figure 6 evaluates the results of the quartile representation for each of the five samples mentioned above. From the data, it can be seen that the EIR-Net neural network not only achieves the phase prediction of the PTA, but also maintains a high accuracy.

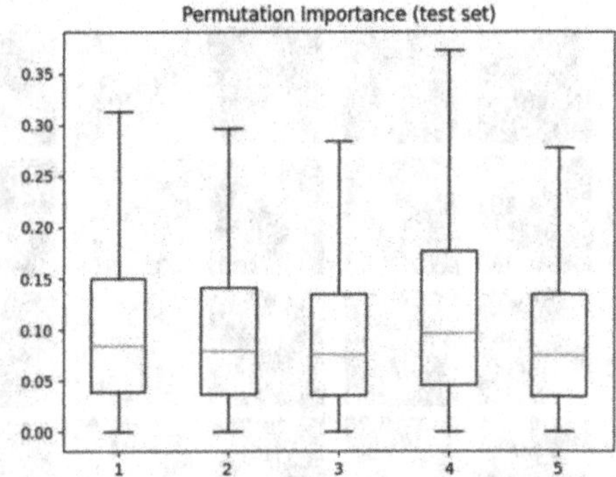

Fig. 6. Quartile description of the average error of the neural network prediction for the previous five samples.

6 Holographic Acoustic Field Reconstruction

The prediction performance of the EIR-Net neural network was reasonably evaluated and discussed in the previous section, but the goal of this study is to generate holographic acoustic fields from the PTA by means of the EIR-Net neural network [17]. Therefore, this section compares the differences between the real and simulated holographic acoustic fields to evaluate the prediction performance of the model.

6.1 Sound Field Reconstruction Process

In order to evaluate the performance of the quality of the EIR-Net neural network based on the generation of holographic acoustic fields from the PTA [18], four sets of multi-focal holographic acoustic field information were randomly selected as input samples from the test set. The samples are placed into the EIR-Net neural network for prediction, and the predicted phases of the transducers in the four sets of PTA are obtained. The prediction results are passed through the forward propagation Eq. (3) to generate simulated holographic acoustic fields from the PTA.

6.2 Analysis of Results

The experiments are shown graphically to obtain the holographic acoustic field using the EIR-Net neural network and to evaluate the accuracy of the reconstruction results. As shown in Fig. 7, the sound pressure intensity and phase distribution in a plane of the simulated holographic acoustic field, as well as the difference maps between the simulated and real holographic acoustic fields, where the sound pressure intensity are normalized for better comparison.

The simulation reconstruction results show that the transducer phase obtained from the EIR-Net neural network (Fig. 7(a)) fully supports the PTA to generate the corresponding holographic acoustic field (Fig. 7(c) and Fig. 7(e)). The experiments also compare the sound pressure intensity and phase difference values between the simulated holographic acoustic field and the real values (Fig. 7(d) and Fig. 7(f)). It can be seen from

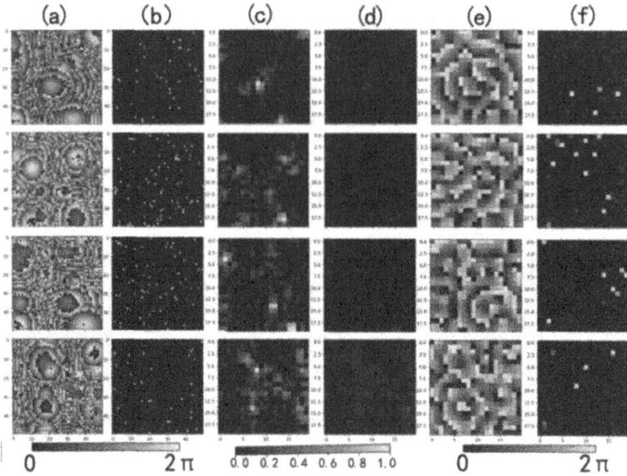

Fig. 7. Cross-sectional plot of the simulated holographic acoustic field generated by the PTA in the z = 1.25 mm plane with a hologram size of 5 × 5 cm^2. The lower chromaticity bar in the plot is the spectral bar, the unit (0,2π) represents the phase, and (0,1) represents the normalized sound pressure intensity. (a) PTA phase distribution predicted by the neural network; (b) Phase error predicted by the neural network; (c) Sound pressure intensity distribution of the simulated holographic acoustic field; (d) Difference plot between simulated and real holographic acoustic field sound pressure intensity; (e) Simulated holographic acoustic field pressure phase distribution; (f) Difference plot between simulated and real holographic acoustic field sound pressure phase.

the figures that the errors between the simulated holographic acoustic field and the real holographic acoustic field are smaller and more similar. Therefore, the EIR-Net neural network method proposed in this paper can not only clearly reconstruct the general outline and detail information of the original holographic acoustic field, but also maintain a high accuracy for the target.

7 Conclusion

In this paper, we propose the EIR-Net neural network, a convolutional neural network (CNN)-based regression network [19], which is used to achieve the solution of mathematically intractable inverse mapping problems. We trained the network with a dataset generated by a simulation method and tested the samples to prove the feasibility of the network. The EIR-Net neural network has higher prediction accuracy in generating holographic acoustic fields based on PTA compared to the latest AcousNet method. In future work, we hope to further explore new methods based on deep learning, especially generative adversarial networks [20], to further improve the prediction performance of neural networks.

References

1. Marzo, A., et al.: Holographic acoustic elements for manipulation of levitated objects. Nat. Commun. **6**, 8661 (2015). https://doi.org/10.1038/ncomms9661

2. Ma, Z., Collins, D. J., Guo, J., Ai, Y.: Mechanical properties based particle separation via traveling surface acoustic wave. Anal. Chem. **88**(23), 11844–11851. (2016). https://doi.org/10.1021/acs.analchem.6b03580
3. Marzo, A., Drinkwater, B.W.: Holographic acoustic tweezers. Proc. Natl. Acad. Sci. U. S. A. **116**(1), 84–89 (2019). https://doi.org/10.1073/pnas.1813047115
4. Zeng, X.Z., McGough, R.: Evaluation of the angular spectrum approach for simulations of near-field pressures. J. Acoust. Soc. Am. **123**(1), 68–76 (2008). https://doi.org/10.1121/1.2812579
5. Plasencia, D.M., Hirayama, R., Montano-Murillo, R., et al.: GS-PAT: high-speed multi-point sound-fields for phased arrays of transducers. ACM Trans. Graph. **39**(4), 1–138 (2020)
6. Zhong, C., Jia, Y., Jeong, D. C., Guo, Y., Liu, S.: AcousNet: a deep learning based approach to dynamic 3D holographic acoustic field generation from phased transducer array. IEEE Robot. Autom. Lett. **7**(2), 666–673 (2022). https://doi.org/10.1109/LRA.2021.3130368
7. Averkiou, M. A., Hamilton, M.F.: Nonlinear distortion of short pulses radiated by plane and focused circular pistons. J. Acoust. Soc. Am. **102**(5), 2539–2548 (1997). https://doi.org/10.1121/1.420308
8. O'Neil, H. T.: Theory of focusing radiators. J. Acoust. Soc. Am. **21**(5), 516–526 (1949). https://doi.org/10.1121/1.1906542
9. Liu, Y.: Efficient modeling of sound source radiation in free-space and room environments. Purdue University (2016)
10. Tsang, P.W.M., Poon, T.C.: Novel method for converting digital Fresnel hologram to phase-only hologram based on bidirectional error diffusion. Opt. Exp. **21**(20), 23680–23686 (2013). https://doi.org/10.1364/OE.21.023680
11. He, K., Zhang, X., Ren, S., Sun, J.: Deep residual learning for image recognition. In: Institute of Electrical and Electronics Engineers. 29th IEEE Conference on Computer Vision and Pattern Recognition: 29th IEEE Conference on Computer Vision and Pattern Recognition (CVPR), 26 June–1 July 2016, Las Vegas, Nevada. pp. 770–778. (2016). https://doi.org/10.1109/CVPR.2016.90
12. Szegedy, C., Liu, W., Jia, Y., Sermanet, P., Reed, S., Anguelov, D., Erhan, D., Vanhoucke, V., Rabinovich, A.: Going deeper with convolutions. In: Institute of Electrical and Electronics Engineers. 2015 IEEE Conference on Computer Vision and Pattern Recognition: 2015 28th IEEE Conference on Computer Vision and Pattern Recognition (CVPR 2015), 7–12 June 2015, Boston, MA, USA, pp. 1–9. https://arxiv.org/pdf/1409.4842.pdf (2015)
13. Wang, Q., et al.: ECA-Net: efficient channel attention for deep convolutional neural networks. In: Institute of Electrical and Electronics Engineers. 2020 IEEE/CVF Conference on Computer Vision and Pattern Recognition: IEEE/CVF Conference on Computer Vision and Pattern Recognition (CVPR 2020), 13–19 June 2020, Seattle, WA, USA, pp. 11531–11539 (2020) https://doi.org/10.1109/CVPR42600.2020.01155
14. Zhao, H., Gallo O., Frosio, I., Kautz, J.: Loss functions for image restoration with neural networks. IEEE Trans. Comput. Imag. **3**(1), 47–57 (2017). https://doi.org/10.1109/TCI.2016.26448652644865
15. Liu, L., Jiang, H., He, P. et al.: On the variance of the adaptive learning rate and beyond. In: International Conference on Learning Representations. https://arxiv.org/pdf/1908.03265.pdf (2020)
16. Melde, K., Mark, A.G., Qiu, T., Fischer, P.: Holograms for acoustics. Nature **537**(7621), 518–522 (2016). https://doi.org/10.1038/nature19755
17. Fushimi, T., Yamamoto, K., Ochiai, Y.: Acoustic hologram optimisation using automatic differentiation. Sci. Rep. **11**(1), 12678 (2021). https://doi.org/10.1038/s41598-021-91880-2
18. Setiadi, D.R.I.M.: PSNR vs SSIM: imperceptibility quality assessment for image steganography. Multimed. Tools Appl. **80**(6), 8423–8444 (2020). https://doi.org/10.1007/s11042-020-10035-zn

19. Wei, C., Ma, X.: Empirical likelihood ratio test for seemingly unrelated regression models. Int. J. Stat. Probab. **10**(3), 1 (2021). https://doi.org/10.5539/ijsp.v10n3p1
20. Liu, Y., Zhao, Q., Lv, Y., Wang, K.: Improved triple generative adversarial nets. Int. J. Comput. Appl. Technol. **59**(2), 114 (2019). https://doi.org/10.1504/IJCAT.2019.098029

A Depth-Guided Attention Strategy for Crowd Counting

Hao Chen[1], Zhan Li[1(✉)], Bir Bhanu[2], Dongping Lu[1], and Xuming Han[1]

[1] Department of Computer Science, Jinan University, Guangdong 510632, China
lizhan@jnu.edu.cn

[2] Department of Electrical and Computer Engineering, University of California, Riverside, CA, USA

Abstract. Crowd counting, an essential technology with numerous applications, often encounters challenges due to non-uniform crowd distributions and noisy backgrounds in congested scenes. To address these issues, this paper proposes the utilization of depth information as an independent indicator. Specifically, we introduce a depth-guided attention strategy (DAS) to fuse depth and crowd density information, effectively modeling the relationship between crowd density and depth of field. Additionally, we propose a depth-guided method to generate the target density map by leveraging the negative correlation between the depth of field and head size in crowd scenes, enabling better supervised learning. To achieve fast inference speed, we design two lightweight crowd counting networks within a knowledge distillation framework that require only a small number of parameters. Furthermore, we propose a two-step network inference algorithm to reduce counting errors. Extensive experiments conducted on four challenging datasets demonstrate that our proposed methods significantly improve counting accuracy over baseline networks.

Keywords: Crowd Counting · Depth Information · Convolutional Neural Network · Lightweight Network

1 Introduction

As urban areas become more centralized, crowd gatherings become more frequent, increasing the risk of accidents. As a result, crowd counting technology has gained increased attention in research due to its ability to estimate the number of people in images or videos, making it applicable in security-related scenarios. However, existing crowd-counting networks face several challenges that must be addressed, including the following three aspects.

The first challenge pertains to the inefficiency of previous approaches that trained an additional depth branch [25] to obtain depth information, which neither saves time nor resources and does not account for the negative impact of background depth information. Second, most crowd counting methods use fixed Gaussian kernels to generate target (ground-truth) density maps from

L. Iliadis et al. (Eds.): ICANN 2023, LNCS 14263, pp. 25–37, 2023.
https://doi.org/10.1007/978-3-031-44204-9_3

dot annotations representing the center positions of heads, but this approach does not account for variations in head size due to differences in depth of field across regions in images. Classical geometry-adaptive Gaussian kernels [10,14,27] assume that crowd density is homogeneous, whereas this is not typically the case in real-world scenarios. Thus, indicators that are independent of crowd distribution are required to generate more robust and realistic target density maps. Third, although most high-performance networks [17,24,25] offer better counting accuracy, they come with the drawbacks of a large model size and low efficiency, making them impractical for deployment in mobile devices or embedded systems.

To address the challenges mentioned above, this study proposes two approaches that utilize depth information in images to enhance crowd counting accuracy. First, we propose a depth-guided attention strategy (DAS) that incorporates depth information and foreground/background segmentation. In the DAS framework, depth information extracted by a depth feature extractor [18] and a mask map produced by a plugin mask branch are used to modify the feature maps extracted by the backbone network. Second, we propose a depth-guided method for generating target density maps and mask maps. Assuming that heads at the same depth of field are of similar size, we leverage the depth value estimated by a pretrained model [18] to fit the size of the Gaussian kernels to the heads. Using depth-guided density maps, we generate smooth mask maps as soft targets to supervise the learning of the mask branch.

To validate the effectiveness of our DAS approach for crowd counting, we construct the depth-guided attention network (DANet) and the depth-guided attention context-aware network (DACAN) by employing two different baselines. Moreover, to achieve a better balance between accuracy and computation time (efficiency), we use DANet as a teacher network in a knowledge distillation framework to construct two lightweight networks: 1/2 mobile depth-guided attention network (1/2-MDANet) and 1/4 Ghost depth-guided attention network (1/4-GDANet). Finally, we propose a two-step network inference algorithm to further improve counting accuracy. The major contributions of this work are summarized as follows:

- We propose a depth-guided attention strategy (DAS) for crowd counting. Using this strategy, we construct two networks called DANet and DACAN. Extensive experimental results show that the proposed DAS effectively improves the performance of different baseline networks.
- We propose a depth-guided method to generate the target density map for supervised learning.
- We propose two lightweight networks, which achieve state-of-the-art performance with an extremely small (850K and 90K) number of parameters.
- We propose a two-step network inference algorithm to decrease counting errors.

2 Related Work

In recent years, there has been a proliferation of crowd counting methods based on convolutional neural networks (CNNs) that have achieved remarkable results by integrating density maps to estimate the number of people. Li et al. [10] proposed the congested scene recognition network (CSRNet), which employs dilated kernels to enlarge receptive fields. Liu et al. [14] proposed the context-aware network (CAN), which adaptively encodes the scale of contextual information required to accurately predict crowd density. Additionally, as image depth affects crowd density, some researchers have explored the effect of depth of field on crowd counting [25]. Furthermore, with the widespread adoption of mobile and embedded devices, it is practical to deploy lightweight models [13,27,29] that balance counting accuracy and computational efficiency.

Supervised learning of crowd counting networks typically involves the use of target density maps, making the performance of CNN-based methods heavily dependent on the methods used to generate target density maps. Zhang et al. [27] proposed a method to generate geometry-adaptive Gaussian kernels based on the distance between each head annotation and its nearest neighbors. Lian et al. [12] later proposed a method to design depth-adaptive kernels. However, these methods rely solely on either spatial neighborhood information or crowd depth information to generate Gaussian kernels. In contrast, our approach incorporates both types of information to generate more realistic target density maps.

3 Methods

3.1 Constructing DANet Using DAS

We utilize the DANet as a case study to demonstrate the efficacy of DAS. Our DANet architecture comprises a backbone network and two branches, namely the density branch and the mask branch, along with two layers, namely the depth transformation layer and the mask transformation layer. Within the framework of DAS, the mask branch generates a mask map to segregate the crowd regions from the image background. Additionally, a pre-trained depth feature extractor produces depth feature maps that are combined with the visual geometry group (VGG) feature maps generated by the backbone network. We obtain the attention feature maps by performing element-wise product between the mask and the summation of the depth and VGG features. Finally, the density branch is employed to establish the relationship between the attention feature maps and the density map. The diagram of the DAS framework is illustrated in Fig. 1.

Backbone Network. Given the exceptional performance of VGG-16 [20] in image feature extraction, we adopt the first 10 layers of VGG-16, which include three pooling layers following the second, fourth, and seventh convolutional layers, as the backbone network. Each pooling layer decreases the size of the input feature maps by half in both height and width. Consequently, when a crowd image with dimensions of $H \times W$ is fed into the backbone network, a collection of VGG feature maps denoted as $F^0(\boldsymbol{x})$ of size $H/8 \times W/8 \times C$ can be acquired, where C is the number of channels.

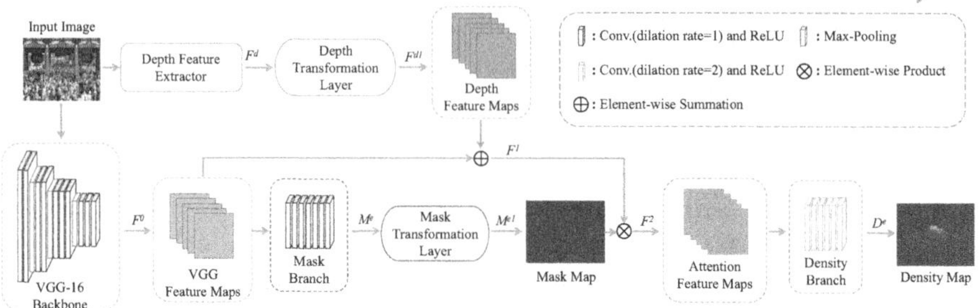

Fig. 1. Overview of DAS framework. The depth feature extractor is pretrained in advance, other parts are the components of DANet.

Introducing Depth Information. As our work primarily focuses on crowd analysis rather than depth estimation, we incorporate a pre-trained depth feature extractor [18] to introduce depth information extracted from crowd images. The depth feature extractor provides a set of depth feature maps denoted as $F^d(\boldsymbol{x})$ upon input of an image. Additionally, we devise a depth transformation layer, implemented as a 1×1 convolution, that reduces the dimensionality of $F^d(\boldsymbol{x})$ to match the channel number of $F^0(\boldsymbol{x})$, generating $F^{d1}(\boldsymbol{x})$. The depth transformation layer is calculated as follows:

$$F^{d1}(\boldsymbol{x}) = Conv_{1\times 1}(F^d(\boldsymbol{x})). \tag{1}$$

Subsequently, we combine $F^{d1}(\boldsymbol{x})$ with $F^0(\boldsymbol{x})$ by element-wise summation to produce combined feature maps, denoted as $F^1(\boldsymbol{x})$:

$$F^1(\boldsymbol{x}) = F^{d1}(\boldsymbol{x}) \oplus F^0(\boldsymbol{x}), \tag{2}$$

where $\oplus$ indicates element-wise summation.

Mask Branch. The mask branch is comprised of seven convolutional layers with a kernel size of three and a dilation rate of one. With the exception of the final layer, each layer is followed by a ReLU function. We use $F^0(\boldsymbol{x})$ as input to the mask branch to estimate a two-dimensional grayscale mask map $M^e(\boldsymbol{x})$ of size $H/8 \times W/8$. To produce a binary mask map, we have designed a simple yet effective mask transformation layer, which can be expressed as follows:

$$M^{e1}(\boldsymbol{x}) = \begin{cases} 1, & if\ M^e(\boldsymbol{x}) \geqslant \varepsilon \\ 0, & if\ M^e(\boldsymbol{x}) < \varepsilon \end{cases}, \tag{3}$$

where ε denotes a preset threshold. Finally, we multiply the mask map $M^{e1}(\boldsymbol{x})$ with the feature maps $F^1(\boldsymbol{x})$ to obtain the attention feature maps $F^2(\boldsymbol{x})$, expressed as:

$$F^2(\boldsymbol{x}) = F^1(\boldsymbol{x}) \otimes M^{e1}(\boldsymbol{x}), \tag{4}$$

where $\otimes$ denotes element-wise multiplication.

Density Branch. The configuration of the density branch is similar to that of the mask branch, except that the dilation rate is changed from one to two in the first six layers. We feed the attention feature maps $F^2(\boldsymbol{x})$ calculated by Eq. 4 into the density branch to estimate a 2D density map $D^e(\boldsymbol{x})$ of size $H/8 \times W/8$. Following most CNN-based methods [10,14,27], the number of people in the input crowd image is estimated by a summation of the pixel values in $D^e(\boldsymbol{x})$.

Network Learning. To optimize the DANet, we use the Euclidean loss for density map estimation and binary cross-entropy loss for mask map estimation, which can be expressed mathematically as follows:

$$\mathcal{L}_{density} = \left\| D^e(\boldsymbol{x}) - D^{GT}(\boldsymbol{x}) \right\|_2^2, \tag{5}$$

$$\mathcal{L}_{mask} = -M^{GT}(\boldsymbol{x}) log M^e(\boldsymbol{x}) - (1 - M^{GT}(\boldsymbol{x})) log(1 - M^e(\boldsymbol{x})), \tag{6}$$

where $D^{GT}(\boldsymbol{x})$ and $M^{GT}(\boldsymbol{x})$ are the ground-truth density map and ground-truth mask map, respectively, which are introduced in Sect. 3.2. $D^e(\boldsymbol{x})$ and $M^e(\boldsymbol{x})$ are the 2D density map and 2D mask map estimated by the DANet, respectively. The total training loss is the summation of the above two losses, expressed as:

$$\mathcal{L}_{total} = \mathcal{L}_{density} + \lambda \mathcal{L}_{mask}, \tag{7}$$

where λ is a trade-off parameter between the two losses.

3.2 Generating Target Density and Mask Maps

Depth-Guided Density Map. The proposed method is grounded on the assumption that people with the same head size are at the same depth of field in a scene. First, we follow [27] to generate a geometry-adaptive Gaussian kernel for each head. Second, since most datasets for crowd counting do not provide depth maps, we utilize the pretrained model MiDaS v3.0 DPT-Large [18] to estimate the corresponding depth map of an input crowd image. To reduce the depth estimation error of each head, we adopt the average value of depth in a neighborhood with adaptive size. Specifically, given a head with location $\boldsymbol{x}_i$ in the depth map, the depth value at the position $\boldsymbol{x}_i$ is estimated by the mean of the depth values of its $m_i \times m_i$ neighborhood, which can be expressed as follows:

$$d_{pi} = \frac{1}{m_i \times m_i} \sum_{k=1}^{m_i \times m_i} D_p(\boldsymbol{x}_{i_k}), \; with \; m_i = \lfloor \gamma \cdot (1 - D_p(\boldsymbol{x}_i)) \rfloor, \tag{8}$$

where m_i is the size of neighborhood of the ith head, γ is a constant coefficient, $\lfloor \cdot \rfloor$ denotes a round down function, and d_{pi} represents the average depth value of the ith head. Because a larger depth of field leads to a smaller head size, which occupies a smaller region of pixels, we set m_i as a negative linear correlation output of the depth value $D_p(\boldsymbol{x}_i)$.

Third, a non-linear function is applied to fit the overall relationship between the standard deviation of each geometry-adaptive Gaussian kernel and the corresponding depth value of each head. Specifically, for each crowd image, this relationship is fitted using Eq. 9. The revised standard deviation σ_{di} of each Gaussian kernel and a general mathematical form of fitting equation $\mathcal{F}$ can be defined as follows:

$$\sigma_{di} = \mathcal{F}(d_{pi}),\ with\, \mathcal{F} = a \cdot d_{pi}^2 + b \cdot d_{pi} + c, \tag{9}$$

where a, b and c are fitting coefficients of the quadratic function $\mathcal{F}$ estimated using the least square method. Finally, we can obtain the depth-guided density map determined by an adaptive Gaussian kernel of each head. Specifically, given a head at location $\boldsymbol{x}_i$, it can be represented as a delta function $\delta(\boldsymbol{x} - \boldsymbol{x}_i)$, and supposing that the crowd image contains N heads in total, the ground-truth depth-guided density map $D^{GT}(\boldsymbol{x})$ of this crowd image can be expressed as:

$$D^{GT}(\boldsymbol{x}) = \sum_{i=1}^{N} \delta(\boldsymbol{x} - \boldsymbol{x}_i) * G_{\sigma_{di}}(\boldsymbol{x}), \tag{10}$$

where $G_{\sigma_{di}}(\boldsymbol{x})$ corresponds to the Gaussian kernel with the revised standard deviation σ_{di} and $*$ indicates the convolution operation.

Target Mask Map. Additionally, we use the depth information as an auxiliary cue to separate crowd regions from the background by producing a target mask map from a depth-guided density map. During the training process, smooth (soft) targets are generally easier for networks to learn than binary (hard) ones. Therefore, instead of directly setting a threshold value to obtain a binary map, a *Tanh* function is employed to convert a depth-guided density map $D^{GT}(\boldsymbol{x})$ to a ground-truth smooth mask map $M^{GT}(\boldsymbol{x})$, which can be defined as follows:

$$M^{GT}(\boldsymbol{x}) = Tanh(K \times D^{GT}(\boldsymbol{x})), \tag{11}$$

where K is a large constant, which is set to 1e8 in our experiment. As most pixel values of head regions in the depth-guided density map tend to be extremely small, we use this *Tanh* function to multiply them by a large factor to change these values to one (representing foreground regions).

3.3 Knowledge Distillation for Lightweight Networks

Lightweight Network Learning. The concept of structured knowledge transfer (SKT) [13] is based on transferring the generalization ability of a high-performance but large "teacher" network to a smaller "student" network. This technique effectively reduces the number of network parameters and computations, which enables the deployment of lightweight crowd counting models on resource-limited devices. In view of this, we propose a teacher-student-based SKT framework to efficiently transfer the depth knowledge in DANet to two lightweight student networks, namely, the mobile depth-guided attention network (MDANet) and Ghost depth-guided attention network (GDANet), where DANet is utilized as a teacher network.

MDANet and GDANet. An MDANet is proposed by replacing all convolutional layers in DANet with residual depthwise separable convolution modules, which is designed by combining depthwise separable convolution [5] and residual learning [4] to efficiently train the model. Meanwhile, we design a GDANet by using Ghost modules [3] as a substitute for the standard convolutional layers in the DANet. We further lighten MDANet and GDANet by reducing the number of channels in the convolutional layers to obtain 1/n-MDANet and 1/n-GDANet, in which '1/n' indicates that the channel number of each convolutional layer (except the last one) is 1/n of the original one in the DANet.

3.4 Two-Step Network Inference Algorithm

We propose a two-step network inference algorithm, as specified in Algorithm 1, to utilize the estimated mask map on both the input crowd image and the feature maps, thereby improving counting accuracy. In the first step, we feed an image $\boldsymbol{x}$ to the backbone network and the mask branch to obtain only the mask map $M^{e1}(\boldsymbol{x})$, without utilizing the depth information. In the second step, we input the crowd image $\boldsymbol{x}$ processed by $M^{e1}(\boldsymbol{x})$ and the depth feature maps $F^d(\boldsymbol{x})$ produced by the depth feature extractor into our network to obtain the density map $D^e(\boldsymbol{x})$.

Algorithm 1: Two-step Network Inference

Input: Input crowd image $\boldsymbol{x}$
Output: Density map $D^e(\boldsymbol{x})$

```
Feed x into the proposed network (1st step) and obtain the transformed mask
  map M^{e1}(x);
x ← x ⊗ M^{e1}(x);
Feed x into the depth feature extractor and obtain depth feature maps F^d(x);
Feed x and F^d(x) into the proposed network (2nd step) and obtain the density
  map D^e(x).
```

4 Experiments

4.1 Datasets

ShanghaiTech. The ShanghaiTech dataset [27] consists of two parts: Part_A (SHA) and Part_B (SHB). SHA contains 482 crowd images, which represents highly congested scenes. Among them, 300 images are used for training, and the remaining 182 images for testing. Meanwhile, SHB contains 716 images, representing sparsely distributed scenes, among which 400 images are used for training and 316 for testing.

UCF_CC_50. UCF_CC_50 [7] is a small dataset containing 50 gray images with different resolutions.As images in this small-scale dataset are not divided for training and testing, we conduct a five-fold cross-validation as most papers do [1,11,28].

UCF-QNRF. UCF-QNRF [8] is a large and challenging dataset of crowd images, including 1535 images (1201 for training and 334 for testing) with 1.25 million dot annotations.

4.2 Implementation Details

To demonstrate the effectiveness of DAS across var ious baseline networks, we introduce DACAN as an additional network with CAN as the baseline. We initialize the weights of the backbone networks in both DANet and DACAN with VGG-16 pretrained on ImageNet, while the weights of the remaining convolutional layers are initialized with a Gaussian distribution of zero mean and 0.01 standard deviation. We employ Stochastic Gradient Descent (SGD) as the optimizer and maintain a fixed learning rate of 1e-7. In contrast, for 1/n-MDANet and 1/n-GDANet, we initialize the weights of all convolutional layers using a Gaussian distribution of zero mean and 0.01 standard deviation, and train them using Adam optimizer with a fixed learning rate of 1e-4. Regarding data augmentation, we crop a patch with a size of 1/4 of the original image without

Table 1. Comparison of the counting error on four datasets.

Methods	Year	SHA		SHB		UCF_CC_50		UCF-QNRF	
		MAE	RMSE	MAE	RMSE	MAE	RMSE	MAE	RMSE
DECCNet [25]	2019	58.6	101.1	7.1	11.4	–	–	107.9	179.0
DM-Count [22]	2020	61.9	99.6	7.4	11.8	211.0	291.5	85.6	148.3
DUBNet [17]	2020	64.6	106.8	7.7	12.5	243.8	329.3	105.6	180.5
TopoCount [1]	2021	61.2	104.6	7.8	13.7	<u>184.1</u>	258.3	89.0	159.0
UOT [16]	2021	58.1	95.9	**6.5**	**10.2**	–	–	<u>83.3</u>	<u>142.3</u>
GL [21]	2021	61.3	95.4	7.3	11.7	–	–	84.3	147.5
AutoScale [24]	2022	60.5	100.4	6.8	11.3	–	–	87.5	147.8
COMAL [28]	2022	59.6	97.1	7.8	12.4	231.9	333.7	102.1	178.3
ChfL [19]	2022	<u>57.5</u>	94.3	6.9	<u>11.0</u>	–	–	**80.3**	**137.6**
MSFFA [11]	2023	59.5	96.3	<u>6.7</u>	11.6	190.2	263.2	94.6	170.6
DMCNet [23]	2023	58.5	**84.6**	8.6	13.7	–	–	96.5	164.0
CSRNet [10] (baseline)	2018	68.2	115.0	10.6	16.0	266.1	397.5	122.8	213.5
DANet (ours)	–	59.7	94.1	7.2	11.7	209.3	291.0	96.7	169.2
		-12.5%	-18.2%	-32.1%	-26.9%	-21.3%	-26.8%	-21.3%	-20.7%
CAN [14] (baseline)	2019	62.3	100.0	7.8	12.2	212.2	**243.7**	107.0	183.0
DACAN (ours)	–	**57.1**	<u>90.1</u>	7.2	12.1	**181.4**	<u>251.8</u>	91.18	151.2
		-8.3%	-9.9%	-7.7%	-0.8%	-14.5%	+3.3%	-14.8%	-17.4%

overlapping, following the approach used in previous studies [10,27]. Additionally, we adopt random flipping and color jittering techniques.

All the proposed networks are implemented and tested by PyTorch on a workstation with an NVIDIA RTX 3090Ti GPU.

We adopt the Mean Absolute Error (MAE) and Root Mean Square Error (RMSE) as evaluation metrics. Lower metric values indicate better results.

5 Results

5.1 Quantitative Evaluation

We compare the proposed networks with several existing methods using four widely used datasets, and report the experimental results on test sets in Table 1 and Table 2. The best and second-best values are shown in **bold** and <u>underlined</u>, respectively.

For SHA, by using DAS, DANet effectively decreases counting errors, indicated by a reduction of 12.5% in MAE and 18.2% in RMSE, compared with that of the baseline network CSRNet. Meanwhile, DACAN achieves the best MAE and second best RMSE. On SHB, compared with CSRNet, DANet achieves a large reduction of 32.1% in MAE and 26.9% in RMSE, respectively. In addition, DANet and DACAN significantly improved the counting performance on the UCF-QNRF and UCF_CC_50 datasets, compared with their baselins. Moreover, DACAN achieves the lowest MAE of 181.4 on the UCF_CC_50 dataset.

We further compare our methods with several state-of-the-art lightweight models in Table 2. The 1/2-MDANet achieves the lowest RMSE on SHA and the second-lowest MAE and RMSE on SHB among all lightweight networks, while

Table 2. Comparison of the counting error on the ShanghaiTech dataset and number of model parameters.

Methods	Year	SHA		SHB		Params (M)
		MAE	RMSE	MAE	RMSE	
MCNN [27]	2016	110.2	173.2	26.4	41.3	<u>0.13</u>
SANet [2]	2018	<u>67.0</u>	<u>104.5</u>	8.4	13.6	1.39
LCNet [15]	2019	93.3	149.0	15.3	25.2	0.86
SKT [13]	2020	71.5	114.4	**7.5**	**11.7**	1.02
DICNN [6]	2021	84.8	133.7	11.3	17.3	0.80
LSANet [29]	2022	**66.1**	110.2	8.6	13.9	0.20
LigMSANet [9]	2022	76.6	121.4	10.9	17.5	0.63
FPANet [26]	2023	70.9	120.6	8.8	15.5	7.77
1/2-MDANet (ours)	–	67.4	**104.1**	<u>7.6</u>	<u>12.7</u>	0.85
1/4-GDANet (ours)	–	70.9	109.7	8.1	13.4	**0.09**
DANet (teacher model, ours)	–	59.7	94.1	7.2	11.7	24.9

the 1/4-GDANet achieves a counting accuracy preferable over most of the other networks with a minimal number of parameters. Compared to the teacher model DANet, the 1/2-MDANet and 1/4-GDANet significantly reduce the parameters from 24.9M to 0.85M (3.4%) and 0.09M (0.36%), respectively.

5.2 Ablation Study

To verify the effectiveness of the depth-guided attention strategy (DAS), the depth-guided density map, and the two-step network inference algorithm, we utilize CSRNet as the baseline and attempt various combinations of these techniques. As shown in Table 3, each technique helps improve the performance of the counting accuracy, and with all techniques incorporated, DANet significantly reduces the MAE value from 68.2 to 59.7 (12.5%) and the RMSE value from 115.0 to 94.1 (18.2%), compared to the baseline CSRNet. We also perform an experiment to verify the significance of depth information in DAS. Without using depth information, we only use a mask to separate out the crowd region to improve counting accuracy, which decreases the MAE value from 68.2 to 65.1. However, when we use DAS with the baseline CSRNet, the MAE value drops to 62.4, indicating the significant importance of depth information in DAS.

Table 3. Effect of the proposed techniques with a CSRNet baseline on SHA.

Techniques	Combinations					
DAS w/o depth					✓	
DAS	✓	✓		✓		
Depth-guided Density Map	✓	✓	✓			
Two-step Inference	✓					
MAE	59.7	61.2	64.7	62.4	65.1	68.2
RMSE	94.1	97.2	100.7	99.5	105.3	115.0

Table 4 presents the effect of different channel numbers of convolutional layers in MDANet and GDANet on counting accuracy. Compared to MDANet, 1/2-MDANet maintains comparable MAE and RMSE values while reducing the number of parameters by approximately 25%. However, when we further reduce the channel number by half to train a 1/4-MDANet, the MAE and RMSE values increase significantly to 72.1 and 111.8, respectively. Moreover, with a decrease in channel number, the MAE and RMSE values of GDANet show a slight increase. Thus, we consider 1/2-MDANet and 1/4-GDANet to achieve the best trade-off between accuracy and efficiency.

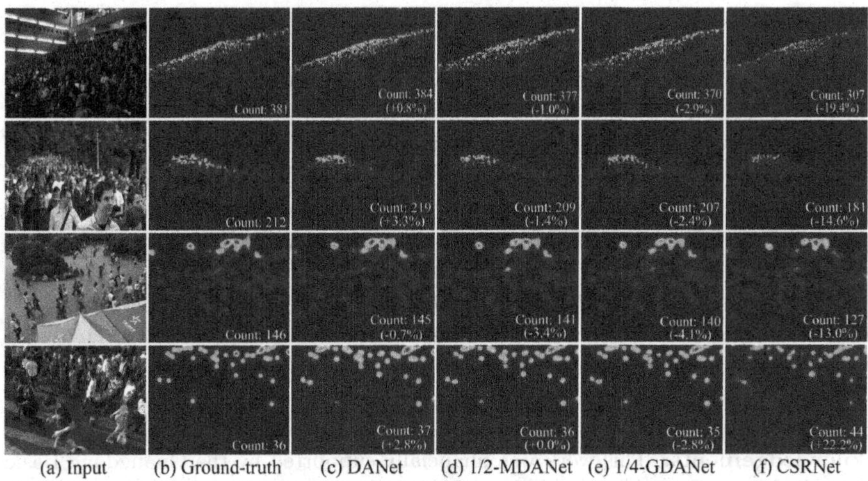

Fig. 2. Comparison of density maps estimated by the proposed networks and CSRNet.

Table 4. Effect of different numbers of channels of each layer in MDANet and GDANet.

Methods	SHA		Params (M)
	MAE	RMSE	
MDANet	66.7	106.3	3.34
1/2-MDANet	67.4	104.1	0.85
1/4-MDANet	72.1	111.8	0.22
GDANet	69.8	109.8	1.41
1/2-GDANet	70.2	112.0	0.36
1/4-GDANet	70.9	109.7	0.09

5.3 Qualitative Results

Figure 2 presents a comparison between the density maps produced by the proposed networks and the baseline network CSRNet. The results indicate that DANet outperforms CSRNet in both dense and sparse crowd scenes, as demonstrated by a higher similarity between our density maps and ground-truth density maps. In addition, the proposed 1/2-MDANet and 1/4-GDANet achieve comparable counting accuracy with a minimal number of parameters. Since the density map estimated by the networks is 1/8 the size of input, we down sample the ground-truth density maps to 1/8 of their original size to ensure better visual contrast.

6 Conclusions

In this paper, we focus on utilizing the crowd depth information to improve crowd counting accuracy. Specifically, we propose a depth-guided attention strategy (DAS), then propose a depth-guided method to generate target density maps. We design DANet and DACAN using different baselines to verify the proposed methods. For a practical consideration, we use knowledge distillation constructing two lightweight networks 1/2-MDANet and 1/4-GDANet. In addition, we propose a two-step network inference algorithm to further decrease counting errors. The quantitative and qualitative comparisons show the superior performance of proposed networks over baselines, highlighting the efficacy of DAS and depth-guided density map. The proposed DAS also could be useful for semantic segmentation and haze removal, which will be explored in our future work.

Acknowledgements. This work was financially supported by the Guangdong Basic and Applied Basic Research Foundation (No. 2022A1515010119) and the National Natural Science Foundation of China (No. 62071201, No. U2031104).

References

1. Abousamra, S., Hoai, M., Samaras, D., Chen, C.: Localization in the crowd with topological constraints. In: AAAI Conference on Artificial Intelligence, vol. 35, pp. 872–881 (2021)
2. Cao, X., Wang, Z., Zhao, Y., Su, F.: Scale aggregation network for accurate and efficient crowd counting. In: European Conference on Computer Vision, pp. 734–750 (2018)
3. Han, K., Wang, Y., Tian, Q., Guo, J., Xu, C., Xu, C.: Ghostnet: more features from cheap operations. In: IEEE Conference on Computer Vision and Pattern Recognition, pp. 1580–1589 (2020)
4. He, K., Zhang, X., Ren, S., Sun, J.: Deep residual learning for image recognition. In: IEEE Conference on Computer Vision and Pattern Recognition, pp. 770–778 (2016)
5. Howard, A.G., et al.: Mobilenets: efficient convolutional neural networks for mobile vision applications. arXiv preprint arXiv:1704.04861 (2017)
6. Hua, C., Xu, K., Tong, T.: Crowd counting with dilated inception convolution. In: International Conference on Computing and Artificial Intelligence, pp. 208–215 (2021)
7. Idrees, H., Saleemi, I., Seibert, C., Shah, M.: Multi-source multi-scale counting in extremely dense crowd images. In: IEEE Conference on Computer Vision and Pattern Recognition, pp. 2547–2554 (2013)
8. Idrees, H., et al.: Composition loss for counting, density map estimation and localization in dense crowds. In: European Conference on Computer Vision, pp. 532–546 (2018)
9. Jiang, G., Wu, R., Huo, Z., Zhao, C., Luo, J.: Ligmsaet: lightweight multi-scale adaptive convolutional neural network for dense crowd counting. Expert Syst. Appl. **197**, 116662 (2022)
10. Li, Y., Zhang, X., Chen, D.: Csrnet: dilated convolutional neural networks for understanding the highly congested scenes. In: IEEE Conference on Computer Vision and Pattern Recognition, pp. 1091–1100 (2018)

11. Li, Z., Lu, S., Dong, Y., Guo, J.: Msffa: a multi-scale feature fusion and attention mechanism network for crowd counting. Visual Comput. **39**(3), 1045–1056 (2023)
12. Lian, D., Li, J., Zheng, J., Luo, W., Gao, S.: Density map regression guided detection network for rgb-d crowd counting and localization. In: IEEE Conference on Computer Vision and Pattern Recognition, pp. 1821–1830 (2019)
13. Liu, L., Chen, J., Wu, H., Chen, T., Li, G., Lin, L.: Efficient crowd counting via structured knowledge transfer. In: ACM International Conference on Multimedia, pp. 2645–2654 (2020)
14. Liu, W., Salzmann, M., Fua, P.: Context-aware crowd counting. In: IEEE Conference on Computer Vision and Pattern Recognition, pp. 5099–5108 (2019)
15. Ma, X., Du, S., Liu, Y.: A lightweight neural network for crowd analysis of images with congested scenes. In: IEEE International Conference on Image Processing, pp. 979–983 (2019)
16. Ma, Z., Wei, X., Hong, X., Lin, H., Qiu, Y., Gong, Y.: Learning to count via unbalanced optimal transport. In: AAAI Conference on Artificial Intelligence, vol. 35, pp. 2319–2327 (2021)
17. Oh, M.h., Olsen, P., Ramamurthy, K.N.: Crowd counting with decomposed uncertainty. In: AAAI Conference on Artificial Intelligence, vol. 34, pp. 11799–11806 (2020)
18. Ranftl, R., Lasinger, K., Hafner, D., Schindler, K., Koltun, V.: Towards robust monocular depth estimation: mixing datasets for zero-shot cross-dataset transfer. IEEE Trans. Pattern Anal. Mach. Intell. **44**, 1623–1637 (2020)
19. Shu, W., Wan, J., Tan, K.C., Kwong, S., Chan, A.B.: Crowd counting in the frequency domain. In: IEEE Conference on Computer Vision and Pattern Recognition, pp. 19618–19627 (2022)
20. Simonyan, K., Zisserman, A.: Very deep convolutional networks for large-scale image recognition. arXiv preprint arXiv:1409.1556 (2014)
21. Wan, J., Liu, Z., Chan, A.B.: A generalized loss function for crowd counting and localization. In: IEEE Conference on Computer Vision and Pattern Recognition, pp. 1974–1983 (2021)
22. Wang, B., Liu, H., Samaras, D., Nguyen, M.H.: Distribution matching for crowd counting. Adv. Neural Inf. Process. Syst. **33**, 1595–1607 (2020)
23. Wang, M., Cai, H., Dai, Y., Gong, M.: Dynamic mixture of counter network for location-agnostic crowd counting. In: Proceedings of the IEEE/CVF Winter Conference on Applications of Computer Vision, pp. 167–177 (2023)
24. Xu, C., et al.: Autoscale: learning to scale for crowd counting. Int. J. Comput. Vision **130**(2), 405–434 (2022)
25. Yang, S.D., Su, H.T., Hsu, W.H., Chen, W.C.: Deccnet: depth enhanced crowd counting. In: IEEE International Conference on Computer Vision Workshops, p. 4521–4530 (2019)
26. , Zhai, W., Gao, M., Li, Q., Jeon, G., Anisetti, M.: Fpanet: feature pyramid attention network for crowd counting. Appl. Intell. 1–18 (2023)
27. Zhang, Y., Zhou, D., Chen, S., Gao, S., Ma, Y.: Single-image crowd counting via multi-column convolutional neural network. In: IEEE Conference on Computer Vision and Pattern Recognition, pp. 589–597 (2016)
28. Zhou, F., et al.: Comal: compositional multi-scale feature enhanced learning for crowd counting. Multimedia Tools Appl., 1–20 (2022)
29. Zhu, F., Yan, H., Chen, X., Li, T.: Real-time crowd counting via lightweight scale-aware network. Neurocomputing **472**, 54–67 (2022)

A Noise Convolution Network for Tampering Detection

Zhiyao Xie[1], Xiaochen Yuan[1(✉)], Chan-Tong Lam[1], and Guoheng Huang[2]

[1] Faculty of Applied Sciences, Macao Polytechnic University, Macau SAR, China
{p2215884,xcyuan,ctlam}@mpu.edu.mo

[2] School of Computer Science and Technology, Guangdong University of Technology, Guangzhou, China
kevinwong@gdut.edu.cn

Abstract. The vulnerability of digital images to tampering is an ongoing information security issue in the multimedia field. Thus, identifying tampered digital images and locating the tampered regions in the images can help improve the security of information dissemination. A deep fusion neural network named NC-Net is designed in this paper, introducing pattern noise as assistance to fully exploit the tampered features present on the tampered image. The incorporation of noise texture information enabled NC-Net to acquire deeper tampered image features during the training phase. The extracted noise is incorporated as a crucial component within the convolutional structure of the model, serving as a potent activation signal for the tampered region. The performance of NC-Net is confirmed through relevant experiments on publicly available tampered datasets, and outstanding results are achieved in comparison to other methods.

Keywords: Tampering Detection · Noise enhancement · Deep Learning · Neural Network

1 Introduction

In the prosperous multimedia era today, digital images are evolved into an indispensable carrier for information dissemination. However, with the rise of increasingly user-friendly image editing software, the integrity and security of digital image information content are becoming increasingly vulnerable to manipulation and misuse. The ease of access to powerful editing tools and the widespread availability of digital images make it increasingly difficult to authenticate the veracity and originality of images, leading to widespread concerns about the accuracy and trustworthiness of visual media. As such, tamper detection techniques become

This work was supported by the Science and Technology Development Fund of Macau SAR (Grant number 0045/2022/A), and the Research project of the Macao Polytechnic University (Project No. RP/FCA-12/2022).

L. Iliadis et al. (Eds.): ICANN 2023, LNCS 14263, pp. 38–48, 2023.
https://doi.org/10.1007/978-3-031-44204-9_4

very important research topics in multimedia security for confirming the authenticity of images. Image forgery can be broadly classified into global forgery and local forgery. Global forgery is a technique that is often used to enhance the quality of an image, such as by increasing the brightness, contrast, or saturation. While this technique can be useful for improving the aesthetics of an image, it can also have drawbacks. One of the biggest disadvantages of global forgery is that it can destroy the unique fingerprint that is generated by the camera hardware and environment when an image is captured. This can make it difficult to determine whether an image has been tampered with, which can be a major challenge for law enforcement and other investigators trying to determine the authenticity of an image. On the other hand, local forgery refers to the alteration of specific regions within an image while leaving other parts unchanged. This technique is often used by malicious individuals to deceive others by creating fake or misleading visual content. In many cases, local forgery is combined with global forgery to try and hide the trace of tampering. The behavior of tampering can vary depending on the intention of the forger and the tools used to manipulate the image. In general, image forgery can be classified into three distinct categories: splicing [5], copy-move [4], and inpainting [21]. Splicing [5] is commonly used to create a composite image that appears to be an original, but in reality, it is made up of different parts that have been stitched together. Copy-move [4] involves copying a specific region of an image and pasting it into another location within the same image and is often used to hide or duplicate objects within an image. Finally, inpainting [21] refers to the process of filling in the gaps left by removing objects from an image. This technique is commonly used to remove unwanted objects from an image or to restore damaged areas. In all three categories, the behavior of tampering is carefully designed to deceive viewers and create a convincing image that appears to be genuine.

In recent years, deep learning-based tampered image analysis techniques emerge as the mainstream approach to coping with this malicious activity. These techniques leverage the power of artificial neural networks and machine learning algorithms to automatically identify and localize areas of an image that are tampered with. Rao et al. [15] proposed an image tampering detection method based on deep learning techniques, which utilizes a steganalysis rich model (SRM) [7] convolutional kernel as a pre-processing initialization layer before ten convolutional layers. The neural network utilized for tampering detection differs significantly from traditional forgery detection methods that rely on semantic content analysis. Instead of looking for changes in the semantic meaning of the image, the neural network focuses on the subtle changes in texture and color that are characteristic of tampered regions. By analyzing the unique texture features and patterns present in the image fingerprint and the destructive effects of tampering on it, tampering detection is highly effective at identifying even the most subtle and sophisticated forgeries. BayarConv2D [2] was proposed in 2018, which effectively suppresses the impact of image semantic content on tampering traces and enables adaptive extraction of image tampering features. The use of local noise features reinforces the distinction between image tampered areas and natural image areas, so deep fusion networks emerge to address the wide variety of image tampering traces. FusionNet [12] was the first actual network to fuse image tampering trace features. It adopts the pre-processing method of splitting the tampered image into patches, which leads to the easy loss of the holistic information of the image, and the model overly focuses on the local transmission of the image. RGB-N [20] supplemented with noise feature streams learns richer tampering track features. Table 1 is a summary of the tamper detection models mentioned above and the structures and techniques they use.

Table 1. Summary of image tampering detection techniques.

Methods	Forensic Clue	Fusion	Structure			Detection Type
			Backbone	Neck	Head	
Rao et al. [15]	+	–	10-Conv	–	FC	Boxes
BayarConv [2]	–	–	5-Conv	–	FC	Boxes
ManTra-Net [17]	+	+	VGG-LSTM	Anomaly	Conv	Objects
BusterNet [16]	–	+	VGG-16	ConcatConv	Conv	Objects
FusionNet [12]	+	+	VGG-16	ConcatConv	Conv	Objects
RGB-N [20]	+	+	VGG-16	RPN	FC	Boxes
Our proposed	+	+	Resnet-C4	Noise-RPN	FC	Boxes

Hence, our contribution is to design a deep neural network model named Noise Convolution Network (NC-Net) that captures the local noise features in the tampered regions of the image. The use of noise features in this paper is not limited to just introducing the loss calculation in the training process like other models, but the noise features are treated as components in the model structure and embedded in the model.

2 Our Methodology

This section presents the framework architecture of NC-Net by leveraging image noise for highlighting abnormal noise traces, scale transformations for finer retention of image tampering information, optional convolution for functioning as a stimulus for the tampering area, and the loss function of how to guide the training.

2.1 The Framework of Proposed Approach

NC-Net enhances the detection of tampering traces by utilizing a noise block that extracts the image texture from the tampered image, enabling the creation of a noise input stream for training. Image noise is a unique characteristic of the image source that represents the quality of camera components used during image acquisition in specific environmental conditions. Recent work utilizes

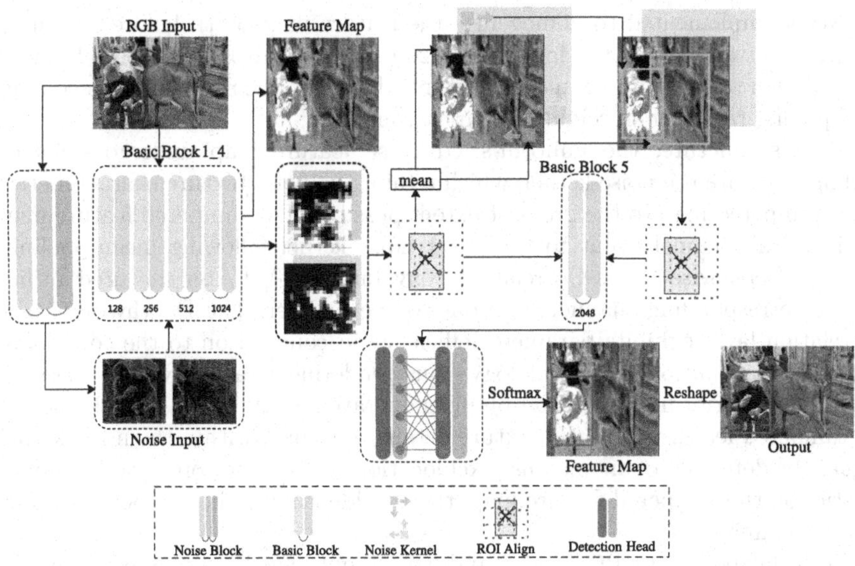

Fig. 1. Flow chart of tampered images detected by NC-Net.

forensic clues of noise in detection [14,19,20]. As a type of texture feature, noise input can provide information about the overall surface properties of a tampered image. A tampered image is usually based on pixel points as a color feature, so the noise input contributes to the RGB input by statistically calculating the regional average feature obtained from multiple pixel points. The high-dimensional feature maps obtained from RGB inputs are rich in semantic information, but tampering with the semantic information in the images is deceptive. If the model relies too much on the semantic content of the image during training, it also shows a bias towards tampered content with semantic logic. This is not consistent with the goal of image tampering detection. The advantage of the regional average feature is to mitigate local bias in the detection. To improve the performance of NC-Net in detecting tampered images, noise features are incorporated into its training process. This is achieved by feeding in the same backbone using the basic block as RGB input, which is processed in a high-dimensional layer with 1024 channels. As shown in Fig. 1, NC-Net is able to better distinguish between relevant tampering information and irrelevant semantic information, which reduces the training bias and improves its ability to accurately detect tampered images.

Despite the size of the manipulated targets in the tampered images, the detection is often supported by the subtle abnormal signals present at the periphery. NC-Net adopts RoI Align [8] to standardize the scaling and reduce information loss in the feature maps caused by pooling. Even though RoI Align [8] was originally intended to standardize the size of proposed boxes on feature maps, it is actually capable of working on feature maps of varying scales. Consequently,

NC-Net is implemented to homogenize the feature maps both before and after the RPN network, resulting in a fixed size of 14×14. RoI Align uses bilinear interpolation to compute virtual pixel points, based on the neighboring incoming pixel points, rather than relying on direct rounding.

At this juncture, the uniform-sized noise feature map undergoes mean-pooling to create the noise kernel, which retains the noise texture characteristics of the tampered map to the greatest extent possible. The tampered feature map has identical channel count to the 1×1 noise kernel following mean-pooling, enabling Depthwise Cross-Correlation convolution [10] to be executed utilizing the corresponding channels in a one-to-one manner. The Depthwise Cross-Correlation layer exhibits parameter efficiency in comparison to the commonly employed convolutional methodology, thus rendering it a lightweight network layer. While performing the pixel-by-pixel operation of the 1×1 noise kernel on the tampered feature map, the texture details contained within the noise kernel trigger the detection of anomalous pixel locations possessing comparable characteristics on the tampered feature map, thereby identifying the tampered regions within the image.

Until this point, the RGB input and noise input have been merged, resulting in the acquisition of an activation feature map through their interoperation. The activated features are utilized by the Region Proposal Network (RPN) to compute the proposal boxes, and its loss function is computed according to the prescribed methodology as follows:

$$L_{RPN}\left(t_i, g_i\right) = \frac{1}{N_{cls}} \sum_i L_{cls}\left(t_i, t_i^*\right) + \lambda \frac{1}{N_{reg}} \sum_i t_i^* L_{reg}\left(g_i, g_i^*\right) \tag{1}$$

where L_{cls} represents the cross entropy loss between the activated features and the ground truth in the RPN, and L_{reg} represents the smooth L_1 loss for regression applied to the proposal boxes. In a forward inference process, each anchor i corresponds to a proposal box that includes a probability t_i of tampering within the region and a probability g_i of four-dimensional box coordinates. The symbols t_i^* and g_i^* donate the positive label and box coordinates derived from the ground truth, respectively. The RPN network utilizes N_{cls} to represent the mini-batch size and N_{reg} to represent the number of anchor locations. To balance the two losses, a hyper-parameter λ is introduced with a value of 10.

During the initial phase of NC-Net, the activated feature map f_a obtained from the output of Basic Block 4 is utilized as the input for the loss function L_{RPN}, whereas the activated feature map f_a^* obtained from the output of Basic Block 5 is utilized as the input for the detection head. Therefore, the composite loss function of NC-Net is the aggregation of the loss incurred by coarse categorization in the RPN network and the loss incurred by precise categorization in the detection head as follows:

$$L_{total} = L_{RPN}\left(f_a\right) + L_{tamper}\left(f_a^*\right) + L_{coordinates}\left(f_a^*\right) \tag{2}$$

By computing the dissimilarity between the detection result from NC-Net and the ground truth, Eq. (2) can reflect the joint probability of detecting the tampered region and the accuracy of the NC-Net in localizing the tampered region.

The parameter L_{tamper} quantifies the likelihood of correctly identifying the tampered area in the final phase detected by the NC-Net. Moreover, the parameter $L_{coordinates}$ represents the precise spatial coordinates of the bounding box that encapsulates the tampered areas in the same phase in NC-Net.

3 Experiments and Evaluations

This section outlines the metrics utilized for assessing the performance of NC-Net in tampering detection. Additionally, it showcases the visual representations of feature maps during detection and the set of detection results, and conducts a comprehensive performance analysis of NC-Net in comparison to other state-of-the-art models using a unified evaluation system. The contributions of NC-Net to tampering detection are demonstrated comprehensively from multiple perspectives.

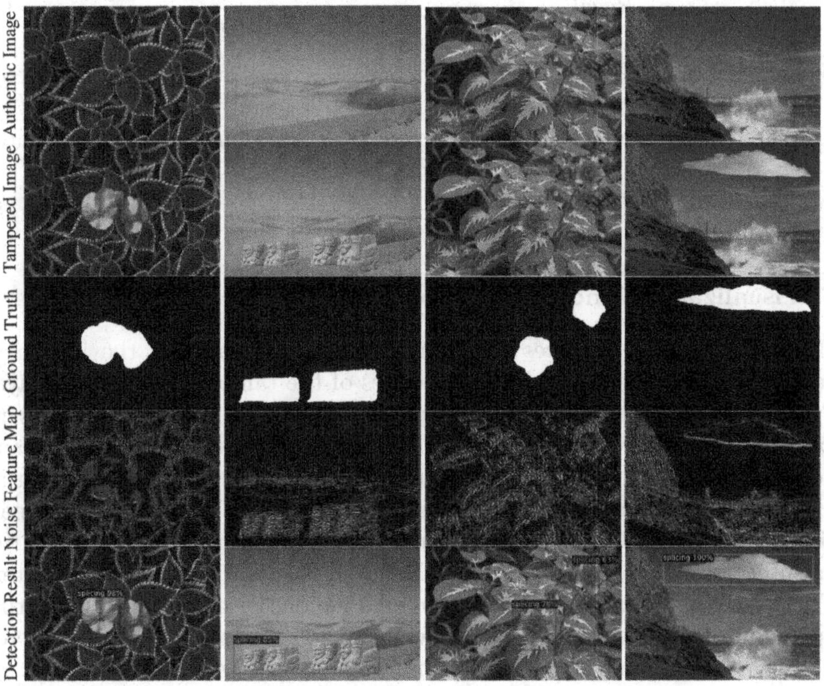

Fig. 2. Noise enhancement feature map used in NC-Net for tampering detection.

3.1 Evaluation Metric

In tampering detection, the term *TruePositives* refers to the accurate identification of the manipulated region. When calculate *TruePositives* involves determining the ratio between the area of the detected bounding box and the area of the smallest ground truth box of more than 75%. Thus, by calculating the proportion of correctly identified tampered regions to the total number of detected results, the precision of tampered regions can be determined as:

$$Precision_{tamper} = \frac{TruePositives}{AllDetections} \tag{3}$$

Recall also known as sensitivity or the rate of *TruePositives*, measures the ability of the model to identify the manipulated region. Therefore, following the ratio between the number of *TruePositives* and the number of tampered regions in the ground truth, the recall of tampered regions can be defined as:

$$Recall_{tamper} = \frac{TruePositives}{AllGround - Truths} \tag{4}$$

The F1 score takes both metrics into account and provides a single score that balances the trade-off between precision and recall. According to Eq. (3) and Eq. (4), the F1 score is the harmonic mean of precision and recall calculated as:

$$F1_{tamper} = \frac{2 * Precision * Recall}{Precision + Recall} \tag{5}$$

3.2 Visualizations and Comparisons

NC-Net utilizes noise features to amplify tampering traces in the image, as demonstrated by the enhanced noise features of the tampered region displayed in Fig. 2. The second row of Fig. 2 displays a tampered image that bears no visible discrepancies from the original image in the first row. Moreover, the tampered image aligns with the underlying semantic logic, further camouflaging its manipulation. The tampered image exhibits noise texture that is readily apparent in the corresponding noise feature map displayed in the fourth row. After being subjected to enhancement by NC-Net, a distinct variance in the noise texture between the tampered and non-tampered regions is conspicuous, indicating the potency of NC-Net in effectively demarcating manipulated and unaltered sections within the image. In the second column in Fig. 2, the noise feature map demonstrates the intensification effect on the tampered area when its color resembles that of the background. The noise feature map in the third column illustrates the enhancement of tampered regions when multiple alterations are present on the image. Lastly, the final column highlights the abnormal edge noise detected in the tampered region.

The visualization outcomes of NC-Net for tampering detection are illustrated in Fig. 3. The results of identifying tampering regions with small objects can be seen in the first three rows, whereas the middle three rows demonstrate the

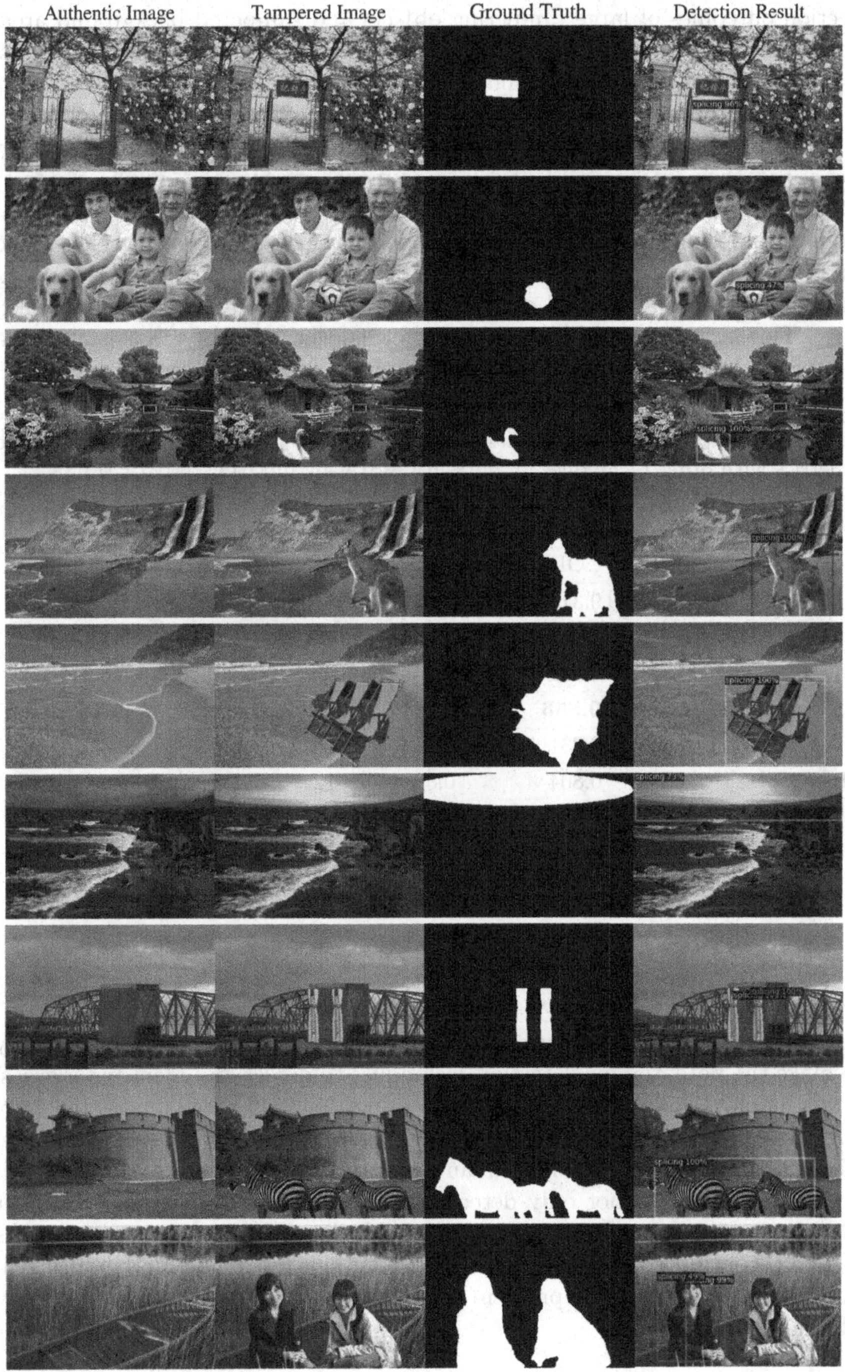

Fig. 3. The detection result outcomes of NC-Net for various categories of tampered image.

detection outcomes of large tampering objects and tampered background area. Additionally, the last three rows display the results of detecting multiple objects, where it is evident that adhered multiple objects are detected as a single object, while separated multiple objects are identified individually.

Table 2 displays the results of benchmarking NC-Net against various cutting-edge approaches, utilizing identical assessment criteria and public datasets CASIA [6] and COLUMBIA [13]. ELA [9] and ADQ [11] are the classic traditional tampering detection algorithms, and the rest are deep learning-based tampering detection models. NC-Net exhibits remarkable superiority in identifying tampering, as almost all of its metrics achieve the highest level of performance. This suggests that NC-Net outperforms other methods in this area and can be considered a highly effective solution for tampering detection.

Table 2. Evaluation and comparison of NC-Net performance by Precision, Recall and F1 metrics with other techniques on dataset CASIA [6] and COLUMBIA [13].

Methods	Precision		Recall		F1	
	CASIA	COLUMBIA	CASIA	COLUMBIA	CASIA	COLUMBIA
ELA [9]	0.086	0.316	0.975	0.961	0.158	0.475
ADQ [11]	0.402	0.367	0.585	**0.998**	0.476	0.536
RGB-N [20]	0.591	0.693	0.548	0.707	0.408	0.697
ManTra-Net [17]	0.821	**0.856**	0.793	0.849	0.692	0.709
LSTM [1]	0.802	0.831	0.783	0.816	0.792	0.823
C2R-CNN [18]	0.581	0.804	0.808	0.612	0.676	0.695
MVSS-Net [3]	–	–	–	–	0.752	0.802
Our proposed	**0.824**	0.802	**0.905**	0.911	**0.845**	**0.839**

4 Conclusion

While digital tools make it easier than ever before to manipulate images, they also make the potential for detection techniques to detect and identify forgeries. NC-Net employs an innovative approach to identifying doctored images by leveraging the hidden feature traces that exist deep within their makeup. These traces, which are imperceptible to the human eye, are readily discernible to NC-Net, allowing the model to not only detect but also enhance and acquire a deeper understanding of these elusive features through the process of deep learning. As technology continues to advance, it is likely that new techniques and models will be developed to combat the problem of image forgery and protect the integrity of digital images.

Acknowledgment. This work was supported by the Science and Technology Development Fund of Macau SAR (grant number 0045/2022/A), and the Research project of the Macao Polytechnic University (Project No. RP/FCA-12/2022).

References

1. Bappy, J.H., Simons, C., Nataraj, L., Manjunath, B.S., Roy-Chowdhury, A.K.: Hybrid LSTM and encoder-decoder architecture for detection of image forgeries. IEEE Trans. Image Process. **28**(7), 3286–3300 (2019). https://doi.org/10.1109/TIP.2019.2895466
2. Bayar, B., Stamm, M.C.: Constrained convolutional neural networks: a new approach towards general purpose image manipulation detection. IEEE Trans. Inf. Forensics Secur. **13**(11), 2691–2706 (2018). https://doi.org/10.1109/TIFS.2018.2825953
3. Chen, X., Dong, C., Ji, J., Cao, J., Li, X.: Image manipulation detection by multi-view multi-scale supervision. In: Proceedings of the IEEE/CVF International Conference on Computer Vision, pp. 14185–14193 (2021)
4. Cozzolino, D., Poggi, G., Verdoliva, L.: Efficient dense-field copy-move forgery detection. IEEE Trans. Inf. Forensics Secur. **10**(11), 2284–2297 (2015)
5. Cozzolino, D., Poggi, G., Verdoliva, L.: Splicebuster: a new blind image splicing detector. In: 2015 IEEE International Workshop on Information Forensics and Security (WIFS), pp. 1–6. IEEE (2015)
6. Dong, J., Wang, W., Tan, T.: Casia image tampering detection evaluation database. In: 2013 IEEE China Summit and International Conference on Signal and Information Processing, pp. 422–426 (2013). https://doi.org/10.1109/ChinaSIP.2013.6625374
7. Fridrich, J., Kodovsky, J.: Rich models for steganalysis of digital images. IEEE Trans. Inf. Forensics Secur. **7**(3), 868–882 (2012)
8. He, K., Gkioxari, G., Dollar, P., Girshick, R.: Mask r-cnn. In: Proceedings of the IEEE International Conference on Computer Vision (ICCV) (2017)
9. Krawetz, N., Solutions, H.F.: A picture's worth. Hacker Fact. Solut. **6**(2), 2 (2007)
10. Li, B., Wu, W., Wang, Q., Zhang, F., Xing, J., Yan, J.: Siamrpn++: evolution of siamese visual tracking with very deep networks. In: Proceedings of the IEEE/CVF Conference on Computer Vision and Pattern Recognition (CVPR) (2019)
11. Lin, Z., He, J., Tang, X., Tang, C.K.: Fast, automatic and fine-grained tampered jpeg image detection via dct coefficient analysis. Pattern Recogn. **42**(11), 2492–2501 (2009)
12. Liu, B., Pun, C.M.: Deep fusion network for splicing forgery localization. In: Proceedings of the European Conference on Computer Vision (ECCV) Workshops (2018)
13. Ng, T.T., Hsu, J., Chang, S.F.: Columbia image splicing detection evaluation dataset. DVMM lab. Columbia Univ CalPhotos Digit Libr (2009)
14. Pan, X., Zhang, X., Lyu, S.: Exposing image splicing with inconsistent local noise variances. In: 2012 IEEE International Conference on Computational Photography (ICCP), pp. 1–10. IEEE (2012)
15. Rao, Y., Ni, J.: A deep learning approach to detection of splicing and copy-move forgeries in images. In: 2016 IEEE International Workshop on Information Forensics and Security (WIFS), pp. 1–6 (2016). https://doi.org/10.1109/WIFS.2016.7823911
16. Wu, Y., Abd-Almageed, W., Natarajan, P.: Busternet: detecting copy-move image forgery with source/target localization. In: Proceedings of the European Conference on Computer Vision (ECCV) (2018)

17. Wu, Y., AbdAlmageed, W., Natarajan, P.: Mantra-net: manipulation tracing network for detection and localization of image forgeries with anomalous features. In: Proceedings of the IEEE/CVF Conference on Computer Vision and Pattern Recognition (CVPR) (2019)
18. Xiao, B., Wei, Y., Bi, X., Li, W., Ma, J.: Image splicing forgery detection combining coarse to refined convolutional neural network and adaptive clustering. Inf. Sci. **511**, 172–191 (2020)
19. Zhou, P., Han, X., Morariu, V.I., Davis, L.S.: Two-stream neural networks for tampered face detection. In: 2017 IEEE Conference on Computer Vision and Pattern Recognition Workshops (CVPRW), pp. 1831–1839. IEEE (2017)
20. Zhou, P., Han, X., Morariu, V.I., Davis, L.S.: Learning rich features for image manipulation detection. In: Proceedings of the IEEE Conference on Computer Vision and Pattern Recognition (CVPR) (2018)
21. Zhu, X., Qian, Y., Zhao, X., Sun, B., Sun, Y.: A deep learning approach to patch-based image inpainting forensics. Signal Process. Image Commun. **67**, 90–99 (2018)

Attention-Based Feature Interaction Deep Factorization Machine for CTR Prediction

Peilin Yang[1,2], Yongliang Han[1,2], Yingyuan Xiao[1,2(✉)], and Wenguang Zheng[1,2]

[1] Engineering Research Center of Learning-Based Intelligent System, Tianjin University of Technology, Tianjin, China
yyxiao@tjut.edu.cn

[2] Tianjin Key Laboratory of Intelligence Computing and Novel Software Technology, Tianjin University of Technology, Tianjin, China

Abstract. Click-Through Rate (CTR) prediction is widely used in many fields, such as web search, recommender systems, etc. Recently, the CTR prediction model using deep learning and attention mechanism technology has achieved remarkable success. However, there are some problems with previous work: (1) Most of the previous works usually consider the significance of features statically, which is not conducive to building personalized recommender systems. (2) Most of the previous works usually used shallow interaction, which was not enough to fully fit each feature to produce better prediction performance. In this paper, a novel model named Attention-based Feature Interaction Deep Factorization Machine (AFI-DeepFM) is proposed for learning more useful features and more comprehensive and rich feature interactions. Specifically, the AFI-DeepFM leverages the convolutional squeeze network to extract the feature information to better dynamically learn more useful features. Besides, the model can also effectively capture the interaction between features using the Kronecker product method. Extensive experiments conducted on the two public datasets demonstrate that the AFI-DeepFM is productive and outperforms the baseline models.

Keywords: Click-through rate · Convolutional squeeze excitation network · Feature interaction · Multilayer perceptron

1 Introduction

CTR prediction is one of the key technologies for promoting business, which uses interaction data between users and advertisements to predict whether users will click on advertisements. The research on CTR prediction is of great significance as it can increase advertising revenue. Many models have been used to CTR prediction, including Field-aware Factorization Machine (FFM) [1] and others. Recently, deep learning based models [2–8, 18, 19] have attracted attention due to

L. Iliadis et al. (Eds.): ICANN 2023, LNCS 14263, pp. 49–60, 2023.
https://doi.org/10.1007/978-3-031-44204-9_5

their high fitting ability. In addition, some models [9–13] use attention networks to dynamically learn more comprehensive and rich feature interactions, thereby improving prediction accuracy. It can be seen that CTR prediction based on neural network has become a research trend.

The present works have been improved, but still faces the some difficulties:

- As far as we know, the features are not isolated, but they are related. For example, when we predict user income, the feature "occupation" is more useful than feature "gender", but the feature "occupation" is largely affected by feature "gender". However, most of the works can not sort out the relationship between the features according to the corresponding scenes.
- Many related works usually use simple methods to calculate feature interactions, such as Hadamard product and inner product. these shallow interaction is not enough to make the features fully fit.

Due to these problems, we put forward a novel model named AFI-DeepFM as an abbreviation for Attention-based Feature Interaction Deep Factorization Machine. Convolutional Squeeze Excitation Network (CSENet) leverages the convolutional squeeze network to capture the connections between features and extract effective feature information, and then applies an excitation network to learn more useful features. Besides, we adopt a new fine-grained method called Kronecker product to calculate feature interactions, which captures embedding dimension correlation more effectively.

The following are the main contributions:

- We propose a novel model named Attention-based Feature Interaction Deep Factorization Machine (AFI-DeepFM), which can learn more useful features and more comprehensive and rich feature interactions. Besides, neural factorization machines can capture nonlinear feature interactions.
- We propose Convolutional Squeeze Excitation Network (CSENet), which serves as an enhanced version of the attention network to better dynamically learn more useful features.
- We adopt a novel interactive way-Kronecker product. Compared with the traditional interactive mode, this method can bring more abundant interactive effects.
- After extensive experimentation, we find that our AFI-DeepFM model outperformed other baseline models on two public datasets.

2 Related Work

We focus on some models that have already exist in CTR prediction. Some of them focus on feature-level interactions between different features, some on the Attention-based feature model.

2.1 Feature-Level Interaction

The xDeepFM [2] is a model that combines explicit and implicit feature interactions. It uses compressed Interaction Network (CIN) to improve the interaction effect. The Operational-aware Neural Network (ONN) [6] combines with FFM model [1] can significantly improve the prediction accuracy. The Feature Generation by Convolutional Neural Network (FGCNN) [3] applies CNN for feature extraction to generate new special features. Co-Action Network(CAN) [16] is used to learn the interaction of explicit pairwise vectors without introducing too many redundant parameters. To increase prediction accuracy, Deep User Match Network(DUMN) [17] adds item behavior to the model to explore the connections between target users and comparable users.

Although the CTR model based on deep learning can improve prediction accuracy, it does not consider the fact that feature interaction has different influence on the prediction value.

2.2 Attention-Based Model

Attention-based models have developed rapidly and have been widely adopted in natural language processing, image detection and other fields and achieve remarkable results. Therefore, attention mechanism has been introduced into CTR field. The FiBiNET [9] uses the Squeeze-Excitation Network to generate embedding with feature importance. The AutoInt [10] utilizes multiple layers of self-attention to capture the interaction between features. The CTR model based on attention that can filter out useful features. By interacting with users and timestamps, deep-representational item network (DRINK) [20] is constructed to represent a series of candidate item information. To dynamically model the characteristics of items, the author proposes a transformer-based multi-representational item network. These features are input into the MLP layer for processing to generate accurate prediction rating. However, most of existing works can not sort out the relationship between the features according to the specific situations.

Based on these observations, inspired by AutoInt [10], FwFM [4], and FGCNN [3], we design the Attention-based Feature Interaction Deep Factorization Machine (AFI-DeepFM) model, which can solve the above problems well.

3 The Proposed Model

This section introduces the architecture of AFI-DeepFM, as shown in Fig. 1. It includes input and embedding layer, the Convolutional Squeeze Excitation Network (CSENet) layer, the interaction layer, Multilayer Perceptron (MLP) layer and the prediction layer. Through the input and embedding layer, the features are transformed into dense embedding features, which provides a basis for subsequent processing. The CSENet layer dynamically learn feature importance. The interaction layer effectively learns the feature second-order interactions. The MLP layer obtains the feature high-order interactions. The prediction layer makes the final prediction.

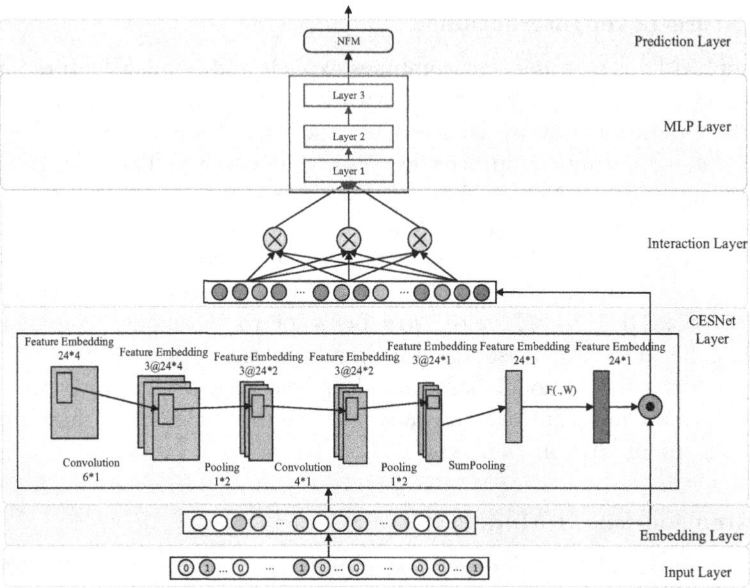

Fig. 1. The architecture of AFI-DeepFM.

3.1 Input and Embedding Layer

CTR models based on deep learning, such as xDeepFM [2], often use sparse inputs and embedding layers. Due to the use of one-hot encoding in the raw input features, the input features become very sparse and high-dimensional. To deal with the problem, the embedding layer outputs a concatenated feature embedding vector $E = [e_1, e_2, .., e_i, ..., e_n]$, where $e_i \in R^D$ represents the embedding vector of the i-th feature, n represents the number of features, while D represents the dimension of the embedding layer.

3.2 Convolutional Squeeze Excitation Network Layer

The purpose of CSENet is to learn more useful features. It can be seen from Fig. 1 that the CSENet layer involves three parts: convolutional squeeze part, excitation part, and re-embedding part. The traditional attention network does not explore the deeper connection between features, such as FiBiNET [9]. Therefore, we first employ the convolutional squeeze network to capture the deep connections between features and extract feature information, and then learn more useful features via the excitation network, and finally reconstruct the embedding vector of each feature.

Convolutional Squeeze Part. We represent each instance as an embedding matrix $E \in R^{n*D}$ and shape it into $I^1 \in R^{n*D*1}$, which is used as the input matrix of the first convolution layer to facilitate the subsequent operation. To explore the relationship between the features, a convolutional layer is obtained by convolving a matrix $W^1 \in R^{k^1*1*1*f^1}$ with *tanh* activation functions. The output of the convolution layer is $O^1 \in R^{n*D*f^1}$, The convolution layer formula is expressed as follows:

$$O^1_{r,c,j} = tanh(\sum_{k=1}^{k^1} I^1_{r+k-1,c,1} W^1_{k,1,1,j}) \tag{1}$$

where $O^1_{:,:,j}$ denotes the j-th filter in the first convolutional layer, r,c are the row and column index of the j-th filter.

After the convolution layer, the max-pooling operation is then adopted to reduce the embedding size. We set q as the width of the pooling layer while the length is 1. The output of the first pooling operation is $S^1 \in R^{n*(D/q)*f^1}$:

$$S^1_{r,c,j} = max(O^1_{r,c*q,j}, ..., O^1_{r,c*q-q+1,j}) \tag{2}$$

where $S^1_{:,:,j}$ denotes the j-th filter in the max-pooling layer. Note that $I^{i+1} = S^i$.

Excitation Part. The result of the convolutional squeeze part is $S \in R^n$:

$$S_{n,1} = \sum_{j=1}^{f^m} S^m_{n,1,j} \tag{3}$$

where $S^m_{n,1,j}$ denotes the j-th filter of the m-th pooling operation. We adopt the excitation network [14] to estimate the significance of the features based on the static vector S. Formally, the importance of features is calculated as below:

$$A = F(S) \ = ReLU(W_2 ReLU(W_1 S)) \tag{4}$$

where $A \in R^n$, the learning parameters are $W_1 \in R^{n*(n/t)}$,$W_2 \in R^{(n/t)*n}$, and t is reduction ration.

Re-Embedding Part. The last step in CSENet is to reconstruct the embedding vector. It does feature-wise multiplication between the original feature embedding E and feature importance vector A and outputs the new embedding $V = [v_1, ..., v_i, ..., v_n]$. The new embedding V formula is as follows:

$$V \ = \ [a_1 * e_1, \ldots, a_i * e_i, \ldots, a_n * e_n] \ = \ [v_1, \ldots, v_i, \ldots, v_n] \tag{5}$$

3.3 Interaction Layer

The goal of the interaction layer is to achieve higher-order interaction of features and perform calculations on this basis. We adopt a completely new method - Kronecker product, to calculate the interaction between features. Compared to traditional methods, Kronecker product matrices are more effective in capturing dimensional correlations, while traditional methods assume that the embedding dimensions are independent. This new method can achieve better data modeling effect. The Kronecker product matrix M_{ij} and interaction results p_{ij} are as follows:

$$M_{ij} = v_i \otimes v_j \tag{6}$$

$$p_{ij} = \sum_{i=1}^{D} \sum_{j=1}^{D} M_{ij} W_{ij} \tag{7}$$

where W_{ij} represents the parameter matrix of Kronecker product matrix M_{ij}, D represents the embedding dimension, and the corresponding positions of W_{ij} and M_{ij} are multiplied and added to obtain the final interaction result. From the Kronecker product matrix M_{ij}, we can find that the Kronecker product has a deeper degree of interaction, each embedding dimension of the feature has a pairwise interaction.

3.4 Prediction Layer

Inspired by [15], we use Neural Factorization Machine (NFM) to learn deeper feature interactions. The specific formula is as follows:

$$f(z) = \frac{1}{2} \left[\left(\sum_{j=1}^{|z|} z_j v_j \right)^2 - \left(\sum_{k}^{|z|} z_k v_k \right)^2 \right] \tag{8}$$

$$\Gamma(f(z)) = h^T \delta_L \left(W_L \left(\cdots \delta_1 \left(W_n f(z) + b_n \right) \cdots \right) + b_L \right) \tag{9}$$

$$\hat{y} = m_0 + \sum_{j=1}^{|z|} m_j z_j + \Gamma(f(z)) \tag{10}$$

where $\hat{y}$ represents the predicted value, z denotes the input, m_o and m_j denote the global deviation and the coefficient of the potential feature respectively. $z_j, z_k \in z$ are the corresponding vectors, $v_j, v_k \in R^s$ denote the embedding vectors. In addition, the model learned parameters include $\theta = \{W_L, h, b_L\}$ and s denotes the embedding dimension. δ_L refers to the $ReLU$.

CTR prediction generally uses cross entropy as the loss function, the specific formula is as follows:

$$loss = -\frac{1}{T} \sum_{i=1}^{T} (y_i log(\hat{y}_i) + (1 - y_i) * log(1 - \hat{y}_i)) \tag{11}$$

where T is the total number of instances.

4 Experiments

4.1 Experimental Setup

Datasets. Avazu: Initially, the Avazu dataset was used in the Kaggle competition. The dataset contains 24 fields, each instance has a label with a value of 0 or 1. In order to carry out the experiment, we randomly select 1 million instances and split them into training sets and test sets according to the ratio of 80%:20%.

Criteo: Many CTR models are evaluated using Criteo dataset. We select 26 discrete features and carried out experiments. To ensure the validity of the experiment, we randomly select 0.6 million instances and split them into training sets and test sets according to the ratio of 80%:20%.

Evaluation Metrics. AUC: The commonly used evaluation index in classification problem is the area under ROC Curve. The range of AUC value is between 0 and 1.

Baseline Methods. To evaluate the performance of the proposed AFI-DeepFM, we compare it with six baseline CTR approaches, **xDeepFM** [2], **FiBiNET** [9], **ONN** [6], **AutoInt** [10], **FwFM** [4], **FGCNN** [3].

Implementation Details. All models are implemented using TensorFlow framework. The embedding vector dimension of the embedding layer is 8. We adopt Adam optimization method [14], and the learning rate is 0.0001, set the minimum batch size of 256 for Avazu and Criteo datasets. For all models with MLP modules, we set the network layer to 2. In AFI-DeepFM, the number of convolutional layers is 2, the convolution kernel size is (6, 1) and (4, 1) respectively, the pooling layer size is (1, 3), and the reduction rate is 3.

4.2 Performance Comparison

Next, we compare the AFI-DeeFM with the models in the baseline algorithms, the specific data are shown in Table 1.

- AFI-DeepFM achieves the best results over the baseline methods. AFI-DeepFM outperforms FGCNN by 0.99% and 8.83% in terms of log loss (0.17% and 3.41% in terms of AUC) and outperforms AtuoInt by 1.32% and 6.89% in terms of log loss (0.09% and 3.16% in term of AUC) on the Avazu and Criteo datasets.
- The AFI-DeepFM successfully reached its forecast target. Compared to the FGCNN model, AFI-DeepFM has a 0.17% increase in AUC on the Avazu, indicating that the importance of the features must be considered. Compared to the FiBiNET model, AFI-DeepFM has a 0.15% increase in AUC on the Avazu, which shows that CSENet's ability to learn more useful features is

Table 1. Comparison between the proposed model with baselines.

Model	Avazu		Criteo	
	Logloss	AUC	Logloss	AUC
xDeepFM	0.398	0.7545	0.5542	0.7159
FwFM	0.3987	0.7544	0.579	0.7041
ONN	0.4176	0.7437	0.6179	0.7064
FGCNN	0.3911	0.7548	0.5788	0.7127
FiBiNET	0.3998	0.755	0.5997	0.6889
AutoInt	0.3944	0.7555	0.5594	0.7052
AFI-DeepFM	**0.3812**	**0.7565**	**0.4905**	**0.7468**

stronger than the traditional attention network. Compared to the AutoInt model, AFI-DeepFM has a 0.1% increase in AUC on the Avazu, which shows that it is significant to consider the connections between features.

- The AFI-DeepFM is more sensitive to discrete data. We can see that the performance of AFI-DeepFM on the Avazu dataset is more stable than that on the Criteo dataset. We believe that we discarded the continuous data in the Criteo dataset during the data preprocessing process.

4.3 Comparison of Different Interaction Methods

We research the impact of different interaction methods on the interaction layer. The AFI-DeepFM-I represents the use of the inner product method, AFI-DeepFM-H represents the use of the Hadamard product method, AFI-DeepFM-B represents the use of the bilinear interaction method, and AFI-DeepFM-K represents the use of the Kronecker product method. The different performances are shown in Table 2.

Table 2. the performance of different interaction methods.

Model	Avazu		Criteo	
	Logloss	AUC	Logloss	AUC
AFI-DeepFM-I	0.3822	0.7550	0.4920	0.7448
AFI-DeepFM-H	0.3815	0.7561	0.4916	0.7452
AFI-DeepFM-B	0.3814	0.7562	0.4914	0.7454
AFI-DeepFM-K	**0.3812**	**0.7565**	**0.4905**	**0.7468**

- Kronecker product has the best performance than the commonly used conventional method. The AFI-DeepFM-K outperforms AFI-DeepFM-B by 0.02% and 0.09% in terms of log loss (0.03% and 0.14% in terms of AUC) on the Avazu and Criteo datasets.

- Compared with the Hadamard product and inner product, the Kronecker product can get a better interaction effect. The AFI-DeepFM-K outperforms AFI-DeepFM-I by 0.1% in terms of AUC and outperforms AFI-DeepFM-H by 0.04% in terms of AUC on the Avazu. Therefore, we conclude that Kronecker product interaction is more subtle and more suitable for feature interactions.

4.4 Hyper-parameter Tuning

The model is studied with superparameter. We try to adjust the following super-parameters: 1) Embedding dimensions; 2) Neuron numbers in each laye of MLP; 3) The number of MLP layers. It should be noted that by default, our network parameters are as described in Sect. 4.

Table 3. The performance of different embedding dimensions.

Embedding dimensions	Avazu		Criteo	
	Logloss	AUC	Logloss	AUC
4	0.3813	0.7562	0.4912	0.7457
6	0.3815	0.7562	0.4911	0.7458
8	**0.3812**	**0.7565**	**0.4905**	**0.7468**
10	0.3813	0.7563	0.4915	0.7455
12	0.3815	0.7562	0.4913	0.7456
16	0.3812	0.7563	0.4913	0.7455

Embedding Part. On Avazu and Criteo datasets, we conducted experiments on embedding vector dimension, and adjusted it from 4 to 16. The results are shown in Table 3.

- AFI-DeepFM performs best when the embedding vector dimension is 8. Interestingly, we also find that the change of embedding vector dimension has little effect on the model performance. After analysis, we guess that it may be because the selected dimensions have small differences and cannot reflect the impact of embedded vector dimensions on performance.

MLP Part. We research the effect of different neuron numbers in each layer and different MLP layers. Some observations are as follows:

- We can see that as the number of MLP layers and the neuron numbers in each laye increase, the performance of the AFI-DeepFM model on the Avazu and Criteo datasets does not vary linearly. We believe that this is caused by the overfitting of the neural network itself.

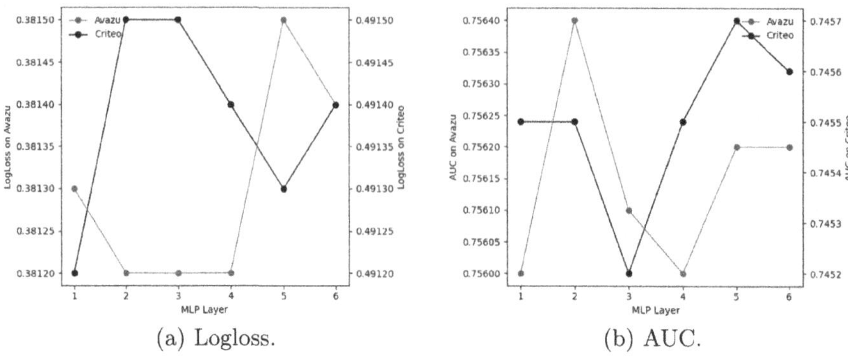

(a) Logloss. (b) AUC.

Fig. 2. Effect of different MLP layers on performance.

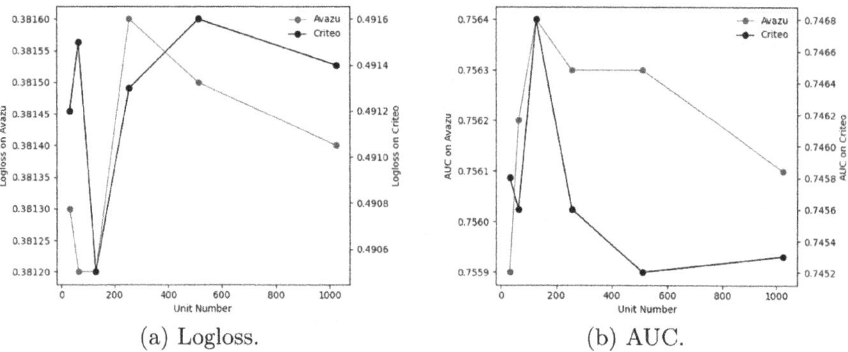

(a) Logloss. (b) AUC.

Fig. 3. Effect of different neuron numbers in each layer of MLP on performance.

- We can find that as the number of MLP layers increases, the fluctuation of the log loss of the AFI-DeepFM model is gentler than the change of the AUC in Fig. 2. Hence, we conclude that the AUC indicator is more sensitive to data and more suitable for the field of CTR prediction. When the number of MLP layers is 2, AFI-DeepFM's log loss and AUC are both optimal on the Avazu and Criteo.
- We figure out that as the number of neuron units increases, the performance of AFI-DeepFM fluctuates significantly, as seen in Fig. 3. Therefore, we state that neuron numbers in each layer affects the performance of the model more than the number of layers. When the neuron numbers in each layer is 128, the log loss and AUC of the AFI-DeepFM are both optimal on the Avazu and Criteo.

5 Conclusion

In response to the shortcomings of current models, we propose a new model called Attention-Based Feature Interaction Deep Factorization Machine (AFI-

DeepFM), aimed at learning more useful features and more comprehensive and rich feature interactions. The AFI-DeepFM utilizes convolutional squeeze excitation network (CSNet) to learn more useful features. The CSENet captures the connections between features by applying convolutional squeeze network, and then learns more useful features using excitation networks to extract feature information. The introduction of convolutional squeeze network enhances the ability of excitation networks to learn more useful features. The AFI-DeepFM uses Kronecker product method to model feature interaction. Kronecker product fully explores the relationship between feature embedding vectors, making feature interactions more delicate and perfect.

Acknowledgements. This work is supported by Tianjin "Project + Team" Key Training Project under Grant No. XC202022.

References

1. Juan, Y., Lefortier, D., Chapelle, O.: Field-aware factorization machines in a real-world online advertising system. In: Proceedings of the 26th International Conference on World Wide Web Companion, pp. 680–688 (2017)
2. Lian, J., Zhou, X., Zhang, F., Chen, Z., Xie, X., Sun, G.: Xdeepfm: combining explicit and implicit feature interactions for recommender systems. In: Proceedings of the 24th ACM SIGKDD International Conference on Knowledge Discovery & Data Mining, pp. 1754–1763 (2018)
3. Liu, B., Tang, R., Chen, Y., Yu, J., Guo, H., Zhang, Y.: Feature generation by convolutional neural network for click-through rate prediction. In: The World Wide Web Conference, pp. 1119–1129 (2019)
4. Pan, J., et al.: Field-weighted factorization machines for click-through rate prediction in display advertising. In: Proceedings of the 2018 World Wide Web Conference, pp. 1349–1357 (2018)
5. Chen, W., Zhan, L., Ci, Y., Yang, M., Lin, C., Liu, D.: FLEN: leveraging field for scalable CTR prediction. arXiv preprint arXiv:1911.04690 (2019)
6. Yang, Y., Xu, B., Shen, S., Shen, F., Zhao, J.: Operation-aware neural networks for user response prediction. Neural Netw. **121**, 161–168 (2020)
7. Guo, W., Tang, R., Guo, H., Han, J., Yang, W., Zhang, Y.: Order-aware embedding neural network for CTR prediction. In: Proceedings of the 42nd International ACM SIGIR Conference on Research and Development in Information Retrieval, pp. 1121–1124 (2019)
8. Du, X., He, X., Yuan, F., Tang, J., Qin, Z., Chua, T.S.: Modeling embedding dimension correlations via convolutional neural collaborative filtering. ACM Trans. Inf. Syst. (TOIS) **37**(4), 1–22 (2019)
9. Huang, T., Zhang, Z., Zhang, J.: Fibinet: combining feature importance and bilinear feature interaction for click-through rate prediction. In: Proceedings of the 13th ACM Conference on Recommender Systems, pp. 169–177 (2019)
10. Song, W., et al.: Autoint: automatic feature interaction learning via self-attentive neural networks. In: Proceedings of the 28th ACM International Conference on Information and Knowledge Management, pp. 1161–1170 (2019)
11. Hong, F., Huang, D., Chen, G.: Interaction-aware factorization machines for recommender systems. In: Proceedings of the AAAI Conference on Artificial Intelligence, vol. 33, pp. 3804–3811 (2019)

12. Zhou, G., et al.: Deep interest evolution network for click-through rate prediction. In: Proceedings of the AAAI Conference on Artificial Intelligence, vol. 33, pp. 5941–5948 (2019)
13. Zhang, J., Huang, T., Zhang, Z.: Fat-deepffm: field attentive deep field-aware factorization machine. arXiv preprint arXiv:1905.06336 (2019)
14. Hu, J., Shen, L., Sun, G.: Squeeze-and-excitation networks. In: Proceedings of the IEEE Conference on Computer Vision and Pattern Recognition, pp. 7132–7141 (2018)
15. Liu, D., Li, J., Du, B., Chang, J., Gao, R.: Daml: dual attention mutual learning between ratings and reviews for item recommendation. In: SIGKDD, pp. 344–352 (2018)
16. Bian, W., et al.: CAN: feature co-action network for click-through rate prediction. In: WSDM, pp. 57–65 (2022)
17. Huang, Z., Tao, M., Zhang, B.: Deep user match network for click-through rate prediction. In: SIGIR, pp. 1890–1894 (2021)
18. Long, L., Yin, Y., Huang, F.: Hierarchical attention factorization machine for CTR prediction. In: DASFAA, pp. 343–358 (2022)
19. Yang, P., et al.: MAN: main-auxiliary network with attentive interactions for review-based recommendation. Appl. Intell. 1–16 (2022)
20. Zhang, J., Lin, F., Yang, C., Wang, W.: Deep multi-representational item network for CTR prediction. In: SIGIR, pp. 2277–2281 (2022)

Block-Level Stiffness Analysis of Residual Networks

Eliska Kloberdanz(✉) and Wei Le

Department of Computer Science, Iowa State University, Ames, IA 50011, USA
{eklober,weile}@iastate.edu

Abstract. Residual Networks (ResNets) can be interpreted as dynamic systems, which are systems whose state changes over time and can be described with ordinary differential equations (ODEs) [13,28]. Specifically, the dynamic systems interpretation views individual residual blocks as ODEs. Numerical techniques for solving ODEs result in an approximation; and therefore contain an error term. If an ODE is *stiff* it is likely that this error is amplified and becomes dominating in the solution calculations, which negatively affects the accuracy of the approximated solution [4]. Therefore, *stiff* ODEs are often numerically unstable. In this paper we leverage the dynamic systems interpretation to perform a novel theoretical analysis of ResNets by leveraging findings and tools from numerical analysis of ODEs. Specifically, we perform block level stiffness analysis of ResNets. We find that residual blocks towards the end of ResNet models exhibit increased stiffness and that there is a statistically significant correlation between stiffness and model accuracy and loss. Based on these findings, we propose that ResNets behave as stiff numerically unstable ODEs.

Keywords: residual networks · numerical stability · ordinary differential equations

1 Introduction

There are three theoretical interpretations of Residual Networks (ResNets): (1) unraveled ResNets, (2) unrolled iterative estimation, and (3) dynamical systems. The unravelled interpretation views ResNets as a collection of 2^n paths along which the input data flows, where n is the number of residual blocks [26]. The unrolled iterative estimation interpretation explains ResNets as iterative approximators, where the first estimate provided by the first layer and is progressively refined by subsequent layers [12]. Finally, the dynamical systems view interprets ResNets as discretized dynamical systems, where ResNets are seen as ordinary differential equations (ODEs) [7,13,21]. Specifically, the dynamical systems interpretation regards ResNets's residual blocks as a series of forward Euler discretizations of an initial value ODE. This connection between residual blocks and ODEs can be leveraged for novel theoretical analyses that further our

L. Iliadis et al. (Eds.): ICANN 2023, LNCS 14263, pp. 61–73, 2023.
https://doi.org/10.1007/978-3-031-44204-9_6

understanding and interpretation of ResNets. In this paper we perform a stiffness analysis of ResNets and their residual blocks by leveraging findings from numerical analysis of ODEs.

Stiffness is an interesting property of an ODE that has important implications. If a differential equation is *stiff*, the solution to the equation will have an unpredictable error that will negatively affect the accuracy of the approximated solution [4]. Therefore, *stiff* ODEs are often numerically unstable and their solutions have accuracy issues [24,25].

There is no rigorous definition of stiffness; however there are certain phenomena that indicate that a problem may be stiff. One way to assess stiffness of an ODE is to analyze the eigenvalues of the Jacobian of the ODE. Specifically, if the eigenvalues of the Jacobian differ greatly in magnitude [3,5] or if a large portion of the eigenvalues have negative real parts [4], it is likely that the ODE is stiff. Unfortunately, there are no specific thresholds regarding what constitutes a high variation in magnitude of eigenvalues or high proportion of eigenvalues with negative real parts.

In this paper we investigate whether ResNets exhibit some of the characteristics that can indicate stiffness. Specifically, we focus on analyzing the eigenvalues of the Jacobian of individual residual blocks with respect to their inputs in ResNet18, ResNet34, and ResNet50. Using these eigenvalues we calculate (1) the stiffness index and (2) proportion of eigenvalues with negative real parts for each residual block and target label, where the stiffness index captures the degree of variation of the eigenvalues magnitude [18].

We find stiffness significantly varies with respect to different residual blocks. Specifically, we find that residual blocks towards the end of the network indicate increased stiffness, i.e.: they have a high stiffness index and also a high proportion of eigenvalues with negative real parts. For example, the last block in ResNet50 has a stiffness index of –35.32 and 31.96% of the eigenvalues of its Jacobian have negative real parts.

We perform a correlation analysis between stiffness and model accuracy/loss and show that they are correlated and that their correlation is statistically significant. In particular, we calculate the pearson correlation, which ranges from –1 to 1, where positive values indicate positive linear relationships and negative values indicate inverse relationships. We also compute the p-value of the correlation coefficients, where a p-value less or equal to 0.05 is considered statistically significant. For example, given ResNet18's last residual block, the stiffness index has a negative correlation with accuracy of –0.36 and the percentage of negative eigenvalues has a positive correlation with loss of 0.34. The stiffness index of the last residual block in ResNet34 has a negative correlation with accuracy of –0.20 and the percentage of negative eigenvalues has a negative correlation with accuracy of –0.38. Finally, given the last block in ResNet50, the correlation between the stiffness index and accuracy is –0.27 and the correlation between the percent of negative eigenvalues and loss is 0.25.

Based on these findings we propose that ResNets can be interpreted as not only as ODEs, but specifically as stiff ODEs, which are numerically unstable.

This interpretation could be another possible explanation of why DNNs are susceptible to adversarial examples.

The rest of this paper is organized as follows. Section 2 provides related work, Sect. 3 provides a detailed explanation of the dynamic systems interpretation of ResNets, which is the basis of this work. Section 4 describes our stiffness analysis, which investigates whether individual residual blocks behave as stiff ODEs. Finally, Sect. 5 reports the results of our analysis and Sect. 6 summarizes our conclusions.

2 Related Work

There is a large body of numerical analysis literature that studies stiffness; however, in this work we are the first ones to connect the concepts of stiffness and ResNets via the dynamical systems interpretation [13,28] to propose that ResNets can be viewed as stiff ODEs. Prior related works primarily focus on the challenges of solving stiff ODEs, which are prone to yielding unreliable results due to their stiffness.

To get an overview of on topic of stiff ODEs, please refer to [24], who provide a review of numerical integration techniques for stiff ODEs. Additionally, [25] describe the meaning of stiffness, why do stiff problems arise, how they can be recognized, and also compare the appropriateness of different solution methods. [17] propose generalized Runge-Kutta methods of order four with stepsize control as a solution method for stiff ODEs. Because stiff ODEs often contain varying time scales, [9] propose heterogeneous multiscale methods for stiff ODEs and show promising stability and convergence results. [10] develop a matrix updating technique that aims to reduce the computational cost of matrix operations needed for solving stiff ODEs. Other works are domain specific such as [29], which proposes a new method for solving stiff ODEs describing the chemical kinetics of reactive flow problems.

One of the most recent works that focuses on solving stiff ODEs is [18], who leverage neural ODEs. Neural ODEs have been introduced by [7] as a form of new continuous depth deep learning models that parametrize ODEs with a neural network and learn the underlying dynamic system. [18] study learning neural ODEs on data generated from two classical stiff systems, ROBER [23] and POLLU [27], which describe the dynamics of species concentrations in stiff chemical reaction systems. They propose a new derivative calculation that can be used for neural network backpropagation and output normalization techniques for learning stiff ODEs with neural ODEs.

The dynamic systems interpretation views ResNets as a discretized forward Euler method, which is known to be a numerically unstable solution to an ODE [22]. [20] leverage this fact to establish a link between numerical stability of ResNets and their adversarial robustness. They propose modifications to the ResNet architecture that effectively replace the numerically unstable forward (explicit) Euler method with backward (implicit) Euler method, which is numerically stable. Their experiments show that the modificantion improves adversarial robustness.

3 Dynamical Systems Interpretation of ResNets

Dynamical system is a system whose state changes with time [1]. Dynamical systems can be discrete or continuous depending on whether the time variable is discrete or continuous. Given a dynamical system defined by function f, time variable t, and state x, an iteration of discrete dynamical system can be described as $x_{t+1} = f(x_t)$, while a continuous system is represented as a differential equation $dx/dt = f'(x)$. Differential equations are especially useful for describing non-linear equations, e.g.: calculating the angular position of a swinging pendulum is a canonical dynamic system that can be solved via differential equations [2].

Prior works [13,28] have shown that ResNets can be interpreted as ordinary differential equations, where ordinary signifies that the differential equation contains a function with respect to only one (as opposed to multiple) independent variable.

The ResNet architecture consists of a convolutional input layer followed by residual blocks with identity skip connections and a fully connected output layer. The skip connections allow ResNets to skip a block; and therefore, find the optimal number of layers. A residual block (Fig. 1a) is the building block of ResNets. It is composed of two convolutional layers and can be defined as:

$$x_{i+1} = F(x_i, W_i) + x_i, \tag{1}$$

where F is the residual module and W_i are its parameters.

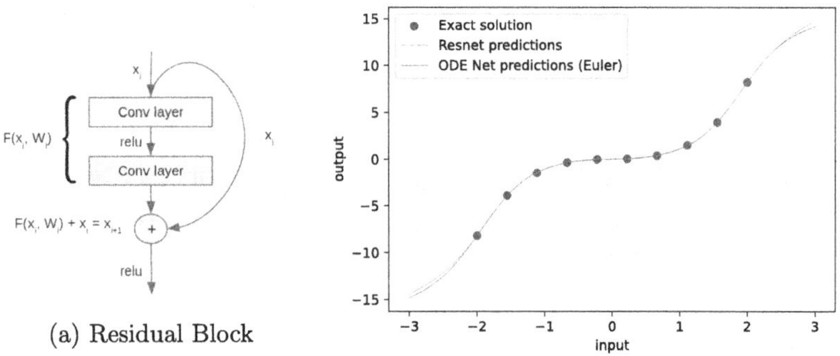

(a) Residual Block

(b) ResNets correspond to ODENets, which replace residual block with ODEs

Fig. 1. ResNets consist of residual blocks and are equivalent to ODENets

Without loss of generality, Eq. 1 can be written as follows with an additional parameter h.

$$x_{i+1} = hF(x_i, W_i) + x_i \tag{2}$$

Eq. 2 can be rearranged as:

$$\frac{x_{i+1} - x_i}{h} = F(x_i, W_i) \tag{3}$$

For a sufficiently small h in Eq. 3, the residual block becomes:

$$x(t) = F(x(t), W(t)), x(0) = x_0 \; for \; 0 \leq t \leq T, \tag{4}$$

where x(0) and x(T) correspond to the input and output feature maps and T to the depth of the residual network. The Euler forward method is an explicit method for solving ODEs using the following formula:

$$x_{i+1} = x_i + hf(x_i, W_i), \tag{5}$$

which has the same form as Eq. 2 and where h represents the step size. The equivalence of ResNets and ODENets can be demonstrated with a simple example shown in Fig. 1b, which compares the results of classical ResNets and ODENets fitted to a randomly generated set of numerical inputs and outputs.

4 Stiffness Analysis of ResNets

4.1 Stiffness

Numerical solution to an ODE is an approximation; and therefore contains an error term. If an ODE is *stiff* it is likely that this error is amplified and becomes dominating in the solution calculations [4]. Therefore, *stiff* ODEs are often numerically unstable. Typically, stiff ODE equations are problems for which explicit methods do not work [14,15].

Stiff systems derive their name from the motion of spring and mass systems that have large spring constants, and are common, for example, in the study of vibrations, chemical reactions, electrical circuits [4], and control theory [17]. There is no rigorous mathematical definition of stiffness; however certain indicators can be used to assess if an ODE is stiff. One of those indicators are the eigenvalues of the Jacobian of the function in the ODE, where the Jacobian is a matrix that consists of first order partial derivatives of a function and is defined in Eq. 6. Residual blocks can be viewed as functions; and therefore, we can compute their Jacobians. Moreover, because the Jacobians of residual blocks are square matrices, we can compute their eigenvalues.

$$\mathbb{J} = \begin{bmatrix} \frac{\partial \mathbf{f}(\mathbf{x})}{\partial x_1} \cdots \frac{\partial \mathbf{f}(\mathbf{x})}{\partial x_n} \end{bmatrix} = \begin{bmatrix} \nabla^T f_1(\mathbf{x}) \\ \vdots \\ \nabla^T f_m(\mathbf{x}) \end{bmatrix} = \begin{bmatrix} \frac{\partial f_1(\mathbf{x})}{\partial x_1} & \cdots & \frac{\partial f_1(\mathbf{x})}{\partial x_n} \\ \vdots & \ddots & \vdots \\ \frac{\partial f_m(\mathbf{x})}{\partial x_1} & \cdots & \frac{\partial f_m(\mathbf{x})}{\partial x_n} \end{bmatrix} \tag{6}$$

Eigenvalues are characteristic scalar values, which have special properties and can be computed only for square matrices via eigenvalue decomposition. Given a square matrix A, if there is a vector $X \in \mathbb{R}^n \neq 0$ such that:

$$AX = \lambda X \tag{7}$$

for some scalar λ, then λ is the eigenvalue of A [19]. Eigenvalue decomposition of a square matrix A yields three matrices: Q, V, and Q^{-1} such that $A = QVQ^{-1}$. In this matrix factorization, Q is a square matrix that contains eigenvectors in its columns, V is a diagonal matrix that contains eigenvalues on its diagonal, and Q^{-1} is simply a transpose of Q.

Stiff ODEs cause severe numerical integration problems and their solutions are typically associated with stability and accuracy problems [24]. Both individual and systems of ODEs can be stiff [6]. An example of a single stiff ODE is:

$$\frac{dy}{dt} = -1000y + 3000 - 2000e^{-t} \tag{8}$$

For an initial value $y(0) = 0$, the analytical solution is:

$$y = 3 - 0.998e^{-1000t} - 2.002e^{-t} \tag{9}$$

Figure 2 compares an approximate and exact solution to the example stiff ODE in Eq. 8. We approximate the solution using an explicit Euler method, but even with a step size as small as 0.0015, the approximate solution is very inaccurate and unstable.

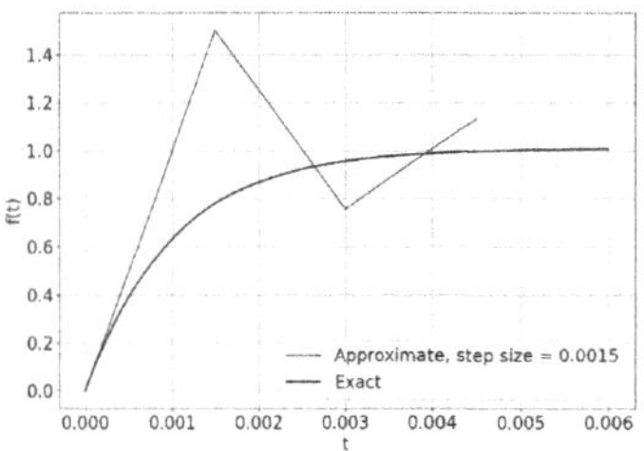

(a) Exact vs approximate solution on a time interval from 0.0 to 0.006

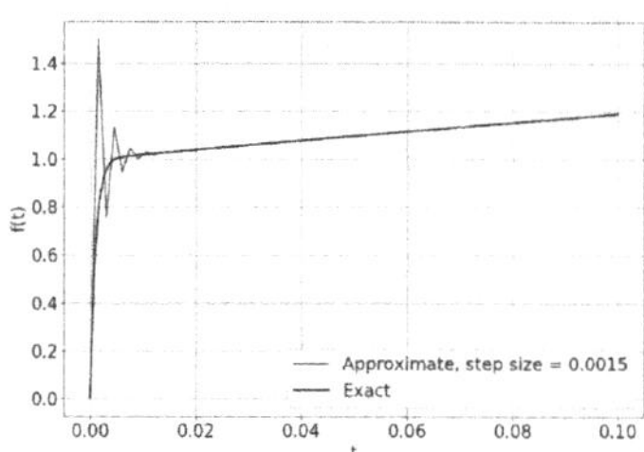

(b) Exact vs approximate solution on a time interval from 0.0 to 0.1

Fig. 2. Solutions to stiff ODEs have accuracy and stability issues

4.2 Stiffness Analysis

In Sect. 3 we have explained how ResNets can be interpreted as a discretized forward Euler method applied to an initial value ODE as per the dynamic systems interpretation [13,28]. Prior works have shown that the forward Euler method is numerically unstable [22] and attempted to modify ResNets to increase their stability [20]. Additionally, the phenomenon of adversarial examples [11] that produce incorrect predictions when passed as inputs into ResNets, can be viewed as a manifestation of numerical instability [8]. Adversarial examples are inputs that have been carefully crafted with the goal of fooling a neural network. They add small virtually imperceivable perturbations to initial inputs such that the inputs appear legitimate and unaltered, but still cause the network to output an incorrect prediction. Numerically stable methods are resilient to small changes in initial data or conditions such that their output does not result in a dramatic change in the solution to the problem [4]. Given these issues and the fact that the explicit methods for solving ODEs are likely to fail if a problem is *stiff*, it is possible that ResNets are stiff and numerically unstable.

To investigate this, we perform a numerical analysis to test whether ResNets exhibit characteristics of stiff ODEs. Specifically, we focus on analyzing the eigenvalues of the Jacobian of each residual block with respect to the block inputs. Using these eigenvalues, for each residual block, we calculate (1) the stiffness index and (2) what proportion of eigenvalues contain negative real parts according to Eqs. 10 and 11 respectively.

Stiffness Index. A problem is stiff if the eigenvalues of the Jacobian of the function described by the ODE differ greatly in magnitude, which can be measured by the stiffness index [18]. The stiffness index is defined in Eq. 10, where λ_i corresponds to the eigenvalues of the Jacobian matrix and Re represent the real part of a complex number.

$$S = \frac{max(Re(\lambda_i))}{min(Re(\lambda_i))} \tag{10}$$

Percent of Eigenvalues with Negative Real Parts. Another indication of stiffness is if majority of those eigenvalues have negative real parts [16]. We calculate this metric as follows.

$$P = \frac{count(Re(\lambda_i) > 0)}{count(\lambda_i)} \tag{11}$$

Computational Complexity. Computing the Jacobian of a residual block and its eigenvalues is computationally expensive. Given a residual block with input and output dimension equal to n : $F : \mathbb{R}^n \rightarrow \mathbb{R}^n$, to obtain the Jacobian matrix of F we need to compute the first partial derivative of each input dimension with respect to each output dimension, which yields a n $\times$ n matrix. Therefore, the larger the inputs and residual blocks, the more computational power is required to compute the Jacobian and its eigenvalues. For example, the first block of both ResNet18 and ResNet34 produces over 268 million Jacobian matrix elements and over 16 million eigenvalues. We have performed experiments on GPUs as much as 80GB memory; however, that was still not sufficient for larger ResNet architectures or larger inputs. For this reason we focus on ResNet18, ResNet34, and ResNet50 that have been pre-trained on CIFAR10. Specifically, we compute the Jacobian of every residual block with respect to each input to perform the analysis.

5 Results

We perform a stiffness analysis of ResNet18, ResNet34 and Resnet50 with CIFAR10 test images, and our results show that residual blocks towards the end of ResNets behave as stiff ODEs. Moreover, we show that stiffness varies with respect to different blocks as opposed to different inputs, which means that stiffness is a property of the model itself. It also implies that our results obtained using CIFAR10 images as inputs generalize across different inputs and reflect on the model as opposed to particular inputs. Additionally, we also show that there is a statistically significant correlation between elevated stiffness and model accuracy/loss.

5.1 ResNet18

ResNet18 contains eight residual blocks and in Table 2 we show that the stiffness index and percentage of eigenvalues with negative real parts spikes in last three blocks. The average block stiffness index is –4.15, but the last residual block shows a significant spike in stiffness of –12.99, which is three times higher than the average. The percentage of negative eigenvalues behaves similarly. The average percentage of negative eigenvalues in a block is 10.04, but this percentage doubles in the last three residual blocks. This indicates that the last three residual blocks of ResNet18 behave as stiff ODEs.

In addition to analyzing stiffness of different blocks we also calculate the average stiffness index and percentage of negative eigenvalues produced by different inputs with different target labels. In Table 3 we show stiffness does not change with respect to different image labels. Based on that we conclude that it is ResNet18 itself that drives stiffness and not its inputs.

Next, we assess the significance of our finding that the last three residual blocks of ResNet18 behave as stiff ODEs by testing if the two stiffness metrics are correlated with ResNet18's accuracy and loss and if those correlations are statistically significant. In Table 1 we show that the increased stiffness in the last three blocks is correlated with ResNet18's accuracy and loss. For example, the last residual block's percentage of negative eigenvalues has a –0.36 correlation with the model accuracy and its stiffness index has a 0.34 correlation with the model loss. The p-value of these correlations is less than 0.05, i.e.: they are statistically significant. This means that higher proportion of negative eigenvalues implies lower accuracy and higher stiffness index implies higher loss.

5.2 ResNet34

ResNet34 contains sixteen blocks and similarly to ResNet18, it is the residual blocks towards the end of the network that exhibit increased stiffness. In Table 5 we show that the last eight blocks show a spike in stiffness index and percentage of negative eigenvalues. The average block stiffness index is –7.84, but it approximately doubles in most of the last eight blocks. For example, the sixteenth block has a stiffness index of –16.82. Similar results can be observed for the

Table 1. ResNet18 correlation analysis between stiffness and accuracy/loss with statistically significant results in bold

block	acc, stiffness index		acc, pct neg eigen values		loss, stiffness index		loss, pct neg eigen values	
	corr	p-value	corr	p-value	corr	p-value	corr	p-value
1	0.00	0.83	−0.01	0.67	0.01	0.76	0.00	0.87
2	0.03	0.06	−0.01	0.45	−0.02	0.19	0.01	0.45
3	−0.01	0.74	**−0.06**	0.00	0.02	0.17	**0.06**	0.00
4	**−0.04**	0.01	**−0.10**	0.00	**0.04**	0.03	**0.10**	0.00
5	0.00	0.97	**−0.14**	0.00	0.01	0.68	**0.13**	0.00
6	**−0.09**	0.00	**−0.38**	0.00	**0.08**	0.00	**0.36**	0.00
7	−0.03	0.08	**−0.18**	0.00	0.02	0.34	**0.18**	0.00
8	**−0.23**	0.00	**−0.36**	0.00	**0.21**	0.00	**0.34**	0.00
all blocks	−0.01	0.15	**−0.07**	0.00	0.01	0.19	**0.07**	0.00

Table 2. ResNet18 stiffness analysis by block with stiffness index and percent of negative eigen values with real parts over 10.00 in bold

block	stiffness index	pct of negative eigen values
1	−2.28	2.82
2	−5.12	2.54
3	−1.28	1.96
4	−4.04	4.33
5	−1.30	4.35
6	−4.94	**19.73**
7	−1.28	**22.65**
8	**−12.99**	**21.92**
all blocks	−4.15	**10.04**

Table 3. ResNet18 stiffness analysis by label

label	stiffness index	pct of negative eigen values
0	−4.31	10.46
1	−4.42	9.71
2	−4.02	10.31
3	−4.00	11.57
4	−4.02	9.80
5	−4.10	10.14
6	−4.07	9.53
7	−4.13	9.20
8	−4.15	9.67
9	−4.31	9.99

percentage of negative eigenvalues in Resnet34's blocks. The average block contains 15.15% of negative eigenvalues, but that percentage is significantly higher in the last 7 blocks. For example the last block's Jacobian matrix has 22.34% of negative eigenvalues and the twelfth and thirteenth blocks have 33.58% and 34.13% respectively.

Table 6 shows that stiffness does not seem to vary with respect to different input labels, which is the same conclusion made in case of ResNet18. Compared to Table 5, which shows a block level analysis, the stiffness index and percentage of negative eigenvalues is virtually constant across different input image labels.

Similarly to ResNet18, we perform a correlation analysis to assess the impact of stiffness observed in the latter half of ResNet34's blocks on its accuracy and loss. Table 4 shows that the residual blocks with increased stiffness have a statistically significant correlation with the model's accuracy and loss. For example, the last block's stiffness index has a −0.20 correlation with the model's accuracy and that the percentage of negative eigenvalues in the last block have a 0.35 correlation with the model's loss.

Table 4. ResNet34: Correlation analysis between stiffness and accuracy/loss with statistically significant results in bold

block	acc, stiffness index		acc, pct neg eigen values		loss, stiffness index		loss, pct neg eigen values	
	corr	p-value	corr	p-value	corr	p-value	corr	p-value
1	**−0.07**	0.02	−0.01	0.74	0.05	0.09	0.00	0.94
2	0.02	0.44	0.01	0.79	−0.03	0.37	−0.01	0.80
3	−0.02	0.42	0.02	0.56	0.02	0.53	−0.02	0.54
4	−0.01	0.73	0.03	0.39	0.00	0.95	−0.02	0.52
5	−0.01	0.82	−0.02	0.48	−0.01	0.82	0.02	0.59
6	**0.06**	0.03	0.00	0.94	**−0.07**	0.03	0.00	0.89
7	0.05	0.09	**−0.12**	0.00	−0.04	0.17	**0.12**	0.00
8	**−0.07**	0.02	**−0.22**	0.00	0.04	0.19	**0.23**	0.00
9	**−0.07**	0.03	**−0.26**	0.00	**0.06**	0.05	**0.26**	0.00
10	**−0.17**	0.00	**−0.32**	0.00	**0.17**	0.00	**0.31**	0.00
11	**−0.22**	0.00	**−0.31**	0.00	**0.21**	0.00	**0.30**	0.00
12	**−0.11**	0.00	**−0.23**	0.00	**0.10**	0.00	**0.22**	0.00
13	0.05	0.08	**−0.21**	0.00	−0.05	0.12	**0.21**	0.00
14	0.04	0.18	−0.05	0.08	−0.02	0.41	**0.08**	0.01
15	**−0.23**	0.00	**−0.34**	0.00	**0.21**	0.00	**0.33**	0.00
16	**−0.20**	0.00	**−0.38**	0.00	**0.18**	0.00	**0.35**	0.00
all blocks	−0.01	0.11	**−0.05**	0.00	0.01	0.13	**0.05**	0.00

Table 5. ResNet34 stiffness analysis by block with stiffness index and percent of negative eigen values with real parts over 10.00 in bold

block	stiffness index	pct of negative eigen values
1	-3.34	3.10
2	-5.24	2.81
3	-5.91	2.78
4	-1.10	2.50
5	-6.00	4.78
6	-5.69	4.10
7	-5.29	5.15
8	-1.73	7.83
9	**-14.56**	**11.91**
10	-9.47	**25.78**
11	**-10.46**	**30.69**
12	**-13.05**	**33.58**
13	**-11.26**	**34.13**
14	-1.85	**25.56**
15	**-13.59**	**25.39**
16	**-16.82**	**22.34**
all blocks	-7.84	**15.15**

Table 6. ResNet34 stiffness analysis by label

label	stiffness index	pct of negative eigen values
0	-7.82	15.94
1	-7.77	14.12
2	-7.79	15.69
3	-7.88	17.14
4	-7.51	15.31
5	-7.98	15.44
6	-7.79	14.58
7	-8.00	14.36
8	-7.96	14.49
9	-7.84	14.42

5.3 ResNet50

Due to computation constraints explained in Sect. 4.2, for ResNet50, a larger architecture, we compute the stiffness index and percentage of negative eigen-

Table 7. ResNet50: Correlation analysis between stiffness and accuracy/loss with statistically significant results in bold

block	acc, stiffness index		acc, pct neg eigen values		loss, stiffness index		loss, pct neg eigen values	
	corr	p-value	corr	p-value	corr	p-value	corr	p-value
16	**−0.27**	0.00	**0.20**	0.00	**0.25**	0.00	**−0.15**	0.00

Table 8. ResNet50 stiffness analysis of last block

block	stiffness index	pct of negative eigen values
16	-35.32	31.96

Table 9. ResNet50 stiffness analysis by label

label	stiffness index	pct of negative eigen values
0	-31.28	31.91
1	-39.61	28.23
2	-32.26	32.79
3	-28.45	35.92
4	-33.27	34.14
5	-34.33	36.37
6	-39.56	27.23
7	-41.05	32.17
8	-37.34	27.77
9	-36.30	33.14

values only for its sixteenth block, which is the last residual block. The last residual block Jacobian is the smallest from all blocks; and is therefore the least computationally expensive. Moreover, the results from our stiffness analysis on both ResNet18 and ResNet34 show that stiff residual blocks reside towards the end of the network architecture.

As shown in Table 8, the stiffness index of the last residual block in ResNet50 is 35.32, which is higher than any block stiffness index in ResNet18 or ResNet34. The percentage of negative eigenvalues is 31.96%, which is also high. Similarly to ResNet18 and ResNet34, Table 9 demonstrates that the stiffness indicators do not significantly vary in response to different inputs. Finally, Table 7 shows that the stiffness index is about 20% correlated with ResNet50's accuracy and loss and that the correlation is statistically significant.

6 Conclusion

In this paper we leverage the dynamic systems interpretation of ResNets that views them as ODEs whose solutions are equivalent to forward Euler discretization of an initial value ODE. We perform a novel stiffness analysis whose results lead to our proposal that ResNets can be interpreted as stiff ODEs. Solutions involving stiff ODEs have numerical problems that cause poor accuracy and stability, because the error term in the approximate solution becomes dominating. While stiffness does not have a rigorous mathematical definition, there are some analyses that can be performed to assess whether its is likely that an ODE is stiff.

In this work we focus on studying the eigenvalues of the Jacobian matrix that is created by computing the first partial derivatives of a residual block with respect to its inputs. Specifically, using the eigenvalues we compute the stiffness index and percentage of negative eigenvalues with real parts for each residual block to perform a stiffness analysis. Our results show that residual blocks towards the end of ResNets exhibit a high stiffness index and high percentage of negative eigenvalues. We also show that stiffness varies with respect to different blocks as opposed to types of inputs, which indicates that stiffness is an inherent property of some residual blocks. To assess the significance of these results we perform a correlation analysis, which indicates that stiffness has a statistically significant correlation with a model's accuracy and loss. Based on these findings we conclude that some residual blocks in ResNets (specifically the ones in the latter half of the architecture) correspond to stiff ODEs. Therefore, we propose that ResNets could viewed not only as ODEs as per the dynamic systems interpretation, but specifically as stiff ODEs, which are numerically unstable. Our stiffness analysis along with instructions for reproducing results are available at: https://anonymous.4open.science/r/Stiffness-Analysis-ResNets-18D2/README.md.

References

1. Arrowsmith, D.K., Place, C.M.: An introduction to dynamical systems (1990)
2. Brin, M., Stuck, G.: Introduction to dynamical systems (2002)
3. Bui, T.D., Bui, T.: Numerical methods for extremely stiff systems of ordinary differential equations. Appl. Math. Model. **3**, 355–358 (1979)
4. Burden, R.L., Faires, J.D., Burden, A.M.: Numerical Analysis. Cengage Learning, Boston (2015)
5. Butcher, J.C.: Numerical methods for ordinary differential equations (2008)
6. Chapra, S.C., Canale, R.P.: Numerical methods for engineers (1986)
7. Chen, T.Q., Rubanova, Y., Bettencourt, J., Duvenaud, D.K.: Neural ordinary differential equations. ArXiv abs/1806.07366 (2018)
8. DeVore, R.A., Hanin, B., Petrova, G.: Neural network approximation. Acta Numer. **30**, 327–444 (2021)
9. Engquist, B., Tsai, Y.H.R.: Heterogeneous multiscale methods for stiff ordinary differential equations. Math. Comput. **74**, 1707–1742 (2005)
10. Enright, W.H.: Improving the efficiency of matrix operations in the numerical solution of stiff ordinary differential equations. ACM Trans. Math. Softw. **4**, 127–136 (1978)
11. Goodfellow, I.J., Shlens, J., Szegedy, C.: Explaining and harnessing adversarial examples. CoRR abs/1412.6572 (2015)
12. Greff, K., Srivastava, R.K., Schmidhuber, J.: Highway and residual networks learn unrolled iterative estimation. ArXiv abs/1612.07771 (2017)
13. Haber, E., Ruthotto, L., Holtham, E.: Learning across scales - a multiscale method for convolution neural networks. ArXiv abs/1703.02009 (2018)
14. Hairer, E., Wanner, G.: Solving Ordinary Differential Equations II. Stiff and Differential-Algebraic Problems, vol. 14, January1996. https://doi.org/10.1007/978-3-662-09947-6
15. Hairer, E., Wanner, G.: Solving ordinary differential equations ii: stiff and differential-algebraic problems (2002)

16. Heath, M.T., Munson, E.: Scientific computing: an introductory survey (1996)
17. Kaps, P., Rentrop, P.: Generalized Runge-Kutta methods of order four with step-size control for stiff ordinary differential equations. Numer. Math. **33**, 55–68 (1979)
18. Kim, S., Ji, W., Deng, S., Ma, Y., Rackauckas, C.: Stiff neural ordinary differential equations. Chaos Interdiscip. J. Nonlinear Sci. **31**(9), 093122 (2021)
19. Layton, W.J., Sussman, M.M.: Numerical linear algebra (2017)
20. Li, M., He, L., Lin, Z.: Implicit Euler skip connections: enhancing adversarial robustness via numerical stability. In: ICML (2020)
21. Lu, Y., Zhong, A., Li, Q., Dong, B.: Beyond finite layer neural networks: bridging deep architectures and numerical differential equations. ArXiv abs/1710.10121 (2018)
22. Press, W.H., Teukolsky, S.A., Vetterling, W.T., Flannery, B.P.: Numerical recipes in c (2nd ed.): the art of scientific computing (1992)
23. Robertson, H.: The Solution of a Set of Reaction Rate Equations, Numerical Analysis: An Introduction, pp. 178–182. Academic Press, Cambridge, Massachusetts (1967)
24. Seinfeld, J.H., Lapidus, L., Hwang, M.: Review of numerical integration techniques for stiff ordinary differential equations. Ind. Eng. Chem. Fundam. **9**, 266–275 (1970)
25. Shampine, L.F., Gear, C.W.: A user's view of solving stiff ordinary differential equations. SIAM Rev. **21**, 1–17 (1979)
26. Veit, A., Wilber, M.J., Belongie, S.J.: Residual networks behave like ensembles of relatively shallow networks. In: NIPS (2016)
27. Verwer, J.G.: Gauss-Seidel iteration for stiff ODEs from chemical kinetics. SIAM J. Sci. Comput. **15**, 1243–1250 (1994)
28. Weinan, E.: A proposal on machine learning via dynamical systems (2017)
29. Young, T.R., Boris, J.P.: A numerical technique for solving stiff ordinary differential equations associated with the chemical kinetics of reactive-flow problems. J. Phys. Chem. **81**, 2424–2427 (1977)

CKNA: Kernel Hyperparameters Optimization Method for Group-Wise CNNs

Rongjin Huang[1], Shifeng Qu[2], Hai Yang[1], and Zhanquan Wang[1](✉)

[1] Institute of Information Science and Engineering, East China University of Science and Technology, Shanghai 200237, China
y30211018@mail.ecust.edu.cn zhqwang@ecust.edu.cn

[2] Key Laboratory of Smart Manufacturing in Energy Chemical Process, Ministry of Education, East China University of Science and Technology, Shanghai 200237, China

Abstract. Traditional CNNs lack specific interpretable indicators for configuring kernel hyperparameters. Practitioners typically tune model performance via tedious trial and error experiments, resulting in longer training time and expensive computational costs. To address this issue, a novel systematic method, namely CKNA, that considers comprehensive kernel hyperparameters to optimize the network architecture is proposed. Firstly, we innovatively define channel-dispersion and pseudo-kernel to characterize behaviors differentiated by kernel values across model layers. Based on these concepts, the kernel scaling algorithm and the flat wave algorithm are proposed to automatically adjust kernel size and numbers, respectively. Furthermore, we decompose the channel-expand and down-sample operations into adjacent layers to break the bottleneck effect existing in kernel elements. CKNA is applied to classic group-wise CNNs, and experimental results on ImageNet demonstrate that the optimized models obtain at least a 5.73% improvement in classification accuracy.

Keywords: Kernel hyperparameter · Network architecture · Group-wise CNNs

1 Introduction

CNN-based visual recognition models are widely used in medical segmentation, autonomous driving, and other domains, which promote great economic advantages. To further improve the performance of the full model, researchers either reconstruct submodules [1] or continually explore better methods for setting hyperparameters. For instance, they support variable learning rates [2], smoother activation functions [3], or even optimize over multiple hyperparameters simultaneously [4].

However, kernel hyperparameters, which play a crucial role in traditional CNNs, have yet to receive sufficient intensive study. Larger kernels with greater Efficient Receptive Field(ERF) capture more comprehensive information but also increase computational cost, small kernels are usually stacked to replace the single large kernel in early works [5,6]. However, stacking small kernels may not deepen the network, but limit the ERF in multi-layer networks [7,8]. Conversely, kernels with a large ERF can be the key driver for downstream tasks [9].

L. Iliadis et al. (Eds.): ICANN 2023, LNCS 14263, pp. 74–85, 2023.
https://doi.org/10.1007/978-3-031-44204-9_7

Typically, the number of channels corresponds to kernels in the CNNs layer, too high or too low will hurt model performance, and simply extending model width cannot produce consistent results [10, 11]. Neural Architecture Search may help explore superior model width but has no clear indicator to aid in tuning kernel numbers setting in different layers.

To address the issues above, we propose a method to optimize network architecture based on kernel hyperparameters. We inspect kernel features among network layers based on visualizing model weights, then define the concepts of pseudo-kernel and channel-dispersion to comprehensively describe kernel distributions, which serve as important indicators to regulate kernel sizes and numbers. We also observe kernel element values in different network layers from an information flow point of view and find that there is a bottleneck effect in certain layers. For this reason, we rebuild network layers containing down-sample and channel-expand operations to expand the value ranges of kernel elements. To further optimize network architectures, the CKNA is validated on group-wise CNNs. Experiments show that CKNA-optimized models achieve a significantly increased accuracy on several datasets.

This paper is organized as follows. Section 2 develops a novel optimization named CKNA, including concept definitions and optimization algorithms of the pseudo-kernel and channel-dispersion, and reconstructs model layers. Section 3 presents the CKNA process and performs extensive experiments. Section 3.2 performs ablation experiments for single-dimensional improvement in classification, including kernel numbers, kernel size, and kernel element values. Section 4 makes a conclusion.

2 CKNA Method

In this section, we introduce the group convolution module and then present issues existing in architectures. Then, we illustrate the CKNA method from three dimensions: kernel size, kernel numbers, and kernel elements in layers. Finally, we summarize the overall flow of CKNA.

2.1 MobileNet Bottle Convolution Module

The typical representative of using group convolution technology is the Mobilenet Bottle Convolution module(MBConv) [11], which performs one-dimensional convolution operations to greatly reduce model parameters. Figure 1 shows an MBConv that performs both down-sample and channel-expand operations, where exp represents the dilatation factor within MBConv.

In Fig. 1, marking input tensor as $[C_0, H, W]$. We begin by using $exp * C_0$ standard kernels with the form of $[C_0, 1, 1]$ to pointwise operation (referred to as PW), followed by $exp * C_0$ group kernels with the form of [1, n, n] for the group-wise convolution operation (referred to as GC). Finally, we use C_1 standard kernels with the shape of $[exp * C_0, 1, 1]$ to complete the down-wise operation (referred to as DW), shrinking the output dimension to the target quantity.

In this paper, we will study the size and number of kernels in CNNs indirectly by studying kernel size and exp in the MBConv.

2.2 Scaling Kernel Size

Visualize Kernel Element Values. In the CNNs, we represent all of the kernels in a single network layer with a shape of $[B, C, n, n]$ as $[B, N]$, and visualize the values of kernel elements in a manner similar to Fig. 2. $N = C \times n \times n$ in the traditional standard convolution kernels, while $N = n \times n$ in the group convolution kernels.

Figure 2 shows the behavioral differences between kernels in different layers. In (a), kernel elements get the largest spread but scatter everywhere. In (b), kernel elements have a moderate range, while the uneven values show a peak shape, with a high center and low edges. As shown in (c), kernel elements distribute relatively sparsely and uniformly, in a narrow domain. (d) random distribution with no obvious pattern.

Pseudo-Kernel. Adjusting kernel size by observing and summarising values distribution between elements would be a common choice, but relying on visuals may suffer from the D-K effect, where the observer's intuitive cognition seriously affects subsequent tuning strategies. To alleviate subjective factors, we propose the concept of pseudo-kernel, which quantifies the set of kernel elements into a single form.

We design hierarchical criteria to compute pseudo-kernels for all kernels with a uniform $[B, C, n_1, n_2]$ in layers at the origin. when $B \times C \geq 100$, we take the mean of the top 10% highest kernel element values to represent that element. when $B \times C < 100$, we choose the mean of the 10 best values. Equation 1 shows the computational formula for the pseudo-kernels W and their element values w. Note that, α, β refer to hyperparameters, $\alpha = 10, \beta = 0.1$.

$$\begin{aligned} W &= \{w_{ij}, 0 < i, j < n, i, j \in N_+\} \\ w_{ij} &= \frac{1}{K} \sum \text{MaxK}\{w_{ij}^{BC}\} \\ K &= \max[\alpha, \beta BC], i, j \in N_+, i \leq n_1, j \leq n_2 \end{aligned} \tag{1}$$

Kernel Scaling Algorithm. Assuming the current kernel size noted as K, we extract kernel elements on the edge of the pseudo-kernel to form a set O, then propose the kernel scaling algorithm(KSA) to scale K as follows, with a threshold defined as $0 < \lambda_1 < \lambda_2 < 1$.

$$\begin{aligned} &\text{if}\, \forall_0 \in O, s.t.\ \text{o} < \lambda_1 \text{ and } K > 3, K \rightarrow K - 2 \\ &\text{elif}\, \exists o \in O, s.t.\text{o} > \lambda_2 \text{ and K} < 7, K \rightarrow K + 2 \end{aligned} \tag{2}$$

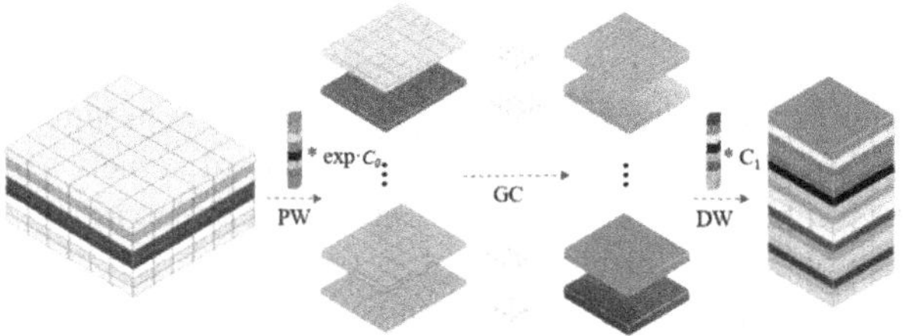

Fig. 1. MBCov module

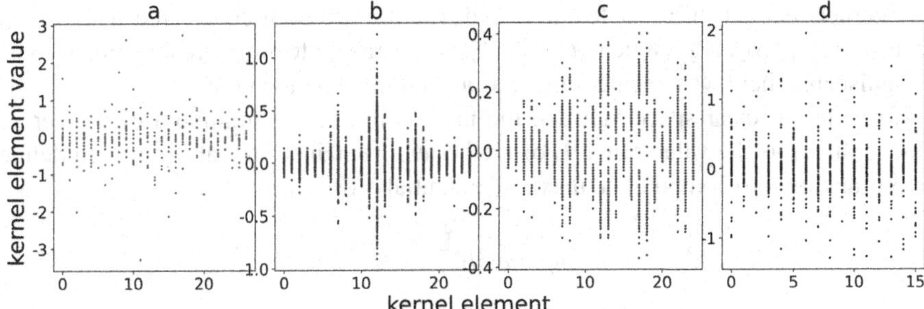

Fig. 2. Kernel element values distribution in layers. The horizontal and vertical axes respectively refer to kernel element numbers and kernel element values, where each dot represents a kernel element. (a) represents a standard kernel with a shape of $[B, C, 3, 3]$. (b) and (c) both represent group kernels with a shape of $[B, 1, 5, 5]$. (d) represents a 1×1 kernel with a shape of $[B, C, 1, 1]$.

Different models have varied λ_1 and λ_2. Here, we set $\lambda_1 = 0.3$, $\lambda_2 = 0.6$. If one more pseudo-kernels meet KSA at the same epoch, we prioritize reducing the kernel size and then expanding from shallow to deep. Taking into account hardware resources and contrasting with the baseline model, the overall parameters in the improved model are approximately equal to that of the original model, with kernel sizes between 7 and 3. Furthermore, if a kernel expanded last epoch satisfies KSA to shrink this epoch, in the current round, we reduce it again but have no operation in the next 2 epochs.

2.3 Setting Suitable Kernel Numbers

As indicated by the distinctive behaviors of the kernel elements shown in Fig. 2, custom processions of input information at various stages require a myriad of kernels among the different layers. On this basis, it is convinced that we can improve the performance of the model by tuning the number of kernels, which facilitates the transmission of information between layers.

Valid Information Point. Individually, We consider each layer as a closed system, referred to as the network layer system(NLS), and calculate its information content via the Shannon entropy [12] as defined in Eq. 3, where $P(\mathbf{x})$ represents the probability of the occurrence of event $\mathbf{x}$, $H(X)$ represents the Shannon entropy.

$$H(X) = -\sum_{x} P(\mathbf{x}) \log_2[P(\mathbf{x})] \tag{3}$$

In NLS, the events correspond to every possible valid value that kernel elements have. Thus, to enrich the NLS information content, we first aim to augment potential valid values for kernel elements.

Assuming that a layer contains two 1×1 kernels with values a and b, and a sufficiently small positive number, denoted as the effective distance ξ. When $|a - b| > \xi$, those kernels extract different features, and a and b are both considered to be Valid information points(VIPs). When $|a - b| \leq \xi$, the extracted features are too similar to be distinguishable, here we consider only a as a valid information point.

We define a linear space between the maximum and the minimum of the kernel element values as the value range $\mathbf{L}$ of the kernels contained in that layer, then define the formulation 4 to compute the maximal potential VIPs Ω_0.

$$\Omega_0 = ceil(\frac{\mathbf{L}}{\xi}) + 1 \tag{4}$$

Assuming a current set S_0 contains n elements in an NLS. When adding a new information factor χ, if $\exists\ s \in S_0, s.t.\ s - \chi < \xi$, ξ cannot change into a VIP. We mark the expected VIPs in the system as $E(n)$ and calculate the increment $f(\Delta n)$ by formulation 6. When S_0 approaches Ω_0, $f(\Delta n)$approaches 0, where χ can hardly transform into a VIP; when S_0 approaches 0, $f(\Delta n)$ approaches 1, χ gets the high probability to convert into a VIP.

$$E(n) = \frac{S_0}{\Omega_0} \cdot S_0 + \frac{\Omega_0 - S_0}{\Omega_0} \cdot (S_0 + 1) = 1 + S_0 - \frac{S_0}{\Omega_0} \tag{5}$$

$$f(\Delta n) = E(n) - S_0 = 1 - \frac{S_0}{\Omega_0} > 0 \tag{6}$$

Furthermore, we define the set including all VIP values in NLS at a certain time as the system state, noted as φ_0. we count φ_0 by formulation 7, then we mark the system state after add χ as φ_1, and define the states increment function as:$\mathbf{F}(\mathbf{\Delta n}) = \varphi_1 - \varphi_0$, which can calculate and organize as formulation 8.

$$\varphi_0 = \frac{\Omega_0!}{(\Omega_0 - S_0)!} \tag{7}$$

$$\mathbf{F}(\mathbf{\Delta n}) = \frac{(\Omega_0 - S_0)!}{(\Omega_0 - E(n))!} - 1 \tag{8}$$

According to Eq. 8, when $\Omega_0 S$ and S_0 are fixed, the larger $E(n)$ is, the higher the growth rate of the state numbers. According to Eqs. 5, the sparser VIPs struggle in the domain, the higher the information increment gets after adding kernel elements. For certain S_0 and $E(n)$, $\Omega_0$and $\mathbf{F}(\mathbf{\Delta n})$ exhibit a positive correlation. the wider $\mathbf{L}$, the higher information increment obtained by χ, as shown in Eqs. 4.

Therefore, we make a conclusion that the sparser kernel elements distribute in the original layer, or the wider range of values, the higher increase in information obtained after expanding the channel numbers.

Channel-Dispersion. We introduce the concept of channel-dispersion (CD) to represent the dispersion of kernel element values distribution in a network layer.

For a lay contained uniform kernel size, we note that kernel as $n \times n$. Let C_{pr} and C_{en} represent channels before and after the convolution operation in sequence. We define (CD) formulation as in Eq. 9, where C_{xki} represents the x-th kernel element value in the k−th dimension of the x−th kernel among C_{en} kernels. The set **E** represents all kernel element values in the current layer, which contains $n \times n$ elements. The hyperparameter ∂ scales the dense differences in kernel values distribution. In this paper, $\partial = 10$. and we use θ to modify CDs by eliminating the tiny kernel elements in pseudo-kernels. Here, $\theta = 0.1$.

$$
\begin{aligned}
CD &= \frac{\partial^2}{C_{en}C_{pr}Ne}\sum_{x=1}^{C_{en}}\sum_{y=1}^{C_{en}}\sum_{k=1}^{C_{pr}}\sum_{i=1}^{n\cdot n}(C_{xki} - C_{yki})^2 \\
Ne &= |\{e \in E : e > \theta\}|
\end{aligned}
\tag{9}
$$

The shallow layer requires relatively fewer kernels to extract coarse-grained information, along with higher CD. In contrast, the deeper layer has greater demand for kernels to process higher dimensional abstract semantic information [13], resulting in relatively lower CD. We convince that CDs in intermediate layers should exhibit a staircase-like pattern with a gradually decreasing dispersion.

Flat Wave Algorithm. Assuming that CD among the CNNs layer are labeled Li from shallow to deep, where i represents the layer depth, $i = 0, 1, 2, ..., l$, and exp_i represents the dilation coefficient in the i-th layer. We propose the Flat Wave Algorithm(FWA) to adjust exp, to orderly decrease the overall CDs. Specific FWA shows as follows.

$$
\begin{aligned}
&\text{if } L_i > \frac{1}{2}(L_{i+1} + L_{i-1}) \cdot (1 + \lambda_3), exp_i \rightarrow exp_i + 1 \\
&\text{elif } L_i < \frac{1}{2}(L_{i+1} + L_{i-1}) \cdot (1 - \lambda_3), exp_i \rightarrow exp_i - 1
\end{aligned}
$$

In particular, The CD on the previous layer of the first layer, and the next layer of the last layer, are replaced with themselves. Similar to the KSA, the λ_3 varies for different models. In this paper, $\lambda_3 = 0.3$. When several exps satisfy FWA at the same time, exp reduction gets the jump on expansion, from shallow to deep layers. At the KSA, parameters in the improved model are roughly equal to the original model, and exps are set between 7 and 2. Specifically, exp in the layer that performs the down-sample operation is no less than 3. Finally, if retrained model is out of the FWA, we stop that exp optimization procession.

2.4 Break Battle Effect Among Kernel Elements

In traditional CNNs [14–16], we mark the layer performs both down-sample(OPds) and channel-expand (OPce) within a single layer as DSCE. In DSCE, kernel element values are similar to (c) in Fig. 2, with a narrow range of element values that are less than half of the adjacent layer. According to Eq. 3 and 4, a shrinking value range L implies a proportional decrease in VIPs, which leads to a reduced NLS entropy and blocks information transmission between layers.

Kernel elements get a relatively small value range in the DSCE is referred to as the "bottleneck effect" existing in the layer. To address this issue, we suggest separating

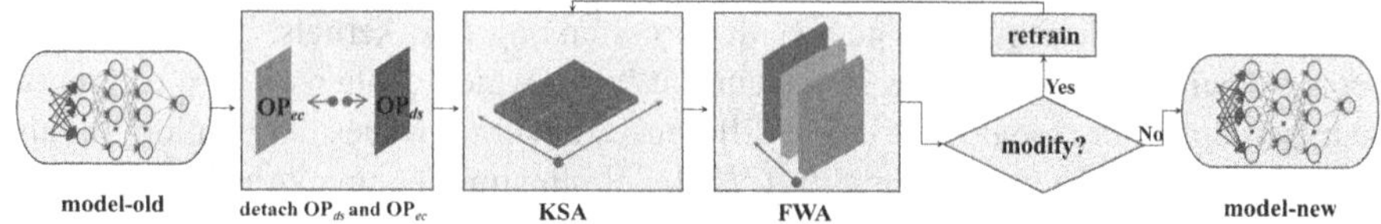

Fig. 3. Procession of CKNA

OPds and OPce, then performing them step by step in contiguous layers. To investigate OPds and OPce run order on model classification accuracy, we performed several experiments and found that only performing OPce before OPds will extend the value range of the down-sample layer, to achieve the intended goal that increasing VIPs within this layer.

Therefore, we optimize model performance from the perspective of breaking the bottleneck effect of the kernel element values, where OPce parts with OPds and performs firstly in different layers, to fluently transmit information between layers.

2.5 Compound Optimizing

We consider the method that exerts comprehensive kernel features to optimize network architecture, as CKNA, which includes kernel size, kernel numbers, and kernel elements. Figure 3 shows the specific optimization process of CKNA.

CKNA begins by detaching OPds and OPce into different adjacent layers, then completes them separately by the order of OPce followed by OPds. Next, we calculate pseudo-kernels to scale kernel size based on KSA, then determine channel numbers based on the PW and DW CDs, and define kernel numbers considering GC CDs and exps accordingly. Kernel features are recalculated after the model is retrained, to adjust the kernel size and quantity until the model keep unchanged. Eventually, the optimization process comes to a tail, a new model is produced.

3 Experiment

In this section, we applied CKNA to group-wise convolution models and obtain comprehensively improved experiments on several datasets represented by ImageNet [17]. All experiments in this paper are performed on the same device with the following hardware configuration: CPU: 12th Gen Intel(R) Core(TM) i9-12900K, GPU model: NVIDIA 3090, GPU quality: 1. The experimental code refers to [18], and all hyperparameters not mentioned in this paper are set to default values.

3.1 CKNA on Group-Wise Convolution Models

To better implement CKNA, we first make partial adaptations to the MobileNetV3-small architecture, which makes extensive use of group-wise convolution, to propose the CKNA-B model as the baseline model, as shown in Table 2.

Table 1. Parts of pseudo-kernels among CKNA-B and CKNA-M

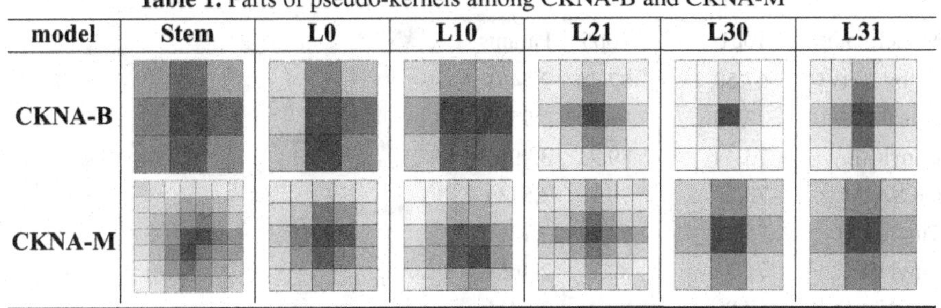

model
Stem
L0
L10
L21
L30
L31
CKNA-B
CKNA-M

Table 2. CKNA-B&CKNA-M architecture

Layer	Operator	SE	CKNA-B					CKNA-M				
			Input	s	exp	kernel	CD	Input	s	exp	kernel	CD
$stem$	Conv2D	–	$224^2 \times 3$	2	–	3×3	109	$224^2 \times 3$	2	–	7×7	17
L_0	MBConv	–	$112^2 \times 16$	2	1	3×3	58 44 58	$112^2 \times \mathbf{24}$	2	4	7×7	11 10 11
L_{10}	MBConv	–	$56^2 \times 16$	2	4.5	3×3	26 34 21	$56^2 \times \mathbf{32}$	2	4	7×7	8.5 7.0 7.3
L_{11}	MBConv	–	$28^2 \times 24$	1	3.7	3×3	12 28 9.5	$28^2 \times \mathbf{40}$	1	6	5×5	2.9 5.8 2.9
L_{20}	MBConv	✓	$28^2 \times 24$	2	4	5×5	15 8.0 10	$28^2 \times \mathbf{40}$	1	4	5×5	6.5 7.8 5.4
L_{21}	MBConv	✓	$14^2 \times 40$	1	6	5×5	3.8 8.4 3.5	$28^2 \times \mathbf{48}$	**2**	3	5×5	3.0 2.9 2.7
L_{22}	MBConv	✓	$14^2 \times 40$	1	6	5×5	3.6 5.9 3.0	$14^2 \times \mathbf{48}$	1	2	3×3	98 25 285
L_{30}	MBConv	✓	$14^2 \times 40$	1	3	5×5	7.9 36 7.0	$14^2 \times \mathbf{48}$	1	7	3×3	2.8 5.3 2.3
L_{31}	MBConv	✓	$14^2 \times 48$	1	3	5×5	3.1 5.8 2.7	$14^2 \times \mathbf{64}$	1	2	3×3	3.9 5.3 2.9
L_{40}	MBConv	✓	$14^2 \times 48$	2	6	5×5	4.8 2.8 3.6	$14^2 \times \mathbf{64}$	1	6	3×3	2.5 4.9 2.2
L_{41}	MBConv	✓	$7^2 \times 96$	1	6	5×5	1.6 3.2 1.4	$14^2 \times 96$	**2**	5	5×5	1.7 1.2 1.6
L_{42}	MBConv	✓	$7^2 \times 96$	1	6	5×5	1.6 1.7 1.4	$7^2 \times 96$	1	5	3×3	1.7 1.1 1.5
L_{50}	Conv2D	–	$7^2 \times 96$	1	–	1×1	– – –	$7^2 \times 96$	1	–	–	– – –
$tail$	SAP+FCx2	–	$7^2 \times 576$	–	–	1×1	– – –	$7^2 \times 576$	–	–	–	– – –

First, we simply decompose OPds and OPce in the last two DSCEs of CKNA-B constrained by GPU memory, then run OPce at L_{20}, L_{40}, then run OPds at L_{21}, L_{41}. Next, we calculate the pseudo-kernel and scale kernel size according to KSA. Finally, we increased channels in the shallow layers and then adjust exp orderly according to FWA. Kernel size and numbers are reset after retaining the model several times according to KSA and FWA, respectively. When kernel features no longer meet CKNA, we cease network adjustment and obtain the final model CKNA-M. Figure 5 shows CKNA-M architecture and parts of pseudo-kernels are shown in Table 1. Figure 5 shows the detailed architecture.

To further demonstrate the generality, we apply CKNA to TinyNet-D and name the enhanced model CKNA-Ti, Table 3 shows implement results. CKNA-Ti obtains amazing gain, and classification accuracy significantly outperforms TinyNet-D by up to 7.09%. we achieve a cross-layer breakthrough beyond TinyNet-C, pushing the performance-bound approach excitingly toward TinyNet-B, as shown in Fig. 4.

Table 3. Imagenet accuracy on models

Model_name	Top1	Top5	Params
Mobilenetv3	67.50	87.38	2.54M
Lcnet-100	72.00	89.49	2.95M
Convit-tiny	73.44	89.71	3.99M
CKNA-M	**73.23**	90.79	**2.51M**
TinyNet-B	75.0	92.2	3.73M
TinyNet-C	71.2	89.7	2.46M
TinyNet-D	67.0	87.38	2.34M
FBNet-B	74.1	–	4.5M
Proxy lessNAS	74.7	92.2	4.1M
CKNA-Ti	**74.09**	91.67	**2.34M**

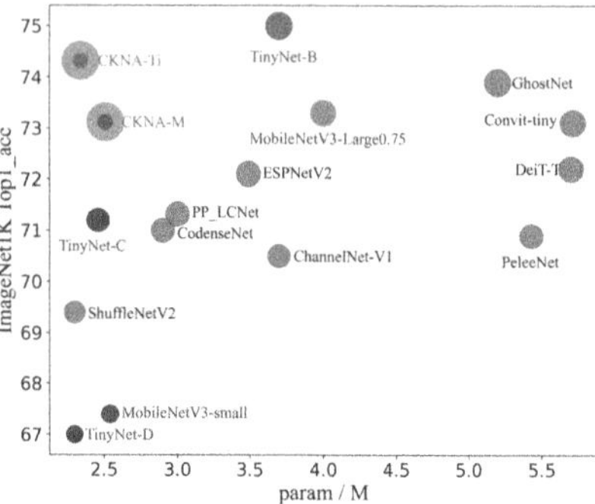

Fig. 4. CNNs vs. Imagenet Accuracy

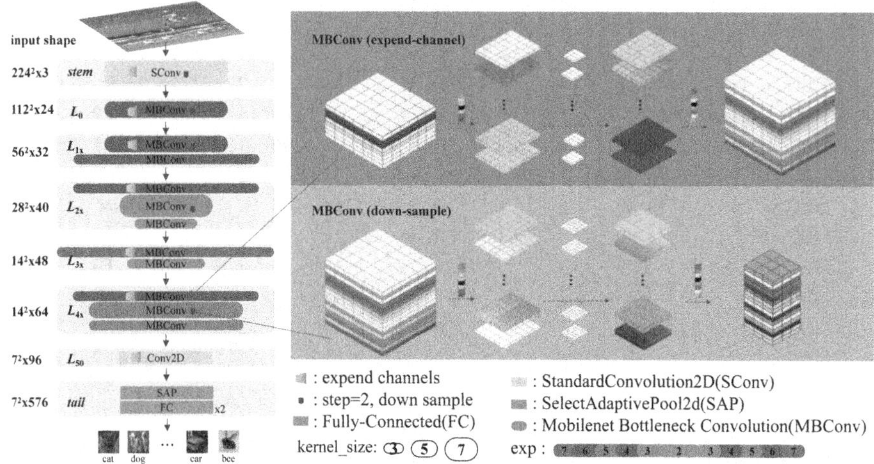

Fig. 5. CKNA-M architecture. The rounded rectangular blocks represent network layers that use the MBConv module, with the length and color representing the exp and the height representing the kernel size. Note that the SE module is omitted. (Color figure online)

Generally, CKNA-X utilizes a staggered combination of different kernel sizes, which contributes to a significantly improved ERF compared to the original model, which uses the smaller kernels first and the larger ones second. By precisely tuning exps at different layers, we approximate CDs among the global network, which is much better than the original one where CDs vary by more than two orders of magnitude.

Table 4. Multi-dataset experiment results

Dataset_name	Train_size	Val_size	Class	CKNA-B	CKNA-M
ImangeNet	1281167	50000	1000	67.99	73.23(+5.24)
CIFAR-100	50000	10000	100	74.32	76.35(+2.03)
Food-101	75750	25250	101	73.07	80.26(+7.19)
Flowers102	2040	6149	102	70.15	74.94(+4.79)
Stanford Cars	8144	8041	196	70.17	80.38(+10.21)
FGVC Aircraft	6667	3333	100	68.35	75.34(+6.08)

Table 5. Imagenet accuracy on models

Model_name	Top1	Top5	Params
MobileNetV3	67.50	–	2.54M
CKNA-B	67.99(+0.49)	87.56	2.54M
CKNA-C	70.76(+3.26)	89.02	2.52M
CKNA-D	71.34(+3.84)	89.59	2.54M
CKNA-K	68.44(+0.94)	87.78	2.54M
CKNA-CD	72.89(+5.39)	90.29	2.54M
CKNA-M	**73.23**(+5.73)	90.79	**2.53M**

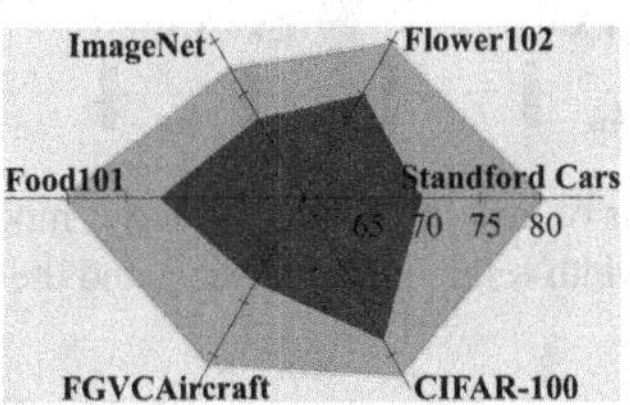

Fig. 6. top_1 accuracy between CKNA-M and CKNA-B on datasets. the blue and orange refer to the performance of CKNA-B and CKNA-M, respectively (Color figure online)

3.2 Multiple Datasets Experiments

We also evaluate and compare CKNA-M to CKNA-B on a list of commonly used datasets [19] as shown in Table 4, where lists both the train and val set sizes as well as the target classes for each dataset (Table 5).

When comparing CKNA-M to CKNA-B on different datasets, we simply tune the output counts to the target classes, while other hyperparameters remain the same. When training on the CIFAR-100, for example, output counts are set to 100, and then re-train directly. Table 4 shows results, and Fig. 6 draws that radar plot.

From Fig. 6, it is clear that in comparison to CKNA-B, CKNA-M achieves a significant increase in classification accuracy, with a huge progress of 5.24% on ImageNet representative and excellent performance on other datasets, especially on the Standford Cars, which achieves an astonishing 10.21% increment. Noted that the image size for the CIFAR100 is only 32×32 pixels, which we simply expand to 224×224 using binary interpolation before feeding into the model with no additional tuning, so the precision of this is somewhat lower than expected.

3.3 Ablation Experiment

In this section, we derive a series of models, by individually improving the kernel size, and the channel numbers, and restructuring the DSCE among CKNA-B cells. We

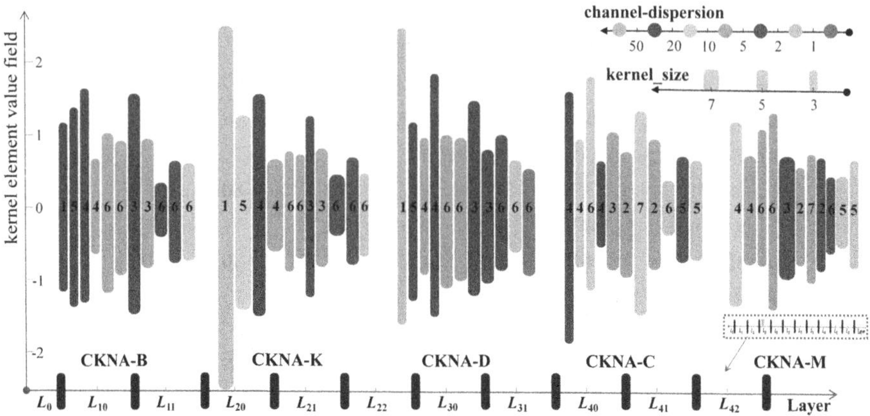

Fig. 7. Parts of lays in CKNA-B's series models. The bars represent the layers, the color refers to CDs, the width refers to kernel size, and the number inside represents exp.

trained and compared these models on ImageNet in order to approximate the model gain from the full viewpoint. Table 4 shows results for CKNA-B series models.

The CDs, the kernel size, and the kernel element value range information of CKNA-B series models are plotted as an information flow diagram shown in Fig. 7, intuitively displaying the process of information flow between layers.CKNA-K and CKNA-C adjust the kernel size and numbers and improve classification accuracies by 0.44% and 2.76%, respectively. This provides that different layers require custom kernel sizes and numbers. CKNA-D decayed OPds and OPce in L_{20} and L_{40} to break the bottleneck effect between layers, obtains a significantly increased value range of kernel elements, ultimately achieves a fabulous high-performance growth of up to 3.14%. CKNA-M combines multi-dimensional improvements, not only eliminating the bottleneck effect of network layers but also setting the kernel sizes and quantities more reasonably, ultimately increasing the overall classification accuracy of the baseline model by 5.73% with fewer parameters. These results strongly certify the effectiveness of the comprehensive kernel optimization network architecture.

4 Conclusion

This paper systematically investigates the configuration of kernel hyper-parameters in CNNs and identifies that the specifically referenced indicator was a missing piece, preventing the models from achieving better accuracy and performance. Innovatively, to address this issue, we propose that CKNA make an explicit kernel assignment based on the comprehensive kernel feature optimization method. By resetting kernel hyper-parameters, enhancement models obtain an excited improvement with fewer parameters on multiple datasets, preliminary validating the new way of designing efficient kernel configuration in group-wise CNNs. In the future, the CKNA is expected to be trained and completed on more CNNs to further verify the generalization performance.

References

1. Dosovitskiy, A., et al.: An image is worth 16 $\times$ 16 words: transformers for image recognition at scale. arXiv preprint arXiv:2010.11929 (2020)
2. Smith, L.N., Topin, N.: Super-convergence: very fast training of neural networks using large learning rates. In: Artificial Intelligence and Machine Learning for Multi-domain Operations Applications, vol. 11006, pp 369–386. SPIE (2019)
3. Misra, D. Mish: a self regularized non-monotonic activation function. arXiv preprint arXiv:1908.08681 (2019)
4. Nematzadeh, S., Kiani, F., Torkamanian-Afshar, M., Aydin, N.: Tuning hyperparameters of machine learning algorithms and deep neural networks using metaheuristics: a bioinformatics study on biomedical and biological cases. Comput. Biol. Chem. **97**, 107619 (2022)
5. Simonyan, K., Zisserman, A.: Very deep convolutional networks for large-scale image recognition. arXiv preprint arXiv:1409.1556 (2014)
6. He, K., Zhang, X., Ren, S., Sun, J.: Deep residual learning for image recognition. In: Proceedings of the IEEE Conference on Computer Vision and Pattern Recognition, pp. 770–778 (2016)
7. Veit, A., Wilber, M.J., Belongie, S.: Residual networks behave like ensembles of relatively shallow networks. Adv. Neural Inf. Process. Syst. **29** (2016)
8. De, S., Smith, S.: Batch normalization biases residual blocks towards the identity function in deep networks. Adv. Neural Inf. Process. Syst. **33**, 19964–19975 (2020)
9. Ding, X., Zhang, X., Han, J., Ding, G.: Scaling up your kernels to 31 $\times$ 31: revisiting large kernel design in CNNs. In: Proceedings of the IEEE/CVF Conference on Computer Vision and Pattern Recognition, pp. 11963–11975 (2022)
10. Zagoruyko, S., Komodakis, N.: Wide residual networks. arXiv preprint arXiv:1605.07146 (2016)
11. Howard, A.G., et al.: Mobilenets: efficient convolutional neural networks for mobile vision applications. arXiv preprint arXiv:1704.04861 (2017)
12. Shannon, C.E.: A mathematical theory of communication. ACM SIGMOBILE Mob. Comput. Commun. Rev. **5**(1), 3–55 (2001)
13. Pascanu, R., Montufar, G., Bengio, Y.: On the number of response regions of deep feed forward networks with piece-wise linear activations. arXiv preprint arXiv:1312.6098 (2013)
14. Zhang, X., Zhou, X., Lin, M., Sun, J.: Shufflenet: an extremely efficient convolutional neural network for mobile devices. In: Proceedings of the IEEE Conference on Computer Vision and Pattern Recognition, pp. 6848–6856 (2018)
15. Ma, N., Zhang, X., Zheng, H.T., Sun, J.: Shufflenet v2: practical guidelines for efficient CNN architecture design. In: Proceedings of the European Conference on Computer Vision (ECCV), pp. 116–131 (2018)
16. Liu, Z., Mao, H., Wu, C.Y., Feichtenhofer, C., Darrell, T., Xie, S.: A convnet for the 2020s. In: Proceedings of the IEEE/CVF Conference on Computer Vision and Pattern Recognition, pp. 11976–11986 (2022)
17. Deng, J., Dong, W., Socher, R., Li, L.J., Li, K., Fei-Fei, L.: Imagenet: a large-scale hierarchical image database. In: 2009 IEEE Conference on Computer Vision and Pattern Recognition, pp. 248–255. IEEE (2009)
18. Wightman, R.: Pytorch image models (2019). https://github.com/huggingface/pytorch-image-models
19. Tan, M., Le, Q.: Efficientnet: rethinking model scaling for convolutional neural networks. In: International Conference on Machine Learning, pp. 6105–6114. PMLR (2019)

Conditional Convolution Residual Network for Efficient Super-Resolution

Yunsheng Guo[1], Jinyang Huang[1], Xiang Zhang[2], Xiao Sun[1], and Yu Gu[3](✉)

[1] School of Computer Science and Information Engineering, Hefei University of Technology, Hefei, Anhui, China
guoyunsheng@mail.hfut.edu.cn, {hjy,sunx}@hfut.edu.cn

[2] School of Computer Science and Engineering, University of Electronic Science and Technology of China, Hefei, Anhui, China
zhangxiang@ieee.org

[3] School of Cybers Science and Technology, University of Science and Technology of China, Hefei, Anhui, China
yugu.bruce@ieee.org

Abstract. With the continuous development of deep learning, single-image super-resolution (SISR) based on convolutional neural networks (CNNs) has made significant progress. Although CNN-based methods have achieved great success, these methods are difficult to apply to edge devices due to the need for large amounts of computing resources. To address this problem, the latest advancements in efficient SISR techniques focus on reducing the number of parameters and multiply-add operations (MAdds). In this paper, we propose a novel Conditional Convolution Residual Network (CCRN) to tackle this challenge. The main idea is to use conditional convolution instead of ordinary convolutional layers for residual feature learning and to combine Contrast-aware Channel Attention (CCA) and Enhanced Spatial Attention (ESA) mechanisms to improve the model's performance. The model's performance is ensured while reducing the computational complexity. Experimental results demonstrate that CCRN has fewer MAdds than existing SISR methods while achieving state-of-the-art performance.

Keywords: Efficient super-resolution · Conditional convolution · Attention mechanism

1 Introduction

Single Image Super-Resolution (SR) is a fundamental task in the field of computer vision, which aims to reconstruct high-resolution (HR) images from low-resolution (LR) images for better visual effects. With the development of deep learning, convolutional neural network-based methods have been widely introduced to the SR field to achieve high-quality super-resolution images. To improve the restoration quality of SR networks, existing SR networks typically employ large-scale models, which result in high computational complexity and make it challenging to apply them in real-world scenarios that require efficiency or real-time implementation, especially on edge devices.

L. Iliadis et al. (Eds.): ICANN 2023, LNCS 14263, pp. 86–97, 2023.
https://doi.org/10.1007/978-3-031-44204-9_8

To design lightweight neural networks, researchers have approached the problem from the perspectives of parameters and computational complexity and adopted different optimization strategies. For example, FSRCNN [1] reduces computation and parameter numbers by using upscaling modules and adhering to reducing the size of convolutions and features. Recursive learning has also been widely applied in many works, such as DRCN [2] and DRRN [3], to further reduce the number of parameters. However, due to their limited representation capabilities, these recursive methods also lead to performance degradation while consuming more computational resources. For instance, DRCN uses 17.9 trillion multiply-add operations (MAdds), while DRRN uses 6.8 trillion, which is difficult to afford for mobile devices. Therefore, to improve efficiency, some researchers have adopted different approaches, such as parameter sharing strategies [2], cascaded networks with grouped convolutions [4], information or feature distillation mechanisms [5], and attention mechanisms [6]. Although these methods employ compact architectures and improve mapping efficiency, there is still redundancy in convolution operations. Hence, researchers have shifted the focus from efficient SR to designing effective modules and dedicated networks to enhance the performance of SR networks further.

In this paper, we propose a novel lightweight super-resolution (SR) network, called Conditional Convolution Residual Network (CCRN). The network significantly reduces the MAdds of the network by optimizing convolution operations and introducing effective attention modules while achieving state-of-the-art performance.

Firstly, CCRN constructs the basic modules using Conditional Convolution [7]. This approach addresses the challenge of increasing model capacity by adding parameters, depth, and channels, which would otherwise result in greater computational demands and deployment difficulty. By inputting the convolution kernel parameters, Conditional Convolution breaks the static convolution characteristics, thereby improving the model's performance more efficiently. Secondly, to ensure the quality of reconstructed images, we introduce attention mechanisms in the process of feature extraction to select important pixel points at a fine-grained level, and better utilize pixel-level information in the image. Specifically, we add Enhanced Spatial Attention (ESA) [8] and Contrast-Aware Channel Attention (CCA) [5] modules at the end of each residual block to achieve this goal. Our proposed CCRN method significantly reduces the model's MAdds while maintaining SR performance in efficiency-oriented SR networks.

Overall, our main contributions can be summarized as follows:

- We introduce conditional convolution to construct basic modules and demonstrate their effectiveness in SR.
- We learn the importance of channels and space with two effective attention modules, ESA and CCA, respectively, and enhance the model's ability.
- The proposed CCRN, which integrates conditional convolution and effective attention modules, significantly reduces the network's computational complexity while maintaining SR performance.

2 Related Work

2.1 Deep Networks for SR

In recent years with the rapid development of deep learning techniques, convolutional neural networks (CNNs) have greatly advanced the development of low-level computer vision tasks [9]. Super-resolution (SR) tasks have also made increasingly significant progress. Since the pioneering work of Dong *et al.* [10], who proposed the SRCNN with a three-layer convolutional neural network that significantly outperformed traditional methods, a series of methods have been proposed to improve SR models. For example, Kim *et al.* proved [11] that deeper networks can achieve better performance by increasing the network depth to 20. Zhang et al. [12] introduced dense connections into the network, further enhancing the model's representation ability. Liang *et al.* [13] proposed a Transformer architecture for image restoration based on Swin Transformer [14], which achieved significant improvement and surpassed the state-of-the-art performance. [15] introduced a channel attention mechanism to utilize global statistics information for better performance.

Most of the above methods improve the quality by using more convolutional layers and attention mechanisms, ignoring resource-limited applications, which limits the practical application of these methods.

2.2 Efficient SR Models

Although the aforementioned methods have made significant progress in performance, most of them come with high computational costs, which has prompted researchers to develop more efficient methods for SR tasks. There have been many works aimed at designing more effective models for SR. Ahn *et al.* [4] proposed CARN-M, which is a residual network with a cascading mechanism that can reduce parameters and computations at the expense of lowered quality. Hui *et al.* proposed an information distillation network [16] that explicitly splits intermediate features for distilling and compressing local long-short path features. Based on IDN [16], IMDN [5] was introduced with a more reasonable feature distillation mechanism and effectively adaptive pruning strategy. By re-examining these distillation mechanisms, Liu *et al.* [17] proposed a novel channel-splitting strategy that utilizes convolutional layers for dimensionality change. Additionally, they designed shallow residual blocks to improve inference performance while maintaining parameter size.

3 Method

3.1 Network Architecture

The overall architecture of our proposed CCRN method is shown in Fig. 1. It inherits the architectures of IMDN and consists of four stages: shallow feature extraction, deep feature extraction, feature fusion, and upsampling module.

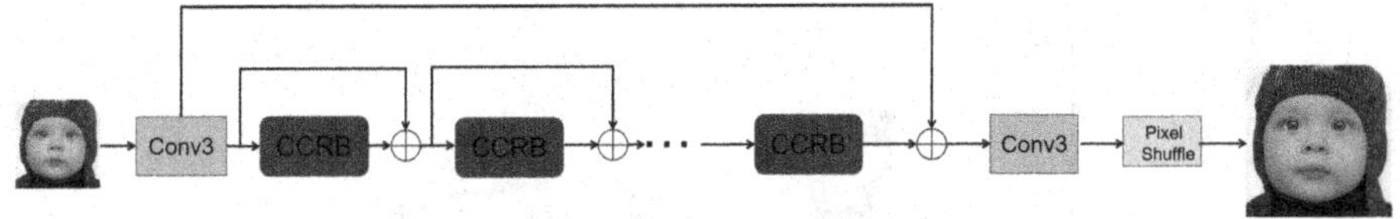

Fig. 1. CCRN Network Architecture

The shallow feature extraction stage involves extracting coarse features from the LR image using a 3×3 convolution operation, which can also be used to supplement the residual information lost in the feature extraction process with subsequent blocks. Given an input image I_{LR}, this feature extraction process can be formulated as:

$$F_0 = L(I_{LR}) \tag{1}$$

where L represents the feature extraction function of the 3×3 convolution, and F_0 is the extracted feature map. Next, we use a cascaded approach with multiple CCRBs for deep feature extraction, which can be formulated as:

$$F_n = H_{CCRB}^n(H_{fuse}(F_{n-1}, F_{n-2})) \tag{2}$$

where $H_{CCRB}^n(\cdot)$ represents the n-th CCRB block, and F_n is the n-th output feature map. $H_{fuse}(\cdot)$ represents the fusion module, and to utilize residuals for learning, the input and output of the n-1 CCRB block are aggregated. In the feature fusion stage, the multi-distilled deep features F_n and the shallow features F_0 are fused together through residual connections.

$$F_{fuse} = H_{fuse}(F_0, F_n) \tag{3}$$

The reconstruction stage can be formulated as follows:

$$F_{rec} = H_{rec}(F_{fuse}) \tag{4}$$

where $H_{rec}(\cdot)$ consists of a 3×3 convolution layer and a pixelshuffle operation. The model is optimized using the L1 and L2 functions, and the specific optimization process is described in the experiments.

3.2 Conditional Convolution Residual Block

Inspired by the IMDB in IMDN, we designed a more efficient conditionally-convolutional residual block (CCRB) with a structure similar to IMDB. The overall architecture of CCRB is shown in Fig. 2(a).

A CCRB generally consists of three stages: feature distillation, feature condensation, and feature enhancement. In the first stage, for the input feature F_{in}, feature distillation can be formulated as:

$$\begin{aligned}
&F_{distilled1}, F_{coarse1} = DL_1(F_{in}), RL_1(F_{in}),\\
&F_{distilled2}, F_{coarse2} = DL_2(F_{coarse1}), RL_2(F_{coarse1}),\\
&F_{distilled3}, F_{coarse3} = DL_3(F_{coarse2}), RL_3(F_{coarse2}),\\
&F_{distilled4} = DL_4(F_{coarse3})
\end{aligned} \tag{5}$$

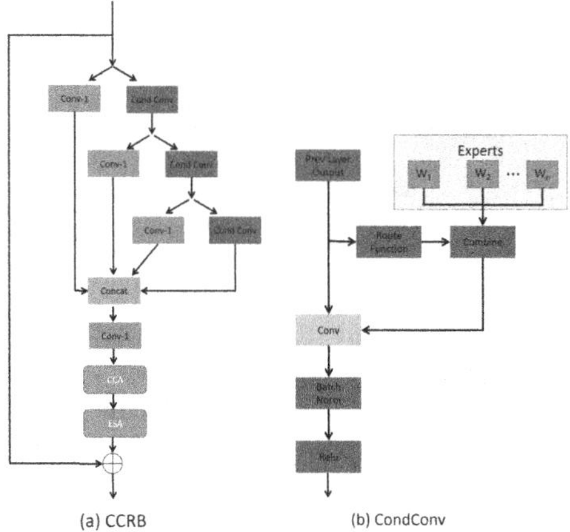

Fig. 2. The architecture of CCRB and CondConv

where DL represents the distillation layer that generates distilled features, and RL represents the refinement layer that further refines coarse features. In the feature condensation stage, the distilled features $F_{distilled1}$, $F_{distilled2}$, $F_{distilled3}$ and $F_{distilled4}$ are concatenated together and then compressed into a feature map with reduced dimensions using a 1×1 convolution.

$$F_{condensed} = H_{linear}(Concat((F_{distilled1}, \cdots, F_{distilled4})) \tag{6}$$

where $F_{condensed}$ is the compressed feature map, and $H_{linear}(\cdot)$ represents a 1×1 convolution layer. For the final stage, in order to enhance the model's representation ability while maintaining efficiency, we introduce a lightweight enhanced spatial attention (ESA) block [8] and a contrast-aware channel attention (CCA) block [5] as part of the CCRB.

$$F_{enhanced} = H_{ESA}(H_{CCA}(F_{condensed})) \tag{7}$$

where $F_{enhanced}$ is the enhanced feature map, $H_{ESA}(\cdot)$ and $H_{CCA}(\cdot)$ respectively represent the ESA and CCA modules, which have been shown to effectively enhance model ability from both spatial and channel perspectives.

3.3 Conditional Convolution

As shown in Fig. 2(b), in CondConv [7] each convolution kernel has the same dimension as the standard convolution kernel parameters. The ability improvement of conventional convolutional layers relies on increasing the kernel size and the number of channels, which further increases the overall computation of the network. However, the CondConv kernel is customized for each input sample, then the obtained kernel is used to perform convolution on that sample to obtain the corresponding output. Specifically, the convolution kernel in CondConv is parameterized by:

$$Output(x) = \sigma((\alpha_1 \cdot W_1 + \cdots + \alpha_n \cdot W_n) * x) \tag{8}$$

Each α is an example-dependent scalar weight computed using a routing function with learning parameters, n is the number of experts, and σ is the activation function. When we adjust the convolution layer to use CondConv, W_i is the same kernel in convolution as in normal convolution. The following routing function is used to compute α. This function is computationally efficient, distinguishes the input examples in a meaningful way, and is easy to interpret. We compute example-dependent routing weights α from layer inputs in three steps: global average pooling, fully connected layers, and sigmoid activation.

$$\alpha = Sigmoid(GlobalAveragePool(x) * R) \tag{9}$$

where R is the learning routing weight matrix that maps the pooled input to n expert weights. Normal convolutional operations operate only on local sensory fields, and the routing function described above allows to use of information from the global context in local operations.

In the previous efficient SR models, the capacity of the regular convolutional layers is generally increased by increasing the kernel height/width of the kernel or the number of input/output channels, but each additional parameter in the convolution requires additional multiplication proportional to the number of pixels in the input feature map, which can be large. This also increases the overall computational effort.

In CCRB we introduce the CondConv layer, where we compute a convolution kernel for each example as a linear combination of n experts before applying the convolution. It is crucial that each convolution kernel is computed only once, but is applied to many different positions in the input image. This means that by increasing n, we can increase the capacity of the network with only a small increase in inference cost; each additional parameter requires only 1 additional multiplication and addition. This greatly reduces the computational cost of increasing the capacity of the network and plays a big role in reducing the MAdds in Efficient SR.

3.4 ESA and CCA

We introduce both the enhanced spatial attention (ESA) module and the contrast-aware channel attention(CCA) module to pay more attention to the features related to the fine details of the image. The ESA mechanism operates at the end of each residual block to enforce features to focus more on the regions of interest. By aggregating these salient features together, we can obtain more representative features. The ESA mechanism as shown in Fig. 3(a) starts with a 1×1 convolutional layer to reduce the channel dimension, making the entire block very lightweight. To further expand the receptive field, we use a stride convolution (with a stride of 2), followed by a max pooling layer. An upsampling

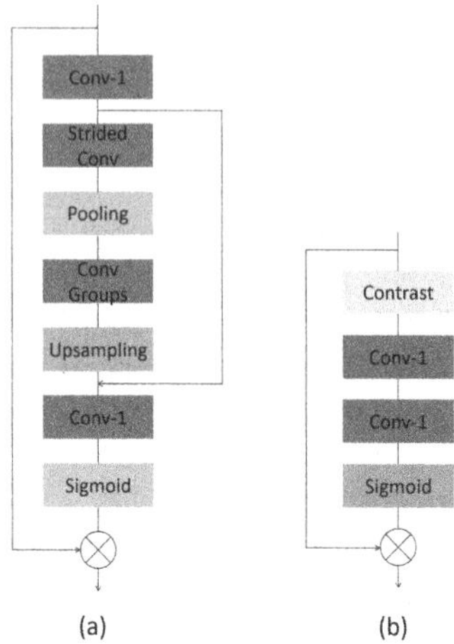

Fig. 3. The architecture of ESA and CCA

layer is employed to restore the spatial dimension, and a 1×1 convolutional layer is used to recover the channel dimension. Finally, an attention mask is generated by a sigmoid layer. To utilize residual information, a skip connection is also employed to directly forward the high-resolution features before spatial downsampling to the end of each block.

In deep neural networks, different channels in different feature maps often represent different objects. Channel attention serves as an object selection process that can adaptively re-calibrate the weights of each channel to determine what to focus on. CCA as shown in Fig. 3(b) utilizes contrastive information, including the sum of mean and standard deviation, to calculate the weights for channel attention.

4 Experiment

4.1 Datasets and Metrics

The training images consisted of 5000 images from LSDIR [18] and 800 images from DIV2K [19]. We employed four standard benchmark datasets, namely, Set5 [20], Set14 [21], B100 [22], Urban100 [23] to evaluate the performance of different methods. The average peak signal-to-noise ratio (PSNR) and structural similarity index measure (SSIM) on the Y channel (i.e., luminance) were used as evaluation metrics.

4.2 Implementation Details of CCRN

The proposed CCRN consists of four CCRB blocks with 48 channels and employs two experts in conditional convolutions. All kernels in the deep convolutions have a size of 3. The batch size is set to 16, and each LR input patch has a size of 48 $\times$ 48. The model is optimized using the Adam optimizer with $\beta 1 = 0.9$ and $\beta 2 = 0.999$. The initial learning rate is set to 1×10^{-4} with drops by half every 200 epochs. We set the total epochs to 2000, first the L1 loss is employed for model optimization with 1000 epochs, and a total of 1×10^6 iterations are performed. Then L2 loss is used to fine-tune the network with 1000 epochs. We implement our model using Pytorch on a GeForce RTX 3090 GPU.

Table 1. Results on method complexity (number of parameters, Multi-Adds). The multi-adds operation is calculated with 320 $\times$ 180 input size.

Method	Params [K]	Multi-Adds[G]
SRCNN	8	52.7
LapSRN	251	29.9
DRRN	298	6796.9
MemNet	678	2662.4
VDSR	665	612.6
IDN	553	31.1
CARN	1592	90.9
IMDN	715	41.0
CCRN (ours)	**752**	**14.15**

4.3 Study of the Basic Module

In our work, each feature extraction part of CCRB consists of three CondConv, and each CondConv can be set with different numbers of experts. We investigated the impact of changing the number of experts in CondConv. As shown in Table 2, with an increase in the number of experts, the SR performance improves, and the model's parameters increase, but the model's MAdds remain stable. This suggests that increasing the number of experts in CondConv can improve the model's performance without affecting the model's computational cost.

Figure 4(b) demonstrate the outputs of feature maps with different layers. All feature maps are from the final CCRB module, each row displays 10 feature maps from the input of the CCA layer, the output of the CCA layer, and the output of the ESA layer, respectively. Through the attention mechanism, we can observe that the details of the image have been further explored, which is beneficial to enhancing the image quality for SR.

Table 2. Ablation results of various experts in CondConv(PSNR/SSIM)

Expert Number	Multi-Adds [G]	Params [K]	Set5 [20]
1	14.15	503	31.55/0.8834
2	14.15	752	31.75/0.8875
3	14.15	1002	31.82/0.8887

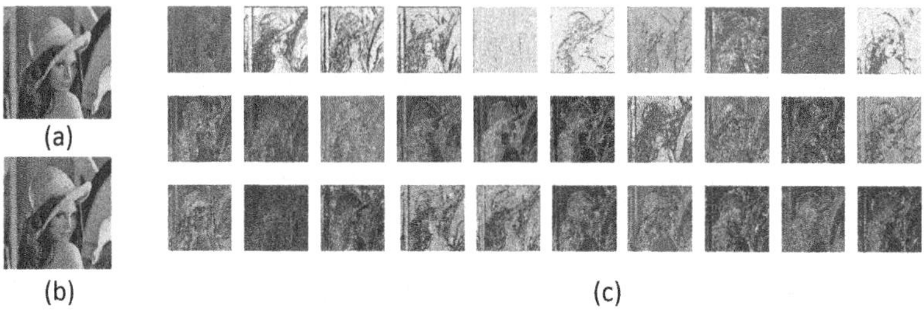

Fig. 4. Illustrations of (a) Low-resolution image (b) Super-resolution image (c) Feature Maps

Table 3. Average PSNR/SSIM for scale ×4 on datasets Set5, Set14, B100, Urban100 with bicubic degradation.(Compared to CARN, which achieves the best PSNR performance, we have obtained comparable results using only one-sixth of the MAdds (multiply-additions) utilized).

Method	B100 [22]	Set5 [20]	Set14 [21]	Urban100 [23]
	PSNR/SSIM	PSNR/SSIM	PSNR/SSIM	PSNR/SSIM
Bicubic	25.96/0.6675	28.42/0.8104	26.00/0.7027	23.14/0.6577
SRCNN	26.90/0.7101	30.48/0.8626	27.50/0.7513	24.52/0.7221
LapSRN	27.32/0.7275	31.54/0.8852	28.09/0.7700	25.21/0.7562
DRRN	27.38/0.7284	31.68/0.8888	28.21/0.7720	25.44/0.7638
MemNet	27.40/0.7281	31.74/0.8893	28.26/0.7723	25.50/0.7630
VDSR	27.29/0.7251	31.82/0.8903	28.01/0.7674	25.18/0.7524
IDN	27.41/0.7297	32.13/0.8937	28.25/0.7730	25.41/0.7632
CARN	**27.58**/0.7349	**32.21**/0.8948	**28.60**/0.7806	**26.07**/0.7837
IMDN	27.56/0.7353	32.13/0.8948	28.58/0.7811	26.04/0.7838
CCRN(ours)	27.43/0.7305	31.75/0.8875	28.42/0.7756	25.69/0.7710

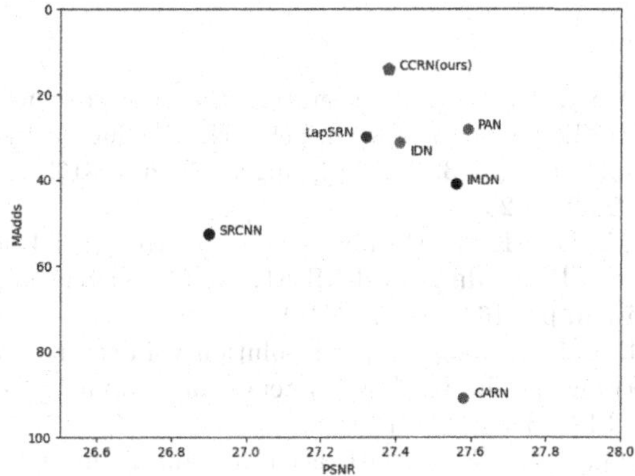

Fig. 5. MAdds and PSNR (based on B100 [22] dataset)

4.4 Result and Discussion

The model complexity comparison and performance evaluation of CCRN and other Efficient SR models, namely, SRCNN [24], LapSRN [25],DRRN [3], MemNet [26], VDSR [11], IDN [16],CARN [4], IMDN [5] on the testing dataset are presented in Table 1 and Table 3 for ×4 scales. The complexity of each model can be found in the second and third columns of Table 1, where the second column shows the number of parameters included in the model, and MAdds represents the number of Multi-Adds in the model, where one Multi-Add represents one multiplication and addition operation. A lower number of Multi-Adds indicates that the model requires less computation and thus has faster computational speed. It can be observed that CCRN has significantly fewer Multi-Adds than all the other models, which implies a great advantage in computational speed. Table 3 also shows that CCRN achieves good performance. Compared to IMDN, which suffers from a 0.13 PSNR loss on B100 [22] at ×4 scale, CCRN requires only one-third of the computation. As shown in Fig. 5. CCRN has the lowest number of Multi-Adds among all SR models while maintaining a high PSNR.

5 Conclusion

In this paper, we propose a lightweight network named Conditional Convolution Residual Network (CCRN) for single image super-resolution. Inspired by the Information Multi-distillation Network (IMDN) and Conditional Convolution (CondConv), the design of CCRN adopts a similar architecture to IMDN but introduces more efficient Conditional Convolution Residual Blocks (CCRB). Furthermore, effective ESA blocks and CCA blocks are used to enhance the representative ability of the model. Extensive experiments demonstrate that our method can achieve the same SR performance as advanced and efficient SR methods with much fewer MAdds, significantly reducing the computational cost of the model required for single image SR.

References

1. Dong, C., Loy, C.C., Tang, X.: Accelerating the super-resolution convolutional neural network. In: Leibe, B., Matas, J., Sebe, N., Welling, M. (eds.) ECCV 2016, Part II. LNCS, vol. 9906, pp. 391–407. Springer, Cham (2016). https://doi.org/10.1007/978-3-319-46475-6_25
2. Kim, J., Lee, J.K., Lee, K.M.: Deeply-recursive convolutional network for image super-resolution. In: Proceedings of the IEEE Conference on Computer Vision and Pattern Recognition, pp. 1637–1645 (2016)
3. Tai, Y., Yang, J., Liu, X.: Image super-resolution via deep recursive residual network. In: Proceedings of the IEEE Conference on Computer Vision and Pattern Recognition, pp. 3147–3155 (2017)
4. Ahn, N., Kang, B., Sohn, K.-A.: Fast, accurate, and lightweight super-resolution with cascading residual network. In: Proceedings of the European Conference on Computer Vision (ECCV), pp. 252–268 (2018)
5. Hui, Z., Gao, X., Yang, Y., Wang, X.: Lightweight image super-resolution with information multi-distillation network. In: Proceedings of the 27th ACM International Conference on Multimedia, pp. 2024–2032 (2019)
6. Chen, H., Gu, J., Zhang, Z.: Attention in attention network for image super-resolution. arXiv preprint arXiv:2104.09497 (2021)
7. Yang, B., Bender, G., Le, Q.V., Ngiam, J.: CondConv: conditionally parameterized convolutions for efficient inference. In: Advances in Neural Information Processing Systems, vol. 32 (2019)
8. Liu, J., Zhang, W., Tang, Y., Tang, J., Wu, G.: Residual feature aggregation network for image super-resolution. In: Proceedings of the IEEE/CVF Conference on Computer Vision and Pattern Recognition, pp. 2359–2368 (2020)
9. He, K., Zhang, X., Ren, S., Sun, J.: Deep residual learning for image recognition. In: Proceedings of the IEEE Conference on Computer Vision and Pattern Recognition, pp. 770–778 (2016)
10. Dong, C., Loy, C.C., He, K., Tang, X.: Image super-resolution using deep convolutional networks. IEEE Trans. Pattern Anal. Mach. Intell. **38**(2), 295–307 (2015)
11. Kim, J., Lee, J.K., Lee, K.M.: Accurate image super-resolution using very deep convolutional networks. In: Proceedings of the IEEE Conference on Computer Vision and Pattern Recognition, pp. 1646–1654 (2016)
12. Zhang, Y., Tian, Y., Kong, Y., Zhong, B., Fu, Y.: Residual dense network for image super-resolution. In: Proceedings of the IEEE Conference on Computer Vision and Pattern Recognition, pp. 2472–2481 (2018)
13. Liang, J., Cao, J., Sun, G., Zhang, K., Van Gool, L., Timofte, R.: SwinIR: image restoration using swin transformer. In: Proceedings of the IEEE/CVF International Conference on Computer Vision, pp. 1833–1844 (2021)
14. Liu, Z., et al.: Swin transformer: hierarchical vision transformer using shifted windows. In: Proceedings of the IEEE/CVF International Conference on Computer Vision, pp. 10012–10022 (2021)
15. Zhang, Y., Li, K., Li, K., Wang, L., Zhong, B., Fu, Y.: Image super-resolution using very deep residual channel attention networks. In: Proceedings of the European Conference on Computer Vision (ECCV), pp. 286–301 (2018)
16. Hui, Z., Wang, X., Gao, X.: Fast and accurate single image super-resolution via information distillation network. In: Proceedings of the IEEE Conference on Computer Vision and Pattern Recognition, pp. 723–731 (2018)

17. Lim, B., Son, S., Kim, H., Nah, S., Lee, K.M.: Enhanced deep residual networks for single image super-resolution. In: Proceedings of the IEEE Conference on Computer Vision and Pattern Recognition Workshops, pp. 136–144 (2017)
18. Li, Y., et al.: LSDIR: a large scale dataset for image restoration (2023)
19. Agustsson, E., Timofte, R.: NTIRE 2017 challenge on single image super-resolution: dataset and study. In: Proceedings of the IEEE Conference on Computer Vision and Pattern Recognition Workshops, pp. 126–135 (2017)
20. Bevilacqua, M., Roumy, A., Guillemot, C., Alberi-Morel, M.L.: Low-complexity single-image super-resolution based on nonnegative neighbor embedding (2012)
21. Zeyde, R., Elad, M., Protter, M.: On single image scale-up using sparse-representations. In: Boissonnat, J.-D., et al. (eds.) Curves and Surfaces 2010. LNCS, vol. 6920, pp. 711–730. Springer, Heidelberg (2012). https://doi.org/10.1007/978-3-642-27413-8_47
22. Martin, D., Fowlkes, C., Tal, D., Malik, J.: A database of human segmented natural images and its application to evaluating segmentation algorithms and measuring ecological statistics. In: Proceedings Eighth IEEE International Conference on Computer Vision, ICCV 2001, vol. 2, pp. 416–423. IEEE (2001)
23. Huang, J.-B., Singh, A., Ahuja, N.: Single image super-resolution from transformed self-exemplars. In: Proceedings of the IEEE Conference on Computer Vision and Pattern Recognition, pp. 5197–5206 (2015)
24. Dong, C., Loy, C.C., He, K., Tang, X.: Learning a deep convolutional network for image super-resolution. In: Fleet, D., Pajdla, T., Schiele, B., Tuytelaars, T. (eds.) ECCV 2014, Part IV. LNCS, vol. 8692, pp. 184–199. Springer, Cham (2014). https://doi.org/10.1007/978-3-319-10593-2_13
25. Lai, W.-S., Huang, J.-B., Ahuja, N., Yang, M.-H.: Deep laplacian pyramid networks for fast and accurate super-resolution. In: Proceedings of the IEEE Conference on Computer Vision and Pattern Recognition, pp. 624–632 (2017)
26. Tai, Y., Yang, J., Liu, X., Xu, C.: MemNet: a persistent memory network for image restoration. In: Proceedings of the IEEE International Conference on Computer Vision, pp. 4539–4547 (2017)

Cross Attention with Deep Local Features for Few-Shot Image Classification

Tengfei Chu, Hao Shen, Jing Lv, and Ming Yang(✉)

Nanjing Normal University, Nangjing, China
{202202020,202202019,05275,myang}@njnu.edu.cn

Abstract. Traditional few-shot learning methods that rely on image-level features have been widely adopted, but they may not be effective in representing the local information of images. Recently, some methods have introduced deep local features that are semantically rich and achieved promising results. However, these methods typically take all local features into consideration, ignoring that some of them, such as sky and grass, are task-irrelevant and may affect the accuracy of image classification. In this thesis, we propose a novel Local Cross Attention Network (LCAN) that aims to learn the query local features that are most relevant to each task. Specifically, we designed a local cross attention mechanism composed of two modules: a query local attention module and a class relevant module. The former is used to determine what kind of query local features to attend by using the spatial and channel information in the query feature, while the latter utilizes the local relationship between the query feature and the support feature to determine which query local features to attend. Extensive experimental on three widely used few-shot classification benchmarks (miniImageNet, tieredImageNet and CUB-200) demonstrate that our proposed method achieves state-of-the-art performance.

Keywords: Few-shot learning · Deep local features · Attention mechanism

1 Introduction

Deep learning based image classification methods [3,8,12,21,26] typically require a large number of labeled samples to optimize model parameters, resulting in better classification accuracy. However, the collection of such samples can be arduous or costly to label, making few-shot learning methods [7,9,18,20,27,28] appealing to researchers. The goal of few-shot learning is to train a model that can generalize well, even with a limited number of examples. Nevertheless, the scarcity of examples for each class presents a challenge in effectively representing class distributions, making this task particularly difficult. To address the challenge of few-shot learning, researchers have proposed various methods, which can be broadly categorized as meta-learning based [2,5,7,13] or metric learning based [4,14,22,25,30] The former uses the meta-learning paradigm to enable

L. Iliadis et al. (Eds.): ICANN 2023, LNCS 14263, pp. 98–110, 2023.
https://doi.org/10.1007/978-3-031-44204-9_9

the model to learn how to learn. These methods often utilize recursive neural networks or long-short-term memory networks to learn memory networks that store knowledge [1,10]. The latter utilizes simpler architectures to learn a deep embedding space that propagates representations. Typically relying on metric learning and the episodic training mechanism [16], these methods have significantly advanced the field of few-shot learning. However, most existing methods utilize image-level features for classification, such as matching networks [16], prototypical networks [11], and relation networks [22]), which may not be effective in representing images in few-shot learning scenarios.

In recent years, DN4 [14], DeepEMD [29], and FRN [24] have started to utilize the semantically rich deep local features in image features to address the problem of few-shot learning, and have achieved promising results. However, these method treats the contributions of all local features to the final classification result as equal, ignoring the fact that the importance of different local features may vary, and thus the contributions of different local features to the classification result may vary as well. Some task-irrelevant, such as background and sky, may mislead the model.

To mitigate the impact of task-irrelevant local features on the classification result, we propose a Local Cross Attention Network (LCAN), which fully utilizes the local similarity relationship between query image and the support set to focus on the query local features relevant to the task. Specifically, we designed a local cross attention mechanism composed of two modules: a query local attention module and a class relevant module. The query local attention module addresses the issue of what kind of query local features to focus on by utilizing convolutional blocks to capture the spatial and channel information of the query feature map. The class relevant module tackles the issue of where to focus on the query local features by leveraging the local relationships between the query and support features. Moreover, we use a differential fusion method to combine the above two modules, so that our LCAN can focus on task-relevant query local features.

The contributions of our thesis are summarized as follows:

(1) We propose a query local attention module and a class relevant module. The former addresses the problem of what kind of query local features to focus on. The latter tackles the problem of where to focus on the query local features.
(2) We propose a differential fusion module to integrate the above modules, which can control the steepness of the output values after merging the two modules.
(3) We conduct extensive experiments on the miniImageNet, tieredImageNet, and CUB-200 datasets, which demonstrate that LCAN outperforms state-of-the-art methods.

2 Related Works

In this section, we focus on related works on metric learning based few-shot learning, which can be roughly divided into two categories: image-level features based and deep local features based methods.

2.1 Image-Level Features Based Methods

Traditional metric learning methods for few-shot learning typically use global average pooling layer on feature maps to obtain image-level features.

MatchingNet [16] uses cosine distance between query and support samples based on these features for classification, while ProtoNet [11] measures the Euclidean distance between the query feature and the class-mean feature for classification. RelationNet [22] employs a neural network as the distance metric to classify query samples.

2.2 Deep Local Features Based Methods

The other category of metric learning based methods is based on deep local features, which contain rich semantic information and are more capable of representing image information.

CovaMNet [15] utilizes these deep local features to represent images through covariance, and proposes covariance metric to calculate the distance between the query sample and support set. DN4 [14] searches for the nearest neighbor of each deep local feature in each class in support set using KNN algorithm to achieve classification of the query set sample. DeepEMD [29] uses Earth Mover's Distance to calculate the optimal matching cost between the query and support set based on the deep local features. FRN [24] reconstructs the query sample by using the deep local features of the support set , and predicts the score of the query sample in that class in support set. Unlike these methods take all query local features into consideration, the proposed LCAN only utilizes task-relevant query local features on classification.

3 Problem Definition

In this paper, we address the N-way K-shot few-shot image classification problem, where N denotes the number of classes and K denotes the number of samples per class. The objective of few-shot image classification is to classify a given query sample into one of the N classes in the support set, given limited training examples. We split a given dataset C into three disjoint datasets: C_{train}, C_{val}, and C_{test}, where each dataset consists of samples from a unique label space.

The model is trained using labeled training data from C_{train} with the episodic training mechanism. In each episodic task, we create a support set A_S and a query set A_Q. The support set A_S consists of N classes, with K samples per class. The objective is to classify the samples in A_Q into one of the classes in the support set A_S. Similarly, we construct episodic tasks from C_{val} and C_{test} for validation and testing.

4 Local Cross Attention Net

As depicted in Fig. 1, the LCAN consists of a deep embedding network Ψ, a local cross attention mechanism Γ, and a metric module Φ. The deep embedding network Ψ extracts deep local features from images in query set and support set, similar to traditional convolutional neural networks (CNN). The local cross attention mechanism Γ uses these local features to learn attention coefficients that indicate the importance of each local feature in the classification process. Finally, the metric module Φ employs the local features and attention coefficients to compute the distance between the query image and the support image.

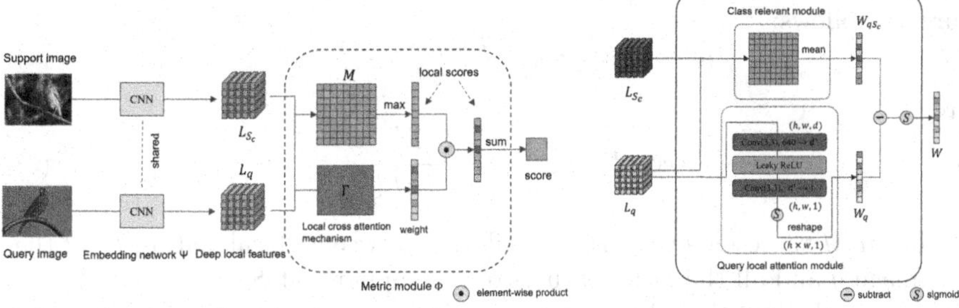

Fig. 1. The network architecture of LCAN, under the 5-way 1-shot setting with an example of a query image and a support image.

Fig. 2. The structure of the local cross attention mechanism Γ.

4.1 Deep Embedding Network Ψ

For a given image X, its corresponding feature map $\Psi(X) \in \mathbb{R}^{h \times w \times d}$ can be obtained through a deep embedding network Ψ, where h and w denote the height and width of the feature map, respectively, and d represents the number of channels in the feature map. From a spatial perspective, the feature map $\Psi(X)$ is composed of $m = h \times w$ d-dimensional feature vectors, which are referred to as deep local features. Therefore, the deep local features extracted from image X through the deep embedding network Ψ can be expressed as:

$$\Psi(X) = [x^1, ..., x^m] \in \mathbb{R}^{d \times m}, \tag{1}$$

where x_i denotes the i-th local feature of image X.

4.2 Local Cross Attention Mechanism Γ

The structure of the local cross attention mechanism Γ is illustrated in Fig. 2, which comprises two modules: the class-relevant module and the query local attention module. The local cross attention mechanism generates attention weights that are employed to weigh the query local scores, enhancing the significance of task-relevant query local features in the metric module and further improving the classification of the query image.

Class Relevant Module. Images belonging to the same class usually have similar target regions. Based on this observation, we propose a class relevant module that utilizes the similarity of local features between images in query set and support set to select the features related to the support image in the query image.

Given a query image q and a support image set S_c of class c, their local features can be extracted by the deep embedding network Ψ. We define $L_q = [L_q^1, ..., L_q^m] \in \mathbb{R}^{d \times m}$ and $L_{S_c} = [L_{S_c}^1, ..., L_{S_c}^m] \in \mathbb{R}^{d \times m}$ as the sets of local features for the query image and support set, respectively, where d is the dimension of each local feature, and m is the number of local features.

To calculate the similarity matrix $M \in \mathbb{R}^{m \times m}$ between the query image and the support set, we use the cosine similarity metric between each pair of local features as follows:

$$M_{i,j} = \cos(L_q^i, L_{S_c}^j), \tag{2}$$

where

$$\cos(L_q^i, L_{S_c}^j) = \frac{L_q^i L_{S_c}^j}{|L_q^i| \cdot |L_{S_c}^j|}. \tag{3}$$

Each row in M represents the cosine similarity between a local feature L_q^i of the query image q and all the local features of the support set S_c.

We then calculate the relevance $W_{qS_c} \in \mathbb{R}^{m \times 1}$ between each local feature in the query image and the support set class c by taking the average of the elements in each row of M:

$$W_{qS_c} = [w_{qS_c}^1, ..., w_{qS_c}^m] \in \mathbb{R}^{m \times 1}, \tag{4}$$

$$w_{qS_c}^i = \frac{1}{m} \sum_{j=1}^{m} M_{i,j}, \tag{5}$$

where $i = 1, ..., m$.

Query Local Attention Module. The specific structure of the query local feature attention module is shown in Fig. 2. Given the feature map $f \in \mathbb{R}^{h \times w \times d}$, a 3×3 convolution $conv1$ is used to learn the channel and spatial information of the feature map f, and compress the channel dimension from d to d' ($d' < d$), while keeping the spatial dimension unchanged during the convolution. Then, a Leaky ReLU activation function σ_1 is used to enhance the module's non-linear expression ability, and another 3×3 convolution $conv2$ is used to learn the channel and spatial information of the feature map f. This allows the attention module of our LCAN to better capture the global information of the feature map f. After the convolution operation, the channel dimension is compressed from d' to 1. After applying the *Sigmoid* function σ_2, the attention coefficients W_q of the query local features can be obtained. All these calculation process can be represented by the following equation:

$$W_q = \sigma_2(Conv2(\sigma_1(Conv1(f)))) \in \mathbb{R}^{h \times w}. \tag{6}$$

For subsequent calculations, W_q is reshaped to:

$$W_q = [w_q^1, ..., w_q^m] \in \mathbb{R}^{m\times 1}, \tag{7}$$

where $m = h \times w$.

Fusion Layer. After the output of the two modules have been calculated, we propose a a differential fusion module to integrate them, which can control the steepness of the output values after merging the two modules. Specifically, the output of the class-relevant module and the query local attention module are fused by subtracting them:

$$w_i = \sigma(w_{qS_c}^i - w_q^i), \tag{8}$$

where $\sigma(x) = \frac{1}{1+exp(-\tau x)}$ is the sigmoid activation function with a parameter τ that can amplify or shrink the input x. Finally, the weights w_i are concatenated into a vector $W \in \mathbb{R}^{m\times 1}$:

$$W = [w_1, \ldots, w_m]. \tag{9}$$

Additionally, the τ parameter in the Sigmoid function can be adjusted to control the steepness of the output. A higher τ value results in a steeper output, while a lower τ value produces a more gradual curve. This allows for more fine-grained control over the weighting of the two modules during fusion.

4.3 Metric Module Φ

After obtaining the similarity matrix $M \in \mathbb{R}^{m\times m}$ between the query image q and the support image S_c using Eq. 2, we use the following equation to obtain the score r_i for the local feature L_q^i of the query image q:

$$r_i = \max(M_{i,1}, ..., M_{i,m}). \tag{10}$$

where, $M_{i,j}$ represents the cosine similarity between the local feature L_q^i and the local features $L_{S_c}^i$. Meanwhile, max represents taking the maximum value.

Next, we multiply the weights w_i obtained from Eq. 9 with the local score r_i of the query image q, resulting in the similarity score R_c between the query image q and the support image S_c:

$$R_c = \sum_{i=1}^{m} w_i \cdot r_i. \tag{11}$$

We obtain the classification probability of the query sample q using a softmax function, and then calculate the image classification loss using the commonly used classification cross-entropy loss in few-shot learning, as shown in the following equation:

$$p(y = c|q) = \frac{exp(R_c)}{\sum_{j=1}^{N} exp(R_j)}, \tag{12}$$

$$loss = \frac{1}{|A_Q|} \sum_{q \in A_Q} -log(p(y = c^* | q)). \tag{13}$$

where, c^* is the true label of the query sample q in the query set A_Q, and we update the network parameters by minimizing the $loss$.

Table 1. Few-shot classification accuracy (%) on miniImageNet and tieredImageNet. †: our re-implemented results, **bold** results indicate the best performance, and underlined results indicate the second-best performance. In addition, the 95% confidence intervals are all below 0.25.

Model	Backbone	miniImageNet		tieredImageNet	
		1-shot	5-shot	1-shot	5-shot
MatchingNet [16]	ResNet-12	63.08	75.99	68.50	80.60
ProtoNet† [11]	ResNet-12	62.67	77.88	68.48	83.46
RelationNet† [22]	ResNet-12	60.97	75.12	64.71	78.41
MetaOptNet [13]	ResNet-12	62.64	78.63	65.99	81.56
TAPNet [28]	ResNet-12	61.65	76.36	63.08	80.26
Meta-Baseline [4]	ResNet-12	63.17	79.26	68.62	83.29
FEAT [25]	ResNet-12	66.78	82.05	70.80	84.79
DSN [20]	ResNet-12	62.64	78.83	67.39	82.85
RFS-Simple [27]	ResNet-12	62.02	79.64	69.74	84.41
DN4† [14]	ResNet-12	66.18	81.28	70.93	83.99
DeepEMD [29]	ResNet-12	65.91	82.41	71.16	86.03
FRN [24]	ResNet-12	66.45	82.83	71.16	86.01
LCAN	ResNet-12	**66.84**	**84.01**	**71.77**	**86.29**

5 Experiment

5.1 Datasets

We conducted experiments on three datasets: miniImageNet [16], tieredImageNet [19], and CUB-200 [17]. Following [14,24,29], miniImageNet consists of 100 classes with 64, 16, and 20 classes used for training, validation, and evaluation respectively. tieredImageNet has 608 classes, with 351, 97, and 160 classes used for training, validation, and evaluation respectively. CUB-200 comprises 200 bird classes, with 100, 50, and 50 classes used for training, validation, and evaluation, respectively. As is commonly implemented, all images in CUB-200 are cropped with the human-annotated bounding boxes.

5.2 Implementation Details

Backbone Network. Our experiments are conducted using ResNet-12 [12] backbones, which is a widely used architecture in the FSL literature. ResNet-12 consists of four residual blocks, each having three convolutional layers with a 3 × 3 kernel. Additionally, a 2 × 2 max-pooling layer is added to the first residual block.

Training Details. We conducted experiments on N-way K-shot tasks. For mini-/tieredImageNet, following literature [14,29], we use the pre-training stage and meta-train our model by using the SGD optimizer with an initial learning rate of 0.0005, which was halved every ten epochs. Meta-training was performed for 40 epochs on miniImageNet and 60 epochs on tieredImageNet. In each epoch, we randomly sampled 200 tasks with a batch size of 1. For CUB-200, we followed the training setting of FRN [24] and trained our model for 600 epochs. The learning rate was scaled down by a factor of 10 at epoch 300, 400, and 500. We trained our model with a 10-way setting for both the 1-shot and 5-shot models. During the test stage, we reported the average accuracy and the corresponding 95% confidence interval over 10,000 tasks.

Table 2. Few-shot classification accuracy (%) on CUB-200 fine-grained dataset. The 95% confidence intervals are all below 0.2.

Model	Backbone	CUB-200	
		1-shot	5-shot
ProtoNet [11]	ResNet-12	82.98	91.38
CTX [6]	ResNet-12	78.47	90.90
DSN [20]	ResNet-12	80.80	91.19
DN4 [14]	ResNet-12	<u>85.44</u>	92.51
DeepEMD [29]	ResNet-12	83.35	91.60
FRN [24]	ResNet-12	83.16	<u>92.59</u>
LCAN	ResNet-12	<u>**85.90**</u>	<u>**93.55**</u>

Table 3. Few-shot classifications (%) in the cross-domain setting: miniImageNet → CUB. †: our re-implemented results.

Model	Backbone	miniImageNet→CUB	
		1-shot	5-shot
MatchingNet+FT [23]	ResNet-10	36.61 ± 0.53	55.23 ± 0.83
RelationNet+FT [23]	ResNet-10	44.07 ± 0.77	59.46 ± 0.71
GNN+FT [23]	ResNet-10	47.47 ± 0.75	66.98 ± 0.68
MetaOptNet [13]	ResNet-12	44.79 ± 0.75	64.98 ± 0.68
ProtoNet [11]	ResNet-12	40.05 ± 0.18	55.29 ± 0.19
DN4† [14]	ResNet-12	<u>53.86 ± 0.21</u>	<u>75.97 ± 0.18</u>
FRN [24]	ResNet-12	51.60 ± 0.21	72.97 ± 0.18
LCAN	ResNet-12	**55.84 ± 0.21**	**78.05 ±0.18**

Table 4. Ablation study on miniImageNet and tieredImageNet. QLAM represents Query Local Attention Module, CRM represents Class Relevant Module.

QLAM	CRM	miniImageNet		tieredImageNet	
		1-shot	5-shot	1-shot	5-shot
✗	✗	66.18	81.28	70.93	83.99
✓	✗	<u>66.41</u>	<u>83.83</u>	71.38	<u>86.11</u>
✗	✓	66.39	83.58	<u>71.52</u>	85.96
✓	✓	**66.84**	**84.01**	**71.77**	**86.29**

Table 5. Ablation study on the local cross attention mechanism factor τ under the 5-way 1-shot task from tieredImageNet.

τ	1	2	3	4	5	6	7	8	9	10
accuracy	71.43	71.50	71.51	71.75	**71.77**	71.43	71.38	71.30	71.24	71.22

5.3 General Few-Shot Classification Results

Table 1 details the comparisons of LCAN with image-level features based methods [4,11,16,22] as well as local feature based methods [14,24,29] on mini-/tieredImag-eNet. As seen from Table 1, our LCAN achieves the highest accuracy on miniImageNet with 66.84% and 84.01% on 5-way 1-shot and 5-way 5-shot tasks, respectively, which make a great improvement compared to the previous image-level feature based methods and local feature based methods.Specially, our LCAN is 3.35%, 2.28% and 1.76% better than DN4, DeepEMD and FRN on the 5-way 5-shot task, respectively. And our LCAN achieves 71.77% and 86.29% on tieredImageNet under 5-way 1-shot and 5-way 5-shot settings, respectively, achieving competitive performance.

5.4 Fine-Grained Few-Shot Classification Results

We follow the same setting as in FRN [24] to train all the models from scratch on the fine-grained dataset. Table 2 evaluates our method on CUB-200. It can be seen that the proposed LCAN obtains significant improvements compared with previous state-of-the-art methods. Specifically, compared with local features based methods (i.e. DN4 [14], DeepEMD [29] and FRN [24]), LCAN is 0.54%, 3.06% and 3.29% better than them under 5-way 1-shot setting.

5.5 Cross-Domain Few-Shot Classification Results

We also evaluate on the challenging cross-domain setting proposed by [23], where models trained on miniImageNet base classes are directly evaluated on test classes from CUB-200. As shown in Table 3, our LCAN outperforms previous state-of-the-art methods. For example, our LCAN is 3.68% and 2.74% better than DN4 on the 5-way 1-shot task and 5-way 5-shot task, respectively.

The reason why our LCAN can achieve these state-of-the-art performances is that LCAN can learn task-related deep local features, strengthen the importance of these features, and alleviate the interference of task-irrelevant local features on the classification of images.

6 Discussion

6.1 Ablation Study

The Impact of Each Module in LCAN. To evaluate the effectiveness of each module in LCAN and compare their impact on the classification performance, comprehensive experiments were conducted on miniImageNet and tieredImageNet datasets. The experimental results, presented in Table 4, demonstrate the performance of different methods, including the ones with each module removed, which are referred to as Baseline. The results show that each module contributes to improving the classification performance when used alone under different scenarios. Moreover, the best performance is achieved when these modules are combined together, indicating that they complement each other to enhance the effectiveness of LCAN.

The Influence on Factor τ. Table 5 shows the results of our experiments on how the classification accuracy is influenced by different values of τ in LCAN. We observed that the classification accuracy initially improves as the value of τ increases, but then begins to deteriorate. This is because when τ is too large, the local cross attention mechanism generates sparse weights, and some irrelevant features may be assigned a weight of zero, which leads to a larger impact of misclassification and thus a decline in classification accuracy. Conversely, when

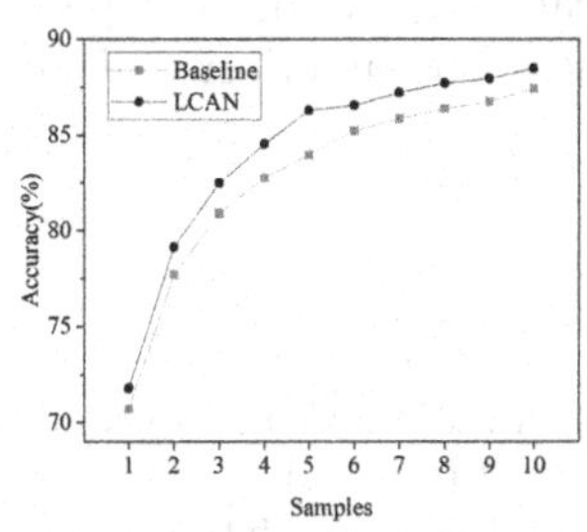

Fig. 3. The effect of the number of samples on classification results, the experiment is based on the tieredImageNet dataset.

Fig. 4. Visualizations of query and support images in 5-way 1-shot tasks. Images (from miniImageNet) at the second column of each pane are from the ground truth class while the four on the far right are the confounding support classes.

τ is too small, the weights may be too similar to each other, making it difficult to distinguish the importance of local features, which also leads to a decline in classification accuracy. Therefore, in all other experiments of LCAN, we selected the optimal value of τ corresponding to the best results, which was set to 5.

The Effect on the Number of Samples. We conducted experiments on the tieredImageNet dataset with 5-way 1-shot, 5-way 2-shot,..., 5-way 10-shot tasks to verify the effect of the number of samples on LCAN. The results are presented in Fig. 3. The experimental results depicted in Fig. 3 indicate that LCAN outperforms Baseline in all scenarios with varying numbers of samples on tieredImageNet. Furthermore, both LCAN and Baseline achieve higher accuracy as the number of samples increases, since the model becomes easier to optimize with more samples.

6.2 Visualization

To better understand the capabilities of our LCAN, we visualized the attention map learned by our method. As shown in Fig. 4, our LCAN effectively concentrates on the most relevant regions of interest, prioritizing the dog over the person in the image. Additionally, we observed that when utilizing ground truth, LCAN can better identify the task-relevant objects in the query image, specifically the back region of the dog. These visualizations provide valuable insights into the inner workings of our model, showcasing its ability to attend to important features and leading to improved classification performance.

7 Conclusion

In this paper, we propose a Local Cross Attention Network (LCAN) for few-shot learning, aiming to learn more discriminative local representations for query images by utilizing the support set. Specifically, a local cross attention mechanism is designed to select task-relevant deep local features. Extensive experimental results on the benchmarks verify the effectiveness and superiority of the proposed LCAN.

References

1. Miller, A., Fisch, A., Dodge, J., Karimi, A.H., Bordes, A., Weston, J.: Key-value memory networks for directly reading document. In: EMNLP (2016)
2. Santoro, A., Bartunov, S., Botvinick, M., Wierstra, D., Lillicrap, T.: Meta-learning with memory-augmented neural networks. In: ICML, pp. 1842–1850 (2016)
3. Krizhevsky, A., Sutskever, I., Hinton, G.E.: ImageNet classification with deep convolutional neural networks, pp. 1097–1105 (2012)
4. Chen, Y., Liu, Z., Xu, H., Darrell, T., Wang, X.: Meta-baseline: exploring simple meta-learning for few-shot learning. In: ICCV, pp. 9062–9071 (2021)

5. Chi, Z., Henghui, D., Guosheng, L., Ruibo, L., Changhu, W., Chunhua, S.: Meta navigator: search for a good adaptation policy for few-shot learning. In: ICCV, pp. 9435–9444 (2021)
6. Doersch, C., Gupta, A., Zisserman, A.: Crosstransformers: spatially-aware few-shot transfer. NIPS **33**, 21981–21993 (2020)
7. Finn, C., Abbeel, P., Levine, S.: Model-agnostic meta-learning for fast adaptation of deep networks. In: ICML, pp. 1126–1135 (2017)
8. García-Ródenas, R., Linares, L.J., López-Gómez, J.A.: On the performance of classic and deep neural models in image recognition. In: ICANN, pp. 600–608 (2017)
9. Hou, R., Chang, H., Ma, B., Shan, S., Chen, X.: Cross attention network for few-shot classification. In: NIPS, vol. 32 (2019)
10. Weston, J., Chopra, S., Bordes, A.: Memory networks. In: ICLR (2015)
11. Jake, S., Kevin, S., Richard, Z.: Prototypical networks for few-shot learning. In: NIPS, pp. 4077–4087 (2017)
12. He, K., Zhang, X., Ren, S., Sun, J.: Deep residual learning for image recognition. In: CVPR, pp. 770–778 (2016)
13. Lee, K., Maji, S., Ravichandran, A., Soatto, S.: Meta-learning with differentiable convex optimization. In: CVPR, pp. 10657–10665 (2019)
14. Li, W., Wang, L., Xu, J., Huo, J., Gao, Y., Luo, J.: Revisiting local descriptor based image-to-class measure for few-shot learning. In: CVPR, pp. 7260–7268 (2019)
15. Li, W., Xu, J., Huo, J., Wang, L., Gao, Y., Luo, J.: Distribution consistency based covariance metric networks for few-shot learning. In: AAAI, pp. 8642–8649 (2019)
16. Oriol, V., et al.: Matching networks for one shot learning. In: NIPS, pp. 3630–3638 (2016)
17. Welinder, P., et al.: Caltech-UCSD birds 200 (2010)
18. Qi, C., Yingwei, P., Ting, Y., Chenggang, Y., Tao, M.: Memory matching networks for one-shot image recognition. In: CVPR, pp. 4080–4088 (2018)
19. Ren, M., et al.: Meta-learning for semi-supervised few-shot classification. In: ICLR (2018)
20. Simon, C., Koniusz, P., Nock, R., Harandi, M.: Adaptive subspaces for few-shot learning. In: CVPR, pp. 4136–4145 (2020)
21. Simonyan, K., Zisserman, A.: Very deep convolutional networks for large-scale image recognition. In: ICLR (2015)
22. Sung, F., Yang, Y., Zhang, L., Xiang, T., Torr, P.H., Hospedales, T.M.: Learning to compare: relation network for few-shot learning. In: CVPR, pp. 1199–1208 (2018)
23. Tseng, H.Y., Lee, H.Y., Huang, J.B., Yang, M.H.: Cross-domain few-shot classification via learned feature-wise transformation. In: ICLR (2020)
24. Wertheimer, D., Tang, L., Hariharan, B.: Few-shot classification with feature map reconstruction networks. In: CVPR, pp. 8012–8021 (2021)
25. Ye, H.J., Hu, H., Zhan, D.C., Sha, F.: Few-shot learning via embedding adaptation with set-to-set functions. In: CVPR, pp. 8808–8817 (2020)
26. Yin, B., Scholte, H.S., Bohté, S.: LocalNorm: robust image classification through dynamically regularized normalization. In: Farkaš, I., Masulli, P., Otte, S., Wermter, S. (eds.) ICANN 2021. LNCS, vol. 12894, pp. 240–252. Springer, Cham (2021). https://doi.org/10.1007/978-3-030-86380-7_20
27. Tian, Y., Wang, Y., Krishnan, D., Tenenbaum, J.B., Isola, P.: Rethinking few-shot image classification: a good embedding is all you need? In: Vedaldi, A., Bischof, H., Brox, T., Frahm, J.-M. (eds.) ECCV 2020. LNCS, vol. 12359, pp. 266–282. Springer, Cham (2020). https://doi.org/10.1007/978-3-030-58568-6_16
28. Yoon, S.W., Seo, J., Moon, J.: TapNet: neural network augmented with task-adaptive projection for few-shot learning. In: ICML, pp. 7115–7123 (2019)

29. Zhang, C., Cai, Y., Lin, G., Shen, C.: DeepEMD: few-shot image classification with differentiable earth mover's distance and structured classifiers. In: CVPR, pp. 12203–12213 (2020)
30. Zhou, M., Li, Y., Lu, H.: Ensemble-based deep metric learning for few-shot learning. In: ICANN, pp. 406–418 (2020)

Deep Video Compression Based on 3D Convolution Artifacts Removal and Attention Compression Module

Zhichen Liu and Jianping Luo(✉)

Guangdong Key Laboratory of Intelligent Information Processing, College of Electronic and Information Engineering, Shenzhen University, Shenzhen, China
2070436028@email.szu.edu.cn, ljp@szu.edu.cn

Abstract. Most research of video compression focuses on how to effectively extract the information between frames and use this information for the subsequent reconstruction. Previous algorithms used 2D convolution to extract information between adjacent frames, but 2D convolution is insufficient in spatio-temporal extraction ability, so we consider using a 3D convolution network to remove artifacts caused by motion compensation. In order to further improve the compression performance, we put the 3D convolution network and the residual compression network into the feature space to reduce the errors caused by inaccurate pixel-level operations. In addition, we also propose a motion compression network based on attention module, so that the network can pay more attention to the complex area of the image. Experimental results show that our model achieves the same or even better performance than other end-to-end video compression models in PSNR and MS-SSIM, even though our method has a much smaller number of parameters.

Keywords: 3D convolution · feature space · attention module

1 Introduction

With the rapid development of the Internet, video information has become the largest source of Internet traffic. Currently, the two widely used video compression standards are H.264 [20] and H.265 [16]. But these traditional video compression methods have been used for many years. They follow a fixed framework, which includes motion estimation, motion compensation, DCT transform and other modules. Each module is designed separately and cannot be optimized jointly. When the first end-to-end video compression framework (DVC) shows comparable performance to traditional methods, it demonstrates the great potential in the field of deep video compression.

Many video compression methods have achieved good results, but most of these methods have complex structure. For example, Yang et al. [22] proposed a hierarchical learning video compression method, which corresponds to different

L. Iliadis et al. (Eds.): ICANN 2023, LNCS 14263, pp. 111–123, 2023.
https://doi.org/10.1007/978-3-031-44204-9_10

decoding qualities of video frames at different layers. Lin et al. [7] proposed a video compression framework with a complex motion estimation and compensation network, it add a very complex multi-frame video enhancement network.

In this paper, we make four improvements to the DVC framework. Firstly, we consider applying 3D convolution to improve the quality of motion compensation frame. Generally speaking, the motion compensation module in deep video compression framework includes a warp operation and its subsequent CNN network to eliminate artifacts caused by warp. However, in the existing motion compensation methods, two adjacent frames are concatenated into a 2D convolution network by a concat operation. In this way, the correlation between two frames is lost, but 3D convolution has powerful spatio-temporal extraction ability and can extract relevant information on time direction well.

Secondly, we make an improvement for motion and residual compression network. In the DVC framework [11], motion and residual compression both use the image compression method proposed in [1]. We introduce the attention module into the compression network, so that it can pay more attention to the complex area of the image.

In addition, considering that the residuals of pixel space will directly affect the final reconstruction quality, so we put the residual compression process into the feature space. Referring to the use of deformable convolution mentioned in [19], it shows that two consecutive frames can be aligned in the feature space. Also in [6], a series of operations are also carried out in the feature space. It shows that it is feasible to implement the above operations in the feature space.

Finally, we also change the encoding direction of video sequences. Considering that in a GOP, the continuous propagation of errors will lead to the degradation of decoding quality, we propose a bidirectional encoding method. It starts with the middle frame of a GOP, encoding in both forward and backward directions. In general, our proposed method mainly has the following contributions:

- Due to the insufficient ability of 2D convolution in spatio-temporal extraction, we try to apply 3D convolution to the motion compensation following network. The spatio-temporal information extracted by 3D convolution is used to eliminate artifacts generated by motion compensation.
- The attention module is introduced into the motion and residual compression network to improve the adaptive compression ability. This module can make the network pay more attention to the complex area of the image and improve the compression efficiency.
- In order to reduce errors caused by inaccurate pixel-level operations, we align adjacent frames in the feature space, and implement 3D convolution and residual compression network in the feature space.

2 Related Work

2.1 Image Compression

At present, some traditional image compression methods include JPEG [18], JPEG2000 [15] and BPG [3] are based on hand-crafted techniques, such as DCT transformation, quantization, etc. These technologies have achieved great compression performance. However, because each module in the compression framework is independent, joint optimization cannot be carried out. So in order to solve this problem, the learning-based image compression method is proposed. In recent years, there are more and more image compression methods based on DNNs. One is the progressive image compression framework based on recurrent neural networks (RNNs) [17] and the other is the image compression framework based on auto-encoder structure based on convolutional neural network (CNN) [1,2]. In this paper, our 3D feature compression uses the method in image compression [1,2].

2.2 Video Compression

At present, video compression methods based on deep learning can be divided into two categories: delay-constrained and non-delay-constrained. For the first category, the compression of the current frame depends only on the previous frame, for example, Lu et al. [11] proposed the first end-to-end video compression framework, it replaces every component in the traditional framework with a neural network and uses a loss function for joint optimization. Lin et al. [7] used multiple previous frames as reference frames. At the same time, the residual refinement network and MV refinement network are added to generate a more accurate current prediction frame. Hu et al. [6] proposed a feature-space video coding network (FVC), it generates predicted features through a deformable compensation module and fuses multi-frame features by using the attention mechanism.

For the second category, there is no limit to the position of the reference frame, which can come from the future. For example, Wu et al. [21] used an RNN-based hierarchical interpolation method for video compression. Yang et al. [22] proposed a hierarchical learned video compression method. Each layer designs in different networks to control the different compression quality.

Our method only relies on one reference frame, which can be either the previous or the next frame. Therefore, we can flexibly switch the encoding mode according to the usage scenario.

3 Proposed Method

Let $V = \{X_1, X_2, ..., X_{t-1}, X_t, ...\}$ denote the video sequence. X_t and X_{t-1} represent the current frame and previous frame. $\hat{X}_t$ and $\hat{X}_{t-1}$ represents reconstructed current frame and previous frame. V_t and R_t represent motion and residuals, $\hat{V}_t$ and $\hat{R}_t$ are their corresponding reconstructed versions. F_t, F_t^{warp} and $\hat{F}_{t-1}$ are the corresponding feature representation of X_t, X_t^{warp} and $\hat{X}_{t-1}$ respectively. X_t^{warp} is the motion compensation frame after warp operation.

3.1 Overview of the Proposed Method

Figure 1 shows our video compression framework. We propose three improvements to the DVC framework. The specific compression workflow of our scheme is introduced as follows.

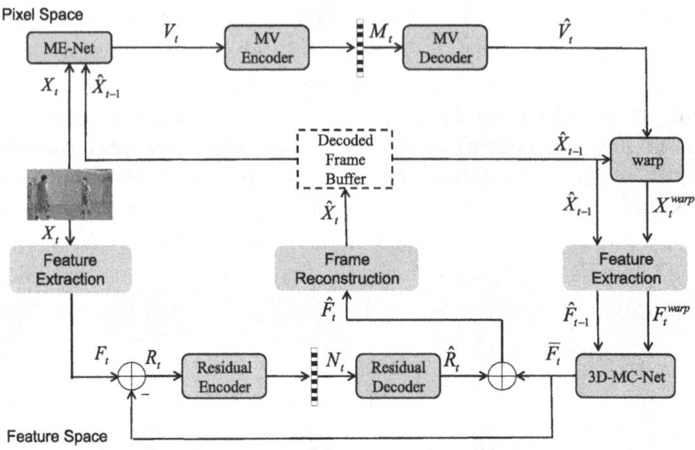

Fig. 1. The overall framework of proposed method.

Step 1 *Motion estimation.* The current frame X_t and the reference frame $\hat{X}_{t-1}$ are fed into a motion estimation network (ME-Net) to extract the motion V_t. In this paper, the ME-Net is based on the optical flow network SpyNet [14].
Step 2 *Compression and decompression of motion.* The motion after compression and quantization can be expressed as $\hat{M}_t$. We use a network based on attention module to compress and decompress motion, more information is provided in Sect. 3.4.
Step 3 *Motion compensation.* The previous reconstructed frame $\hat{X}_{t-1}$ is warped to the motion compensation frame X_t^{warp} based on the motion information $\hat{V}_t$.
Step 4 *Feature extraction.* We use a feature extraction network to convert X_t, X_t^{warp} and $\hat{X}_{t-1}$ into their corresponding feature representations F_t, F_t^{warp} and $\hat{F}_{t-1}$. The structure of the feature extraction network is shown in Fig. 2(a).

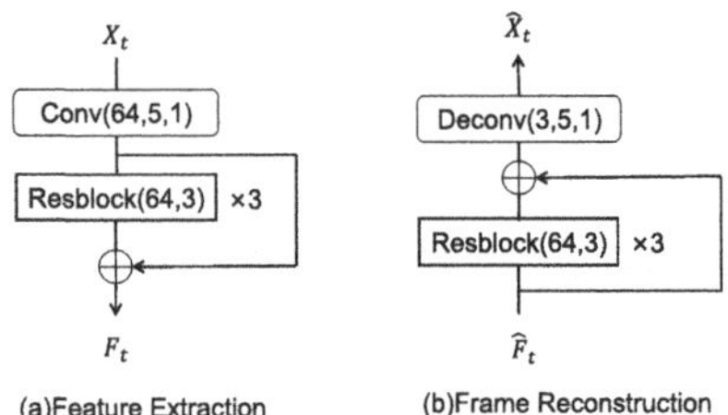

Fig. 2. (a) is Feature Extraction network, (b) is Frame Reconstruction network.

Step 5 *Feature prediction.* Based on the feature $\hat{F}_{t-1}$, we use a feature prediction network to improve the quality of motion compensation feature F_t^{warp} and output the predict feature $\overline{F}_t$. The feature prediction network corresponds to 3D-MC-Net in Fig. 1. More information is provided in Sect. 3.3.

Step 6 *Residual calculation, compression and decompression.* Residual refers to the difference between the predicted feature $\overline{F}_t$ and the original feature F_t, which can be expressed by the formula: $R_t = F_t - \overline{F}_t$. The residual after compression and quantization can be expressed as $\hat{N}_t$. The network has the same structure as the motion compression network. More information is provided in Sect. 3.4.

Step 7 *Feature reconstruction.* After decompressing the residual $\hat{R}_t$, the reconstructed feature $\hat{F}_t$ can be obtained by adding $\hat{R}_t$ to the predicted feature $\overline{F}_t$. It can be expressed by the formula: $\hat{F}_t = \overline{F}_t + \hat{R}_t$.

Step 8 *Frame reconstruction.* The frame reconstruction network restores the feature $\hat{F}_t$ of feature space to the frame $\hat{X}_t$ of pixel space. The structure of frame reconstruction network is shown in Fig. 2(b).

3.2 3D Convolution Network

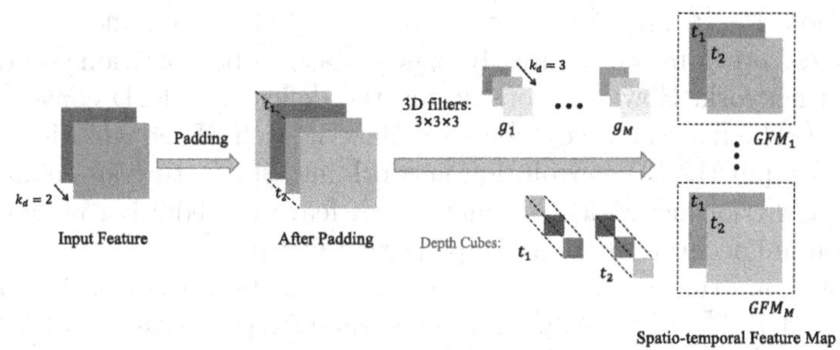

Fig. 3. 3D convolutional network.

2D convolution extracts the spatial features of a single still image. Compared with 2D convolution, 3D convolution add the depth dimension. A 3D filter can be expressed as $k_d \times k_h \times k_w$, k_d, k_h and k_w denotes depth, height and width respectively. In this paper, the input depth of frame sequence is 2, and the 3D convolution kernel is $3 \times 3 \times 3$. As shown in Fig. 3, the k_d of 3D filter is set to 3. t_1 and t_2 in the figure are two cubes in the depth direction. The 3D filter $g_1, ..., g_M$ generates its corresponding spatio-temporal feature map by sliding at t_1 and t_2 cubes. The depth of the spatio-temporal feature map is 2, which corresponds to t_1 and t_2 respectively. Similarly, different 3D filters can generate different spatio-temporal feature map. The $GFM_1, ..., GFM_M$ are M spatio-temporal feature map generated by 3D filters $g_1, ..., g_M$ respectively.

3.3 Feature Prediction Network

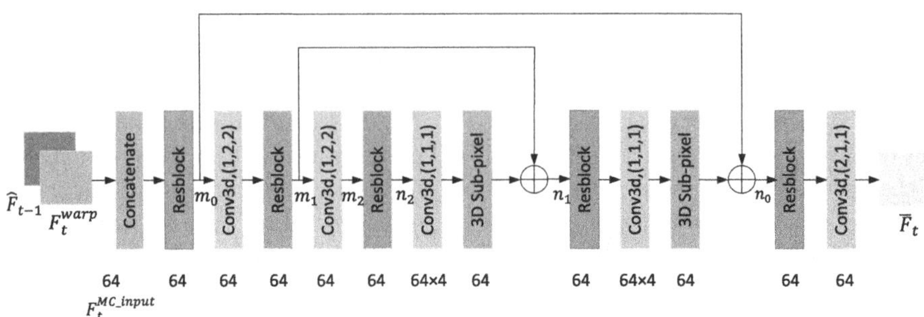

Fig. 4. 3D convolutional feature prediction network structure.

After converting motion compensation frame X_t^{warp} and previous reconstruction frame $\hat{X}_{t-1}$ into the feature space, we can get the corresponding feature representation F_t^{warp} and $\hat{F}_{t-1}$. To remove the artifacts on motion compensation frames, previous work directly concatenates adjacent frames into a 2D convolution network. However, considering the deficiency of 2D convolution in spatio-temporal extraction, we hope to replace it with 3D convolution. In this paper, we also put the 3D convolution network into the feature space and name it feature prediction network. The purpose of feature prediction network is to obtain the more accurate motion compensation feature $\overline{F}_t$.

Figure 4 shows the structure of our feature prediction network. We concatenate $\hat{F}_{t-1}$ and F_t^{warp} in terms of time dimensions and denote it as $F_t^{MC\_input}$. The input of feature prediction network is the concatenation result $F_t^{MC\_input}$, which can be expressed as $D \times H \times W \times C$. D, H, W and C represent depth, height, width and number of channels respectively. The whole prediction network includes two down-sampling and two up-sampling processes. Since the Resblock network does not change the image size, we skip the Resblock structure for analysis. The down-sampling process can be expressed by the following formula:

$$F_t^{MC\_input} \longrightarrow m_0 \tag{1}$$

$$m_{i-1} \downarrow_2 \longrightarrow m_i \qquad i = 1, 2 \tag{2}$$

m_0, m_1 and m_2 are the output of the corresponding convolution layer respectively, where $\downarrow_2$ indicates 2 times of down-sampling. We use a convolution with stride of 2 to implement the down-sampling process.

In addition, we also add a feature fusion operation to the 2 times of up-sampling process. The feature fusion process can be summarized as follows: firstly, the feature n_i of layer i is sent to the 3D convolution network to expand the number of channels to four times. Then we reduce its number of channels and expand its size for two times through the 3D sub-pixel convolution network

[13]. Finally, the expanded feature n_i and m_{i-1} are added to obtain feature n_{i-1} through lateral connection. The process can be expressed by symbols as follows:

$$n_i \uparrow^2 \quad + \quad m_{i-1} \longrightarrow \quad n_{i-1} \quad i = 1, 2 \tag{3}$$

$$n_0 \overset{Depth \quad Reduction}{\longrightarrow} \overline{F}_t \tag{4}$$

where $\uparrow^2$ indicates 2 times of up-sampling. Up-sampling is achieved by 3D sub-pixel convolution, which is extension of 2D sub-pixel operation. For 3D sub-pixel convolution, a tensor with the size of $D \times H \times W \times s^2C$ can be reshaped to $D \times sH \times sW \times C$. s represents the magnification of the image.

Finally, the depth of n_0 is reduced by a 3D convolution network, and the final squeeze output dimension is $H \times W \times C$.

3.4 Motion Compression Network

In the DVC framework, motion and residual compression both use the image compression method proposed by Ballte et al. [1]. The only difference is that the convolution kernel size is set to 5×5 in the residual compression network. In our method, we add an attention module based on the structure in Fig. 5(a) and the improved motion compression network is shown in Fig. 5(b).

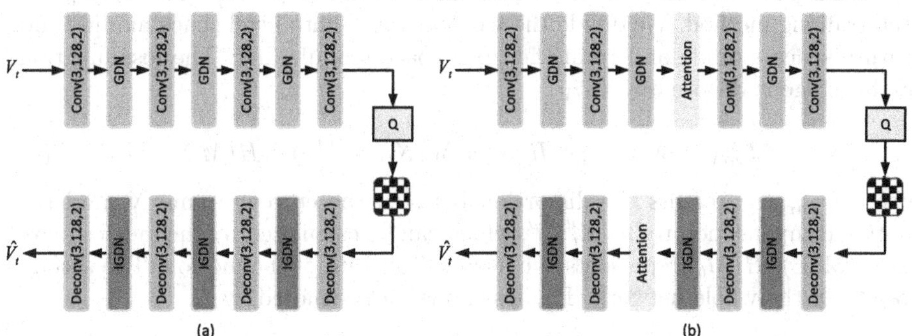

Fig. 5. (a) is the motion compression model structure of DVC and (b) is the improved motion compression model structure.

The attention module in Fig. 5(b) is refers to the attention structure mentioned in the image compression method [4] and is simplified based on Liu et al. [9]. Attention module can make the network pay more attention to the complex area of the image, so as to improve the compression performance of the network. The proposed structure of the attention module is shown in Fig. 6(a), which consists of two branches. The main branch is stacked with three residual blocks to generate features, while the mask branch is stacked with a series of residual blocks, convolution layers and S activation functions.

$$M = sigmoid(F(X)) \tag{5}$$

X represents the input, $F(\cdot)$ represents the convolution operation and M represents attention mask. The value of M is between 0 and 1, and then M multiplies the feature map generated by the main branch to realize the adaptive allocation of image features.

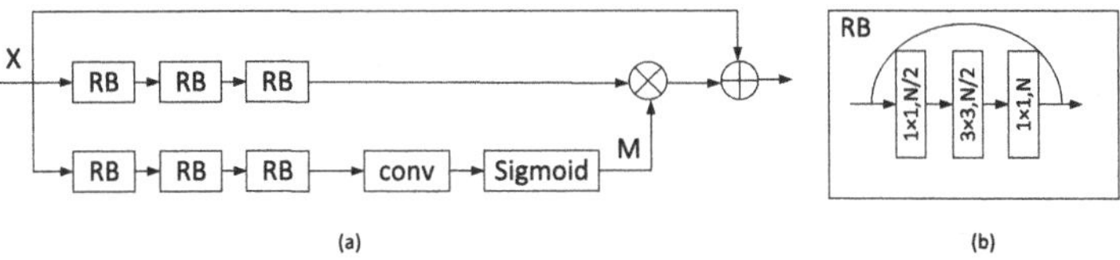

Fig. 6. (a) is the structure of attention module, (b) is the structure of RB module.

3.5 Training Strategy

Loss Function. The purpose of video compression task is to make the distortion and compression bit rate as low as possible, but the reduction of bit rate will inevitably increase the distortion. Therefore, we should reasonably balance the relationship between the two in the loss function. In this paper, we use a step-by-step training method. We divide the whole network into pixel space module and feature space module and train the pixel space module first. The loss function at this stage is denoted by L_{MV}:

$$L_{MV} = \lambda D_{warp} + R_{MV} = \lambda d(X_t, X_t^{warp}) + H(\hat{M}_t) \tag{6}$$

where D_{warp} represents the distortion between the current frame X_t and the motion compensation frame X_t^{warp}, which can be calculated by the mean square error (MSE). $H(\hat{M}_t)$ represents the encoded bit rate of the motion. The second step train the whole network. The loss function is denoted by L:

$$L = \lambda D_{recon} + R_{ALL} = \lambda d(X_t, \hat{X}_t) + H(\hat{M}_t) + H(\hat{N}_t) \tag{7}$$

where D_{recon} represents the distortion between the current frame X_t and the reconstructed frame $\hat{X}_t$, which can be calculated by mean square error (MSE) or multi-scale structural similarity (MS-SSIM), corresponding to PSNR model and MS-SSIM model respectively. $H(\hat{N}_t)$ represents the encoded bit rate of the residual. λ is an adjustable parameter, which is used to weigh the relationship between bit rate and distortion.

Quantization and Bit Rate Estimation. Because the whole network is end to-end trained and the quantization operation is not differential, we use the method of adding noise in [1] to replace quantization. In the real training process, the bit rate is estimated by calculating the entropy of potential representation.

In this paper, we use CNN network in [1] to estimate the distribution of potential representation $\hat{M}_t$ and $\hat{N}_t$. After calculating its entropy, we feed the estimated bit rate of potential representation into the loss function.

4 Experiments

4.1 Experimental Setup

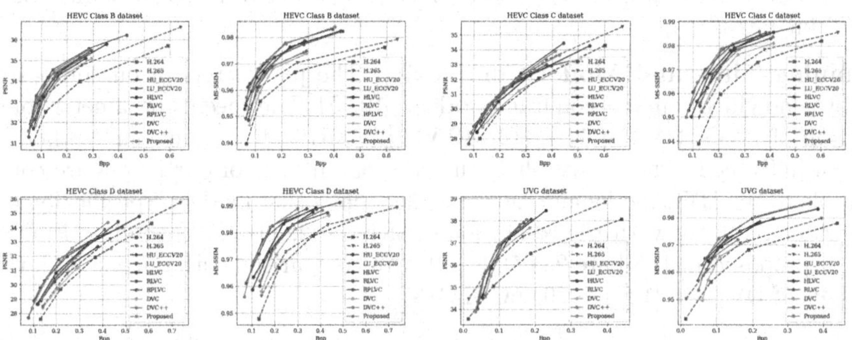

Fig. 7. PSNR and MS-SSIM performance comparison between proposed method and H.264 [20], H.265 [16], DVC [11], DVC++ [12], HLVC [22], RLVC [22], HU_ECCV20 [5], LU_ECCV [10], RPLVC [8].

Datasets. We train our model by using the Vimeo-90k dataset, which contains 89800 independent sequences, and each sequence contains 7 consecutive frames. The batch size is set as 4 and the resolution of training images is 256×256. Our test data includes UVG dataset and HEVC dataset(ClassB, ClassC, and ClassD).

Evaluation Metrics. We use PSNR and MS-SSIM to evaluate the compression quality of the model. At the same time, we use bits per pixel (Bpp) to represent the coding bit rate of potential representation $\hat{M}_t$ and $\hat{N}_t$. Bpp is calculated as follows: firstly, calculating the total bits required to compress video frame, then dividing by its resolution.

Implementation Details. We use Adam as the optimizer and set the initial learning rate as 0.0001. The batch size is set as 4 and the resolution of training images is 256×256. Specially, in order to minimize error propagation, our I-frame is not the first frame in a GOP, but the (GOP-1)/2 frame in a GOP. After the I-frame is encoded, we encode rest frames from the front and back two directions to further improve the encoding and decoding efficiency.

Experimental Results. In this paper, we make some improvements to the DVC model and compare it with the traditional video compression methods,

H.264 [20] and H.265 [16]. The H.264 and H.264 encoding follow the settings in DVC and use FFmpeg with a very fast mode. In the rate-distortion graph shown in Fig. 7, we show the results of some deep video compression models in recent years. We test it on HEVC and UVG datasets respectively. Figure 7 shows that our method outperforms the baseline method DVC [11] and its enhanced version DVC++ [12] on all datasets. In addition, with a smaller number of parameters, our model still shows better PSNR and MS-SSIM performance than the other deep video compression models mentioned above. The comparison results of specific parameter numbers are shown in Table 1. Compared with H.264 and H.265, our method also achieves better results in terms of PSNR and MS-SSIM at all bit rates.

Running Time and Model Complexity. The parameters of our proposed end-to-end video compression framework are 10.5M. The specific parameter comparison of DVC [11], DVC++ [12], RLVC [22], RPLVC [8] and our method is shown in Table 1. The results show that the parameters of our model are comparable to the DVC model and much smaller than other models. Specifically, for the video sequence with the resolution of 384 × 192, the corresponding FLOPs of our proposed method are 234.5GFLOPs. In comparison with our method, the FLOPs of DVC++ [12] are 294.6GFLOPs.

Table 1. Comparison of model parameters.

Model	DVC	DVC++	RLVC	RPLVC	Proposed
parameters(M)	**10.1**	**29.4**	**16.7**	**27.1**	**10.5**

4.2 Ablation Study and Model Analysis

We respectively conduct four ablation experiments and test them on the HEVC ClassD. The test results are shown in Fig. 8. At the same time, BDBR and BD-PSNR were used to calculate the performance gap of the ablation model. The results are shown in Table 2. In addition, we also ensure that the number of parameters in the comparison models is roughly the same. The specific comparison results of the number of parameters are shown in Table 2.

Feature Extraction and Frame Reconstruction Network. In our method, residual compression network are implemented in feature space. The transformation between pixel space and feature space is realized by feature extraction and frame reconstruction network. In order to verify the validity of these networks, we directly remove these two networks. The result after deletion is shown in Fig. 8 named as ABL No-Feature with red line. Table 2 shows the specific values, and the baseline corresponding to the proposed method in Fig. 8. It shows that after removing the feature extraction and frame reconstruction networks,

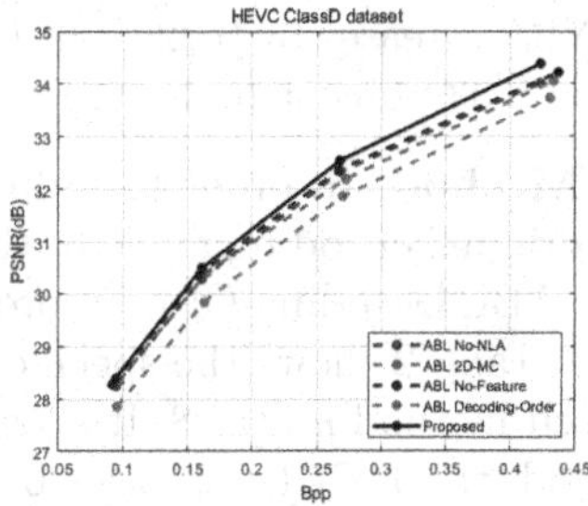

Fig. 8. In ablation experiment, we compared the experimental results under the following four settings: ABL No-Feature, ABL 2D-MC, ABL No-NLA and ABL Decoding-Order. (Color figure online)

Table 2. BDBR and BD-PSNR performances for different setting when compared with proposed model.

Model	BDBR(%)	BD-PSNR(dB)	Parameters(M)
ABL No-Feature	**3.21**	**−0.12**	**9.1**
ABL 2D-MC	**7.43**	**−0.28**	**10.1**
ABL No-NLA	**5.63**	**−0.22**	**10.6**
ABL Decoding-Order	**19.15**	**−0.68**	**10.5**

the PSNR decreases by 0.12dB at the same bit rate and the required bit rate increases by 3.21 percent under the same PSNR.

Feature Prediction Network. Considering the inadequacy of 2D convolution in time dimension extraction, we choose 3D convolution to implement motion compensation network. At the same time, we transfer this network from the pixel space to the feature space and call it the feature prediction network in our model. In order to verify whether 3D convolution plays a certain role in improving video compression performance, we compare the results of 2D convolution and 3D convolution. As shown in Fig. 8, the green line ABL 2D-MC represents the results of using 2D convolution network. Table 2 shows the specific values, and the baseline corresponding to the proposed method in Fig. 8. It shows that when use the 2D convolution, the PSNR decreases by 0.28dB at the same bit rate and the required bit rate increases by 7.43 percent under the same PSNR.

Attentional Motion Compression Network. Compared with DVC, we add an attention module to the motion compression network. In order to verify whether the attention module can effectively improve the video compression performance, we replace the attention module with the ordinary convolution layer. In Fig. 8, the blue line ABL No-NLA represents the result of adding the ordinary convolution layer. Table 2 shows the specific values, and the baseline corresponding to the proposed method in Fig. 8. It shows that when not use the attentional module, the PSNR decreases by 0.22dB at the same bit rate and the required bit rate increases by 5.63 percent under the same PSNR.

Bidirectional Encoding Method. In order to reduce the influence of error propagation, we change the original encoding mode to the bidirectional encoding mode. In Fig. 8, the grey line ABL Decoding-Order represents the results of using bidirectional encoding mode. Table 2 shows the specific values, and the baseline corresponding to the proposed method in Fig. 8. It shows that when not use the bidirectional encoding method, the PSNR decreases by 0.68dB at the same bit rate and the required bit rate increases by 19.15 percent under the same PSNR.

5 Conclusion

In this paper, we propose a video compression network based on 3D convolution and feature space residual compression. Firstly, based on the insufficient ability of 2D convolution in terms of spatio-temporal extraction, we apply a 3D convolution network to improve the quality of motion compensation frame. Then, we put the 3D convolution network and residual compression network into the feature space, so as to reduce the direct influence of inaccurate pixel-level errors on decoded frames. Finally, we also add an attention module to the motion compression network, so that the network can pay more attention to the complex area of the image. The experimental results show that our video compression algorithm is better than most of the current deep video compression algorithms in PSNR and MS-SSIM, even though the number of parameters is much smaller than others.

Acknowledgements. This work was supported by the National Natural Science Foundation of China under Grant 62176161, and the Scientific Research and Development Foundations of Shenzhen under Grant JCYJ20220818100005011 and 20200813144831001.

References

1. Ballé, J., Laparra, V., Simoncelli, E.P.: End-to-end optimized image compression. arXiv preprint arXiv:1611.01704 (2016)
2. Ballé, J., Minnen, D., Singh, S., Hwang, S.J., Johnston, N.: Variational image compression with a scale hyperprior. arXiv preprint arXiv:1802.01436 (2018)
3. Bellard, F.: BPG image format (2014). Volume 1, 2 (2016)
4. Cheng, Z., Sun, H., Takeuchi, M., Katto, J.: Learned image compression with discretized gaussian mixture likelihoods and attention modules. In: Proceedings of the IEEE/CVF Conference on Computer Vision and Pattern Recognition, pp. 7939–7948 (2020)
5. Hu, Z., Chen, Z., Xu, D., Lu, G., Ouyang, W., Gu, S.: Improving deep video compression by resolution-adaptive flow coding. In: Vedaldi, A., Bischof, H., Brox, T., Frahm, J.-M. (eds.) ECCV 2020. LNCS, vol. 12347, pp. 193–209. Springer, Cham (2020). https://doi.org/10.1007/978-3-030-58536-5_12

6. Hu, Z., Lu, G., Xu, D.: FVC: a new framework towards deep video compression in feature space. In: Proceedings of the IEEE/CVF Conference on Computer Vision and Pattern Recognition, pp. 1502–1511 (2021)
7. Lin, J., Liu, D., Li, H., Wu, F.: M-LVC: multiple frames prediction for learned video compression. In: Proceedings of the IEEE/CVF Conference on Computer Vision and Pattern Recognition, pp. 3546–3554 (2020)
8. Liu, C., Sun, H., Katto, J., Zeng, X., Fan, Y.: Learned video compression with residual prediction and loop filter. arXiv preprint arXiv:2108.08551 (2021)
9. Liu, H., Chen, T., Guo, P., Shen, Q., Cao, X., Wang, Y., Ma, Z.: Non-local attention optimized deep image compression. arXiv preprint arXiv:1904.09757 (2019)
10. Lu, G., et al.: Content adaptive and error propagation aware deep video compression. In: Vedaldi, A., Bischof, H., Brox, T., Frahm, J.-M. (eds.) ECCV 2020. LNCS, vol. 12347, pp. 456–472. Springer, Cham (2020). https://doi.org/10.1007/978-3-030-58536-5_27
11. Lu, G., Ouyang, W., Xu, D., Zhang, X., Cai, C., Gao, Z.: DVC: an end-to-end deep video compression framework. In: Proceedings of the IEEE/CVF Conference on Computer Vision and Pattern Recognition, pp. 11006–11015 (2019)
12. Lu, G., Zhang, X., Ouyang, W., Chen, L., Gao, Z., Xu, D.: An end-to-end learning framework for video compression. IEEE Trans. Pattern Anal. Mach. Intell. **43**(10), 3292–3308 (2020)
13. Luo, J., Huang, S., Yuan, Y.: Video super-resolution using multi-scale pyramid 3D convolutional networks. In: Proceedings of the 28th ACM International Conference on Multimedia, pp. 1882–1890 (2020)
14. Ranjan, A., Black, M.J.: Optical flow estimation using a spatial pyramid network. In: Proceedings of the IEEE Conference on Computer Vision and Pattern Recognition, pp. 4161–4170 (2017)
15. Skodras, A., Christopoulos, C., Ebrahimi, T.: The jpeg 2000 still image compression standard. IEEE Signal Process. Mag. **18**(5), 36–58 (2001)
16. Sullivan, G.J., Ohm, J.R., Han, W.J., Wiegand, T.: Overview of the high efficiency video coding (HEVC) standard. IEEE Trans. Circuits Syst. Video Technol. **22**(12), 1649–1668 (2012)
17. Toderici, G., et al.: Full resolution image compression with recurrent neural networks. In: Proceedings of the IEEE Conference on Computer Vision and Pattern Recognition, pp. 5306–5314 (2017)
18. Wallace, G.K.: The JPEG still picture compression standard. IEEE Trans. Consum. Electron. **38**(1), xviii-xxxiv (1992)
19. Wang, X., Chan, K.C., Yu, K., Dong, C., Change Loy, C.: EDVR: video restoration with enhanced deformable convolutional networks. In: Proceedings of the IEEE/CVF Conference on Computer Vision and Pattern Recognition Workshops (2019)
20. Wiegand, T., Sullivan, G.J., Bjontegaard, G., Luthra, A.: Overview of the H. 264/AVC video coding standard. IEEE Trans. Circ. Syst. Video Technol. **13**(7), 560–576 (2003)
21. Wu, C.Y., Singhal, N., Krahenbuhl, P.: Video compression through image interpolation. In: Proceedings of the European Conference on Computer Vision (ECCV), pp. 416–431 (2018)
22. Yang, R., Mentzer, F., Gool, L.V., Timofte, R.: Learning for video compression with hierarchical quality and recurrent enhancement. In: Proceedings of the IEEE/CVF Conference on Computer Vision and Pattern Recognition, pp. 6628–6637 (2020)

Deep-Learning Based Three Channel Defocused Projection Profilometry

Tianbo Liu(✉)

Shenzhen International Graduate School, Tsinghua University, Shenzhen 518055, China
liutb21@mails.tsinghua.edu.cn

Abstract. Speeding up the process of fringe projection profilometry to make it more suitable for dynamic three-dimensional measurement is one of the targets of structured light research. In this work, based on the fact that the frame rate of the projector can be much higher than that of the camera, we propose a three-channel binary defocused projection method to break through the speed bottleneck of the camera. Three sequential phase-shifting binary patterns are projected in a defocused way by the three color channels of the projector respectively during one camera's exposure time. To tackle the issue of color crosstalk, a deep-learning based end-to-end fringe rectification method is first introduced. As a result, only three camera shots are required for single scene reconstruction. Through experiments in three static scenes and one dynamic scene, we demonstrate that our method substantially speeds up the reconstruction rate with an acceptable range of accuracy loss. In addition, given the limited available datasets in the fringe projection profilometry field, a new dataset is also released.

Keywords: Fringe projection · 3D shape reconstruction · Structured light · Dynamic measurement

1 Introduction

Fringe projection is a widely adopted technique for three-dimensional (3D) shape reconstruction which can be broadly categorized into Fourier transform profilometry (FTP) and phase shifting profilometry (PSP) [1,2].

The **FTP** utilizes only a single high-frequency fringe pattern, and the phase is extracted by applying a properly designed band-pass filter in the frequency domain [3]. Though it has the advantage of requiring only a single shot to recover the 3D shape, **its measuring accuracy is limited** [4].

On the other hand, the phase-shift (PS) reconstruction process, which is more accurate, involves three steps: projecting fringes with an equal phase difference to obtain the warped relative phase, calculating the absolute phase using techniques such as gray code [5] or multi-frequency heterodyne [6], and obtaining the 3D shape with calibration information.

L. Iliadis et al. (Eds.): ICANN 2023, LNCS 14263, pp. 124–135, 2023.
https://doi.org/10.1007/978-3-031-44204-9_11

While the **PS** method provides improved accuracy, it requires multiple shots. Therefore it is **not suitable for dynamic measurements** [7]. Two approaches have been proposed to address this limitation and accelerate the PS process: increasing the projecting speed and reducing the number of required patterns (Fig. 1).

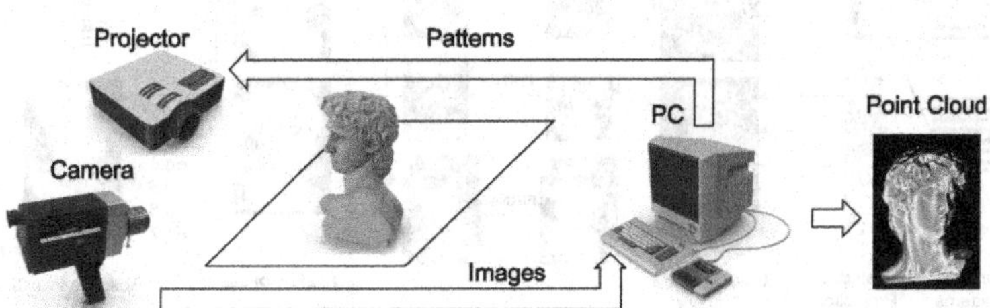

Fig. 1. A typical fringe projection profilometry system. The implementation of the fringe projection profilometry system involves a Personal Computer (PC) as the central unit for generating the projected patterns, controlling the camera and projector, and processing the captured images. A physical cable synchronizes the camera and projector, and the processed images are used to generate point clouds of the target scene.

To enhance the speed of the projection, **binary defocus** was introduced in literature [8]. As professional projectors are capable of projecting binary patterns much more quickly than 8-bit patterns, this approach utilized a defocused projector and binary patterns generated through a dithering algorithm, to imitate the standard system with 8-bit patterns and a focused projector. However, the quality of the imitation can be greatly impacted by the defocus level of the projector, which significantly **decreases the accuracy of the system** [9].

To reduce the number of required patterns, the **color-coded projection** methods were proposed [10–12]. This approach encodes three separate fringe patterns in the red, blue, and green channels of a 24-bit color pattern, which is then projected by the projector and captured by the camera as a single color image. The information on the three fringes is contained within the three color channels of the captured image. However, challenges of **color cross-talk** between color channels arise, which needs extra efforts to be solved.

Recently, various **deep-learning based approaches** have been proposed [13–17]. Feng *et al.* [14] were pioneers in incorporating deep learning into PSP in order to reduce the number of required fringes. They developed two convolutional neural networks (CNN) that were capable of predicting the relative phase from a single fringe projection. Over the years, numerous studies have proposed to substitute parts or the entirety of the traditional PS process. Neural networks help us reduce the number of required patterns, which consequently speed up the reconstruction process. However, it is noteworthy that these approaches have only focused on 8-bit patterns, thereby **not fully utilizing the speed capability** of the projector.

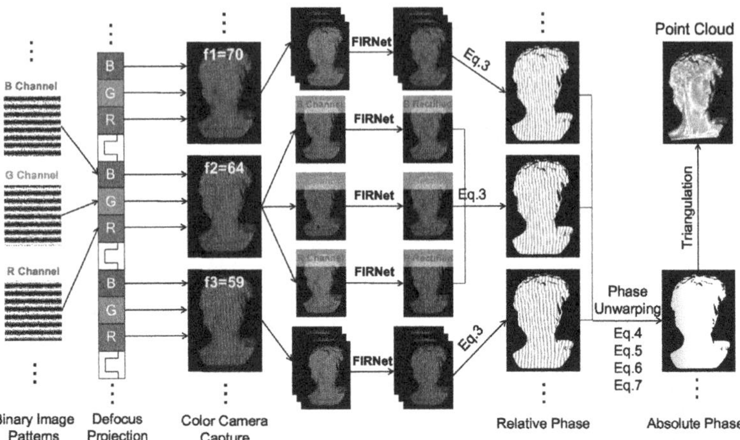

Fig. 2. An overview of the system. The binary PS fringes are encoded into three color channels of a defocused projector. Each color channel's projection averages the exposure time of the camera, so the final captured image is one color image. The captured color image is subjected to channel-wise separation and further processed by the FIRNet to be rectified. The relative phase is generated using the PS algorithm, while the absolute phase is determined through 3-frequency heterodyne algorithm. The final calculation of the three-dimensional coordinates of the points is achieved through trigonometry, aided by the calibration information.

To solve the problems mentioned above, we propose a deep-learning based three-channel binary fringe projection method that **combines the advantages of binary defocus and color-coded projection**. As illustrated in Fig. 2, three binary patterns with equal phase differences are projected successively in a defocused manner, by the three color channels of the projector within a single camera exposure time. To better analyze the captured image, we employ neural networks, referred to as the Fringe Image Rectification Network (FIRNet), which is trained to rectify the color cross-talk and non-standard defocus model of the image. Additionally, a background estimation network is employed to eliminate extraneous noise in the image. A total number of 9 binary patterns are projected and 3 color images are captured to generate point clouds of a single scene.

The major contributions of our work are the following:

- We speed up the reconstruction process by incorporating the binary defocus and color-coded projection techniques, making PS methods more appropriate for dynamic 3D measurements.
- Unlike previous works [11,18], we don't require additional cameras or patterns to address the issues of color-crosstalk, by introducing neural networks.
- A new dataset is released, which gives new vigor to structured light research.

2 The Proposed Deep-Learning Based Fringe Projection Profilometry

The proposed method begins by encoding nine binary fringes into three color channels and capturing three 24-bit color images. Next, the captured images are separated into their individual color channels and the fringes are rectified by the FIRNet. Three warped phases with different frequencies are obtained through the application of a 3-step PS technique, and the absolute phase is determined by the 3-frequency heterodyne algorithm. Finally, with the aid of calibration information, the three-dimensional coordinates of the points can be calculated through the use of trigonometry.

2.1 Relative Phase Obtaining

Supposing the $A(x, y)$ and $B(x, y)$ are the background and projection intensity for pixel (x, y). The nth captured PS fringe pattern can be concluded as

$$I_n(x,y) = A_n(x,y) + B_n(x,y)\cos[\phi(x,y) - \frac{2\pi n}{N}], \tag{1}$$

where N represents the number of PS steps. If A_n stays the same during the whole process, according to the orthogonality of trigonometric functions,

$$\sum_{n=0}^{N-1} A_n(x,y)\sin\frac{2\pi n}{N} = 0. \tag{2}$$

With Eq. (1) and Eq. (2), the warped relative phase $\phi(x, y)$ can be computed by

$$\phi(x,y) = \arctan\frac{\sum_{n=0}^{N-1} I_n(x,y)\sin\frac{2\pi n}{N}}{\sum_{n=0}^{N-1} I_n(x,y)\cos\frac{2\pi n}{N}}. \tag{3}$$

In this methodology, three binary patterns of equal frequency and equal-difference phases ($\frac{2\pi}{3}$) are generated. The dithering algorithm [20,21] is then utilized to convert these 8-bit patterns into corresponding binary patterns. In contrast to previously utilized color-coded projection techniques that project color patterns directly, the proposed method utilizes the individual red, green, and blue channels of the projector to successively project three binary patterns in a sequential and defocused manner. Through a single exposure of the camera, the sequential projections of three channels are captured, resulting in a color image that can be decomposed into its corresponding R, G, and B channels. This system presents two advantages. First, binary defocus allows the projector to circumvent the speed limitation of projecting 8-bit patterns (120 Hz), as it can project binary patterns at the fastest speed of 4225 Hz. Second, color-coded projection reduces the number of images required for reconstruction, as one color image contains the information of three fringes. To set up this system, the projector must operate at a rate three times faster than that of the color camera. The 3-step PS algorithm was chosen to calculate the relative phase, which is depicted in Eq. (3).

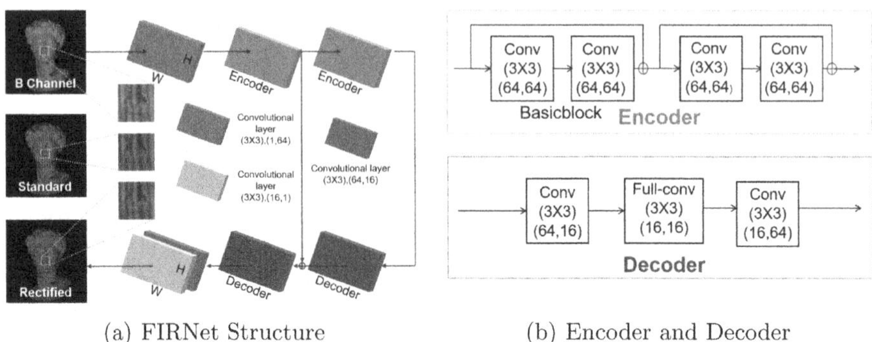

(a) FIRNet Structure (b) Encoder and Decoder

Fig. 3. The proposed neural network is an end-to-end solution for the rectification of raw fringes, whose structure is shown in Fig. 3(a). The architecture of the encoder and decoder are illustrated in Fig. 3(b).

2.2 Rectification of Fringes

Influenced by the color cross-talk and imprecision in the defocus projection model, each channel of the raw image are of poor quality, which is illustrated in Fig. 4. Owing to the noise, the sinusoidal fringes lack sufficient clarity and exhibit an unstable intensity distribution. Additionally, the background intensity (A(x,y)) of each channel exhibits significant variation, which renders Eq. (2) and Eq. (3) invalid.

The FIRNet, which functions as an end-to-end fringe rectification component, is designed to address the aforementioned issues. The FIRNet takes raw fringe patterns as input and utilizes a corrected fringe pattern, which shares the same phase and frequency but is projected with 8-bit patterns, to guide the network training. Given that fringe rectification is a novel task that requires the ability of semantic segmentation, we selected the LinkNet [23] as the backbone network. The LinkNet is a compact neural network specifically designed for real-time semantic segmentation. Given that our reconstruction task places a higher emphasis on the precision of the fringe rectification, modifications were made to the LinkNet to make it more suitable for our task. The architecture of our FIRNet is depicted in Fig. 3.

In order to retain the particulars of the fringes, the present methodology withdraws all max-pooling layers in the LinkNet. Furthermore, the 4-layer encoder-decoder structure is reduced to two, in order to minimize the number of parameters in the network. The input of the FIRNet is a raw fringe pattern with $(W \times H \times 1)$ pixels. The encoder begins with an initial block which performs convolution on the input image with a kernel of size $(3 \times 3 \times 1)$ and a stride of 1. To balance the model size and feature extraction capability of the encoder, the Resnet18 [24] model was chosen as the encoder, as opposed to more complex models. Two encoders are sequentially connected, each of which has 64 filters. The later portion of the encoder consists of residual blocks and is represented as encoder block. There are two sequentially connected decoders. The deconvolutional layers are reserved for future expansion of the image in the event that max-pooling layers are added to reduce the number of parameters in the model. It is worth noting that the first encoder's output is connected directly to the input of the second decoder to preserve more spatial information of the raw fringe. The detailed structure of the encoder and decoder is illustrated in Fig. 3(b). After the Encoder-decoder module, there are two convolution layers with a kernel of size $(3 \times 3 \times 1)$ and a stride of 1 to reduce the number of channels to 1, which achieves the end-to-end rectification.

In Fig. 4, it can be observed that, due to the effect of color cross-talk, the sinusoidal characteristics of the fringes are influenced. However, the FIRNet effectively restores the fringe and background intensity in the raw image by rectifying the $A(x, y)$ values of each channel to be similar, thus improving the reliability of the relative phase calculation and enhancing the accuracy of the reconstruction process.

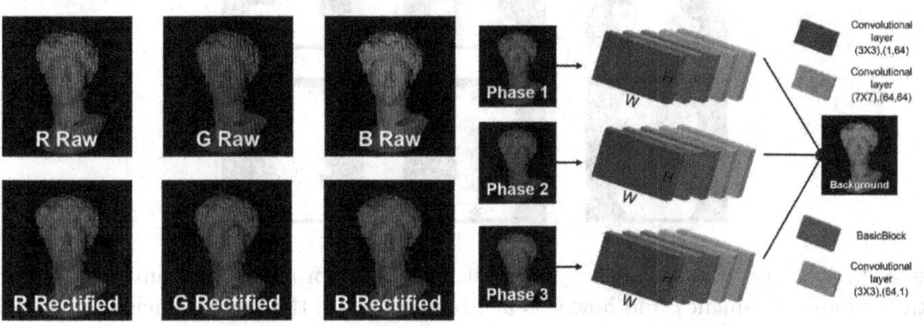

(a) Rectification Results (b) Background Estimation CNN

Fig. 4. (a) is a comparison of the raw and rectified images, demonstrating the efficacy of the FIRNet in terms of the improvement of brightness uniformity and fringe quality. (b) demonstrates the detailed structure of the background estimation CNN.

2.3 Background Estimation

In the traditional method of distinguishing the projected region, researchers typically projected pure white and black patterns respectively, and captured two images. Subsequently, a threshold is established to generate a mask based on the brightness difference between the two images. Inspired by [14], to circumvent the need for projecting these two patterns, we use a deep-learning based method for background estimation, as depicted in Fig. 4(b).

The input to the network is the rectified fringe pattern, and the output is the estimated background. The fringe pattern is processed through a convolution layer with a kernel size of $(3 \times 3 \times 1)$ and a stride of 1, which increases the number of channels to 64. Followed by two basic blocks of ResNet18 with 64 channels for further adjustment of the input image. A convolution layer with a kernel size of $(7 \times 7 \times 1)$ is utilized to expand the receptive field. Finally, a $(3 \times 3 \times 1)$

kernel is employed to reduce the number of channels to 1, thereby achieving background prediction. Since one color image contains three fringes, to obtain a more precise background, the outputs of the three fringes are averaged. By setting an intensity threshold, the projected region can be distinguished and most of the noise outside of the region can be eliminated.

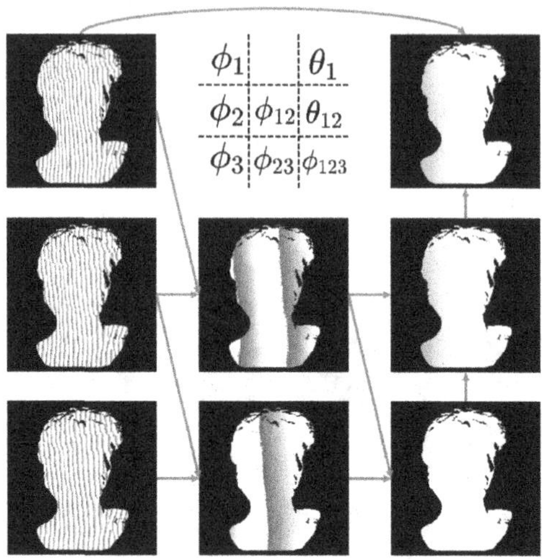

Fig. 5. Process for unwrapping the phase. It depicts the process of obtaining the fringe with the lowest frequency and how it is utilized to unravel the relative phase. The label for each subfigure is in the second picture.

2.4 Absolute Phase Calculation

We choose 3-steps PS to recover the warped phase and a three-frequency heterodyne algorithm to unwrap it. In general, 9 binary patterns are projected with a defocused projector and converged into 3 color patterns for one frame reconstruction. Two-frequency heterodyne can be described as

$$\phi_{12} = \phi_1 - \phi_2 \quad if(\phi_1 > \phi_2), \tag{4}$$

$$\phi_{12} = \phi_1 - \phi_2 + 2\pi \quad if(\phi_1 < \phi_2), \tag{5}$$

where ϕ_{12} means new relative phase with lower frequency. ϕ_{123}, which covers the whole width of the fringe pattern, can be calculated in the same way. From the original phase, we choose the ϕ_1 with the highest frequency as a base for unwrapping. The formulas are as follows:

$$\theta_{12} = \phi_{12} + 2\pi * Round(\frac{\phi_{123} * \lambda_{23}/\lambda_{123} - \phi_{12}}{2\pi}), \tag{6}$$

$$\theta_1 = \phi_1 + 2\pi * Round(\frac{\theta_{12} * \lambda_1/\lambda_{12} - \phi_1}{2\pi}). \quad (7)$$

Additionally, the unwrapping process for the three-frequency heterodyne algorithm is depicted in Fig. 5. The unwrapped absolute phase, denoted as θ_1, is obtained through Eq. (6) and Eq. (7). Utilizing calibration information, 3D point clouds can be calculated through the application of trigonometry.

3 Results and Evaluation

3.1 Device Settings and Training Details

We have developed a system for fringe projection and acquisition, comprising a specialized projector (LightCrafter 4500, with a resolution of 912×1140) and an industrial-grade camera (Basler acA720-520uc, with a resolution of 720×540). The system utilizes a trigger line to synchronize the camera and projector. The LightCrafter 4500 is capable of projecting binary patterns and 8-bit patterns at maximum frequencies of 4225 Hz and 120 Hz, respectively. Additionally, the camera's maximum acquisition rate is 520 Hz. We performed simultaneous calibration of the camera and projector by projecting both phase-shifting and Gray code patterns, which limits the pixel error in the camera to 0.06 pixels and the error in the projector to 0.6 pixels. The networks were trained using a GTX 3090 GPU for 200 epochs, utilizing the ADAM optimizer and a mean squared error loss function. The learning rate was set as 10^{-5}.

3.2 Dataset

Totally, 120 sets of data were collected from various scenes. In each scene, three color images were acquired at frequencies 70, 64, and 59, as depicted in Fig. 2, while the projector was set in a defocused state. Additionally, a standard 3-step PS pattern with the same three frequencies was recorded in a total of 9 instances, with the projector set in a focused state. Furthermore, one image was captured with no light source present, and another image was captured with a fully white pattern projected. The dataset was divided into a training set and a testing set, with a ratio of 4:1, and the division was done randomly. Our code and dataset are available at https://github.com/FantastLiu/deep-learning-based-Three-Channel-Binary-Fringe-Defocused-Projection-Profilometry.

3.3 Baselines

We selected benchmarks including accurate traditional approaches and deep-learning based methods published in recent years. According to the rate of reconstruction, the methods can be classified into low speed (denoted by '[L]' in italics) and high speed (denoted by '[H]' in italics).

6PS-GC*[L]* [5]: 6-step PS unwarped by gray code. 12 Patterns were projected focused with the fastest speed of 120 Hz.

3PS-3FP*[L]* [6]: 3-step PS unwarped by 3-frequency heterodyne technique. All 9 patterns were projected focused with the fastest speed of 120 Hz.
3PS-DE*[L]* [8]: Contrast to the 3PS-3FP, we projected binary patterns in a defocused manner. The projecting speed was set to be 510 Hz.
L-GC*[L]* [13]: Using one fringe pattern to predict the relative phase. All 7 Patterns were projected focused with the fastest speed of 120 Hz.
L-SR*[H]* [15]: A learning-based single-shot reconstruction method. One 24-bit color pattern was projected focused with the fastest speed of 120 Hz.
Ours*[H]*: Except for the projection method, all settings and patterns were the same as 3PS-DE. The projector worked at the rate of 1530 Hz, which is 3 times higher than the camera.

It is noteworthy that, the projector and camera must be strictly synchronized. The speed of the algorithm, measured in frames per second (FPS), is determined by the projection rate divided by the number of captures required. All methods were implemented at the highest speed using the chosen projector and camera in this study.

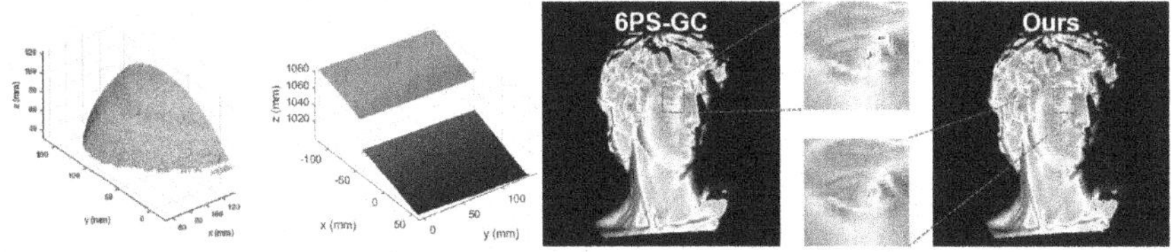

(a) Standard Semi-sphere and Steps (b) David Plaster

Fig. 6. (a) is a standard model for a semi-sphere with 100 mm diameter and steps with 30 mm height. (b) represents 'David plaster' reconstruction result.

Table 1. Semi-sphere and steps reconstruction results table.

Method	Semi-sphere			Steps			Frame Rate
	MAE	*MSE*	*Diameter*	*MAE*	*MSE*	*Height*	
6PS-GC*[L]* [5]	0.5943	0.5873	99.9584	0.9478	0.8875	30.0432	10
3PS-3FP*[L]* [6]	0.8476	0.7786	99.9888	1.0345	0.9967	29.8761	13.33
3PS-DE*[L]* [8]	0.8874	0.8452	99.9678	1.2587	1.1936	29.8424	56.67
L-GC*[L]* [13]	0.6389	0.6025	100.0475	1.0783	1.0121	30.8264	17.14
L-SR*[H]* [15]	0.9379	0.9078	99.9875	1.3974	1.2866	30.4127	120
Ours*[H]*	0.9032	0.8739	100.0348	1.1985	1.1126	29.8974	170

[1] *[L]* means the low speed method, *[H]* means the high speed method.
[2] The units for MAE, MSE, Diameter, and Height are mm.
[3] The unit for Frame Rate is fps.

3.4 Experiment and Comparative Analysis

In order to verify the feasibility of our proposed method, four scenarios were evaluated which were not present in the training dataset. The first and second scenarios involved the reconstruction of a standard semi-sphere with a diameter of 100 mm and a standard step with a height of 30 mm. We created reference models of semi-spheres and steps as shown in Fig. 6(a), and assessed the accuracy of the reconstruction by evaluating the Mean Absolute Error(MAE), Mean Squared Error(MSE), diameter, and height of the reconstructed models against the reference models. The results, as presented in Table 1, indicate that our method successfully controlled the MAE, MSE, diameter, and height error to within 1%, while also achieving a significant increase in processing speed. In comparison to the learning-based approach L-SR*H*, this method demonstrates a simultaneous improvement in accuracy and speed.

$$MAE = \sum_{i=1}^{D} |x_i - y_i| \quad MSE = \sum_{i=1}^{D} (x_i - y_i)^2 \tag{8}$$

Table 2. 'David plaster' reconstruction results table

Method	MAE(mm)	MSE(mm)	*Frame Rate*(fps)
6PS-GC*[L]* [5]	X*	X*	10
3PS-3FP*[L]* [6]	1.3683	1.2693	13.33
3PS-3FP(de)*[L]* [8]	1.5463	1.4982	56.67
L-GC*[L]* [13]	1.4645	1.3956	17.14
L-SR*[H]* [15]	1.8792	1.9986	120
Ours*[H]*	1.5982	1.5099	170

[1] The results obtained using the 6PS-GCL serve as the benchmark.
[2] *[L]* means the low speed method, *[H]* means the high speed method.

The third scenario aimed to evaluate the ability of our method to restore detailed features. The reconstruction of a 'David plaster' model was performed, and the results were compared to those obtained using 6PS-GCL, the most accurate technique in our experiment. As illustrated in Fig. 6(b), our method demonstrated a strong ability to restore detailed features, particularly in the outline of the eye socket and pupil of the left eye. Also, Table 2 demonstrates the remarkable capacity of our method to expedite the reconstruction process while maintaining accuracy.

Finally, the dynamic measurement capacity of our method was evaluated by recording the process of a ping-pong ball bouncing on a blanket. The results, as shown in Fig. 7, demonstrate that our method was able to accurately capture the rising and falling motion of the ping-pong ball while accurately preserving its shape.

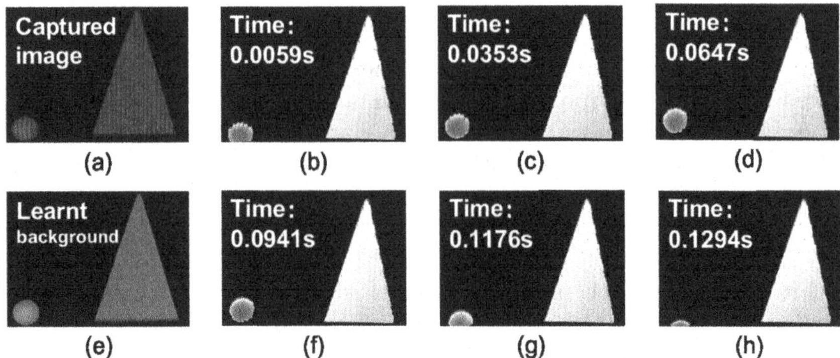

Fig. 7. Ping-pong Bouncing on a Table. (a) is one of the captured images with color fringes. (b)-(d) and (f)-(h) are point clouds of some scenes reconstructed from the whole bouncing process. (e) is the background predicted by the proposed CNN.

4 Conclusion

In this research, we propose a deep-learning based color fringe projection profilometry technique that fully utilizes the potential of the projector's speed. By utilizing only three color images, one frame reconstruction can be completed. We introduce a neural network that simultaneously addresses the issues of projector defocus and color cross-talk from the camera. This results in a substantial acceleration of the recovery process while maintaining accuracy. Our future works will focus on further improvements in speed and precision with the aid of deep-learning technology.

References

1. Gorthi, S.S., Rastogi, P.: Fringe projection techniques: whither we are? Opt. Lasers Eng. **48**, 133–140 (2010). ARTICLE
2. Chao, Z., et al.: Phase shifting algorithms for fringe projection profilometry: a review. Opt. Lasers Eng. **109**, 23–59 (2018)
3. Takeda, M., Mutoh, K.: Fourier transform profilometry for the automatic measurement of 3-D object shapes. Appl. Opt. **22**(24), 3977–3982 (1983)
4. Su, X.Y., Chen, W.J., Zhang, Q.C., Cao, Y.P.: Dynamic 3-D shape measurement method based on FTP. Opt. Lasers Eng. **36**, 49–64 (2001)
5. Sansoni, G., Carocci, M., Rodella, R.: Three-dimensional vision based on a combination of gray-code and phase-shift light projection: analysis and compensation of the systematic errors. Appl. Opt. **38**(31), 6565–6573 (1999)
6. Li, E.B., Peng, X., Xi, J., Chicharo, J.F., Yao, J.Q., Zhang, D.W.: Multi-frequency and multiple phase-shift sinusoidal fringe projection for 3D profilometry. Opt. Exp. **13**(5), 1561–1569 (2005)
7. Zhang, S.: High-speed 3D shape measurement with structured light methods: a review. Opt. Lasers Eng. **106**, 119–131 (2018)

8. Lei, S., Zhang, S.: Flexible 3-D shape measurement using projector defocusing. Opt. Lett. **34**(20), 3080–3082 (2009)
9. Zhang, S.: Flexible 3D shape measurement using projector defocusing: extended measurement range. Opt. Lett. **35**(7), 934–936 (2010)
10. Zhang, S.: Rapid and automatic optimal exposure control for digital fringe projection technique. Opt. Lasers Eng. **128**, 106029 (2020)
11. Yapin, W., et al.: Single-shot phase measuring profilometry based on color binary grating with intervals. Opt. Commun. **451**, 268–275 (2019)
12. Zhang, Z.H.: Review of single-shot 3D shape measurement by phase calculation-based fringe projection techniques. Opt. Lasers Eng. **50**(8), 1097–1106 (2012)
13. Zuo, C., et al.: Deep learning in optical metrology: a review. Light Sci. Appl. **11**(1), 1–54 (2022)
14. Feng, S., et al.: Fringe pattern analysis using deep learning. Adv. Photonics **1**(2), 025001 (2019)
15. Qian, J., et al.: Single-shot absolute 3D shape measurement with deep-learning-based color fringe projection profilometry. Opt. Lett. **45**(7), 1842–1845 (2020)
16. Hieu, N., et al.: hNet: single-shot 3D shape reconstruction using structured light and h-shaped global guidance network. Results Opt. **4**, 100104 (2021)
17. Yan, K., et al.: Fringe pattern denoising based on deep learning. Opt. Commun. **437**, 148–152 (2019)
18. Pan, J., Huang, P.S., Chiang, F.P.: Color phase-shifting technique for three-dimensional shape measurement. Opt. Eng. **45**(1), 013602 (2006)
19. Zhang, X., Gai, S., Da, F.: Fast three-dimensional measurement based on three channel binary fringe defocused projection. Laser Optoeletronics Prog. **57**(23), 231201 (2020)
20. Cho, W., et al.: A dithering algorithm for local composition control with three-dimensional printing. Comput.-Aided Des. **35**(9), 851–867 (2003)
21. Dai, J., Li, B., Zhang, S.: High-quality fringe pattern generation using binary pattern optimization through symmetry and periodicity. Opt. Lasers Eng. **52**, 195–200 (2014)
22. Chaurasia, A., Culurciello, E.: LinkNet: exploiting encoder representations for efficient semantic segmentation. In: 2017 IEEE Visual Communications and Image Processing (VCIP). IEEE (2017)
23. Zhou, L., Zhang, C., Wu, M.: D-LinkNet: LinkNet with pretrained encoder and dilated convolution for high resolution satellite imagery road extraction. In: Proceedings of the IEEE Conference on Computer Vision and Pattern Recognition Workshops (2018)
24. He, K., et al.: Deep residual learning. Image Recognition 7 (2015)

Depthwise Convolution with Channel Mixer: Rethinking MLP in MetaFormer for Faster and More Accurate Vehicle Detection

Zhiwei Lu[1,2], Li Kang[1,2(✉)], and Jianjun Huang[1,2]

[1] College of Electronics and Information Engineering, Shenzhen University, Shenzhen 518060, China
luzhiwei2021@email.szu.edu.cn, kangli@szu.edu.cn

[2] Guangdong Key Laboratory of Intelligent Information Processing, Shenzhen, China

Abstract. Vehicle detection is an important task in intelligent traffic monitoring and autonomous driving. However, vehicle detection not only requires fast detection speed, but also presents a challenge due to detection of small targets under occlusion and illumination. Although some current approaches introduce lightweight networks to improve detection speed or Transformer to improve accuracy, they still struggle to achieve an excellent balance between speed and accuracy. To address these issues, this paper proposes a simple yet effective MetaFormerd-based vehicle detection model, which is constructed based on depthwise convolution with channel mixer (DWCM), using depthwise convolution as the token mixer and replacing the MLP residual block with a channel mixer (CM) module to boost feature reuse. The DWCM module enables enhanced feature extraction capabilities and can be applied to different detection models to improve vehicle detection performance. In extensive experiments, the proposed model not only achieves 38.0% AP on MS COCO, but also achieves 64.2% AP50 and 45.8% AP on UA-DETRAC with 278FPS on a RTX 2080Ti, which is significantly faster and more accurate than the state-of-the-art YOLO detectors without bells and whistles. Furthermore, the proposed CM-based model is more promising than the MLP-based model for vehicle detection which shows the superior potential of CM structure.

Keywords: Vehicle Detection · MetaFormer · Channel Mixer · YOLO

1 Introduction

Vehicle detection is an important research direction, which is mainly used in the fields of intelligent traffic monitoring and autonomous driving. Compared

Supported by National Natural Science Foundation of China (No. 81960312,62171287), Shenzhen Science and Technology Program (No. JCYJ20220818100004008).

L. Iliadis et al. (Eds.): ICANN 2023, LNCS 14263, pp. 136–147, 2023.
https://doi.org/10.1007/978-3-031-44204-9_12

with traditional vehicle detection algorithms, deep learning-based vehicle detection algorithms have better generalization capability and performance, which gradually become the mainstream method for vehicle detection. Deep learning-based vehicle detection algorithms are generally divided into two types: two-stage detection algorithms and one-stage detection algorithms. Two-stage detection algorithms represented by RCNN series [1–4] first generate candidate regions using selective search or RPN, and then perform classification and localization in the candidate regions. These methods are relatively slow due to the need to generate a large number of candidate regions, and is not suitable for deployment on devices with limited computing power. In contrast, one-stage detectors such as SSD [5], YOLO [6–8], RetinaNet [9] and [10], etc. without the stage of generating candidate regions detect targets directly on the image, which have faster detection speed compared with two-stage object detectors.

YOLO detectors provide a better trade-off between speed and accuracy and are the most commonly used detectors in industrial deployments. Jocher et al. [11] proposes SPPF and Focus, improving inference speed with similar accuracy compared with YOLOv4 [12]. Unlike YOLOv2-YOLOv5 [7,8,11,12], Ge et al. [13] adopted anchor-free mechanism and introduced decoupled head to improve consistency in classification and localization tasks. Since then, Li et al. [14] proposed introduced more re-parameterization module RepVGG [15] with self-distillation and RepOptimizer [16] to build detection models specifically designed for industrial deployment. Wang et al. [17] not only investigated the performance of the model re-parameterization in relation to the residual structure, but also introduced auxiliary detection heads for coarse prediction allowing leader detection head to process finer information. More recently, Glenn et al. [18] combined the design concepts of efficient layer aggregation networks and the bottleneck module to design more powerful feature extraction networks. Additionally, they also introduced TAL [19] to alleviate the misalignment problem of classification and localization task and enhance localization accuracy with the help of DFL [20].

In addition to the direct use of the above general detectors in vehicle detection, some methods use lightweight backbone networks such as MobileNets [21–23], ShuffleNets [24,25], EffienctNet [26] and GhostNet [27] to reduce the computation and number of parameters in the network to further enhance the speed on mobile end edge device. In addition, as the Transformer has shown excellent performance in the field of computer vision, some researches [28,29] combined Transformer with convolution to enhance model capacity and capture long-range dependencies. However, there are still some problems with these works: 1) some lightweight models, despite the reduced floating-point operations (FLOPs) and number of parameters, fail to get a significant speed improvement and still poorly achieve the speed-accuracy trade-off. 2) Transformer, despite its ability to increase model capacity and global perceptual field, is slow and difficult to train, which usually requires pre-training on large datasets and adding more data augmentation The performance tends to be poor when trained directly on small datasets.

MetaFormer [30] is a general achitecture of Vision Transformer [31], which consists of two residual modules, the first residual module uses token mixer to extract association information between different tokens, and the second residual module uses channel MLP for feature extraction in the channel dimension, as shown in Fig. 1. Self-attention improve the capability of global modelling, but is computationally intensive when applied to object detection and is more difficult to detect in real time on edge devices. Yu W. et al. [32] suggested that using identity mapping or pooling layers as token mixers can still achieve satisfactory performance. Therefore, in order to achieve higher speed and accuracy, we propose a lightweight vehicle detection model based on MetaFormer architecture, using depthwise convolution as the token mixer, which is more efficient compared with self-attention. Furthermore, we propose a channel mixer (CM) module to replace the channel MLP module with residual connections to reduce the computational effort of the MLP part of MetaFormer and improve the network's ability by remaining more texture information in upper-layer feature. Our model not only achieves higher accuracy than the state-of-the-art detectors in YOLO series on MS COCO, but also outperforms them significantly in terms of accuracy and speed on UA-DETRAC.

The contribution of this paper can be summarized as follows: 1) The channel MLP in MetaFormer structure is replaced with CM for faster and more accurate vehicle detection. Based on this DWCM is constructed using depthwise convolution as token mixer, which show the superior performance compared with popular networks. 2) We combine DWCM module and YOLOv8 to propose a vehicle detection model which significantly outperforms state-of-the-art detectors in YOLO series in terms of speed and accuracy on UA-DETRAC. 3) DWCM is implemented in different detectors and significantly improves vehicle detection accuracy.

2 Methods

2.1 Brief View of MetaFormer

MetaFormer is a general architecture abstracted from Transformer, which consists of an input embedding, two residual modules respectively consisting of a token mixer and a channel MLP. The input embedding first transforms the input feature map I into N tokens of feature dimension C:

$$X = \text{Input\_Embedding}(I). \tag{1}$$

The embedded tokens are fed into duplicated MetaFormer blocks for feature extraction, as shown in Fig. 1. Each layer of MetaFormer contains two residual modules with a normalization layer at the beginning, such as Layer Normalization (LN) or Batch Normalization (BN). The first residual module interacts with different tokens through a token mixer, which can be identity mapping, self-attention, spatial MLP. It can be expressed as

$$Y_1 = \text{Token\_Mixer}(\text{Norm}(X)) + X, \tag{2}$$

where Norm is normalization layer. The second residual module contains a two-layer MLP with an activation function. The channel MLP projects features to higher dimensions for filtering, i.e., the channel dimension is expanded from C to rC and then compressed back to C which can be expressed as

$$Y_2 = \sigma(\mathrm{Norm}(Y_1 W_1) W_2) + Y_1, \tag{3}$$

where $\sigma(\cdot)$ is activation function. W_1, W_2 are learnable parameters of linear projection layer.

2.2 Depthwise Convolution with Channel Mixer

Based on the MetaFormer structure, we use a 3×3 depthwise convolution which is more efficient than self-attention as the token mixer to extract feature information in spatial dimensions.

$$F_S = \delta(\mathrm{BN}(\mathrm{DW}(X))), \tag{4}$$

where $\delta(\cdot)$ is LeakyReLU and $\mathrm{DW}(\cdot)$ is depthwise convolution.

MLP in MetaFormer mainly performs channel feature information extraction, which may not occupy as much computation compared to self-attention. However, if the token mixer is simple operation such as depthwise convolution and pooling layer, FLOPs of channel MLP occupies a major part of the network's computation. The success of DenseNet and CSPNet show that concatenation operation in channel dimension retains more feature information than element summation which helps to improve model performance. In the recent object detectors [11,12,17,18] more concatenation operation is adopted to enhance feature reuse. This structure has been criticized for the increase in computation and memory requirements due to the expansion of the number of channels. However, in MetaFormer it is the expansion of the number of channels that is needed to extract richer and more diverse feature information. Therefore, we improve channel MLP with residual connection part of MetaFormer by proposing a channel mixer (CM) module to reduce the computational effort while achieving better performance, as shown in Fig. 1.

The first linear projection layer expands the channels to $(r-1)C$ and the generated channel diversity feature F_C is concatenated with the upper spatial extraction feature F_S to obtain the mixed feature O_1 which retains more texture information in the upper-layer feature while obtaining rich and diverse generated information. O_1 is then passed through a linear projection layer for channel number compression to filter out the feature information of interest O_2:

$$F_C = \delta(\mathrm{BN}(\mathrm{Conv}_1(F_S))), \tag{5}$$

$$O_1 = \mathrm{Concat}(F_C, F_S), \tag{6}$$

$$O_2 = \delta(\mathrm{BN}(\mathrm{Conv}_2(O_1))), \tag{7}$$

where Conv_1 and Conv_2 are 1×1 convolutions. The normalization layer in CM is BN, which is more commonly used in CNNs and more efficient than LN. To balance efficiency and accuracy, the expansion ratio is set to 2 in our model.

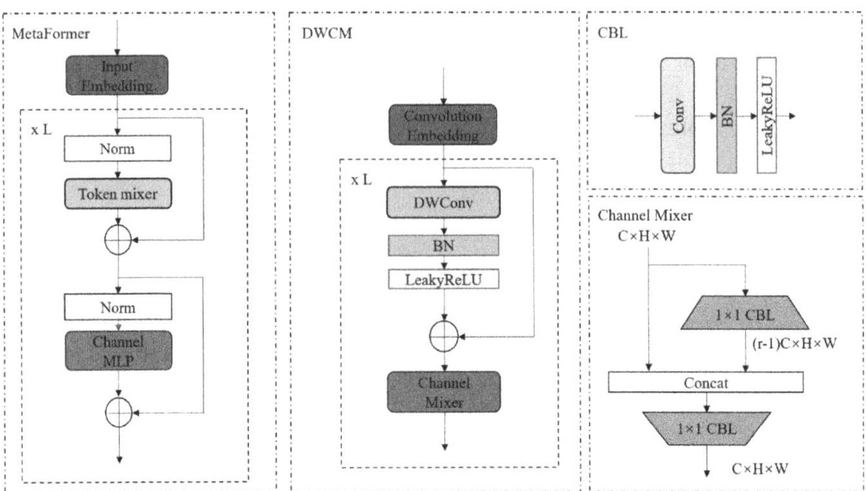

Fig. 1. The structure of MetaFormer and DWCM.

2.3 Detection Model

Our detection model is proposed based on DWCM and YOLOv8, the overall structure of which is shown in Fig. 2. The backbone network is composed of convolution stem and four stages, where the stem is a 6 × 6 CBS, and then each stage contains a 3 × 3 CBS with a stride of 2 as input embedding for downsampling. CBS is a convolution layer followed by BN and SiLU activatition. The channel dimension of each stage is 48, 96, 192 and 384. The output of the final stage of the backbone passes through the SPPF to capture multi-scale receptive field by three cascaded 5 × 5 maximum pooling layers, as shown in Fig. 2.

The neck and the detection head are similar to YOLOv8, except that the C2f [18] modules are replaced with our DWCM modules. Since the focus of classification and localization tasks is often different, where classification tasks focus more on the texture information at the center of the target and localization tasks focus more on the feature information at the edges, coupled detection heads fail to predict exactly with both high confidence classification and accurate localization. The introduction of the decoupled head in YOLOv8 achieves a significant improvement, where each branch contains two 3 × 3 CBS to extract task-specific feature, the first of which compress the number of channels to reduce FLOPs, as shown in Fig. 2.

For the loss function, the common binary cross-entropy (BCE) is used as the loss function for the classification task. For the localization task, CIoU and DFL [20] are used as the loss functions. DFL provides more information and accurate location predictions by modelling the general distribution of the prediction locations, forcing the network to quickly focus on values near the target location. The overall loss function is a weighted sum of the three:

$$L_{total} = \alpha L_{BCE} + \beta L_{DFL} + \gamma L_{CIoU}, \tag{8}$$

where α, β, γ are the weighting coefficients. As dynamic label assignment can further improve the consistency of classification and localization, TAL [19] is introduced to balance classification scores and localization accuracy.

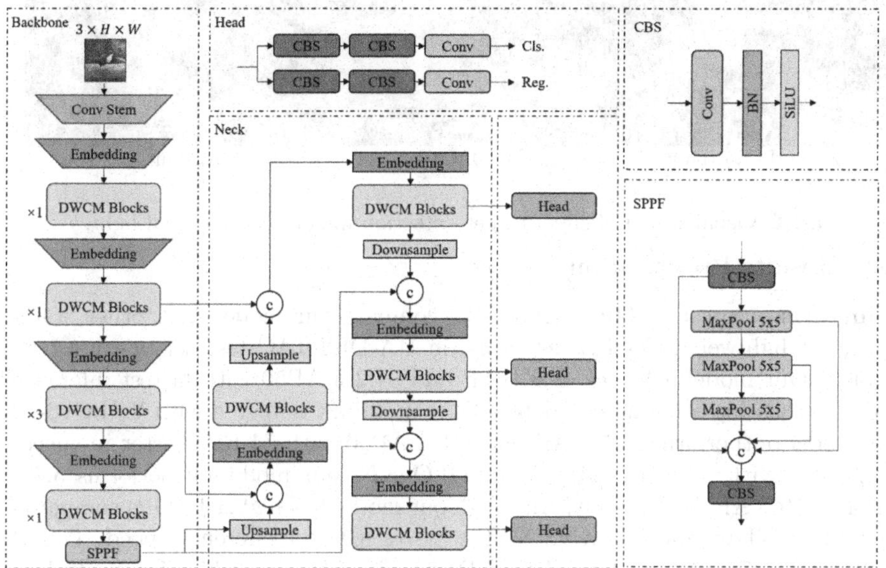

Fig. 2. The overall architecture of our detection model.

3 Experiment

3.1 Implement Details

Our model is trained and validated on the UA-DETRAC and MS COCO. UA-DETRAC is a large-scale vehicle detection and tracking dataset with a training set of 82,085 images and a test set of 56,167 images, consisting of 60 and 40 video frame sequences, respectively. UA-DETRAC has a total of four categories: car, bus, van and others, covering four different weather scenarios: sunny, night, cloudy and rainy. MS COCO is a commonly used dataset in object detection, which contains 118k images for the training set train2017 and 5k images of the validation set val2017.

For MS COCO dataset, our model is trained by an SGD optimizer with momentum of 0.937 for 300 epochs, a batchsize of 32, an initial learning rate of 0.01, and cosine annealing after 3 epochs of warm-up training with a warm-up momentum of 0.8. The data augmentations are similar with YOLOv8, using masic, mixup, random flipping, etc. The training conditions are an RTX 3090Ti, Pytorch version 1.12.1 and cuda version 11.3. For the UA-DETRAC dataset, the hyperparameters remain the same except that batchsize = 16 and epoch is set to 50. The inference speed is measured on a RTX 2080Ti except special indication.

(a) YOLOv7-Tiny (b) YOLOv8-N (c) Ours

Fig. 3. Visualization of small target detection under occlusion and light.

3.2 Results Presentation

Comparison on UA-DETRAC. We compare our model with other state-of-the-art lightweight YOLO detectors on UA-DETRAC test set, as shown in Table 1. Our model achieves 45.8% AP and 64.2% AP50 with fastest inference speed, surpassing other detectors by a large margin. Compared with YOLOv6-N, our model outperforms 3.1% AP and 4.1% AP50 with 74 FPS faster in speed. Compared with YOLOv7-Tiny and YOLOv8-N, our model outperforms 3.7% AP and 2.0% AP, respectively. Although our model has higher FLOPs compared to YOLOv7-Tiny and YOLOv8-N, it achieves a faster inference speed. This is because yolov7 and yolov8 use the CSPNet design ideology, which is less efficient than our model because of its higher memory access time despite its lower FLOPs and parameters.

Figure 3 is visualization of small target detection under occlusion and light. Our model detects more small targets and achieves higher accuracy than other detectors in the presence of light interference.

Table 1. Comparisons on UA-DETRAC.

Method	Size	AP	AP50	AP of each category				FLOPs	Parameters	FPS
				car	bus	van	others			
YOLOX-T	640	43.3%	59.9%	57.5%	61.4%	41.6%	12.6%	12.4G	4.5M	192
YOLOv5-N	640	41.7%	58.6%	55.1%	55.9%	41.4%	14.3%	4.2G	1.8M	259
YOLOv5-S	640	44.9%	62.0%	58.1%	61.0%	44.9%	15.5%	16.0G	7.0M	217
YOLOv6-N	640	42.7%	60.1%	52.0%	58.2%	42.6%	18.2%	11.0G	4.1M	204
YOLOv7-Tiny	640	42.1%	60.9%	55.7%	59.0%	39.2%	14.3%	13.1G	6.1M	208
YOLOv8-N	640	43.8%	60.2%	56.5%	58.1%	42.2%	18.0%	8.2G	3.0M	254
Ours	640	45.8%	64.2%	57.0%	62.4%	41.1%	22.9%	13.5G	5.0M	278

Comparison on COCO. Table 2 shows a comparison of our model with state-of-the-art YOLO models on the COCO dataset. For a fair comparison, we provide detection results for two input resolutions, 416 × 416 and 640 × 640, respectively. For an input resolution of 416 × 416, our model outperforms YOLOv4-Tiny [33] by 11.4% AP and 15.0% AP75. In addition, it outperforms YOLOX-T by 0.6% AP and is 1.5 times faster.

For an input resolution of 640 × 640, our model outperforms other detectors in terms of accuracy and inference speed. Compared with YOLOv5-N, our model is 10.0% AP higher. If we compared our model with YOLOv6-N, our model significant outperforms in small target detection by 1.9% AP_S. Furthermore, our model outperforms YOLOv7-Tiny and YOLOv8-N by 0.5% and 1.1% AP_S, respectively.

Table 2. Comparisons on COCO.

Method	Size	AP	AP50	AP75	AP_S	AP_M	AP_L	FLOPs	Parameters	Latency
YOLOv4-Tiny	416	22.0%	42.1%	20.7%	10.2%	26.3%	30.9%	6.9G	6.1M	2.7 ms
YOLOX-T	416	32.8%	50.3%	34.7%	13.9%	36.0%	50.9%	6.5G	5.1M	5.2 ms
Ours	416	33.4%	48.8%	35.7%	13.5%	35.9%	50.8%	5.7G	3.0M	3.4 ms
YOLOv5-N	640	28.0%	46.1%	29.2%	14.1%	32.1%	36.6%	4.5G	1.9M	3.9 ms
YOLOv5-S	640	37.4%	56.8%	40.2%	21.1%	42.2%	49.0%	16.5G	7.1M	4.7 ms
YOLOv6-N	640	37.5%	53.1%	40.5%	17.7%	41.8%	55.1%	11.4G	4.7M	4.8 ms
YOLOv7-Tiny	640	37.4%	55.2%	40.3%	19.1%	41.8%	52.7%	13.7G	6.2M	4.6 ms
YOLOv8-N	640	37.3%	52.6%	40.5%	18.5%	41.0%	53.6%	8.7G	3.2M	3.9 ms
Ours	640	38.0%	54.3%	41.4%	19.6%	41.6%	52.9%	13.6G	5.0M	3.7 ms

Comparisons of DWCM Network and Popular Networks. To validate the effectiveness of DWCM, we used YOLOv5-S as baseline and replaced its backbone with our network, keeping the neck consistent. As shown in Table 3, our model significantly outperforms in terms of speed and accuracy compared with other lightweight models. The inference speed on GPU and CPU is measured on RTX 2080Ti and i7-8700k respectively.

Although MobileNetv3 and ShuffleNetv2 reduce FLOPs and parameters to improve the inference speed on CPU, their low parallelism and high memory access consumption make them not as fast on the GPU. Compared with MobileNetv3, our model is 3.0% AP and 109 FPS faster than MobileNetv3 on GPU. Compared with ShuffleNetv2, our model is 3.3% AP and 3.9% AP50 more accurate with faster inference speed. In addition, our model outperforms EfficientNet and EfficientFormer [34] by 3.7% and 2.7% AP50 respectively, with significant faster inference speed.

DWCM in Different Object Detectors. In addition, we constructed a deeper network model using DWCM based on the number of blocks (2, 2, 6, 2) in PoolFormer_S12 [30] and applied this to the different detectors. The performance of different models is shown in Fig. 4 and Table 4. For fair comparison, the

Table 3. The performance of different networks.

Method	Size	AP	AP50	FLOPs	Parameters	Latency		FPS	
						GPU	CPU	GPU	CPU
YOLOv5-S_Mobilenetv3_small	640	40.4%	60.4%	7.3G	4.6M	6.2 ms	39.5 ms	161	25.3
YOLOv5-S_Shufflenetv2_1×	640	40.1%	58.2%	8.0G	4.2M	7.7 ms	45.7 ms	130	21.9
YOLOv5-S_Efficientnetv1	640	41.9%	58.4%	14.4G	9.1M	9.2 ms	63.3 ms	109	15.8
YOLOv5-S_EfficientFormerv1	640	42.3%	59.4%	27.4G	15.0M	7.2 ms	140.1 ms	139	7.1
YOLOv5-S_PoolFormer_S12	640	38.6%	54.3%	35.7G	15.0M	7.0 ms	162.6 ms	143	6.2
YOLOv5-S_DWCM	640	43.4%	62.1%	10.6G	4.9M	3.7 ms	42.9 ms	270	23.3

number of channels is kept the same as the original network model. The pooling layer is also used as token mixer to compare the performance of the MetaFormer model based on the CM structure and the MLP structure at an expansion ratio of 4, as shown in Table 4. Using the pooling layer as the token mixer, the CM-based model in YOLOv5-S and YOLOX-T achieves 1.7% and 1.4% higher AP than the MLP-based model, respectively. Meanwhile, using the DWCM module, the improved YOLOX boosted 4.1% AP and 5.3% AP50 compared to the baseline with faster inference speed. In YOLOv7-Tiny, the DWCM-based model not only improves by 2.3% AP and 3.5% AP50 compared to the baseline, but also improves by 2.5% AP and 3.3% AP50 compared to the MLP-based model, with less computation and faster inference.

Table 4. The performance of DWCM in different detectors.

Detectors	Size	Token Mixer	Channel Mixer	FLOPs	Parameters	AP	AP50	FPS
YOLOv5-S	640	✗	✗	16.0G	7.0M	44.9%	62.0%	217
YOLOv5-S	640	DWConv	✗	20.9G	9.0M	44.8%	63.4%	175
YOLOv5-S	640	DWConv	✓	18.4G	8.0M	45.7%	64.2%	202
YOLOv5-S	640	AvgPool	✗	30.8G	12.8M	40.5%	56.3%	185
YOLOv5-S	640	AvgPool	✓	28.5G	11.8M	42.2%	59.1%	192
YOLOX-T	640	✗	✗	12,4G	4.5M	43.3%	59.5%	144
YOLOX-T	640	DWConv	✗	17.7G	6.1M	42.9%	60.0%	151
YOLOX-T	640	DWConv	✓	16.4G	5.6M	47.4%	65.2%	166
YOLOX-T	640	AvgPool	✗	23.3G	8.4M	40.3%	57.5%	159
YOLOX-T	640	AvgPool	✓	22.0G	7.7M	41.7%	57.9%	163
YOLOv7-Tiny	640	✗	✗	13.1G	6.1M	42.1%	60.9%	208
YOLOv7-Tiny	640	DWConv	✗	17.8G	7.6M	41.9%	61.1%	169
YOLOv7-Tiny	640	DWConv	✓	15.4G	6.7M	44.4%	64.4%	178

Figure 5 shows the confusion matrix for different detection models with DWCM. The introduction of the DWCM reduces the probability of false negative (FN), especially for the others category, which is a difficult category to detect because of the small number of objects and less consistent variation in appearance features. Although the classification error rate increases for some categories, the hazard of missed detection is higher than that of classification

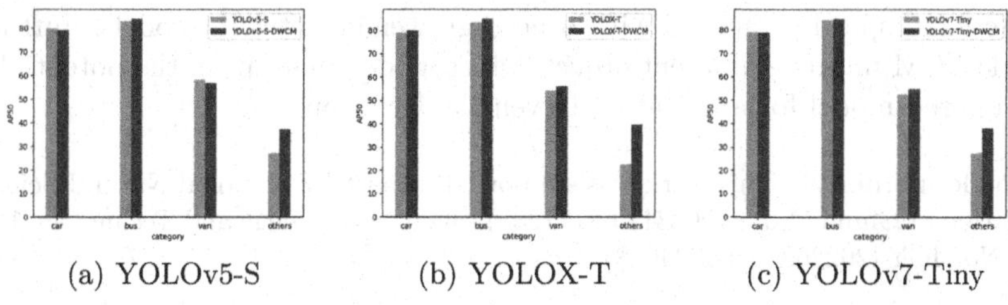

(a) YOLOv5-S (b) YOLOX-T (c) YOLOv7-Tiny

Fig. 4. The performance of DWCM in different detectors.

error in vehicle detection. Overall, DWCM improves the detection performance of difficult categories and reduces the rate of missed detections thereby improving vehicle target detection performance.

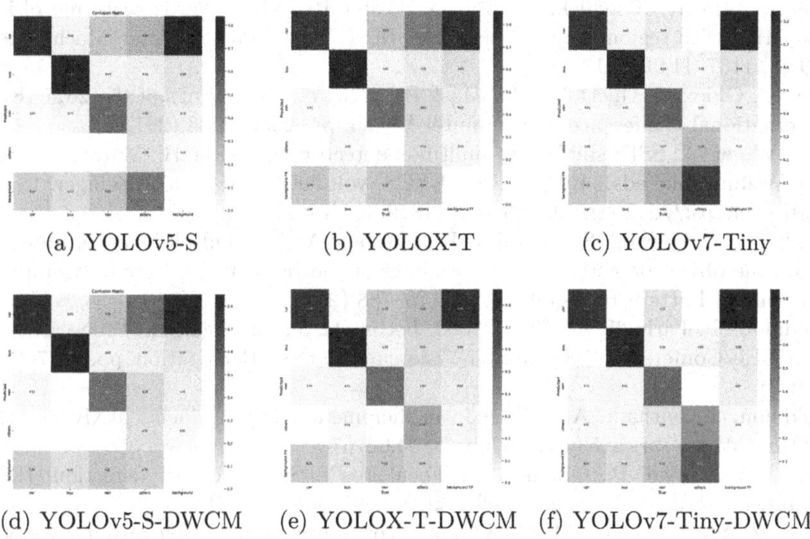

(a) YOLOv5-S (b) YOLOX-T (c) YOLOv7-Tiny

(d) YOLOv5-S-DWCM (e) YOLOX-T-DWCM (f) YOLOv7-Tiny-DWCM

Fig. 5. Confusion Matrix of different models.

4 Conclusion

In order to achieve a faster and more accurate vehicle detection model, we first use depthwise convolution as the token mixer based on MetaFormer structure, and then propose a simple yet effective CM module to replace the channel MLP residual module and construct the DWCM module. Our vehicle detection model is proposed based on DWCM without bells and whistles, outperforming the state-of-the-art detectors in YOLO series on UA-DETARC and MS COCO. Additionally, extensive experiment results show that the DWCM better balance between accuracy and speed compared with other lightweight network models. Furthermore, DWCM improve different object detectors demonstrating the potential of our proposed model for application in vehicle detection.

Acknowledgements. This work was supported in part by National Natural Science Foundation of China (No. 81960312,62171287), Shenzhen Science and Technology Program (No. JCYJ20220818100004008).

References

1. Girshick, R., Donahue, J., Darrell, T., Malik, J.: Rich feature hierarchies for accurate object detection and semantic segmentation. In: Proceedings of the IEEE Conference on Computer Vision and Pattern Recognition, pp. 580–587 (2014)
2. Girshick, R.: Fast R-CNN. In: Proceedings of the IEEE International Conference on Computer Vision, pp. 1440–1448 (2015)
3. Ren, S., He, K., Girshick, R., Sun, J.: Faster R-CNN: towards real-time object detection with region proposal networks. IEEE Trans. Pattern Anal. Mach. Intell. **39**(6), 1137–1149 (2017)
4. He, K., Gkioxari, G., Dollár, P.: Mask R-CNN. In: Proceedings of the 2017 IEEE International Conference on Computer Vision, pp. 2980–2988 (2017)
5. Liu, W., et al.: SSD: single shot multibox detector. In: Leibe, B., Matas, J., Sebe, N., Welling, M. (eds.) ECCV 2016. LNCS, vol. 9905, pp. 21–37. Springer, Cham (2016). https://doi.org/10.1007/978-3-319-46448-0_2
6. Redmon, J., Divvala, S., Girshick, R., Farhadi, A.: You only look once: unified, real-time object detection. In: Proceedings of the IEEE Conference on Computer Vision and Pattern Recognition, pp. 779–788 (2016)
7. Redmon, J., Farhadi, A.: YOLO9000: better, faster, stronger. In: Proceedings of the IEEE Conference on Computer Vision and Pattern Recognition, pp. 6517–6525 (2017)
8. Redmon, J., Farhadi, A.:YOLOv3: an incremental improvement. arXiv preprint (2018). https://arxiv.53yu.com/abs/1804.02767
9. Lin, T.Y., Goyal, P., Girshick, R.: Focal loss for dense object detection. IEEE Trans. Pattern Anal. Mach. Intell. **42**(2), 2999–3007 (2017)
10. Tian, Z., Shen, C., Chen, H.: FCOS: fully convolutional one-stage object detection. In: 2019 IEEE/CVF International Conference on Computer Vision (ICCV), pp. 9626–9635 (2019)
11. Glenn, J.: YOLOv5 release v6.2. https://github.com/ultralytics/yolov5/releases/tag/v6.2
12. Bochkovskiy, A., Wang, C., Liao, H.: YOLOv4: optimal speed and accuracy of object detection. arXiv preprint (2020). https://doi.org/10.48550/arXiv.2004.10934
13. Ge, Z., Liu, S., Wang, F.: YOLOX: exceeding YOLO series in 2021. arXiv preprint (2021). https://doi.org/10.48550/arXiv.2107.08430
14. Li, C., Li, L., Jiang, H.: YOLOv6 v3.0: a full-scale reloading. arXiv preprint (2023). https://doi.org/10.48550/arXiv.2301.05586
15. Ding, X., Zhang, X., Ma, N., Han, J., Ding, G., Sun, J.: RepVGG: making VGG-style ConvNets great again. In: 2021 IEEE/CVF Conference on Computer Vision and Pattern Recognition, pp. 13733–13742 (2021)

16. Ding, X., et al.: Re-parameterizing your optimizers rather than architectures. In: Proceedings of International Conference on Learning Representations, pp. 13733–13742 (2021)
17. Wang, C., Bochkovskiy, A., Liao, H.Y.M.: YOLOv7: trainable bag-of-freebies sets new state-of-the-art for real-time object detectors. In: 2023 IEEE/CVF Conference on Computer Vision and Pattern Recognition (2023). https://doi.org/10.48550/arXiv.2207.02696
18. Glenn, J.: Ultralytics YOLOv8. https://github.com/ultralytics/ultralytics
19. Feng, C., Zhong, Y., Gao, Y., Scott, M., Huang, W.: TOOD: task-aligned one-stage object detection. In: 2021 IEEE/CVF International Conference on Computer Vision, pp. 3490–3499 (2021)
20. Li, X., Lv, C., Wang, W., Li, G., Yang, L., Yang, J.: Generalized focal loss: towards efficient representation learning for dense object detection. IEEE Trans. Pattern Anal. Mach. Intell. **45**(3), 3139–3153 (2023)
21. Howard, A.: MobileNets: efficient convolutional neural networks for mobile vision applications. arXiv preprint (2017). https://doi.org/10.48550/arXiv.1704.04861
22. Sandler, M., Howard, A., Zhu, M., Zhmoginov, A., Chen, L.: MobileNetV2: inverted residuals and linear bottlenecks. In: 2018 IEEE/CVF Conference on Computer Vision and Pattern Recognition, pp. 4510–4520 (2018)
23. Howard, A.: Searching for MobileNetV3. In: 2019 IEEE/CVF International Conference on Computer Vision, pp. 1314–1324 (2019)
24. Zhang, X., Zhou, X., Lin, M., Sun, J.: ShuffleNet: an extremely efficient convolutional neural network for mobile devices. In: 2018 IEEE/CVF Conference on Computer Vision and Pattern Recognition, pp. 6848–6856 (2018)
25. Ma, N., Zhang, X., Zheng, H.-T., Sun, J.: ShuffleNet V2: practical guidelines for efficient CNN architecture design. In: Proceedings of the European Conference on Computer Vision, pp. 116–131 (2018)
26. Tan, M., Le, Q.V.: EfficientNet: rethinking model scaling for convolutional neural networks. In: Proceedings of the International Conference on Machine Learning (2019). https://doi.org/10.48550/arXiv.1905.11946
27. Han, K., et al.: GhostNets on heterogeneous devices via cheap operations. Int. J. Comput. Vision **130**(4), 1050–1069 (2022). https://doi.org/10.1007/s11263-022-01575-y
28. Chen, Y.: Mobile-former: bridging MobileNet and transformer. In: 2022 IEEE/CVF Conference on Computer Vision and Pattern Recognition, pp. 5260–5269 (2022)
29. Mehta, S., Rastegari, M.: MobileViT: light-weight, general-purpose, and mobile-friendly vision transformer. In: Proceedings of International Conference on Learning Representations (2021). https://doi.org/10.48550/arXiv.2110.02178
30. Yu, W.: MetaFormer is actually what you need for vision. In: 2022 IEEE/CVF Conference on Computer Vision and Pattern Recognition, pp. 10809–10819 (2022)
31. Dosovitskiy, A., Beyer, L., Kolesnikov, A.: An image is worth 16×16 words: transformers for image recognition at scale. In: International Conference on Learning Representations (2010). https://doi.org/10.48550/arXiv.2010.11929
32. Yu, W.: MetaFormer baselines for vision. arXiv preprint (2022).https://doi.org/10.48550/arXiv.2210.13452
33. Wang, C., Bochkovskiy, A., Liao, H.: Scaled-YOLOv4: scaling cross stage partial network. In: 2021 IEEE/CVF Conference on Computer Vision and Pattern Recognition, pp. 13024–13033 (2021)
34. Li, Y., et al.: EfficientFormer: vision transformers at MobileNet speed. arXiv preprint (2022). https://doi.org/10.48550/arXiv.2206.01191

DLUIO: Detecting Useful Investor Opinions by Deep Learning

Yi Xiang[1], Yujie Ding[1,2], and Wenting Tu[1(✉)]

[1] School of Information Management and Engineering, Shanghai University of Finance and Economics, Shanghai, China
dingyujie2@myhexin.com, tu.wenting@mail.shufe.edu.cn

[2] Hithink RoyalFlush Information Network Co., Ltd., Hangzhou, Zhejiang, China

Abstract. In recent years, due to the increasing popularity of investment microblogging platforms (e.g., Stocktwits), a critical challenge is to detect useful investor opinions and use them to make wise trading decisions. Conventional work in this subject always relies on some human-defined rules or traditional machine learning algorithms. However, the exploration of deep neural networks which have yielded immense success on many real-world applications on detecting useful investor opinions has received relatively few attention. In this paper, we propose *DLUIO*, a *D*eep *L*earning framework to detect *U*seful *I*nvestor *O*pinions. *DLUIO* uses a deep neural network to measure the quality of investor opinions by considering author impact, stock characteristics and text information simultaneously. Comparing to previous work depending on human-defined rules to generate features related to authors, stocks or microblog content, *DLUIO* employs deep neural networks to learn their representations automatically. Moreover, we propose a strategy to generate portfolios by utilizing prediction results obtained by *DLUIO*. Extensive data analysis and experiments show that *DLUIO* can bring us high-yield portfolios.

Keywords: Stock prediction · Deep learning · Social-media mining

1 Introduction

In recent years, people have released their investment opinions in the form of microblogs on the Internet without restriction, leading to a large volume of investment opinions posted by real investors. A challenging task is to detect useful investor opinions to help people invest [7,10,11,18]. In addition, the technique of deep neural networks are widely used to identify practical information from the vast social network platforms data [3,9,13]. Thus, the relatively attractive research field at present is to automatically find useful investor opinions and make wise investment decisions.

In the early research, a large number of working relies on human-defined rules or simple statistical methods to generate investment indicators from massive

L. Iliadis et al. (Eds.): ICANN 2023, LNCS 14263, pp. 148–160, 2023.
https://doi.org/10.1007/978-3-031-44204-9_13

investor opinions. [2] collected a large volume (i.e., 1.5 million) of messages from Yahoo Finance and Raging Bull platforms to study the predictive power of online messages for the stock market. Finally, they found that stock turnovers could be predicted by the volume of messages. The analysis in [6] is performed on a collection of queries submitted to a popular search engine. Their work shows that the dynamics of query volume can identify early warnings of financial risk. Besides searching behavior, the public emotion (e.g., joy, sadness) revealed on social-media platforms is another indicator commonly used for stock prediction. [5] investigated whether collective mood states on Twitter are related to the value of the Dow Jones Industrial Average (DJIA). They find that certain mood states are indeed predictive of the DJIA closing values. [19] explored the relationship between hope and fear on the one hand and the Dow Jones, NASDAQ, and S&P 500 on the other hand. Their results indicate that the level of tweet emotionality was significantly related to all three aggregated indicators. Recently, in [20], through the study on over 10 million stock-relevant tweets from Weibo, both correlation analysis and causality test show that five attributes of the stock market in China can be competently predicted by various online emotions, like disgust, joy, sadness, and fear.

At present, some researches study the task of identifying investment experts or high-quality investor opinions, which have a similar goal to ours. In previous work, [4] utilized the chi-square test to detect expert investors by considering the performances of investors' viewpoints in past opinions. Compared to their work, our approach infers the quality of specific opinions rather than users. For estimating the qualities of investment opinions, we not only consider the author's past performance but also explore other information. Moreover, [15,16] employed machine learning modeling the quality of the social media data, especially from the opinion authors, related stock, and textual data. Specifically, they designed multiple factors/features about opinion authors, related stock, and textual data and applied linear regression to predict opinion qualities. Compared to their work, *DLUIO* does not need pre-defined hand-picked features. The deep neural network can learn which features to optimally place on which level on its own.

In this paper, a novel neural network named *DLUIO* is proposed to mine credible opinions and help us to select stocks with profitable returns. The neural network in *DLUIO* takes author, stock, and textual data as input information and learns representations of these kinds of information automatically. Moreover, *DLUIO* considers interaction information among author, stock, and textual data by designing neural networks to model second-order factors. Specifically, *DLUIO* first uses a fully connected layer to embed the author, stock, and textual data. Then, interaction layers construct interactive information based on these pieces of information. Finally, the representation vectors and interaction vectors will be used to predict the credibility of opinions.

In the rest of this paper, we define some notations and introduce the background of our work in Sect. 2. Then, we describe our methodology in Sect. 3. Experiments are presented in Sect. 5. Conclusions and directions for future work are given in Sect. 6.

2 Task Formulation

The primary purpose of our work is to mine useful information in investor opinions to help people predict the stock price and establish investment strategies. A typical opinion presents the viewpoint ("Bullish" or "Bearish") on a stock. "Bullish" ("Bearish") viewpoints indicate that investors believe that the price of the stock will rise (drop) in the future. Obviously, people will gain investment income if they can identify which opinions are correct. To benefit from deep learning techniques, we formulate the task of identifying useful opinions as a machine learning problem:

In our study, we assign the correct/wrong label y for each opinion x. Suppose opinion x's viewpoint is that the price of stock s will rise in the near future. Here, we use Δd to denote the number of days according to what is "near the future". Then, the label of opinion x is defined as

$$y_{(x)} = \begin{cases} 1 & if \quad \dfrac{p^d_{\Delta d}(s^x) - p^d(s^x)}{p^d(s^x)} > 0 \\ 0 & else \end{cases} \tag{1}$$

where $p^d(x)$ and $p^d_{\Delta d}(x)$ are the current (i.e., price on day d) and future prices of stock mentioned in x (i.e., price on day $d + \Delta d$). On the other hand, supposing opinion x's viewpoint is that the price of stock s will drop in the near future, the label of opinion x is

$$y_{(x)} = \begin{cases} 1 & if \quad \dfrac{p^d_{\Delta d}(s^x) - p^d(s^x)}{p^d(s^x)} < 0 \\ 0 & else \end{cases} \tag{2}$$

Suppose we plan to invest in stocks on a trading day d_c. For historical opinions posted before $d_c - \Delta d$, we know their actual labels. However, for opinions posted on d_c, we do not know their actual labels. Our task is to train a model by using historical opinions with actual labels to predict labels of opinions posted on d_c. Then, we could know which stocks may go up after Δd days and make wise investment decisions.

3 Our Methodology

According to the task formulation described in Sect. 2. We need to train a model to estimate $y_{(o)}$. Recall that a typical investor opinion includes stock, author and text information, the prediction function should consider these three kinds of information simultaneously:

$$\hat{y}(x) = f(x_{stock}, x_{author}, x_{doc}), \tag{3}$$

where x_{author}, x_{stock} and x_{doc} are representations that indicate stock, author, and text information, respectively.

3.1 First-Order Model with Textual Embedding

A baseline method to predict the target variable by multiple factors is to treat the factors independently and use linear models to combine them:

$$\hat{y}(x) = \alpha + \beta_S \cdot x_{stock} + \beta_A \cdot x_{author} + \beta_D \cdot x_{doc} + \epsilon \tag{4}$$

Considering that author and stock variables are categorical, x_{stock}, x_{author} can be represented by one-hot encoding techniques. Thus, we have $\beta_S \in R^S, \beta_A \in R^A$. However, x_{doc} represents textual information in opinions and is needed to be encoded by text-encoding methodologies.

3.2 Second-Order Model with Factorization Mechanism

Obviously, the first-order model introduced above ignores the interaction among author, stock, and textual information. In this part, we will introduce how we improve it into a second-order model inspired by the Factorization machines(FM) model [12,17].

The factorization mechanism(FM) is a popular model to carry out all interactions between each pair of features. The principle is:

$$\hat{y}_{FM} = \alpha_0 + \underbrace{\sum_{i=1}^{n} \alpha_i x_i}_{\text{first-order information}} + \underbrace{\sum_{i=0}^{n} \sum_{j=i+1}^{n} \hat{\alpha}_{ij} x_i x_j}_{\text{second-order information}} \tag{5}$$

where, the α_0 is the global bias, the α_i represents the weighted for each input feature x_i, and the $\hat{\alpha}_{i,j}$ represent the weighted interactions information between each pair of features x_i, x_j. Beside, $\hat{\alpha}_{i,j} = v_i^T v_j$, the $v_i \in R^l$ is the embedding vector for each feature, and l is the embedding length. In this paper, the $i \in \{author, stock, document\}$, and the $x_i \in R^{n_i}$, then the input length is $n = n_{author} + n_{stock} + n_{document}$. For example, the $x_{stock,i}$ is the element which value is 1 in stock one-hot encoding, $x_{author,j}$ is the element which value is 1 in author one-hot encoding, and the interaction operation of $x_i x_j$, if the opinion refers to the $x_{stock,i}$ and $x_{author,j}$ at the same time, then the interaction information $\hat{\alpha}_{i,j}$ would be obtained, otherwise, the interaction is invalid information.

3.3 Deep Learning Framework to Detect Useful Investor Opinions (DLUIO)

In this part, we introduce our methodology named *DLUIO* to model the first-order and second-order information of authors, stocks, and textual data through a novel neural network. As shown in Fig. 1, *DLUIO* uses embedding layers in neural networks to learn vectors v_{author}, v_{stock}. The embedding layers take inputs with the category indices x_{author}, x_{stock} and convert them into dense vectors v_{author}, v_{stock}. Besides v_{author}, v_{stock}, we also need v_{doc} to represent textual information. In *DLUIO*, v_{doc} comes from the Word2Vec method which is a communal

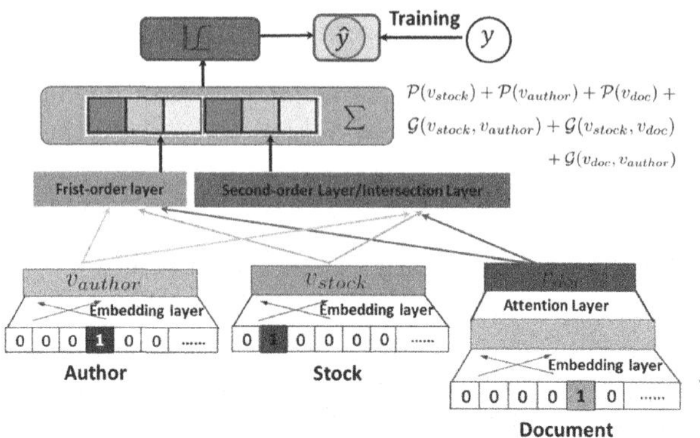

Fig. 1. The network structure of *DLUIO*.

method to model words as a dense and low-dimensional vector to capture the semantics. Then, the representation of a sentence can be regarded as an aggregation of many word vectors. Moreover, for obtaining v_{doc}, the attention mechanism is also used to aggregate the sentence embedding. Specifically, we first encode the words into a vector, a document can describe as a sequence of words, and the textual can represent by $w_{1:n} = [w_1, w_2, \ldots w_n] \in R^{d \times n}$, where the $w_k \in R^n$ is the embedding vector of k-th word. According to the attention mechanism, the different words are given different weights u_w, and the different weights integrate the words. Since it is not all elements of the sentence vector are useful for the sentence representation, therefore, we trying to use an attention mechanism to aggregate the sentence vector for each textual. The textual embedding $\beta_D * v_{doc}$ at Eq. (4) can gain as follow functions:

$$\alpha_{it} = \frac{\exp\left(w_{it}^{\top} u_w\right)}{\sum_t \exp\left(w_{it}^{\top} u_w\right)}; \quad d_i = \sum_t \alpha_{it} w_{it}; \quad v_{doc_i} = relu(d_i) \tag{6}$$

where, the $u_w \in R^n$ is the weight of each word, w_{it} denote the t-th element for the i-th word embedding, $relu(\cdot)$ is a non-linear activation function, then the $v_{doc} \in R^{\|D\|}$ is obtained by the attention mechanism.

After *DLUIO* learns vectors v_{author}, v_{stock} and v_{doc}, it will begin to learn first-order information $\mathcal{P}(v_{stock}), \mathcal{P}(v_{author})$ and $\mathcal{P}(v_{doc})$. Specifically, *DLUIO* converts v_{author}, v_{stock} and v_{doc} into $\mathcal{P}(v_{stock}), \mathcal{P}(v_{author})$ and $\mathcal{P}(v_{doc})$ by fully connected (FC) layers with activation function $relu(\cdot)$:

$$\mathcal{P}(x) = w^{\top} relu(x) \tag{7}$$

As discussed in Sect. 3.2, both first-order and second-order information should be considered. Thus, the decision function should be

$$f(x) = \alpha + \underbrace{\mathcal{P}(v_{stock}) + \mathcal{P}(v_{author}) + \mathcal{P}(v_{doc})}_{\text{first-order information}} + \underbrace{f(s, a, d)}_{\text{second-order information}} + \epsilon \tag{8}$$

where, the $f(s,a,d)$ is the second-order information that will be built by the interaction layer in our neural network. Specifically, the interaction layer will model three kinds of interaction information: $(stock, author)$ interaction, $(stock, doc)$ interaction, and $(doc, author)$ interaction information. We use $\mathcal{G}(\cdot)$ to denote the function to learn second-order information and it is also corresponding to fully connected (FC) layers with activation function $relu(\cdot)$:

$$\mathcal{G}(x,y) = w^{\top} relu(\tanh(x) \odot \tanh(y)) \tag{9}$$

Here activation functions $tanh(\cdot)$ is used by avoiding the optimization problem caused by extreme value and retaining useful information at the element dot operation. Then, we have

$$\begin{aligned} &f(s,a,d) = \\ &\mathcal{G}(v_{stock}, v_{author}) + \mathcal{G}(v_{stock}, v_{doc}) + \mathcal{G}(v_{doc}, v_{author}) \end{aligned} \tag{10}$$

Considering that the target variable y is binary, we need to use activation function $sigmoid(\cdot)$ to obtain the final prediction:

$$\hat{y}(x) = sigmoid(f(x)) \tag{11}$$

4 Portfolio Generation by *DLUIO*

In this part, we discuss how to generate a portfolio to invest in each trading day by using our methodology *DLUIO*. Suppose we plan to invest in stocks on a trading day d. We train a *DLUIO* model with historical opinions posted before $d - \Delta d$. Then, for each opinion, x posted on d, the output $\hat{y}(x)$ represents the probability of the viewpoint ("Bullish" or "Bearish") in this opinion is correct. Now, we change $\hat{y}(x)$ to the stock score which can indicate how to invest the stock. First, we employ min-max scaling to normalize the values:

$$\hat{y}_{norm}(x) = \frac{\hat{y}(x) - \mathbf{min}(\hat{\mathbf{y}})}{\mathbf{max}(\hat{\mathbf{y}}) - \mathbf{min}(\hat{\mathbf{y}})} \tag{12}$$

where $\mathbf{max}(\hat{\mathbf{y}})$ and $\mathbf{min}(\hat{\mathbf{y}})$ denote the maximum and minimum values of $\hat{y}(\cdot)$ for all opinions posted on day d. Then, we calculate the score for the opinion x as:

$$\text{score}(x) = v_x \cdot (2\hat{y}_{norm}(x) - 1) \tag{13}$$

where

$$v_x = \begin{cases} 1 \quad if \quad \text{the viewpoint in } x \text{ is Bullish} \\ -1 \quad else \quad \text{the viewpoint in } x \text{ is Bearish} \end{cases} \tag{14}$$

Based on the above transformation, each opinion scores score(x) should be in $[-1, 1]$. The large absolute value of the score encourages us to trust the viewpoint in the opinion. The sign of the score indicates that the viewpoint is Bullish or Bearish.

Then, for each stock that is tradable on the day d, we add up scores assigned by all opinions related to the stock. Specifically, denoting opinions posted on day d and related to stock s as $\mathrm{X_s}$. The stock score for s is:

$$\mathrm{score}(s) = \sum_{x \in \mathrm{X_s}} \mathrm{score}(x) \tag{15}$$

The stock scores can help us to determine which stocks are worth investing. If $\mathrm{score}(s) > 0$ and its value is large, we should buy the stock the day d and sell it after Δd days. On the other side, If $\mathrm{score}(s) < 0$ and its value is small, we should short stocks (i.e., we "borrow" stocks to "sell" them on the day d and then "buy back" the borrowed stocks on the day $d + \Delta d$. In sum, the whole procedure of making a trading decision on each trading day is summarized by Procedure 1.

Algorithm 1. Portfolio generation (on day d).

Require:
$\mathrm{X}_{\mathrm{tr}}^{d}$ = Training opinions (posted before day $d - \Delta d$)
$\mathrm{X}_{\mathrm{te}}^{d}$ = Test opinions (posted on day d)
$\mathcal{S}_d$ = stocks tradable at time t on day d
N_l = how many stocks we plan to long
N_s = how many stocks we plan to short
Ensure:
$\mathcal{S}_d^l$ = N_l stocks we will long (on day d)
$\mathcal{S}_d^s$ = N_s stocks we will short (on day d)
Learn *DLUIO* model M with $(\mathbf{x}_{\mathrm{tr}}, y_{\mathrm{tr}}) \in \mathrm{X}_{\mathrm{tr}}^{d}$;
for all $s \in \mathcal{S}_d$ **do**
  Extract $\mathrm{X_s}$ (i.e., opinions related to s);
  for all $x \in \mathrm{X_s}$ **do**
    Using M to test x and get $\hat{y}(x)$;
  end for
  calculate $\mathrm{score}(s)$ by equations 12-15;
end for
Rank stocks in $\mathcal{S}_d$ according to $\mathrm{score}(s)$ and select top N_l stocks as $\mathcal{S}_d^l$;
Rank stocks in $\mathcal{S}_d$ according to $-\mathrm{score}(s)$ and select top N_s stocks as $\mathcal{S}_d^s$.

5 Experiments

5.1 Data Collection and Preparation

To evaluate our method and verify that it has practical application value, we collect investment opinions from Stocktwits [1] mentioned in Sect. 2. By obtaining permission from StockTwits, we collected 13,771,091 messages that have one hashtag and explicit sentiment label. The opinions were posted by 175, 841 users in 2018 or 2019 and related to 6,930 stocks traded on the New York Stock Exchange (NYSE), National Association of Securities Dealers Automated Quotations (NASDAQ) or American Stock Exchange (AMEX). Moreover, we collected market data from the Wharton Research Data Services (WRDS)[1].

5.2 Experimental Setup

In our experiments, we simulate trades at the time near the closing time of stock markets. Thus we use closing prices to calculate $\mathcal{R}(o)$. We performed continuous trading from Jan 2019 to Dec 2019 (opinions posted in 2018 are applied for training). We skip the first two weeks in January and the last two weeks in December to reduce the influence of the New Year and Christmas holidays. During the trading procedure, we continuously update the set of training data. Considering that opinions posted long ago may not reflect the latest expertise of users, we only employ opinions of investor u in a recent year as the "historical sentiments" to calculate $\hat{\mathcal{E}}(u)$. We do not ignore transaction fees in our simulation. We assume the rate of transaction fees is 0.25%, which is commonly used in other work [8,14].

5.3 Evaluation Metrics

To evaluate the performance of the methods in recommending stocks, we regard the recommended stocks as equally-weighted portfolios and analyze the performances of the portfolios by the following evaluation metrics.

- **Cumulative Return** Cumulative return is an important and commonly employed evaluation metric in investment evaluation. We trade stocks in the recommended portfolios and perform continuous trading from the beginning of 2019 to the end of 2019. Specifically, on a trading day d, each method generates $\mathcal{S}^r$ and $\mathcal{A}^r$. After the holding period Δd, the investment return from $\mathcal{S}^r$ and $\mathcal{A}^r$ is denoted as $\mathrm{r}(\mathcal{S}^r, \mathcal{A}^r)$ and it equals to:

$$\frac{1}{\mathcal{N}(\mathcal{S}^r)}\left(\sum_{s_i \in \mathcal{S}_l^r} \frac{p^d_{\Delta d}(s_i) - p^d(s_i)}{p^d(s_i)} + \sum_{s_j \in \mathcal{S}_s^r} \frac{p^d(s_j) - p^d_{\Delta d}(s_j)}{p^d(s_j)}\right). \tag{16}$$

  where $\mathcal{S}_l^r$ and $\mathcal{S}_s^r$ are recommended stocks that correspond to *Long* actions and *Short* actions, respectively. The next iteration of trading begins. After all trading sessions, the cumulative return is used to evaluate the recommendation methods. If holding periods are not short, the times of the portfolio reallocation might be very small. Thus, we start continuous trading on each tradable day from 2019-01-02 to 2019-01-02+Δd. For example, if we plan to perform monthly trading (i.e., Δd = 1 month, we set it to 20 trading days in our experiments), we can start continuous trading on the first tradable

[1] https://wrds-www.wharton.upenn.edu/.

day of 2019-01-02 and then portfolio reallocation occurs a month later. Thus, only 11 points of cumulative returns exist. For a more precise evaluation, we start continuous trading on the tradable days 2019-01-02, 2019-01-03, $\cdots$, and 2019-01-30, respectively. We obtain 20 sequences of cumulative returns. For each portfolio reallocation, we apply the average value of the corresponding cumulative returns in all sequences as the result.

- **Maximum Drawdown** Maximum drawdown (MMD) is the maximum loss from a peak to a following bottom and measures how sustained a loss can be. MMD is a key indicator for assessing the risk of a given stock screening strategy. The specific formula for MMD is

$$\begin{aligned} \text{MMD} &= \max \frac{(\text{Peak Value} - \text{Trough Value})}{\text{Peak Value}} \\ &= \max \frac{(P_x - V_x)}{P_x} \end{aligned} \tag{17}$$

  where P_x indicates the maximum net value of the portfolio before timestamp x and V_x is the net value of the portfolio at timestamp x.
- **Daily Return** We also show the average performance of the portfolios recommended on each test day. Specifically, for testing $\mathcal{S}^r$ and $\mathcal{A}^r$ generated on day d, we divide the return $\mathrm{r}(\mathcal{S}^r, \mathcal{A}^r)$ by the length of the holding periods as the *investment return on a single day*:

$$\mathrm{r_d}(\mathcal{S}^r, \mathcal{A}^r) = \frac{\mathrm{r}(\mathcal{S}^r, \mathcal{A}^r)}{|\Delta d|}. \tag{18}$$

  where $|\Delta d|$ indicates the length (i.e., number of days) of the holding period Δd. The average value of the *daily investment return* on all test days is denoted as the **Daily Return**:

$$\textbf{Daily Return} = \frac{1}{\mathcal{N}^d} \sum_{d=1}^{\mathcal{N}^d} \mathrm{r_d}(\mathcal{S}^r, \mathcal{A}^r). \tag{19}$$

Baseline Methods. In our experiments, we compared the effectiveness of CBRDQ and other baseline approaches in aggregating investor sentiments and recommending stocks. The competitors include

- **Buy-and-hold SPY: Buy-and-hold SPY** applies a "**Buy-and-hold**"strategy on the "SPDR S&P 500 Trust ETF" (NYSE Arca: **SPY**). Since SPY is designed to track the S&P 500 stock market index, the comparison will indicate whether a competitive method outperforms the broader markets.
- **FollowExpert:** Bar-Haim et al. [4] uses statistical methods to design a method for identifying expert investors from stock microblogging messages. In the experiments, we use their method to calculate investor expertise and select stocks to invest.

- **TradML:** Tu et al. [15,16] propose a stock recommendation system by using traditional machine learning to predict the qualities of investor opinions. In their work, author, stock, and textual information are represented by human-designed features such as the number of high-quality opinions posted by the author before. However, *DLUIO* uses the technique of deep learning to learn representations of the author, stock, and textual information automatically. In our experiments, we denote Tu's work as "Traditional Machine Learning" (abbreviated to TradML)
- **DLUIO (our method):** In *DLUIO*, the dimension of embedding is 100, and the optimizer is Adam. The learning rate for the word embedding part is 0.0001, and the rest part of the model is 0.001, dropout is 0.3, the value of regularization parameter λ is 0.0001. Since the word embedding is obtained by the pre-training model, thus, the learning rate is smaller than the rest part of the model. Moreover, we use the dataset from 2018-01 to 2018-11 to pre-train the word embedding. Besides, we regularize the all parameters of the model except for the parameters in the embedding layer.

5.4 Experimental Results

In this part, we will evaluate *DLUIO* and baseline methods introduced in Sect. 5.3. Note that there are several human-defined parameters (i.e., N_l, N_s and Δd) in trading strategies. First, we fix $\Delta d = 1$ day and show results corresponding to different methods with varied sizes of portfolios. As Table 1 presents

Table 1. Performances for different portfolio sizes (when $\Delta d = 1$ day and TR = 0.25%).

Size of $\mathcal{S}_c^{\tau}$	Performance Metrics	Methods			
		Buy-and-hold SPY	FollowExpert	TradML	DLUIO (our method)
$N_l = N_s = 5$	Cumulative Return	0.23	0.36	0.36	1.48
	Maximum Drawdown	6.62	16.71	32.35	12.59
	Daily Return	0.09	0.40	0.41	0.67
$N_l = N_s = 6$	Cumulative Return	0.23	0.07	0.11	1.15
	Maximum Drawdown	6.62	21.58	33.23	15.13
	Daily Return	0.09	0.29	0.32	0.60
$N_l = N_s = 7$	Cumulative Return	0.23	0.04	0.26	1.11
	Maximum Drawdown	6.62	20.04	24.30	14.01
	Daily Return	0.09	0.28	0.37	0.59
$N_l = N_s = 8$	Cumulative Return	0.23	0.04	0.12	0.89
	Maximum Drawdown	6.62	18.74	25.36	13.57
	Daily Return	0.09	0.28	0.32	0.54
$N_l = N_s = 9$	Cumulative Return	0.23	−0.01	0.18	0.78
	Maximum Drawdown	6.62	15.14	22.18	11.24
	Daily Return	0.09	0.26	0.34	0.51
$N_l = N_s = 10$	Cumulative Return	0.23	−0.01	0.27	0.71
	Maximum Drawdown	6.62	11.97	22.33	11.29
	Daily Return	0.09	0.26	0.37	0.49

Table 2. Performances of *DLUIO* corresponding to different portfolio sizes and Δd.

Size of S_c^T	Performance Metrics	Δd		
		1 day	1 week	1 month
$N_l = N_s = 5$	Cumulative Return	1.48	0.86	−0.02
	Maximum Drawdown	12.59	16.40	9.07
	Daily Return	0.67	0.32	0.03
$N_l = N_s = 6$	Cumulative Return	1.15	0.65	−0.00
	Maximum Drawdown	15.13	14.89	8.99
	Daily Return	0.60	0.26	0.04
$N_l = N_s = 7$	Cumulative Return	1.11	0.65	−0.02
	Maximum Drawdown	14.01	12.96	8.94
	Daily Return	0.59	0.26	0.03
$N_l = N_s = 8$	Cumulative Return	0.89	0.67	−0.03
	Maximum Drawdown	13.57	10.65	9.13
	Daily Return	0.54	0.27	0.02
$N_l = N_s = 9$	Cumulative Return	0.78	0.64	−0.02
	Maximum Drawdown	11.24	10.30	9.11
	Daily Return	0.51	0.26	0.01
$N_l = N_s = 10$	Cumulative Return	0.71	0.61	−0.02
	Maximum Drawdown	11.29	9.49	9.09
	Daily Return	0.49	0.26	0.01

the performances of different methods when portfolio size is varied while Δd and TR are fixed. From the results in Table 1, we discover that:

- When the portfolio includes 10 stocks ($N_l = N_s = 5$), the cumulative return of FollowExpert, TradML and *DLUIO* outperform Buy-and-hold SPY, which encourages us to select stocks by algorithms.
- In most cases, *DLUIO* provides users with the largest investment return (measured by cumulative return and daily return) while the investment risk (measured by maximum drawdown) is not very high.
- The smaller is the value of N_l and N_s, the better are the performances of *DLUIO*, which implies that *DLUIO* can be used to sort stocks.

Then, for analyzing the influence of Δd. We let Δd = 1 day, 1 week or 1 month (corresponds to daily trading, weekly trading or monthly trading. From the results shown in Table 2, we can determine that

- *DLUIO* can be used for daily trading and weekly trading. For monthly trading, the performance is not good. The possible reason is that the viewpoints in investor opinions posted on Stocktwits are about the short-term performances of stocks.

6 Conclusion and Future Work

In this paper, we studied how to use deep learning to access the credibility of investor opinions and generate profitable portfolios. Compared to conventional approaches, our *DLUIO* learns representations and interaction information about authors, stocks, or microblog content in investor opinions. Comparative experiments based on the real-world dataset demonstrate the effectiveness of our model. In the future, we plan to study the use of other classical neural networks structures such as convolutional neural networks and graph neural networks to improve *DLUIO*.

References

1. Stocktwits (2008). http://www.stocktwits.com
2. Antweiler, W., Frank, M.Z.: Is all that talk just noise? The information content of internet stock message boards. J. Financ. **59**(3), 1259–1294 (2004)
3. Araci, D.: FinBERT: financial sentiment analysis with pre-trained language models. arXiv preprint arXiv:1908.10063 (2019)
4. Bar-Haim, R., Dinur, E., Feldman, R., Fresko, M., Goldstein, G.: Identifying and following expert investors in stock microblogs. In: Proceedings of the 2011 Conference on Empirical Methods in Natural Language Processing, pp. 1310–1319 (2011)
5. Bollen, J., Mao, H., Zeng, X.: Twitter mood predicts the stock market. J. Comput. Sci. **2**(1), 1–8 (2011)
6. Bordino, I., Battiston, S., Caldarelli, G., Cristelli, M., Ukkonen, A., Weber, I.: Web search queries can predict stock market volumes. PLoS ONE **7**(7), e40014 (2012)
7. Chang, J., Tu, W.: A stock-movement aware approach for discovering investors' personalized preferences in stock markets. In: 2018 IEEE 30th International Conference on Tools with Artificial Intelligence (ICTAI), pp. 275–280. IEEE (2018)
8. Das, P., Johnson, N., Banerjee, A.: Online lazy updates for portfolio selection with transaction costs. In: Twenty-Seventh AAAI Conference on Artificial Intelligence (2013)
9. Devlin, J., Chang, M.W., Lee, K., Toutanova, K.: BERT: pre-training of deep bidirectional transformers for language understanding. arXiv preprint arXiv:1810.04805 (2018)
10. Gottschlich, J., Hinz, O.: A decision support system for stock investment recommendations using collective wisdom. Decis. Support Syst. **59**, 52–62 (2014)
11. Nguyen, T.H., Shirai, K., Velcin, J.: Sentiment analysis on social media for stock movement prediction. Expert Syst. Appl. **42**(24), 9603–9611 (2015)
12. Rendle, S.: Factorization machines. In: 2010 IEEE International conference on data mining, pp. 995–1000. IEEE (2010)
13. Rousidis, D., Koukaras, P., Tjortjis, C.: Social media prediction: a literature review. Multimed. Tools Appl. **79**(9), 6279–6311 (2020)
14. Ruf, J., Xie, K.: The impact of proportional transaction costs on systematically generated portfolios. SIAM J. Financ. Math. **11**(3), 881–896 (2020)
15. Tu, W., Cheung, D.W., Mamoulis, N., Yang, M., Lu, Z.: Investment recommendation using investor opinions in social media. In: Proceedings of the 39th International ACM SIGIR Conference on Research and Development in Information Retrieval, pp. 881–884 (2016)

16. Tu, W., Yang, M., Cheung, D.W., Mamoulis, N.: Investment recommendation by discovering high-quality opinions in investor based social networks. Inf. Syst. **78**, 189–198 (2018)
17. Xiao, J., Ye, H., He, X., Zhang, H., Wu, F., Chua, T.S.: Attentional factorization machines: learning the weight of feature interactions via attention networks. arXiv preprint arXiv:1708.04617 (2017)
18. Xu, Y., Keselj, V.: Stock prediction using deep learning and sentiment analysis. In: 2019 IEEE International Conference on Big Data (Big Data), pp. 5573–5580. IEEE (2019)
19. Zhang, X., Fuehres, H., Gloor, P.A.: Predicting stock market indicators through twitter "i hope it is not as bad as i fear". Procedia-Soc. Behav. Sci. **26**, 55–62 (2011)
20. Zhou, Z., Zhao, J., Xu, K.: Can online emotions predict the stock market in China? In: Cellary, W., Mokbel, M.F., Wang, J., Wang, H., Zhou, R., Zhang, Y. (eds.) WISE 2016. LNCS, vol. 10041, pp. 328–342. Springer, Cham (2016). https://doi.org/10.1007/978-3-319-48740-3_24

Dynamic Obstacle Avoidance for Unmanned Aerial Vehicle Using Dynamic Vision Sensor

Xiangyu Zhang[1], Junbo Tie[2], Jianfeng Li[2], Yu Hu[2], Shifeng Liu[3], Xinpeng Li[2], Ziteng Li[2], Xintong Yu[2], Jingyue Zhao[1], Zhong Wan[1,2], Guangda Zhang[1], and Lei Wang[1(✉)]

[1] Defense Innovation Institute, Academy of Military Science, Beijing, China
leiwang@nudt.edu.cn
[2] The College of Computer Science and Technology, National University of Defense Technology, Changsha, China
[3] Phytium Technology Co., Ltd., Nanjing, China

Abstract. Obstacle avoidance in dynamic environments is a critical issue in unmanned aerial vehicle (UAV) applications. Current solutions rely on deep reinforcement learning (DRL), which requires significant computing power and energy and limits UAVs with limited onboard computing resources. A combination of dynamic vision sensor (DVS) and spiking neural network (SNN) can be used for fast perception and low energy consumption. This work proposes an obstacle avoidance framework that uses DVS and SNN-based object detection algorithms to identify obstacles and a lightweight action decision algorithm to generate action commands. Simulation experiments show that the UAV can avoid 70% of dynamic obstacles, with an estimated power consumption of 1.5 to 13.5 milliwatts, and an overall delay up to 7% lower than that of reinforcement learning methods.

Keywords: Unmanned aerial vehicles · Dynamic vision sensor · Spiking neural network · Object detection · Dynamic obstacle avoidance

1 Introduction

UAVs can complete flight missions via prepared programs, remote control equipment, or autonomous navigation systems. UAVs are usually equipped with sensors, cameras, and other equipment, allowing them to perform various tasks. Obstacle avoidance is one of the key tasks of UAV motion planning. The unknown, open, and highly dynamic nature of environments increases the complexity of UAV obstacle avoidance navigation. In UAV obstacle avoidance research, compared to the use of high-precision sensors like LiDAR, UAVs that use traditional vision sensors have lower cost, smaller volume, lighter weight, and more complex obstacle avoidance methods. Recent research on visual obstacle

L. Iliadis et al. (Eds.): ICANN 2023, LNCS 14263, pp. 161–173, 2023.
https://doi.org/10.1007/978-3-031-44204-9_14

avoidance proposes to use DRL to guide UAV to avoid obstacles [8]. However, the high energy consumption of the algorithm limits the continuous obstacle avoidance endurance of the UAVs with limited computing resources.

DVS [5] is a novel type of vision sensor that boasts a high frame rate, low latency, low power consumption, and high dynamic range. The pixels on the DVS are highly sensitive to changes in light intensity, which allows them to asynchronously output events when the light intensity changes exceed a threshold. This characteristic makes DVS ideal for sensing dynamic objects, presenting a new sensor option for dynamic obstacle avoidance of UAVs. On the other hand, SNNs [7] have a similar working mechanism that can effectively process the asynchronous sparse event flow generated by DVS. SNNs can leverage the low power consumption and strong adaptability of neuromorphic computing. Therefore, combining DVS and SNN is a compelling choice for UAV obstacle avoidance.

Previous studies [11,12,15] have used a combination of DVS and SNNs for UAV dynamic obstacle avoidance, with different approaches such as a unique bionic model [11] and SNN-based DRL techniques [12,15]. These methods have shown great potential of combining DVS and SNNs for UAV dynamic obstacle avoidance, but there are few attempts at this combination in existing work, and some methods have inherent disadvantages such as requiring repetitive training and generating rough trajectories. This work aims to explore various obstacle avoidance schemes using this combination.

This work builds upon a previous static obstacle avoidance framework [13], adapting it to include DVS and SNN algorithms respectively for dynamic obstacle perception and detection. By leveraging the DVS's capability for dynamic object perception and the energy-efficient properties of the SNN algorithm, this work proposes an SNN-based object detection algorithm to process the DVS event frames. The action decision algorithm quickly generates action commands to the flight control system using predefined rules based on depth information and object detection results. The main focus of this work is to explore the joint application of DVS and SNN object detection, provide a new solution for neuromorphic computing applied to UAV obstacle avoidance tasks, and use prior knowledge to detect dynamic obstacles and generating smoother trajectories using customized obstacle avoidance decisions. Our contributions are summarized as follows:

- This paper presents a UAV dynamic obstacle avoidance framework that uses DVS for obstacle perception and neuromorphic computing for obstacle detection, which can successfully avoid most of the dynamic obstacles and achieves a delay slightly lower than that of the reinforcement learning-based obstacle avoidance scheme.
- This paper uses the conversion method to obtain the SNN-based object detection algorithm and optimizes its parameters by evaluating its performance. The optimized algorithm can reduce energy consumption by up to three to four orders of magnitude compared to the baseline method before conversion, according to the energy consumption estimation method.

– This paper proposes an obstacle avoidance action decision algorithm based on the depth information of static obstacles and the position information of dynamic obstacles, which generates flexible speed commands for the obstacle avoidance of static and dynamic obstacles.

2 Background and Related Works

2.1 Object Detection Applications Using SNN

Compared to artificial neural networks (ANNs), SNN-based algorithms are more energy-efficient due to their event-driven nature, but present challenges in training. Due to the difficulty of calculating the gradient of spiking signals, some works use conversion methods to convert trained ANNs to SNNs [10]. Seijoon Kim et al. [4] presented the first work on converting an ANN object detection algorithm to an SNN, named Spiking-YOLO, and demonstrated its energy efficiency advantage and comparable accuracy. This work uses an open-source implementation of Spiking-YOLO [2] as a basis for object detection in obstacle avoidance framework and makes corresponding optimization and comparison.

2.2 UAV Obstacle Avoidance Schemes Using DVS and SNN

UAV obstacle avoidance methods using DVS and SNN utilize DVS's sensitivity to dynamic objects and SNN's high energy efficiency. LGMD-based SNN [1] has been used to detect objects sensed by DVS and output speed commands [11]. SNN-based DRL obtained from the conversion method [12] and the direct training SNN method [15] with DVS perception have also been attempted in UAVs obstacle avoidance. However, research on the combination of DVS and SNN for UAV obstacle avoidance is still preliminary, and more exploration is needed to investigate different energy-efficient obstacle avoidance frameworks using various SNN algorithms to process DVS event streams.

3 Proposed Methods

3.1 Framework for Obstacle Avoidance

This work refers to the static obstacle avoidance framework composed of object detection and obstacle avoidance planning proposed by the work [13] and modifies the framework to reduce power consumption and provide a new ability to avoid dynamic obstacles.

Specifically, this work proposes a UAV obstacle avoidance framework that supports both static and dynamic obstacle avoidance, as shown in Fig. 1. The framework mainly consists of three parts: environment perception, SNN-based object detection algorithms that detect dynamic obstacles, and action decision algorithms that generate action commands, where the algorithms are implemented as nodes based on ROS.

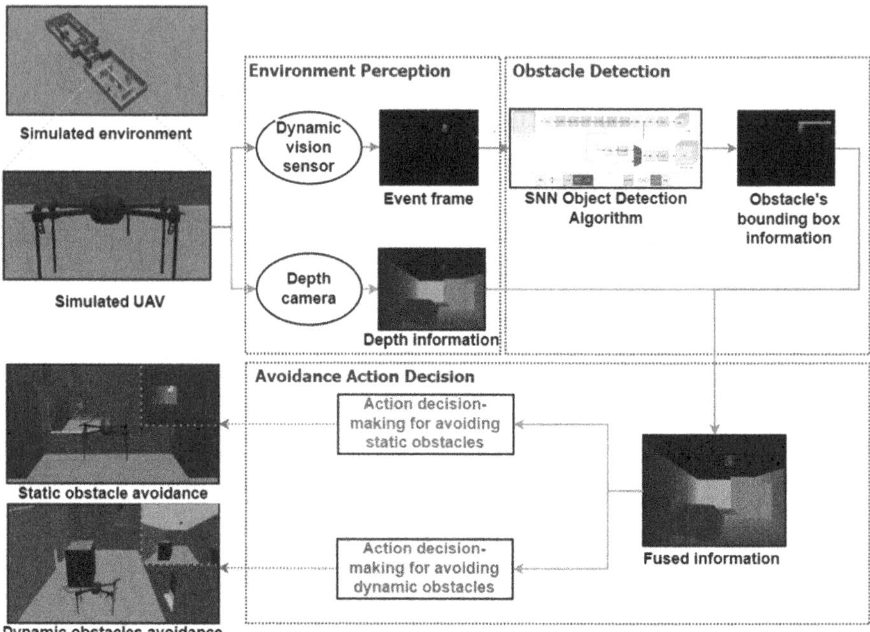

Fig. 1. The obstacle avoidance scheme's architecture and workflow. The obstacle avoidance scheme works as follows: The UAV senses the environment using DVS and depth cameras. The SNN object detection algorithm detects any dynamic obstacles in the DVS event frame. The action decision algorithm processes the fusion information of the detection results and depth information, determines the object types of the obstacles, and generates different action commands for the UAV's flight controller.

Initially, UAV perceives the environment and obtains information by using DVS and depth camera. In the obstacle detection stage, the SNN object detection algorithm processes the event frame and detects dynamic obstacles. After fusing the dynamic obstacle's bounding box information and depth information, the action decision-making algorithm implements different obstacle avoidance strategies according to the obstacle type and produces different actions to avoid these obstacles.

3.2 SNN-Based Object Detection Algorithm

The SNN-based object detection algorithm utilizes neuromorphic computing to process the event frame stream obtained by DVS and detects dynamic objects with polarity in the image. This work trains YOLOv3-tiny with our designed dynamic obstacle dataset and converts it to SNN-YOLOv3-tiny. Specifically, this work uses the method proposed in [2] to replace the non-convolution operations in the model with convolution operations, and then use spiking neurons to perform convolution operation and ultimately obtain the SNN object detection model.

It is important to note that the dynamic obstacle avoidance task requires the UAV to avoid obstacles with faster relative speed than static obstacle avoidance tasks. Therefore, it requires lower obstacle avoidance delay for better performance. In the obstacle avoidance framework of this work, the SNN object detection algorithm has the longest processing time. To meet the requirements of UAV dynamic obstacle avoidance tasks, it is necessary to reduce the delay of the object detection part to maximize the detection speed of the obstacle avoidance framework.

This work improves the detection speed of the algorithm by optimizing the model parameters. After analysis, the detection speed is most affected by the parameters of time step and image size, where the time step refers to the discrete-time unit used to simulate network behavior. Furthermore, these two parameters affect both detection accuracy and other properties such as precision and recall. Therefore, this study needs to balance the detection speed and performance according to the weights in the obstacle avoidance task. This work proposes a scoring formula (1) to compare different parameter combinations and select the most suitable parameter combination for UAV obstacle detection.

$$Score = Detect\_FPS/30 * (F1\_score * 50\% + mAP50 * 50\%) \tag{1}$$

where Detect_FPS represents the rate of the SNN-based object detection algorithm. When detecting obstacles, the detection ratio directly affects the proportion of image processing, so the detection ratio has the highest weight. Secondly, both correct prediction rate and accuracy of obstacle position are equally important, so this work assigns 50% weight to both F1-score and mAP-50 metrics.

3.3 Action Decision-Making Algorithm

The obstacle avoidance action decision-making algorithm utilizes information such as the current attitude of the UAV, destination coordinates, and distance to detect obstacles to send actions to the flight controller based on pre-defined rules. This work considers two scenarios for avoiding obstacles: static and dynamic. Different action decision rules are designed for each scenario.

In static obstacle avoidance, the depth camera provides continuous depth information, and the algorithm calculates a danger index by counting the number of pixels whose depth is less than the customized threshold. The action decision algorithm adjusts the UAV's attitude, destination coordinates, and yaw angle to retreat or steer, depending on the danger index and distance ahead. Once the distance is sufficient and the danger index drops below the threshold, the algorithm directs the UAV forward.

In the dynamic obstacle avoidance task, the action decision-making algorithm receives real-time object detection results and depth information and then adopts a pre-defined optimal obstacle avoidance strategy based on the object detection results. This study defines the warning area in the drone's field of view, and

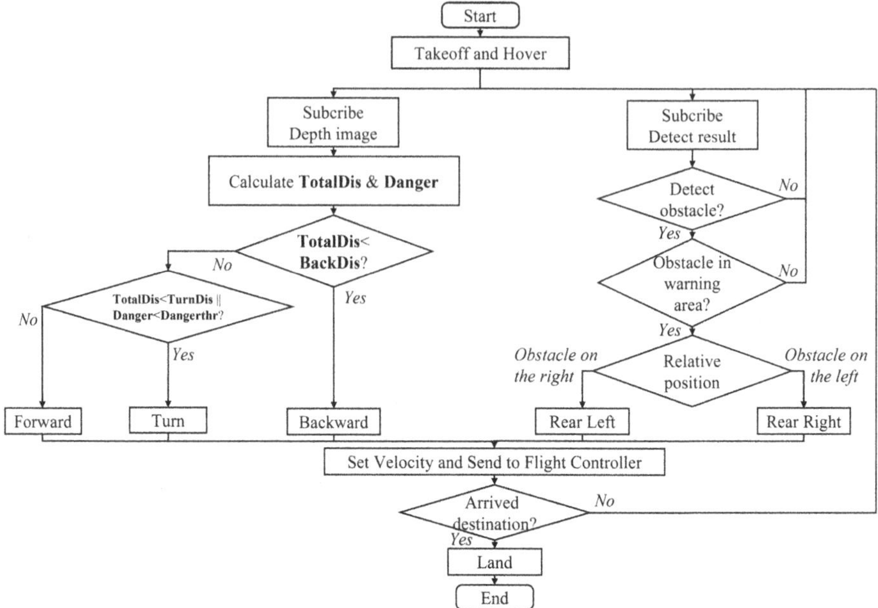

Fig. 2. The flowchart of the obstacle avoidance action decision-making algorithm. Action decision-making calculates depth information to generate different actions at different distances at low flight speed to avoid static obstacles and generates avoidance actions at high flight speed based on the position of dynamic obstacles. TotalDis is the overall distance to the obstacle ahead, Danger is the number of pixels on the sensor when the distance is too close. BackDis, TurnDis, and Dangerthr are custom thresholds.

when the bounding box of the obstacle intersects with the warning area, the drone will take evasive action in the opposite direction to the obstacle.

Figure 2 shows the flowchart of the obstacle avoidance action decision-making process. The decision-making process analyzes depth information and bounding box information and executes different avoidance strategies. The decision-making process generates different speed commands through the flowchart at a fixed rate depending on the selected strategy. These speed commands are used to jointly control the flight of the UAV and avoid different obstacles.

4 Experiments and Results

This section includes two major experiments of UAV obstacle avoidance and SNN-based object detection. The UAV obstacle avoidance experiment explores the performance of the overall obstacle avoidance framework in both static and dynamic scenes. The SNN object detection algorithm experiment involves optimizing model parameters and comparing their performance with the baseline algorithm. Table 1 shows the deployment environment for the two experiments.

Table 1. Experiments environment.

Experiment	OS	DL library	CPU	GPU	Memory capacity
Drone obstacle avoidance	Ubuntu 18.04	PyTorch 1.11.0	Intel Core i7-12700KF	Nvidia RTX 3070Ti 8 GB	16 GB
SNN object detection	CentOS 7.5	PyTorch 1.3.0	Intel Xeon E5-2630 v4	Nvidia Tesla V100 32 GB	64 GB

When optimizing the parameters of the object detection model, testing a variety of parameter combinations requires high GPU memory, so it is divided into two environments.

4.1 Implementation and Experiment Setup

To evaluate the performance of UAV obstacle avoidance against static and dynamic obstacles, this work establishes an experiment environment of obstacle avoidance based on the XTDrone simulation platform [14]. XTDrone is a versatile simulation platform for UAVs that is based on PX4, ROS, and Gazebo. Algorithms deployed on drones are packaged as ROS nodes, and messages are transmitted between nodes in the form of topics.

A more complex obstacle avoidance scene was created by adding richer environmental elements. The indoor static scene covers an area of approximately 220 square meters and includes multiple walls with windows that divide the space. For dynamic obstacles, this work followed the approach of using thrown basketballs as dynamic obstacles in the work [6] based on XTDrone.

To meet the requirements of the obstacle avoidance framework, this work configured the UAV simulation model accordingly. This work chose the iris quadrotor UAV simulation model from the PX4 model library with a depth camera plugin. The depth camera plugin produces RGB and depth images at a rate of 30 FPS, with an image size of $640 * 480$. For the simulated implementation of DVS, this work utilized the ESIM simulator [9] to process the RGB video stream acquired by the depth camera, which results in a DVS event frame stream where positive polarity pixels are red, negative polarity pixels are blue, and non-polarity pixels are black. This study also used the ESIM simulator to convert the image stream recorded by an ordinary camera during the obstacle avoidance process.

To detect dynamic obstacles, this work created a basketball dataset for training and evaluating the object detection algorithm. The basketballs were labeled, resulting in a dataset of 2314 images. The dataset includes images captured by common cameras and images processed as event frames, with each constituting 50% of the dataset and labeled as CAM and DVS classes, respectively.

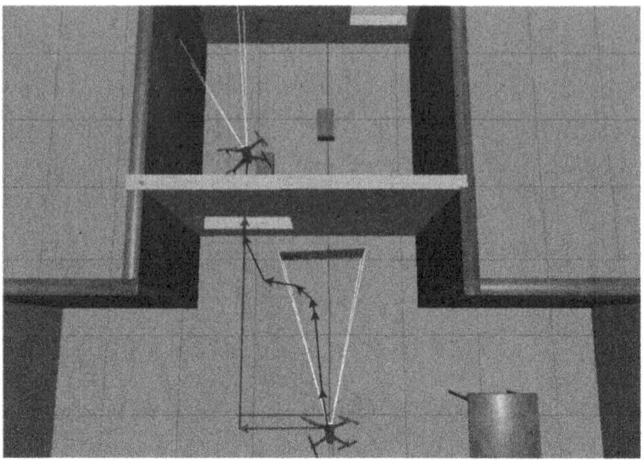

Fig. 3. Trajectory map of the UAV passing through the window, where the green line is the trajectory of the UAV when it passes through the window in the work [6], and the red line is the trajectory of this work. (Color figure online)

4.2 Obstacle Avoidance Experiments in Simulated Environment

This work evaluated the obstacle avoidance framework's performance using the software simulation platform XTDrone. Two separate experiments were conducted to test its effectiveness in avoiding static and dynamic obstacles. A video demo of the experiment is available at https://youtu.be/0xgSFU7AdiM.

Static Obstacles Avoidance. The experiment was designed to test the UAV's ability to pass through the window, a more challenging task than avoiding isolated static obstacles. UAV was placed on the ground 3 m away from the wall, and its take-off position was randomly set within 3 m in the experiment. This work ran 10 experiments, and the drone successfully passed through the window in all attempts. As shown in Fig. 3, the red trajectory of the UAV using the obstacle avoidance method in this work is smoother and is more achievable to the flight controller than the green trajectory of the method in work [6].

Dynamic Obstacles Avoidance. This experiment focused on testing the obstacle avoidance framework's ability to avoid a basketball thrown at a medium distance. The basketball is thrown at a height of 2 m, with a throwing angle of 50° from the ground, and a speed of 7.2 m/s. This work conducted two types of experiments, hovering obstacle avoidance and motion obstacle avoidance.

The hovering obstacle avoidance experiment evaluated the proposed obstacle avoidance framework's delay and avoidance capability. The UAV took off vertically and hovered 5.5 m away from the flight path of a basketball. The basketball was visible to the drone for 0.4 s, and collision with the basketball would occur 1.2 s after it was thrown. In 10 experiments, the drone successfully avoided the basketball 7 times.

Table 2. Decision delay of obstacle avoidance algorithms.

Obstacle Avoidance Decision Algorithm	Object detection delay(ms)	Action decision delay (ms)	Total delay (ms)
Actor-Critic Algorithm	-	-	55–65
Proposed method	54–57	2–3	**56–60**

In obstacle avoidance experiments with failed attempts, it was observed that starting from a position too close to the wall resulted in collisions during obstacle avoidance. It should be noted that when the UAV is limited by its viewing angle, it may not receive sufficient distance information, posing a potential collision risk during emergency obstacle avoidance. This is a common challenge for most fixed-angle visual obstacle avoidance methods, including the method proposed in this study.

In this experiment, we measured the delay of the obstacle avoidance action decision and compared it with the Actor-Critic reinforcement learning algorithm [6]. The proposed algorithm exhibited a slightly lower delay compared to reinforcement learning algorithms, with a reduction of up to 7% (Table 2).

The motion obstacle avoidance experiment aims to test the versatility of the obstacle avoidance framework in handling various obstacle avoidance tasks. This work set the coordinates behind the throwing point of the basketball as the destination for the drone, which flies to the destination while avoiding a suddenly thrown basketball. The event frame stream is fed into the obstacle avoidance framework, and the drone's flight in the absence of the basketball is also verified.

The experimental result in the video demo shows that the UAV with this obstacle avoidance framework can avoid the thrown basketball in time, while still flying towards the destination after avoiding it. This proves that the proposed obstacle avoidance framework can flexibly generate action commands for various tasks and endow the drone with obstacle avoidance capabilities.

4.3 Performance of SNN-Based Object Detection Algorithm

Parameter Selection in Object Detection Based on SNN. In Sect. 3.2, this paper proposed and utilized a scoring formula (1) to comprehensively evaluate the performance of the SNN-YOLOv3-tiny model under different parameter combinations, to select the optimal parameters for UAV dynamic obstacle avoidance tasks. Table 3 presents the detection performance and scores of the SNN-YOLOv3-tiny model under 12 parameter combinations, with the highest scoring combinations highlighted in bold for different classes in the dataset.

Table 3. Performance and scores of SNN-YOLOv3-tiny under different parameter combinations and sensor perception methods. The best combination of parameters in each sensor perception method is bolded.

	timestep	16		32		64		128	
imgsz	Class	CAM	DVS	CAM	DVS	CAM	DVS	CAM	DVS
320	P	0%	100%	0%	100%	100%	99.3%	**100%**	98.5%
	R	0%	0.319%	0%	26.5%	1.07%	88.6%	**78.8%**	98.1%
	mAP-50	0%	39.8%	0%	88%	87.1%	98.3%	**99.3%**	99.4%
	delay(ms)	28.6		46.6		78		**142.6**	
	score	0%	23.56%	0%	46.46%	19.06%	41.01%	**21.91%**	23.11%
416	P	0%	100%	0%	**100%**	100%	98.4%	100%	92.9%
	R	0%	0.319%	0%	**54.3%**	11.3%	96.9%	90.3%	99.9%
	mAP-50	0%	60.7%	0.9%	**99.1%**	95.0%	99.3%	99.5%	99.3%
	delay(ms)	35.6		**57.8**		103.6		182.8	
	score	0%	28.72%	0.26%	**48.87%**	18.55%	31.68%	17.72%	17.83%
640	P	0%	100%	100%	100%	100%	94.2%	100%	87.9%
	R	0%	0.319%	0.3%	38.8%	51.9%	94.6%	92%	99.4%
	mAP-50	0%	43.3%	19.7%	98.2%	92.3%	98.4%	97.3%	98.8%
	delay(ms)	73.8		101.2		172.8		334.0	
	score	0%	9.92%	3.34%	25.38%	15.49%	18.60%	9.64%	9.59%

Different parameters have varying effects on detection delay and performance. Image size mainly affects detection speed, while the time step has a greater impact on detection performance. Increasing both the time step and image size leads to slower detection. Doubling the image size reduces detection speed by 135% while doubling the time step reduces detection speed by 60–80%. Thus, image size has a greater impact on detection speed, while the time step has a significant impact on detection performance. The influence of image size on detection performance is unstable.

It should be noted that the algorithm models exhibit significant differences in detecting images of different categories under different parameters. When the time step is low, the algorithm is less sensitive to ordinary camera data but can detect DVS data. When the time step is high, the algorithm's detection performance for DVS data is also significantly better than that for ordinary camera data. Dynamic objects are more evident in event frames compared to ordinary camera images, and simpler object features are easier to extract in shorter time steps.

The detection results of various categories are evaluated under diverse parameter combinations using (1). The performance of the best scores in different classes has been bolded in Table 3, but the best scores vary widely. Therefore, compared with ordinary cameras, SNN-YOLOv3-tiny is more suitable for detect-

Table 4. Comparison of the performance and power consumption on detecting DVS event-frame images between YOLOv3-tiny (baseline) and SNN-YOLOv3-tiny (this work) with optimal parameters.

Object Detection Algorithm	F1-score	mAP-50	Delay (ms)	Operations of single inference	Operation type	Single operation power consumption(pJ)	Single inference power consumption(J)	Power consumption(mW)
baseline	93.4%	99.5%	3.2	6.97E+09	FP32 MAC	4.6	0.032	10666.6
					INT32 MAC	3.2	0.022	7333.3
this work	70.4%	99.1%	57.8	8.67E+08	FP32 AC	0.9	7.80E-04	13.5
					INT32 AC	0.1	8.67E-05	1.5

ing event frames captured by DVS on UAV, which verifies the high adaptability of the combination of DVS and SNN.

Performance Comparison Between the SNN-Based and Baseline Object Detection Algorithms. This work compared the detection performance and energy consumption of SNN-YOLOv3-tiny under optimal parameters with the YOLOv3-tiny algorithm baseline for the DVS event frame. This work estimates energy consumption using the method from [3] and compares the energy consumption of different algorithms by multiplying the estimated energy consumption per operation with the total number of operations. The comparison results are shown in Table 4.

The algorithm's power consumption evaluation showed that SNN-YOLOv3-tiny, using 32-bit floating-point (FP32) operations, consumed only 2.5% of the energy used by YOLOv3-tiny for a single inference and only 1.3‰ of its energy consumption for continuous detection. When using 32-bit integer (INT32) operations, the energy consumption for a single inference was only 4‰ of YOLOv3-tiny's, and the power consumption was only 0.2‰ of YOLOv3-tiny's. The SNN-based algorithm model also showed good detection accuracy for DVS data.

In summary, compared with the baseline, SNN-YOLOv3-tiny with optimized parameters sacrifices detection delay and accuracy without compromising the effectiveness of dynamic obstacle avoidance, but significantly improves energy efficiency with the SNN mechanism. This shows the value of neuromorphic computing in UAV obstacle avoidance.

5 Conclusion

This work explores the application of DVS and SNN in UAV dynamic obstacle avoidance tasks, employing a framework that integrates DVS and SNN to perceive and detect obstacles, and also incorporates a customized action decision-making algorithm to process information such as the position and depth of obstacles and output corresponding actions. This paper focuses on evaluating and optimizing the parameter combinations of SNN-based obstacle detection algorithms and designing lightweight obstacle avoidance decision-making methods. The experiments utilize a software simulation platform to test the feasibility of this framework and evaluate the success rate, power consumption, and delay of the obstacle avoidance algorithm. The results demonstrate the proposed obstacle avoidance algorithm's high energy efficiency, low delay, and flexibility.

Future work will concentrate on the integration of real-time DVS output event streams with the object detection SNN algorithm, as well as implementing the object detection SNN algorithm on a neuromorphic hardware accelerator, paving the way for the combined use of DVS and SNN object detection algorithms in real-world drone applications.

Acknowledgements. This research has received funding from National Natural Science Foundation of China Youth Fund Project (61802427, 62102437, 62102439, 62102438), Young Talent Support Project (2020-JCJQ-QT-038), Beijing Science and Technology Rising Star Project (Z211100002121116) and the National Natural Science Foundation of China (61802427, 61832018).

References

1. Blanchard, M., Rind, F.C., Verschure, P.F.: Collision avoidance using a model of the locust LGMD neuron. Robot. Auton. Syst. **30**(1–2), 17–38 (2000)
2. Chen, W.: Pytorch-spiking-yolov3 (2021). https://github.com/cwq159/PyTorch-Spiking-YOLOv3
3. Horowitz, M.: 1.1 computing's energy problem (and what we can do about it). In: 2014 IEEE International Solid-State Circuits Conference Digest of Technical Papers (ISSCC), pp. 10–14. IEEE (2014)
4. Kim, S., Park, S., Na, B., Yoon, S.: Spiking-yolo: spiking neural network for energy-efficient object detection. In: Proceedings of the AAAI Conference on Artificial Intelligence, vol. 34, pp. 11270–11277 (2020)
5. Lichtsteiner, P., Posch, C., Delbruck, T.: A 128×128 120 DB 15μs latency asynchronous temporal contrast vision sensor. IEEE J. Solid-State Circuits **43**(2), 566–576 (2008)
6. Lu, J., Wu, X., Cao, S., Wang, X., Yu, H.: An implementation of actor-critic algorithm on spiking neural network using temporal coding method. Appl. Sci. **12**(20), 10430 (2022)
7. Maass, W.: Networks of spiking neurons: the third generation of neural network models. Neural Netw. **10**(9), 1659–1671 (1997)
8. Ouahouah, S., Bagaa, M., Prados-Garzon, J., Taleb, T.: Deep-reinforcement-learning-based collision avoidance in UAV environment. IEEE Internet Things J. **9**(6), 4015–4030 (2021)
9. Rebecq, H., Gehrig, D., Scaramuzza, D.: ESIM: an open event camera simulator. In: Conference on Robot Learning, pp. 969–982. PMLR (2018)
10. Rueckauer, B., Lungu, I.A., Hu, Y., Pfeiffer, M., Liu, S.C.: Conversion of continuous-valued deep networks to efficient event-driven networks for image classification. Front. Neurosci. **11**, 682 (2017)
11. Salt, L., Indiveri, G., Sandamirskaya, Y.: Obstacle avoidance with LGMD neuron: towards a neuromorphic UAV implementation. In: 2017 IEEE International Symposium on Circuits and Systems (ISCAS), pp. 1–4. IEEE (2017)

12. Salvatore, N., Mian, S., Abidi, C., George, A.D.: A neuro-inspired approach to intelligent collision avoidance and navigation. In: 2020 AIAA/IEEE 39th Digital Avionics Systems Conference (DASC), pp. 1–9. IEEE (2020)
13. Wang, D., Li, W., Liu, X., Li, N., Zhang, C.: UAV environmental perception and autonomous obstacle avoidance: a deep learning and depth camera combined solution. Comput. Electron. Agric. **175**, 105523 (2020)
14. Xiao, K., Tan, S., Wang, G., An, X., Wang, X., Wang, X.: XTDrone: a customizable multi-rotor UAVs simulation platform. In: 2020 4th International Conference on Robotics and Automation Sciences (ICRAS), pp. 55–61. IEEE (2020)
15. Zanatta, L., Barchi, F., Bartolini, A., Acquaviva, A.: Artificial versus spiking neural networks for reinforcement learning in UAV obstacle avoidance. In: Proceedings of the 19th ACM International Conference on Computing Frontiers, pp. 199–200 (2022)

Empirical Study on the Effect of Residual Networks on the Expressiveness of Linear Regions

Xuan Qi, Yi Wei, Xue Mei(✉), Ryad Chellali, and Shipin Yang

Nanjing Tech University, Nanjing 211816, China
{mx,spyang}@njtech.edu.cn

Abstract. Residual networks have achieved success across various industries. Currently, the research on the working mechanism of residual networks mainly focuses on shallow sub-networks, while knowledge about many other aspects remains limited. Deep neural networks based on the ReLU (Rectified Linear Unit) activation function partition the input space into piecewise linear regions, and thus, for a residual network with ReLU activation, the number of linear regions can quantify its expressive power. In this paper, we first visualize the linear regions of residual networks in two dimensions to understand how the number of linear regions evolves in residual networks. Moreover, we aim to compare the actual expressive power and input representation capabilities of residual networks by analyzing the number of linear regions in two-dimensional inputs between residual networks and non-residual networks. Our research findings indicate that, under consistent external parameters and conditions, residual networks generally exhibit stronger linear regions expression and input representation capabilities than non-residual networks in most cases.

Keywords: Residual networks · Linear regions · Expressiveness

1 Introduction

In recent years, numerous models featuring diverse residual network structures have achieved remarkable success in various computer vision and deep learning tasks. These residual architectures leverage residual learning frameworks to train deeper networks and enhance the accuracy of predictions. Residual networks are widely acknowledged for their exceptional performance in deep neural network frameworks for image classification, such as ResNet [7], Inception-ResNet [20], DenseNet [11], SKNet [12], and SENet [9]. Similarly, they have also proven to be effective in addressing object detection challenges, as demonstrated in frameworks like Faster R-CNN [16], DSSD [3], Scaled-YOLOv4 [23], and KDEM [18]. Furthermore, the aforementioned deep neural network frameworks exhibit exceptional performance on popular public datasets. As a result, residual models have emerged as the predominant models for feature extraction in images and videos.

L. Iliadis et al. (Eds.): ICANN 2023, LNCS 14263, pp. 174–185, 2023.
https://doi.org/10.1007/978-3-031-44204-9_15

Despite some researchers having endeavored to explore the working mechanism of residual networks since 2015, relevant studies concerning the expressiveness of linear regions in residual networks are still wanting.

In this study, we aim to transform residual networks into mappings of the input space. Residual networks utilize piecewise linear activation function ReLU to fit a variety of different linear functions. For standard networks that use piecewise linear activation function, we can transform the input space into various linear convex regions [5,21]. The final classification outcome is based on the arrangement of linear functions layer by layer within the residual network structure (based on multi-classification). Figure 1 showcases the comprehensive correlation among the linear regions, input data sets, and activation status of the residual network, all mapped in a two-dimensional input space, with different color blocks representing linear regions formed by distinct linear functions within the residual network. Additionally, each neuron in the residual network can partition the input space into two regions along the hyperplane. With the combined effect of numerous neurons, a larger region can be segmented into smaller ones. Therefore, each region comprises linear functions that represent the final multi-classification result, with the predicted label being selected as the maximum value among the linear function results. In residual networks with ReLU activation, the neurons in the later layer divide the linear regions already created by the previous layer. Thus, the linear functions are arranged layer by layer, resulting in the generation of a large number of linear regions when the residual network is in operation. Hence, the arrangement of residual networks with residual connections is similar to DNNs with the piecewise linear activation function ReLU but without residual connections. Figure 3 shows the arrangement of the internal linear convex regions in the residual network and the network without residual connections. Both networks utilize the *make moons* dataset with 16 neurons in each hidden layer, 100 epochs, and equivalent training settings. We count the number of linear regions in each layer of the networks. As the number of layers increases, the neurons in each layer merge the linear boundaries of the previous layer and divide them into higher-level linear region patterns. According to the results, we observed that Fig. 3(a) generates more linear regions than Fig. 3(b).

To our knowledge, our work is the first to study the structure and evolution of linear regions of residual networks. We attempt to address several fundamental empirical questions:

Q1. How do the linear regions based on two-dimensional inputs evolve during the training of residual networks? And how does the number of linear regions of residual networks vary with different network configurations?

Q2. Which network, residual or non-residual, has stronger ability to express inputs under the same conditions? And which network, residual or non-residual, has stronger ability to express linear regions in practice under the same conditions?

We evaluated three sets of residual and non-residual networks with different numbers of neurons on two-dimensional data randomly generated between -1 and

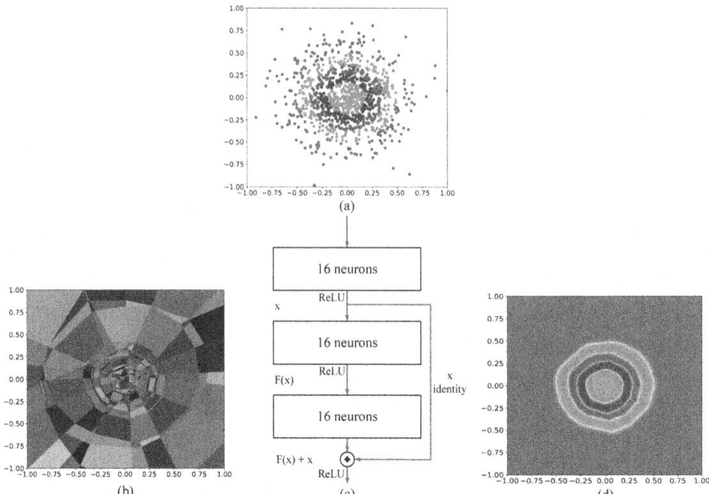

Fig. 1. (a) The two-dimensional input data set *make gaussian quantiles*. (b) Visualization of the linear regions. (c) The residual network structure used for training (100 epochs). (d) Visualization of the decision boundary, where the distribution of the five colored linear regions fits five types of data. The white area can be approximately viewed as the decision boundary of the residual network. (Color figure online)

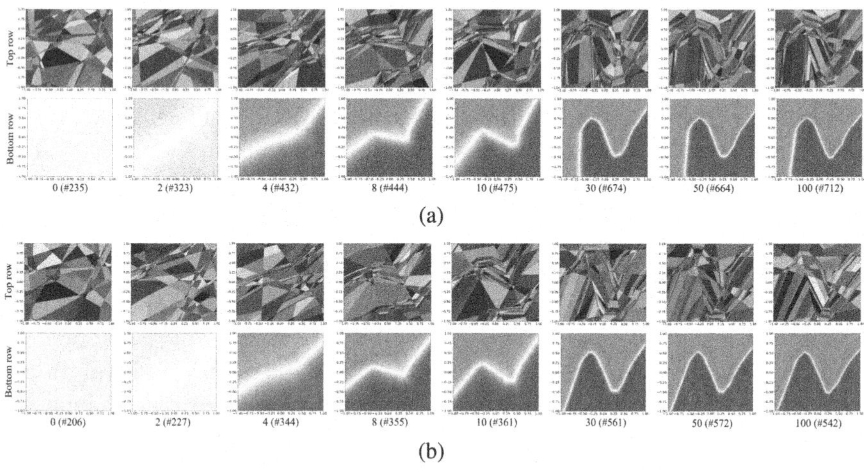

Fig. 2. Top row: Visualization of the linear regions. Bottom row: Visualization of decision boundaries, the blue and red regions in the visualization results represent two different data distributions of the network input, and the white area can be approximated as the decision boundary. (a) Evolution and visualization results of Fig. 3(a) network. (b) Evolution and visualization results of Fig. 3(b) network. (Color figure online)

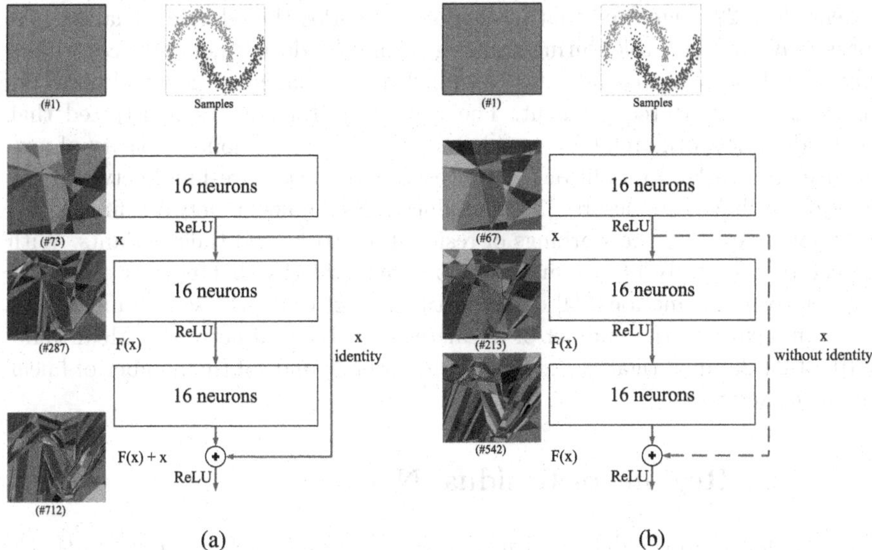

Fig. 3. (a) The process of linear convex region arrangement in the residual network. (b) The process of linear convex region arrangement in the network without residual connections.

1 for various samples, and the main results can be summarized as follows. Q1: In the case of two-dimensional input, the residual network and the non-residual network evolve linear regions layer by layer as shown in Fig. 3, while the evolution of the linear regions at different epochs of the residual network and the non-residual network can be observed in Fig. 2, both networks trained for R epochs, for $R = 0, 2, 4, 8, 10, 30, 50, 100$. In addition, the quantity and density of linear regions in residual networks are mainly correlated with the number of neurons. Increasing the number of neurons results in more numerous and denser linear regions. Q2: In most cases, residual networks have a stronger ability to express linear regions and inputs compared to networks without residual connections.

2 Related Work

Currently, there are many design approaches for residual network models, which share a common feature of utilizing "shortcut connections". The success of residual networks has prompted many researchers to explore their operating mechanisms. In 2016, [7] presented ResNet for the first time at the CVPR conference. By introducing shortcut connections across layers, ResNet effectively solved the challenges of gradient vanishing and exploding during deep neural network training, resulting in increased network depth and expressive capacity. Shortly after, at the ECCV conference, [8] suggested that residual networks could effectively address the issues of network degradation and gradient dispersion, further elaborating on the reasons behind the success of residual networks. The research presented in [22] suggested that in residual networks, the relatively shallow networks play a critical role during training, while the deeper networks contribute only a small amount of gradient. [1] studied the mechanism of residual networks based on the shattered gradient. The results of [13] have demonstrated that the residual network architecture enhances the representational capacity of narrow deep networks. In addition, [17] investigated whether residual networks are superior to linear predictors. [19] introduced a shallow subnetwork first (SSF) argument to explain the workings of residual networks and their variants. With respect to the study of the linear regions in networks that employ piecewise linear activation functions, [4] explored the impact of depth, width, and activation complexity on the number of linear regions of neural networks. Meanwhile, [2,10,14,24,25] investigated the upper and lower bounds of the number of linear regions of networks.

3 Linear Regions of Residual Networks

The residual networks discussed in this paper are all based on the ReLU [15] activation function, which is defined as follows:

$$ReLU(x) = \max(0, x), \tag{1}$$

when the input x is greater than 0, the output of ReLU function is x. Conversely, when x is less than or equal to 0, the output is 0 and the corresponding node is inactive and does not contribute to the output. During gradient back propagation, the derivative of ReLU is:

$$ReLU'(x) = \begin{cases} 1, & \text{if } x > 0, \\ 0, & \text{otherwise} . \end{cases} \tag{2}$$

If x is greater than 0, the gradient equals 1; otherwise, the gradient will vanish. Let us consider a residual network with N ReLU layers, assuming L^n is the number of neurons with n layers, where n is the number of ReLU layers. Therefore, the output of each L^n is

$$z^n = \{z_l^n, l \in L^n\}, \tag{3}$$

$$z_l^n = (\mathbf{w}_l^n)^T \hat{z}^{n-1} + \mathbf{b}^n, \quad l \in L^n, n \leq N. \tag{4}$$

The result of the previous layer through the ReLU activation layer in a residual network is as follows, where $\mathbf{b}^r$ represents the bias of layer r.

$$\hat{z}^{r-1} = \max\left(0, z^{r-1}\right). \tag{5}$$

Therefore, residual networks with ReLU activation can be expressed as:

$$f(x) = \max\left(0, \mathbf{w}_N^T \max\left(0, \mathbf{w}_{N-1}^T \max(0, \ldots) + \mathbf{b}^{N-1}\right) + \mathbf{b}^N\right), \tag{6}$$

referring to (6), residual networks with ReLU activation can be seen as a connected piecewise linear function. As a result, every neuron in a residual network with ReLU activation can be represented as a piecewise linear function of the input $x \in \mathbb{R}^d$:

$$f_l^n(x) = (\mathbf{K}_l^n)^T x + \mathbf{b}_l^n, \quad l \in L^n, \tag{7}$$

where d is the dimension of the input, and the linear weight and bias of the current neuron input are denoted by $\mathbf{K}_l^n$ and $\mathbf{b}_l^n$, respectively.

We have discussed the linear expression of neurons in residual networks with ReLU activation based on input, where each linear inequality forms a convex region. We define the linear regions of residual networks with ReLU activation as follows:

Definition 1 (adapted from [6]) Let P be a residual network with input dimension d_{in} and fix ε, a vector of trainable parameters for P. Define

$$S_P(\varepsilon) := \left\{x \in \mathbb{R}^{d_{\text{in}}} \mid \nabla P(\cdot; \varepsilon) \text{ is discontinuous at } x\right\}. \tag{8}$$

The linear regions of P at ε are the connected parts of input without S_P:

$$\text{linear regions } (P, \varepsilon) = \left\{x \mid x \in \mathbb{R}^{d_{\text{in}}}, x \notin S_P(\varepsilon)\right\}. \tag{9}$$

4 Experiments

The experimental framework we used is Pytorch, where we represent each neuron in the network as linear functions based on inputs. The linear functions of each neuron in the network can be obtained through forward propagation. The dataset used in the experiment consists of two-dimensional data, as two-dimensional input data is easy to visualize. We use eight different sets of two-dimensional datasets with varying sample sizes. The datasets are uniformly generated between -1 and 1, and the labels are randomly generated, dividing the data into two classes: 0 or 1. Our random samples consist of 200, 500, 1000, 2000, 3000, 5000, 7000, and 10000, respectively. Figure 4(a) shows the distribution of random data with different sample sizes. In terms of network parameters and configuration, we utilized the network structures shown in Fig. 3(a) and Fig. 3(b) to verify the linear region expression capabilities of residual networks and networks without residual connections. Additionally, we utilized Adam as the optimizer, set the batch size to 32, the loss function to Cross Entropy, and a learning rate of 0.001.

Figure 4 and Table 1 show the number of linear regions and visualization results trained for 10000 epochs using 8 sets of two-dimensional random samples. We can intuitively observe some commonalities between the residual and non-residual networks, as the complexity of the sample space increases, the number of linear regions segmented by the network first increases and then decreases. We empirically believe that the reason for this phenomenon is that, within the limit of the total amount of data that the network can express, the model needs to increase the number of linear regions to express more irregular discrete data. However, when the total input surpasses the limit, such as when the sample size reaches 3000, the number of linear regions significantly decreases. Additionally,

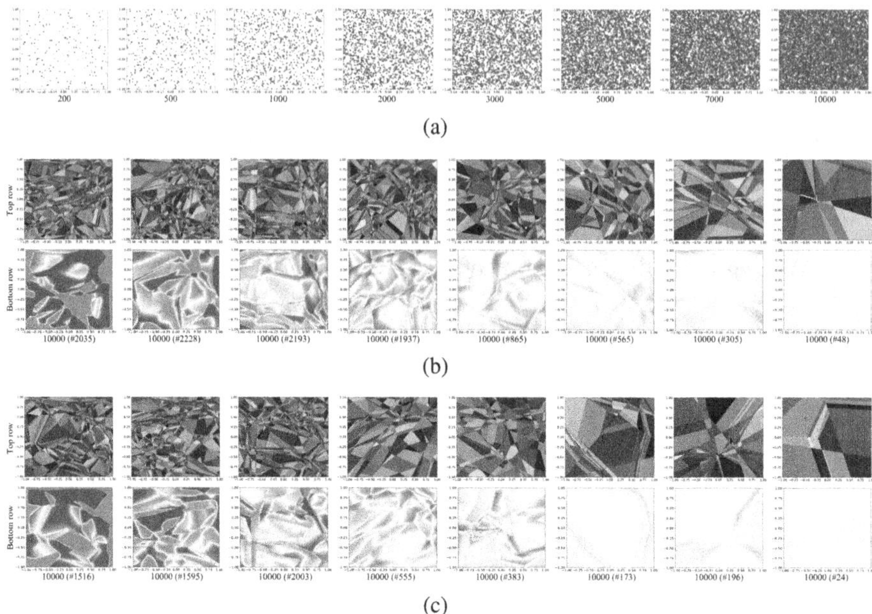

Fig. 4. Top row: Visualization of the linear regions. Bottom row: Visualization of decision boundaries, the blue and red regions represent two different data distributions of the network input, and the white regions can be approximated as the decision boundary. (a) Two-dimensional random inputs with sample size m, for $m = 200, 500, 1000, 2000, 3000, 5000, 7000, 10000$. (b) The number of linear regions and visualization results expressed by the residual network in Fig. 3(a). (c) The number of linear regions and visualization results expressed by the non-residual network in Fig. 3(b). (Color figure online)

Table 1. The number of linear regions of the residual network and non-residual network in Fig. 3 with input two-dimensional random datasets with sample size m and trained for 10000 epochs, for $m = 200, 500, 1000, 2000, 3000, 5000, 7000, 10000$.

Networks	Samples							
	200	500	1000	2000	3000	5000	7000	10000
Fig. 3(a)	2035	2228	2193	1937	865	565	305	48
Fig. 3(b)	1516	1595	2003	555	383	173	196	24

there is a noticeable difference in the ability of the residual and non-residual networks to express linear regions, according to the number of linear regions we have counted and visualization results, under the same conditions of network input, number of neurons, and training parameters, the residual network has a stronger ability to express linear regions and input than the non-residual network in most cases.

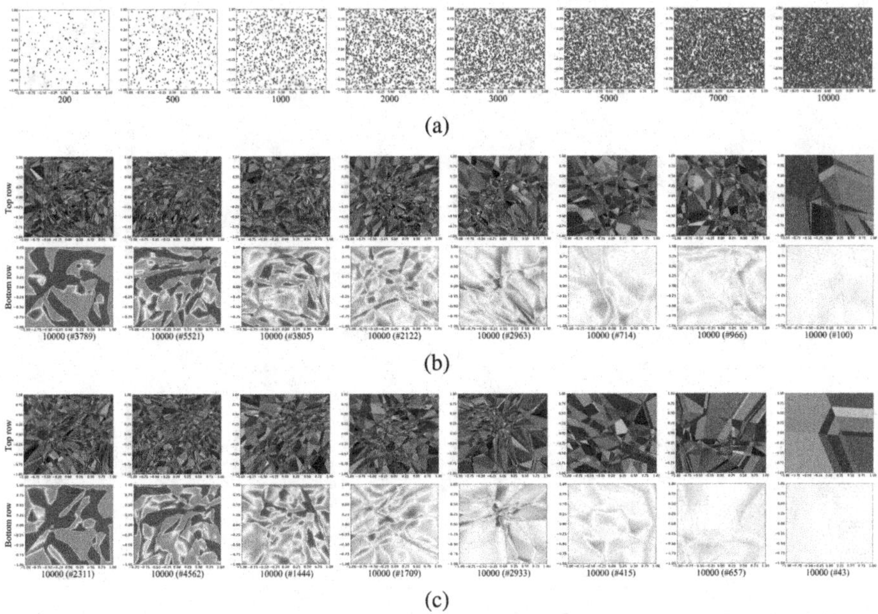

Fig. 5. Top row: Visualization of the linear regions. Bottom row: Visualization of decision boundaries, the blue and red regions represent two different data distributions of the network input, and the white regions can be approximated as the decision boundary. (a) Two-dimensional random datasets with sample size m, for $m = 200, 500, 1000, 2000, 3000, 5000, 7000, 10000$. (b) The number of linear regions and visualization results expressed by the residual network in Fig. 3(a) (32 neurons). (c) The number of linear regions and visualization results expressed by the non-residual network in Fig. 3(b) (32 neurons). (Color figure online)

Table 2. The number of linear regions of the residual network and non-residual network in Fig. 3 (32 neurons) with input two-dimensional random datasets with sample size m and trained for 10000 epochs, for $m = 200, 500, 1000, 2000, 3000, 5000, 7000, 10000$.

Networks	Samples							
	200	500	1000	2000	3000	5000	7000	10000
Fig. 3(a) (32 neurons)	3789	5521	3805	2122	2963	714	966	100
Fig. 3(b) (32 neurons)	2311	4562	1444	1709	2933	415	657	43

To further demonstrate the ability of residual networks to express input and linear regions, we conducted additional experiments with two different sets of neuron numbers while keeping the network training parameters constant. We modified the number of neurons in each layer for both residual and non-residual networks shown in Fig. 3. Figure 5 and Table 2 illustrate the experimental outcomes when the number of neurons in each layer of the networks shown in Fig. 3 was set to 32. Similarly, Fig. 6 and Table 3 demonstrate the experimental find-

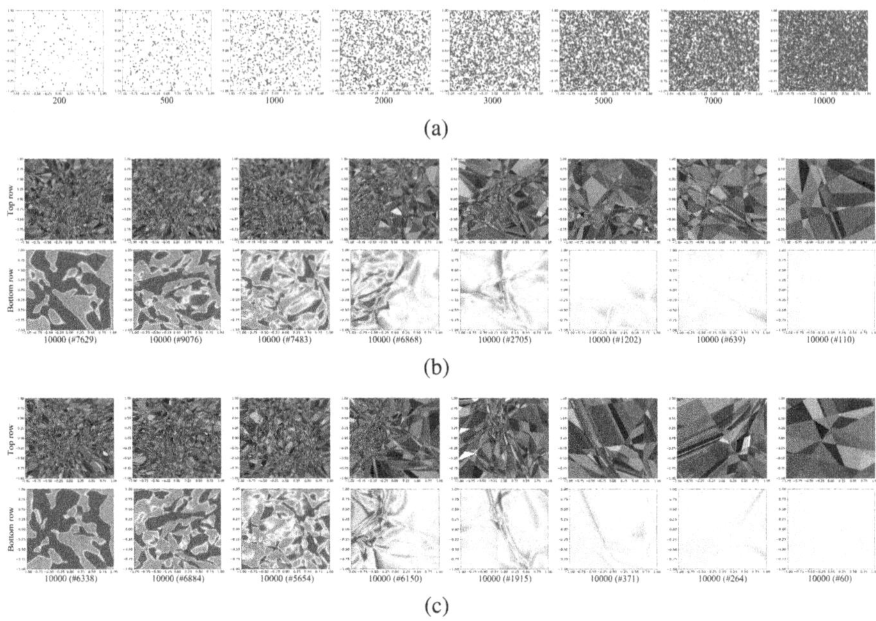

Fig. 6. Top row: Visualization of the linear regions. Bottom row: Visualization of decision boundaries, the blue and red regions represent two different data distributions of the network input, and the white regions can be approximated as the decision boundary. (a) Two-dimensional random datasets with sample size m, for $m = 200, 500, 1000, 2000, 3000, 5000, 7000, 10000$. (b) The number of linear regions and visualization results expressed by the residual network in Fig. 3(a) (64 neurons). (c) The number of linear regions and visualization results expressed by the non-residual network in Fig. 3(b) (64 neurons). (Color figure online)

Table 3. The number of linear regions of the residual network and non-residual network in Fig. 3 (64 neurons) with input two-dimensional random datasets with sample size m and trained for 10000 epochs., for $m = 200, 500, 1000, 2000, 3000, 5000, 7000, 10000$.

Networks	Samples							
	200	500	1000	2000	3000	5000	7000	10000
Fig. 3(a) (64 neurons)	7629	9076	7483	6868	2705	1202	639	110
Fig. 3(b) (64 neurons)	6338	6884	5654	6150	1915	371	264	60

ings when the number of neurons in each layer of the networks in Fig. 3 was increased to 64. Furthermore, the accuracy of the three sets of networks trained on two-dimensional random data is shown in Fig. 7. According to the number of linear regions we have counted and visualization results, under the same conditions of network input, number of neurons, and training parameters, we obtained the same results as before, that is, the residual network has a stronger ability to express linear regions and input than the non-residual network in most cases.

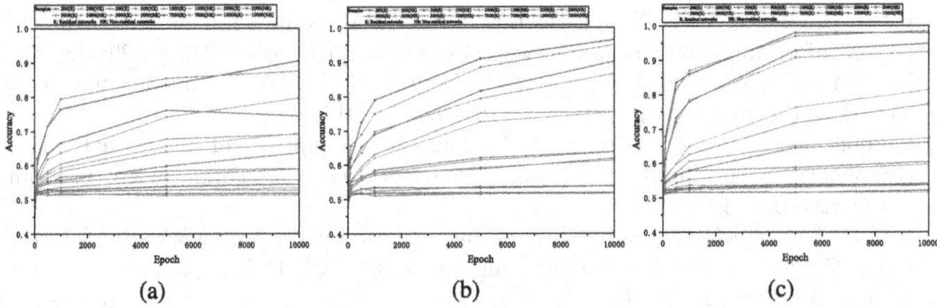

Fig. 7. Accuracy of three sets of networks trained with different samples of 2D random data. (a) The networks in Fig. 3. (b) Each layer of Fig. 3 contains 32 neurons. (c) Each layer of Fig. 3 contains 64 neurons.

5 Conclusion

The working mechanism of residual networks based on ReLU activation functions remains poorly understood. In this study, we investigated a key property of residual networks, namely their ability to express the number of linear regions, which serves as a representative measure of the function complexity they can effectively learn.

We conducted a series of experiments to investigate how the linear regions of residual networks evolve during the training process and how changing network parameters affects the expression of linear regions of residual networks. Additionally, we provided two-dimensional input-based residual network linear region visualization results, including the network's layer-by-layer linear region evolution process and the linear region evolution process at different epochs. In particular, we have empirically observed that under the same conditions of network input, neuron number, and training parameters, the residual network generally exhibits stronger linear region and input expression capabilities compared to non-residual networks.

Our work provides an opportunity to enhance our understanding of the residual networks by studying how their linear regions evolve. In the future, we plan to (i) generalize and prove our results in two and higher dimensions, and (ii) investigate the relationship between the decision boundaries of residual networks and their linear region expression capabilities.

Acknowledgements. This work was supported by the National Natural Science Foundation of China (Grant No. 61973334).

References

1. Balduzzi, D., Frean, M., Leary, L., Lewis, J., Ma, K.W.D., McWilliams, B.: The shattered gradients problem: if ResNets are the answer, then what is the question? In: International Conference on Machine Learning, pp. 342–350. PMLR (2017)

2. Chen, H., Wang, Y.G., Xiong, H.: Lower and upper bounds for numbers of linear regions of graph convolutional networks. arXiv preprint arXiv:2206.00228 (2022)
3. Fu, C.Y., Liu, W., Ranga, A., Tyagi, A., Berg, A.C.: DSSD: deconvolutional single shot detector. arXiv preprint arXiv:1701.06659 (2017)
4. Goujon, A., Etemadi, A., Unser, M.: The role of depth, width, and activation complexity in the number of linear regions of neural networks. arXiv preprint arXiv:2206.08615 (2022)
5. Hanin, B., Rolnick, D.: Complexity of linear regions in deep networks. In: International Conference on Machine Learning, pp. 2596–2604. PMLR (2019)
6. Hanin, B., Rolnick, D.: Deep RELU networks have surprisingly few activation patterns. In: Advances in Neural Information Processing Systems, vol. 32 (2019)
7. He, K., Zhang, X., Ren, S., Sun, J.: Deep residual learning for image recognition. In: Proceedings of the IEEE Conference on Computer Vision and Pattern Recognition, pp. 770–778 (2016)
8. He, K., Zhang, X., Ren, S., Sun, J.: Identity mappings in deep residual networks. In: Leibe, B., Matas, J., Sebe, N., Welling, M. (eds.) ECCV 2016. LNCS, vol. 9908, pp. 630–645. Springer, Cham (2016). https://doi.org/10.1007/978-3-319-46493-0_38
9. Hu, J., Shen, L., Albanie, S., Sun, G., Wu, E.: Squeeze-and-excitation networks. IEEE Trans. Pattern Anal. Mach. Intell. **42**(8), 2011–2023 (2020). https://doi.org/10.1109/TPAMI.2019.2913372
10. Hu, Q., Zhang, H., Gao, F., Xing, C., An, J.: Analysis on the number of linear regions of piecewise linear neural networks. IEEE Trans. Neural Netw. Learn. Syst. **33**(2), 644–653 (2020)
11. Huang, G., Liu, Z., Van Der Maaten, L., Weinberger, K.Q.: Densely connected convolutional networks. In: Proceedings of the IEEE Conference on Computer Vision and Pattern Recognition, pp. 4700–4708 (2017)
12. Li, X., Wang, W., Hu, X., Yang, J.: Selective kernel networks. In: Proceedings of the IEEE/CVF Conference on Computer Vision and Pattern Recognition, pp. 510–519 (2019)
13. Lin, H., Jegelka, S.: ResNet with one-neuron hidden layers is a universal approximator. In: Advances in Neural Information Processing Systems, vol. 31 (2018)
14. Montúfar, G., Ren, Y., Zhang, L.: Sharp bounds for the number of regions of maxout networks and vertices of minkowski sums. SIAM J. Appl. Algebra Geom. **6**(4), 618–649 (2022)
15. Nair, V., Hinton, G.E.: Rectified linear units improve restricted Boltzmann machines. In: Proceedings of the 27th International Conference on Machine Learning (ICML-10), pp. 807–814 (2010)
16. Ren, S., He, K., Girshick, R., Sun, J.: Faster R-CNN: towards real-time object detection with region proposal networks. IEEE Trans. Pattern Anal. Mach. Intell. **39**(6), 1137–1149 (2017). https://doi.org/10.1109/TPAMI.2016.2577031
17. Shamir, O.: Are ResNets provably better than linear predictors? In: Advances in Neural Information Processing Systems, vol. 31 (2018)
18. Shan, S., Xiong, E., Yuan, X., Wu, S.: A knowledge-driven enhanced module for visible-infrared person re-identification. In: Pimenidis, E., Angelov, P., Jayne, C., Papaleonidas, A., Aydin, M. (eds.) ICANN 2022, Part I. Lecture Notes in Computer Science, vol. 13529, pp. 441–453. Springer, Cham (2022)
19. Sun, T., Ding, S., Guo, L.: Low-degree term first in ResNet, its variants and the whole neural network family. Neural Netw. **148**, 155–165 (2022)
20. Szegedy, C., Ioffe, S., Vanhoucke, V., Alemi, A.: Inception-v4, inception-ResNet and the impact of residual connections on learning. In: Proceedings of the AAAI Conference on Artificial Intelligence, vol. 31 (2017)

21. Tseran, H., Montufar, G.F.: On the expected complexity of maxout networks. Adv. Neural. Inf. Process. Syst. **34**, 28995–29008 (2021)
22. Veit, A., Wilber, M.J., Belongie, S.: Residual networks behave like ensembles of relatively shallow networks. In: Advances in Neural Information Processing Systems, vol. 29 (2016)
23. Wang, C.Y., Bochkovskiy, A., Liao, H.Y.M.: Scaled-YOLOv4: scaling cross stage partial network. In: Proceedings of the IEEE/CVF Conference on Computer Vision and Pattern Recognition, pp. 13029–13038 (2021)
24. Wang, Y.: Estimation and comparison of linear regions for relu networks. In: International Joint Conference on Artificial Intelligence (2022)
25. Xiong, H., Huang, L., Yu, M., Liu, L., Zhu, F., Shao, L.: On the number of linear regions of convolutional neural networks. In: International Conference on Machine Learning, pp. 10514–10523. PMLR (2020)

Energy Complexity Model for Convolutional Neural Networks

Jiří Šíma[1(✉)], Petra Vidnerová[1], and Vojtěch Mrázek[2]

[1] Institute of Computer Science of the Czech Academy of Sciences, Prague, Czechia
{sima,petra}@cs.cas.cz

[2] Faculty of Information Technology, Brno University of Technology, Brno, Czechia
mrazek@fit.vutbr.cz

Abstract. The energy efficiency of hardware implementations of convolutional neural networks (CNNs) is critical to their widespread deployment in low-power mobile devices. Recently, a plethora of methods have been proposed providing energy-optimal mappings of CNNs onto diverse hardware accelerators. Their estimated power consumption is related to specific implementation details and hardware parameters, which does not allow for machine-independent exploration of CNN energy measures. In this paper, we introduce a simplified theoretical energy complexity model for CNNs, based on only two-level memory hierarchy that captures asymptotically all important sources of power consumption of different CNN hardware implementations. We calculate energy complexity in this model for two common dataflows which, according to statistical tests, fits asymptotically very well the power consumption estimated by the Time/Accelergy program for convolutional layers on the Simba and Eyeriss hardware platforms. The model opens the possibility of proving principal limits on the energy efficiency of CNN hardware accelerators.

Keywords: Convolutional neural networks · Energy complexity · Dataflow

1 Introduction

Deep neural networks (DNNs) represent a cutting-edge machine learning technology with countless applications in artificial intelligence (AI). In many cases such as smart glasses and mobile phone apps, DNNs have to be implemented in low-power hardware operated on batteries. In contrast, the inference process of already trained DNNs which typically consist of tens of layers, hundreds of thousands of neurons, and tens of millions of weight parameters, is computationally very demanding and highly-energy consuming. Thus, it is often accelerated efficiently in hardware employing massive parallelism in order to meet real-time requirements and energy constraints, which is critical to the widespread deployment of DNNs in mobile AI applications. For instance, in error-tolerant applications such as image classification, the use of approximate computing methods [4] (e.g. low float precision, approximate multipliers) can save enormous amount of energy at the cost of only a small loss in accuracy.

L. Iliadis et al. (Eds.): ICANN 2023, LNCS 14263, pp. 186–198, 2023.
https://doi.org/10.1007/978-3-031-44204-9_16

Recently, there have been great advances in techniques [8] that enable energy-efficient DNN processing on a variety of hardware platforms (e.g. GPUs, FPGAs, in-memory computing architectures) which reduce the computational cost of DNNs through hardware design and/or approximation of DNN models. For a given hardware implementation of DNN, the actual power consumption of the inference process can be measured or analytically estimated using physical laws. However, it depends on parameters and constants related to the specific hardware architecture and its evaluation varies for different hardware implementations, which prevents for machine-independent exploration of DNN energy measures.

Some computer programs [5,9] can optimize the power consumption for a particular DNN on various hardware platforms using different dataflow mapping methods. It has been empirically observed that the energy cost of evaluating DNNs mainly consists of two components, the computation energy and the data energy where the later can be 70% of the total cost [10]. The *computation energy* is needed for performing arithmetic operations, especially the so-called multiply-and-accumulate (MAC) operations ($S \leftarrow S+wy$ on floats S, w, y), which are used for computing weighted sums of inputs in neurons. The *data energy* is required for moving data inside a memory hierarchy (i.e. the dataflow) in hardware implementations of DNNs, which is related to the number of memory accesses.

The aim of this study is to introduce a theoretical hardware-independent model of energy complexity for DNNs that abstracts from their hardware implementation details and ignores specific aspects and constants of real machines, while preserving the asymptotic energy complexity of DNN inference. The use of abstract computational models (such as Turing machines) is fundamental to the field of computational complexity theory to define robust complexity measures (e.g. commonly associated with the usage of the big O notation), to identify efficient algorithms and to establish their principal limits by proving lower bounds.

In this paper, we define an energy complexity measure for convolutional neural networks (CNNs) which are widely used DNN models. The computation energy is naturally determined by the number of MACs during the CNN inference, multiplied by a non-uniform circuit constant related to the number of bits in floating-point operations. To define the data energy of CNN, we introduce an abstract computational model which is composed of only two memory levels called *DRAM* and *Buffer*. The CNN parameters and states are stored in DRAM while arithmetic operations are performed only over numerical data stored in Buffer which is of a limited capacity. The main idea behind this model is that the three arguments of each MAC operation (i.e. float values of an input, weight, and accumulated output) carried out in evaluating a given CNN, must occur together at one time in Buffer. This process requires a certain number of data transfers between DRAM and Buffer which defines the data energy measure.

The energy complexity model of CNNs is exploited for calculating the theoretical energy in the context of two common energy-efficient dataflows under realistic Buffer capacity constraints. For the first dataflow, an output value of each neuron is accumulated in Buffer and written to DRAM only once, and for the second one, any input to each neuron is read into Buffer only once. In both cases, each weight of the CNN is read into Buffer only once. The two dataflows provide upper bounds on energy complexity of the inference process for each convolutional layer separately in terms of its parameters.

The upper bounds on energy complexity are compared to the actual power consumption of evaluating CNNs on the Simba [6] and Eyeriss [2] hardware platforms which is estimated by using the Timeloop/Accelergy software tool [5,9]. The used platforms have been chosen as prominent examples of accelerators based on the systolic array of processing elements which are often implemented in practice as they are general and not tied to a specific CNN. The program optimizes the energy over dataflow mappings onto a given hardware platform. It turns out that the theoretical upper bounds fit asymptotically very well the empirical power consumptions, when the depth, feature map size, filter size, and stride of convolutional layers are varied each separately, which is validated by the statistical linearity and quadraticity tests. Hence, the simplified energy complexity model captures asymptotically all important sources of energy consumption that are common to diverse hardware implementations of CNNs. The model can also be exploited for proving lower bounds on energy complexity of CNNs in order to establish asymptotic limits on energy efficiency of any CNN hardware accelerators. The optimal energy bounds have already been proven for fully-connected layers [7] as a special case and starting point for convolutional layers.

The paper is organized as follows. After a formal definition of CNNs in Sect. 2, the energy complexity model for CNNs is introduced in Sect. 3 where the computation energy is calculated and a trivial lower bound on the data energy is shown. Section 4 presents two common energy-efficient dataflows which provide upper bounds on the data energy. Section 5 validates the energy complexity model by comparing the theoretical energy bounds for AlexNet-like architectures to its power consumption estimated by the Timeloop/Accelergy program for the Simba and Eyeriss hardware platforms. Section 6 summarizes the results.

2 Convolutional Neural Networks

In order to define an energy complexity measure, we first formalize and introduce notations for a *convolutional neural network* (CNN) $\mathcal{N}$. Its *multi-layered* architecture can be described by a directed acyclic graph (V, E) whose vertices in V, called *macro-units*, are matrices of neurons, while its directed edges in $E \subset V \times V$ are incident on macro-units whose neurons are connected. The macro-units are grouped into $D+1$ disjoint *layers*, indexed by level $\lambda = 0, \ldots, D$, starting with the zeroth *input* layer, followed by *hidden* layers, and ending with the *output* layer $Y \subset V$ at the level D. We assume that the edges are only between adjacent layers, which means macro-units in any layer $\lambda \in \{0, \ldots, D-1\}$ can only be connected to macro-units in the subsequent layer $\lambda + 1$. Denote $f_{\leftarrow} = \{g \in V \mid (g, f) \in E\}$ and $f^{\rightarrow} = \{h \in V \mid (f, h) \in E\}$ for any macro-unit $f \in V$.

Each layer $\lambda \in \{0, \ldots, D\}$ is composed of $d_\lambda > 0$ macro-units which are $m_\lambda \times n_\lambda$ matrices of neurons arranged in $m_\lambda > 0$ rows and $n_\lambda > 0$ columns, representing so-called *feature maps*. The parameters m_λ, n_λ, and d_λ are usually called the *height*, *width*, and *depth* of layer λ, respectively. In addition, each non-input layer $\lambda \in \{1, \dots, D\}$ is characterized by the size $r_\lambda \times s_\lambda$ of its so-called *receptive fields* which are rectangular (usually square) local regions in feature maps represented by $g \in f_\leftarrow$ in layer $\lambda - 1$ from which the connections lead to individual neurons in a macro-unit f belonging to layer λ. Thus, each neuron in f is associated with a specific receptive field of the same size, representing its scanning window to feature maps $g \in f_\leftarrow$ in the preceding layer $\lambda - 1$, which assumes $0 < r_\lambda \le m_{\lambda-1}$ and $0 < s_\lambda \le n_{\lambda-1}$. The length of vertical or horizontal shifts of the scanning window on feature map g for adjacent neurons in matrix f, is given by a so-called *stride* $\sigma_\lambda > 0$ in terms of the number of rows or columns in g, respectively, which is a parameter unique to the layer λ.

In order to compensate for under representing the neurons that are located at the edge of feature maps, the macro-units $g \in f_\leftarrow$ in layer $\lambda - 1$ are formally extended by π_λ rows and π_λ columns (of zero-state neurons) both from above and below, and to the left and right, respectively, where the parameter π_λ called *padding* satisfies $0 \le \pi_\lambda \le \max(r_\lambda, s_\lambda)$, which results in their extended formal size $(m_{\lambda-1} + 2\pi_\lambda) \times (n_{\lambda-1} + 2\pi_\lambda)$. Altogether, the size $m_\lambda \times n_\lambda$ of feature maps in the λth layer can be calculated as

$$m_\lambda = \left\lceil \frac{m_{\lambda-1} - r_\lambda + 2\pi_\lambda}{\sigma_\lambda} \right\rceil + 1\,, \quad n_\lambda = \left\lceil \frac{n_{\lambda-1} - s_\lambda + 2\pi_\lambda}{\sigma_\lambda} \right\rceil + 1 \tag{1}$$

in terms of the size $m_{\lambda-1} \times n_{\lambda-1}$ of feature maps in layer $\lambda - 1$.

Apart from input and output layers, we distinguish three types of layers in CNNs, which are called convolutional, pooling, and fully connected layers. In particular, the first $C < D$ hidden layers in $\mathcal{N}$ include general *convolutional* layers, at times interlaced with *(max) pooling* layers from $\Pi \subset \{1, \dots, C\}$. We assume that any non-input layer $\lambda \in \{1, \dots, D\} \setminus \Pi$ that is not pooling, is fully connected with the preceding layer $\lambda - 1$ at the macro-unit level, which means that for every macro-unit f in this layer λ, the set $f_\leftarrow$ contains all macro-units from layer $\lambda - 1$, and hence $|f_\leftarrow| = d_{\lambda-1}$. On the other hand, any macro-unit f in a pooling layer $\lambda \in \Pi$ has only one incoming edge that leads from unique macro-unit g in the preceding layer $\lambda - 1$, that is, $f_\leftarrow = \{g\}$ and $d_\lambda = d_{\lambda-1}$, and the feature map represented by g is partitioned into square non-overlapping receptive fields associated with f, which means $\sigma_\lambda = r_\lambda = s_\lambda$ and $\pi_\lambda = 0$. The remaining layers on the top of $\mathcal{N}$ from level $C + 1$ through D are usual *fully connected* layers of single neurons which constitute trivial feature maps f of size 1×1, that is, $m_\lambda = n_\lambda = \sigma_\lambda = 1$ and $\pi_\lambda = 0$ for every $\lambda = C + 1, \dots, D$. Each neuron f in the (so-called *flattening*) layer $C + 1$ is a trivial macro-unit that collects its inputs from all neurons in the Cth layer, which means the receptive fields of f coincide with feature maps represented by $g \in f_\leftarrow$, that is, $r_{C+1} = m_C$ and $s_{C+1} = n_C$, whereas $r_\lambda = s_\lambda = 1$ for every $\lambda = C + 2, \dots, D$.

Every macro-unit $f \in V$ in a non-pooling layer $\lambda \in \{1, \dots, D\} \setminus \Pi$ is associated with a real *bias* $b_f \in \mathbb{R}$, whereas any edge $(g, f) \in E$ leading from $g \in f_\leftarrow$ to f is labeled with a so-called *filter* (or *kernel*) $\mathbf{W}_{fg} \in \mathbb{R}^{r_\lambda \times s_\lambda}$ which is an $r_\lambda \times s_\lambda$

matrix with real entries $w_{fg}(i,j)$ for every $i=1,\ldots,r_\lambda$ and $j=1,\ldots,r_\lambda$. The *state (output)* $\mathbf{Y}_f \in \mathbb{R}^{m_\lambda \times n_\lambda}$ of any macro-unit $f \in V$ is an $m_\lambda \times n_\lambda$ matrix with real entries $y_f(k,\ell)$ for every $k=1,\ldots,m_\lambda$ and $\ell=1,\ldots,n_\lambda$. We formally define $y_f(k,\ell)=0$ if $k<1$ or $k>m_\lambda$ or $\ell<1$ or $\ell>n_\lambda$ for padding neurons in f.

At the beginning of a computation, an external input is presented to $\mathcal{N}$ by setting the states $\mathbf{Y}_f$ of macro-units f in the input layer. In general step, assume that for a macro-unit $f \in V$ in a layer λ, the states $\mathbf{Y}_g$ have been computed for every $g \in f_{\leftarrow}$. First assume that $\lambda \in \{1,\ldots,D\} \setminus \Pi$ is not a pooling layer. Then the *excitation* $\boldsymbol{\Xi}_f \in \mathbb{R}^{m_\lambda \times n_\lambda}$ of f, which is an $m_\lambda \times n_\lambda$ matrix with real entries $\xi_f(k,\ell)$ for every $k=1,\ldots,m_\lambda$ and $\ell=1,\ldots,n_\lambda$, is evaluated as

$$\xi_f(k,\ell) = b_f + \sum_{g\in f_{\leftarrow}} \sum_{i=1}^{r_\lambda} \sum_{j=1}^{s_\lambda} w_{fg}(i,j)\, y_g\big((k-1)\sigma_\lambda - \pi_\lambda + i\,,(\ell-1)\sigma_\lambda - \pi_\lambda + j\big) \quad (2)$$

for every $k=1,\ldots,m_\lambda$ and $\ell=1,\ldots,n_\lambda$. The state $\mathbf{Y}_f$ of f in the hidden layer $\lambda<D$ is computed by applying the *rectified linear activation function* (ReLU) to its excitation $\boldsymbol{\Xi}_f$ element-wise, that is,

$$y_f(k,\ell) = \max\big(0\,,\xi_f(k,\ell)\big) \quad \text{for every } k=1,\ldots,m_\lambda \text{ and } \ell=1,\ldots,n_\lambda\,. \quad (3)$$

For the output layer $\lambda=D$, the state $\mathbf{Y}_f=(y_f(1,1))=y_f$ of trivial macro-unit f with $m_\lambda=n_\lambda=1$ is computed as the *softmax function* of excitations $\boldsymbol{\Xi}_h = (\xi_h(1,1))=\xi_h$ for every output neuron $h\in Y$, that is, $y_f = e^{\xi_f}/(\sum_{h\in Y} e^{\xi_h}) \in (0,1)$. For the pooling layer $\lambda \in \Pi$ which satisfies $\sigma_\lambda = r_\lambda = s_\lambda$ and $\pi_\lambda = 0$, the state $\mathbf{Y}_f$ of f with $f_{\leftarrow}=\{g\}$, is computed as $y_f(k,\ell) = \max_{i,j\in\{1,\ldots,r_\lambda\}} y_g\big((k-1)r_\lambda + i\,,(\ell-1)r_\lambda + j\big)$ for every $k=1,\ldots,m_\lambda$ and $\ell=1,\ldots,n_\lambda$.

3 Energy Complexity Model

In this section, we introduce a simplified hardware-independent energy complexity model for evaluating a CNN defined in Sect. 2, which captures the main sources of power consumption in practical hardware implementations of CNNs. This model has a memory hierarchy with only two levels, called *DRAM* and *Buffer*, as schematically depicted in Fig. 1. The DRAM memory has an unlimited capacity (corresponding to a large, slow, and cheap memory) which is used for storing the entire CNN $\mathcal{N}$ including its filters $\mathbf{W}_{fg}$ and current states $\mathbf{Y}_f$ for all $f\in V$ and $g\in f_{\leftarrow}$. In contrast, the Buffer memory has a limited capacity of B bits (corresponding to a small, fast, and expensive memory) over which arithmetic operations are implemented, especially the *multiply-and-accumulate (MAC)* operations $S \leftarrow S + wy$ for evaluating excitations (2) of $\mathcal{N}$ where w, y, and S is a filter weight, a neuron state from a previous-layer feature map, and a partial sum accumulating an output of a current-layer neuron, respectively. Thus, in order to perform a MAC operation, the respective float values of its three arguments must simultaneously occur in Buffer which means they must

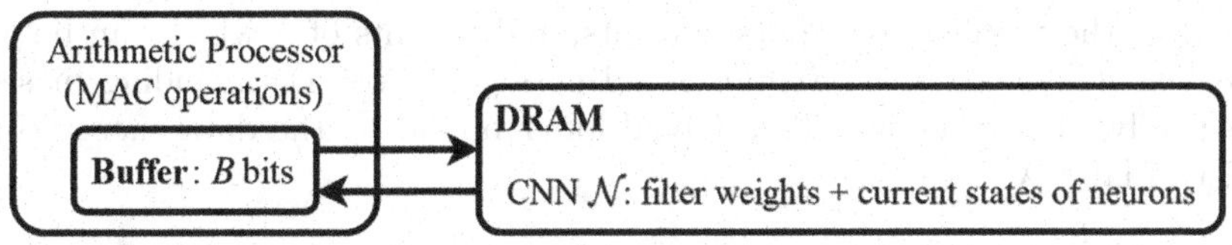

Fig. 1. The energy complexity model

be read from DRAM into Buffer at some point. On the other hand, the results of MACs are later written to DRAM due to the limited Buffer capacity. This requires (read/write) accesses to DRAM memory, which are energy consuming.

As has been discussed in Sect. 1, the energy complexity of evaluating $\mathcal{N}$ consists of the *computation energy* and the *data energy* [10]:

$$E = E_{\text{comp}} + E_{\text{data}} \tag{4}$$

which are related to the number of MACs and the number of DRAM accesses, respectively. For simplicity, we do not consider the energy optimization across multiple layers as e.g. in [1], which means energy complexity (4) is defined as a simple sum of energy costs over separate convolutional and fully-connected layers in $\mathcal{N}$ only, while the less energy-intensive max pooling layers are omitted:

$$E = \sum_{\lambda \in \{1,\ldots,D\} \setminus \Pi} \left(E^{\lambda}_{\text{comp}} + E^{\lambda}_{\text{data}} \right) \tag{5}$$

where $E^{\lambda}_{\text{comp}}$ is the computation energy and $E^{\lambda}_{\text{data}}$ is the data energy for evaluating a convolutional (or fully-connected) layer λ. For a particular layer $\lambda \in \{1,\ldots,D\} \setminus \Pi$, single-neuron states in layer $\lambda - 1$, λ, and corresponding filter weights are called *inputs*, *outputs*, and *weights of layer* λ, respectively.

The computation energy $E^{\lambda}_{\text{comp}}$ is defined as the number of MACs in layer $\lambda \in \{1,\ldots,D\} \setminus \Pi$, multiplied by a parameter C_b that depends on the number of bits b in floating-point MAC operations. This dependence is apparently not uniform (e.g. not linear) since the design of a MAC circuit inside a microprocessor differs for each b, which means there is no program generating a MAC circuit for each b (i.e. a nonuniformity assumption known from circuit complexity theory). The number of MACs in layer λ equals to the number $d_\lambda m_\lambda n_\lambda$ of single-neuron excitations (2) in layer λ (i.e. the number of outputs of λ), multiplied by the number $d_{\lambda-1} r_\lambda s_\lambda$ of inputs to λ that contribute to each of these excitations, which gives

$$E^{\lambda}_{\text{comp}} = C_b \, d_\lambda m_\lambda n_\lambda \, d_{\lambda-1} r_\lambda s_\lambda \,. \tag{6}$$

The data energy $E^{\lambda}_{\text{data}}$ is defined as the number of read and write accesses to DRAM when evaluating layer $\lambda \in \{1,\ldots,D\} \setminus \Pi$, multiplied by the number b of bits in a floating-point representation of numbers to be transferred between DRAM and Buffer. This energy complexity can be split into three components that count the DRAM accesses separately for the inputs, outputs, and weights:

$$E^{\lambda}_{\text{data}} = E^{\lambda}_{\text{inputs}} + E^{\lambda}_{\text{outputs}} + E^{\lambda}_{\text{weights}} \,. \tag{7}$$

Obviously, the numbers of inputs, outputs, and weights of λ which can be calculated as $d_{\lambda-1}m_{\lambda-1}n_{\lambda-1}$, $d_\lambda m_\lambda n_\lambda$, and $d_\lambda(d_{\lambda-1}r_\lambda s_\lambda + 1)$ (including biases), respectively, altogether provide a trivial lower bound on the data energy complexity of layer λ:

$$E_{\text{data}}^{\lambda} \geq b\,(d_{\lambda-1}m_{\lambda-1}n_{\lambda-1} + d_\lambda m_\lambda n_\lambda + d_\lambda(d_{\lambda-1}r_\lambda s_\lambda + 1)) \tag{8}$$

since all the inputs and weights must be read into Buffer at least once and all the evaluated outputs are eventually written to DRAM.

4 Upper Bounds on Energy Complexity

In the following two subsections, we present two common dataflows for evaluating a convolutional layer $\lambda \in \{1, \ldots, D\} \setminus \Pi$ and calculate their theoretical data energy complexity $E_{\text{data}}^{\lambda}$. In the first dataflow, each output is written to DRAM only once and in the second one, each input is read into Buffer only once, while each weight (including bias) is read into Buffer just one time in both dataflows, that is,

$$E_{\text{weights}}^{\lambda} = b\,d_\lambda(d_{\lambda-1}r_\lambda s_\lambda + 1)\,. \tag{9}$$

We will assume a sufficiently large capacity of Buffer:

$$B \geq b\,(2m_\lambda n_\lambda + 1)\,. \tag{10}$$

Moreover, let $K = \{1, \ldots, r_\lambda\} \times \{1, \ldots, s_\lambda\}$ be a set of all kernel indices in layer λ and for any $(i_0, j_0) \in K$, define a subset of K,

$$[(i_0, j_0)] = \{(i_0 + k\sigma_\lambda, j_0 + \ell\sigma_\lambda) \in K \mid k, \ell \in \mathbb{Z}\} \tag{11}$$

where σ_λ is a corresponding stride and $\mathbb{Z}$ denotes the set of integers. Observe that the set $P = \{[(i_0, j_0)] \mid (i_0, j_0) \in K\}$ creates a partition of K which consists of $|P| = \sigma_\lambda^2$ disjoint parts $[i, j]$ for every $i = 1, \ldots, \sigma_\lambda$ and $j = 1, \ldots, \sigma_\lambda$.

4.1 The Dataflow with Write-Once Outputs

We describe the dataflow in which each output is written to DRAM only once. For each macro-unit f in layer λ, one after the other, its excitation Ξ_f of size $m_\lambda n_\lambda$ floats is accumulated in Buffer (cf. its capacity (10)) according to (2) as follows. At the beginning, the bias b_f is read into Buffer (corresponding to 1 DRAM access inside the parentheses in (9)), which initializes the evaluation of Ξ_f. Then for each macro-unit $g \in f_{\leftarrow}$ and for each part $[(i_0, j_0)]$ of the partition P, one by one, the collection of $m_\lambda n_\lambda$ inputs to f,

$$y_g\big((k-1)\sigma_\lambda - \pi_\lambda + i_0\,, (\ell-1)\sigma_\lambda - \pi_\lambda + j_0\big) \tag{12}$$

for every $k = 1, \ldots, m_\lambda$ and $\ell = 1, \ldots, n_\lambda$, is read into Buffer with space left still for at least one float according to (10), which is reserved for one weight.

The indices of inputs in (12), $(k_1-1)\sigma_\lambda - \pi_\lambda + i_0 = (k_2-1)\sigma_\lambda - \pi_\lambda + i$ and $(\ell_1-1)\sigma_\lambda - \pi_\lambda + j_0 = (\ell_2-1)\sigma_\lambda - \pi_\lambda + j$ coincide for some $k_1, k_2 \in \{1,\ldots,m_\lambda\}$, $\ell_1, \ell_2 \in \{1,\ldots,n_\lambda\}$, and $(i,j) \in K$ iff $i = i_0 + k\sigma_\lambda$ and $j = j_0 + \ell\sigma_\lambda$ for $k = k_1 - k_2$ and $\ell = \ell_1 - \ell_2$ iff $(i,j) \in [i_0, j_0]$ due to (11). This means that in (2) each input (12) from this collection is multiplied only by weights $w_{fg}(i,j)$ such that $(i,j) \in [i_0, j_0]$, which are read one by one into Buffer and the respective MACs are performed. The partition P ensures that each weight and each input is read into Buffer only once for one macro-unit f over all parts of P and $g \in f_{\leftarrow}$, which implies (9). After the excitation Ξ_f is eventually evaluated, the state $\mathbf{Y}_f \in \mathbb{R}^{m_\lambda \times n_\lambda}$ of macro-unit f is computed according to (3) and written to DRAM.

Altogether, each output is thus written to DRAM only once, which gives

$$E^\lambda_{\text{outputs}} = b\, d_\lambda m_\lambda n_\lambda \,, \tag{13}$$

while each input is read once for every macro-unit f in layer λ, which implies

$$E^\lambda_{\text{inputs}} = b\, d_\lambda d_{\lambda-1} m_{\lambda-1} n_{\lambda-1} \,. \tag{14}$$

The dataflow provides the following upper bound on the data energy of layer λ:

$$E^\lambda_{\text{data}} \le b\, d_\lambda \left(d_{\lambda-1} m_{\lambda-1} n_{\lambda-1} + m_\lambda n_\lambda + d_{\lambda-1} r_\lambda s_\lambda + 1\right) \tag{15}$$

according to (7), (14), (13), and (9), which differs only in the number of DRAM accesses for reading inputs by factor d_λ from the trivial lower bound (8).

In addition, we will introduce an alternative dataflow of the same data energy (15), provided that Buffer capacity is bounded as

$$B \ge b\left(m_\lambda n_\lambda + r_\lambda s_\lambda + 1\right) , \tag{16}$$

cf. (10). For each macro-unit f in layer λ, one after the other, its excitation Ξ_f of size $m_\lambda n_\lambda$ floats is accumulated in Buffer according to (2), starting with the bias b_f which is read into Buffer to initialize the evaluation of Ξ_f. Next, for each $g \in f_{\leftarrow}$, one by one, the filter $\mathbf{W}_{fg} \in \mathbb{R}^{r_\lambda \times s_\lambda}$ of size $r_\lambda s_\lambda$ is first read into Buffer, followed by single inputs $y_g(k_0, \ell_0)$, one after the other, for every $k_0 = 1,\ldots,m_{\lambda-1}$ and $\ell_0 = 1,\ldots,n_{\lambda-1}$. For each such an input $y_g(k_0, \ell_0)$, all partially evaluated excitations $\xi_f(k,\ell)$ such that $k_0 = (k-1)\sigma_\lambda - \pi_\lambda + i$ and $\ell_0 = (\ell-1)\sigma_\lambda - \pi_\lambda + j$ for some $(i,j) \in K$, are updated in Buffer by performing MACs with corresponding weights $w_{fg}(i,j)$ etc. After Ξ_f is eventually evaluated, the corresponding output $\mathbf{Y}_f \in \mathbb{R}^{m_\lambda \times n_\lambda}$ is computed by (3) and written to DRAM. Clearly, each weight and each input is read into Buffer once for one macro-unit f, which proves the upper bound (15) also for this alternative dataflow.

4.2 The Dataflow with Read-Once Inputs

We describe the dataflow in which each input is read into Buffer only once. For each macro-unit g in layer $\lambda - 1$ and each part $[(i_0, j_0)]$ of the partition P, one after the other, the collection (12) of $m_\lambda n_\lambda$ inputs are read into Buffer to accumulate excitations Ξ_f for every $f \in g^{\rightarrow}$ according to (2) as follows. For each macro-unit $f \in g^{\rightarrow}$, one by one, either its bias b_f is read into Buffer to initialize the evaluation of Ξ_f at the beginning (when the very first collection (12) is in Buffer) or its partially evaluated excitation Ξ_f of size $m_\lambda n_\lambda$ floats is read into Buffer, over which the respective MACs are performed. For this purpose, the corresponding weights $w_{fg}(i,j)$ such that $(i,j) \in [i_0, j_0]$ are one by one read into Buffer. Then, either the partially evaluated excitation Ξ_f is written to DRAM, or at the end when Ξ_f is completely evaluated (after the very last collection (12) over all pairs of macro-units g and parts of P, is in Buffer), Ξ_f is used for computing the state $\mathbf{Y}_f \in \mathbb{R}^{m_\lambda \times n_\lambda}$ of macro-unit f according to (3), which is written to DRAM. The dataflow is thus implemented within Buffer capacity (10).

Moreover, the partition P ensures that each weight (including bias) as well as each input is read into Buffer only once, which implies (9) and

$$E^{\lambda}_{\text{inputs}} = b\, d_{\lambda-1} m_{\lambda-1} n_{\lambda-1}\,, \tag{17}$$

respectively. Any accumulated excitation is read (except for its initialization by a bias at the beginning) and written once for each of the $d_{\lambda-1}$ macro-units in layer $\lambda - 1$ and each part of the σ_λ^2 parts of partition P, which gives

$$E^{\lambda}_{\text{outputs}} = b\left(2d_{\lambda-1}\sigma_\lambda^2 - 1\right) d_\lambda m_\lambda n_\lambda\,. \tag{18}$$

Hence, this dataflow provides another upper bound on the data energy of layer λ:

$$E^{\lambda}_{\text{data}} \le b\left(d_{\lambda-1} m_{\lambda-1} n_{\lambda-1} + \left(2d_{\lambda-1}\sigma_\lambda^2 - 1\right) d_\lambda m_\lambda n_\lambda + d_\lambda \left(d_{\lambda-1} r_\lambda s_\lambda + 1\right)\right) \tag{19}$$

according to (7), (17), (18), and (9). This bound is comparable to (15) if the number of single neurons in layers λ and $\lambda - 1$ is roughly the same, that is, $d_{\lambda-1} m_{\lambda-1} n_{\lambda-1} \approx d_\lambda m_\lambda n_\lambda$, since $\sigma_\lambda^2 m_\lambda n_\lambda \approx m_{\lambda-1} n_{\lambda-1}$ according to (1). Nevertheless, the multiplicative constant 2 of leading term $d_\lambda d_{\lambda-1} m_{\lambda-1} n_{\lambda-1}$ in (19), which is caused by storing partially evaluated excitations into DRAM, makes the upper bound (15) more tight than (19).

5 Experimental Validation

In this section, we compare the theoretical energy complexity introduced in Sect. 3 to the real power consumption estimated by the Timeloop/Accelergy software tool [5,9] for evaluating DNN accelerator designs. The Timeloop finds an optimal mapping of a convolutional layer specified by its parameters onto a given hardware platform in terms of power consumption estimated by Accelergy which reports the energy statistics. Namely, we have employed Simba [6] and Eyeriss [2] as the target platforms onto which convolutional layers with increasing architectural parameters (i.e. not filter weights) have been mapped. All configuration files used in experiments are publicly available at Github[1].

[1] https://github.com/PetraVidnerova/timeloop-accelergy-test.

Table 1. Required Buffer Capacities for AlexNet Convolutional Layers in Kilobytes.

λ	1	2	3	4	5
$m_\lambda = n_\lambda$	55	27	13	13	13
d_λ	64	192	384	256	256
$r_\lambda = s_\lambda$	11	5	3	3	3
σ_λ	4	1	1	1	1
(10): $2m_\lambda^2 + 1$	6051	1459	339	339	339
$b = 8$ bits	5.91 kB	1.42 kB	0.33 kB	0.33 kB	0.33 kB
$b = 16$ bits	11.82 kB	2.85 kB	0.66 kB	0.66 kB	0.66 kB
$b = 32$ bits	23.64 kB	5.7 kB	1.32 kB	1.32 kB	1.32 kB
(16): $m_\lambda^2 + r_\lambda^2 + 1$	3147	755	179	179	179
$b = 8$ bits	3.07 kB	0.74 kB	0.17 kB	0.17 kB	0.17 kB
$b = 16$ bits	6.15 kB	1.47 kB	0.35 kB	0.35 kB	0.35 kB
$b = 32$ bits	12.29 kB	2.95 kB	0.7 kB	0.7 kB	0.7 kB

The computation energy reported by Timeloop/Accelergy corresponds directly to the number of MACs calculated in (6) for E_{comp}^λ where C_b is the energy per one MAC operation which was estimated as $C_8 = 0.56\,pJ$ and $C_{16} = 2.20\,pJ$ for 8-bit Simba and 16-bit Eyeriss architectures, respectively.

For a convolutional layer λ, we measure empirical dependencies of the optimal data energy separately on its depth d_λ, input feature map size $m_{\lambda-1} = n_{\lambda-1}$, kernel size $r_\lambda = s_\lambda$, and stride σ_λ (starting with the parameter values of the first AlexNet layer), by using the Timeloop/Accelergy framework for the Simba and Eyeriss architectures. These dependencies are then compared to corresponding asymptotic upper bounds on E_{data}^λ in the energy complexity model:

$$E_{\text{data}}^\lambda = O\left(d_\lambda\right)\,,\; E_{\text{data}}^\lambda = O\left(m_{\lambda-1}^2\right)\,,\; E_{\text{data}}^\lambda = O\left(r_\lambda^2\right)\,,\; E_{\text{data}}^\lambda = O\left(\sigma_\lambda^{-2}\right)\,, \quad (20)$$

which are derived from (15) for individual variables (when the other independent parameters are considered to be constant) by using the approximation $m_{\lambda-1}^2 \approx \sigma_\lambda^2 m_\lambda^2$ due to (1). Nevertheless, the asymptotic bounds (20) assume a sufficient Buffer capacity satisfying (10) or (16). Table 1 shows required Buffer capacities for AlexNet convolutional layers in kilobytes (kB) which appear in an order of magnitude to be realistic to common hardware architectures such as Eyeriss [2].

Figure 2 presents the results of experimental comparison of energy-efficient CNN hardware implementations to our theoretical energy complexity model. By using the Timeloop/Accelergy tool applied to the Simba and Eyeriss hardware architectures, the optimal values of their data energy consumption have been estimated for AlexNet-like convolutional layers λ with increasing parameters d_λ, $m_{\lambda-1} = n_{\lambda-1}$, $r_\lambda = s_\lambda$, and σ_λ, each separately. These parameters serve as independent variables in regression analysis where the relationships between the data energy and the independent variables are modeled as functions with asymptotics (20), including multiplicative and additive coefficients c_2 and c_1,

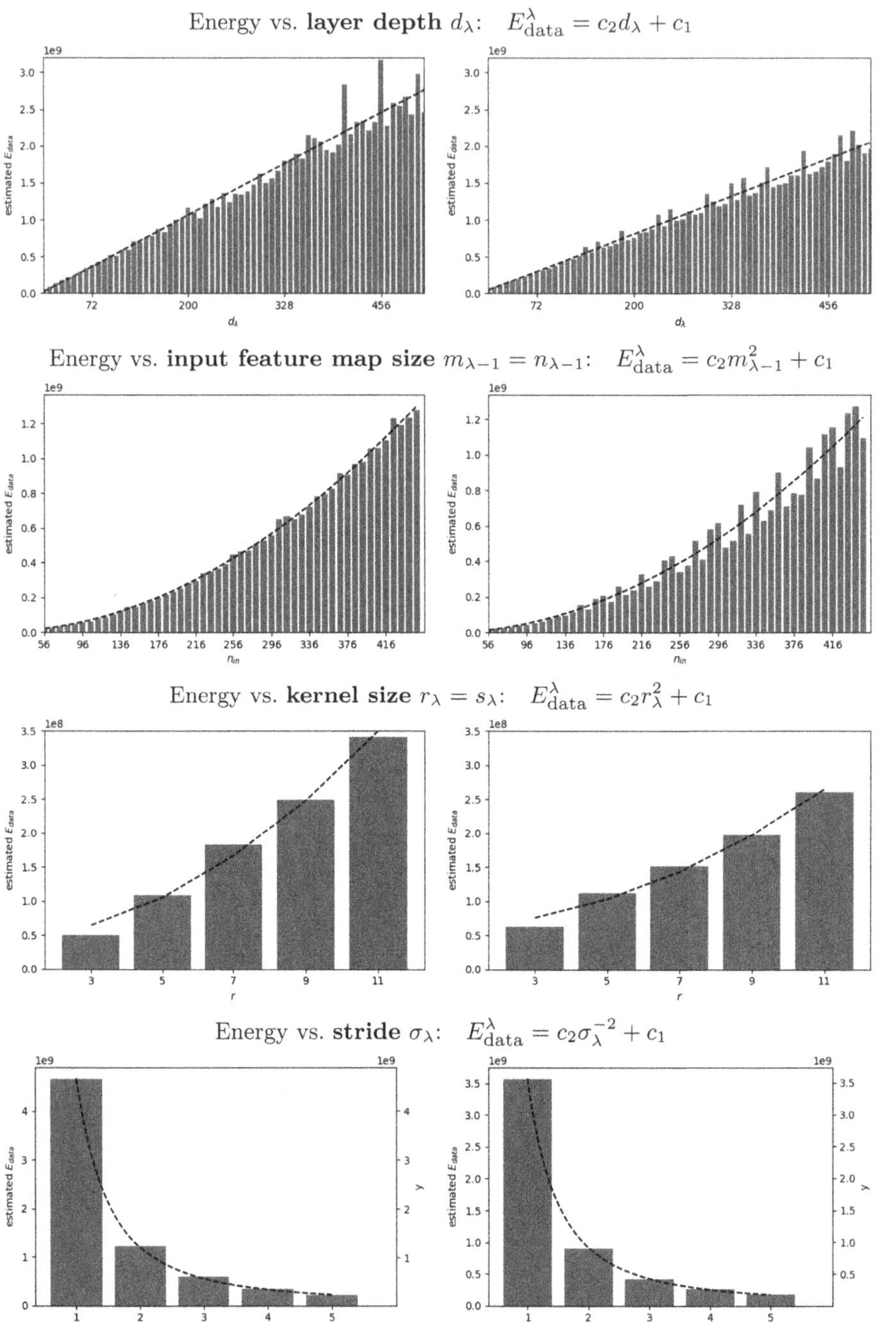

Fig. 2. The data energy estimates by Timeloop/Accelergy (displayed by bars) for AlexNet-like convolutional layer λ with increasing parameters d_λ, $m_{\lambda-1}$,r_λ, and σ_λ, each separately (from top to bottom), on the Simba (left) and Eyeriss (right) architectures, which fit the asymptotic trends (20) in the energy complexity model (dashed lines).

respectively. As depicted in Fig. 2, these coefficients are approximated by the method of least squares so that the theoretical data energy $E_{\text{data}}^{\lambda}$ (dashed lines) fits energy estimates by Timeloop/Accelergy (displayed by bars), which confirms the asymptotic trends (20) in the energy complexity model. In addition, the energy complexity model has been validated by statistical tests using quadratic regression with the function model $ax^2 + bx + c$ for independent variable x to be d_λ, $m_{\lambda-1}$, r_λ, and σ_λ^{-1}, respectively. These statistical tests have approved the linearity in d_λ (p-value 0.556 accepting the null hypothesis of $a = 0$) and the quadraticity in $m_{\lambda-1}$ r_λ, and σ_λ^{-1} (p-value 0.000, 0.001, and 0.000, respectively, rejecting the null hypothesis of $a = 0$).

6 Conclusion

In this paper, we have introduced a hardware-independent energy complexity model for CNNs that captures asymptotically all important sources of power consumption of their diverse hardware implementations. Upper bounds on energy complexity have been derived in this model for two common energy-efficient dataflows. The underlying theoretical asymptotic trends have been validated by statistical tests to fit the energy consumption estimated by the Timeloop/Accelergy program for CNNs of AlexNet-like architectures on the Simba and Eyeriss hardware platforms. In future research we plan to prove matching lower bounds on the data energy for convolutional layers. Partial results along this direction have already been achieved for a special case of fully-connected layers [7]. The proposed model thus allows to determine the principal limits to which heuristic optimizers e.g. based on evolutionary algorithms [3] can reach.

Acknowledgements. The research was supported by the Czech Science Foundation grant GA22-02067S and the institutional support RVO: 67985807 (J. Šíma, P. Vidnerová). We thank Jan Kalina for his advice on statistical tests.

References

1. Alwani, M., et al.: Fused-layer CNN accelerators. In: Proceedings of the IEEE/ACM MICRO 2016, pp. 22:1–22:12 (2016). https://doi.org/10.1109/MICRO.2016.7783725
2. Chen, Y., Emer, J.S., Sze, V.: Eyeriss: A spatial architecture for energy-efficient dataflow for convolutional neural networks. In: Proceedings of the ACM/IEEE ISCA 2016, pp. 367–379 (2016). https://doi.org/10.1109/ISCA.2016.40
3. Kao, S.C., Krishna, T.: GAMMA: Automating the HW mapping of DNN models on accelerators via genetic algorithm. In: Proceedings of the ACM/IEEE ICCAD 2020, pp. 44:1–44:9 (2020). https://doi.org/10.1145/3400302.3415639
4. Mittal, S.: A survey of techniques for approximate computing. ACM Comput. Surv. **48**(4), 62:1–62:33 (2016). https://doi.org/10.1145/2893356
5. Parashar, A., et al.: Timeloop: A systematic approach to DNN accelerator evaluation. In: Proceedings of the IEEE ISPASS 2019, pp. 304–315 (2019). https://doi.org/10.1109/ISPASS.2019.00042

6. Shao, Y.S., et al.: Simba: Scaling deep-learning inference with multi-chip-module-based architecture. In: Proceedings of the IEEE/ACM MICRO 2019, pp. 14–27 (2019). https://doi.org/10.1145/3352460.3358302
7. Šíma, J., Cabessa, J.: Energy complexity of fully-connected layers. In: Proceedings of the IWANN 2023. LNCS 14134, Part I, Springer, Berlin (2023)
8. Sze, V., Chen, Y., Yang, T., Emer, J.S.: Efficient Processing of Deep Neural Networks. Synthesis Lectures on Computer Architecture. Morgan & Claypool Publishers (2020). https://doi.org/10.2200/S01004ED1V01Y202004CAC050
9. Wu, Y.N., Emer, J.S., Sze, V.: Accelergy: An architecture-level energy estimation methodology for accelerator designs. In: Proceedings of the IEEE/ACM ICCAD 2019 (2019). https://doi.org/10.1109/ICCAD45719.2019.8942149
10. Yang, T., Chen, Y., Emer, J.S., Sze, V.: A method to estimate the energy consumption of deep neural networks. In: Proceedings of the IEEE ACSSC 2017, pp. 1916–1920 (2017). https://doi.org/10.1109/ACSSC.2017.8335698

Enhancing the Interpretability of Deep Multi-agent Reinforcement Learning via Neural Logic Reasoning

Bokai Ji[1], Guangxia Li[1(✉)], and Gang Xiao[2]

[1] School of Computer Science and Technology, Xidian University, Xi'an, China
jibokai@stu.xidian.edu.cn, gxli@xidian.edu.cn
[2] National Key Laboratory for Complex Systems Simulation, Beijing, China
searchware@qq.com

Abstract. Explaining the decision-making policies of deep reinforcement learning is challenging owing to the black-box nature of neural networks. We address this challenge by combining deep learning models and symbolic structures into a neural-logic model that reasons in the form of neural logic programming. The proposed explainable multi-agent reinforcement learning algorithm performs reasoning in a symbolic-represented environment using multi-hop reasoning, a relational path-searching method that uses prior symbolic knowledge. Furthermore, to alleviate the partial observability problem in multi-agent systems, we devised an explainable history module using an attention mechanism to incorporate past experiences while preserving interpretability. Experimental studies demonstrate that the proposed method can effectively learn close-to-optimal policies while generating expressive rules to explain the decisions. Particularly, it can learn more abstract concepts than conventional neural network approaches.

Keywords: reinforcement learning · multi-agent · neural logic programming

1 Introduction

Reinforcement learning provides a computational model of how intelligent agents can learn by interacting with their environment. Its integration with deep neural networks has led to an active research area called deep reinforcement learning, whose recent successes in robotics, computer games, and natural language processing have significantly impressed the public. Although most deep reinforcement learning methods involve a single-agent, many real-world tasks involve multiple agents acting together in a shared environment. This naturally falls into multi-agent reinforcement learning (MARL), which is more challenging than its single-agent counterpart. Because all agents in the MARL system act and learn concurrently, their transitions and rewards do not depend only on

This work was supported by the Fund of State Key Laboratory, China under Grant No. XM2020XT1006.

L. Iliadis et al. (Eds.): ICANN 2023, LNCS 14263, pp. 199–210, 2023.
https://doi.org/10.1007/978-3-031-44204-9_17

the current state of a single-agent. This makes the environment nonstationary from the perspective of any agent; thus, it invalidates the Markov assumption that most single-agent reinforcement learning algorithms depend on. Furthermore, the observation and action spaces grow exponentially as the number of agents increases, making single-agent algorithms computationally infeasible in the MARL setting.

In addition to these challenges, MARL methods are often criticized for failing to explain their actions and decisions in human-understandable terms. The lack of interpretability is largely ascribed to the underlying deep neural networks. Neural networks embody the spirit of the connectionist approach, which believes that artificial intelligence can be derived through the interconnections of neuron-like processing units, similar to how the human brain functions. The connectionist approach has always been criticized for using excessive data and computing power for training. The trained models cannot be effectively generalized and are largely opaque to humans. By contrast, its symbolic counterpart presumes that intelligence can be achieved by manipulating symbols through rules and logic operating on those symbols; thus, it can be easily interpreted. As the limitations of using either symbolic or connectionist approaches in isolation have already been identified, some argue that the two approaches must be hybridized, particularly when attempting to enhance the interpretability of deep MARL models.

Inductive logic programming (ILP), a classical symbolic machine learning approach that uses logic programs (sets of logical rules) to induce hypotheses from examples, has been implemented in a gradient-compatible form (i.e., differentiable inductive logic programming (DILP) [1]) to build a hybrid neural-symbolic end-to-end reinforcement learning system [3]. Despite its promising performance in terms of interpretability and generalizability, ILP and its neural-compatible form, DILP, suffer from scalability problems. For instance, their rule search space grows exponentially with the length of the rule [9]. Although they are limited to small-scale problems, most ILP-based methods have high computing costs, particularly when multiple agents are involved [5]. Alternatively, multi-hop reasoning learns first-order logic rules through a relational path search over a knowledge graph [8,9]. Because relations are represented as sparse matrices and reasoning steps are implemented by matrix multiplication, multi-hop reasoning is highly efficient and differentiable. It can be integrated with the connectionist approach to form a neural-logic network that is computationally tractable and explainable.

In this study, we applied multi-hop reasoning to the MARL setting to devise an efficient MARL algorithm with good interpretability. Similar to the existing multi-hop reasoning-based learning method [9], the proposed algorithm induces policies from background knowledge via a set of neural-logic modules and provides explainable chain-like rules. We further alleviated the nonstationary problem in MARL by incorporating global and historical information of the environment during learning. Global information sharing among agents was achieved through centralized training with distributed execution architecture that learns high-level communication across agents. Although long short-term memory (LSTM) has been applied to record historical information [6], it tends to distort the semantics of symbolic representation. Thus, we proposed a linear explainable history module that uses an attention mechanism to preserve interpretability. The proposed algorithm was evaluated in a multi-agent collaborative environment with a deep Q-network (DQN) as the baseline. The experimental results demonstrate that our method learns interpretable policies at a more abstract level and outperforms the DQN in terms of return and convergence speed.

2 Preliminary

2.1 First Order Logic

A typical first-order logic system comprises three components: entities, predicates, and formulas. Predicates describe the relationships among the entities. For instance, $In(bird, tree)$ means that a *bird* is in the *tree*, where *bird* and *tree* are entities. This expression can be generalized to $In(X, Y)$, where X and Y are logical variables that specify the entities. An atom $\alpha = P(t_1, t_2, \ldots, t_n)$ is the basic unit in first-order logic, where t denotes the terms that can be variables or entities. When all the terms in α are constants, α becomes a ground truth. Formulas are combinations of atoms using logical connectives $\{\wedge, \vee, \neg\}$, which match the logic *and*, *or*, and *not*, respectively. A formula becomes a clause when it fits the restricted form $\alpha \leftarrow \alpha_1 \wedge \alpha_2 \wedge \ldots \wedge \alpha_n$, where α is the head atom, and $\alpha_1 \wedge \alpha_2 \wedge \ldots \wedge \alpha_n$ are the body atoms. A grounded clause implies that all body atoms are grounded. Because body atoms are connected with the $\wedge$ connective in a clause, the head atom holds when all the body atoms hold.

Learning such first-order logic clauses helps humans read, understand, and verify the decisions made by algorithms. One approach that can achieve this goal is ILP, which induces clausal theories from examples and background knowledge through the inductive construction of first-order logic. Specifically, ILP aims to develop hypotheses from examples and synthesize new knowledge from experience. Examples and background knowledge are represented as a set of atoms. These atoms can be viewed as a graph, in which the nodes and edges are the entities and edges are corresponding predicates, respectively.

2.2 Multi-hop Reasoning

As solving the ILP problem can be cast as searching rules on the graph, it is considered closely related to multi-hop reasoning, which attempts to search for rules over the background knowledge. The rules that multi-hop reasoning searches for are chain-like rules in the following form:

$$query(x, x') \leftarrow R_1(x, z_1) \wedge R_2(z_1, z_2) \wedge \ldots \wedge R_n(z_n, x'). \quad (1)$$

Specifically, multi-hop reasoning aims to search for a reasoning path between entities x and x' on the background knowledge, given $query(x, x')$. This reasoning process can be considered as a series of matrix multiplications [8]. Consider a background knowledge with a set of entities $\mathcal{X}$ and a set of predicates $\mathcal{P}$. This can be represented by $|\mathcal{P}|$ adjacency matrices $M_1, \ldots, M_{|\mathcal{P}|} \in \{0,1\}^{|\mathcal{X}| \times |\mathcal{X}|}$. For any predicate $P(i,j)$ where i and j are arbitrary entities in the environment, $M(i,j) = 1$ if $P(i,j)$ is true; otherwise, $M(i,j) = 0$. Let v_x be the one-hot encoding of entity x. The t-th hop of reasoning can be computed as

$$\mathbf{v}^0 = \mathbf{v}_x \tag{2a}$$

$$\mathbf{v}^t = M^t \mathbf{v}^{t-1} \tag{2b}$$

where M^t denotes the chosen matrix in the t-th step of reasoning, and $\mathbf{v}^{t-1}$ denotes the path vector that encodes the inference above. After T reasoning steps, the reasoning quality can be computed as

$$score(x, x') = \mathbf{v}_x^T (\prod_{t=1}^{T} M^t) \mathbf{v}_{x'} \tag{3}$$

where T denotes the maximum length of reasoning. With the help of the attention mechanism, the reasoning process can be relaxed to consider all possible lengths and reasoning steps; that is,

$$\mathcal{K}(\mathbf{S}_\psi, \mathbf{S}_\varphi) = \sum_{t'=1}^{T} s_\psi^{(t')} (\prod_{t=1}^{t'} \sum_{k=1}^{\mathcal{P}} s_{\varphi,k}^{(t)} \mathbf{M}_k) \tag{4}$$

where $s_{\varphi,k}^{(t)}$ denotes the predicate attention weight of P_k in the t-th hop reasoning, $S_\psi^{(t')}$ represents the path attention weight of length t', and $|\mathcal{P}|$ is the number of predefined predicates.

3 Methodology

3.1 Problem Setting

We consider a fully cooperative MARL setting, in which n agents collaborate to achieve a goal. It can be formed as a partially observable Markov game containing a set of states $\mathcal{S}$ corresponding to the entire environment, a collection of action sets $\mathcal{A}_1, \ldots, \mathcal{A}_n$ (one for each agent in the environment), and a collection of observation sets $\mathcal{H}_1, \ldots, \mathcal{H}_n$ representing each agent's individual observations of the environment. The observations are represented in terms of first-order logic using a set of entities $\mathcal{X}$ and a set of predicates $\mathcal{P}$. They are subsequently transformed into $|\mathcal{P}|$ adjacency matrices $M_1, \ldots, M_{|\mathcal{P}|}$, similar to the multi-hop reasoning learning. In each round, agent i chooses an action by using a stochastic policy $\pi_{\theta_i} : \mathcal{H}_i \times \mathcal{A}_i \mapsto [0,1]$ and receives a team reward $r : \mathcal{S} \times \mathcal{A}_1 \times \cdots \times \mathcal{A}_n \mapsto \mathbb{R}$. Subsequently, a transition to a new state occurs according to the transition function $P : \mathcal{S} \times \mathcal{A}_1 \times \cdots \times \mathcal{A}_n \mapsto \mathcal{S}$, and new observations $h_i : S \mapsto \mathcal{H}_i$ are perceived simultaneously. The goal of MARL is to maximize the discounted cumulative team reward $G = \sum_{t=0}^{T} \gamma \cdot r_t$, where γ is the discount factor and T is the horizon of the game. In addition, we generated chain-like first-order logic rules that can explain agent actions during the learning process.

3.2 Framework

We proposed an explainable multi-agent reinforcement learning (EMARL) algorithm using the value-decomposition network (VDN) [7]. Figure 1 illustrates a simplified version of this architecture involving two agents. Building on two independent DQN-style agents with individual observations, and action-value functions (Q functions), it combines the two Q functions into a joint function. During the centralized training phase, a single team reward is given. Each agent adjusts its own action-value function $\tilde{Q}_i$ to optimize the team reward by backpropagating the gradient of the joint Q function through deep neural networks. Meanwhile, each agent can only access its local observations and make greedy decisions with respect to its own value function $\tilde{Q}_i$ in the decentralized execution phase.

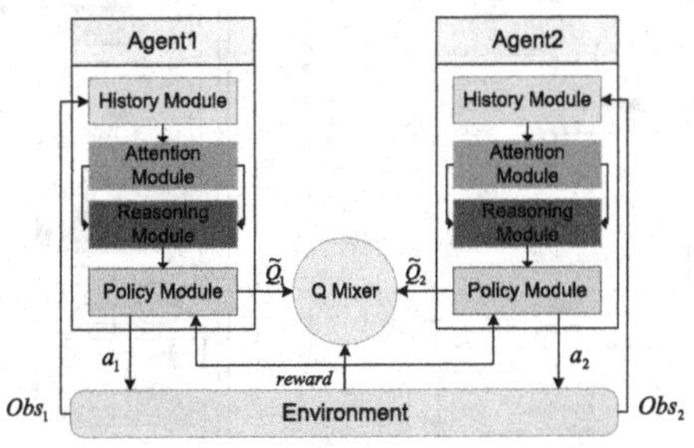

Fig. 1. Value-decomposition network [7] used by the explainable multi-agent reinforcement learning algorithm.

We devised a value-decomposition-compatible agent that can overcome the challenges of MARL (i.e., partial observability and a nonstationary environment) while providing chain-like logic rules to preserve interpretability. Each agent is composed of history, attention, reasoning, and policy modules. The history module takes the current observation as input and concatenates it with several past observations stored in a history buffer. The attention module receives a hybrid observation generated by the history module, selects predicates for each reasoning step by generating predicate attentions, and determines the length of the reasoning path according to the path attention. Using the predicate and path attentions, the reasoning module encodes the selected information into a reasoning matrix M_{reason}, which is forwarded to the policy module to produce a Q-value distribution of actions. Chain-like logic rules can be extracted by selecting predicates and paths with the maximum attention weights. These rules can be used to explain an agent's decision-making policies at any stage of the learning process, although meaningful explanations tend to emerge when the learning process converges. These modules are described in detail in the following section.

3.3 History Module

It has been demonstrated that the DQN underperforms in the MARL setting because agents can only access incomplete state information. Incorporating historical observations can alleviate this problem [2], and LSTM was used for this purpose in a previous study [7]. However, LSTM is unsuitable for our method, as it would distort the semantics of symbolic representation and interfere with model interpretation. Thus, we proposed using an attention mechanism to provide historical information while preserving the semantics of symbolic representation. This was performed by additively aggregating k historical and current

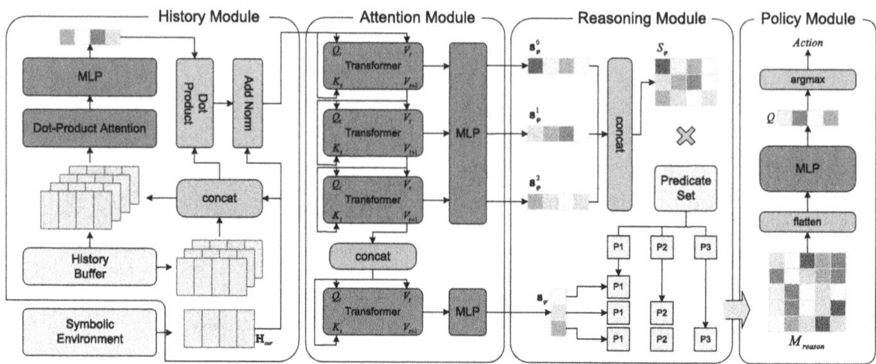

Fig. 2. Anatomy of the devised agent for the explainable multi-agent reinforcement learning algorithm.

observations according to their self-attention weights. Because the observations are represented by predicates using adjacency matrices and addition is a linear operation, the semantics of the predicates are naturally preserved.

As shown in Fig. 2, the history module takes an agent's current observation $\mathbf{H}_{cur} \in \{0,1\}^{|\mathcal{P}|\times|\mathcal{X}|\times|\mathcal{X}|}$ as input and concatenates it with k historical observations from a history buffer to form a total observation (i.e., $\mathbf{H}_{tot} \in \{0,1\}^{(k+1)\times|\mathcal{P}|\times|\mathcal{X}|\times|\mathcal{X}|}$). We reshaped $\mathbf{H}_{tot}$ into a matrix $H_{in} \in \{0,1\}^{(k+1)\times|\mathcal{P}||\mathcal{X}|^2}$ and considered it as a sequence of observation vectors. Naturally, each vector in this sequence represents an observation at a specific time step. Subsequently, we applied the dot-product attention (DPA) to H_{in} by assuming $Q, K, V = H_{in}$ and computing

$$S_h = softmax(\frac{QK^\top}{\sqrt{d}}), \text{ and } V' = SV \tag{5}$$

where d and S_h denote the length of the observation vector and attention matrix, respectively. We obtained weights $\mathbf{s}_h$, which describes the importance of observations at different time steps, by obtaining S_h through a multilayer perceptron (MLP). Finally, we generated a mixed observation blending $k+1$ observations as $\hat{H}_{in} = \mathbf{s}_h H_{in}$ and emphasized the current observation by performing a residual operation, resulting in a hybrid observation $H_{hybrid} = \ln(\hat{H}_{in}) + H_{cur}$. The hybrid observation $H_{hybrid} \in \mathbb{R}^{|\mathcal{P}|\times|\mathcal{X}|^2}$ can be considered as a sequence of predicates of length $|\mathcal{P}|$.

3.4 Attention Module

The attention module uses a stack of transformer encoder blocks to generate the attention weights. Instead of a discrete selection of predicates, soft picking is performed through a weighted combination of all candidate reasoning paths. For a neural-logic system with a maximum of T reasoning steps, we utilized $T+1$ layers of transformer encoder blocks, following the approach in [8]. Specifically, the first T layers correspond to the reasoning steps, whereas the last layer selects a reasoning path of an appropriate length from those generated by the previous T layers.

The predicate attention mechanism works as follows: We initialized Q_φ^0, K_φ^0, and V_φ^0 as H_{hybrid}, respectively. Subsequently, for every reasoning step $t \in [1, T]$, we used DPA to compute $V_\varphi^{t'}$ and the predicate attention matrix $\hat{S}_\varphi^{t'}$ with Q_φ^t, K_φ^t, and V_φ^t. To obtain the predicate attention weights for each reasoning step, we passed $\hat{S}_\varphi^{t'}$ through a multilayer perceptron (MLP), following the same approach used in the history module to compress S_h. Finally, feedforward networks were used to compute Q_φ^{t+1}, K_φ^{t+1}, and V_φ^{t+1} based on $V_\varphi^{t'}$. We concatenated the T resulting vectors $\mathbf{s}_\varphi^1, \ldots, \mathbf{s}_\varphi^T$ to obtain a predicate attention weight S_φ that encodes the soft selection of predicates across all reasoning steps.

To determine the most appropriate reasoning path among all candidates, we attempted to generate a path attention vector $\mathbf{s}_\psi$ that measures the appropriateness of different reasoning paths. Because the output V_φ^{t+1} of the t-th layer encodes information about the previous t reasoning steps, the outputs of the previous T layers $[V_\varphi^1, \ldots, V_\varphi^T]$ was collected into a three-dimensional tensor $\mathbf{M}_{path} \in \mathbb{R}^{T \times |\mathcal{P}| \times |\mathcal{X}|^2}$. We reshaped $\mathbf{M}_{path}$ into matrix $M_{path} \in \mathbb{R}^{T \times |\mathcal{P}||\mathcal{X}|^2}$, which represents a sequence of vectors of length $|\mathcal{P}||\mathcal{X}|^2$, each corresponding to a different reasoning path length. The path attention matrix S_ψ was generated as follows. We considered Q_ψ, K_ψ, and V_ψ to be the inputs to the DPA function. Subsequently V_ψ' and S_ψ was calculated by applying DPA to Q_ψ, K_ψ, and V_ψ. Similar to S_φ, the path attention weight vector $\mathbf{s}_\psi$ of length T was obtained by compressing $S_\psi \in \mathbb{R}^{T \times T}$ using an MLP.

3.5 Reasoning Module

Inspired by the multi-hop reasoning method [8], we proposed the identification of chain-like first-order logic rules by utilizing background knowledge that includes predicates and entities from observations. Recall that the multi-hop reasoning method requires a chain-like rule of length T with the following form:

$$Action(z_0, z_T) \leftarrow P_1(z_0, z_1) \wedge P_2(z_1, z_2) \wedge \ldots \wedge P_T(z_{T-1}, z_T). \qquad (6)$$

We relaxed this constraint by allowing an arbitrary number of entities to be assigned to the head atom *Action*, thereby facilitating the representation of a diverse range of RL actions regardless of the number of objects involved.

Another problem with chain-like rules is their limited expression abilities, resulting in their failure to represent even simple policies in some cases. For example, consider a toy problem in which an agent seeks a button on a plane. The policy "pressing the button when reaching it" can be expressed as $Press() \leftarrow At(X, Y) \wedge Button(X, Y)$, where X and Y are logic variables for the X- and Y-positions, respectively. Although it appears to be simple, this policy cannot be represented by chain-like rules because the former essentially depends on measuring two coordinates belonging to the same axis (e.g., whether X_{agent} is equal to X_{button}), whereas the latter can only express the relations between X and Y.

To solve this problem, we extended the chain-like rule by adding a set of transposed adjacency matrices to the background knowledge as in

$$\hat{\mathcal{M}} = \mathcal{M} \cup \{M^T : M \in \mathcal{M}\} \tag{7}$$

where $\mathcal{M}$ and M denote the background knowledge set and predicate adjacency matrix, respectively. With the help of the transposed adjacency matrices, we can represent the above policy as a chain-like rule: $Press() \leftarrow At(X,Y) \wedge Button^{\top}(Y,X) \wedge At(X,Y)$ or $Press() \leftarrow At^{\top}(Y,X) \wedge Button(X,Y) \wedge At^{\top}(Y,X)$. In the above expression, we used the transpose symbol to represent the flipped predicate. For example, $Bigger(X,Y)$ means X is bigger than Y, whereas the notation $Bigger^{\top}(X,Y)$ has the opposite meaning; that is, Y is bigger than X.

To this end, we focused on path attention $\mathbf{s}_{\psi}$, predicate attention S_{φ}, and a collection of predicates. The aim is to select an appropriate predicate for each reasoning step and pick an appropriate path of reasoning. The process that encodes the soft selection of predicates and paths into matrix M_{reason} can be formulated as follows:

$$M_{reason} = \sum_{t'=1}^{T} \mathbf{s}_{\psi}^{t'} (\prod_{t=1}^{t'} \sum_{k=1}^{2|\mathcal{P}|} \mathbf{s}_{\varphi,k}^{t} M_k), \text{ and } M_k \in \hat{\mathcal{M}} \tag{8}$$

where $s_{\varphi,k}^{t}$ and $S_{\psi}^{t'}$ denote the predicate attention weight of P_k in the t-th reasoning step and the path attention of length t', respectively.

3.6 Policy Module

The policy module generates reinforcement learning policies regarding M_{reason} as an embedded observation. Similar to DQN, the policy module derives an optimal policy π^* by approximating the action value function $Q^{\pi^*}(h,a)$ using an MLP as follows:

$$Q(h,a) = MLP(M_{reason}) \tag{9}$$

In particular, it learns by minimizing the loss

$$L(\theta) = \mathbb{E}_{h,a,r,h'}[Q(h,a|\theta) - y] \tag{10a}$$

$$y = r + \gamma \max_{a'} \bar{Q}(s',a') \tag{10b}$$

where $\bar{Q}$ is the target Q function, whose parameters are periodically updated with the parameter of Q function, r is the true reward of the time step, and γ is the discount factor.

In summary, the core of the proposed algorithm is a special designed interpretable deep Q-network that uses symbolic observations as input. It begins with a history module that aggregates current and historical observations to address the partial observation problem. The downstream attention module uses the hybrid observation to softly select appropriate predicates and paths. Human-readable rules can be extracted by selecting the predicates and paths with the maximum attention weight. The reasoning module further encodes these selections in a reasoning matrix, on which the policy module's decision depends.

4 Experimental Results

4.1 Experiment Setup

Fig. 3. The checker environment.

We evaluated the proposed method using a simplified variant of the checker environment, which is a classic multi-agent task developed in [4]. As shown in Fig. 3, the checker environment is composed of 6×3 grids, where the fruits (apples and lemons) are scattered. The two agents denoted by $A1$ and $A2$ act by choosing to move up, down, left, or right to reach a specific fruit. Once reached, the fruit disappears (i.e., it has been eaten), and a reward is given to the agent team. Interestingly, the reward is not generated evenly but is determined by the agent per se. One agent is sensitive: a team reward of 10 is given when it eats an apple, and a penalty of -10 is imposed when it eats a lemon. The other agent is less sensitive: a team reward of 1 and a penalty of -1 are obtained when it eats an apple and a lemon, respectively. The game ends when all the apples have been eaten by the agents. Therefore, two agents must cooperate and collect them tactically to maximize the overall team reward.

The optimal policy for the two agents as a whole is to let the sensitive agent eat all the apples but not the lemons. However, the sensitive agent cannot achieve this optimal policy on its own because the apples and lemons are arranged alternately. Thus, the less sensitive agent should collect lemons that stand between the sensitive agent and its target apples. Such a setting creates a conflict of interest between the individual agent and the group (because attaining apples is more beneficial from the perspective of the less sensitive agent) and demands sophisticated policies that can coordinate two agent actions.

The environment was represented by a set of predicates: $Zero(X)$, $Last(X)$, $Successor(X,Y)$, $Apple(X,Y)$, $Lemon(X,Y)$, $Type(X)$ and $Current(X,Y)$. Entities include the coordinate numbers $\{0,1,2,3,4,5\}$ and agent type identifiers $\{sensitive, insenitive\}$. Specifically, the predicates $Zero(X)$, $Successor(X,Y)$, and $Last(X)$ offer the fundamental knowledge of coordinates in the environment by denoting the minimum coordinate as $Zero(0)$, maximum coordinate as $Last(5)$, and the coordinates order as $Successor(1,0), Successor(2,1)$,..., $Successor(5,4)$. The predicates $Apple(X,Y)$ and $Lemon(X,Y)$ describe the presence of apples and lemons at position (X,Y), respectively. The predicate $Type(X)$ indicates whether an agent is sensitive or not. In addition, agent actions are represented by predicates $Up()$, $Down()$, $Left()$, and $Right()$, which indicate the direction of agent's movement.

To evaluate the proposed EMARL method, we first conducted an ablation study to demonstrate the effect of its two key parts: VDN architecture and interpretable history module. We then benchmarked EMARL with a fully connected DQN to demonstrate its competitive performance in multi-agent reinforcement learning. RL methods in terms of returns (i.e., discounted cumulative rewards) were evaluated; a higher return value indicates better performance. In addition, we considered a method that is interpretable if it can produce logical rules. The capacity of the history buffer for EMARL and the maximum length of the reasoning path were set to 4 and 3, respectively. The experiment was conducted four times with different random seeds, and the average return is reported.

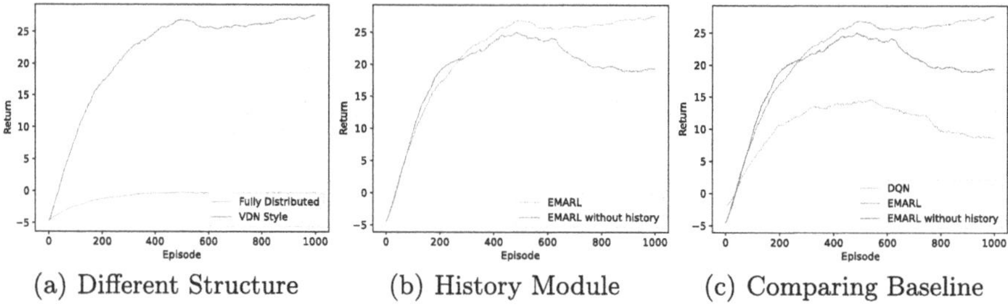

(a) Different Structure (b) History Module (c) Comparing Baseline

Fig. 4. Learning curves of different methods and tasks. The vertical and horizontal axes represent the return of each episode and the number of episodes, respectively. (a) shows the comparison between the fully distributed structure and VDN structure. (b) proves the validity of the history module. (c) demonstrates that EMARL outperforms the baseline in both tasks.

4.2 Results and Analysis

Ablation Study. We first demonstrated the effectiveness of centralized training with distributed execution scheme, specifically, the VDN architecture [7] by comparing the proposed EMARL with a variant whose agents work in a fully distributed manner. For a fair comparison, we banned the two methods from accessing historical observations so that the performance difference comes only from the underlying structure (i.e., VDN vs. fully distributed). Figure 4(a) depict the variation in episodic returns during 1,000 episodes. The VDN-based method substantially outperforms the distributed approach; that is, the former's return (i.e., cumulative reward) continues to increase, whereas the latter has never achieved a positive value. The underperformance of the distributed approach can be attributed to the inherent partial observation trait of MARL and the previously discussed nonstationary problem. This result highlights the effectiveness of centralized training with distributed execution scheme for multi-agent learning.

To evaluate the contribution of the proposed history module to EMARL, we conducted an ablation study by removing it and assessing the performance of the remaining parts. Figure 4(b) shows the trend of episodic return with/without a history module. The effect of the history module is clear as shown by the curve of the full-featured EMARL that is above the other. A closer look at the curve without a history module reveals that its policy initially converges at first but subsequently diverges, whereas the full-featured EMARL does not encounter this problem. This is not surprising because incorporating information from past observations can help agents make better policies when they are not fully aware of the entire environment and their partner's actions. Thus, we conclude that the proposed history module not only improves the learning performance but also alleviates the partial observation problem and stabilizes the training process indirectly.

Learning Performance. We further compared EMARL with a fully connected DQN as the baseline. All methods were trained using the VDN architecture. Figure 4(c) shows that EMARL outperforms DQN by scoring twice as much as the DQN. This implies that EMARL can capture the rich semantics of symbolic representations and more easily address complex problems than DQN. Considering that cooperation among agents is essential for most multi-agent systems, we conclude that the proposed EMARL is effective for solving multi-agent reinforcement learning problems.

Table 1. Logic Rules Extracted from Attention Weights

1.$Up() \leftarrow Apple^{\top}(X,Y) \wedge Successor(Y,Z) \wedge Current(Z,U)$
2.$Down() \leftarrow Last(X) \wedge Current(X,Y) \wedge Apple^{\top}(Y,Z)$
3.$Right() \leftarrow Last(X) \wedge Current(X,Y) \wedge Lemon^{\top}(Y,Z)$
4.$Down() \leftarrow Last(X) \wedge Current(X,Y) \wedge Lemon^{\top}(Y,Z)$

Interpretability. We evaluated the interpretability of EMARL by constructing chain-like logic rules using attention weights and subsequently analyzing them. The most representative logic rules that can describe the learned policies for the checker environment are listed in Table 1. The first rule indicates that an agent moves up when an apple is in front of it. The second rule implies that when an agent is at the top of the map and an apple is in the same column, the agent moves down to approach the apple, as there is no way for the apple to be above it. Similarly, we can interpret the agent actions corresponding to the third and fourth rules as escaping from or approaching a lemon, depending on their type (i.e., *sensitive* or *insensitive*). Note that the predicate $Type(X)$ does not appear in the two rules because the entities *sensitive* and *insensitive* cannot connect to the axis entities under the multi-hop reasoning framework. However, this does not pose a problem for EMARL, because the agent-type information can be manually incorporated, as we know from which agent the rule is extracted. By analyzing these rules, we can observe that the agents trained with EMARL can reason through abstract concepts (e.g., approaching an apple, as shown by the first two rules) rather than relying solely on the spatial position of the object, similar to most classical RL methods. Thus, we conclude that the proposed EMARL method is interpretable and can learn more abstract concepts, with the potential to improve the generalizability of the learned model.

5 Conclusion

In this paper, we present an explainable multi-agent reinforcement learning algorithm that performs reasoning in a symbolically represented environment to simultaneously generate chain-like logic rules with the policy-learning process. This is the first attempt to apply multi-hop reasoning to MARL with centralized training with distributed execution architecture. To alleviate the partial observability and nonstationary problems of multi-agent systems, we proposed an explainable history module that uses an attention mechanism to incorporate past experiences while preserving interpretability. The results demonstrate that the proposed method can effectively learn nearly optimal policies while generating expressive rules to explain its decisions. More importantly, the study shows that a symbolic-neural approach can learn more abstract concepts than pure neural networks, thereby providing an alternative perspective for improving the generalizability of machine learning systems.

References

1. Evans, R., Grefenstette, E.: Learning explanatory rules from noisy data. J. Artif. Intell. Res. **61**, 1–64 (2018)
2. Hausknecht, M.J., Stone, P.: Deep recurrent Q-learning for partially observable MDPs. In: 2015 AAAI, pp. 29–37 (2015)
3. Jiang, Z., Luo, S.: Neural logic reinforcement learning. In: Proceedings of the 36th International Conference on Machine Learning, ICML 2019. Proceedings of Machine Learning Research, vol. 97, pp. 3110–3119 (2019)
4. Leibo, J.Z., Zambaldi, V.F., Lanctot, M., Marecki, J., Graepel, T.: Multi-agent reinforcement learning in sequential social dilemmas. In: Proceedings of the 16th Conference on Autonomous Agents and MultiAgent Systems, AAMAS 2017, pp. 464–473 (2017)
5. Li, G., Xiao, G., Zhang, J., Liu, J., Shen, Y.: Towards relational multi-agent reinforcement learning via inductive logic programming. In: Artificial Neural Networks and Machine Learning - ICANN 2022–31st International Conference on Artificial Neural Networks, vol. 13530, pp. 99–110 (2022)
6. Sorokin, I., Seleznev, A., Pavlov, M., Fedorov, A., Ignateva, A.: Deep attention recurrent q-network. CoRR (2015)
7. Sunehag, P., et al.: Value-decomposition networks for cooperative multi-agent learning based on team reward. In: Proceedings of the 17th International Conference on Autonomous Agents and MultiAgent Systems, AAMAS 2018, pp. 2085–2087 (2018)
8. Yang, F., Yang, Z., Cohen, W.W.: Differentiable learning of logical rules for knowledge base reasoning. In: Advances in Neural Information Processing Systems, vol. 30, pp. 2319–2328 (2017)
9. Yang, Y., Song, L.: Learn to explain efficiently via neural logic inductive learning. In: 8th International Conference on Learning Representations, ICLR 2020 (2020)

Evidential Robust Deep Learning for Noisy Text2text Question Classification

Haoran Wang[1], Jiyao Wang[2], Yuqiu Chen[1], Zehua Peng[3], and Zuping Zhang[1](✉)

[1] Central South University, Changsha, China
{whrannnnn,chenyq99,zpzhang}@csu.edu.cn

[2] The Hong Kong University of Science and Technology, Guangzhou, China
jwanggo@connect.ust.hk

[3] Sichuan University, Chengdu, China
2021223045143@stu.scu.edu.cn

Abstract. Text2text question classification (TQC) is a foundational task in the question classification (QC) field, with a wide range of applications in both industry and academia, such as intelligent customer service systems. Conventional QC tasks typically rely on one or more user-provided keywords to classify questions. In contrast, TQC problems involve categorizing semantically similar standard questions, which are then represented in short text format. However, due to the limited availability of TQC datasets, the process of manual labeling often results in noisy labels that do not accurately reflect the true class of a question, introducing bias into the training data. Noisy labels can lead to unreliable and uncertain supervised signals, which have a significant negative impact on the performance of models. To tackle these challenges, we propose the Evidential Robust Deep Learning (ERDL) framework, which integrates TQC Contrastive Loss (TCL) and TQC Evidential Learning Loss (TEL) to achieve accurate semantic similarity and handle noisy data in the TQC dataset. Notably, TEL is a novel loss function based on evidential learning that models the output as a Dirichlet distribution to capture the uncertainty resulting from noisy data. We evaluated our framework using four noisy TQC datasets and found that it outperformed relevant baselines, as indicated by the experimental results.

Keywords: Text2text question classification · Evidential learning · Noisy label

1 Introduction

Text-to-Text Question Classification (TQC) aims to classify questions by using short texts written in the same language as the input question. These short texts

H. Wang, and J. Wang—Equal Contribution.

L. Iliadis et al. (Eds.): ICANN 2023, LNCS 14263, pp. 211–222, 2023.
https://doi.org/10.1007/978-3-031-44204-9_18

are pre-existing questions that correspond to each category of questions. TQC has the potential to categorize user inquiries in a similar manner to standard questions and can be applied in various areas, such as customer service systems [12]. However, TQC also faces some challenges, including increased model complexity and cost, as well as potential bias resulting from manual annotation.

Standard classification methods typically include traditional text classification and text matching [10,28]. In traditional text classification, each class is represented as a one-hot or probability distribution vector, learned through mapping the input to classes using feed-forward layers like Multilayer Perceptrons (MLPs) [20]. Although cross-entropy loss functions [22] are commonly used for traditional text classification, they are not suitable for TQC due to the large number of label classes. Text matching [16], which employs similarity measure functions to jointly model two texts, is not sufficient for TQC since the outputs can be influenced by varying metrics [21]. With TQC questions being sorted into predefined short text classes, traditional text matching alone is inadequate.

While deep neural networks have demonstrated exceptional performance, they require meticulously labeled data [17], which can be both costly and time-consuming [23]. Using non-expert sources may reduce labeling expenses, but it may also generate unreliable and noisy labels [15]. Noisy labels can render supervised signals unreliable, but there are existing robust models that can address this issue, such as T-revision [30], Robust Early-learning [31], Active Passive Loss [14], Curriculum Learning [13], and Bi-tempered Loss [1]. These models perform well on their respective datasets and frequently employ loss functions in conjunction with softmax. However, softmax provides class probability estimates in the form of point estimates, which can introduce uncertainty issues [24]. Noisy labels can result in biased estimates and exacerbate uncertainties.

To address the challenge of noisy labels in the TQC problem, we propose an **E**vidential **R**obust **D**eep **L**earning Framework (ERDL) depicted in Fig. 1 to learn the similarity and uncertainty within the TQC dataset. Firstly, our framework generates embedding representations for input text and standard answers using the pre-trained MP-Net [27]. Simultaneously, to minimize the distance between positive samples while maximizing the distance between negative samples, our framework employs a novel loss function called TQC Evidential Loss (TEL) $\mathcal{L}_{tel}$, designed based on an evidential learning paradigm to capture the uncertainty introduced by noisy data, thereby addressing the uncertainty problem. The supervised contrastive loss is adapted from NT-Xent [5] and utilized in this work, known as TQC Contrastive Loss (TCL) $\mathcal{L}_{tcl}$. This loss function also enables both uniformity and tolerance for different samples in high-dimensional spaces. By integrating TCL and TEL, the model can effectively learn from TQC noisy data. Specifically, the model is designed to capture the uncertainty introduced by noisy data. TEL models the evidence based on the similarity between the input text and the standard answer, subsequently parameterizing the evidence as a Dirichlet distribution. The evidence represents the neural network's estimate of the corresponding samples for the respective classes. Our main contributions are summarized as follows:

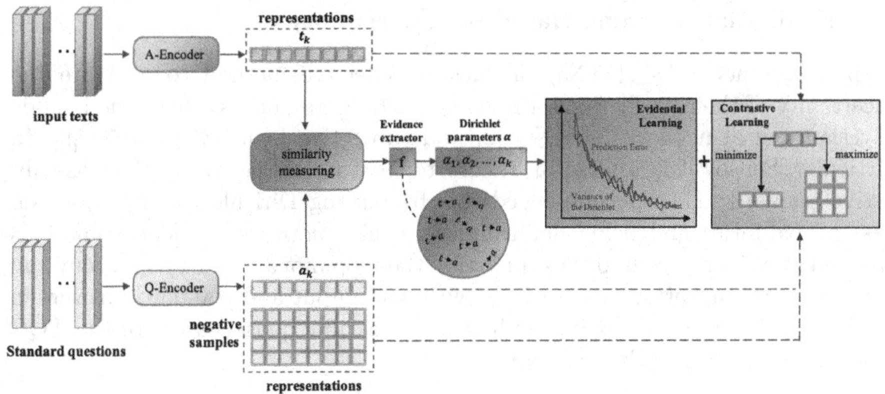

Fig. 1. The overview of the model structure.

- We incorporate evidential learning into TQC problems and present a deep learning framework that builds on the TQC approach. Our framework is designed to be plug-and-play, effectively tackling TQC tasks while ensuring reliable performance even under high label-side noise.
- We have developed a new loss function called TQC Evidential Loss (TEL) using evidential learning. This function effectively addresses the issue of uncertainty caused by noisy data in the model. Additionally, we have combined this loss function with the contrast loss function, which is based on NT-Xent's variant design. This fusion significantly enhances the model's training performance on TQC noisy data.
- Our framework was extensively experimentally compared on four TQC noisy datasets, and the results demonstrate that our approach outperforms all relevant baseline models in this study.

2 Related Work

2.1 Learning from Noisy Labels

Deep learning networks can achieve high performance, but they often encounter issues with unreliable annotations. To address this, robust training methods such as Robust Regularization [26], weight decay [11], and batch regularization [6] have been developed. Additionally, there are several typical models, including Bilevel learning [7], annotator confusion, and Robust-Early learning [31]. To cope with noisy data, the Robust Loss Function proposes a robust loss function such as robust MAE [3] and generalized cross entropy [33]. The TQC task is more challenging than regular classification because it involves increased classes and semantic information.

2.2 Evidential Learning Based on Uncertainty

Deep neural networks (DNNs) [3] lack an effective method to evaluate the uncertainty of their predictions. Previous attempts to address this issue include Bayesian neural networks (BNNs) [2] and subjective logic (SL) theory [9]. In particular, Sensoy [24] applied SL theory to treat neural net predictions as subjective opinions. They accomplished this by placing Dirichlet distributions on class probabilities and using deterministic neural networks to learn functions that collect evidence from data supporting these opinions. In this paper, our aim is to model the uncertainty associated with user input and standard answers in the TQC dataset. We do this to enhance the learning performance of the TQC model when dealing with noisy data.

3 Approach

3.1 Preliminaries

In our TQC problem, given a training data set $\{(t_i, q_i)\}_{i=1}^{N}$, t_i represents the i-th user input text, while q_i is the i-th matching standard problem. $\mathcal{T}$ denotes the total set of the user's input texts, and $\mathcal{Q}$ is the set of all standard questions. The similarity of $\{(t_i, q_i)\}$ could be measured through $S\left(q(t_i), a(q_i)\right)$, where q and a are the MP-Net encoder that embeds the input texts and standard questions into the feature representation, which is respectively. And $S\left(*\right)$ is the similarity metric. In the Natural Language Processing (NLP) task, the text is usually mapped as a high-dimensional embedding. Cosine similarity is a better measure of the distance between two vectors in a high-dimensional space, so we use cosine similarity as the similarity metric. To clear the representation, we denote $S\left(q, t\right)$ as $S\left(t_i, q_i\right)$ in the following.

Due to limited TQC datasets, manual data labeling is crucial. To tackle introduced noise, we propose TEL loss based on evidential learning, capturing model uncertainty. We also employ NT-Xent contrastive loss. By fusing these two losses, we greatly improve model training on TQC noisy data. The overall objective function for the N-sample batch is:

$$\mathcal{L} = \sum_{i=1}^{N} \lambda \mathcal{L}_{tcl}\left(t_i, q_i\right) + \frac{1}{N} \sum_{i=1}^{N} \mathcal{L}_{tel}\left(t_i, q_i\right) \tag{1}$$

$\mathcal{L}_{tel}$ is the evidential loss function to capture the uncertainty that noisy data introduce into the model, and $\mathcal{L}_{tcl}$ is the contrastive loss function. The above loss function is used for the training of the model.

$$\lambda = \begin{cases} 1, & \text{if } \arg\max\left(\boldsymbol{p}_i\right) \text{is the ground truth} \\ 0, & \text{otherwise} \end{cases} \tag{2}$$

where $\boldsymbol{p}_i$ is the probability distribution of the sample derived from its corresponding Dirichlet distribution.

3.2 Theory of Evidential Uncertainty

The algorithm we developed to model uncertainty in noisy data is rooted in the Dempster-Shafer Theory of Evidence (DST) [4], which provides a Bayesian extension of subjective probability. To parameterize the DST's concept of belief mass, we draw on the framework of subjective logic (SL) [8], which employs a Dirichlet distribution to quantify belief mass and uncertainty within a well-defined theoretical framework.

Specifically, SL defines a frame of K mutually exclusive singletons (e.g., class labels) that own a non-negative belief mass for each singleton $k = 1, \ldots, K$ and provide an overall uncertainty mass of u. The above $K + 1$ mass values are all non-negative and sum up to one, and $u \geq 0$ and $b_k \geq 0$ i.e.

$$u + \sum_{k=1}^{K} b_k = 1 \tag{3}$$

where b_k for the sample k can be computed by the evidence for the sample. b_k represents the kth output out of softmax, which represents the mass of beliefs for the kth class. And u represents the quality of uncertainty for a particular output. e_k can be viewed as the evidence of the kth output, where $e_k \geq 0$. Then we can compute the belief b_k and the uncertainty $u \geq 0$ with $S = \sum_{i=1}^{K} (e_i + 1)$.

$$b_k = \frac{e_k}{S} \quad \text{and} \quad u = \frac{K}{S} \tag{4}$$

Evidence e_k is extracted from the similarity measuring, which we have generated by calculating the similarity between the input t_i and target q_i and subsequently scaling it using the exponential function. Subsequently, we parameterize the distribution belief mass as a Dirichlet distribution with $\alpha_k = e_k + 1$. From the parameters of the formed Dirichlet distribution, subjective opinions using $b_k = (\alpha_k - 1)/S$ can be obtained. Here, $S = \sum_{i=1}^{K} \alpha_i$ represents the Dirichlet strength. Unlike the traditional sense of softmax that assigns one probability to each sample. This method outputs a Dirichlet distribution that represents the density of each such probability assignment. Specifically, it represents a probability density function (pdf) used to calculate the possible values of the probability mass function (pmf) $\mathbf{p}$. It has k parameters $\boldsymbol{\alpha} = [\alpha_1, \ldots, \alpha_K]$ and is given as follow.

$$D(\mathbf{p} \mid \boldsymbol{\alpha}) = \begin{cases} \frac{1}{B(\boldsymbol{\alpha})} \prod_{i=1}^{K} p_i^{\alpha_i - 1}, & \text{for } p \in S_K \\ 0, & \text{otherwise} \end{cases} \tag{5}$$

where $\mathcal{S}_K$ is the K-dimensional simplex,

$$\mathcal{S}_K = \left\{ \mathbf{p} \mid \sum_{i=1}^{K} p_i = 1 \text{ and } 0 \leq p_1, \ldots, p_K \leq 1 \right\} \tag{6}$$

where $B(\alpha)$ is the K-dimensional multinomial beta function. Thus, with the above modeling setup, the output expectation probability of the kth singleton is derived from the average of his corresponding Dirichlet distribution.

$$\widehat{p}_{\mathbf{k}} = \frac{\alpha_{\mathbf{k}}}{\mathbf{S}} \tag{7}$$

3.3 TQC Evidential Learning Loss

In this part, for any user input $\mathbf{t_i}$, the variable $\mathbf{y_i}$ represents the ground truth class in one-hot form. The variable $\boldsymbol{\alpha}_i$ denotes the Dirichlet density parameter on the predictor. Then the sum of squares loss (LS) is utilized to bring the query probability close to the ground truth, and this loss function can be labeled as follows.

$$\begin{aligned}\mathcal{L}_{tel}\left(\boldsymbol{\alpha}_i, \boldsymbol{y}_i\right) &= \int \left\|\boldsymbol{y}_i - \boldsymbol{p}_i\right\|_2^2 \frac{1}{B\left(\boldsymbol{\alpha}_i\right)} \prod_{j=1}^{K} p_{ij}^{\alpha_{ij}-1} d\boldsymbol{p}_i \\ &= \sum_{j=1}^{K} \left(y_{ij} - \mathbb{E}\left[p_{ij}\right]\right)^2 + \operatorname{Var}\left(p_{ij}\right) \\ &= \sum_{j=1}^{K} \left(y_{ij} - \hat{p}_{ij}\right)^2 + \frac{\hat{p}_{ij}\left(1-\hat{p}_{ij}\right)}{\left(S_i+1\right)}\end{aligned} \tag{8}$$

where $\mathbb{E}\left[p_{ij}\right]$ is the are the expectation of p_{ij}, and $\operatorname{Var}\left(p_{ij}\right)$ is the variance of the p_{ij}.

With the above equation, we can minimize the expected probability by making it as close to the ground truth as possible. The last two components of this loss function were obtained from the above analysis. The goal is to minimize this loss function so that the expected probability is as close to the ground truth as possible.

3.4 Contrastive Learning Loss

Using NT-Xent, our model reduces the distance between positive samples while increasing the distance between negative samples. During the training phase, we pass the user-input text t and its matching standard question q into two text encoders that have been trained with MP-Net. This generates a representation of t and q, denoted as $\mathbf{e^t}$ and $\mathbf{e^q}$ respectively, where $e, r \in R^{N \times d}$, N is the batch size, and d is the dimension of the feature vector. During inference, we use the representation of the user's input text $\mathbf{e_i^t}$ as the anchor point and the representation of its corresponding standard question $\mathbf{e_i^q}$ as the positive point. The loss function expects to find the corresponding point in $N-1$ negative samples within the batch. The specific loss function is shown below.

$$\mathcal{L}_{\text{con}}\left(t_i, q\right) = -\log\left(\frac{\exp\left(\mathrm{S}\left(t_i, q_i\right)/\tau\right)}{\sum_{j=1}^{N} 1_{[j \neq i]} \exp\left(\mathrm{S}\left(t_i, q_j\right)/\tau\right)}\right) \tag{9}$$

where τ control the temperature and 1 is the indicator.

4 Experiment

4.1 Dataset

In the TQC task, we utilized a total of four datasets, all of which were formatted in text2text style [29]. Our datasets consist of COVID-Q and TREC-small, both of which contain multi-class questions that conform to TQC specifications and have short text class labels. COVID-Q pertains to COVID-19 questions, with classes such as propagation and prevention. TREC-small covers people, location, and digital information. For real-world applications, CB-Balance and CB-imbalance were collected to train the bank's customer information service systems.

To generate noisy data, we randomly selected a proportion of IDs, replaced the corresponding standard question IDs with randomly selected questions, and generated noisy label data accordingly.

Table 1. Results of comparison experiments with baseline models in COVID-Q and TREC small

Model		COVID-Q								TREC10-smal							
		Noisy Ratio															
		20%		*40%*		*60%*		*80%*		*20%*		*40%*		*60%*		*80%*	
		Acc	F1	Acc	F1	Acc	F1	Acc	F1	Acc	F1	Acc	F1	Acc	F1	Acc	F1
Traditional Classification Model	NC	45.66	38.95	27.25	30.70	25.30	2.69	4.34	0.55	13.40	20.58	13.00	11.76	3.40	3.59	2.40	0.11
	HC	49.38	56.02	34.88	31.21	27.21	11.32	8.00	6.36	16.33	21.74	15.17	13.88	7.55	3.46	3.66	3.41
	DSSM	59.79	59.13	57.89	45.32	54.31	43.31	48.89	37.21	60.45	45.13	52.45	40.14	31.36	26.87	27.13	23.99
	LSHRGMN	61.37	60.52	58.31	56.01	56.98	49.29	49.42	42.35	68.00	57.88	53.24	51.00	33.26	29.12	30.74	26.13
Noisy-label Processing Model	Label Smoothing	57.93	54.24	55.54	52.79	43.86	40.31	7.04	0.88	74.40	63.76	66.80	61.73	57.40	53.29	43.60	45.66
	GCE	67.81	64.99	62.28	56.83	61.38	56.75	23.95	21.27	81.40	71.86	74.40	66.54	69.40	56.60	66.20	55.51
	Co-teaching+	68.00	68.09	64.22	62.37	60.92	59.00	27.32	26.44	82.90	70.27	76.55	66.10	72.54	60.00	69.22	56.27
	Active Passive Loss	70.81	68.81	66.92	65.96	61.83	59.40	28.59	29.52	82.80	71.09	79.20	69.45	78.40	62.25	75.20	60.20
	Robust-Early Learning	73.17	70.32	69.50	68.99	66.01	60.01	55.40	54.18	84.02	70.90	82.02	68.55	80.02	65.67	77.67	62.80
	ERDL	**76.95**	**78.20**	**71.56**	**70.10**	**70.36**	**69.07**	**64.22**	**63.25**	**85.00**	**71.59**	**84.40**	**70.20**	**81.40**	**67.18**	**81.00**	**65.43**

Notes: In this table and the following tables, the best results are bolded in **black**, and the underline __ marks the second best results.

4.2 Implementation Details

Using MP-Net, we obtain embedding parameters. Two independent encoders encode user input text and standard problem, respectively. An attention-pooling layer generates an overall sentence representation. Feature truncation and rejection ratios are set at 0.1, with a contrast loss function temperature τ of 0.1. The batch size is 64, and the learning rate is 0.0001. We used Python 3.8, PyTorch 1.9.1, and Transformers 2.1.1 for the experimental environment. Experiments were run on an Ubuntu 18.04 system with an RTX3090 graphics card and 24268 MB of memory.

Table 2. Results of comparison experiments with baseline models in CB-imbalance and CB-balance

Model		CB-balance								CB-imbalance							
		Noisy Ratio															
		20%		*40%*		*60%*		*80%*		*20%*		*40%*		*60%*		*80%*	
		Acc	F1	Acc	F1	Acc	F1	Acc	F1	Acc	F1	Acc	F1	Acc	F1	Acc	F1
Traditional Classification Model	NC	10.55	0.44	10.34	0.27	7.32	0.36	4.80	0.11	0.52	0.34	0.26	0.31	0.21	0.13	0.10	0.00
	HC	14.31	6.13	13.18	4.14	8.19	2.13	6.20	0.20	9.76	8.13	9.13	5.09	3.40	1.20	1.10	1.00
	DSSM	56.19	31.99	50.88	26.32	53.18	22.19	38.88	26.66	59.99	51.68	49.32	49.19	43.21	35.28	29.13	18.77
	LSHRGMN	59.38	36.12	53.18	28.14	56.22	27.14	53.00	29.32	65.65	53.31	51.13	52.14	55.13	38.22	42.77	28.87
Noisy-label Processing Model	Label Smoothing	52.32	17.50	50.00	13.04	48.73	13.00	33.33	5.99	55.47	42.29	51.30	38.54	47.40	36.39	30.47	20.82
	GCE	65.82	31.87	64.98	29.06	61.60	28.31	55.27	19.71	2.52	2.37	2.04	1.34	1.16	0.27	0.30	0.10
	Co-teaching+	66.65	39.17	64.02	35.12	63.65	31.87	58.18	21.09	59.67	53.19	52.59	41.22	46.19	34.78	38.52	27.13
	Active Passive Loss	71.52	41.70	70.46	37.03	67.09	31.96	59.70	20.90	65.63	54.10	54.43	41.55	47.66	35.52	40.10	29.76
	Robust-Early Learning	77.28	62.32	70.99	57.17	68.01	54.38	60.38	52.38	70.11	64.77	60.88	55.38	56.23	50.02	47.18	48.23
	ERDL	**89.66**	**85.97**	**86.50**	**78.42**	**85.23**	**77.09**	**80.38**	**74.77**	**76.30**	**66.26**	**76.04**	**65.57**	**73.18**	**64.48**	**70.31**	**58.05**

4.3 Comparison Experiments

In this article's experiments, we use two evaluation metrics to comprehensively assess the model's fitting ability: accuracy, and F1-score. In order to verify the superiority of our algorithm on the TQC, we have conducted experiments on four data sets and compared them with the baselines.

Naive Classification, in the model, MP-Net is used for encoding, no target text is modeled, and cross-entropy loss is used for optimization. **Hierarchy Classification** [18] output is generated by a hierarchical softmax method to generate a classification probability vector. **DSSM** [25](i.e., Deep Structured Semantic Models) represents text as a vector. The model has mainly been used in text similarity matching scenarios. **Label Smoothing** [19] reduce overfitting by estimating label noise marginalization during training, and avoid full probability assignment to noisy data. **Generalized cross-entropy**(GCE) [33] is proposed to fuse the MAE and CE (Cross-Entropy) loss functions. **Co-teaching+** [32] is further upgraded by borrowing Decoupling's "Update by Disagreement" strategy. **Active passive loss (APL)** [14] is to Maximize the probability of belonging to a class & minimize the probability of belonging to other classes. **Robust-Early Learning** [31], the core idea of Robust-Early Learning is to divide the parameters into critical and non-critical parameters.

We compared our framework to the baseline using four noisy datasets. The results in Table 1 and Table 2 demonstrate that our framework achieved optimal performance with a high percentage improvement across all four datasets, particularly when trained with our proposed loss function on the TQC noisy dataset. Our framework outperforms the best-performing baseline model on TREC10-small, improving both Acc and F1 values by 66.5% and 61.7% respectively at noise levels ranging from 60% to 80%. Additionally, on CB-balance, our framework maintains a 30% improvement in Acc and a 61% improvement in F1 across four different noise ratios compared to the original best-performing baseline model, LSHRGMN.

Our framework demonstrates superior performance compared to the baseline model under conditions of noisy labeling, as evidenced by the results presented in Tables 1 and 2. Specifically, our approach shows improved accuracy on the TQC dataset. Moreover, on the CB Balance dataset, our algorithm's effectiveness increases as the proportion of noise increases. At 80% noise, our Acc and F1 boosting ratios reach 24.8% and 29.9%, respectively. Similarly, on both the CB Imbalance and COVID-Q datasets, the model's boosting effect becomes more pronounced with higher noise proportions.

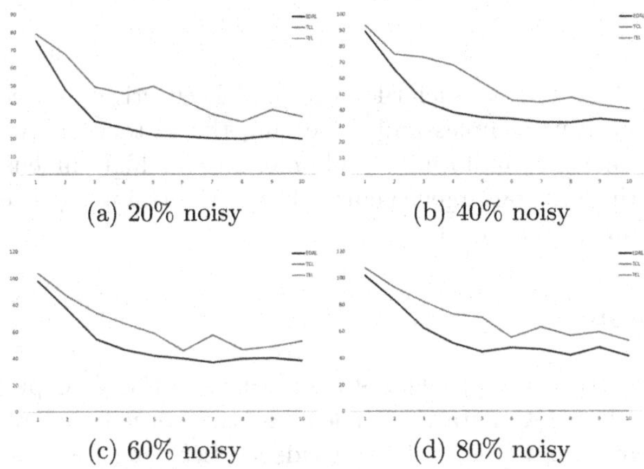

(a) 20% noisy (b) 40% noisy

(c) 60% noisy (d) 80% noisy

Fig. 2. The convergence curve of the noisy data, where the gray curve representing the evidential learning loss converges to zero. (Color figure online)

4.4 Ablation Study

In order to fully verify the validity of the model, we compared our framework with two other model variants, the model with only the loss of $\mathcal{L}_{tel}$ added and the model with only the $\mathcal{L}_{tcl}$ loss added; in order to verify the validity of the two loss functions separately. The experimental results are shown in Table 3 and Table 4.

Table 3. Results of Ablation Study in COVID-Q and CB-imbalance

Model	Covid-Q								CB-imbalance							
	20%		*40%*		*60%*		*80%*		20%		40%		60%		80%	
	Acc	*F1*	*Acc*	*F1*	*Acc*	*F1*	*Acc*	*F1*	*Acc*	*F1*	*Acc*	*F1*	*Acc*	*F1*	*Acc*	*F1*
ERDL	**76.95**	**78.20**	**71.56**	**70.10**	**70.36**	**69.07**	**64.22**	**63.25**	**76.30**	**66.19**	**76.02**	**65.57**	**73.18**	**64.48**	**70.31**	**58.05**
$\mathcal{L}_{tcl}$	72.90	72.76	69.01	66.58	65.12	66.18	53.14	51.44	73.44	63.63	72.66	61.13	69.01	58.77	67.45	55.28
$\mathcal{L}_{tel}$	43.99	42.09	43.86	42.09	38.02	39.18	37.57	37.05	52.86	40.41	50.78	40.00	50.26	39.67	50.00	39.26

Effect of the $\mathcal{L}_{tel}$. We first compare the model with $\mathcal{L}_{tel}$ removed. It can be seen that the performance of the model decreases to some extent with the removal of $\mathcal{L}_{tel}$, with percentage level decreases in both ACC and F1. This also verifies the effectiveness of $\mathcal{L}_{tel}$ for the model. In addition, as shown in Fig. 2, the rate of convergence of the loss during the training process has decreased.

Table 4. Results of Ablation Study in TREC10-small and CB-balance

Model	CB-balance								TREC10-small							
	20%		*40%*		*60%*		*80%*		20%		40%		60%		80%	
	Acc	*F1*	*Acc*	*F1*	*Acc*	*F1*	*Acc*	*F1*	*Acc*	*F1*	*Acc*	*F1*	*Acc*	*F1*	*Acc*	*F1*
ERDL	**89.66**	**85.97**	**86.50**	**78.42**	**85.23**	**77.09**	**80.38**	**74.77**	**85.00**	**71.59**	**84.40**	**70.20**	**81.40**	**67.18**	**81.00**	**65.43**
$\mathcal{L}_{tcl}$	86.29	76.61	85.23	75.07	80.59	74.64	75.74	65.24	77.60	67.10	77.40	63.61	75.20	61.59	67.00	53.90
$\mathcal{L}_{tel}$	39.87	43.63	38.61	42.07	37.34	40.75	36.71	39.96	34.20	24.11	32.20	24.05	30.00	22.22	29.20	21.58

Effect of the $\mathcal{L}_{tcl}$. $\mathcal{L}_{tcl}$ is crucial for the model, effectively reducing the distance between positive samples and increasing the distance between negative samples, thus balancing uniformity and tolerance in high-dimensional space. Figure 2 shows the loss convergence curve during the training process with limited discussion due to poor effect.

5 Conclusion

In this paper, we study the problem of noisy labels in the TQC problem, where noisy labels in the TQC dataset can lead to the degradation of model performance. We propose a Robust Deep Evidence Learning framework to tackle the challenge. It learns TQC dataset similarity and captures noise uncertainty. Extensive experimental comparisons validate our framework on four noisy TQC datasets. The current TQC dataset is restricted and cannot train the model on a bigger dataset. Also, no other loss functions were experimented with except for the contrastive one. Future plans include gathering a larger dataset and attempting additional loss functions to combine with the evidential learning loss.

References

1. Amid, E., et al.: Robust bi-tempered logistic loss based on Bregman divergences. In: Advances in Neural Information Processing Systems, vol. 32 (2019)
2. Gal, Y., Ghahramani, Z.: Bayesian convolutional neural networks with Bernoulli approximate variational inference. arXiv preprint arXiv:1506.02158 (2015)
3. Ghosh, A., Kumar, H., Sastry, P.S.: Robust loss functions under label noise for deep neural networks. In: Proceedings of the AAAI Conference on Artificial Intelligence, vol. 31, no. 1 (2017)
4. Gordon, J., Shortliffe, E.H.: The Dempster-Shafer theory of evidence. In: Rule-Based Expert Systems: The MYCIN Experiments of the Stanford Heuristic Programming Project, vol. 3, pp. 832–838 (1984)
5. Hjelm, R.D., et al.: Learning deep representations by mutual information estimation and maximization. arXiv preprint arXiv:1808.06670 (2018)
6. Ioffe, S., Szegedy, C.: Batch normalization: accelerating deep network training by reducing internal covariate shift. In: International Conference on Machine Learning, pp. 448–456. PMLR (2015)
7. Jenni, S., Favaro, P.: Deep bilevel learning. In: Proceedings of the European Conference on Computer Vision (ECCV), pp. 618–633 (2018)
8. Jøsang, A.: Subjective Logic, vol. 3. Springer, Cham (2016). https://doi.org/10.1007/978-3-319-42337-1

9. Jøsang, A.: Subjective Logic: A Formalism for Reasoning Under Uncertainty. Springer, Cham (2018). https://doi.org/10.1007/978-3-319-42337-1
10. Kowsari, K., et al.: Text classification algorithms: a survey. Information **10**(4), 150 (2019)
11. Krogh, A., Hertz, J.: A simple weight decay can improve generalization. In: Advances in Neural Information Processing Systems, vol. 4 (1991)
12. Liu, P., et al.: Multi-timescale long short-term memory neural network for modelling sentences and documents. In: Proceedings of the 2015 Conference on Empirical Methods in Natural Language Processing, pp. 2326–2335 (2015)
13. Lyu, Y., Tsang, I.W.: Curriculum loss: Robust learning and generalization against label corruption. arXiv preprint arXiv:1905.10045 (2019)
14. Ma, X., et al.: Normalized loss functions for deep learning with noisy labels. In: International Conference on Machine Learning, pp. 6543–6553. PMLR (2020)
15. Mason, W., Suri, S.: Conducting behavioral research on Amazon's mechanical turk. Behav. Res. Methods **44**(1), 1–23 (2012)
16. Minaee, S., et al.: Deep learning-based text classification: a comprehensive review. In: ACM Computing Surveys (CSUR), pp. 1–40. vol. 54, no. 3, pp. 1–40 (2021)
17. Paolacci, G., Chandler, J., Ipeirotis, P.G.: Running experiments on amazon mechanical turk. Judgment Decis. Making **5**(5), 411–419 (2010)
18. Peng, H., et al.: Incrementally learning the hierarchical softmax function for neural language models. In: Proceedings of the AAAI Conference on Artificial Intelligence, vol. 31, no. 1 (2017)
19. Pereyra, G., et al.: Regularizing neural networks by penalizing confident output distributions. arXiv preprint arXiv:1701.06548 (2017)
20. Pinkus, A.: Approximation theory of the MLP model in neural networks. Acta Numer **8**, 143–195 (1999)
21. Rao, J., et al.: Bridging the gap between relevance matching and semantic matching for short text similarity modeling. In: Proceedings of the 2019 Conference on Empirical Methods in Natural Language Processing and the 9th International Joint Conference on Natural Language Processing (EMNLP-IJCNLP), pp. 5370–5381 (2019)
22. Rubinstein, R.: The cross-entropy method for combinatorial and continuous optimization. Methodol. Comput. Appl. Probab. **1**, 127–190 (1999)
23. Scott, C., Blanchard, G., Handy, G.: Classification with asymmetric label noise: consistency and Maximal Denoising. In: Conference on Learning Theory, pp. 489–511. PMLR (2013)
24. Sensoy, M., Kaplan, L., Kandemir, M.: Evidential deep learning to quantify classification uncertainty. In: Advances in Neural Information Processing Systems, vol. 31 (2018)
25. Shen, Y., et al.: Learning semantic representations using convolutional neural networks for web search. In: Proceedings of the 23rd International Conference on World Wide Web, pp. 373–374 (2014)
26. Song, H., et al.: Learning from noisy labels with deep neural networks: a survey. IEEE Trans. Neural Netw. Learn. Syst. (2022)
27. Song, K., et al.: MPNeT: masked and permuted pre-training for language understanding. Adv. Neural. Inf. Process. Syst. **33**, 16857–16867 (2020)
28. Wang, J., et al.: Multi-aspect co-attentional collaborative filtering for extreme multi-label text classification. Knowl. Based Syst. **260**, 110110 (2023)
29. Wang, J., et al.: Preciser comparison: augmented multi-layer dynamic contrastive strategy for text2text question classification. Neurocomputing **544**, 126299 (2023)

30. Xia, X., et al.: Are anchor points really indispensable in label-noise learning? In: Advances in Neural Information Processing Systems, vol. 32 (2019)
31. Xia, X., et al.: Robust early-learning: Hindering the memorization of noisy labels. In: International Conference on Learning Representations (2020)
32. Yu, X., et al.: How does disagreement help generalization against label corruption? In: International Conference on Machine Learning. PMLR, pp. 7164–7173 (2019)
33. Zhang, Z., Sabuncu, M.: Generalized cross entropy loss for training deep neural networks with noisy labels. In: Advances in Neural Information Processing Systems, vol. 31 (2018)

FBPFormer: Dynamic Convolutional Transformer for Global-Local-Contexual Facial Beauty Prediction

Qipeng Liu, Luojun Lin(✉), Zhifeng Shen, and Yuanlong Yu

Fuzhou University, Fuzhou 35010, China
ljlin@fzu.edu.cn

Abstract. Facial Beauty Prediction (FBP) is subjective and varies from person to person, which makes it difficult to obtain a unified and objective evaluation. Previous efforts adopt conventional convolution neural networks to extract local facial features and calculate corresponding facial attractiveness scores, ignoring the global facial features. To address this issue, we propose a dynamic convolution vision transformer named FBPFormer which aims to focus on both local facial features and the global facial information of the human face. Specifically, we first build a lightweight convolution network to produce pseudo facial attribute embedding. To inject the global facial information into the transformer, the parameters of encoders are dynamically generated by the embedding of each instance. Therefore, these dynamic encoders can fuse and further fuse local facial features and global facial information while encoding query, key, and value vectors. Furthermore, we design an instance-level dynamic exponential loss to dynamically adjust the optimization objectives of the model. Extensive experiments show our method achieves competitive performance, demonstrating its effectiveness in the FBP task.

Keywords: Face beauty prediction · Vision transformer · Dynamic convolution

1 Introduction

Facial Beauty Prediction (FBP) aims to use a machine to objectively evaluate the face attractiveness score instead of individual subjective evaluation with large differences. Benefiting from a lot of psychological research [4,29,31] and advances in deep learning [12], we can use machines to objectively evaluate the attractiveness of human faces instead of high-cost artificial subjective assessment. It has a wide range of applications in practice, such as social recommendation systems [30], facial make-up recommendations [1,22], facial beautification [16], and so on. The key issue in FBP is how to obtain a face beauty model that conforms to the public aesthetic.

L. Iliadis et al. (Eds.): ICANN 2023, LNCS 14263, pp. 223–235, 2023.
https://doi.org/10.1007/978-3-031-44204-9_19

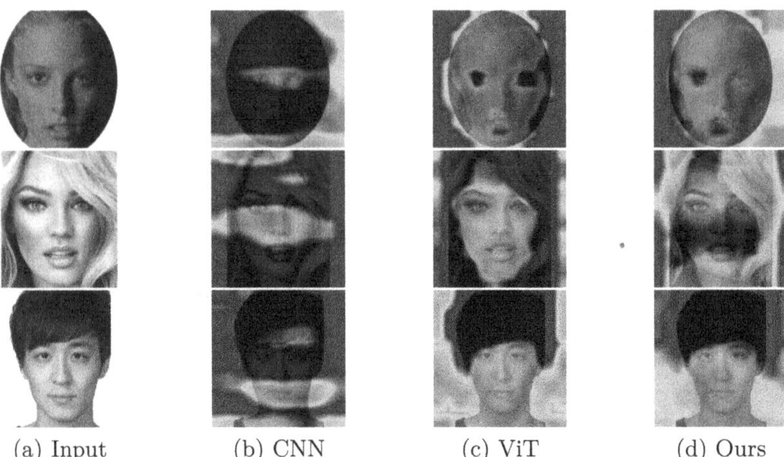

Fig. 1. Grad-CAM [32] results for the difference between convolution neural network (CNN) and vision transformer (ViT). Following [21], the visual attention of CNN is based on the AlexNet. The result demonstrates that ViT pays more attention to the global feature of a human face and CNN focuses on the local features. Our method can aggregate global-local-contextual information.

Early works adopt conventional machine learning techniques [3,9,10] to predict facial beauty scores. With the popularity of deep learning, some researchers choose convolution neural networks (CNNs) to build facial beauty prediction models and achieve great performance, such as six-layer convolution neural networks [34], R^2-ResNeXt [18] and R^3CNN [20]. However, as shown in Fig. 1(b), the weakness of the above methods is that CNNs mainly resort to learning the local features but lack attention to the global features of the face in face beauty task. Instead, the vision transformers (ViTs) can utilize the global public features of the face to make a comprehensive evaluation of the beauty, which is more in line with human nature, such as the overall skin texture [27] and face contour, as shown in Fig. 1(c).

Local facial attributes are personalized, such as the shape of the mouth, eyes, and nose, which have different effects on different faces and play a critical role in FBP. However, the attribute information of the human face is not been explicitly considered in previous methods for FBP. Therefore, the P-AaNet [21] consisting of a set of dynamic filters, introduces the local facial attribute information by using pseudo-attribute embedding to adaptively adjust filter parameters. The pseudo-attribute embedding is produced by a lightweight feature extraction network with down-sampling. Different faces correspond with different convolution kernel parameters, which allows the dynamic convolution to fully exploit the local features of each face.

Global facial features such as skin texture, facial symmetry, and the distribution of facial organs are important indicators of facial attractiveness [11]. Vision transformers, with their powerful global modeling capabilities, have been shown the great performance, outperforming traditional CNNs in a range of computer vision tasks, including image classification [6] and object detection [38]. The vision transformer (ViT) is made up of several blocks with global multi-head self-attention (MSAs), which enhances the modeling power of high-order spatial information interactions and makes it an ideal choice for FBP.

In this paper, we present a novel approach to the FBP task built on the dynamic convolutional transformer, named FBPFormer, which combines the MSA of the block with dynamic convolution called the dynamic convolution block. The dynamic convolutional adaptive acquisition of personalized face information and the adaptive high-order global spatial modeling capabilities of the ViT enable the creation of more comprehensive and objective models of FBP. The FBPFormer adjusts its MSAs based on personalized facial attributes for each instance, allowing it to handle variations across different attributes. Furthermore, we design an instance-level dynamic exponential loss to dynamically adjust the optimization objectives of the model, so that hard samples can receive more attention in the later training period. Additionally, some research [26] suggests that the hidden dimension of blocks should be kept high for better representation while we believe that the hidden dimension should be decreased in the FBP task. Experimental results experiments show that the FBPFormer achieves advanced performance on the SCUT-5500 dataset. The main contributions of our work are summarized as follows:

(1) A novel dynamic convolution transformer network named FBPFormer is proposed to address the problem of lack of utilization of global public face information in previous FBP works. To the best of our knowledge, our method is the first work to apply the ViT with dynamic convolution to the FBP task.
(2) A lightweight dynamic convolution layer is designed for the ViT to obtain better results without increasing the number of parameters in the model.
(3) An instance-level dynamic exponential loss is proposed to adjust the optimization objective of the model to focus more on hard samples with large losses in the later training period.
(4) The proposed FBPFormer explores the possibility that FBP can be objectively evaluated from the perspective of deep learning and achieves competitive results on the SCUT-FBP5500 dataset, which will bring new implications to the FBP community and aesthetic cognitive psychology.

2 Related Work

Facial Beauty Prediction. Based on the classic pattern recognition process, early work on FBP was successful by combining manual features with shallow predictors. The hand-crafted features comprise the geometric features (e.g.,geometric ratios and landmark distances) and textural features (e.g., LBP-/Gabor-/SIFT-like features) [28,36]. However, these handcrafted features are low-level features that are difficult to obtain discriminative facial representation. Recent years, some researchers have been using CNN to assess facial beauty automatically by using local key features of the face [2,19,33]. Because of the hierarchical nonlinear transformation, the CNN-based FBP models have been proven to be superior to the previous traditional methods.

Dynamic Convolution. The traditional convolution assumes that all samples share the same convolution kernel parameters, but dynamic convolution can generate convolution kernel parameters adaptively based on each sample, so it has better generalization performance [35] treats the convolutional kernel parameters as linear combinations of multiple expert weights [25] adaptivly weights the convolutional kernel parameters by utilizing dynamic activation vectors [37] generates a set of coefficients adaptively, fusing the fixed convolution into a dynamic convolution kernel.

Vision Transformer. Due to its outstanding global context modeling capabilities, the vision transformer has achieved state-of-the-art performance for many computer vision tasks, such as image classification, object detection, and image segmentation. Swin Transformer [23] adopts the hierarchical construction method commonly used in CNN to build the hierarchical Transformer and introduces the locality idea to perform self-attention calculation in the window region without coincidence, greatly increasing the sensation field of ViT. ConViT [8] simulated the locality of CNN through the gated positional self-attention (GPSA) layer and then made the layer pay attention to the location information through a gated parameter. CoT [15] uses a convolution layer to extract the local feature information of the image, so as to make full use of the static context information inside the key.

In this paper, we integrate the advantages of convolution neural networks and vision transformers by introducing dynamic convolution into the vision transformer, so as to realize efficient utilization of local and global facial information and obtain more accurate facial beauty evaluation.

3 Proposed Method

In this section, we first provide an overview of the FBPFormer framework, then introduce the details of the dynamic convolution encoder block and explain why this design is chosen. Finally, we describe the feature extraction network and dynamic convolutional self-attention in detail.

3.1 Overview

Figure 2 shows the fundamental building block of our model. The dynamic convolution block consists of two main components: a dynamic multi-head self-attention module that integrates personalized face information with high-order global spatial information of faces, and a parameter generator that adaptively generates convolution kernel parameters based on the input face image to encode the query, key, and value vectors in the transformer.

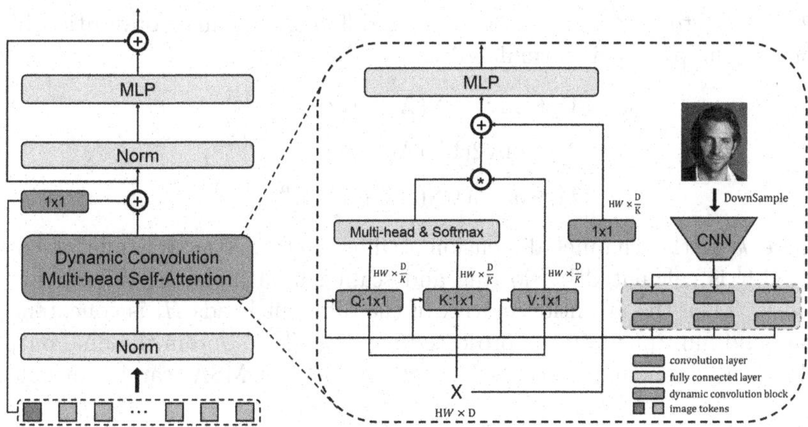

Fig. 2. The overall structure of dynamic convolution block. The dynamic multi-head self-attention module is in blue. The core of the dynamic convolution part is highlighted in green. The embedding network is used to downsample the original image, and the parameters of Q, K, and V encoders are adaptively generated by the generator (gray). The CLS token is the yellow token in the input sequence. (Color figure online)

More specifically, we encode the query Q, key K, and value V vectors by performing different dynamic convolution layers on them separately. We then compute the attention matrix using the encoded vectors. It is important to note that the kernel parameters of the dynamic convolution layers are controlled adaptively using facial attributes. The parameter generator updates the kernel weights by using the attributes embedding as input. This embedding is derived from the original image through a shallow convolution network.

3.2 Dynamic Convolution Block

Dynamic Multi-head Self-Attention. The ViT model makes full use of the self-attention mechanism in natural language processing (NLP). Unlike NLP, where words are embedded into vectors, ViT converts images into discrete patches through convolution, and the dimensions of the patches are always kept the same size in each block. However, high-dimensional embedding can introduce unnecessary noise to the model during training. To address this issue, we propose a dynamic convolution attention block that computes the channel attention of features and eliminates unnecessary parts. Given the input feature $X \in \mathbb{R}^{n \times d}$, which is also the output of the previous $l-1$th block, $Q \in \mathbb{R}^{n \times d}$, $K \in \mathbb{R}^{n \times d}$ and $V \in \mathbb{R}^{n \times d}$ represents the output directly from a multi-layer perceptron (MLP) block in the normal ViT block. This process can be written as follows:

$$Q, K, V = \text{Split}(\text{MLP}(\text{LN}(X_{l-1})) \in \mathbb{R}^{n \times 3d}), \tag{1}$$

where n, d are the length and channel dimension of the vector, respectively, and $\text{LN}(\cdot)$ is the layer normalization [14]. In our dynamic convolution attention block, the Q, K, V vectors are generated by three different dynamic convolution block $\text{DyConv}(\cdot)$, the process is formulated as

$$\begin{aligned} \hat{Q} &= \text{DyConv1}(\text{LN}(X_{l-1})) \in \mathbb{R}^{n \times (d/k)}, \\ \hat{K} &= \text{DyConv2}(\text{LN}(X_{l-1})) \in \mathbb{R}^{n \times (d/k)}, \\ \hat{V} &= \text{DyConv3}(\text{LN}(X_{l-1})) \in \mathbb{R}^{n \times (d/k)}, \end{aligned} \tag{2}$$

where k is the channel dimension scaling factor. The dynamic attention matrix W^O is calculated by dotting and scaling by a factor of $\sqrt{d_k}$ among Q, K, and V. Then the attention matrix of the different heads H_i is concatenated together and multiplied by the projected matrix W^O to obtain the final output. Finally, the dynamic multi-head self-attention block (DMSA) can be formulated as

$$\text{DyAttention}(\hat{Q}, \hat{K}, \hat{V}) = \text{Softmax}\left(\frac{\hat{Q} \cdot \hat{K}^\top}{\sqrt{d_k}}\right)\hat{V}, \tag{3}$$

$$\begin{aligned} \text{DyMultiHead}(Q, K, V) &= \text{Concat}(H_1, H_2, \cdots, H_h)W^O, \\ \text{where } \mathrm{H_i} &= \text{DyAttention}(\hat{Q}_i, \hat{K}_i, \hat{V}_i). \end{aligned} \tag{4}$$

Besides, there exists a residual connection in the dynamic attention block. We use a 1-D convolution layer to transform the dimension of the input to match that of the output of the DMSA module. This allows us to combine global high-order spatial information interaction with adaptive face personalized attribute information in high-dimensional space, which can be written as

$$\hat{\mathbf{X}}_l = \text{DMSA}\left(\text{LN}\left(\mathbf{X}_{l-1}\right)\right) + \text{Conv}(\mathbf{X}_{l-1}), \tag{5}$$

$$\hat{\mathbf{X}}_l = \text{MLP}\left(\text{LN}\left(\hat{\mathbf{X}}_l\right)\right) + \hat{\mathbf{X}}_l. \tag{6}$$

Parameter Generator. We adopt the dynamic convolution with filter regeneration manner to generate the parameters of QKV encoders. Specifically, the filter regeneration in our method consists of two parts: the feature extraction network and the parameter generator. The purpose of the feature extraction network is to extract the local semantic information from the original image to compensate for the lack of local information in the ViT model. We use global average pooling to downsample the image, then convolution layers with kernel sizes of 7×7 and 5×5 are deployed to extract the local semantic information. Suppose we have an input image I_{img}, the dynamic filter parameters of adaptive convolutional layer W_n^l generated by the parameter generator can be formulated as follows:

$$W_n^l = \mathcal{G}^l\left(\mathcal{E}\left(I_{img}\right)\right), \quad \ell = 1 \ldots L \tag{7}$$

where l indicates the l- th block in the transformer, $\mathcal{G}^l(\cdot)$ is the l-th parameter generator and $\mathcal{E}(\cdot)$ is an embedding network shared by all parameter generators.

3.3 Dynamic Exponential Loss

To better explore the potential information of hard samples with large losses, we propose an instance-level dynamic exponential loss (DELoss). It could be written as:

$$Loss(x_i) = (Y_i - y_i)^{n - \frac{Y_i - y_i}{\mathrm{Max}(Y-y)}} \tag{8}$$

where Y_i and y_i are the corresponding ground truth label and prediction of the ith sample x_i in the batch, respectively. $\mathrm{Max}(Y - y)$ is the maximum value of $Y_i - y_i$. The n is set to 2. The DELoss is equal to the MSE loss when $Y_i - y_i$ is close to 0 and degrades to L1 loss when the loss of the sample is the largest of the current batch. In this way, the loss size of different samples can be dynamically adjusted. When training losses tend to converge, more attention will be paid to hard samples with larger losses, and more potential facial beauty semantic information can be mined.

4 Experiments

4.1 Experiment Settings

We evaluate our method on the SCUT-FBP5500 [17] dataset. This dataset includes 5500 facial images that are labeled by 75 raters with 5 rating scores ranging from 1 to 5. The ground-truth score for each image is the average score of 75 ratings. We adopt the five-fold cross-validation strategy to evaluate our method. Specifically, the dataset is divided equally into 5 folds, and we test each fold with the remaining 4 folds as the training set. Following the previous studies [21], Pearson Correlation (PC), Maximum Absolute Error (MAE), and Root Mean Square Error (RMSE) are used to measure the performance. Results of the aforementioned metrics and corresponding averaged ones are reported. We compare our method with different CNNs and ViTs such as ConvNeXt, Swin-Transformer, etc.

4.2 Implementation Details

The structure of FBPFormer is similar to the ViT-B and consists of 12 blocks with the initial dimension $d = 768$. It is worth noting that we use the ImageNet [5] pre-training model in our experiments and initialize the fully-connected layers of FBPFormer randomly to make the comparison model perform optimally. The input images are first resized to 256×256 and then randomly cropped to 224×224 to feed the model. We update the model parameters by using mini-batch Stochastic Gradient Descent (SGD) with the learning rate of 1e-3, the momentum of 0.9 and the weight decay of 5e$-$4. The max epoch is set to 40 with the batch size of 32. During the testing phase, we apply a 224×224 center crop to each image before feeding it into the model and embedding network.

4.3 Comparison with Other Transformers and CNNs

We take the ViT as the baseline method for the experiments and compare our method with other convolution-based or transformer-based methods on the SCUT-FBP5500 dataset. Since our Dynamic ViT achieved the best results with a channel dimension scaling factor $k = 64$, we maintain this setting in the comparison below. The results of the 5-fold cross-validation in terms of PC, MAE, and RMSE are shown in Table 1. It shows that our FBPFormer can achieve even higher performance compared to Swin-Transformer and ConvNeXt, the best existing transformer and convolution neural network, and obtain the highest correlation of 0.9183, minimum errors with MAE of 0.2053.

Table 1. The FBP results of five-fold cross-validation on the SCUT-FBP5500 dataset.

PC	1	2	3	4	5	Average
R^3CNN [19]	0.9143	0.9143	0.9136	0.9146	**0.9217**	0.9142
ResNet-101 [13]	0.8966	0.8939	0.8863	0.8954	0.8988	0.8942
ConvNeXt-B [24]	0.8671	0.9088	0.9071	0.9130	0.9109	0.9014
RIRG+SCA [2]	0.8990	0.8939	0.9020	0.8999	0.9067	0.9003
ViT-B [7]	0.8875	0.8941	0.8992	0.8930	0.8976	0.8943
Swin-B [23]	0.9042	0.9053	0.9134	**0.9209**	0.9087	0.9105
ConViT-B [8]	0.9006	0.8983	0.9085	0.9068	0.9091	0.9047
FBPFormer	**0.9181**	**0.9184**	**0.9184**	0.9197	0.9167	**0.9183**
MAE	1	2	3	4	5	Average
R^3CNN [19]	0.2109	0.2152	0.2126	0.2130	0.2085	0.2130
ResNet-101 [13]	0.2309	0.2327	0.2466	0.2424	0.2462	0.2398
ConvNeXt-B [24]	0.2704	0.2148	0.2235	0.2187	0.2318	0.2318
RIRG+SCA [2]	0.2300	0.2284	0.2257	0.2345	0.2251	0.2287
ViT-B [7]	0.2462	0.2404	0.2401	0.2422	0.2384	0.2414
Swin-B [23]	0.2350	0.2211	0.2219	0.2141	0.2260	0.2236
ConViT-B [8]	0.2320	0.2355	0.2303	0.2293	0.2260	0.2306
FBPFormer	**0.2011**	**0.2046**	**0.2074**	**0.2068**	**0.2067**	**0.2053**
RMSE	1	2	3	4	5	Average
R^3CNN [19]	0.2767	0.2895	0.2837	0.2804	**0.2701**	0.2800
ResNet-101 [13]	0.3032	0.3124	0.3307	0.3146	0.3200	0.3162
ConvNeXt-B [24]	0.3551	0.2876	0.2960	0.2855	0.2984	0.3045
RIRG+SCA [2]	0.3020	0.3081	0.3013	0.3039	0.2916	0.3014
ViT-B [7]	0.3206	0.3122	0.3121	0.3138	0.3099	0.3137
Swin-B [23]	0.3027	0.2984	0.2939	0.2797	0.2973	0.2944
ConViT-B [8]	0.3036	0.3078	0.3010	0.2996	0.2989	0.3022
FBPFormer	**0.2715**	**0.2726**	**0.2760**	**0.2720**	0.2752	**0.2734**

4.4 Ablation Studies

Different Scaling Factors k of DMSA Module. To verify the effectiveness of the channel scaling in the dynamic convolution block, we compare the DMSA module under different channel dimension scaling factors k on the FBP-5500 dataset in terms of MAE, RMSE, and PC performance, and compare it with the ViT model that removes the last block (ViT-B/11). As shown in Tables 2, we can draw the following conclusions: (1) The DMSA module achieves the best results with a smaller number of channels (1/64) and parameters (1/6) of the original ViT block. (2) Even when the channels of the dynamic convolution blocks are reduced to 64 times the original ViT, our FBPFormer still outperforms the ViT model, which demonstrates the usefulness of the dynamic convolution block.

Table 2. Comparison of DMSA module with different scaling factor k on SCUT-FBP5500 dataset.

Network	Scaling Factor	Params	PC	MAE	RMSE
ViT-B	-	6.75M	0.8943	0.2414	0.3137
ViT-B/11	-	-	0.9088	0.2304	0.2972
FBPFormer	$k = 16$	6.95M	0.9173	0.2103	0.2756
FBPFormer	$k = 32$	3.48M	0.9178	0.2063	0.2772
FBPFormer	$k = 64$	1.75M	**0.9183**	**0.2053**	**0.2734**

Different Position of Dynamic Convolution Block. To explore the effect of the dynamic convolution block at different positions in the ViT, we conduct experiments on the SCUT-FBP5500 dataset, where the dynamic convolution block is located in each of the last three layers of the transformer. The scaling factor k of the DMSA modules used in the experiment is 64. As shown in Table 3, the dynamic convolution block in the 12-th block outperforms other positions and achieves better results than the baseline ViT-B in different positions when the number of parameters is reduced from 85.6M to 66.3M (about 19% reduction).

Table 3. Comparison of Dynamic Convolution Block in different position on SCUT-FBP5500 dataset.

Position	Model Params	PC	MAE	RMSE
12th	80.4M	**0.9183**	**0.2053**	**0.2734**
11th	73.3M	0.9168	0.2091	0.2763
10th	66.3M	0.9147	0.2168	0.2795

Effectiveness of DMSA Module and DELoss. To prove the effectiveness of the FBPformer, we conduct ablation studies on the DMSA module with different channel scaling factors and DELoss. As shown in Table 4, we can conclude that the proposed DMSA works well on different channels of the block, and the dynamic convolution located at the last block with a scaling factor of $k = 64$ and DELoss provides the best performance.

4.5 Visualization

We use t-SNE to obtain low-dimensional embedding from the high-dimensional CLS token of the output of ViT. The visualization shows that the dynamic vision transformer can better distinguish the features of the face in each fractional segment. For example, we can easily find the classification boundary that separates most between the blue [2, 3) and orange [3, 4) segments (Fig. 3).

Table 4. Ablation studies of DMSA Module and DELoss on SCUT-FBP5500 dataset.

Scaling Factor	w/ DMSA	w/ DELoss	PC	MAE	RMSE
$k = 32$	×	×	0.9071	0.2257	0.2948
$k = 32$	✓	×	0.9090	0.2210	0.2900
$k = 32$	✓	✓	0.9178	0.2063	0.2772
$k = 64$	×	×	0.9092	0.2215	0.2893
$k = 64$	✓	×	0.9102	0.2203	0.2886
$k = 64$	✓	✓	**0.9183**	**0.2053**	**0.2734**

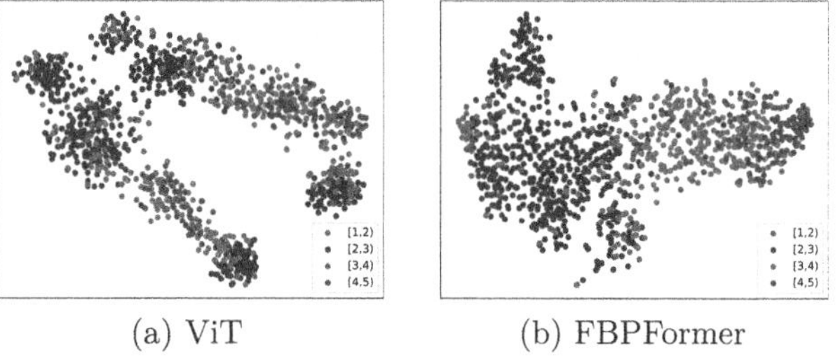

(a) ViT (b) FBPFormer

Fig. 3. The t-SNE is adopted to visualize the distribution of ViT (a) and ours (b). The facial beauty score is divided into 4 non-overlapping ranges marked by different colors. It shows that the FBPFormer could obtain more distinguishable features than ViT.

5 Conclusion

In this paper, we propose a dynamic convolution transformer, named FBPFormer for facial beauty prediction. Our FBPFormer uses a dynamic convolutional neural network in the ViT architecture. By introducing pseudo facial attributes as prior knowledge to adaptively update the parameters of the Q, K, and V encoders, FBPFormer can acquire more distinctive features of faces with different scores. It achieves competitive results compared to well-established baselines on the SCUT-FBP5500 dataset and only requires a simple learning rate strategy with the SGD optimizer. Finally, there is currently a lack of large-scale datasets for facial beauty evaluation, so we will continue to search for more datasets and optimize our network structure in the future.

Acknowledgements. This work was supported by the Fujian Provincial Natural Science Foundation (No. 2022J05135); and the National Natural Science Foundation of China (No. U21A200672).

References

1. Alashkar, T., Jiang, S., Wang, S., Fu, Y.: Examples-rules guided deep neural network for makeup recommendation. In: AAAI, pp. 941–947 (2017)
2. Cao, K., Choi, K.N., Jung, H., Duan, L.: Deep learning for facial beauty prediction. Information **11**(8), 391 (2020)
3. Chen, Y., Mao, H., Jin, L.: A novel method for evaluating facial attractiveness. In: 2010 International Conference on Audio, Language and Image Processing, pp. 1382–1386. IEEE (2010)
4. Cross, J.F., Cross, J.: Age, sex, race, and the perception of facial beauty. Dev. Psychol. **5**(3), 433 (1971)
5. Deng, J., Dong, W., Socher, R., Li, L.J., Li, K., Fei-Fei, L.: ImageNet: a large-scale hierarchical image database. In: 2009 IEEE Conference on Computer Vision and Pattern Recognition, pp. 248–255. IEEE (2009)
6. Ding, M., Xiao, B., Codella, N., Luo, P., Wang, J., Yuan, L.: Davit: dual attention vision transformers. arXiv preprint arXiv:2204.03645 (2022)
7. Dosovitskiy, A., et al.: An image is worth 16x16 words: transformers for image recognition at scale. arXiv preprint arXiv:2010.11929 (2020)
8. d'Ascoli, S., Touvron, H., Leavitt, M.L., Morcos, A.S., Biroli, G., Sagun, L.: Convit: improving vision transformers with soft convolutional inductive biases. In: International Conference on Machine Learning, pp. 2286–2296. PMLR (2021)
9. Eisenthal, Y., Dror, G., Ruppin, E.: Facial attractiveness: beauty and the machine. Neural Comput. **18**(1), 119–142 (2006)
10. Fan, J., Chau, K., Wan, X., Zhai, L., Lau, E.: Prediction of facial attractiveness from facial proportions. Pattern Recogn. **45**(6), 2326–2334 (2012)
11. Fink, B., Neave, N.: The biology of facial beauty. Int. J. Cosmet. Sci. **27**(6), 317–325 (2005)
12. Hadji, I., Wildes, R.P.: What do we understand about convolutional networks? arXiv preprint arXiv:1803.08834 (2018)
13. He, K., Zhang, X., Ren, S., Sun, J.: Deep residual learning for image recognition. In: Proceedings of the IEEE Conference on Computer Vision and Pattern Recognition, pp. 770–778 (2016)

14. Lei Ba, J., Kiros, J.R., Hinton, G.E.: Layer normalization. ArXiv e-prints pp. arXiv-1607 (2016)
15. Li, Y., Yao, T., Pan, Y., Mei, T.: Contextual transformer networks for visual recognition. arXiv preprint arXiv:2107.12292 (2021)
16. Liang, L., Jin, L., Li, X.: Facial skin beautification using adaptive region-aware masks. IEEE Trans. Cybern. **44**(12), 2600–2612 (2014)
17. Liang, L., Lin, L., Jin, L., Xie, D., Li, M.: SCUT-FBP5500: a diverse benchmark dataset for multi-paradigm facial beauty prediction. ICPR (2018)
18. Lin, L., Liang, L., Jin, L.: R^2-ResNeXt: a ResNeXt-based regression model with relative ranking for facial beauty prediction. In: 2018 24th International Conference on Pattern Recognition (ICPR), pp. 85–90. IEEE (2018)
19. Lin, L., Liang, L., Jin, L.: Regression guided by relative ranking using convolutional neural network (R^3 CNN) for facial beauty prediction. IEEE Trans. Affect. Comput. **13**(1), 122–134 (2019)
20. Lin, L., Liang, L., Jin, L.: Regression guided by relative ranking using convolutional neural network (R^3CNN) for facial beauty prediction. IEEE Trans. Affect. Comput. **13**, 122–134 (2019)
21. Lin, L., Liang, L., Jin, L., Chen, W.: Attribute-aware convolutional neural networks for facial beauty prediction. In: IJCAI, pp. 847–853 (2019)
22. Liu, L., Xing, J., Liu, S., Xu, H., Zhou, X., Yan, S.: Wow! you are so beautiful today! ACM Trans. Multimedia Comput. Commun. Appl. (TOMM) **11**(1s), 20 (2014)
23. Liu, Z., et al.: Swin transformer: hierarchical vision transformer using shifted windows. In: Proceedings of the IEEE/CVF International Conference on Computer Vision, pp. 10012–10022 (2021)
24. Liu, Z., Mao, H., Wu, C.Y., Feichtenhofer, C., Darrell, T., Xie, S.: A convnet for the 2020s. In: Proceedings of the IEEE/CVF Conference on Computer Vision and Pattern Recognition, pp. 11976–11986 (2022)
25. Ma, N., Zhang, X., Huang, J., Sun, J.: WeightNet: revisiting the design space of weight networks. In: Vedaldi, A., Bischof, H., Brox, T., Frahm, J.-M. (eds.) ECCV 2020. LNCS, vol. 12360, pp. 776–792. Springer, Cham (2020). https://doi.org/10.1007/978-3-030-58555-6_46
26. Park, N., Kim, S.: How do vision transformers work? In: The Tenth International Conference on Learning Representations, ICLR 2022, Virtual Event, April 25–29, 2022. OpenReview.net (2022). https://openreview.net/forum?id=D78Go4hVcxO
27. Perrett, D.I., et al.: Effects of sexual dimorphism on facial attractiveness. Nature **394**(6696), 884 (1998)
28. Ren, Y., Geng, X.: Sense beauty by label distribution learning. In: IJCAI, vol. 17, pp. 2648–2654 (2017)
29. Rhodes, G., et al.: The evolutionary psychology of facial beauty. Annu. Rev. Psychol. **57**, 199 (2006)
30. Rothe, R., Timofte, R., Van Gool, L.: Some like it hot-visual guidance for preference prediction. In: CVPR, pp. 5553–5561 (2016)
31. Rubenstein, A.J., Langlois, J.H., Roggman, L.A.: What makes a face attractive and why: the role of averageness in defining facial beauty (2002)
32. Selvaraju, R.R., Cogswell, M., Das, A., Vedantam, R., Parikh, D., Batra, D.: Grad-cam: visual explanations from deep networks via gradient-based localization. In: Proceedings of the IEEE International Conference on Computer Vision,p pp. 618–626 (2017)

33. Xie, D., Liang, L., Jin, L., Xu, J., Li, M.: SCUT-FBP: a benchmark dataset for facial beauty perception. In: IEEE International Conference on Systems, Man, and Cybernetics, pp. 1821–1826 (2015)
34. Xu, J., Jin, L., Liang, L., Feng, Z., Xie, D., Mao, H.: Facial attractiveness prediction using psychologically inspired convolutional neural network (PI-CNN). In: 2017 IEEE International Conference on Acoustics, Speech and Signal Processing (ICASSP), pp. 1657–1661. IEEE (2017)
35. Yang, B., Bender, G., Le, Q.V., Ngiam, J.: Condconv: conditionally parameterized convolutions for efficient inference. Advances in Neural Information Processing Systems, vol. 32 (2019)
36. Zhang, D., Chen, F., Xu, Y.: Computer Models for Facial Beauty Analysis. Springer, Cham (2016). https://doi.org/10.1007/978-3-319-32598-9
37. Zhang, Y., Zhang, J., Wang, Q., Zhong, Z.: Dynet: dynamic convolution for accelerating convolutional neural networks. arXiv preprint arXiv:2004.10694 (2020)
38. Zhu, X., Su, W., Lu, L., Li, B., Wang, X., Dai, J.: Deformable DETR: deformable transformers for end-to-end object detection. arXiv preprint arXiv:2010.04159 (2020)

Heavy-Tailed Regularization of Weight Matrices in Deep Neural Networks

Xuanzhe Xiao[1], Zeng Li[1(✉)], Chuanlong Xie[2], and Fengwei Zhou[3]

[1] Southern University of Science and Technology, Shenzhen 518055, People's Republic of China
12132907@mail.sustech.edu.cn, liz9@sustech.edu.cn

[2] Beijing Normal University, Zhuhai 519087, People's Republic of China
clxie@bnu.edu.cn

[3] Huawei Noah's Ark Lab, Hong Kong, People's Republic of China
fzhou@connect.ust.hk

Abstract. Unraveling the reasons behind the remarkable success and exceptional generalization capabilities of deep neural networks presents a formidable challenge. Recent insights from random matrix theory, specifically those concerning the spectral analysis of weight matrices in deep neural networks, offer valuable clues to address this issue. A key finding indicates that the generalization performance of a neural network is associated with the degree of heavy tails in the spectrum of its weight matrices. To capitalize on this discovery, we introduce a novel regularization technique, termed **Heavy-Tailed Regularization**, which explicitly promotes a more heavy-tailed spectrum in the weight matrix through regularization. Firstly, we employ the Weighted Alpha and Stable Rank as penalty terms, both of which are differentiable, enabling the direct calculation of their gradients. To circumvent over-regularization, we introduce two variations of the penalty function. Then, adopting a Bayesian statistics perspective and leveraging knowledge from random matrices, we develop two novel heavy-tailed regularization methods, utilizing Power-law distribution and Fréchet distribution as priors for the global spectrum and maximum eigenvalues, respectively. We empirically show that heavy-tailed regularization outperforms conventional regularization techniques in terms of generalization performance.

Keywords: Heavy-Tailed Regularization · Deep Neural Network · Random Matrix Theory

1 Introduction

Deep neural networks (DNN) have shown remarkable performance in recent years, achieving unprecedented success in various fields such as computer vision, natural language processing, and recommendation systems [6,10,11,25]. However, there is still a lack of clear understanding of how neural networks generalize. Efforts to construct a generalization framework for DNNs have incorporated

L. Iliadis et al. (Eds.): ICANN 2023, LNCS 14263, pp. 236–247, 2023.
https://doi.org/10.1007/978-3-031-44204-9_20

various mathematical tools from conventional learning theory [3–5,24]. Nevertheless, the majority of these approaches have been found to exhibit certain limitations. For example, the VC dimension and Rademacher complexity have been deemed inadequate in offering a satisfactory explanation for the generalization performance of DNNs [26]. The uniform-convergence-based generalization bounds may fail to elucidate generalization in deep learning due to their vacuous generalization guarantee [20].

One might consider that the weight matrices of a DNN serve as a representation of its generalization capabilities for the following reasons: from a theoretical standpoint, the parameters contained within the weight matrices are intricately connected to the model's output space, input data, optimization algorithm, etc.; Additionally, in practical scenarios, access to trained models often comes with limited information regarding training and testing data, which can be attributed to the highly compartmentalized nature of the industry. Recently, Martin and Mahoney [16] introduced a perspective grounded in random matrix theory (RMT) to elucidate the generalization behavior of deep neural networks. They studied the empirical spectral distribution (ESD) of weight matrices in deep neural networks and observed a *5+1 phase of regularization* – throughout the training process, the ESDs of the weight matrices initially conform well to the Marchenko-Pastur (MP) law, gradually deviate from it, and ultimately approach a Heavy-Tailed (HT) distribution [14,16]. This regularization phenomenon is referred to as *Implicit Self-Regularization.* Furthermore, this theory suggests that large, well-trained DNN architectures should exhibit Heavy-Tailed Self-Regularization, meaning that the spectra of their weight matrices can be well-fitted by a heavy-tailed distribution. Building on Martin and Mahoney's work, Meng and Yao [19] discovered that the complexity of the classification problem could influence the weight matrices spectra of DNNs. These theories offer a novel perspective for exploring the generalization of DNNs.

In addition to the aforementioned studies, several works have advocated the positive impact of heavy tails of weight matrices on the generalization of neural networks from the perspective of stochastic gradient descent (SGD). Zhou et al. [27] pointed out that the time required for both SGD and Adam to escape sharp minima is negatively related to the heavy-tailedness of gradient noise. They further explained that the superior generalization of SGD compared to Adam in deep learning is due to Adam's gradient calculation being smoothed by the exponential moving average, resulting in lighter gradient noise tails compared to SGD. Hodgkinson et al. [12] presented a similar finding, demonstrating that, within a stochastic optimization problem, multiplicative noise and heavy-tailed stationary behavior enhance the capacity for basin hopping during the exploratory phase of learning, in contrast to additive noise and light-tailed stationary behavior. Simsekli et al. [22] approximated the trajectories of SGD using a Feller process and derived a generalization bound controlled by the Hausdorff dimension, which is associated with the tail properties of the process. Their results suggest that processes with heavier tails should achieve better generalization. Barsbey et al. [2] argued that the heavy-tailed behavior present in the weight matrices of a neural network contributes to network compressibility, thereby enhancing the network's generalization capabilities. Taken together, these results suggest that the heavy tail of weight matrices is a fundamental factor for the improved generalization of DNNs under SGD.

An intuitive notion arising from these theories is that the presence of heavy tails of weight matrices during DNN training is crucial for achieving favorable generalization performance. However, previous studies provide a limited understanding of how to enhance the heavy-tailed behavior in neural networks. In this study, our focus lies in regularizing DNNs to facilitate more rapid and pronounced heavy-tailed behavior. To this end, we introduce an explicit regularization technique called **Heavy-Tailed Regularization**. We empirically demonstrate that models trained with heavy-tailed regularization display superior generalization performance compared to those trained with conventional methods.

Contribution of This Paper

1. We propose a regularization framework termed *Heavy-Tailed Regularization*. This proposal is motivated by prior research, which has shown that the heavy-tailed behavior of weight matrices in neural networks can improve their generalization capabilities.
2. We develop four distinct heavy-tailed regularization methods, including (a) Weighted Alpha regularization, (b) Stable Rank regularization, (c) Power-law Prior, and (d) Fréchet Prior. The first two methods are inspired by existing complexity measures for neural networks, while the latter two are informed by insights from random matrix theory (RMT) and Bayesian statistics.
3. We made comparison with conventional methods on widely used datasets including KMNIST and CIFAR10. Numerical experiments show that the heavy-tailed regularization approaches are efficient and outperform competing conventional regularization methods.

2 Heavy-Tailed Regularization

2.1 Definition

Consider a DNN $f_{\mathbf{W}} : \mathcal{X} \rightarrow \mathcal{Y}$ with L layers and with weight matrices of its fully connected layers $\mathbf{W} = \{\mathbf{W}_1, \mathbf{W}_2, \cdots, , \mathbf{W}_L\}$ and data sample set $S = \{(x_1, y_1), (x_2, y_2) \cdots, (x_N, y_N)\}$ with sample size N.

Denote $l(f(x), y)$ the loss of example $(x, y) \in \mathcal{X} \times \mathcal{Y}$ under model $f_{\mathbf{W}}$. The optimization problem of the DNN can be viewed as a problem of minimizing the empirical risk with a penalty term:

$$\min_{\mathbf{W}} \quad \mathcal{L}(x, y) = \frac{1}{N} \sum_{i=1}^{N} l(f(x_i), y_i) + \lambda \sum_{l=1}^{L} p_l(\mathbf{W}_l), \tag{1}$$

where λ is a tuning parameter and $p_l(\cdot)$ is a penalty function on the weight matrices.

Here, we propose a class of regularization methods called **Heavy-Tailed Regularization**, which refers to the regularization methods that are conducive to making the model's weight matrices more heavy-tailed. To achieve this goal, $p_l(\cdot)$ is supposed to be a complex measure of the model that reflects the degree of the heavy-tailed behavior of the model, and it decreases as the tails get heavier.

To describe the degree of heavy tails of the spectra of the weight matrices, it is critical to estimate the tail index α. In statistics, estimating the tail index is a tricky issue. Denote the data points $\{x_i, 1 \le i \le n\}$ and assume the data come from a heavy-tailed distribution with density function $p(x) \sim cx^{-\alpha}$, i.e., its p.d.f. is comparable with *power-law* $x^{-\alpha}$ as $x \to \infty$. A general method to estimate the tail index α is the Hill estimator (HE), which can be used for general power-law settings. If the data is sorted in increasing order, the HE can be written by:

$$\hat{\alpha} = 1 + \frac{k}{\left(\sum_{i=1}^{k} \ln \frac{x_{n-i+1}}{x_{n-k}}\right)}, \tag{2}$$

where k is a tuning parameter. There is a trade-off depending on the value of k between the bias and variance of the estimator. In this study, we use HE with $k = \frac{n}{2}$ for tail index estimation.

2.2 Weighted Alpha Regularization

Motivated by Martin and Mahoney's work [15,17,18], the *Weighted Alpha* (also called *AlphaHat*) is used in our regularization approach. In their theory, there is a strong linear correlation between the test accuracy and the Weighted Alpha of models. The Weighted Alpha is defined as:

$$\text{Weighted Alpha}(\mathbf{W}) = \sum_{l=1}^{L} \alpha_l \log \lambda_{\max,l}, \tag{3}$$

where α_l is the tail index of all the positive eigenvalues of $\mathbf{S}_l = \mathbf{W}_l^T \mathbf{W}_l$, and $\lambda_{\max,l}$ is the maximum eigenvalue of $\mathbf{S}_l$. In Martin and Mahoney's theory, only the performance of Weighted Alpha on different architectures of large-scale, pre-trained, state-of-the-art models was discussed. While we are interested in how this metric changes during the training process of DNNs. Here, we conducted some experiments and obtained evidence that Weighted Alpha is *negatively correlated* with test accuracy. Thus, the penalty function $p_l(\cdot)$ can be written as

$$p_l(\mathbf{W}_l) = \alpha_l \cdot \log \lambda_{\max,l}. \tag{4}$$

In fact, we do not need to penalize the weighted alpha throughout the training process. Our goal is to impose a heavy-tailed perturbation in the stochastic optimization, which only requires us to activate the regularization in the early stages or intermittently. Otherwise, it will be over-regularized. On the other hand, for practical reasons, we can terminate the regularization at some point to avoid high computational costs. Therefore, we provide two additional variants of the penalty function as follows:

1. Decay Weighted Alpha:

$$p_l(\mathbf{W}_l) = d(\lfloor e/m \rfloor) \cdot \alpha_l \cdot \log \lambda_{\max,l}, \tag{5}$$

where e is the current epoch number, m is the frequency of decay, and $d(\cdot)$ is a decreasing function called the *decay function.* The decay function is called *power decay* when $d(x) = x^{-k} I_{\{} x^{-k} > t\}$ and called *exponential decay* when $d(x) = \exp(-kx) I_{\{} \exp(-kx) > t\}$ for the hyperparameter k and t. The adoption of this penalty function means that the regularization is activated only in the early epochs and becomes weaker with training.
2. Lower Threshold Weighted Alpha:

$$p_l(\mathbf{W}_l) = \alpha_l \cdot \log \lambda_{\max,l} \cdot I\left\{\sum_{l=1}^{L} \alpha_l \cdot \log \lambda_{\max,l} \geqslant t\right\}, \tag{6}$$

where t is a hyperparameter, $I\{\cdot\}$ is the indicator function. The adoption of this penalty function means that the regularization is activated only when the Weighted Alpha is above a predetermined lower threshold t, i.e., the model falls short of the degree of the heavy tail we expect.

2.3 Stable Rank Regularization

Stable rank is a classical metric in deep learning, which is defined as

$$\text{stable}(\mathbf{W}_l) = \frac{||\mathbf{W}_l||_F^2}{||\mathbf{W}_l||_2^2}. \tag{7}$$

It has been verified that the stable rank decreases as the training of DNNs [16]. Several recent studies [4,21] also shows that the generalization error can be upper bounded by $O\left(\prod_i ||\mathbf{W}_i||_2^2 \sum_i \text{stable}(\mathbf{W}_i)\right)$, which implies that a smaller $\sum_i \text{stable}(\mathbf{W}_i)$ leads to a smaller generalization error. In light of this, the penalty function for the stable rank regularization can be written as $p_l(\mathbf{W}_l) = \text{stable}(\mathbf{W}_l)$, and thus the optimization problem can be written as

$$\min_{\mathbf{W}} \quad \mathcal{L}(x, y) = \sum_{i=1}^{N} l(f(x_i), y_i) + \lambda \sum_{l=1}^{L} \frac{||\mathbf{W}_l||_F^2}{||\mathbf{W}_l||_2^2} \tag{8}$$

Note that $||\mathbf{W}||_F^2$ is the sum of square singular values of $\mathbf{W}$ and $||\mathbf{W}||_2$ is the maximum singular value of $\mathbf{W}$. Recall the random matrix theory, when the matrix is heavy-tailed, the maximum eigenvalue is far off the global spectrum. Combined with Martin's 5+1 phase transition theory [16], a smaller stable rank of the weight matrix leads to stronger heavy-tailed self-regularization.

Similar to the weighted alpha regularization, in order to avoid over-regularization, we can also add decay and upper threshold to stable rank regularization as follows:

1. Decay Stable Rank:

$$p_l(\mathbf{W}_l) = d(\lfloor e/m \rfloor) \cdot \frac{\|\mathbf{W}_l\|_F^2}{\|\mathbf{W}_l\|_2^2}. \tag{9}$$

2. Lower Threshold Stable Rank:

$$p_l(\mathbf{W}_l) = \frac{\|\mathbf{W}_l\|_F^2}{\|\mathbf{W}_l\|_2^2} \cdot I\left\{\sum_{l=1}^{L} \frac{\|\mathbf{W}_l\|_F^2}{\|\mathbf{W}_l\|_2^2} \geqslant t\right\}. \tag{10}$$

2.4 Heavy Tailed Regularization from a Bayesian Perspective

Here, we propose two heavy-tailed regularization methods from a Bayesian perspective. Let us view the deep neural network as a probabilistic model $P(\mathbf{y}|\mathbf{x}, \mathbf{W})$, where $\mathbf{x} \in \mathcal{X} = \mathbb{R}^p$ is the input and $\mathbf{y} \in \mathcal{Y}$ is the output probability assigned by the neural network. $\mathbf{W} = \{\mathbf{W}_1, \cdots, \mathbf{W}_L\}$ is the set of weight matrices of the neural network. Given a training sample set $S = \{(x_1, y_1), (x_2, y_2) \cdots, (x_N, y_N)\}$ with sample size N, a common method for estimating the weights $\mathbf{W}$ is the maximum likelihood estimation (MLE):

$$\mathbf{W}^{\text{MLE}} = \arg\max_{\mathbf{W}} \sum_{i=1}^{N} \log P(y_i | x_i, \mathbf{W}). \tag{11}$$

Specifically, for a multi-classification task, the probabilistic model is usually a multinomial distribution, and then the MLE can be written as

$$\mathbf{W}^{\text{MLE}} = \arg\max_{\mathbf{W}} \sum_{i=1}^{N} y_i \log f_{\mathbf{W}}(x_i). \tag{12}$$

From a Bayesian perspective, if we want to introduce the heavy-tailed regularization upon the model, we can assign a heavy-tailed prior upon the probabilistic model and then find the maximum a posteriori (MAP) rather than MLE:

$$\mathbf{W}^{\text{MAP}} = \arg\max_{\mathbf{W}} \log P(\mathbf{y} | \mathbf{x}, \mathbf{W}) + \log P(\mathbf{W}). \tag{13}$$

Thus, it is important to choose a reasonable prior $P(\mathbf{W})$ for the weights which can make the weights more heavy-tailed.

Recall the Random Matrix Theory for the heavy-tailed matrices, if a random matrix is heavy-tailed, its limiting spectral distribution (LSD) is supposed to be power-law [7–9] and its largest eigenvalue is supposed to be Fréchet distribution [1,23]. Therefore, it is easy to consider that prior distribution can be set as Power-law or Fréchet distribution when we introduce prior knowledge of the global spectrum or maximum eigenvalue.

Now we introduce the heavy-tailed prior upon the model. Firstly we consider the prior of global spectra of weight matrices. When the weight matrices are heavy-tailed, the LSD is power-law, so the prior distribution can be set as

$$P(\mathbf{W}) = \prod_{l=1}^{L} P(\mathbf{W}_l) \propto \prod_{l=1}^{L} \prod_{j=1}^{K_l} \lambda_{l,j}^{-\alpha_l}, \tag{14}$$

where α_l is the tail index of the power-law of square singular value of weight matrix $\mathbf{W}_l$ in the l-th layer of the neural network, $\lambda_{l,j}$ is the j-th square singular value of $\mathbf{W}_l$. K_l is the number of singular values of $\mathbf{W}_l$ that is considered to be from a heavy-tailed distribution. K_l is a hyperparameter and we choose K_l as half the size of $\mathbf{W}_l$ in our study. Substituting this into (13), we have the following optimization problem:

$$\mathbf{W}^{\mathrm{MAP}} = \arg\max_{\mathbf{W}} \sum_{i=1}^{N} y_i \log f_{\mathbf{W}}(x_i) - \sum_{l=1}^{L} \sum_{j=1}^{K_l} \alpha_l \log \lambda_{l,j} \tag{15}$$

Secondly, we consider the prior of the maximum square singular value of the weight matrices. When the weight matrices are heavy-tailed, the distribution of maximum square singular value is Fréchet distribution, so the prior distribution can be set as

$$P(\mathbf{W}) = \prod_{l=1}^{L} P(\mathbf{W}_l) = \prod_{l=1}^{L} \exp\left(-\lambda_{\max,l}^{-\alpha_l}\right). \tag{16}$$

where α_l is the tail index of $\mathbf{W}_l$ and $\lambda_{\max,l}$ is the maximum square singular value. Similarly, substituting this into (13), we have the following optimization problem:

$$\mathbf{W}^{\mathrm{MAP}} = \arg\max_{\mathbf{W}} \sum_{i=1}^{N} y_i \log f_{\mathbf{W}}(x_i) - \sum_{l=1}^{L} \lambda_{\max,l}^{-\alpha_l}. \tag{17}$$

So far we derive two forms of MAP but we have some problems to solve: How to determine the hyperparameters $\boldsymbol{\alpha} = \{\alpha_l, 1 \le l \le L\}$, and how to solve this maximization problem. In Empirical Bayes, the hyperparameter is determined by maximizing the marginal likelihood of the data, that is

$$\boldsymbol{\alpha} = \arg\max_{\boldsymbol{\alpha}} \log \int P(\mathbf{y}, \mathbf{W} \,|\mathbf{x}, \boldsymbol{\alpha})\, \mathrm{d}\mathbf{W}. \tag{18}$$

It's apparently impossible since the integral is intractable. According to Mandt et al., [13], the SGD can be seen as a variational expectation maximization (VEM) method for Bayesian inference. The maximization problems in (15) and (17) are equivalent to the following minimization problem:

$$\min_{\mathbf{W}} \quad \mathcal{L}(x, y) = \frac{1}{N} \sum_{i=1}^{N} l(f(x_i), y_i) + \sum_{l=1}^{L} \sum_{j=1}^{K_l} \alpha_l \log \lambda_{l,j}, \tag{19}$$

$$\min_{\mathbf{W}} \quad \mathcal{L}(x, y) = \frac{1}{N} \sum_{i=1}^{N} l(f(x_i), y_i) + \sum_{l=1}^{L} \lambda_{\max,l}^{-\alpha_l}, \tag{20}$$

where $l(f(x), y) = -y \log f(x)$ is the cross entropy loss. The hyperparameters $\boldsymbol{\alpha}$ can be optimized when the SGD is seen as a type of VEM algorithm. Instead of the MLE, the Hill estimator is a better choice to estimate the hyperparameters $\boldsymbol{\alpha}$. When the tuning parameter is added, the (19) and (20) can be modified as:

$$\min_{\mathbf{W}} \quad \mathcal{L}(x, y) = \frac{1}{N} \sum_{i=1}^{N} l\left(f\left(x_i\right), y_i\right) + \mu \sum_{l=1}^{L} \sum_{j=1}^{K_l} \hat{\alpha}_l \log \lambda_{l,j}, \tag{21}$$

$$\min_{\mathbf{W}} \quad \mathcal{L}(x, y) = \frac{1}{N} \sum_{i=1}^{N} l\left(f\left(x_i\right), y_i\right) + \mu \sum_{l=1}^{L} \lambda_{\max,l}^{-\hat{\alpha}_l}, \tag{22}$$

where $\hat{\alpha}_l$ is the Hill estimator of the l-th layer weight matrix.

Note that (21) and (22) are the special cases of (1) when $p_l(\mathbf{W}) = \alpha_l \cdot \sum_j \log \lambda_{j,l}$ and $p_l(\mathbf{W}) = \lambda_{\max,l}^{\alpha_l}$. Since the penalty terms are similar to the weighted alpha, these regularization terms can be considered as variants of Weighted Alpha. According to the priors used in these regularizations, we call the (21) **Heavy-Tailed Regularization under Power-law Prior** and the (22) **Heavy-Tailed Regularization under Fréchet Prior**.

3 Experiment

In this section, we experimentally demonstrate the performance of Heavy-Tailed Regularization on multi-classification tasks. To verify the effectiveness of heavy-tailed regularization, we employed the Weighted Alpha Regularization and Stable Rank Regularization with their variants, and the heavy-tailed regularization under the Power-law and Fréchet spectral prior. Here all the tail index is replaced by its Hill estimator with $k = \frac{n}{2}$, where n is the size of corresponding weight matrix. In our experiment, we used the following training methods to compare with the heavy-tailed regularization approach:

1. Vanilla problem (Base): We considered the original model without any explicit regularization.
2. Weight Decay: We considered the most commonly used explicit regularization in (1) where $p_l(\mathbf{W}) = \frac{1}{2}||\mathbf{W}||_F^2$.
3. Spectral Norm Regularization: We considered another explicit regularization method with regards to the spectrum which penalty function $p_l(\mathbf{W}) = \frac{1}{2}||\mathbf{W}||_2^2$.

All the experiments here are based on mini-batch SGD and learning rate decay. In our experiments, we used the following four settings on the model and dataset:

1. The Three Layer Neural Network (FC3) on KMNIST and CIFAR10.
2. The LeNet5 on CIFAR10.
3. The ResNet18 on CIFAR10.

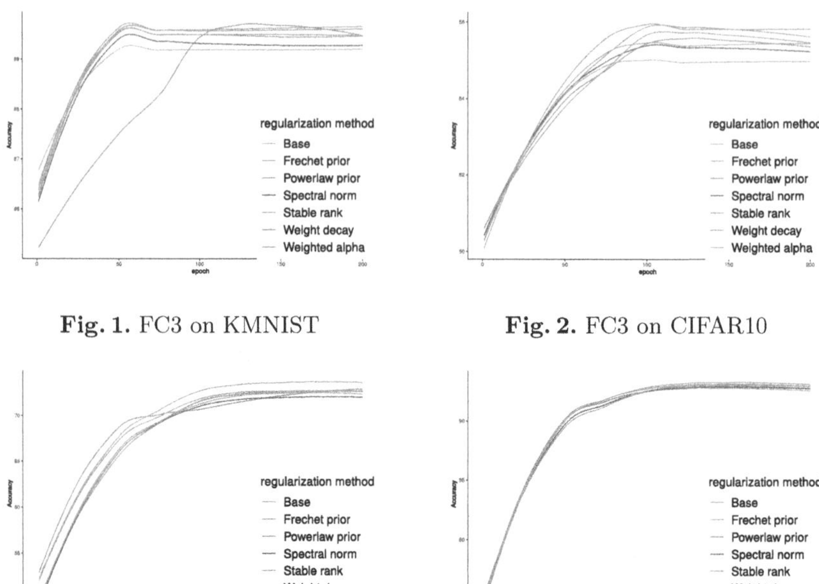

Fig. 1. FC3 on KMNIST

Fig. 2. FC3 on CIFAR10

Fig. 3. LeNet5 on CIFAR10

Fig. 4. ResNet18 on CIFAR10

3.1 FC3

In the first place, we train the neural network with three hidden layers on the KMNIST and CIFAR10 dataset for 200 epochs. The KMNIST dataset is adapted from Kuzushiji Dataset and is a drop-in replacement for the MNIST dataset. The image size of the KMNIST dataset is 28 $\times$ 28. The CIFAR10 dataset consists of 60000 color images whose size is 32 $\times$ 32. The CIFAR10 dataset is more complex than the KMNIST dataset so the CIFAR10 dataset is more difficult to be classified correctly. Because the image size of these two datasets varied, we use two types of three-layer neural networks with different sizes for each dataset. For the KMNIST dataset, we use the network with sizes of layers $\mathbf{n} = [784, 128, 128, 128, 10]$; For the CIFAR10 dataset, we use the network with sizes of layers $\mathbf{n} = [3072, 512, 256, 256, 10]$.

The results are shown in Fig. 1, 2 and Table 1. The heavy-tailed regularizations all show better accuracies than the vanilla problem both on the KMNIST dataset and the CIFAR10 dataset. The Fréchet prior achieves the best test accuracy on the KMNIST dataset, and the stable rank with lower threshold of $t = 15$ achieves the best test accuracy on the CIFAR10 dataset.

3.2 LeNet5

Secondly, we train the LeNet5 on the CIFAR10 dataset for 200 epochs. The LeNet5 is a famous and classical convolutional neural network (CNN) architec-

Table 1. The average (± standard error) of test accuracy of FC3 with different regularization methods on the KMNIST and CIFAR10 dataset

Network	Dataset	Method	β	Test accuracy
FC3	KMNIST	base		89.19 ± 0.020
		weight decay	5.00×10^{-4}	89.44 ± 0.037
		spectral norm	0.0001	89.27 ± 0.013
		weighted alpha[a]	5.00×10^{-5}	89.60 ± 0.011
		stable rank[b]	1.00×10^{-4}	89.48 ± 0.008
		Power-law prior	5.00×10^{-4}	89.58 ± 0.175
		Fréchet prior	$\mathbf{2.00} \times 10^{-5}$	$\mathbf{89.64 \pm 0.173}$
	CIFAR10	base		54.97 ± 0.039
		weight decay	5.00×10^{-4}	55.56 ± 0.092
		spectral norm	0.0001	55.27 ± 0.003
		weighted alpha[a]	1.00×10^{-4}	55.72 ± 0.053
		stable rank[b]	$\mathbf{1.00} \times 10^{-4}$	$\mathbf{55.82 \pm 0.041}$
		Power-law prior	5.00×10^{-5}	55.44 ± 0.038
		Fréchet prior	5.00×10^{-5}	55.45 ± 0.029

[a] We use power decay weighted alpha with $k = 2$.
[b] We use lower threshold stable rank with $t = 1$.

Table 2. The average (± standard error) of test accuracy of LeNet5 with different regularization methods on the CIFAR10 dataset

Network	Dataset	Method	β	Test Accuracy
LeNet5	CIFAR10	base		72.42 ± 0.213
		weight decay	5.00×10^{-4}	72.62 ± 0.277
		spectral norm	0.0001	71.98 ± 0.275
		weighted alpha[a]	0.004	72.61 ± 0.300
		stable rank	**0.1**	$\mathbf{73.63 \pm 0.193}$
		Power-law prior	7.00×10^{-4}	72.61 ± 1.061
		Frechet prior	5.00×10^{-5}	72.58 ± 0.270

[a] We use power decay weighted alpha with $k = 2$.

ture. The results are shown in Fig. 3 and Table 2. The heavy-tailed regularization also all shows better accuracy than the vanilla problem both on the CIFAR10 dataset. As shown in the table, the stable rank with $\beta = 0.1$ achieves the best test accuracy.

3.3 ResNet18

Thirdly, we train the ResNet18 on the CIFAR10 dataset for 200 epochs. The ResNet is a CNN architecture which greatly advanced the SOTA in various computer vision tasks. In this experiment, we add one linear layer with size

Table 3. The average (± standard error) of test accuracy of ResNet18 with different regularization methods on the CIFAR10 dataset

Network	Dataset	Method	β	Test accuracy
ResNet18	CIFAR10	base		92.65 ± 0.066
		weight decay	5.00×10^{-4}	93.15 ± 0.087
		spectral norm	0.0001	92.78 ± 0.069
		weighted alpha	5.00×10^{-5}	93.04 ± 0.045
		stable rank	$\mathbf{5.00} \times 10^{-4}$	$\mathbf{93.19 \pm 0.049}$
		Power-law prior	1.00×10^{-4}	92.85 ± 0.111
		Frechet prior	3.00×10^{-5}	93.07 ± 0.086

of 512×128 before the linear layer in the origin ResNet18 architecture. The results are shown in Fig. 4 and Table 3. As shown in the table, the stable rank with $\beta = 5 \times 10^{-4}$ achieves the best test accuracy.

Acknowledgements. Zeng Li's research is partially supported by NSFC (National Nature Science Foundation of China) Grant NO. 12101292, NSFC Grant NO. 12031005, Shenzhen Fundamental Research Program JCYJ20220818100602005.

References

1. Auffinger, A., Ben Arous, G., Péché, S.: Poisson convergence for the largest eigenvalues of heavy tailed random matrices. In: Annales de l'IHP Probabilités et Statistiques, vol. 45, pp. 589–610 (2009)
2. Barsbey, M., Sefidgaran, M., Erdogdu, M.A., Richard, G., Simsekli, U.: Heavy tails in SGD and compressibility of overparametrized neural networks. Adv. Neural. Inf. Process. Syst. **34**, 29364–29378 (2021)
3. Bartlett, P., Maiorov, V., Meir, R.: Almost linear VC dimension bounds for piecewise polynomial networks. Adv. Neural. Inf. Process. Syst. **11** (1998)
4. Bartlett, P.L., Foster, D.J., Telgarsky, M.J.: Spectrally-normalized margin bounds for neural networks. Adv. Neural. Inf. Process. Syst. **30** (2017)
5. Bartlett, P.L., Mendelson, S.: Rademacher and Gaussian complexities: risk bounds and structural results. J. Mach. Learn. Res. **3**(Nov), 463–482 (2002)
6. Chen, Q., Zhao, H., Li, W., Huang, P., Ou, W.: Behavior sequence transformer for e-commerce recommendation in Alibaba. In: Proceedings of the 1st International Workshop on Deep Learning Practice for High-Dimensional Sparse Data (2019). https://doi.org/10.1145/3326937.3341261, http://dx.doi.org/10.1145/3326937.3341261
7. Davis, R.A., Heiny, J., Mikosch, T., Xie, X.: Extreme value analysis for the sample autocovariance matrices of heavy-tailed multivariate time series. Extremes **19**(3), 517–547 (2016). https://doi.org/10.1007/s10687-016-0251-7
8. Davis, R.A., Mikosch, T., Pfaffel, O.: Asymptotic theory for the sample covariance matrix of a heavy-tailed multivariate time series. Stochast. Process. Appl. **126**(3), 767–799 (2016)

9. Davis, R.A., Pfaffel, O., Stelzer, R.: Limit theory for the largest eigenvalues of sample covariance matrices with heavy-tails. Stochast. Process. Appl. **124**(1), 18–50 (2014)
10. Galassi, A., Lippi, M., Torroni, P.: Attention in natural language processing. IEEE Trans. Neural Netw. Learn. Syst. **32**(10), 4291–4308 (2020). https://doi.org/10.1109/tnnls.2020.3019893, http://dx.doi.org/10.1109/tnnls.2020.3019893
11. He, K., Zhang, X., Ren, S., Sun, J.: Deep residual learning for image recognition. In: Proceedings of the IEEE Conference on Computer Vision and Pattern Recognition, pp. 770–778 (2016)
12. Hodgkinson, L., Mahoney, M.: Multiplicative noise and heavy tails in stochastic optimization. In: International Conference on Machine Learning, pp. 4262–4274. PMLR (2021)
13. Mandt, S., Hoffman, M.D., Blei, D.M.: Stochastic gradient descent as approximate Bayesian inference. arXiv preprint arXiv:1704.04289 (2017)
14. Martin, C.H., Mahoney, M.W.: Traditional and heavy-tailed self regularization in neural network models. arXiv preprint arXiv:1901.08276 (2019)
15. Martin, C.H., Mahoney, M.W.: Heavy-tailed universality predicts trends in test accuracies for very large pre-trained deep neural networks. In: Proceedings of the 2020 SIAM International Conference on Data Mining, pp. 505–513. SIAM (2020)
16. Martin, C.H., Mahoney, M.W.: Implicit self-regularization in deep neural networks: evidence from random matrix theory and implications for learning. J. Mach. Learn. Res. **22**(165), 1–73 (2021)
17. Martin, C.H., Mahoney, M.W.: Post-mortem on a deep learning contest: a Simpson's paradox and the complementary roles of scale metrics versus shape metrics. arXiv preprint arXiv:2106.00734 (2021)
18. Martin, C.H., Peng, T.S., Mahoney, M.W.: Predicting trends in the quality of state-of-the-art neural networks without access to training or testing data. Nat. Commun. **12**(1), 1–13 (2021)
19. Meng, X., Yao, J.: Impact of classification difficulty on the weight matrices spectra in deep learning and application to early-stopping. arXiv preprint arXiv:2111.13331 (2021)
20. Nagarajan, V., Kolter, J.Z.: Uniform convergence may be unable to explain generalization in deep learning. Adv. Neural Inf. Process. Syst. **32** (2019)
21. Neyshabur, B., Bhojanapalli, S., Srebro, N.: A PAC-Bayesian approach to spectrally-normalized margin bounds for neural networks. arXiv preprint arXiv:1707.09564 (2017)
22. Simsekli, U., Sener, O., Deligiannidis, G., Erdogdu, M.A.: Hausdorff dimension, heavy tails, and generalization in neural networks. Adv. Neural. Inf. Process. Syst. **33**, 5138–5151 (2020)
23. Soshnikov, A.: Poisson statistics for the largest eigenvalues of Wigner random matrices with heavy tails. Electron. Commun. Probab. **9**, 82–91 (2004)
24. Vapnik, V., Levin, E., Le Cun, Y.: Measuring the VC-dimension of a learning machine. Neural Comput. **6**(5), 851–876 (1994)
25. Vaswani, A., et al.: Attention is all you need. ArXiv abs/1706.03762 (2017)
26. Zhang, C., Bengio, S., Hardt, M., Recht, B., Vinyals, O.: Understanding deep learning (still) requires rethinking generalization. Commun. ACM **64**(3), 107–115 (2021)
27. Zhou, P., Feng, J., Ma, C., Xiong, C., Hoi, S.C.H., et al.: Towards theoretically understanding why SGD generalizes better than Adam in deep learning. Adv. Neural. Inf. Process. Syst. **33**, 21285–21296 (2020)

Interaction of Generalization and Out-of-Distribution Detection Capabilities in Deep Neural Networks

Francisco Javier Klaiber Aboitiz[1], Robert Legenstein[1], and Ozan Özdenizci[1,2(✉)]

[1] Institute of Theoretical Computer Science, Graz University of Technology, Graz, Austria
f.j.klaiberaboitiz@student.tugraz.at, {robert.legenstein,ozan.ozdenizci}@igi.tugraz.at

[2] TU Graz - SAL Dependable Embedded Systems Lab, Silicon Austria Labs, Graz, Austria

Abstract. Current supervised deep learning models are shown to achieve exceptional performance when data samples used in evaluation come from a known source, but are susceptible to performance degradations when the data distribution is even slightly shifted. In this work, we study the interaction of two related aspects in this context: (1) out-of-distribution (OOD) generalization ability of DNNs to successfully classify samples from unobserved data distributions, and (2) being able to detect strictly OOD samples when observed at test-time, finding that acquisition of these two capabilities can be at odds. We experimentally analyze the impact of various training data related texture and shape biases on both abilities. Importantly, we reveal that naive outlier exposure mechanisms can help to improve OOD detection performance while introducing strong texture biases that conflict with the generalization abilities of the networks. We further explore the influence of such conflicting texture bias backdoors, which lead to unreliable OOD detection performance on spurious OOD samples observed at test-time.

Keywords: Deep neural networks · generalization · out-of-distribution detection · outlier exposure · texture and shape bias

1 Introduction

Deep neural networks (DNNs) have achieved outstanding performance on various image processing tasks over the last decades. However, their degree of success is generally conditioned to the particularities of the test-time evaluated data, as models tend to become vulnerable when tested on unfamiliar images that do

This work has been supported by the "University SAL Labs" initiative of Silicon Austria Labs (SAL) and its Austrian partner universities for applied fundamental research for electronic based systems.

L. Iliadis et al. (Eds.): ICANN 2023, LNCS 14263, pp. 248–259, 2023.
https://doi.org/10.1007/978-3-031-44204-9_21

not belong to the same data distribution as the samples used to train it. This particularly hinders the generalization ability of DNNs in several settings [7,23]. To the contrary, in practical real-world use, the environments and datasets that such models will encounter are often dynamic and frequently change, hence this lack of adaptability constitutes a relevant problem.

Given this circumstance, two desirable capabilities for a DNN arise in order to handle such challenges. Firstly, one would ideally like to have strong *test-time generalization ability*, defined as the capacity to extrapolate to instances out of the training data distribution. In addition, one would also ideally like to distinguish between in-distribution (ID) images that belong or relate to the source training set, and OOD ones that come from a different distribution. This property is often desirable in various applications since it would enable easier categorization of potential misclassifications under uncertain decision making by a deployed DNN. Overall, this points towards the other widely-studied DNN capability, *out-of-distribution (OOD) detection* [21,27].

Although it would be desirable to acquire both capabilities in a trained DNN, state-of-the-art algorithms do not necessarily satisfy them simultaneously, but often interact in conflicting ways depending on the characteristics of the datasets used to train and evaluate them. In this work, we firstly experimentally study if DNNs trained with increased color and texture information become more shape- and less texture-biased, consistently with previous studies [4,10,22]. Accordingly, we show that these networks successfully generalize to instances that are of lesser color or texture complexity, and subsequently become more effective in categorizing such images as ID using various state-of-the-art OOD detection methods that harness internal decision making characteristics of DNNs [8,9,16,17]. Importantly, we reveal that using outlier exposure [9] for more reliable OOD detection can introduce strong texture biases to DNNs during optimization, conflicting with their generalization abilities associated with stronger shape bias. We explore this phenomenon experimentally in depth and expose that this vulnerability extends to unreliable OOD detection on spurious OOD samples.

2 Background

Out-of-Distribution Generalization: Neural networks tend to exploit so-called *shortcuts* during optimization by learning easier and pixel-wise more obvious correlations [3], which leads models not to rely more on complex, yet more correct, environmental features than the ones used in train-time. In this context, training datasets might introduce such shortcut biases for the image classification task, which consist in the repetitive presence of certain non-semantic features (i.e., colors or textures) in the samples belonging to some class that are not truly related to the real class of an image [25]. Hence, during optimization, DNNs can acquire biases that might (mistakenly) make them learn to tag instances that present specific colors/textures to a particular class. More broadly, this impacts their generalization performance on out-of-distribution test samples [3,7].

One well-known example introduces the problem of background bias in DNNs, where predictions are found to occasionally rely on the information in the background of the object to be classified rather than the actual content [26]. This problem is strictly coupled with the diversity of observed training set samples in terms of their objects' presence in a variety of backgrounds. There are several explored methodologies on improving DNNs to overcome such challenges. Mainly these methods rely on data augmentation or manipulation during training.

A relevant line of work aims to improve test-time out-of-distribution generalization capabilities by increasing the shape-bias of networks in their decision making [15,20,26]. In particular, [4] and [22] proposed exploiting stylized and counterfactual images during training in which the color/texture content of foreground and background become arbitrary, such that only the shapes of objects are clearly perceived and eventually learned by the model.

Out-of-Distribution Detection: One other limitation of deep neural networks is their tendency to become overconfident in their predictions on unseen data samples [27]. In various neural network applications, being able to recognize whether a prediction is reliable or not is a desirable property, since one can reduce the potential impact of a misclassification by anticipating its occurrence. In this context, out-of-distribution detection is defined as the capability to identify whether an input image belongs to the same source domain as those used for training, or is instead observed from an unobserved test data domain and the resulting predictions might be unreliable [21].

Several OOD detection algorithms that exploit DNN prediction confidences have been developed to date [21,27]. These algorithms initially rely on the conventional approach to training a DNN for classification, which involves using exclusively in-distribution data where each image is labeled as one of the available classes. A recent state-of-the-art alternative named outlier exposure (OE) [9] has been proposed as an improvement, which consists of utilizing arbitrary OOD data with different content during training towards making unconfident decisions for such samples and thus making it easier to detect similar OOD images at test-time. This approach has been found beneficial in several scenarios, overcoming to some degree the trade-off problem by improving the OOD detection capability of a model. Various improvements to these methods have also been developed over the past years [18,24]. In Sect. 3.2 we describe in detail the benchmark OOD detection methods of particular interest [8,9,16,17].

3 Experiments

3.1 Datasets and Models

We performed our experiments in the context of digit classification from RGB colored images. This choice was mainly motivated based on the fact that digits should be clearly identifiable solely by their shape, in contrast to other categorization tasks where textures or backgrounds could potentially also be useful. We synthetically crafted seven variants of the well-known handwritten MNIST digits dataset [14]. We also experimented with the Street View House Numbers (SVHN) dataset [19] which consists of a real-world digit classification task.

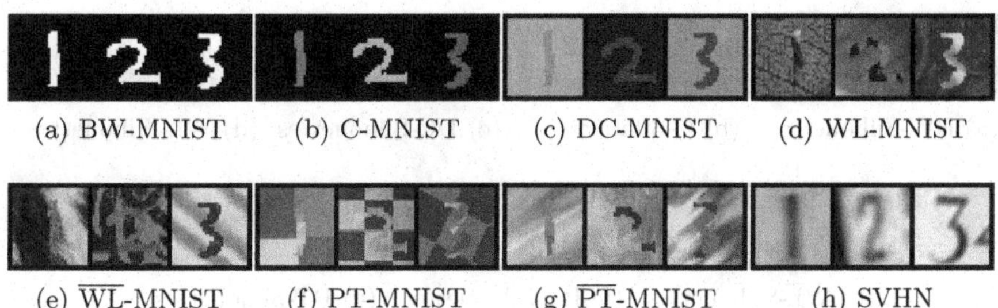

Fig. 1. Digit classification datasets used in our experiments with various foreground and background colors and textures. (Color figure online)

Generated data samples are illustrated in Fig. 1: (a) **Binarized MNIST**, where each grayscale MNIST image was thresholded by 0.5 in pixel value and images were still represented in three color channels. (b) **Colored MNIST**, where for each image the foreground was randomly assigned a color from a list of 10 predefined colors with a slight additional intensity variation. (c) **Double Colored MNIST**, where each image was randomly assigned a foreground-background color pair among the 90 possible combinations. (d) **Wildlife MNIST**, where each image was assigned a foreground-background texture pair from a list of 10 foreground striped animal skin textures and 10 background textures of veined plant leaves [22]. (e) **Wildlife-flip MNIST**, where we swapped the assigned foreground and background pair of each image in wildlife MNIST. (f) **Patterned MNIST**, where each image was assigned a foreground-background texture pair from a list of 10 foreground smeared paintings and 10 chequered background textures retrieved from the Describable Textures Dataset [1]. (g) **Patterned-flip MNIST**, where we swapped the assigned foreground and background pair of each image in patterned MNIST.

During dataset generation we ensured that for every class, each foreground-background color or texture pair was represented by an approximately equal number of instances, in order to prevent any class-associative dataset bias in our experiments. We considered samples from the CIFAR-10 [12] dataset while training models with outlier exposure to be the strictly OOD examples. All images were represented within the same normalization range in $[-1, 1]$.

Additionally we also generated synthetic *spurious OOD* evaluation datasets of 10,000 samples that did not contain any digits, but consisted of the same binarized, colored, double-colored, wildlife and patterned contextual cues. Firstly we created seven **Silhouettes** dataset variants (see Fig. 2), which contained images with the shape of the silhouettes of different animals or objects from ten categories (i.e., umbrella, starfish, anchor, lamp, ibis, pigeon, butterfly, dragonfly, guitar, sea horse). These categories were hand-selected and customized from the Caltech 101 Silhouettes Dataset [2]. Similarly, we created seven **Omniglot** dataset variants (see Fig. 3), which contained images of handwritten alphabet

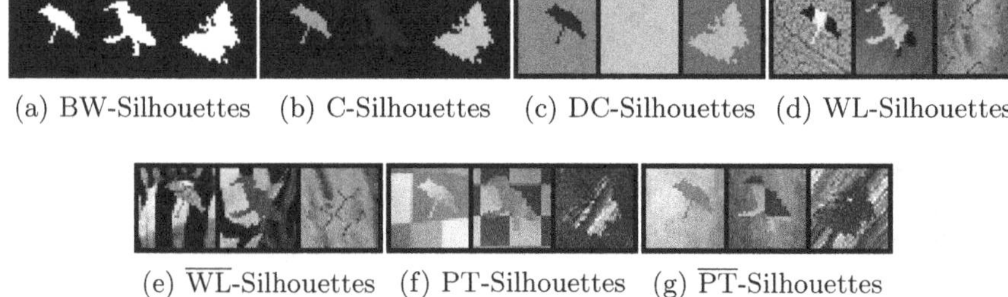

(a) BW-Silhouettes (b) C-Silhouettes (c) DC-Silhouettes (d) WL-Silhouettes

(e) $\overline{\text{WL}}$-Silhouettes (f) PT-Silhouettes (g) $\overline{\text{PT}}$-Silhouettes

Fig. 2. Silhouettes variant datasets used in our experiments with various foreground and background colors and textures. (Color figure online)

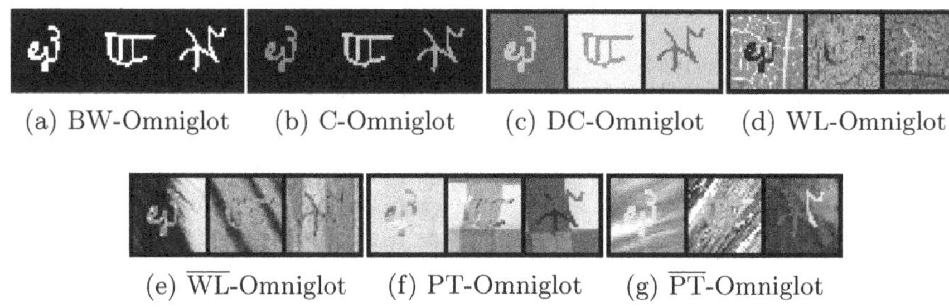

(a) BW-Omniglot (b) C-Omniglot (c) DC-Omniglot (d) WL-Omniglot

(e) $\overline{\text{WL}}$-Omniglot (f) PT-Omniglot (g) $\overline{\text{PT}}$-Omniglot

Fig. 3. Omniglot variant datasets used in our experiments with various foreground and background colors and textures. (Color figure online)

characters from various different languages. We arbitrarily selected a subset of 10,000 images from the original Omniglot dataset [13].

We used a ResNet-18 architecture in all our experiments [6]. Parameter updates during training were performed using an Adam optimizer [11] with a learning rate of 0.001 and a weight decay parameter of 0.0001. Training of a model lasted for at most 50 epochs using mini-batches of size 32, and terminated via early stopping based on a validation set loss.

3.2 Benchmark Out-of-Distribution Detection Methods

Maximum Softmax Probability: Seminal work by [8] proposes to use the *maximum softmax probability* (MSP) for each prediction to categorize each sample as in- or out-of-distribution depending on whether this softmax probability assigned confidence is greater or lower than some threshold. For a given neural network f and input sample x, the MSP score is then calculated as in Eq. (1).

$$\text{Score}_{\text{MSP}}(x; f) = \max_{i \in K} \frac{\exp(f_i(x))}{\sum_{j=1}^{K} \exp(f_j(x))}, \tag{1}$$

where $f_i(x)$ indicates the logit value for the i-th class across K classes.

Energy-Based OOD Detection: Subsequent work from [17] alternatively proposes to harness all obtained logit values by the model to compute an energy function and an associated *energy score* for OOD detection as in Eq. (2).

$$\text{Score}_{\text{Energy}}(x; f) = \log \sum_{i \in K} \exp\left(f_i(x)\right). \tag{2}$$

This formulation views DNNs with a softmax output activation simultaneously as energy-based models that estimate the probability density $p(x)$ through the Gibbs distribution, where the energy for a given input pair (x, y) is represented by the negative of the y-th logit value, $E(x, y) = -f_y(x)$ [5]. Overall, this score estimates prediction uncertainty such that the higher the total energy, the lower score will be, and also the confidence on the sample being ID.

Input Perturbation Based OOD Detection (ODIN): This method proposed by [16] exploits perturbed versions of each image before computing scores. Specifically, as obtained via Eq. (3), ODIN relies on the assumption that small modifications in the direction of the gradient tend to increase the MSP of ID samples more than OOD samples, hence the MSP score of these perturbed instances would now yield more reliable OOD detection scores.

$$\begin{aligned} &\text{Score}_{\text{ODIN}}(x; f) = \text{Score}_{\text{MSP}}(\overline{x}; f) \\ &\text{where} \quad \overline{x} = x - \epsilon \text{sign}(-\nabla_x \log(\text{Score}_{\text{MSP}}(x; f))). \end{aligned} \tag{3}$$

Outlier Exposure (OE): One of the most widely-acknowledged improvements to existing OOD detection methods by [9] proposes to extend the conventional training loss function by not only taking into account in-distribution data but also arbitrary out-of-distribution samples whose labels do not relate to the ID ones and always considered equiprobable. Specifically, OE was shown to improve the performance of any existing OOD detection score measure by changing the model training procedure with the proposed loss function in Eq. (4).

$$\mathbb{E}_{(x,y)\sim D_{\text{ID}}}[\mathcal{L}(f(x), y)] + \lambda \cdot \mathbb{E}_{\tilde{x}\sim D_{\text{OOD}}^{\text{OE}}}[\mathcal{L}_{\text{OE}}(f(\tilde{x}), \tilde{y}))], \tag{4}$$

where $\mathcal{L}_{\text{OE}}$ minimizes the cross-entropy loss from $f(\tilde{x})$ to the uniform distribution for $\tilde{y}$. This way the model assigns uniform probability across all classes for arbitrary OOD instances, in order to better distinguish between ID and OOD samples using confidence score based metrics.

3.3 Evaluation Metrics

We used two conventionally adopted metrics to evaluate the OOD detection performance of the previously described approaches based on their respective score measures. Firstly we used **AUROC** as a threshold-independent metric that calculates the area under the receiver operating characteristic curve. For

Table 1. Classification accuracies of evaluated models. Light gray boxes indicate evaluations on ID test sets and test sets with simpler complexities where strong generalization is observed. Dark gray boxes with bold values indicate evaluations on a (ID) test set with the foreground-background texture flip.

Training dataset	Loss function	Testing dataset							
		BW-MNIST	C-MNIST	DC-MNIST	WL-MNIST	$\overline{\text{WL}}$-MNIST	PT-MNIST	$\overline{\text{PT}}$-MNIST	SVHN
BW-MNIST	Classic	98.29	65.32	24.09	21.53	15.03	16.84	17.59	20.59
	with OE	97.62	62.38	31.92	30.91	16.04	21.28	24.94	17.14
C-MNIST	Classic	98.71	98.65	14.85	15.87	17.34	16.00	14.07	10.97
	with OE	84.60	98.32	11.54	17.85	15.78	13.17	13.43	13.80
DC-MNIST	Classic	97.94	97.69	97.99	56.80	51.32	49.66	54.23	37.26
	with OE	93.34	96.37	97.97	68.91	68.80	55.92	59.62	20.44
WL-MNIST	Classic	98.60	98.03	97.77	98.12	**92.99**	87.52	87.51	22.25
	with OE	97.04	89.54	77.14	95.55	**43.21**	53.55	63.12	26.82
PT-MNIST	Classic	95.06	90.88	95.54	88.00	87.54	97.50	**81.49**	32.58
	with OE	39.78	50.33	78.14	57.80	71.82	95.67	**52.17**	34.45
SVHN	Classic	70.27	69.96	68.93	29.99	31.32	32.83	30.96	93.27
	with OE	43.38	47.34	39.19	23.62	22.22	25.39	24.77	92.12

this metric, a perfect OOD detector would obtain an AUROC score of 100%. Secondly we used the metric **false positive rate at 95% of true positive rate (FPR95)**, which estimates the ratio of OOD (negative) samples that are misclassified as in-distribution (positive) when the true positive rate is as high as 95%. For this metric, a better OOD detector obtains lower FPR95 scores.

4 Experimental Results

4.1 Improving OOD Generalization by Increasing Shape Bias

Our evaluations on model generalization with training and test sets of increasing color and texture complexities are shown in Table 1. We observe that models trained with a specific foreground-background combination using the classic cross-entropy loss function generalizes well to test images with lower complexities (see light gray boxes in Table 1) due to their gradually increasing shape bias and reduced color/texture bias, consistently with previous studies [4,22].

On the other hand, we observed (somewhat expected) side effects of increasing the shape bias of the model to foster generalization, which is the reduced OOD detection capability on simpler MNIST-variants. We depict this in Tables 2, 3 and 4 consistently across MSP, Energy and ODIN score based methods, for models trained with the classic loss function. To illustrate with an example, in Table 2 with the MSP scores, DC-MNIST models trained with the classic loss achieve lower AUROC and higher FPR95 on test sets with simpler complexities (AUROC/FPR95: 46.79/94.70 on BW, 54.03/93.39 on C), than test sets with higher complexities (AUROC/FPR95: 90.16/37.81 on WL, 92.77/31.76 on $\overline{\text{WL}}$, 92.22/31.40 on PT, 90.33/36.87 on $\overline{\text{PT}}$). These results are also mostly consistent for models using other MNIST-variant training sets, as well as in Tables 3 and 4. This outcome shows that these less complex test sets are now considered to be ID, whereas the model did not precisely observe such samples during training.

Table 2. Evaluations of out-of-distribution sample detection in terms of AUROC (↑) and FPR95 (↓) metrics using *MSP score function* on the MNIST dataset variants and SVHN. We indicate AUROC values of 50.00 and FPR95 values of 95.00 obtained for ID cases with a dash (–).

Training dataset	Loss function	Out-of-distribution detection testing dataset																	
		BW-MNIST		C-MNIST		DC-MNIST		WL-MNIST		$\overline{\text{WL}}$-MNIST		PT-MNIST		$\overline{\text{PT}}$-MNIST		SVHN		CIFAR-10	
		AUROC	FPR95	AUROC	FPR95	AUROC	FPR95	AUROC	FPR95	AUROC	FPR95	AUROC	FPR95	AUROC	FPR95	AUROC	FPR95	AUROC	FPR95
BW-MNIST	Classic	–	–	78.65	77.03	94.60	18.65	95.47	27.15	97.16	13.43	96.62	14.97	97.01	12.05	94.75	32.27	97.19	13.60
	with OE	–	–	83.21	66.81	99.77	1.40	99.90	0.60	100.0	0.03	100.0	0.03	99.95	0.26	99.96	0.19	100.0	0.00
C-MNIST	Classic	47.12	95.54	–	–	99.17	0.81	98.60	3.55	98.15	8.17	98.91	2.27	98.70	2.94	98.80	2.67	98.62	3.46
	with OE	83.36	60.97	–	–	96.75	25.33	99.62	1.10	99.44	2.77	99.32	3.07	99.11	4.60	100.0	0.00	100.0	0.00
DC-MNIST	Classic	46.79	94.70	54.03	93.39	–	–	90.16	37.81	92.77	31.76	92.22	31.40	90.33	36.87	97.21	13.28	96.84	20.53
	with OE	98.47	5.24	83.70	71.62	–	–	95.65	23.38	94.88	24.52	97.31	14.42	94.99	21.72	99.92	0.30	100.0	0.00
WL-MNIST	Classic	50.78	95.81	58.27	92.71	55.65	92.69	–	–	76.67	77.34	81.31	68.09	78.14	70.13	91.89	78.77	98.37	5.58
	with OE	41.75	97.39	62.28	85.51	71.33	68.18	–	–	**95.97**	**25.19**	92.79	38.13	86.71	47.40	98.06	12.16	100.0	0.00
PT-MNIST	Classic	80.25	81.68	71.14	83.51	54.61	92.37	77.24	72.80	74.17	73.59	–	–	85.47	57.39	92.50	49.82	97.89	11.00
	with OE	98.67	9.77	98.53	11.09	71.30	61.68	91.47	31.59	88.85	50.36	–	–	**95.17**	**27.84**	97.83	14.29	100.0	0.00
SVHN	Classic	79.69	76.04	80.17	74.17	79.49	76.57	89.49	57.12	89.15	58.33	89.30	57.81	89.50	57.96	–	–	96.12	27.5
	with OE	92.43	47.32	91.95	41.65	94.11	29.81	97.55	16.09	96.86	21.31	96.37	23.80	97.27	18.29	–	–	100.0	0.00

Table 3. Evaluations of out-of-distribution sample detection in terms of AUROC (↑) and FPR95 (↓) metrics using *Energy score function* on the MNIST dataset variants and SVHN. We indicate AUROC values of 50.00 and FPR95 values of 95.00 obtained for ID cases with a dash (–).

Training dataset	Loss function	Out-of-distribution detection testing dataset																	
		BW-MNIST		C-MNIST		DC-MNIST		WL-MNIST		$\overline{\text{WL}}$-MNIST		PT-MNIST		$\overline{\text{PT}}$-MNIST		SVHN		CIFAR-10	
		AUROC	FPR95	AUROC	FPR95	AUROC	FPR95	AUROC	FPR95	AUROC	FPR95	AUROC	FPR95	AUROC	FPR95	AUROC	FPR95	AUROC	FPR95
BW-MNIST	Classic	–	–	68.00	84.83	83.21	87.48	86.19	77.05	89.51	72.25	89.16	70.65	89.09	77.35	79.05	94.21	92.97	54.41
	with OE	–	–	91.90	35.13	100.0	0.10	100.0	0.05	100.0	0.00	100.0	0.00	100.0	0.03	100.0	0.00	100.0	0.00
C-MNIST	Classic	47.34	95.48	–	–	98.88	0.68	98.48	3.21	98.19	6.99	98.82	2.06	98.51	2.64	98.47	3.10	98.42	4.63
	with OE	91.91	31.22	–	–	99.20	1.81	99.97	0.04	99.96	0.07	99.91	0.00	99.95	0.00	98.84	4.31	99.77	0.94
DC-MNIST	Classic	47.10	94.48	54.36	92.84	–	–	91.21	31.03	93.69	25.76	93.10	25.64	91.31	30.85	97.41	10.36	96.81	19.78
	with OE	99.91	0.00	89.79	49.14	–	–	97.88	11.29	97.24	12.92	98.77	5.95	97.01	13.18	100.0	0.05	100.0	0.00
WL-MNIST	Classic	50.65	95.78	58.37	91.49	56.13	91.65	–	–	76.34	73.06	81.36	63.15	78.23	66.57	92.39	67.76	99.24	1.85
	with OE	36.92	99.59	61.92	81.53	73.73	59.21	–	–	**98.22**	**8.09**	95.78	18.88	89.62	31.96	99.28	3.83	100.0	0.00
PT-MNIST	Classic	80.49	76.02	70.43	82.18	54.18	91.68	78.66	66.85	75.31	68.60	–	–	86.88	48.78	91.99	46.49	99.07	3.99
	with OE	99.88	0.00	99.84	0.51	73.16	52.95	93.76	18.37	93.50	28.97	–	–	**97.81**	**9.94**	99.34	3.48	100.0	0.00
SVHN	Classic	79.20	75.63	79.55	75.08	77.80	79.03	91.00	44.72	90.39	46.63	90.05	48.86	90.70	46.47	–	–	97.15	15.11
	with OE	96.70	20.35	95.21	24.85	95.96	18.53	98.92	5.85	98.61	7.43	98.30	9.55	98.77	6.58	–	–	10.00	0.00

Table 4. Evaluations of out-of-distribution sample detection in terms of AUROC (↑) and FPR95 (↓) metrics using *ODIN score function* on the MNIST dataset variants and SVHN. We indicate AUROC values of 50.00 and FPR95 values of 95.00 obtained for ID cases with a dash (–).

Training dataset	Loss function	Out-of-distribution detection testing dataset																	
		BW-MNIST		C-MNIST		DC-MNIST		WL-MNIST		$\overline{\text{WL}}$-MNIST		PT-MNIST		$\overline{\text{PT}}$-MNIST		SVHN		CIFAR-10	
		AUROC	FPR95	AUROC	FPR95	AUROC	FPR95	AUROC	FPR95	AUROC	FPR95	AUROC	FPR95	AUROC	FPR95	AUROC	FPR95	AUROC	FPR95
BW-MNIST	Classic	–	–	76.08	82.17	93.30	53.17	94.31	42.07	96.18	28.03	95.60	26.60	95.98	30.63	93.16	60.53	95.04	37.43
	with OE	–	–	81.27	68.63	99.66	2.27	99.88	0.80	99.98	0.03	99.99	0.00	99.94	0.33	99.93	0.47	100.0	0.00
C-MNIST	Classic	48.57	95.10	–	–	98.81	2.90	97.30	13.20	96.97	15.63	97.86	9.73	97.67	9.77	97.60	12.67	97.40	16.17
	with OE	74.74	83.67	–	–	99.03	5.13	99.09	4.97	98.21	10.67	98.83	6.10	99.42	3.37	99.81	1.20	100.0	0.00
DC-MNIST	Classic	49.89	93.17	55.29	93.90	–	–	84.86	62.17	88.29	50.67	88.50	46.93	84.49	59.33	93.84	35.43	94.62	36.83
	with OE	98.45	7.43	81.42	73.27	–	–	92.56	37.90	91.94	34.07	95.77	22.73	91.73	33.33	99.72	1.40	100.0	0.00
WL-MNIST	Classic	56.81	94.10	72.49	78.60	73.22	76.90	–	–	73.19	79.70	79.34	67.93	71.23	81.63	90.08	82.93	91.74	49.40
	with OE	42.52	97.00	61.24	83.37	77.93	54.87	–	–	**97.16**	**14.23**	93.49	29.77	86.65	43.43	94.94	27.83	99.85	0.50
PT-MNIST	Classic	88.48	59.43	80.41	70.47	66.97	81.47	76.02	74.17	74.32	72.37	–	–	82.98	63.43	86.64	78.13	91.50	49.97
	with OE	99.84	0.40	99.69	1.43	76.46	52.43	91.64	24.47	90.28	40.37	–	–	**95.18**	**23.73**	96.42	20.00	100.0	0.00
SVHN	Classic	91.29	42.20	89.69	46.47	80.52	69.77	91.34	40.73	91.88	38.87	90.39	43.87	90.62	42.17	–	–	96.48	18.80
	with OE	98.03	11.87	96.75	17.53	96.73	15.77	98.62	7.70	98.51	7.60	97.83	11.67	98.47	8.37	–	–	99.98	0.03

Table 5. Experiments on varying the degree of outlier exposure regularization via λ. Accuracies for models trained on WL-MNIST and PT-MNIST are presented for evaluations on ID and flipped test sets.

Training dataset	Testing dataset	Outlier exposure regularization weight					
		$\lambda = 0.00$	$\lambda = 0.15$	$\lambda = 0.25$	$\lambda = 0.50$	$\lambda = 0.75$	$\lambda = 1.00$
WL-MNIST	WL-MNIST	98.12	97.38	97.29	95.55	97.26	97.04
	$\overline{\text{WL}}$-MNIST	92.99	28.19	48.59	43.21	53.76	45.01
PT-MNIST	PT-MNIST	97.50	96.12	94.03	95.67	96.42	94.91
	$\overline{\text{PT}}$-MNIST	81.49	65.56	58.62	52.17	73.15	30.97

Finally, we also observe that with improved generalization, models lead to more false positives to be made on SVHN test samples (e.g., see increased FPR95 metrics in Table 4 with classic loss for WL-MNIST: 82.93, PT-MNIST: 78.13), which signals slightly higher shape-biases to recognize real-world digit images.

4.2 Influence of Outlier Exposure

We investigate the impact the OE (with $\lambda = 0.5$) with respect to models trained with the classic cross-entropy loss. Firstly, in Tables 2, 3 and 4, we observe an improvement of OOD detection performance with increased AUROC and decreased FPR95 metrics in most training-testing combinations, with major improvements in cases where models trained on the classic loss function could not achieve a good performance (e.g., WL-MNIST trained model on the PT-MNIST test set in Table 4 improves an AUROC/FPR95 of 79.34/67.93 (classic) to 93.49/29.77 with OE). Note that these results are consistently obtained for all score functions which reinforces the idea of this enhancement. Note that on the SVHN and CIFAR-10 test sets, OE leads to nearly perfect performance.

One of the most important and conflicting observations is the large increase in AUROC and decrease in FPR95 values from classic to OE, for models trained on WL and PT, when tested on $\overline{\text{WL}}$ and $\overline{\text{PT}}$. These results are highlighted in Tables 2, 3, 4 with dark gray boxes and bold values. While the $\overline{\text{WL}}$ and $\overline{\text{PT}}$ test sets consist of the same textures and digits, simply swapping the foreground and background texture order at test-time significantly decreases the OOD detection performance of the models if they are trained with OE using samples from CIFAR-10 (i.e., a WL-MNIST trained model now tends to detect samples from $\overline{\text{WL}}$ as OOD). This indicates that OE steers the models to be more biased to the textures particularly used for the foreground and background. Note that contrarily, both WL and PT models were in fact trained to have higher shape bias due to the rich texture and color exposure during training. A similar degradation of generalization performance for WL- and PT-MNIST models on $\overline{\text{WL}}$ and $\overline{\text{PT}}$ test sets is also observed in terms of classification accuracies in Table 1 (see dark gray boxes with bold values). We did not observe a significant impact of OE for models trained on BW-, C-, DC-MNIST and SVHN.

We performed ablations on the degree of OE on scenarios where a notable impact due to OE has been observed. Specifically, we take into account models trained on WL and PT for $\lambda \in \{0, 0.15, 0.25, 0.5, 0.75, 1.0\}$, and tested on $\overline{\text{WL}}$ and $\overline{\text{PT}}$. Results presented in Table 5 show that using OE tends to consistently make the models more texture biased, regardless of our default choice of $\lambda = 0.5$.

4.3 Evaluations on Spurious OOD Examples

We performed a final set of OOD detection evaluations on our generated spurious OOD test sets based on Silhouettes and Omniglot, presented in Tables 6 and 7. These test sets share the foreground and background colors and textures with the MNIST ones, but the shape content do not correspond to the digits.

Our main observations are highlighted in dark gray boxes with bold values. We observe that models trained on MNIST variants using OE are now more vulnerable in their OOD detection capabilities with respect to a classic loss-based training approach. We reveal that using OE during training can lead to ×2–3 higher false positives to be made (as measured by the increased FPR95) on successfully detecting spurious OOD test samples. We find this to be another experimental indicator result of these models trained with OE to (adversely) have higher texture biases. Importantly, this conflicting impact of OE was restricted to test cases which specifically contained same spurious features. We did not observe this when models were tested on an OOD variant different from the one used for training (e.g., C-MNIST model tested on BW-, DC-, WL-, $\overline{\text{WL}}$-, PT- or $\overline{\text{PT}}$-Silhouettes or Omniglot). In these cases OOD detection performance was naturally higher, and even improved with respect to the classic setting.

5 Discussion

In this work, we experimentally studied the interaction and trade-off between generalization and OOD detection capabilities in deep neural networks. We have shown that shape and texture biases introduced via the training data can be an important factor that determines how the degree of success is shared between both abilities. In this context, we particularly explored outlier exposure to overcome this problem and improve OOD detection without compromising its generalization capacity. While this approach was found successful in several settings by improving OOD detection capability, it was also shown to have vulnerabilities in certain circumstances. By simply swapping the foreground and background textures at test-time for strongly generalizing models, we showed that OE introduces strong texture bias artifacts to trained models. We explored this hypothesis in depth with additional evaluations on spurious OOD data, and showed that OE can even lead to unreliable OOD detection when spurious OOD instances are considered. Overall, we believe that the choice of outlier samples during training can significantly improve usability of OE, in particular if one considers spurious OOD examples as the outliers during optimization.

Table 6. Evaluations of spurious OOD sample detection using MSP scores, in terms of AUROC (↑) and FPR95 (↓) metrics on the Silhouettes dataset variants.

Training dataset	Loss function	Out-of-distribution detection testing dataset													
		BW-Silhouettes		C-Silhouettes		DC-Silhouettes		WL-Silhouettes		$\overline{\text{WL}}$-Silhouettes		PT-Silhouettes		$\overline{\text{PT}}$-Silhouettes	
		AUROC	FPR95	AUROC	FPR95	AUROC	FPR95	AUROC	FPR95	AUROC	FPR95	AUROC	FPR95	AUROC	FPR95
BW-MNIST	Classic	97.48	**13.78**	92.93	40.29	96.43	12.12	96.64	19.52	97.22	12.61	97.00	12.51	97.35	8.66
	with OE	96.20	**25.40**	92.81	28.07	100.0	0.00	100.0	0.03	100.0	0.00	100.0	0.00	100.0	0.00
C-MNIST	Classic	95.63	25.98	95.78	**25.00**	99.62	1.03	99.11	2.25	98.95	3.89	99.37	1.22	99.36	1.52
	with OE	97.24	19.64	91.82	**51.95**	99.23	3.24	99.64	1.63	98.93	6.88	99.75	1.51	99.76	1.17
DC-MNIST	Classic	97.67	11.85	97.79	10.80	97.43	**13.20**	98.66	4.15	98.63	4.37	98.59	4.48	98.57	4.70
	with OE	99.89	0.07	98.67	7.39	95.52	**31.75**	98.92	5.84	98.87	6.39	98.25	11.70	98.52	9.35
WL-MNIST	Classic	97.79	10.50	97.85	10.00	97.61	12.26	97.49	**12.89**	98.14	7.85	98.19	7.28	98.06	8.06
	with OE	91.76	53.80	93.83	42.70	95.94	28.43	93.35	**46.10**	97.72	15.89	97.59	16.94	97.34	18.37
PT-MNIST	Classic	98.07	9.39	96.48	23.23	97.04	17.88	97.93	10.90	97.80	11.60	96.96	**18.14**	98.37	7.16
	with OE	99.58	2.14	99.68	1.73	96.86	21.37	98.89	7.48	98.65	8.99	93.96	**42.78**	98.43	9.89
SVHN	Classic	89.49	54.54	91.17	49.16	92.02	47.03	92.48	49.20	92.29	49.33	92.34	48.91	92.50	48.29
	with OE	98.89	7.86	98.28	12.32	97.95	13.09	98.31	12.14	98.05	13.83	98.08	13.65	98.46	10.75

Table 7. Evaluations of spurious OOD sample detection using MSP scores, in terms of AUROC (↑) and FPR95 (↓) metrics on the Omniglot dataset variants.

Training dataset	Loss function	Out-of-distribution detection testing dataset													
		BW-Omniglot		C-Omniglot		DC-Omniglot		WL-Omniglot		$\overline{\text{WL}}$-Omniglot		PT-Omniglot		$\overline{\text{PT}}$-Omniglot	
		AUROC	FPR95	AUROC	FPR95	AUROC	FPR95	AUROC	FPR95	AUROC	FPR95	AUROC	FPR95	AUROC	FPR95
BW-MNIST	Classic	96.58	**18.25**	96.58	18.25	96.08	13.22	96.58	18.25	96.97	14.55	96.59	16.73	97.05	9.78
	with OE	95.24	**29.96**	85.99	47.01	100.0	0.00	100.0	0.00	99.95	0.15	100.0	0.00	100.0	0.00
C-MNIST	Classic	96.93	16.43	97.03	**15.77**	99.21	0.55	98.67	2.44	98.55	5.77	99.12	0.91	98.76	2.35
	with OE	97.11	15.54	96.43	**20.42**	97.21	19.75	99.66	0.93	99.36	2.48	99.41	2.00	99.13	3.29
DC-MNIST	Classic	93.93	30.11	95.23	24.64	95.18	**25.72**	97.68	11.53	97.81	10.97	97.47	13.50	97.74	11.48
	with OE	99.96	0.05	99.31	2.47	94.84	**27.15**	99.30	2.44	99.22	3.10	99.20	3.05	99.13	3.93
WL-MNIST	Classic	97.13	15.71	97.07	15.61	96.84	17.05	96.94	**16.77**	97.40	13.22	97.89	9.87	97.65	11.62
	with OE	90.80	54.32	91.64	50.70	95.62	28.45	93.77	**41.71**	98.47	9.84	97.71	16.21	97.54	16.49
PT-MNIST	Classic	96.74	20.10	96.13	26.10	95.90	25.45	97.22	16.08	96.91	18.17	95.75	**24.94**	97.55	13.44
	with OE	100.0	0.00	100.0	0.08	96.10	25.17	98.79	8.03	98.35	11.44	93.14	**44.86**	98.85	7.31
SVHN	Classic	92.05	48.54	92.41	46.09	92.48	44.82	92.95	47.23	92.28	48.25	92.57	46.96	92.46	49.58
	with OE	98.52	10.58	98.44	10.46	98.36	10.96	98.97	7.14	97.53	17.21	98.35	11.49	98.62	9.56

References

1. Cimpoi, M., Maji, S., Kokkinos, I., Mohamed, S., Vedaldi, A.: Describing textures in the wild. In: Proceedings of the IEEE Conference on Computer Vision and Pattern Recognition (2014)
2. Fei-Fei, L., Fergus, R., Perona, P.: Learning generative visual models from few training examples: an incremental Bayesian approach tested on 101 object categories. Computer Vision and Pattern Recognition Workshop (2004)
3. Geirhos, R., et al.: Shortcut learning in deep neural networks. Nat. Mach. Intell. **2**(11), 665–673 (2020)
4. Geirhos, R., Rubisch, P., Michaelis, C., Bethge, M., Wichmann, F.A., Brendel, W.: ImageNet-trained CNNs are biased towards texture; increasing shape bias improves accuracy and robustness. arXiv preprint arXiv:1811.12231 (2018)
5. Grathwohl, W., Wang, K.C., Jacobsen, J.H., Duvenaud, D., Norouzi, M., Swersky, K.: Your classifier is secretly an energy based model and you should treat it like one. In: International Conference on Learning Representations (2020)
6. He, K., Zhang, X., Ren, S., Sun, J.: Deep residual learning for image recognition. In: Proceedings of the IEEE Conference on Computer Vision and Pattern Recognition, pp. 770–778 (2016)

7. Hendrycks, D., Dietterich, T.: Benchmarking neural network robustness to common corruptions and perturbations. arXiv preprint arXiv:1903.12261 (2019)
8. Hendrycks, D., Gimpel, K.: A baseline for detecting misclassified and out-of-distribution examples in neural networks. arXiv preprint arXiv:1610.02136 (2016)
9. Hendrycks, D., Mazeika, M., Dietterich, T.: Deep anomaly detection with outlier exposure. In: International Conference on Learning Representations (2019)
10. Hermann, K., Chen, T., Kornblith, S.: The origins and prevalence of texture bias in convolutional neural networks. Adv. Neural. Inf. Process. Syst. **33**, 19000–19015 (2020)
11. Kingma, D.P., Ba, J.: Adam: a method for stochastic optimization. In: International Conference on Learning Representations (2015)
12. Krizhevsky, A.: Learning multiple layers of features from tiny images. Master's thesis, University of Toronto (2009)
13. Lake, B.M., Salakhutdinov, R., Tenenbaum, J.B.: Human-level concept learning through probabilistic program induction. Science **350**(6266), 1332–1338 (2015)
14. LeCun, Y.: The MNIST database of handwritten digits (1998)
15. Lee, S., Hwang, I., Kang, G.C., Zhang, B.T.: Improving robustness to texture bias via shape-focused augmentation. In: Proceedings of the IEEE/CVF Conference on Computer Vision and Pattern Recognition, pp. 4323–4331 (2022)
16. Liang, S., Li, Y., Srikant, R.: Enhancing the reliability of out-of-distribution image detection in neural networks. arXiv preprint arXiv:1706.02690 (2017)
17. Liu, W., Wang, X., Owens, J., Li, Y.: Energy-based out-of-distribution detection. Adv. Neural. Inf. Process. Syst. **33**, 21464–21475 (2020)
18. Moon, J.H., Ahn, N., Sohn, K.A.: Decomposing texture and semantics for out-of-distribution detection (2022). https://openreview.net/forum?id=UYDtmk6BMf5
19. Netzer, Y., Wang, T., Coates, A., Bissacco, A., Wu, B., Ng, A.Y.: Reading digits in natural images with unsupervised feature learning (2011)
20. Ryali, C., Schwab, D.J., Morcos, A.S.: Learning background invariance improves generalization and robustness in self-supervised learning on ImageNet and beyond. In: NeurIPS 2021 Workshop on ImageNet: Past, Present, and Future (2021)
21. Salehi, M., Mirzaei, H., Hendrycks, D., Li, Y., Rohban, M.H., Sabokrou, M.: A unified survey on anomaly, novelty, open-set, and out-of-distribution detection: solutions and future challenges. arXiv preprint arXiv:2110.14051 (2021)
22. Sauer, A., Geiger, A.: Counterfactual generative networks. In: International Conference on Learning Representations (2021)
23. Shen, Z., et al.: Towards out-of-distribution generalization: a survey. arXiv preprint arXiv:2108.13624 (2021)
24. Sun, Y., Ming, Y., Zhu, X., Li, Y.: Out-of-distribution detection with deep nearest neighbors. In: International Conference on Machine Learning (2022)
25. Tommasi, T., Patricia, N., Caputo, B., Tuytelaars, T.: A deeper look at dataset bias. In: Csurka, G. (ed.) Domain Adaptation in Computer Vision Applications. ACVPR, pp. 37–55. Springer, Cham (2017). https://doi.org/10.1007/978-3-319-58347-1_2
26. Xiao, K., Engstrom, L., Ilyas, A., Madry, A.: Noise or signal: the role of image backgrounds in object recognition. arXiv preprint arXiv:2006.09994 (2020)
27. Yang, J., Zhou, K., Li, Y., Liu, Z.: Generalized out-of-distribution detection: a survey. arXiv preprint arXiv:2110.11334 (2021)

Long-Distance Pipeline Intrusion Warning Based on Environment Embedding from Distributed Optical Fiber Sensing

Chengyuan Zhu[1,2], Yanyun Pu[1], Zhuoling Lyu[1], Jiren Qian[3], and Kaixiang Yang[1](✉)

[1] Zhejiang University, Hangzhou 310007, Zhejiang, China
yangkaixiang@zju.edu.cn
[2] The Huzhou Institute of Zhejiang University, Huzhou 313000, Zhejiang, China
[3] Zhejiang Zheneng Natural Gas Operation Co.,Ltd., Hangzhou, China

Abstract. Pipeline is one of the most important transportation modes of oil and gas. However, it is different from the single-scene environments in fields such as security and high-speed railway, as the environment along the length of long-distance pipelines is complex and variable, including plains, mountains, and lakes. Different geological conditions have different effects on the transmission of vibrations, which poses great challenges to the external perception of distributed optic fiber sensing (DOFS) systems. At the same time, the similarity of different external activity signal characteristics also greatly affects the recognition performance of DOFS systems. Mechanical construction activities along the pipeline have posed a serious threat to the safety of pipelines. In this paper, an intrusion warning ensemble model based on environmental embedding is developed on the latest novel distributed optic fiber hardware system (ϕ-OTDR), named Surroundings-Embedding Ensemble Learning (SEEL). Environmental embedding technology captures the fine-grained differences in spatial environment between different defense areas. At the same time, ensemble learning technology reduces the negative impact of random noise and environmental interference. A large amount of data collected in the actual environment is used for comparison experiments. The results show that this model can achieve more accurate intrusion detection accuracy and has a wider practical application range by effectively fusing environmental information. In addition, the effectiveness of the new component designed is verified through ablation experiments.

Keywords: Oil and gas pipeline · ϕ-OTDR · Environment embedding · Ensemble learning

This work was supported in part by the school-enterprise cooperation project from Zhejiang Province Natural Gas Operating Co., Ltd. No. YXSCZ2020148, in part by the National Natural Science Foundation of China No. U21A20478, 62106224.

L. Iliadis et al. (Eds.): ICANN 2023, LNCS 14263, pp. 260–271, 2023.
https://doi.org/10.1007/978-3-031-44204-9_22

1 Introduction

Oil and gas resources are essential for a country's economic development, and long-distance pipelines are the primary physical carrier for transporting oil, natural gas, and other resources. However, oil and gas pipelines are located in an open natural and social environment, which is prone to various hazards, such as natural disasters, human activities, and terrorist attacks [1]. These hazards can cause pipeline rupture and leakage, significantly impacting human life, property, and health. Foreign invasion has become one of the most important risks among all types of risks. To address these risks, various measures are taken for the security monitoring of pipelines. However, traditional radar, infrared, and other detection methods cannot achieve long-distance detection [2–4].

The distributed optical fiber intrusion monitoring system research mainly focuses on signal data processing, feature extraction, and pattern recognition [5–7,24]. Ma et al. improved the Signal-to-noise ratio (SNR) of the signal based on EMD, and significantly improved the event recognition rate [8]. Xu et al. extracted the short-term energy ratio, short-term horizontal crossover rate, vibration duration, and power spectrum energy ratio as features from the vibration signal [9]. They used a support vector machine (SVM) to identify the four signals of knocking, knocking, shaking and squeezing, reaching a recognition accuracy of 90%. Taking advantage of the nonlinear and non-stationary characteristics of optical fiber sensor signals, Meng et al. used the XGBoost model to identify the collected signals. They achieved a recognition accuracy of 98.5% in the laboratory environment [10]. However, most existing studies have not considered the influence of spatial environment information on intrusion discrimination [11,12]. The natural environment and manufactured environment around the defense area have an essential influence on the modal distribution of the vibration waveform. For example, the average amplitude of the waveform in the defense area near the farmland is about 50. In contrast, the average amplitude of the defense area around the high speed can reach 2000. The same model cannot effectively perform intrusion detection on farmland and defense areas near high speed, which significantly limits the reusability and practicability of the model [13].

This paper proposes a new ensemble learning detection model for distributed optical fiber intrusion events based on environmental embedding based on the above observations. The model thoroughly mines the environmental information around the defense area and efficiently characterizes it. At the same time, ensemble learning technology is used to suppress the adverse effects of random noise and environmental interference to achieve higher intrusion detection accuracy. The main contributions of this paper are as follows:

(1) The environment embedding technology is proposed to efficiently characterize the natural and artificial environments in which the defense area is located. The full-spatial distribution of intrusion events can be modeled by fusing the environment embedding vector and the time series feature vector. To the best of our knowledge, this is the first work in the field of distributed

optical fiber intrusion warning to discuss environmental factors using embedding techniques.

(2) Given the massive disadvantage of random noise and environmental interference, an ensemble learning model SEEL (Surroundings-Embedding Ensemble Learning) based on environmental embedding and time-series features is designed, dramatically improving the generalization ability and practicability of the model.

(3) The real defense area data is collected and cleaned to form a standard data set. A large number of data experiments are carried out on the data set to verify the effectiveness of the proposed model framework.

The rest of this paper is organized as follows: The second section presents the basics of distributed fiber-optic vibration sensing systems. The third section describes the implementation of the environment embedding technology and the implementation of ensemble learning models. The fourth section will verify the effectiveness of the proposed model framework on real datasets and analyze the effectiveness of each novel setting. The fifth section will give the conclusion and prospects.

2 Long-Distance Phase-Sensitive Distributed Optical Fiber Vibration Sensing System

A distributed optical fiber vibration sensing system is developed by deploying fiber optic sensors along the pipeline [14]. ϕ-OTDR technology is used to detect the intensity of backward Rayleigh scattered light in the optical fiber, and the vibration source is classified based on the difference in interference waveform. Figure 1 shows the components of the distributed optical fiber vibration sensing system. The system architecture includes ultra-narrow linewidth lasers, acoustooptic modulators, fiber amplifiers, couplers, distributed sensing fibers, photodetectors, and a data acquisition card. Firstly, the sensing fiber is laid alongside the oil and gas pipeline network in a large area, and each sensing unit is set as a defense area. The other components are integrated into the chassis. After the laser source with narrow linewidth is switched from continuous light to pulsed light by the modulator, it is sent to the sensing fiber through the circulator [15]. The Rayleigh backscattered light output from the circulator's other end is received by the photodetector and transmitted to the computer through the data acquisition card. The signal is further processed for display. This distributed optical fiber vibration sensing system has the advantages of high accuracy, high reliability, and high efficiency [16]. It can effectively detect pipeline vibration signals and locate the source of vibration. The system has a wide application prospect in the fields of oil and gas pipeline safety monitoring, port and facility monitoring, and offshore platform monitoring.

When the sensing fiber is disturbed, the optical phase of the disturbed position will change due to the elastic optical effect. As a result, the phase of the backscattered light at the corresponding position will change, and the inner pulse

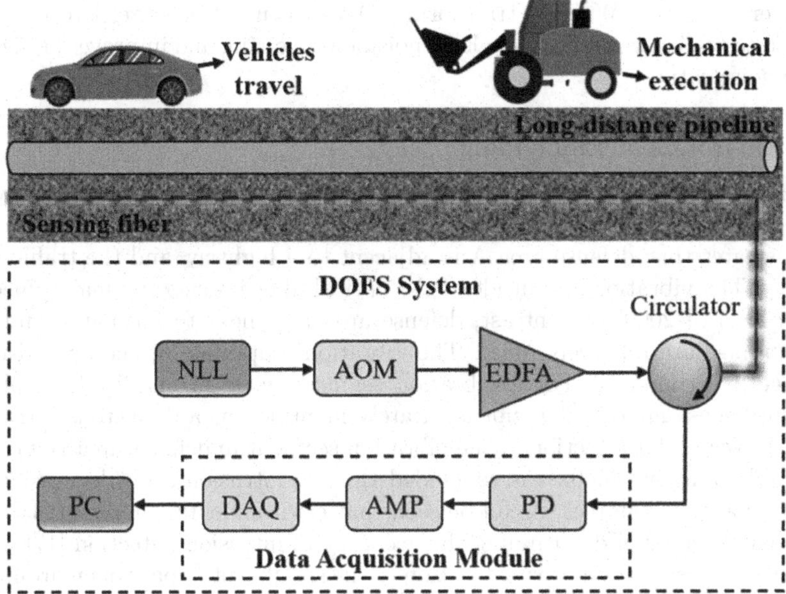

Fig. 1. Distributed optic fiber vibration sensing system.

width of the interference light intensity of the scattered light will also change accordingly. The main parameters of the system are as follows: the center wavelength of the ultra-narrow linewidth laser is 1550 nm, the linewidth is 3 kHz, the total length of the distributed optical fiber is 48 km, the signal loss is 0.27 dB/km, and the data acquisition frequency is 2 kHz

3 Data Preprocessing and Model Building

3.1 Data Preprocessing

Since there are some random noises in the distributed optical fiber sensing system, such as system noise and environmental interference, it is necessary to perform noise reduction processing on the ϕ-OTDR waveform to improve the signal-to-noise ratio of the system. Many studies have proven that the method based on wavelet decomposition can effectively reduce the noise of waveform data. In this paper, the wavelet decomposition and reconstruction methods are used to preprocess the original data. The specific implementation steps are as follows:

(1) Discrete wavelet transform (DWT) is applied to the initially distributed fiber waveform signal to obtain wavelet coefficients.
(2) The appropriate threshold rule is selected to modify the wavelet coefficients, which is realized by the soft threshold in this paper.

(3) Inverse Discrete Wavelet Transform (IDWT) is used for wavelet reconstruction to realize waveform signals' denoising processing and improve the signal-to-noise ratio.

3.2 Environment Embedding

The natural and man-made environments surrounding a defense area have a significant impact on the waveform distribution of events. A specific example demonstrates this: defense area A is adjacent to a highway, and the traffic flow is heavy. The vibration amplitude of the optical fiber is generally maintained at a high level of 2000. In contrast, defense area B is next to farmland, and the surroundings are relatively quiet. The vibration amplitude of the optical fiber is generally around 50. For a vibration segment with an amplitude of about 2000 in defense area A, it is not accurately identified as a dangerous intrusion event. However, for a section of the vibration segment in defense area B with an amplitude of about 2000, it is concluded that an intrusion event has occurred. From the above examples, it can be seen that environmental characteristics are an essential factor in determining the accuracy of intrusion detection [17].

Existing work does not pay attention to the significant impact of environmental characteristics and hopes to use more complex models to distinguish event modes, significantly limiting the accuracy and practicality of intrusion detection. Inspired by the word embedding work in natural language processing, this paper proposes the defense area environment embedding technology. This technology effectively represents the natural and artificial environments surrounding the defense area in an abstract and efficient manner, significantly improving the discrimination accuracy of the model [18].

Embedding is a distributed representation method that converts original input data into a linear combination of a series of features. This approach solves the problem of overly large representation dimensions and provides a very efficient representation ability. Embedding technology is widely used in natural language processing, where it is widely applied to represent basic characters and words. Embedding technology based on one-hot encoding trains entity embedding vectors with the help of meaningful sequence prediction tasks. Compared to one-hot encoding, the embedding vector has the characteristics of flexible dimension setting and high feature abstraction. For example, trained word embedding can achieve the effect of Formula (1) in natural language processing.

$$E(e) - E(m) \approx E(q) - E(w) \tag{1}$$

where E(x) is the embedding vector of word x. E(e), E(m), E(q), and E(w) represents "Emperor", "Man", "Queen" and "Woman" respectively.

In the distributed optical fiber system, it is theoretically feasible to set category-based one-hot encoding for each defense area. For example, categories such as expressways, highways, farmland, and factories can be set. Then, the one-hot encoding can be determined according to the surrounding environment of a specific defense area. However, this method of extracting environmental features is inefficient and has limited accuracy, due to the following reasons:

(1) It takes a lot of human resources and material resources to survey the surrounding environment of many defense areas.
(2) The optimal category setting cannot be determined.
(3) This method introduces human bias.

Based on the above observations, this paper proposes an environment embedding technology to set a reasonable and efficient environment representation vector for a specific defense area. The specific implementation steps are as follows:

(1) Extract the daily defense area alarm sequence. If there are few alarm events, the alarm threshold can be set. In this paper, the alarm threshold is 2000.
(2) Set the window length k to slice the alarm sequence. k is an odd number, which ensures that there is the same number of defense areas on both sides of the central defense area of the slice.
(3) Perform sequence prediction tasks. The prediction model uses the defense areas on both sides of the sequence to predict the middle defense area and train a three-layer neural network to obtain the environmental embedding vector of the defense area.

The approach involves selecting the alarm sequences based on factual observations, such as the frequently alarmed defense areas near 8:00 am being located near areas with high traffic flow, such as highways or expressways. The environmental embedding vector can cross the "roadside", "high-speed side", and other surface location features, and then deeply explore the high-level abstract characteristics of "large traffic flow", which has more representation and generalization capabilities. An essential parameter in the environment embedding technology is the dimension e, which determines the dimension of the obtained embedding vector. The larger the dimension within a specific range, the more information it contains. In this paper, the parameter e is set to 8 by default.

3.3 Ensemble Learning Model SEEL

To suppress random noise interference and effectively integrate time series and environment information, an ensemble learning model SEEL based on environment embedding and time-series features is proposed. Figure 2 shows its model architecture. SEEL consists of four parts, namely time series feature distillation module, environmental feature distillation module, spatiotemporal feature discrimination module and fusion module. Next, the specific implementation details are introduced in detail.

The input of SEEL is the environment embedding vector and the time series feature vector. Section 3.2 introduces the method of obtaining the environment embedding vector in detail. The time series feature vector is obtained by calculating the eigenvalues of the windowed waveform and combining them. Table 1 shows the detailed information of the features. The time series feature distillation module is used to extract high-level temporal features. The environment embedding vector is introduced based on a multi-layer network to assist super-vision, which helps focus on more useful high-level temporal features. The structure of the environmental feature distillation module is the same as that of the time series feature distillation module, except that the roles are exchanged, and the environmental features are distilled with the help of time series features. The spatiotemporal feature discrimination module combines the time series feature vector and the environment embedding vector as input and obtains the probability value through the n layers of XGBoost models [19]. The introduction of this module can significantly improve the final discrimination accuracy. To avoid the interference of random noise, this paper takes n = 10. The fusion module receives the outputs of the first three modules and performs feature fusion through a multi-layer neural network. At the same time, the residual connection and regularization technology are used to improve the representation ability of the model. The last layer of the neural network uses the sigmoid activation function to ensure that the predicted probability value of the output is distributed between 0 and 1.

Table 1. Timing feature types and definitions.

Number	Features	Definitions
1	Peak value	$Max(X)$
2	Minimum	$Min(X)$
3	Energy	$Sum(X)$
4	Mean	$\frac{1}{n}\sum_{i=1}^{n} x_i$
5	Variance	$\frac{1}{n}\sum_{i=1}^{n} (x_i - \bar{x})^2$
6	Peak-to-peak	$Max(X) - Min(X)$
7	Peak-to-peak square	$(Max(X) - Min(X))^2$
8	Peak-to-peak root value	$\sqrt{\text{Max}(X) - \text{Min}(X)}$
9	Standard deviation	$\sqrt{\frac{1}{n}\sum_{i=1}^{n} (x_i - \bar{x})^2}$
10	Skewness	$\frac{1}{n}\sum_{i=1}^{n} \left(\frac{x_i - \bar{x}}{\sqrt{x_{var}}}\right)$
11	Shape factor	X_{RMS}/X_{arv}
12	Impulse factor	X_{PK}/X_{arv}
13	Crest factor	X_{PK}/X_{RMS}

4 Experimental Result and Analysis

4.1 Experimental Setup

In this paper, one year's record data was extracted from a continuously running distributed fiber optic system database in Zhejiang Province. After data cleaning and preprocessing, the standard dataset Dataset-OTDR was formed. Table 2 shows the basic information about the data set.

This paper selects the following four commonly used models as the baseline to compare with SEEL.

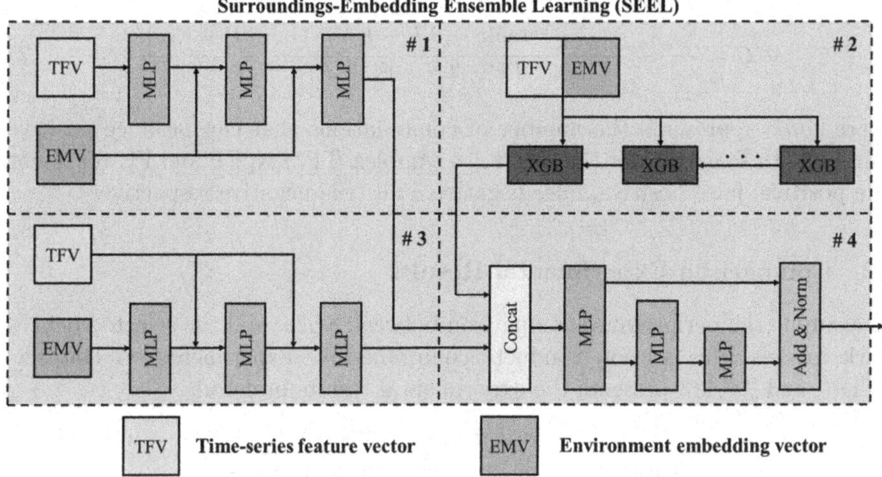

Fig. 2. The structure of SEEL model.

Table 2. Timing feature types and definitions.

Number	Index	Parameter
1	Sampling time	2021.01-2021.12
2	Sampling frequency	4 Hz
3	Window length	120
4	Positive sample size	10000
5	Negative sample size	15000

(1) Least Squares Support Vector Machine (LSSVM) [20]: LSSVM is an improved SVM model and is widely used in industrial data-driven modeling tasks.
(2) Extreme Gradient Boosting (XGBoost) [19]: XGBoost is an improved model based on gradient decision tree (GBDT), which uses second-order Taylor expansion to optimize the target value and has a solid fitting ability.
(3) Back Propagation Neural Network (BPNN) [21]: BPNN can automatically ad-just the network weights through error backpropagation. In theory, it can ap-proximate any nonlinear function with arbitrary precision, and is widely used in distributed optical fiber intrusion detection tasks.
(4) Long Short-Term Memory Network (LSTM) [22]: Recurrent Neural Network (RNN) is often used in time-series data modeling tasks due to its special iterative structure, and LSTM alleviates the long-term dependency problem on its basis. Currently, LSTM is still the mainstream model in sequence modeling tasks.

In this paper, Area Under Curve (AUC) is used as the evaluation index of the classification results [23]. As shown in the formula (2):

$$AUC = \frac{\sum_{i \in \text{positiveClass}} \text{rank}_i - (TP + FN) \cdot (1 + TP + FN)/2}{TP + \text{TN} + \text{FP} + FN} \tag{2}$$

where $rank_i$ represents the number of combinations that can produce positive samples with score greater than negative samples. TP, FN, FP and FN represent true positive, false positive, false negative, and true negative respectively.

4.2 Comparison Experimental Results

To examine the performance comparison between SEEL and the selected benchmark models, this section conducts comprehensive experiments on Dataset-OTDR, and Table 3 presents the experimental results in detail.

Table 3. Comparative experimental results.

Number	Model	AUC
1	LSSVM	0.8912
2	XGBoost	0.9541
3	BPNN	0.9386
4	LSTM	0.9274
5	SEEL	0.9762

As can be seen from Table 3, SEEL has superior performance beyond the baseline. Compared with XGBoost, which has the highest accuracy in the baseline, SEEL has an AUC improvement of 2.21%, which thoroughly verifies the progressive nature of the SEEL model.

4.3 Analysis of Ablation Experiments

The effectiveness of the model often relies on those well-designed novel modules. In this section, the effectiveness of the novel design in SEEL is verified by ablation experiments. First, the ablation model is defined:

(1) SEEL-#1: The #1 module in the SEEL model is the environmental feature distillation module model.
(2) SEEL-#2: The #2 module in the SEEL model is a spatial-temporal feature discrimination module model.
(3) SEEL-#3: The #3 module in the SEEL model is the time series feature distillation module model.
(4) SEEL-#3-rs: The environment embedding vector supervision part is removed in SEEL-#3.

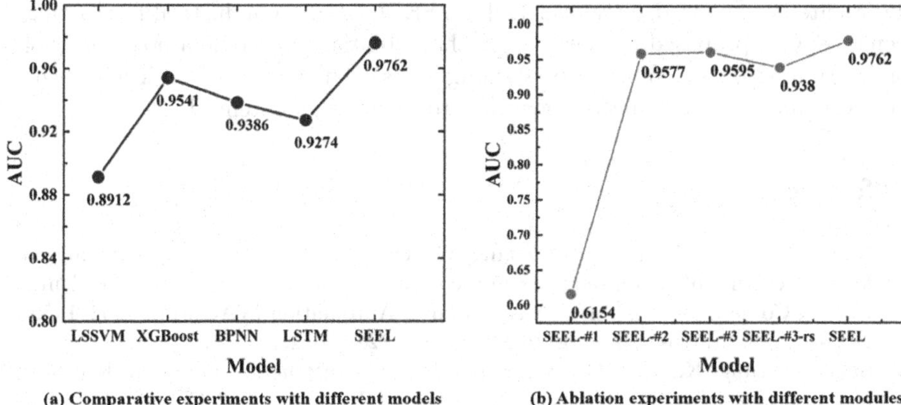

Fig. 3. Comparison of experimental results.

The trained ablation model is compared with SEEL on Dataset-OTDR, and Table 4 shows the detailed comparison results. As shown in Fig. 3, in-depth analysis of the experimental results shows that the AUC of the ablation model is significantly lower than that of SEEL, which indicates that the fusion strategy of SEEL significantly improves the model performance. In addition, compared with SEEL-#3-rs, the performance index of SEEL-#3 is improved by 2.15%, which verifies the robust improvement of the fine-grained environment representation vector for the task of warning classification.

Table 4. Ablation experimental results.

Number	Model	AUC
1	SEEL-#1	0.6154
2	SEEL-#2	0.9577
3	SEEL-#3	0.9595
4	SEEL-#3-rs	0.9380
5	SEEL	0.9762

5 Conclusion

In this paper, we propose a novel SEEL framework for distributed optical fiber early warning tasks. By fusing fine-grained environment representation vectors and performing model fusion strategy, SEEL outperforms all baseline models in terms of performance. Furthermore, many ablation experiments have verified the effectiveness of the designed novel components. In future work, we plan to investigate the knowledge transfer task on SEEL for more industrial forecasting scenarios. Our proposed framework has the potential to become a powerful tool for distributed optical fiber early warning tasks, and our future work will focus on developing more advanced algorithms to realize this potential.

References

1. Xiang, X., Shen, J., Yang, K., Zhang, G., Qian, J., Zhu, C.: Daily natural gas load forecasting based on sequence autocorrelation. In: 2022 37th Youth Academic Annual Conference of Chinese Association of Automation (YAC), pp. 1452–1459, Beijing (2022). https://doi.org/10.1109/YAC57282.2022.10023872
2. Shen, J., Yang, K., Zhu, C., et al.: Third-party construction intrusion detection of natural gas pipelines based on improved YOLOv. In: 2022 Chinese Automation Congress (CAC), pp. 1844–1849, Xiamen (2022). https://doi.org/10.1109/CAC57257.2022.10054804
3. Yang, Y., Li, Y., Zhang, H.: Pipeline safety early warning method for distributed signal using bilinear CNN and LightGBM. In: Proceeding of the IEEE International Conference on Acoustics, Speech, and Signal Processing (ICASSP 2021), Toronto (2021)
4. Zhu, C., Yang, K., Yang, Q., et al.: A comprehensive bibliometric analysis of signal processing and pattern recognition based on distributed optical fiber. Measurement **206**, 112340 (2022)
5. Yang, Y., Zhang, H., Li, Y.: Long-distance pipeline safety early warning: a distributed optical fiber sensing semi-supervised learning method. IEEE Sens. J. **21**(17), 19453–19461 (2021)
6. Yang, Y., Zhang, H., Li, Y.: Pipeline safety early warning by multifeature-fusion CNN and LightGBM analysis of signals from distributed optical fiber sensors. IEEE Trans. Instrum. Meas. **70**(2514213), 1–13 (2021)
7. Yang, Y., Li, Y., Zhang, T., Zhou, Y., Zhang, H.: Early safety warnings for long-distance pipelines: a distributed optical fiber sensor machine learning approach. In: Proceeding of the Thirty-Fifth AAAI Conference on Artificial Intelligence (AAAI 2021), pp. 14991–14999 (2021)
8. Ma, F., Wang, X., Liu, X., et al.: Application of segmentation threshold method and wavelet threshold denoising based on EMD in ϕ-OTDR system. In: International Conference on Information Optics and Photonics, Beijing (2018)
9. Xu, C., Guan, J., Bao, M., Lu, J., Ye, W.: Pattern recognition based on enhanced multifeature parameters for vibration events in ϕ-OTDR distributed optical fiber sensing system. Microw. Opt. Technol. Lett. **59**(12), 3134–3141 (2017)
10. Meng, H., Wang, S., Gao, C., Liu, F.: Research on recognition method of railway perimeter intrusions based on ϕ-OTDR optical fiber sensing technology. IEEE Sens. J. **21**(8), 9852–9859 (2021)
11. Zhu C., Yang, K., Yang, Q., Pu, Y., Jiang, H.: Visibility and meteorological parameter model based on rashomon regression analysis. In: 2022 12th International Conference on Information Science and Technology (ICIST), pp. 367–373, Kaifeng (2022). https://doi.org/10.1109/ICIST55546.2022.9926838
12. Yang, K., Shi, Y., Yu, Z., Yang, Q., Sangaiah, A.K., Zeng, H.: Stacked one-class broad learning system for intrusion detection in industry 4.0. IEEE Trans. Ind. Inform. **19**(1), 251–260 (2023). https://doi.org/10.1109/TII.2022.3157727

13. Liu, G., Si, J., Meng, W., Yang, Q., Li, C.: wind turbine fault detection with multimodule feature extraction network and adaptive strategy. IEEE Trans. Instrum. Meas. **72**(3504613), 1–13 (2023). https://doi.org/10.1109/TIM.2022.3227606
14. Lu, Y., Zhu, T., Chen, L., et al.: Distributed vibration sensor based on coherent detection of phase-OTDR. J. Lightwave Technol. **28**(22), 3243–3249 (2010)
15. Hong, R., et al.: Enlarging dynamic strain range in UWFBG array based ϕ-OTDR assisted with polarization signal. IEEE Photonics Technol. Lett. **33**(18), 994–997 (2021). https://doi.org/10.1109/LPT.2021.3079186
16. Yang, K., Yu, Z., Chen, C.-L.-P., et al.: Incremental weighted ensemble broad learning system for imbalanced data. IEEE Trans. Knowl. Data Eng. **34**(12), 5809–5824 (2022)
17. Yang, K., Yu, Z., Wen, X., et al.: Hybrid classifier ensemble for imbalanced data. IEEE Trans. Neural Netw. Learn. Syst. **31**(4), 1387–1400 (2020). https://doi.org/10.1109/TNNLS.2019.2920246
18. Boom, D., Cedric, S., et al.: Representation learning for very short texts using weighted word embedding aggregation. Pattern Recogn. Lett. **80**, 150–156 (2016)
19. Chen, T., He, T., Benesty, M., et al.: Xgboost: extreme gradient boosting. R Package Version **1**(4), 1–4 (2015)
20. Samui, P., Kothari, D.-P.: Utilization of a least square support vector machine (LSSVM) for slope stability analysis. Scientia Iranica **18**(1), 53–58 (2011)
21. Wang, L., Zeng, Y., Chen, T.: Back propagation neural network with adaptive differential evolution algorithm for time series forecasting. Expert Syst. Appl. **42**(2), 855–863 (2015)
22. Sherstinsky, A.: Fundamentals of recurrent neural network (RNN) and long short-term memory (LSTM) network. Physica D: Nonlinear Phenomena **404**, 132306 (2020). https://doi.org/10.1016/j.physd.2019.132306
23. Yang, K., Liu, Y., Yu, Z., et al.: Extracting and composing robust features with broad learning system. IEEE Trans. Knowl. Data Eng. **35**(4), 3885–3896 (2023)
24. Zhu, C., Pu, Y., Yang, K., et al.: Distributed optical fiber intrusion detection by image encoding and SwinT in multi-interference environment of long-distance pipeline. IEEE Trans. Instrum. Meas. **72**, 1–12 (2023)

LSA3D: Lightweight Separate Asynchronous 3D Convolutional Neural Network for Gait Recognition

Jianyu Chen[1,2], Zhongyuan Wang[1(✉)], Kangli Zeng[1], Jinsheng Xiao[3], and Zhen Han[1]

[1] National Engineering Research Center for Multimedia Software, School of Computer Science, Wuhan University, Wuhan, China
wzy_hope@163.com

[2] China and Guangdong Laboratory of Artificial Intelligence and Digital Economy (SZ), Shenzhen, China

[3] School of Electronic Information, Wuhan University, Wuhan, China

Abstract. Gait recognition is gaining attention as an emerging biotechnology for identifying subjects from a remote distance. Existing works have confirmed that modeling the motion trajectory of the subject is the key to gait recognition. Considering the motion continuity in the gait sequences, 3D CNN is a suitable and powerful tool for extracting spatiotemporal features. However, directly stacking 3D convolutions to extract sequence features will increase the model complexity and the number of parameters. To address the above issues, we propose a lightweight separated asynchronous 3D convolutional neural network (LSA3D) for gait recognition. Unlike common stacked 3D architecture, our network adopts the reverse pyramid design pattern, i.e., the top uses 3D convolution to extract internal features with rich spatiotemporal information, and the bottom uses separated asynchronous convolution to exploit deeper interactions between features. Experiments on the CASIA-B and OUMVLP gait recognition datasets show that LSA3D outperforms the state-of-the-art gait recognition methods.

Keywords: Gait recognition · global and local features · convolutional neural networks

1 Introduction

Gait recognition is a unique biometric technology that identifies subjects by analyzing their walking conditions. Unlike other identification technologies such as face, iris, and fingerprint recognition, gait recognition can be performed without the cooperation of the subject and therefore has great potential for application in the field of public security and criminal surveillance. Although the rapid development of gait recognition in recent years, it is still disturbed by some objective

L. Iliadis et al. (Eds.): ICANN 2023, LNCS 14263, pp. 272–282, 2023.
https://doi.org/10.1007/978-3-031-44204-9_23

factors, such as the walking speed of subjects, self-obscuration caused by subjects carrying bags and wearing coats, and camera view changes.

Many approaches have attempted to solve solutions to the above challenges in a cross-view premise. These existing methods can be classified into model-based methods and silhouette-based methods. Among them, model-based methods focus on detecting salient changes in skeletal joints by reconstructing the model on the subject. Since model-based methods are susceptible to the influence of pose estimation accuracy, the recognition performance remains to be improved. In contrast, the silhouette-based method is gradually becoming the mainstream gait recognition method due to its simplicity and easy recognition. Early silhouette methods have focused on template modeling, where multiple gait silhouettes are first compressed onto a single image to obtain a gait template, and then feature extraction is performed on the template. However, these methods neglect to model the periodicity of gaits, which leads to the loss of temporal information. To learn the motion patterns of subjects during their gait cycle, some researchers have proposed to directly extract features from the original gait silhouette sequences, which can preserve the necessary temporal information while focusing on the appearance information. For example, GaitNet [16] used an automatic encoder to extract features from gait sequences and exploited long short-term memory networks to model motion representations in the sequences. GaitSet [1] treated gait sequences as an unordered set to extract spatiotemporal features, which can achieve better performance based on improved flexibility in gait recognition. GaitPart [4] presented a fine-grained learning model for each body part and demonstrated its effectiveness experimentally.

Furthermore, to collaboratively extract spatiotemporal features. MT3D [6] extracted features at different temporal scales using 3D CNN at the sequence level to learn the gait silhouette information better. 3DLocal [5] proposed a new 3D local operation method to extract local features of body parts in an adaptive spatiotemporal scale. Compared with 2D CNN-based gait recognition methods, 3D CNN-based methods show superior performance in terms of recognition accuracy. However, the model complexity and real-time inference capability are severely limited, thus requiring high hardware devices in terms of storage and processing power.

To address the above issues, in this paper, we propose a lightweight separated asynchronous 3D convolutional neural network for gait recognition. Specifically, inspired by [10,13,14] in action recognition, we propose a novel lightweight separated asynchronous 3D convolutional block to simulate 3D convolution, which ensures collaborative extraction of information from spatiotemporal multi-dimensions while fully considering the information interaction of each individual dimension in the spatiotemporal domain. Moreover, our method focuses on modeling local inter-limb motion and learning global semantic information in the silhouettes. This modality ensures the network learns more complementary feature information to improve gait recognition performance.

In general, the contributions of this work can be summarized as follows.

- We propose a novel lightweight separated asynchronous 3D convolutional neural network (LSA3D) for gait recognition. The structure supports the micromotion representation of local limbs and focuses on the global semantic information of silhouettes.
- In LSA3D, we propose a new separated asynchronous 3D block to learn spatiotemporal information. By decoupling the spatiotemporal dimensions, this unit achieves a performance comparable to 3D convolution while reducing the number of parameters. To our knowledge, it is a novel attempt based on lightweight 3D convolution.
- Experiments on the CASIA-B [15] and OUMVLP [12] gait datasets confirm that our LSA3D outperforms the state-of-the-art gait methods both in performance and the number of parameters, thus meeting the demand for lightweight gait recognition.

2 Related Work

With the development of deep learning techniques, gait recognition performance has significantly improved and progressively enhanced the feasibility of monitoring under social surveillance. Currently, gait recognition methods are generally classified as model-based and appearance-based methods. Model-based methods are 3D reconstructions of human form and structure and therefore require high image quality. Appearance-based methods can extract feature information directly from the silhouettes and are relatively more flexible, so they are gradually becoming the mainstream methods for gait recognition nowadays. These methods can be further divided into template-based and sequence-based methods based on data processing forms. For example, Shiraga et al. [11] proposed GEINet, which extracts spatial features from gait templates. Although the gait template can integrate information from gait sequences of various lengths, it loses the temporal information between sequences in the compression process. In contrast, the sequence-based approach can preserve the spatiotemporal information in the gait sequences. For example, Chao et al. [1] proposed a gait backbone named GaitSet, which retains part of the temporal information while extracting spatial information in the set by treating the gait sequence as unordered. Notably, some of the latest gait methods then use a 3D CNN architecture to extract the spatiotemporal information in the gait sequences. Among them, Lin et al. [6] proposed an MT3D network, which designed a hybrid 2/3D module to extract spatiotemporal features and then introduced a frame pooling algorithm for normalization to improve feature representation. Huang et al. [5] focused on the different changes of each part during the walking of the subject and proposed 3DLocal networks for adaptive spatiotemporal modeling of local limbs with multiple 3D convolutions. Compared with 2D CNN methods, these methods generally significantly improve recognition performance but inevitably introduce many parameters in the computational process and are limited in real-time inference capability.

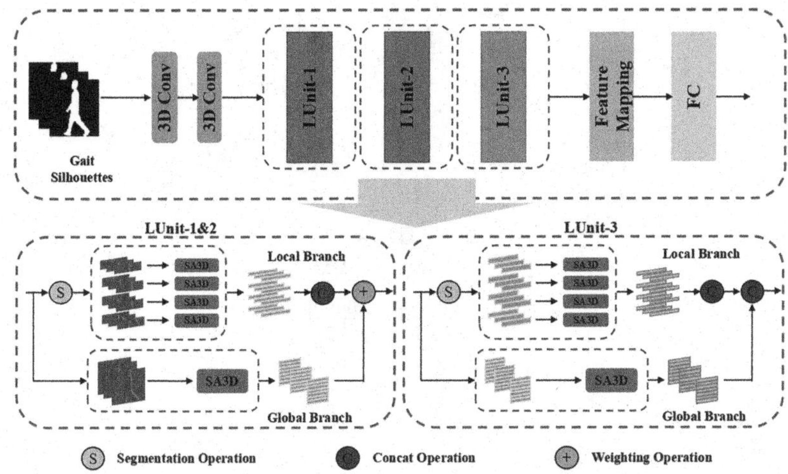

Fig. 1. The complete framework of our proposed LSA3D. It consists of three units that use 3D convolution to extract gait features from global and local perspectives, and two different kinds of units are built depending on the fusion modality.

3 Methodology

3.1 Problem Elicitation and Overview

We first propose two related problems based on existing works on gait recognition, propose a solution based on the issues and design a network structure. Specifically, we have to consider the issues:

- *How to economically and efficiently model the appearance and motion representations of subjects*: Considering the continuity of gait trajectories, 3D CNN is more suitable than 2D CNN for extracting gait spatiotemporal features. However, the network stacking multiple 3D convolutions will inevitably cause parameter explosion. Therefore, designing a lightweight 3D CNN structure can reduce redundant parameters with guaranteed performance.
- *How to ensure that the complete silhouette information of the subject is learned*: Existing gait recognition methods use either global or local manner to model silhouettes. Given the singular nature of silhouette maps, combining global and local modeling is an effective strategy for learning the complete silhouette information of subjects.

3.2 Lightweight Separate Asynchronous 3D CNN

Through detailed investigation, we have found that 3D CNN-based networks are more suitable for extracting features in gait sequences. Some mature methods such as MT3D [6], 3DLocal [5], and GaitGL [7] also further prove this theory, and these methods achieve a more significant breakthrough in recognition performance than 2D CNNs, especially under complex environments. However, these

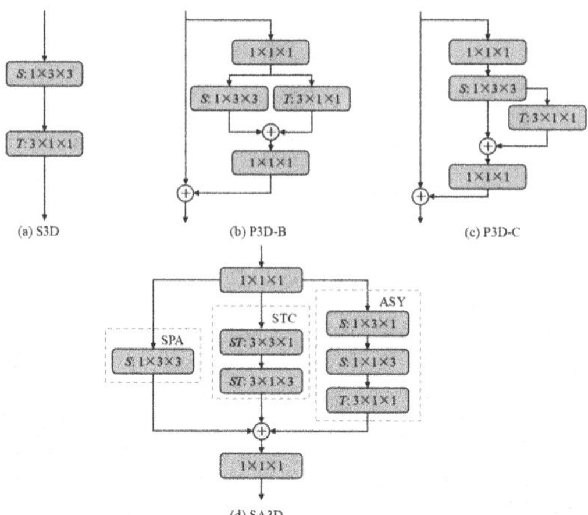

Fig. 2. The complete structure of our proposed SA3D. Among them, (a)–(c) [10,13] are the existing separation structures which use R(2+1)D patterns.

methods either use hybrid 2/3D convolution or directly use 3D convolution to construct the network, which improves the recognition accuracy but has a high computational burden and severely reduces the real-time inference capability. Considering the advantages of 3D convolutional cooperative extraction of spatiotemporal domain features, it is worthwhile to investigate how to simulate the 3D convolutional feature capability based on a reduced amount of parameter computation. Given that the 3D convolution contains three dimensions T, H, and W, where T denotes the temporal dimension and H, W denotes the height and width in the spatial dimension. Theoretically, combining these three dimensions in an exhaustive mode can consider the interaction between the feature information to the maximum extent. Motivated by [10,13,14], we propose a new lightweight separated asynchronous 3D convolutional unit block for collaborative extracting spatiotemporal features of gait sequences to meet the lightweight gait recognition requirements with guaranteed performance. The detailed structure of our SA3D unit is reported in Fig. 2.

Furthermore, existing gait work has proposed global or local feature modeling approaches. Although these approaches have achieved some success, however, any individual feature extraction approach has certain limitations, i.e., global feature modeling fails to take into account the more fine-grained motion changes of local limbs during movement, and local feature modeling ignores the contextual semantic relations present in the global silhouettes. Therefore, an effective combination of the two can enhance the completeness of gait modeling. We borrow the network architecture in GaitGL [7] and embed SA3D to model the spatiotemporal features between global and local in gait sequences. In Fig. 1, we have presented the detailed structure of our proposed lightweight independent asynchronous 3D convolutional neural network.

4 Experiments

4.1 Experimental Settings

Datasets. We conduct extensive experiments on two publicly available gait recognition datasets.

- **CASIA-B.** The CASIA-B [15] is the most commonly available in gait recognition, which captures 13640 gait sequences of 124 subjects. Among them, each subject includes 11 views, and each view consists of 10 sequences, respectively. Specifically, it contains 6 sequences for normal walking (NM), 2 for bagging (BG), and 2 for clothing (CL). For a fair comparison, during training and testing, we follow the protocol in [1], where the first 74 subjects are trained, and the remaining 50 subjects are tested. During testing, NM#1-4 serve as the gallery and the remaining sequences as probes.
- **OUMVLP.** The OUMVLP [12] dataset is the largest gait dataset available, which consists of 10,307 subjects. Among them, each subject has 14 views with a 15° interval for each view, with specific distribution areas of [0°–90°] and [180°–270°]. It is worth noting that this dataset contains only samples of subjects walking normally. During the testing, we divide the first sequence as a gallery and the rest as probes.

Implementation Details. We have followed the data preprocessing method in [1] to normalize the gait silhouettes, i.e., the image sizes of the two datasets are cropped to 64×44. The sampling batch size is (P, K), where the CASIA-B dataset is set to (8, 8), and the OUMVLP dataset is set to (8, 16). In the training phase, the initial number of frames for each batch is configured as 30 frames. We choose Adam as the optimization function for the training process with an initial learning rate of 1e−4. Among them, the training iterations are 80K on the CASIA-B dataset and 210K on the OUMVLP dataset, where the learning rate is adjusted to 1e−5 at 150K iterations.

4.2 Comparison with State-of-the-Art Methods

Evaluation Analysis on CASIA-B. We have compared the proposed methods on the CASIA-B dataset with the state-of-the-art gait recognition methods. Among them, we classify these methods into two categories: 2D CNN-based methods and 3D CNN-based methods. Table 1 reports the comparison of LSA3D with these methods in three gait walking conditions. Specifically, compared with all 2D CNN methods, we can notice that LSA3D has significantly higher recognition accuracy than these methods in the three gait conditions, especially in the two conditions of BG and CL, where the improvement is more pronounced. Moreover, compared with 3D CNN methods, our LSA3D still has advantages in recognition accuracy under multiple walking conditions. For example, our method outperforms MT3D by 1.7% (81.5% vs. 83.2%) in the CL condition.

Table 1. Comparative performance of LSA3D with other gait recognition methods on CASIA-B, where the same view situation is excluded(† denotes our reproduction under equivalent conditions).

Gallery NM#1-4						0°–180°											Mean
Probe	Architecture	Method	Venue	Year	Resolution	0°	18°	36°	54°	72°	90°	108°	126°	144°	162°	180°	
NM#5-6	2D CNN	GaitNet [16]	IEEE T-PAMI	2022	64×44	93.1	92.6	90.8	92.4	87.6	95.1	94.2	95.8	92.6	90.4	90.2	92.3
		GaitSet [1]	IEEE T-PAMI	2022	64×44	91.1	99.0	99.9	97.8	95.1	94.5	96.1	98.3	99.2	98.1	88.0	96.1
		GaitPart [4]	CVPR	2020	64×44	94.1	98.6	99.3	98.5	94.0	92.3	95.9	98.4	99.2	97.8	90.4	96.2
		RPNet [9]	IEEE T-CSVT	2022	64×44	95.1	99.0	99.1	98.3	95.7	93.6	95.9	98.3	98.6	97.7	90.8	96.6
	3D CNN	MT3D [6]	ACM-MM	2020	64×44	95.7	98.2	99.0	97.5	95.1	93.9	96.1	98.6	99.2	98.2	92.0	96.7
		GaitGL† [7]	ICCV	2021	64×44	96.0	98.0	99.1	97.8	95.8	94.2	97.6	98.7	99.3	98.8	93.0	97.1
		LSA3D(ours)	-	-	64×44	**95.8**	**98.4**	**99.1**	**97.9**	**96.9**	**95.1**	**97.1**	**98.8**	**98.7**	**99.1**	**94.5**	**97.4**
BG#1-2	2D CNN	GaitNet [16]	IEEE T-PAMI	2022	64×44	88.8	88.7	88.7	94.3	85.4	92.7	91.1	92.6	84.9	84.4	86.7	88.9
		GaitSet [1]	IEEE T-PAMI	2022	64×44	86.7	94.2	95.7	93.4	88.9	85.5	89.0	91.7	94.5	95.9	83.3	90.8
		GaitPart [4]	CVPR	2020	64×44	89.1	94.8	96.7	95.1	88.3	84.9	89.0	93.5	96.1	93.8	85.8	91.5
		RPNet [9]	IEEE T-CSVT	2022	64×44	92.3	96.6	96.6	94.5	91.9	87.6	90.7	94.7	96.0	93.9	86.1	92.8
	3D CNN	MT3D [6]	ACM-MM	2020	64×44	91.0	95.4	97.5	94.2	92.3	86.9	91.2	95.6	97.3	96.4	86.6	93.0
		GaitGL† [7]	ICCV	2021	64×44	92.8	96.0	96.9	95.4	94.1	90.2	92.4	96.6	97.7	96.4	89.5	94.4
		LSA3D(ours)	-	-	64×44	**92.3**	**96.2**	**97.2**	**95.3**	**94.1**	**90.4**	**93.3**	**96.0**	**97.5**	**97.2**	**90.2**	**94.5**
CL#1-2	2D CNN	GaitNet [16]	IEEE T-PAMI	2022	64×44	50.1	60.7	72.4	72.7	74.6	78.4	70.3	68.2	53.5	44.1	40.8	62.3
		GaitSet [1]	IEEE T-PAMI	2022	64×44	59.5	75.0	78.3	74.6	71.4	71.3	70.8	74.1	74.6	69.4	54.1	70.3
		GaitPart [4]	CVPR	2020	64×44	70.7	85.5	86.9	83.3	77.1	72.5	76.9	82.2	83.8	80.2	66.5	78.7
		RPNet [9]	IEEE T-CSVT	2022	64×44	75.6	87.1	88.3	83.1	78.8	78.0	79.9	82.7	83.9	78.9	66.6	80.3
	3D CNN	MT3D [6]	ACM-MM	2020	64×44	76.0	87.6	89.8	85.0	81.2	75.7	81.0	84.5	85.4	82.2	68.1	81.5
		GaitGL† [7]	ICCV	2021	64×44	74.7	87.7	89.5	86.6	82.7	77.9	83.5	85.5	85.5	83.1	69.8	82.4
		LSA3D(ours)	-	-	64×44	**75.2**	**90.1**	**91.2**	**88.4**	**82.8**	**77.7**	**84.1**	**85.7**	**87.0**	**84.1**	**68.8**	**83.2**
Avearge	2D CNN	GaitNet [16]	IEEE T-PAMI	2022	64×44	77.3	80.7	84.0	86.5	82.5	88.7	85.2	85.5	77.0	73.0	72.6	81.2
		GaitSet [1]	IEEE T-PAMI	2022	64×44	79.1	89.4	91.3	88.6	85.1	83.8	85.3	88.0	89.4	87.8	75.1	85.7
		GaitPart [4]	CVPR	2020	64×44	84.6	93.0	94.3	92.3	86.5	83.2	87.3	91.4	93.0	90.6	80.9	88.8
		RPNet [9]	IEEE T-CSVT	2022	64×44	87.7	94.2	94.7	92.0	88.8	86.4	88.8	91.9	92.8	90.2	81.2	89.9
	3D CNN	MT3D [6]	ACM-MM	2020	64×44	87.6	93.7	95.4	92.2	89.5	85.5	89.4	92.9	94.0	92.3	82.2	90.4
		GaitGL† [7]	ICCV	2021	64×44	87.8	93.9	95.2	93.3	90.9	87.4	91.2	93.6	94.2	92.8	84.1	91.3
		LSA3D(ours)	-	-	64×44	**87.8**	**94.9**	**95.8**	**93.9**	**91.3**	**87.7**	**91.5**	**93.5**	**94.4**	**93.5**	**84.5**	**91.7**

Even compared with our original backbone network GaitGL [7], LSA3D outperforms it by 0.8% (82.4% vs. 83.2%). These comparison results also indicate that our proposed lightweight 3D method outperforms existing 3D CNNs in terms of recognition accuracy while meeting the demand for lightweight gait recognition.

Evaluation Analysis on OUMVLP. We have further compared the recognition performance of LSA3D with other state-of-the-art methods on the OUMVLP dataset, and Table 2 reports the detailed comparisons. Specifically, compared to MvGGAN [3], the average recognition accuracy of our method is much better than 29.7% (58.4% vs. 88.1%); compared to the representative GaitSet [1], our method outperforms it by more than 0.2% (87.9% vs. 88.1%) in the equivalent situation. Even compared with the latest PRNet [9], our method still outperforms it by 3.1% (85.0% vs. 88.1%) with multiple views in the same situation. It can be seen that our proposed method still has a competitive ability on large gait recognition datasets.

4.3 Ablation Study

Analysis of SA3D Block. We have performed a detailed ablation experimental analysis of the LSA3D blocks and report the comparative results in Table 3. In Table 3, it can be seen that the average recognition accuracy of the three

Table 2. Comparative performance of LSA3D with other gait recognition methods on OUMVLP, where the same view situation is excluded.

Method	Year	Venue	Probe View														Mean
			0°	15°	30°	45°	60°	75°	90°	180°	195°	210°	225°	240°	255°	270°	
MvGGAN [3]	2021	IEEE T-IP	52.6	62.8	63.9	57.5	55.4	61.3	61.9	54.8	58.8	59.3	58.5	56.6	57.5	56.8	58.4
GPAN [2]	2022	IEEE T-BIOM	69.9	81.2	87.1	87.4	81.6	85.2	82.7	73.0	79.4	85.9	85.8	80.0	83.6	80.6	81.7
GaitSet [1]	2022	IEEE T-PAMI	81.3	88.6	90.2	90.7	88.6	89.1	88.3	83.1	87.7	89.4	89.7	87.8	88.3	86.9	87.9
PRNet [9]	2022	IEEE T-CSVT	73.5	84.4	89.6	89.8	86.3	87.4	86.0	76.3	83.2	88.6	88.9	85.7	86.4	84.4	85.0
LSA3D(ours)	–	–	**82.0**	**88.5**	**90.5**	**90.8**	**89.7**	**89.8**	**89.0**	**86.5**	**86.3**	**89.4**	**89.5**	**88.1**	**88.1**	**85.9**	**88.1**

Table 3. Effects of ablation of SA3D blocks on CASIA-B and comparison with backbone. SPA denotes the spatial branch, STC denotes the spatiotemporal cooperative branch, and ASY represents the asynchronous convolution branch.

Setting	Method	Parameters	Rank-1 Accuracy (%)			
			NM	BG	CL	Mean
(-)	Backbone	3.10M	97.1	94.4	82.4	91.3
(a)	SPA	1.90M	95.8	91.3	76.5	87.9
(b)	SPA+STC	2.33M	97.0	93.7	82.8	91.2
(c)	SPA+ASY	2.20M	96.8	92.7	80.2	89.9
(d)	**SPA+STC+ASY**	**2.77M**	**97.4**	**94.5**	**83.2**	**91.7**
Convolutional Unit Architecture						
Setting	1×3×3	3×3×1	3×1×3	3×1×1	1×3×1	1×1×3
(a)	✔					
(b)	✔	✔	✔			
(c)	✔			✔	✔	✔
(d)	✔	✔	✔	✔	✔	✔

gait walking conditions achieves 87.9% when feature extraction is performed only in the spatial dimension. When fusing the spatiotemporal collaborative extraction branch, the average recognition accuracy can be improved by 3.3% (87.9% vs. 91.2%). After merging asynchronous convolutional branches, the average recognition accuracy is enhanced by 2.0% (87.9% vs. 89.9%) based on the scheme (a). Finally, when we interact spatial branch, spatiotemporal cooperative branch, and asynchronous convolutional branch, the average gait recognition performance reaches 91.7%, which is another 0.5% (91.2% vs. 91.7%) improvement over the previous optimal performance scheme (b), while the number of parameters only increases by 0.44M. Compared to the original backbone [7], when replacing the original 3D convolution with SA3D, our method reduces the parameters by 0.33M while maintaining better average recognition accuracy. It is worth mentioning that our approach greatly improves the real-time inference capability of the network during training and testing.

Analysis of Global and Local Learning. Considering the potentially rich spatiotemporal characteristics of gait sequences, employing either global or local

Table 4. Effects on network performance with global and local feature modeling on CASIA-B.

Method	Rank-1 Accuracy (%)			
	NM	BG	CL	Mean
Global	96.6	92.6	80.4	89.9
Local	95.4	91.5	79.5	88.8
Global&Local	**97.4**	**94.5**	**83.2**	**91.7**

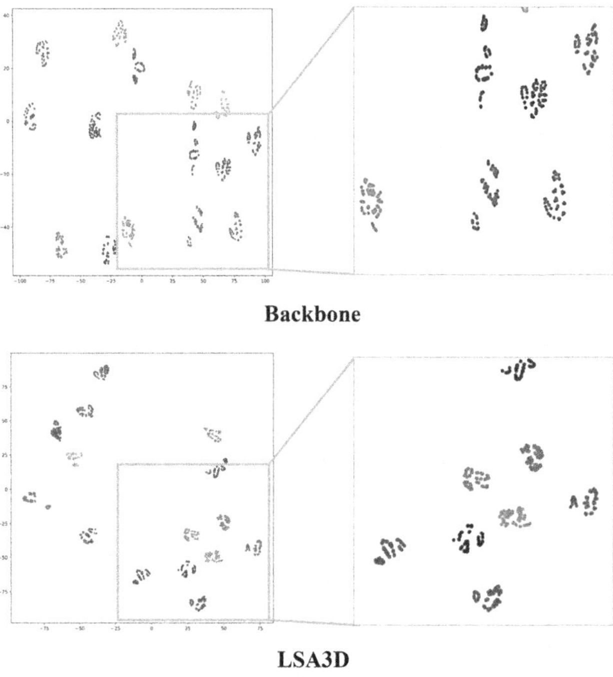

Fig. 3. Visualization of feature distribution of LSA3D and backbone on CASIA-B.

silhouette modeling solitary may lead to a partial loss of information. Thus, our network models the gait sequence both globally and locally. Table 4 reports the experimental results of the network in modeling gait sequences independently and coordinatively, respectively. Among them, LSA3D achieves an average recognition accuracy of 89.9% in the three gait walking conditions with only global modeling. When employing local modeling, LSA3D achieved an average recognition accuracy of 88.8%. In contrast, the average recognition accuracy improves significantly by 1.8% (89.9% vs. 91.7%) compared to global modeling and 2.9% (88.8% vs. 91.7%) compared to local modeling with the combination of them. These results also demonstrate the necessity and practicality of modeling the features of gait sequences both globally and locally.

4.4 Feature Visualization

We visualize the distribution of subject features of LSA3D with its backbone network in Fig. 3, where the visualization operation is performed by t-SNE [8], and the samples are collected from the test set of CASIA-B with 15 subjects. In Fig. 3, the feature distribution of our backbone is displayed on the left, while the right shows the feature distribution of the LSA3D method. Visual observation shows that the backbone features are relatively dense between different individuals, which may lead to subtle recognition errors. In contrast, the distribution of our method is relatively scattered among different individuals, and the feature distribution of the same category is denser, making it easier to distinguish and recognize.

5 Conclusion

In this paper, we propose a lightweight separated asynchronous 3D neural convolutional network to achieve gait recognition in complex environments. Specifically, we have designed a plug-and-play separated asynchronous 3D convolutional block for learning the spatiotemporal information in gait sequences. By replacing the 3D convolution in the original backbone, our proposed LSA3D network can reduce the number of parameters and guarantee performance. Moreover, our network models the appearance and motion of the gait sequence globally and locally, which can ensure that the network learns the complete interaction information and improve the recognition capabilities. Extensive experiments on the gait recognition datasets CASIA-B and OUMVLP have validated the effectiveness of LSA3D.

Acknowledgements. This work was supposed in part by the National Natural Science Foundation of China (U1903214, 62071339, 61872277, 62072347) and in part by the Open Research Fund from Guangdong Laboratory of Artificial Intelligence and Digital Economy (SZ) (GML-KF-22-16).

References

1. Chao, H., Wang, K., He, Y., Zhang, J., Feng, J.: Gaitset: cross-view gait recognition through utilizing gait as a deep set. IEEE Trans. Pattern Anal. Mach. Intell. **44**(7), 3467–3478 (2022)
2. Chen, J., Wang, Z., Yi, P., Zeng, K., He, Z., Zou, Q.: Gait pyramid attention network: toward silhouette semantic relation learning for gait recognition. IEEE Trans. Biometrics Behav. Identity Sci. **4**(4), 582–595 (2022). https://doi.org/10.1109/TBIOM.2022.3213545
3. Chen, X., Luo, X., Weng, J., Luo, W., Li, H., Tian, Q.: Multi-view gait image generation for cross-view gait recognition. IEEE Trans. Image Process. **30**, 3041–3055 (2021)
4. Fan, C., et al.: Gaitpart: temporal part-based model for gait recognition. In: Proceedings of the IEEE/CVF Conference on Computer Vision and Pattern Recognition, pp. 14225–14233 (2020)

5. Huang, Z., et al.: 3d local convolutional neural networks for gait recognition. In: Proceedings of the IEEE/CVF International Conference on Computer Vision, pp. 14920–14929 (2021)
6. Lin, B., Zhang, S., Bao, F.: Gait recognition with multiple-temporal-scale 3d convolutional neural network. In: Proceedings of the 28th ACM International conference on Multimedia, pp. 3054–3062 (2020)
7. Lin, B., Zhang, S., Yu, X.: Gait recognition via effective global-local feature representation and local temporal aggregation. In: Proceedings of the IEEE/CVF International Conference on Computer Vision, pp. 14648–14656 (2021)
8. Van der Maaten, L., Hinton, G.: Visualizing data using t-SNE. J. Mach. Learn. Res. **9**(11), 2579–2605 (2008)
9. Qin, H., Chen, Z., Guo, Q., Jonathan, Wu., Q.M., Lu, M.: RPNet: gait recognition with relationships between each body-parts. IEEE Trans. Circ. Syst. Video Technol. **32**(5), 2990–3000 (2022)
10. Qiu, Z., Yao, T., Mei, T.: Learning spatio-temporal representation with pseudo-3d residual networks. In: Proceedings of the IEEE International Conference on Computer Vision, pp. 5533–5541 (2017)
11. Shiraga, K., Makihara, Y., Muramatsu, D., Echigo, T., Yagi, Y.: Geinet: view-invariant gait recognition using a convolutional neural network. In: 2016 International Conference on Biometrics, pp. 1–8. IEEE (2016)
12. Takemura, N., Makihara, Y., Muramatsu, D., Echigo, T., Yagi, Y.: Multi-view large population gait dataset and its performance evaluation for cross-view gait recognition. IPSJ Trans. Comput. Vis. Appl. **10**(1), 1–14 (2018). https://doi.org/10.1186/s41074-018-0039-6
13. Xie, S., Sun, C., Huang, J., Tu, Z., Murphy, K.: Rethinking spatiotemporal feature learning: speed-accuracy trade-offs in video classification. In: Proceedings of the European Conference on Computer Vision (ECCV), pp. 305–321 (2018)
14. Yang, H., et al.: Asymmetric 3d convolutional neural networks for action recognition. Pattern Recognit. **85**, 1–12 (2019)
15. Yu, S., Tan, D., Tan, T.: A framework for evaluating the effect of view angle, clothing and carrying condition on gait recognition. In: 18th International Conference on Pattern Recognition, vol. 4, pp. 441–444 (2006)
16. Zhang, Z., Tran, L., Liu, F., Liu, X.: On learning disentangled representations for gait recognition. IEEE Trans. Pattern Anal. Mach. Intell. **44**(1), 345–360 (2022)

MADNet: EEG-Based Depression Detection Using a Deep Convolution Neural Network Framework with Multi-dimensional Attention

Shuyu Chen, Yangzuyi Yu, and Jiahui Pan(✉)

South China Normal University, Guangzhou, China
panjiahui@m.scnu.edu.cn

Abstract. Major depressive disorder (MDD) is a common and serious mental health problem that has received increasing attention from both researchers and clinicians. Electroencephalography (EEG)-based automatic diagnosis of MDD has been explored in previous studies, but feature extraction remains an area for improvement. We propose a novel deep learning approach for the automated detection of MDD. For feature extraction, a multi-dimensional attention mechanism is used to extract features from a simple pre-processed EEG signal to enhance spatio-temporal feature learning. We randomly divided EEG data from 26 MDD patients and 26 healthy controls into training and testing sets for network training and testing, respectively. Our method achieved the highest accuracy of 95.14% in subject-based data classification experiments compared to other methods. As a result of its simplicity and convenience, the method proposed in this study has the potential to be utilized as a tool for assisting in the daily diagnosis of depression.

Keywords: Automated detection of MDD · EEG signals · Deep learning · Multi-dimensional attention

1 Introduction

Depression is a prevalent mental health disorder that affects a significant portion of the population. However, since an individual's mental state cannot be directly measured, current diagnostic tools typically use the Patient Health Questionnaire (PHQ-9) [8], the Hamilton Rating Scale for Depression (HAM-D) [11] and the Beck Depression Inventory (BDI) [2] to determine whether someone is depressed. However, the interpretation of these questionnaire scores relies on the psychiatrist or counselor, leading to potential subjectivity and a greater risk of misdiagnosis. There is a pressing need to find a more objective way of assessing whether someone is depressed.

Electroencephalography (EEG) is an electrical biometric method measures the electrical activity of the brain. This technique records complex brain signals and provides a wealth of information about various regions of the brain [17]. The

L. Iliadis et al. (Eds.): ICANN 2023, LNCS 14263, pp. 283–294, 2023.
https://doi.org/10.1007/978-3-031-44204-9_24

abnormal shape of the EEG signal is expressed as a change in the signal pattern of the patient's particular state. The EEG measurements reflect the biological activity of the brain to accurately detect abnormalities in the brain [3], so this method is objective and reliable.

Additionally, since EEG signals vary in activity at different times, and are formed by the activity of nerve cells in the brain recorded at different locations on the surface of the scalp [9], and since it is known from existing studies [7] that changes in brain activity and structure have been observed in people with depression, both the temporal and spatial characteristics are important in using EEG to differentiate people suffering from MDD from normal individuals.

Therefore, we propose a novel convolutional network employing a multi-dimensional attention mechanism for EEG-based assisted diagnosis of MDD, called "MADNet". The main contributions of this paper are as follows:

- We propose a novel EEG-based auxiliary diagnostic framework for MDD, encompassing preprocessing, feature extraction, and classification.
- We design a multi-dimensional and comprehensive feature extraction method for feature engineering, utilizing a convolutional module based on channel and spatial attention mechanisms for local spatio-temporal feature learning, as well as a multiheaded self-attention module for global feature learning, to comprehensively extract valid features from EEG signals.
- Our proposed model demonstrates high accuracy of 95.14% in classifying MDD patients and normal individuals by EEG signals.

The remainder of the paper is organized as follows. The related work is presented in Sect. 2. The proposed method is described in detail in Sect. 3. The experimental setup and results are presented in Sect. 4. Finally, we discuss carefully and draw conclusions in Sect. 5.

2 Related Work

Related work in this field can be broadly categorized into two approaches.: deep learning(DL) methods based on hand-crafted features and DL methods based on raw data. This section presents work related to these two categories.

Acharya et al. [1] presented an automated model for detecting depression from electroencephalography (EEG) signals using deep learning (DL). While the model demonstrated promising results when trained and tested on data from the same subjects, its accuracy in identifying depression in untrained individuals may be uncertain. This highlights a potential limitation of the method, as it may not be widely applicable beyond the specific population used in the study. Li et al. [10] trained a CNN-based model to identify mild depression in clinical practice, using spectrograms from 128-channel EEG recordings as input. However, the 128-electrode device is costly and time-consuming to install. Wang et al. [19] achieved relatively higher performance than other methods by using a CNN network mixed with GRU and introducing an attention mechanism to extract the power spectral density (PSD) from the raw data as model input. However, since depression affects both superficial and deep brain structures [14], the use of hand-crafted features may not fully capture depression-related information. One study [6] mapped wavelet coherence between channels onto images as part of their constructed 2D CNN architecture and achieved high accuracy. However, this approach is difficult to apply in practice, as using wavelet coherence for detection requires high-end equipment and is both time-consuming and costly. Rafie et al. [13] proposed a modular time series network based on InceptionTime, which was trained on EEG signals using the potential power of InceptionTime for multidimensional time series data with different length scales, and achieved 91.67% accuracy.

While these studies have made important contributions to the field of EEG-based depression detection, there are limitations to each method. In particular, some require expensive equipment or time-consuming preprocessing, while others may not capture all relevant information about depression. To address these limitations, we designed a deep learning model for MDD classification based on EEG that can run without pre-extracted features and uses a multi-dimensional attention mechanism to allow the model to learn multiple aspects of information in the EEG to improve overall accuracy. Additionally, we established a 19-channel EEG-based and subject-based experimental protocol that avoids pre-extracted features and trains and tests the network on different subjects without the need for expensive equipment or complex procedures. Our proposed method aims to overcome the limitations of previous approaches while maintaining high accuracy in depression detection using EEG data.

3 Materials and Methodology

3.1 Overview

We propose a new framework, called Multi-dimensional Attention Net (MADNet), that combines channel spatial attention-based convolution and Transformer for classifying EEG data from depressed and normal individuals. MADNet is a deep learning model for EEG analysis with 3 components: The channel spatial attention-based convolution module to extract local temporal and spatial features. The self-attention module for extracting global temporal and spatial features by identifying long-range dependencies using multiheaded self-attention mechanism. The classifier module that uses extracted features for making predictions in various EEG-related tasks. The overall framework is shown in Fig. 1.

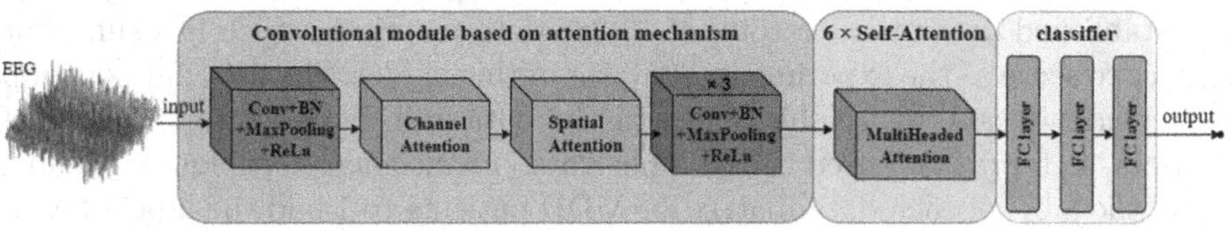

Fig. 1. Proposed framework of MADNet.

3.2 Materials and Preprocessing

The EEG dataset of MDD patients and healthy controls(HCs) used in this study is a publicly available dataset collected by Mumtaz [12] and commonly used as an experimental dataset to classify normal and MDD individuals. It included 34 MDD patients and 30 HCs, all recruited from Hospital Universiti Sains Malaysia (HUSM). All MDD patients were carefully screened to ensure that they had not been diagnosed with any other significant mental health problems or had any history of conditions associated with psychiatric disorders. The Ethics Committee approved the study and informed consent was obtained from all subjects before participating. Subjects with cumulative scores > 7 on the Hospital Anxiety and Depression Scale (HADS), a questionnaire used to measure symptoms of anxiety and depression, were considered to have MDD. In comparison, 30 subjects with no history of psychiatric disorders were selected as HCs. EEG data were collected using the International 10–20 system [4] with a sampling rate of 256 Hz. A total of 20 channels (Fp1, F3, C3, P3, O1, F7, T3, T5, Fz, Fp2, F4, C4, P4, O2, F8, T4, T6, Cz, Pz and A1–A2) of original data were collected. Three types of EEG data were collected: five minutes of eye closed (EC) resting state, five minutes of eye open (EO) resting state, and task (TASK) state.

In this study, 19 channels except A1–A2 were selected as experimental data in the dataset since A1–A2 was used as the reference electrode for all channels. Due to the presence of more noise in the eye open state, we chose the eye closed resting state data. Additionally, due to the presence of some subjects without closed-eye resting data, only 26 subjects each from MDD patients and HCs could be selected as experimental subjects. Before using the data, the 19 selected channels were extracted. To ensure the accuracy and clarity of the data, several filters were applied. A bandpass filter with a range of 0.1 Hz to 70 Hz was used to remove low frequency noise and uncorrelated signal. Additionally, a 50 Hz notch filter was applied to eliminate baseline noise. Finally, Z score normalization was used to reduce fluctuations and non-smoothness.

$$x_o = \frac{x_i - \mu}{\sqrt{\sigma^2}}, \tag{1}$$

where x_i represents the bandpass filtered data while x_o denotes the output of standardization. The mean and variance, represented by μ and σ^2 respectively, are calculated using the training data and then directly applied to the test data.

The data were segmented into matrices of 4 s inc, with a 75% overlap between adjacent matrices. Each matrix is 4 s of 19-channel data, and since the sampling rate is 256 Hz, the shape of each data matrix is (19, 1024). The structure of the matrix is shown in Fig. 2. There are 294 data matrices for each subject, so the established dataset has a total of 15,288 data matrices, which is a sufficient number to serve as the experimental dataset of this model. The 75% data overlap helps eliminate any phase shift effect in the data and increases the number of matrices, so there is no need to use other data enhancement techniques. Finally, we set the label of each data matrix for MDD patients to 1 and the label of each data matrix for HC subjects to 0. The labels of the data matrices were used as the ground truth for training and testing the MADNet model.

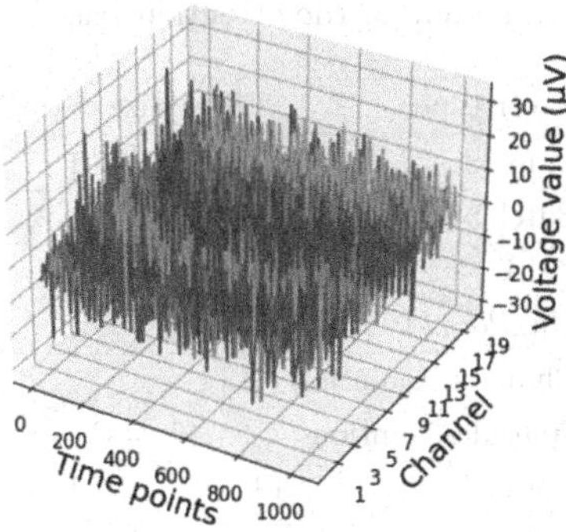

Fig. 2. Graphical representation of the EEG data used in the proposed method. The x-axis represents the time point (1024 time points in total for 4 s), the y-axis represents the channel in which it is located, and the z-axis is the voltage value (μV) of the corresponding channel at that time point.

3.3 Network Architecture

As shown in Fig. 1, MADNet comprises three modules: the attention-based convolution module, multiheaded self-attention module, and classifier module. The input is the EEG data preprocessed as described above. The output is the classification of whether the subject suffers from depression or not.

The Attention-Based Convolution Module. As detailed in Table 1, this module comprises four convolution modules, two attention modules, and a dropout layer, where each convolution module contains a convolution layer, a batch normalization layer, a maximum pooling layer and a RELU activation layer. We extract local features in the input signal by convolutional operations, use the batch normalization layer to normalize the convolutionally extracted results to speed up model convergence, reduce the spatial dimension of the data while preserving important feature information by the maximum pooling layer, and finally increase the nonlinear expressiveness of the model by the rectified linear (ReLU) activation function layer.

Inspired by [20], we designed the attention mechanism-based convolution module consisting of the channel attention module and the spatial attention module. The model employs two attention modules that enable it to better capture channel and spatial information in the data. These modules calculate the attention feature map sequentially along two separate dimensions - channel and space. The attention map is then multiplied with the input feature map, allowing the model to adaptively optimize its features and more effectively capture channel and spatial information in the data. The formula for the attention modules is shown below.

$$\mathcal{F}_{\mathrm{CA}}(x) = \sigma(W_2\sigma(W_1(\mathrm{Concat}(\mathrm{AvgPool}(x), \mathrm{MaxPool}(x))))) \cdot x \tag{2}$$

$$\mathcal{F}_{\mathrm{SA}}(x) = \sigma(W_s[\mathrm{AvgPool}(x), \mathrm{MaxPool}(x)]) \cdot x \tag{3}$$

Table 1. Detailed parameters of the attention-based convolution module

S.No	Layer name	Layer type	Filter Size	Stride x	Stride y	Output size
1	Conv1	Conv2d	1×5	1	2	$128 * 1 * 510$
2	BN1	BatchNorm2d				$128 * 1 * 510$
3	R1	ReLU				$128 * 1 * 510$
4	MP1	MaxPool2d	1×2	1	2	$128 * 1 * 255$
5	Channel Attention	Channel Attention				$128 * 1 * 1$
6	Spatial Attention	Spatial Attention				$128 * 1 * 255$
7	Conv2	Conv2d	1×5	1	2	$64 * 1 * 126$
8	BN2	BatchNorm2d				$64 * 1 * 126$
9	R2	ReLU				$64 * 1 * 126$
10	MP2	MaxPool2d	1×2	1	2	$64 * 1 * 63$
11	Conv3	Conv2d	1×5	1	2	$64 * 1 * 30$
12	BN3	BatchNorm2d				$64 * 1 * 30$
13	R3	ReLU				$64 * 1 * 30$
14	MP3	MaxPool2d	1×2	1	2	$64 * 1 * 15$
15	Conv4	Conv2d	1×3	1	2	$32 * 1 * 7$
16	BN4	BatchNorm2d				$32 * 1 * 7$
17	R4	ReLU				$32 * 1 * 7$
18	MP4	MaxPool2d	1×2	1	2	$32 * 1 * 3$
19	D1	Dropout				$32 * 1 * 3$

where σ represents the sigmoid function, x represents the input feature map, $AvgPool$ and $MaxPool$ represent the global average pooling and global max pooling operations, $Concat$ represents the tensor concatenation along the channel dimension, W_1, W_2 and W_s represent the weights of three convolutional layers, $\mathcal{F}_{\mathrm{SA}}$ and $\mathcal{F}_{\mathrm{CA}}$ represent the channel and spatial attention module, respectively.

To ensure the robustness of the model and prevent overfitting to the training data, a dropout layer is incorporated. This improves the generalization of the model so that it performs better on new data. The attention-based convolution module helps the model selectively attend to relevant features while filtering out extraneous noise, thereby enabling it to learn more appropriate local characteristics.

Multiheaded Self-attention Module. Since neural activity is coherent and the EEG signal varies over time, context-sensitive features assist the model in the extraction of features from the data matrices. Inspired by [18], we have incorporated a self-attention module into our model to extract global spatial features in the data. This complements the limited receptive field of the attention-based convolution module described above. The self-attention mechanism can simultaneously focus on the changes and correlations between EEG signals across time and electrodes and can more accurately learn the differences in EEG signals between normal individuals and MMD patients. The architecture of the self-attention module we used is shown in Fig. 3:

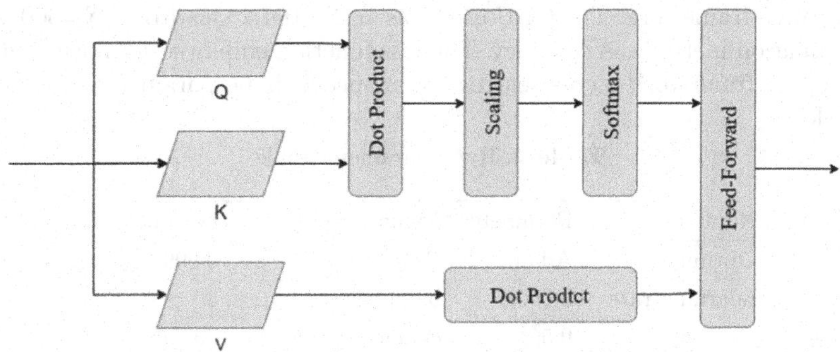

Fig. 3. Structure of the self-Attention module

The features derived from the preceding module are transformed into uniform three copies, designated as query (Q), key (K), and value (V). Subsequently, the dot product operation is performed on Q and K to obtain their similarity scores. The features obtained by dot product are scaled to avoid gradient disappearance, this process facilitates stable training. The output is obtained as a weighting matrix, i.e., attention weights, by the Softmax function. Then, the attention weights use dot product over V [18]. In order to enhance the model's capacity for fitting the data, two fully connected feed-forward layers have been appended to the network. In this study, a multi-headed self-attention mechanism is used, and this process can be mathematically expressed as

$$\mathrm{MHA}(Q, K, V) = Concact[head_0; \cdots ; head_{10}] \tag{4}$$

$$head_i = Softmax\left(\frac{Q_i K_i^T}{\sqrt{d_k}}\right) V_i \tag{5}$$

where MHA represents multi-headed attention, $Concat$ represents the concatenation, while Q_l, K_l, and $V_l \in R^{m \times \frac{k}{h}}$ denote the Q, K, and V matrices in the i-th head, d_k denotes the dimensionality of the K_l.

Classifier Module. Subsequent to the attention-based convolution and multi-headed self-attention modules, a classifier module comprising three fully connected layers was incorporated into the architecture to serve as the classifier module.

In summary, the pre-processed EEG data are segmented into 4-s, 75% overlapping data matrices, which serve as model inputs, The data were then sequentially passed through an attention-based convolution module and then through a 6-layer self-attention module before the classification results were output using a fully connected layer.

4 Experiments and Results

4.1 Experiment Settings

In this study, we wrote the code using Python 3.10, and ran the DL model using the PyTorch framework. The GPU used was an NVIDIA Quadro RTX 4000, and the evaluation metric was accuracy. The loss function employed for optimization of the entire framework is cross-entropy. Our specific hyperparameters are shown in Table 2.

Table 2. Hyperparameter table

Name	Parameter	Name	Parameter
Optimizer	Adam	$\beta 2$	0.999
Learning rate	0.0001	batch_size	3
$\beta 1$	0.5	epochs	30
Depth of MHA	6	num_head of MHA	10

4.2 Training and Testing of the Network

In this paper, we conducted two types of experiments: sample split data-based experiments and subject split data-based experiments.

In the sample split data-based experiments, all the data matrices are split, with 80% being used as the training set and 20% as the test set, and the performance is evaluated based on the samples from all the test sets. Overall, there are 12230 samples being used for network training, and 3058 samples for testing.

In the subject split data-based experiments, the training and test sets were divided according to the subjects. The 52 subjects, comprising 26 individuals diagnosed with depression and 26 controls, were partitioned into 10 distinct groups. This partitioning ensured an equal representation of depressed and normal subjects in each group and precluded the possibility of data leakage between the training and test sets, thereby mitigating the potential for overfitting. Of these ten groups, six contained data from six subjects, and the remaining four groups contained data from four subjects each. We then trained the network using tenfold cross-validation. One group in each fold was used as the test set, each data matrix from the remaining nine groups was randomly scrambled as a training set, and performance was evaluated against samples from all test sets.

4.3 Results

Sample Split Data-Based Experimental Results. For the purpose of performing sample-based classification, a total of 3508 data matrices from both MDD and HC subjects were evaluated using the trained network. The resulting confusion matrix is illustrated in Fig. 4. Analysis of the confusion matrix reveals that the proposed method achieves an accuracy of 99.38%, indicating that the network is highly effective in classifying the test data.

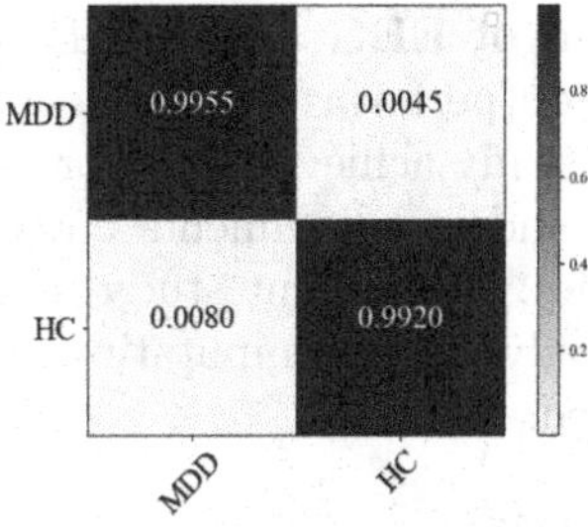

Fig. 4. Confusion matrix for experiments based on sample split data

Subject Split Data-Based Experimental Results. The ten fold cross-validation test results for the subject split data-based experiments are presented in Table 3. In the subject split data-based experiments, the model proposed in this study still performed better. The subject data in the training set will not appear in the test set, thus avoiding overfitting due to data leakage.

Table 3. Results of a tenfold cross-validation test for experiments based on subject segmentation data

Fold	Acc (%)	Fold	Acc (%)
1	100	6	98.8
2	72.4	7	100.0
3	99.26	8	100.0
4	90.64	9	100.0
5	92.46	10	97.79
Average	95.14		

Table 4. Results and comparison between experiments based on sample classification and those based on subject classification

Ref	Year	Total subjects		Channels	Features	Classification Method	Cross Validation	Acc%
		MDD	HC					
[5]	2020	33	30	19	EEG Bands	Sample Based	5	97.56
[16]	2021	21	24	64	EEG Signals	Sample Based	–	99.10
[15]	2021	18	15	19	EEG Signals	Sample Based	10	99.37
						Subject Based	10	91.40
[19]	2022	16	16	16	PSD	Sample Based	–	99.33
[13]	2022	34	30	19	EEG Signals	Subject Based	10	91.67
Ours	2023	26	26	19	EEG Signals	Sample Based	10	99.38
						Subject Based	10	95.14

Performance Comparison of EEG and DL-Base MDD Diagnosis. As shown in Table 4, MADNet outperforms the previously proposed networks, and the model proposed in this study achieves superior results both in experiments based on sample split data and in experiments based on subject split data. In addition, unlike other studies, the present study used the raw EEG signal for diagnosis. As a result, not only is the computational cost reduced, but also the preprocessing time is reduced.

4.4 Ablation Experiments

The structure of MADNet was determined through an ablation study. In the first ablation study, we evaluated the effects of the channel and spatial attention mechanism and the multi-headed self-attention mechanism on the performance of MADNet. The **Only convolution** only uses convolution layers, the **No channel attention and spatial attention module** uses only convolution layers and the multiheaded self-attention module, the **No multiheaded attention module** uses only the convolution module based on the channel and spatial attention mechanism, and **MADNet** uses both the convolution module based on the channel and spatial attention mechanism and the multiheaded self-attention module, focusing on both local and global spatio-temporal features. The results of the first ablation study are shown in Fig. 5. In the second ablation study, we evaluated the effect of Z score normalization on MADNet performance. The results of the second ablation study is shown in Table 5.

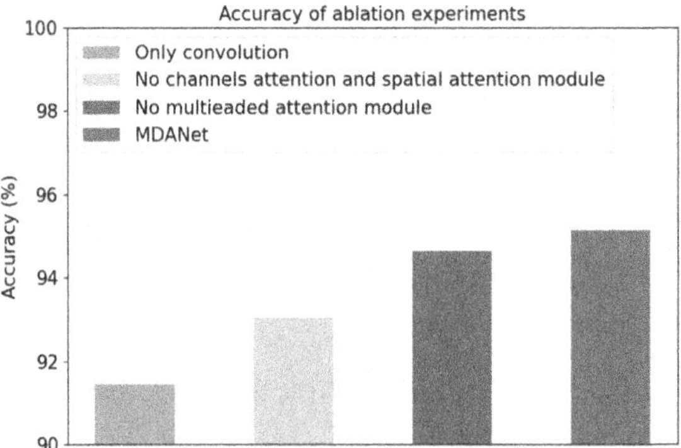

Fig. 5. Results of the first ablation study

Table 5. Results of the second ablation study

Ablation experiments	Acc%
Not use Z score normalization	93.28
Use Z score normalization	95.14

5 Discussion and Conclusion

To apply a neural network for EEG-based depression detection in real-life applications, the overall process must be simple and efficient. Therefore, we propose MADNet, a neural network that effectively discriminates between depressed patients and healthy individuals by leveraging a multi-dimensional attention mechanism to comprehensively extract features from EEG signals. The proposed framework employs a few simple pre-processing steps, such as bandpass filtering and Z score normalization. Additionally, in the deep learning framework, important local features are learned using a convolutional module based on channel and spatial attention mechanisms, and global correlations are learned using a multiheaded self-attention module. The overall process proposed in this study is therefore simple and convenient and can be use as a tool for assisting in the daily diagnosis of depression.

However, the proposed model has certain drawbacks; for example, MADNet requires 19 EEG channels for classification, and attaching 19 acquisition channels to the head is a tedious task. Using fewer EEG channels for classification could be considered in future research. On the other hand, each depressed person has a different degree of illness, and some depressed people may have very small brain changes, while MADNet assumes that depression causes significant changes in the brain, which may lead to MADNet not being able to accurately determine whether the subject is depressed or not. Therefore, the MADNet proposed in this study should be considered as a tool to assist in diagnosing depression on a daily basis.

This study successfully employed the MADNet neural network to classify subjects as depressed or non-depressed based on EEG data. We confirmed the effectiveness of multi-dimensional focused extraction of EEG signals. The proposed MADNet also outperformed other baseline methods. In experiments based on sample-split data, our model achieved an accuracy of 99.38%, and in experiments based on subject-split data, it yielded an accuracy of 95.14% using ten fold cross-validation. Overall, our model shows good performance. Future research could explore different domains, tasks, and methods.

Acknowledgement. This work was supported in part by the National Natural Science Foundation of China under grant 62076103 and the Special Innovation Project of Colleges and Universities in Guangdong Province under grant 2022KTSCX035.

References

1. Acharya, U.R., Oh, S.L., Hagiwara, Y., Tan, J.H., Adeli, H., Subha, D.P.: Automated EEG-based screening of depression using deep convolutional neural network. Comput. Methods Program. Biomed. **161**, 103–113 (2018)
2. Beck, A.T., Steer, R.A., Brown, G.K., et al.: Beck Depression Inventory. Harcourt Brace Jovanovich, New York (1987)
3. Goudiaby, B., Othmani, A., Nait-ali, A.: EEG biometrics for person verification. In: Nait-ali, A. (ed.) Hidden Biometrics. Series in BioEngineering, pp. 45–69. Springer, Singapore (2020). https://doi.org/10.1007/978-981-13-0956-4_3

4. Jasper, H.H.: Ten-twenty electrode system of the international federation. Electroencephalogr. Clin. Neurophysiol. **10**, 371–375 (1958)
5. Kang, M., Kwon, H., Park, J.H., Kang, S., Lee, Y.: Deep-asymmetry: asymmetry matrix image for deep learning method in pre-screening depression. Sensors **20**(22), 6526 (2020)
6. Khan, D.M., Masroor, K., Jailani, M.F.M., Yahya, N., Yusoff, M.Z., Khan, S.M.: Development of wavelet coherence EEG as a biomarker for diagnosis of major depressive disorder. IEEE Sens. J. **22**(5), 4315–4325 (2022)
7. Korgaonkar, M.S., Fornito, A., Williams, L.M., Grieve, S.M.: Abnormal structural networks characterize major depressive disorder: a connectome analysis. Biol. Psychiat. **76**(7), 567–574 (2014)
8. Kroenke, K., Spitzer, R.L., Williams, J.B.: The PHQ-9: validity of a brief depression severity measure. J. Gen. Intern. Med. **16**(9), 606–613 (2001)
9. Kumar, J.S., Bhuvaneswari, P.: Analysis of electroencephalography (EEG) signals and its categorization-a study. Procedia Eng. **38**, 2525–2536 (2012). https://doi.org/10.1016/j.proeng.2012.06.298
10. Li, X., et al.: EEG-based mild depression recognition using convolutional neural network. Med. Biol. Eng. Comput. **57**, 1341–1352 (2019)
11. Lukasiewicz, M., et al.: Young mania rating scale: how to interpret the numbers? Determination of a severity threshold and of the minimal clinically significant difference in the emblem cohort. Int. J. Methods Psychiatr. Res. **22**(1), 46–58 (2013)
12. Mumtaz, W., Qayyum, A.: A deep learning framework for automatic diagnosis of unipolar depression. Int. J. Med. Inform. **132**, 103983 (2019)
13. Rafiei, A., Zahedifar, R., Sitaula, C., Marzbanrad, F.: Automated detection of major depressive disorder with EEG signals: a time series classification using deep learning. IEEE Access **10**, 73804–73817 (2022)
14. Sapolsky, R.M.: Depression, antidepressants, and the shrinking hippocampus. Proc. Natl. Acad. Sci. **98**(22), 12320–12322 (2001)
15. Seal, A., Bajpai, R., Agnihotri, J., Yazidi, A., Herrera-Viedma, E., Krejcar, O.: DeprNet: a deep convolution neural network framework for detecting depression using EEG. IEEE Trans. Instrum. Meas. **70**, 1–13 (2021)
16. Sharma, G., Parashar, A., Joshi, A.M.: DepHNN: a novel hybrid neural network for electroencephalogram (EEG)-based screening of depression. Biomed. Signal Process. Control **66**, 102393 (2021)
17. Siuly, S., Li, Y., Zhang, Y.: Electroencephalogram (EEG) and its background. In: Siuly, S., Li, Y., Zhang, Y. (eds.) EEG Signal Analysis and Classification. HIS, pp. 3–21. Springer, Cham (2016). https://doi.org/10.1007/978-3-319-47653-7_1
18. Vaswani, A., et al.: Attention is all you need. In: Advances in Neural Information Processing Systems, vol. 30 (2017)
19. Wang, Z., Ma, Z., Liu, W., An, Z., Huang, F.: A depression diagnosis method based on the hybrid neural network and attention mechanism. Brain Sci. **12**(7), 834 (2022)
20. Woo, S., Park, J., Lee, J.Y., Kweon, I.S.: CBAM: convolutional block attention module. In: Proceedings of the European Conference on Computer Vision (ECCV), pp. 3–19 (2018)

Maintenance Automation Using Deep Learning Methods: A Case Study from the Aerospace Industry

P. J. Mayhew[1,2](✉), H. Ihshaish[2], I. Deza[2], and A. Del Amo[1]

[1] GE Aerospace, Bishops Cleeve, Cheltenham, UK
Peter.Mayhew@ge.com

[2] School of Computing and Creative Technologies UWE, Bristol, UK

Abstract. In this study, state-of-the-art AI models are employed to classify aerospace maintenance records into categories based on the fault descriptions of avionic components. The classification is performed using short natural language text descriptions provided by specialised repair engineers. The primary goal is to conduct a more comprehensive analysis of a complex and lengthy maintenance dataset, with the objective of determining the likelihood of failures in non-critical components of airplanes.

Various methodologies are used, including two vectorisation models to natural language representation, as well as several machine learning algorithms such as BiGRU and BiLSTM, to identify repair and replacement event likelihood from the provided corpora. The resulting performance of the deployed models provide a very high F1 score overall, indicating models' ability to learn repair patterns from the, typically complex, engineering description of components with high confidence.

Two case studies are conducted. The first for a binary classification, with several models achieving an average F1 score of around 95%. In the second case, a multi-class classification is performed for four different classes, with the BiLSTM model achieving the highest performance, accurately predicting the validation set with a 95.2% F1 score.

The misclassified samples were manually inspected, and it was found that in many cases, the relevant information was simply missing from the text due to errors or omissions by description authors. Only 12% of the misclassified samples were found to be due to errors made by the model, resulting in an effective accuracy rate of $\sim$ 99.4%.

Keywords: NLP · Aerospace · Maintenance

1 Introduction

Product reliability is important for all industries including Aerospace, Automotive, Oil and Gas, Healthcare to reduce the risk of unscheduled failures [3,29].

Supported by GE Aerospace: www.geaerospace.com.

L. Iliadis et al. (Eds.): ICANN 2023, LNCS 14263, pp. 295–307, 2023.
https://doi.org/10.1007/978-3-031-44204-9_25

Products with poor reliability will increase downtime and result in reduced customer satisfaction. Manufacturers may also incur increased warranty costs and risk receiving fines if the reliability is below contractual requirements. Therefore, companies are looking towards new methods to monitor product health; to identify failure trends and implement corrective actions. For example, fitting a more durable capacitor on a power supply can have a direct impact on improving the production yield rate and in-service reliability.

Monitoring product health and reliability data is a time consuming task [26]. Categorising customer returns is subjective because the text records are unstructured, contain technical jargon, and prone to human typographic mistakes. As a result, maintenance records are often underused in industry [15,26]. This presents a huge challenge in industry and companies are looking towards automated tools such as natural language processing (NLP) and machine learning methods to help in many incidences [19,25].

NLP has been applied in several industries, safety report [1,3,18,28–30], IT systems, [32], Commercial equipment [31], Customer Feedback [10] and clinical applications [7–9,11–14,16,17,22,24] to automatically classify electronic records. Each industry has difficulties classifying the data due to misspellings, jargon, domain specific terminology and abbreviations.

Applying NLP to the maintenance records would reduce this workload on engineers, and allow a consistent approach to reduce human bias. There are different ways to categorise customer returns, such as by failure modes, no fault found rate, safety concerns, human factors, unscheduled/scheduled removals.

This study evaluates categorising the records by the type of repair performed. Specifically, categorising by the sub-assemblies/components replaced during the maintenance activity. The reason is the data is readily available, and can be used as a performance indicator of module failures. Training a model to predict what components will be replaced based on the fault description also gives us additional information to forecast spares provisioning so the material is available for future customer returns. This reduces the repair turn around time.

Modern electronics and electromechanical assemblies have highly complex hierarchical structures; which consistent of many sub-assemblies and components. In the aerospace industry, the display instruments fitted to the aircraft cockpit are called Line Replaceable Units (LRU). If the aircraft reports a fault condition, the technician can quickly diagnose and removed the suspect LRU from the aircraft using Fault Tree Analysis. The suspect LRU is returned to the manufacturing repair organisation for evaluation and repair. For civil aerospace products, the repair activity is performed in accordance with component maintenance manuals (CMM) which contain instructions on how to test the equipment and lists the bill of material, which is a list of spare parts that can be ordered to perform the repair. This CMM allows *module level repair* or *component level repair*.

Module level repair involves swapping complex assemblies with known working assemblies to diagnose the failure. For example, swapping a power supply or graphics card. This is generally a quick method to diagnose the direct cause of failure.

Component level repair involve studying assembly drawings and schematics to troubleshoot i.e. a printed circuit assembly to a single component, such as a capacitor, diode, integrated circuit. This has the advantage of reducing scrap rate, but complex faults can take significantly more man hours to diagnose, which drives up the repair cost.

The rest of this discussion shall focus on civil products which have module level repair. However, the reader should be aware that the methods described can also be applied to component level repair.

In this paper, fault descriptions in the maintenance records are categorised using binary and multi-label classifiers to predict which sub-assemblies need to be replaced.

2 Methodology

Two case studies are considered in this work, the first to analyse the maintenance records containing fault descriptions as short text and predict if a single assembly is replaced. The second case study uses the same maintenance records, and predicts the replacement of two assemblies, which are encoded as four categories. Thus, predicting if neither is replaced, if either is replaced, or both are replaced simultaneously.

Two datasets are used. The first is the *maintenance records* containing text descriptions and unique *repair numbers*. The second contains a list of *material issued (assemblies)* from stores to the repair job. Both datasets contains a *repair number* and joined using a one to many relationship.

Categorising the repairs based on every replacement part is unpractical because this can lead to thousands of categories. Some assemblies are replaced more frequently than others, and some not at all. Therefore, this variability will result in a heavily unbalanced dataset. To reduce imbalance, sub-assemblies replaced infrequently (<100 times) over 22 years are dropped. Common parts such as screws, washers, security labels were also dropped as they are generally replaced as part of the repair process.

It is worth mentioning that this method is suitable for a *mature* product with a long service history. Relatively new products would lack this historical data and another method would need to be considered.

The records contain spelling errors, grammar errors, domain specific jargon, and missing data. These challenges are also identified by [6,23,29]. The fault description text was cleansed and pre-processed using general NLP techniques.

As a baseline, the text was encoded using Term Frequency- Inverse Document Frequency (TF-IDF). Six binary classifiers were trained to predict if a single sub-assembly were replaced based on the fault text description from 7098 records. More complex language models such as BERT have been considered. They would require longer training times, longer computation times, and much more data to learn the jargon and domain specific language. Therefore, whilst we do not discount using BERT, simpler solutions such as TF-IDF are sufficient as the baseline of our methodology.

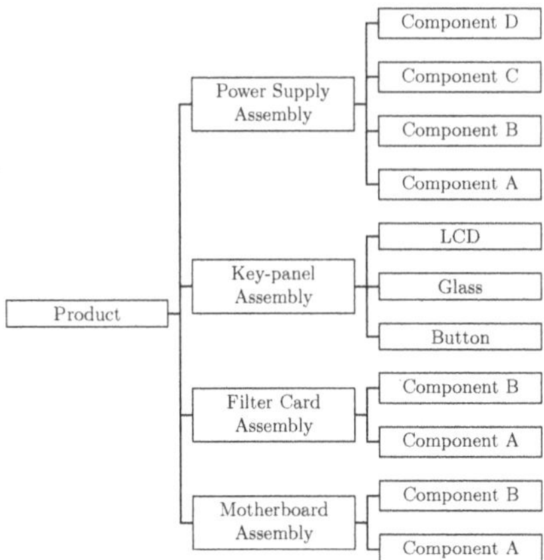

Fig. 1. Block diagram showing hierarchical structure of a product. On the left is the *finished* product. Middle is the sub-assemblies, PCBs, complex parts, and on the right is surface mount components.

A second case study encodes the text using word embedding [2,20,21]. A multi label classifier using a Bidirectional Long-Short Term Memory (BiLSTM) and Bidirectional Gated Recurrent Unit (BiGRU) are trained to predict if two sub-assemblies were/were not replaced. We chose word embedding as a comparison to TF-IDF because it can capture semantic meaning of the text.

10-fold cross validation was applied to evaluate the models performance.

The hierarchical BOM structure of a product is illustrated in Fig. 1 to show the relationship between the finished product, sub-assembly and components

2.1 Model Training

The data was split into 80% training data and 20% test data throughout this paper. From the training data, 5% was used for validation. Stratified sampling was used to split the categories; to reduce the sampling bias and give the best representation of each category.

Six binary classifiers were trained; Random Forests, Multinomial Naive Bayes (NB), SGD Classifier, Support Vector Machines, Logistic Regression and K Nearest Neighbours (KNN) to predict the replacement of either the processor assembly or the key-panel. The popular Term Frequency - Inverse Document Frequency (TF-IDF) was used. This method is limited as it considers the terms to be independent and does not use the semantic similarity between words. The results are shown in Sect. 3.1.

Secondly, two multi label classifiers are compared; Bidirectional LSTM, and a Bidirectional GRU. These ML architectures have the advantage in real world applications to feed sentences as a vectorised word sequence, which contains information from the past and present to produce a more meaningful output

Table 1. List of Sub Assemblies to categorise and number of occurrences in the dataset

Category	Assembly Replaced	Qty
0	Processor Assembly	1486
1	Key panel Assembly	208
2	Processor and Key panel Assembly	707
3	No parts replaced	4697

from the text descriptions. The fault descriptions were vectorised using a pre-trained GloVe Word vectors [27] from Stanford University to capture the text semantics. The embedding contained 6 billion tokens with 50 dimensions[1] The results are shown in Sect. 3.2.

Both models were trained using categories 0–2 from Table 1. Then both models retrain on categories 0–3. The reason is that Category 3 is 66% of the total dataset; which will heavily bias the results. These repairs have no parts issued to the job, or the repair only replaced components which have been filtered from our dataset, such as screws, labels etc. If the F1 score of the models has not changed significantly then this will be a good indication that the model has trained on all categories, and not just category 3.

The BiLSTM model was retrained over 19 epochs, before there was no further reduction in the loss value. The dataset included categories 0–2 from Table 1. The BiLSTM model retrained over 15 epochs, using all categories 0–3 from Table 1. The results are shown in Sect. 3.2.

The BiGRU model was trained using the same dataset over 24 epochs on categories 0–2 from Table 1., categories and pre-trained GloVe word embedding as detailed in Sect. 3.2. The BiGRU model retrained over 15 epochs for categories 0–3 from Table 1. The results are shown in Sect. 3.2.

3 Results

3.1 Case Study 1 - Predict Single Assembly Replacement

The performance results of the six binary classification models are summarised in Table 2. The SVM produced the highest F1 accuracy score of 95%.

3.2 Case Study 2 - Predict Combined Assembly Replacement

BiLSTM Model. The BiLSTM was trained using categories 0–2, and the classification report is summarised in Table 3. The test set had a weighted F1 score of 95.2% and a loss of 15.9%. There was 458 true matches, and 23 false matches.

The receiver operating characteristic curve (ROC) measured the quality of the models predictions is shown in Fig. 2.

[1] Website https://nlp.stanford.edu/projects/glove/.

Table 2. Comparison of six binary classifier to predict the replacing the Key-panel Assembly and the processor assembly on the right hand side

	Key-Panel Assembly			Processor Assembly		
Classifier	Not R'plcd	R'plcd	F1-score	Not R'plcd	R'plcd	F1-score
RandomForest	0.97	0.87	0.92	0.96	0.94	0.95
MultinomialNB	0.89	0.38	0.64	0.93	0.91	0.92
SGDClassifier	0.98	0.91	0.94	0.96	0.95	0.95
SVM	0.98	0.92	0.95	0.96	0.94	0.95
LogisticRegression	0.97	0.86	0.91	0.96	0.95	0.95
KNN	0.95	0.78	0.86	0.94	0.92	0.94

Table 3. BiLSTM Classification Report to predict replacing the key-panel (Category 0), processor (Category 1), both (Category 2)

Category	Precision	Recall	F1-score	Support
0	0.958	0.977	0.968	306
1	0.950	0.927	0.938	41
2	0.938	0.903	0.920	134
avg/total	0.952	0.952	0.952	481

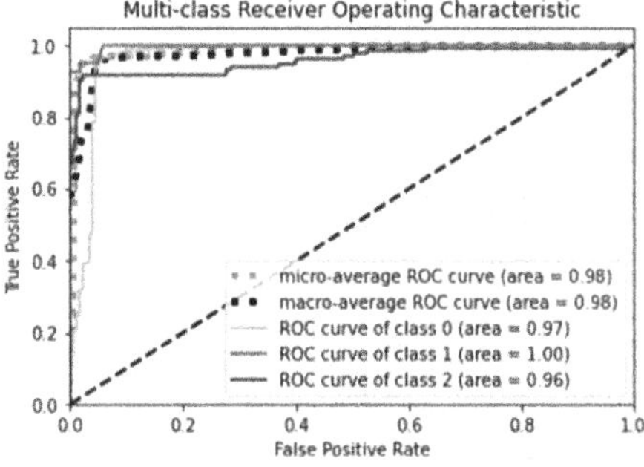

Fig. 2. ROC Curve for BiLSTM for three categories. This shows a high AUC, meaning the model has very high separability for each category. By comparison, the black dotted line shows an AUC of 0.5 (random chance)

The BiLSTM model was retrained using categories 0–3. The test set had a weighted F1 score of 93.3% accuracy and a loss of 22.3%. Comparing the true and predicted categories showed 1326 true matches, and 94 false matches. The classification report is summarised in Table 4 and the receiver operating characteristic curve (ROC) measuring the quality of the models predictions is shown in Fig. 3.

Table 4. BiLSTM Classification Report to predict replacing the key-panel (Category 0), processor (Category 1), both (Category 2), or no parts replaced (Category 3)

Category	Precision	Recall	F1-score	Support
0	0.888	0.936	0.911	297
1	0.680	0.810	0.739	42
2	0.816	0.915	0.863	141
3	0.984	0.941	0.962	940
avg/total	0.939	0.934	0.935	1420

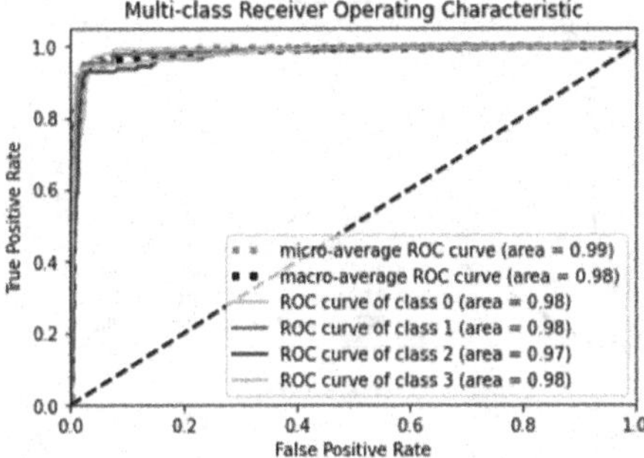

Fig. 3. ROC Curve for BiLSTM for four categories. This shows a high AUC, meaning the model has very high separability for each category. By comparison, the black dotted line shows an AUC of 0.5 (random chance)

The cross validation results using 10-folds was 94.03% avg to categorise groups 0–3 and 97.57% avg with category 3 dropped.

BiGRU Model. The BiGRU was trained using categories 0–2. The test set had a weighted F1 score of 93.5% and a loss of 21.6%. Comparing the true and predicted categories showed 450 true matches, and 31 false matches.

The classification report is summarised in Table 5 and the receiver operating characteristic curve (ROC) measuring the quality of the models predictions is shown in Fig. 4.

The BiGRU model was retrained using categories 0–3. The test set had a weighted F1 score of 93.8% accuracy and a loss of 20.9%. Comparing the true and predicted categories showed 1332 true matches, and 88 false matches.

The classification report is summarised in Table 6 and the receiver operating characteristic curve (ROC) measuring the quality of the models predictions is shown in Fig. 5. The Area Under the Curve (AUC) is very high, meaning the model has a high measure of separability for each category. The black dotted line is an example AUC of 0.5 which would be random chance.

The cross validation results using 10-folds was 94.26% avg to categorise groups 0–3 and 97.79% avg with category 3 dropped.

Table 5. BiGRU Classification Report to predict replacing the key-panel (Category 0), processor (Category 1), or both (Category 2)

Category	Precision	Recall	F1-score	Support
0	0.958	0.964	0.961	306
1	0.844	0.927	0.884	41
2	0.914	0.873	0.893	134
avg/total	0.936	0.936	0.935	481

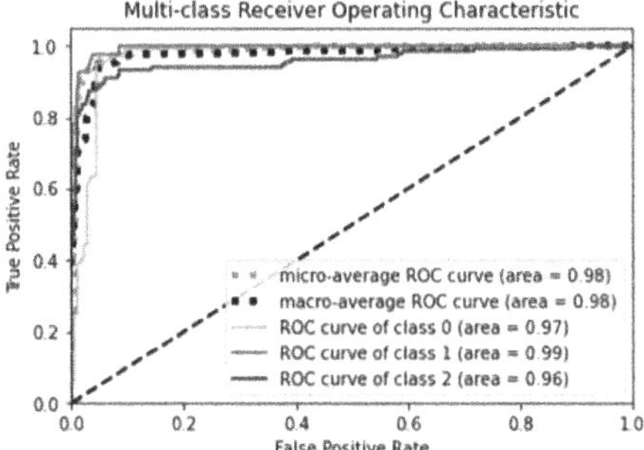

Fig. 4. ROC Curve for BiGRU with three categories. This shows a high AUC, meaning the model has very high separability for each category. By comparison, the black dotted line shows an AUC of 0.5 (random chance)

Table 6. BiGRU Classification Report to predict replacing the key-panel (Category 0), processor (Category 1), both (Category 2), or no parts replaced (Category 3)

Category	Precision	Recall	F1-score	Support
0	0.900	0.936	0.917	297
1	0.698	0.881	0.779	42
2	0.823	0.922	0.870	141
3	0.986	0.944	0.964	940
avg/total	0.943	0.938	0.940	1420

4 Manual Review of Errors in the Models

The 94 mis-classified records were manually reviewed, which gave us the following additional information:

- 17 records has the fault description "No fault stated". This resulted in the model classifying the records as "no parts replaced". However, sub-assemblies were replaced during the maintenance activity.

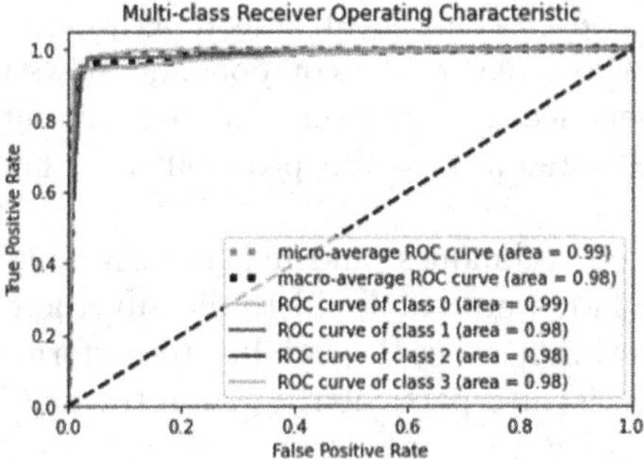

Fig. 5. ROC Curve for BiGRU with four categories. This shows a high AUC, meaning the model has very high separability for each category. By comparison, the black dotted line shows an AUC of 0.5 (random chance)

Table 7. Comparison of the multilabel classifiers to predict replacing the key-panel (Category 0), processor (Category 1), both (Category 2), or no parts replaced (Category 3)

Model	Categories	F1-score
BiLSTM	0–2	95.2%
BiLSTM	0–3	93.3%
BiGRU	0–2	93.5%
BiGRU	0–3	93.8%

- 55 records contained text description detailing faults of specific sub-assemblies that needed to be replaced. However, there was no parts issued to the repair job. This is either because the decision was changed and the record not updated, or the entries have missing data.
- 9 records has a fault description which did not correlate to material issued to the job. For example; the text described a faulty key-panel. However, both key-panel and processor was replaced.
- 2 records were outliners. A Liquid Crystal Display (LCD) and interface card was replaced and the model was not trained on these parts
- 11 records were manually confirmed to be true mis-classifications.

Therefore, 88% of the mis-classified records was a result of poorly described fault descriptions, or missing data. Only 12% was truly mis-classified by the model. Therefore, if the data quality is improved by accurate fault descriptions, and material issued to the job, then one can expect to see a higher F1 score (Table 7).

5 Conclusions

Based on the results of this study, it can be concluded that ML/AI models can effectively classify aerospace maintenance records from text description into workable categories based on component fault descriptions. The use of descriptions from engineers who replaced the components allows for a comprehensive analysis of the maintenance dataset using an thus far untapped data source, enabling a better understanding of the probability of failures in non-critical components of airplanes.

Various vectorisation techniques, and machine learning algorithms, including BiGRU and BiLSTM, were employed to classify the dataset. The models achieved high F1 scores, indicating their ability to perform this task effectively. The BiLSTM model performed particularly well in the multi-class classification, achieving a 95.2% F1 score.

It was found that errors or omissions by the person filling out the reports were a significant source of misclassified samples, with only 12% of the misclassified samples attributed to errors made by the model. This highlights the importance of ensuring accurate and complete information is provided in maintenance reports.

The dataset contains further text features, such as customer reported faults, or incoming inspection, which were not evaluated in this paper. The analysis of these texts can provide essential information to further improve the models' accuracy, and fill in missing data.

Overall, this study demonstrates the potential of AI models to improve the analysis of complex maintenance datasets and provide valuable insights into the dataset in use with the aim of improving reliability and lowering costs of airplanes' maintenance.

In order to validate the findings of the presented methods further one would need to consider the method of data augmentation to improve the imbalance issues in the presented data set. Future results should consider SMOTE [5] and MLSMOTE [4], among others.

Going forwards, we plan on predicting the numbers of repairs coming into the repair shop based on historical data, and what repairs we expect; which will provide an advantage to the repair shop and the customer. The benefit is that stock inventory can be provisioned in advance to reduce turn around time for the customer.

Acknowledgements. The completion of this research project would not have been possible without the contributions and support of many individuals at UWE and GE. I am grateful to all those who played a role in the success.

References

1. Agovic, A., Shan, H., Banerjee, A.: Analyzing aviation safety reports: from topic modeling to scalable multi-label classification. In: Proceedings of the 2010 Conference on Intelligent Data Understanding, CIDU 2010, pp. 83–97. Citeseer (2010)

2. Bojanowski, P., Grave, E., Joulin, A., Mikolov, T.: Enriching word vectors with subword information. Trans. Assoc. Comput. Linguist. **5**, 135–146 (2017). https://doi.org/10.1162/tacl_a_00051
3. Candell, O., Karim, R., Söderholm, P.: eMaintenance-Information logistics for maintenance support (2009). https://doi.org/10.1016/j.rcim.2009.04.005
4. Charte, F., Rivera, A.J., Del Jesus, M.J., Herrera, F.: MLSMOTE: approaching imbalanced multilabel learning through synthetic instance generation. Knowl. Based Syst. **89**, 385–397 (2015). https://doi.org/10.1016/j.knosys.2015.07.019
5. Chawla, N.V., Bowyer, K.W., Hall, L.O., Kegelmeyer, W.P.: SMOTE: synthetic minority over-sampling technique. J. Artif. Intell. Res. **16**, 321–357 (2002). https://doi.org/10.1613/jair.953, http://arxiv.org/abs/1106.1813
6. Devaney, M., Ram, A., Qiu, H., Lee, J.: Preventing failures by mining maintenance logs with case-based reasoning (2005)
7. Do, B.H., Wu, A.S., Maley, J., Biswal, S.: Automatic retrieval of bone fracture knowledge using natural language processing. J. Digit. Imaging **26**(4), 709–713 (2013). https://doi.org/10.1007/s10278-012-9531-1
8. Elhadad, N., Zhang, S., Driscoll, P., Brody, S.: Characterizing the sublanguage of online breast cancer forums for medications, symptoms, and emotions. In: AMIA ... Annual Symposium Proceedings / AMIA Symposium. AMIA Symposium 2014, pp. 516–525 (2014). https://www.ncbi.nlm.nih.gov/pmc/articles/PMC4419934/
9. Ford, E., Carroll, J.A., Smith, H.E., Scott, D., Cassell, J.A.: Extracting information from the text of electronic medical records to improve case detection: a systematic review. J. Am. Med. Inform. Assoc. **23**(5), 1007–1015 (2016). https://doi.org/10.1093/jamia/ocv180
10. Grivel, L.: Customer feedbacks and opinion surveys analysis in the automotive industry. text mining and its applications to intelligence. CRM Knowl. Manage. 249–257 (2005). https://doi.org/10.2495/978-1-85312-995-7/13
11. Heinze, D.T., Morsch, M.L., Holbrook, J.: Mining free-text medical records. Proceedings. In: AMIA Symposium, pp. 254–258 (2001). https://doi.org/10.1016/j.procir.2019.02.098
12. Jensen, K., et al.: Analysis of free text in electronic health records for identification of cancer patient trajectories. Sci. Rep. **7**(1), 46226 (2017). https://doi.org/10.1038/srep46226
13. Kang, N., Singh, B., Afzal, Z., van Mulligen, E.M., Kors, J.A.: Using rule-based natural language processing to improve disease normalization in biomedical text. J. Am. Med. Inform. Assoc. **20**(5), 876–881 (2013). https://doi.org/10.1136/amiajnl-2012-001173
14. Lucini, F.R., et al.: Text mining approach to predict hospital admissions using early medical records from the emergency department. Int. J. Med. Inform. **100**, 1–8 (2017). https://doi.org/10.1016/j.ijmedinf.2017.01.001
15. Lyall-Wilson, B., Kim, N., Hohman, E.: Modeling human factors topics in aviation reports (2019). https://doi.org/10.1177/1071181319631095
16. Maguire, F.B., et al.: A text-mining approach to obtain detailed treatment information from free-text fields in population-based cancer registries: a study of non-small cell lung cancer in California. PLoS ONE **14**(2), e0212454 (2019). https://doi.org/10.1371/journal.pone.0212454
17. Marafino, B.J., Davies, J.M., Bardach, N.S., Dean, M.L., Dudley, R.A.: N-gram support vector machines for scalable procedure and diagnosis classification, with applications to clinical free text data from the intensive care unit. J. Am. Med. Inform. Assoc. **21**(5), 871–875 (2014). https://doi.org/10.1136/amiajnl-2014-002694

18. Marev, K., Georgiev, K.: Automated aviation occurrences categorization. In: ICMT 2019–7th International Conference on Military Technologies, Proceedings, pp. 1–5 (2019). https://doi.org/10.1109/MILTECHS.2019.8870055
19. McKenzie, A., Matthews, M., Goodman, N., Bayoumi, A.: Information extraction from helicopter maintenance records as a springboard for the future of maintenance text analysis. In: García-Pedrajas, N., Herrera, F., Fyfe, C., Benítez, J.M., Ali, M. (eds.) IEA/AIE 2010. LNCS (LNAI), vol. 6096, pp. 590–600. Springer, Heidelberg (2010). https://doi.org/10.1007/978-3-642-13022-9_59
20. Mikolov, T., Chen, K., Corrado, G., Dean, J.: Efficient estimation of word representations in vector space. In: 1st International Conference on Learning Representations, ICLR 2013 - Workshop Track Proceedings (2013). https://arxiv.org/abs/1301.3781
21. Mikolov, T., Sutskever, I., Chen, K., Corrado, G., Dean, J.: Distributed representations of words and phrases and their compositionality. In: Advances in Neural Information Processing Systems cs.CL, pp. 1–9 (2013). https://arxiv.org/abs/1310.4546
22. Moreno Sandoval, A., Díaz, J., Campillos Llanos, L., Redondo, T.: Biomedical term extraction: NLP techniques in computational medicine. Int. J. Interact. Multimedia Artif. Intell. **5**(4), 51 (2019). https://doi.org/10.9781/ijimai.2018.04.001
23. Navinchandran, M., Sharp, M.E., Brundage, M.P., Sexton, T.B.: Studies to predict maintenance time duration and important factors from maintenanceworkorder data. In: Proceedings of the Annual Conference of the Prognostics and Health Management Society, PHM, vol. 11 (2019). https://doi.org/10.36001/phmconf.2019.v11i1.792
24. Nguyen, A., Moore, D., McCowan, I., Courage, M.J.: Multi-class classification of cancer stages from free-text histology reports using support vector machines. In: Annual International Conference of the IEEE Engineering in Medicine and Biology - Proceedings, vol. 2007, pp. 5140–5143. IEEE, United States (2007). DOIurl10.1109/IEMBS.2007.4353497
25. Paul, S.: NLP tools used in civil aviation: a survey (2018). https://doi.org/10.26483/ijarcs.v9i2.5559
26. Pelt, M., Stamoulis, K., Apostolidis, A.: Data analytics case studies in the maintenance, repair and overhaul (MRO) industry. In: MATEC Web of Conferences, vol. 304, p. 04005 (2019). https://doi.org/10.1051/matecconf/201930404005
27. Pennington, J., Socher, R., Manning, C.D.: GloVe: global vectors for word representation. In: EMNLP 2014–2014 Conference on Empirical Methods in Natural Language Processing, Proceedings of the Conference, pp. 1532–1543. Association for Computational Linguistics, Doha, Qatar (2014). https://doi.org/10.3115/v1/d14-1162
28. Robinson, S.D., Irwin, W.J., Kelly, T.K., Wu, X.O.: Application of machine learning to mapping primary causal factors in self reported safety narratives (2015). https://doi.org/10.1016/j.ssci.2015.02.003
29. Sexton, T., Hodkiewicz, M., Brundage, M.P., Smoker, T.: Benchmarking for keyword extraction methodologies in maintenance work orders. In: Proceedings of the Annual Conference of the Prognostics and Health Management Society, PHM. Philadelphia, PA (2018). https://doi.org/10.36001/phmconf.2018.v10i1.541
30. Tanguy, L., Tulechki, N., Urieli, A., Hermann, E., Raynal, C.: Natural language processing for aviation safety reports: from classification to interactive analysis. Comput. Ind. **78**, 80–95 (2016). https://doi.org/10.1016/j.compind.2015.09.005

31. Wang, J., Li, C., Han, S., Sarkar, S., Zhou, X.: Predictive maintenance based on event-log analysis: a case study. IBM J. Res. Dev. **61**(1), 121–132 (2017). https://doi.org/10.1147/JRD.2017.2648298
32. Zhang, K., Xu, J., Min, M.R., Jiang, G., Pelechrinis, K., Zhang, H.: Automated IT system failure prediction: a deep learning approach. In: Proceedings - 2016 IEEE International Conference on Big Data, Big Data 2016, pp. 1291–1300. IEEE (2016). https://doi.org/10.1109/BigData.2016.7840733

MCASleepNet: Multimodal Channel Attention-Based Deep Neural Network for Automatic Sleep Staging

Yangzuyi Yu, Shuyu Chen, and Jiahui Pan(✉)

South China Normal University, Guangzhou, China
panjiahui@m.scnu.edu.cn

Abstract. Sleep staging is significant for the capture of sleep patterns and the assessment of sleep quality. Although previous studies attempted to automatically detect sleep stages and achieved high classification performance, several challenges remain: 1) How to correctly classify the sleep stages end-to-end. 2) How to capture the representations and sleep transition rules effectively. 3) How to capture the sleep features adaptively from multimodal data for sleep staging. To address these problems, a multimodal channel attention-based sleep staging network named MCASleepNet is proposed. Specifically, the proposed network is a mixed model composed of a dual-stream convolutional neural network (CNN) structure, a solitary long short-term memory (LSTM) module and a multimodal channel attention module. The dual-stream CNN structure is designed for the extraction of sleep representation characteristics from multimodal data. Meanwhile, the LSTM module is developed to learn transition rules between sleep stages. In addition, the multimodal channel attention module is developed to extract meaningful features of specific sleep stages from multimodal sleep data, electroencephalogram (EEG) and electrooculogram (EOG) signals. The sleep staging experiment demonstrates that the MCASleepNet proposed in this study exceeds the state-of-the-art baseline methods, with an overall accuracy of 89.1% and a macro F1 score of 84.4 on the publicly available Sleep-EDF dataset.

Keywords: sleep stages · electroencephalogram · long short-term memory · multimodal channel attention

1 Introduction

Sleep staging is significant for the capture of sleep patterns and the assessment of sleep quality [1]. Sleep staging can measure sleep architecture, observe characteristic sleep waves and understand sleep cycle variability in humans. Effective and feasible sleep assessment is of vital importance for the identification of sleep disorders and timely intervention [12]. To obtain sleep data, sleep researchers use polysomnography (PSG) to record brain, eye and muscle activity during sleep, which can be observed and illustrate sleep features in long-term monitoring [2].

L. Iliadis et al. (Eds.): ICANN 2023, LNCS 14263, pp. 308–319, 2023.
https://doi.org/10.1007/978-3-031-44204-9_26

Brain activities are recorded as an electroencephalogram (EEG) and eye movements as an electrooculogram (EOG). At present, there are two commonly used sleep staging standards and sleep quality scales: the guidelines of Rechtschaffen and Kales (R&K) [15] and the American Academy of Sleep Medicine (AASM) [7]. Generally, sleep experts performing manual sleep staging divide sleep data into 30 s sleep epochs and classify them into different sleep stages: wake (W), nonrapid eye movement (NREM) sleep and rapid eye movement (REM) sleep. Specifically, according to the R&K standard, NREM sleep can be further divided into four stages, N1, N2, N3 and N4. According to the AASM standard, N3 and N4 are combined and marked as stage N3. However, the subjective nature of manual sleep staging by a sleep specialist can limit the accuracy of the sleep assessment, and manual staging requires a high level of clinician experience and is time consuming. Therefore, automated sleep staging models have become popular, and many studies have proposed various automated sleep staging methods around these issues to improve the accuracy and objectivity of staging and reduce latency and time consumption, and these methods have obtained state-of-the-art performance [8,14,16].

To achieve automatic sleep staging, several related studies have proposed classification methods using EEG and/or EOG have been proven to be effective. However, several challenges remain:

Unimodal sleep signals and manually extracted sleep features are used to classify sleep stages. Fraiwan et al. [5] proposed an automated sleep staging method based on time-frequency analysis of single-channel EEG signals, using a random forest classifier. Hassan et al. [6] proposed a deep learning model for sleep staging and converted raw PSG signals into time-frequency images as training data. Although the above methods resulted in highly accurate classification, the distribution of features varies from dataset to dataset, the manual feature extraction method is only specific to a particular dataset and may require prior knowledge. Furthermore, information may be lost in the original sleep data after conversion. Single-channel EEG show similar features in different sleep periods, reducing the accuracy of classification. For example, the next stage of the stage wake is the stage N1, so the two periods have similar EEG oscillations that can easily be confused [7]. Manual sleep staging typically classifies sleep stages by combining features from multiple modalities, such as complementary features of EEG and EOG at different times, to reduce the impact of conflicting features of a single modality on staging as described above. Therefore, multimodal raw EEG and EOG are used for sleep staging, and deep learning method is applied to achieve end-to-end classification and reduce manual intervention.

The hybrid model of a convolutional neural network (CNN) and a recurrent neural network (RNN) is used to learn sleep signal representations and sleep transition rules. During sleep, different sleep stages are characterized by different sleep physiological electrical signals, which are characterized by information including different frequencies, wave amplitudes and spatio-temporal distribution characteristics. The sleep transition rules are a cyclical transition between NREM and

REM sleep, with NREM sleep moving sequentially from stage N1 to N4 [7]. Supratak et al. [16] developed a two-stream CNN composed of two different convolutional filter sizes to exploit temporal and frequency features from different scales, following a bidirectional LSTM to extract sequential information. Furthermore, Xu et al. [18] compared LSTM networks with four classical CNNs and observed that LSTM models have better classification performance than CNNs. Since CNN is not as effective as LSTM for learning temporal features of EEG, this paper design a dual-stream CNN for learning EEG and EOG representations, rather than dedication a branch to learning temporal features of EEG. To improve computational efficiency and reduce computational resources, a single LSTM is used in this paper to learn sleep transition rules.

The feature fusion method and attention mechanism are applied to sleep signal modalities. The complementarity of the EEG and the EOG is reflected in that the features of the EEG are similar in different periods, but there are different features in the EOG to distinguish that period, or the opposite. Using the complementary features of EEG and EOG in different sleep stages can effectively distinguish sleep stages. To capture multimodal sleep features, most deep learning models usually use concatenate operations [11,13]. However, the dominance of different modalities making decisions is different in different stages of sleep, which also ignores the mutuality between EEG and EOG. In addition, many sleep staging network use only unimodal and temporal-spatial attention mechanisms [3,4,10]. The use of hybrid models for multimodal feature extraction with the channel attention mechanism for multimodal fusion are less common. Therefore, this paper proposes a multimodal channel attention mechanism to fuse multimodalities and focus more on the characteristics of different modal contributions to specific sleep stages.

To solve the above-mentioned challenges, we propose a deep neural network for sleep staging called the Multimodal Channel Attention Sleep Network (MCASleepNet). Overall, the main contributions of the proposed MCASleepNet are summarized as follows:

- A hybrid network consisting of a dual-stream CNN structure and a solitary LSTM module is developed. The CNN structure is beneficial for capturing significant features of EEG and EOG signals at the same time. The LSTM module is designed to learn sleep transition rules depending on the former and later stages. The hybrid network can prevent repeated learning of temporal features and reduce model parameters compared to other computationally complex RNNs.
- A multimodal channel attention module is proposed to effectively integrate multimodal physiological signal features learned from CNN. Benefiting from this module, MCASleepNet can adaptively obtain valuable characteristics from EEG and EOG signals.
- Experimental results show that MCASleepNet achieves state-of-the-art performance in terms of an average accuracy of 89.1% and MF1-score of 84.4 on the Sleep-EDF dataset. In addition, compared with the benchmark method,

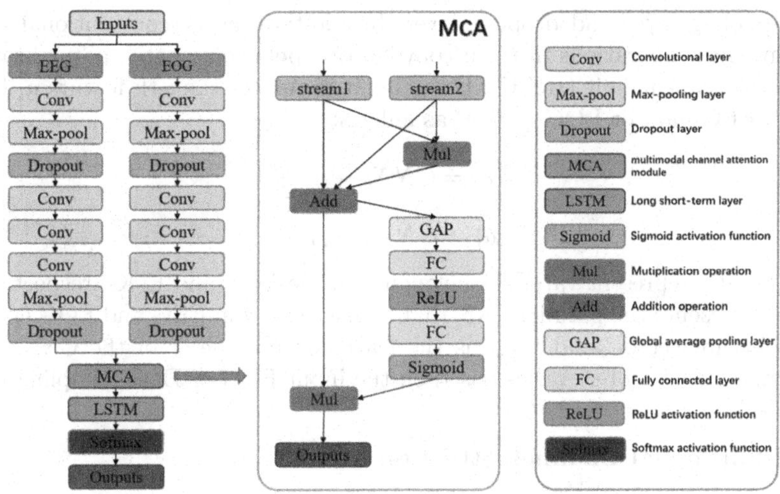

Fig. 1. Sleep stage network architecture of MCASleepNet.

our model parameters are minimal, which has great potential to automatically assist sleep physicians in sleep staging.

2 Multimodal Channel Attention-Based Network for Sleep Staging

The overall architecture of MCASleepNet is shown in Fig. 1. We introduce the procedure of each part in detail in the following. The proposed sleep staging network mainly consists of 3 parts: (1) To achieve representation learning, we propose a dual-stream CNN structure. (2) To adaptively obtain valuable characteristics from multimodal signals, we design a multimodal channel attention module. (3) To implement sequence learning, we develop a solitary LSTM module.

2.1 Representation Learning

In the dual-stream CNN structure, the convolutional layer close to the input is used to learn specific shallow features of the original data to reduce manual intervention and prevent partial information loss. The input data e_i[input dimension, 1, 1] are passed through a one-dimensional convolution layer, where the input dimension is the sampling rate × epoch duration. The shallow features are fed into the max pooling and dropout layers to reduce dimension and select information, which can deepen the follow features.

In order to learn the deeper features of the EEG and EOG, the obtained shallow features are fed into 3 successive convolutional layers, interleaved with a max-pooling layer and dropout layer. In addition, every convolutional layer performs three operations in turn: convolution operations, batch normalization and rectified linear unit (ReLU). Formally, it computes the i-th feature a_i from the i-th EEG data or EOG data e_i as follows:

$$a_i^l = CNN_{\theta_l}(e_i^l) \tag{1}$$

$$a_i^s = CNN_{\theta_s}(e_i^s) \tag{2}$$

where l and s represent variables belonging to the EEG and EOG, respectively. CNN_θ represents the parallel CNN that transforms from EEG and EOG epochs into a feature vector, and theta is the learnable parameter of the CNN. It is noted that the size of a_i varies based on the input EEG or EOG sampling rate.

2.2 Multimodal Channel Attention Module

In the multimodal channel attention module, the resulting dual-stream features are first fused. In contrast to direct multimodal fusion using the concatenate operation, multiplication allows a higher confidence level for important modal features and a lower confidence level for irrelevant features. Then it is added to the input features to obtain a fused feature map $X_{fuse} \in R^{C\times H\times W}$, where C denotes the total channel number, and H and W denote the height and weight of features, respectively, which has a combined confidence level and avoids loss of the original features.

After GlobalAveragePooling (GAP) compression and reshaping, a feature map of size $1\times 1\times C$ is obtained, which reduces the spatial dimensionality of the fused features and allows the model to focus on the global information. A non-linear transformation is performed by two successive fully connected (FC) layers with ReLU and sigmoid activation functions, and the weighting coefficients for the channel wise are calculated. Finally the features are recalibrated and the feature map learned by the attention module is multiplied by the input features to obtain the new feature map $X_{att}^{'} \in R^{C\times H\times W}$. The model adjusts the weights of features by modal channel attention, allowing the model to better learn the correlation and important features of sleep EEG and EOG between channels, improving the model's fitting ability. Formally, the modality fusion component and the channel-wise attention component are defined as follows:

$$X_{fuse} = a_i^l + a_i^s + (a_i^l \cdot a_i^s) \tag{3}$$

$$X_{att} = FC_S(FC_R(GAP(X_{fuse}))) \tag{4}$$

$$X_{att}^{'} = X_{fuse} \cdot X_{att} \tag{5}$$

where X_{fuse} is the fused feature map and $\cdot$ is the element-wise multiplication. FC_R and FC_S represent the fully connected layer with the ReLU and Sigmoid activation function, respectively.

2.3 Sequence Learning

Sleep transition rules are important global temporal information to classify sleep stages. The model can improve its accuracy by obtaining important information from previous input samples. To further improve the usability of the model and to reduce the redundancy of the model, a unidirectional LSTM module is used in this paper to capture the temporal features of the sleep signal.

In the unidirectional LSTM module, the module learns the temporal information between each epoch from the EEG and EOG signals and learns the sleep transition rules for each sleep stage [7]. To keep the size of the input data constant $X_i \in R^{C \times H \times W}$, the number of neurons and the hidden size of the forward LSTM are set to the same value with W as 128. there are N sequentially arranged fused feature vectors from the MCA module, denoted as $\{X_1 ..., X_n\}$. The i-th feature X_i is processed as follows:

$$h_i, c_i = LSTM_\theta(h_{i-1}, c_{i-1}, X_i) \tag{6}$$

where $LSTM_\theta$ is the LSTM with the sequence of features X_i as input, theta represents the learnable parameters of the LSTM, h_i and c_i are the vectors of hidden states and cell states about X_i obtained by unidirectional LSTM layer processing, and h_{i-1} and c_{i-1} are the hidden states and cell states obtained by processing the sequence of features X_{i-1}. h_0 and c_0 are initialized to $\vec{0}$.

After the above part of training and updating of weights, we input the output information of the LSTM layer to the softmax layer with 5 neurons, which calculate the predicted value and output the label corresponding to the maximum value as the final sleep stage classification.

3 Experiments and Results

3.1 Dataset

Sleep-EDF Dataset. In Sleep-EDF [9], there are 39 PSG records from an age effect study in healthy subjects (SCs) aged 25–34. There were 20 subjects in total, 10 males and 10 females. PSG records of approximately 20 h are available for each subject, except for subject 13, whose one recording was lost due to equipment failure. All records contain EEG data from Fpz-Cz and Pz-Oz electrode locations, EOG data from horizon only, chin EMG and event markers. Specifically, the sleep records are divided into 30-s epochs and labeled into one of eight categories: W, N1, N2, N3, N4, REM, MOVEMENT, and UNKNOWN by sleep specialists according to the R&K standard [15].

In this study, stages N3 and N4 were combined into a single stage, N3, according to the AASM standard [7], and the MOVEMENT and UNKNOWN categories were removed. We adopt Fpz-Cz EEG and HEOG channels with a sampling rate of 100 Hz to train and test our sleep staging model. All sleep stages are labeled $\{0, 1, 2, 3, 4\}$ in the following order: W, N1, N2, N3, N4, REM. Specifically, to increase the amount of data and avoid overfitting, each EEG and EOG epoch was randomly intercepted for 30 s starting 3 s forward or backward along the time axis. In addition, since it was desired to study the effect of raw sleep data on sleep staging, no preprocessing techniques were used in this experiment.

3.2 Baseline Methods

The proposed model is compared with the following baseline methods:

- DeepSleepNet [16]: A sleep staging network based on a single-channel CNN-BiLSTM network using raw sleep signals.
- SeqSleepNet [13]: An automatic sleep staging model composed of parallel filterbank layers and based on an end-to-end RNN network.
- SleepEEGNet [11]: A seq2seq sleep staging network consisting of CNNs to learn local features and to capture long short-term context dependencies.
- TinySleepNet [17]: A sleep staging model using CNN to learn time-invariant features and a unidirectional LSTM to learn sleep transition rules.
- SalientSleepNet [8]: A sleep staging multimodal network using EEG and EOG as data sources using U^2-Net.

3.3 Experiment Settings

The healthy control group contained 20 subjects in the Sleep-EDF dataset who were selected for offline analysis of data and 20-fold cross-validation. In each iteration of the experiment, one subject was used as the test set, and the rest of the subjects' data were divided into a training set and a validation set with 17 and 2 subjects, respectively. The data differ for each fold of cross-validation and ensure that the test set is isolated from the data in the training and validation sets. The detailed hyperparameter settings are shown in Table 1.

The overall performance of the proposed model is evaluated by the accuracy (ACC) and macro averaging F1-score (MF1). Each sleep stage class is measured by F1-score (F1), which combines precision and recall metrics. The accuracy does not adequately reflect the predictive power of the model due to the different proportions of different sleep stages in the sleep cycle; for example, stage N1 has the smallest amount of data in the whole dataset at 6.34%. MF1 was examined equally for each category, and its value was influenced by the rare category. The MF1 score was chosen as the measure for comparison with the baseline in this study.

$$ACC = \frac{\sum_{i=1}^{n} TP_i}{N} \tag{7}$$

$$MF1 = \frac{\sum_{i=1}^{n} F1_i}{N} \tag{8}$$

where TP_i is the true positives of class i, $F1_i$ is the F1-score of each sleep stage class i, n is the number of sleep stages, and N is the total number of epochs in the test set.

Table 1. The hyperparameters used for experiments

Parameter	Value	Parameter	Value
Optimizer	Adam	Max-pool kernel size	8,4
Learning rate	0.0001	kernel_size	8
$\beta 1$	0.9	Padding	same
$\beta 2$	0.999	batch_size	15
ϵ	1e-8	Training epochs	200
Regularization	TRUE	EarlyStopping patience	100
Input dim	3000	sampling_rate	100
Conv.filters	128	n_folds	20

3.4 Experimental Results

The experimental results of MCASleepNet after 20-fold cross-validation were produced as a confusion matrix, as shown in Fig. 2. Each row and column indicates the classification results by the sleep experts and the proposed model, respectively. The main diagonal line in the matrix indicates the number of samples correctly identified by the proposed model. From Fig. 2, it can be seen that the percentage of correct predictions for each sleep stage is higher than the other values in the peer rows and columns. The results showed that satisfactory results were obtained for the classification of all sleep stages except the N1 stage. This may be because N1 has the least number of samples, resulting in poor classification, but it can be seen from Table 2 that N1 has the best classification performance compared to the baseline models.

The proposed model was compared with four baseline methods on a publicly available dataset, as shown in Table 2. The results show that this paper's model achieves the best accuracy of overall performance compared with the baseline models. To validate the effectiveness of the proposed two-stream model, the same two-channel (HEOG and Fpz-Cz) input signals from the Sleep-EDF dataset were fed into the baseline models for 20-fold cross-validation. The results showed that this model had an overall staging accuracy of 89.1%, which was higher than that of all baseline methods. It also performed the best in MF1 and each sleep stage classification. The results demonstrated that MCASleepNet has good sleep staging ability. Figure 3 shows a comparative hypnogram of manual scoring by a sleep expert and automatic scoring by MCASleepNet on the sleep-EDF dataset of SC4032E0. In addition, due to the use of the solitary LSTM module, the present model has a smaller number of parameters than the two-stream baseline model using RNNs with a similar structure. The number of parameters for DeepSleepNet is about 21 M, which is approximately 3 times more than MCASleepNet (about 7 M). The number of parameters for SeqSleepNet and SleepEEGNet is not available in their published literature, we thus did not compare them. Since TinySleepNet is not a two-stream network and SalientSleepNet is not a hybrid model, we do not compare the number of model parameters with them here.

Table 2. The performance of automatic staging on Sleep-EDF datasets

Models	Channel	Overall performance		Per-class performance (F1-score)				
		Accuracy (%)	*MF1*	*W*	*N1*	*N2*	*N3*	*REM*
DeepSleepNet [16]	Fpz-Cz	82.0	76.9	84.7	46.6	86.0	85.0	82.0
SeqSleepNet [13]	Fpz-Cz	86.0	79.6	91.9	47.8	87.2	85.7	86.2
SleepEEGNet [11]	Fpz-Cz	84.3	79.7	89.2	52.2	86.8	85.1	85.0
TinySleepNet [17]	Fpz-Cz	85.4	80.5	90.1	51.4	88.5	**88.3**	84.4
SalientSleepNet [8]	Fpz-Cz &EOG	87.5	83.0	92.3	56.2	89.9	87.2	89.2
Our method	Fpz-Cz &EOG	**89.1**	**84.4**	**93.3**	**60.4**	**90.0**	88.2	**90.1**

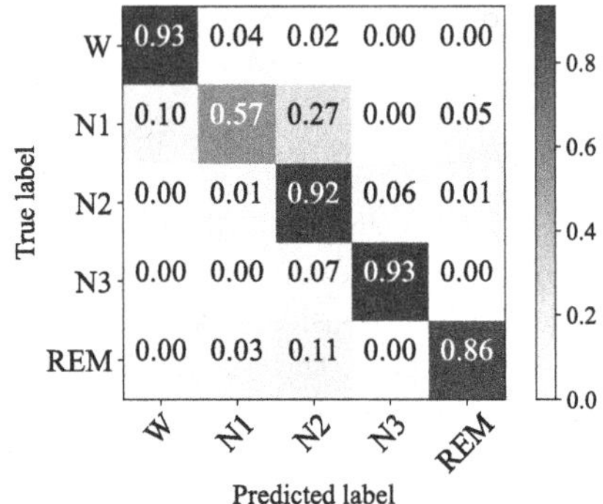

Fig. 2. The confusion matrix based on MCASleepNet for Sleep-EDF dataset.

To demonstrate the usefulness of the multimodal channel attention module for EEG and EOG complementary and contradictory feature extraction, we randomly visualized the EEG and EOG signals in half of the predicted results for different periods, using data from Subject SC4032E0, as shown in Fig. 4. All authenticity regarding the presence of EEG and EOG signal characteristics in each sleep stage is based on the AASM standard [7]. For example, as shown in Fig. 4, we can see the presence of rapid eye movements with large amplitudes and sharp initial offsets in both the W (caused by blinking) and REM stages of the EOG. However, there are high-frequency EEGs in the W stage but low-frequency EEGs in the REM stage, and these features work together to improve the predictive accuracy of the classification model so that EEG and EOG have complementary features. In the adjacent W and N1 stages, the features are similar and can easily be confused when staging. Both have high-frequency brain waves, so using only the EEG as a training feature can easily reduce predictive performance due to conflicting features in a single modality. However, as shown in Fig. 4, the EOG in stage N1 has a lower amplitude and a slow initial deflection, which is slow eye movement (SEM). Combining the EEG and EOG features makes it easier to distinguish stage N1 from stage W. In stage N3, low-frequency, high-amplitude waves called slow waves appear in the EEG. In stage N2, there are k-complex waves and sleep spindles. These are the characteristic

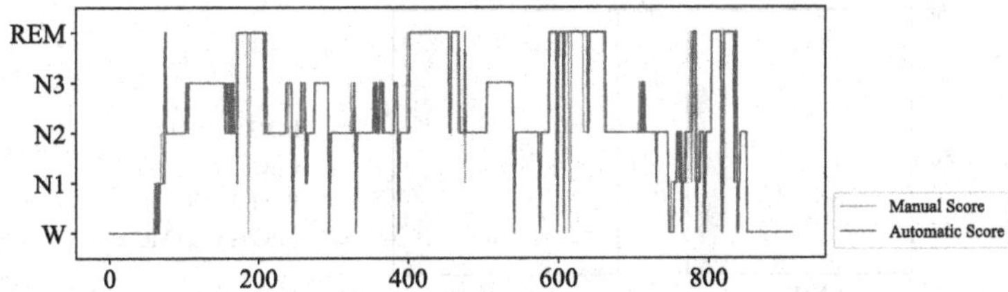

Fig. 3. Example of a comparison hypnogram manually scored by a sleep expert (red) and automatically scored by MCASleepNet (blue) in the SC4032E0 sleep-EDF dataset. (Color figure online)

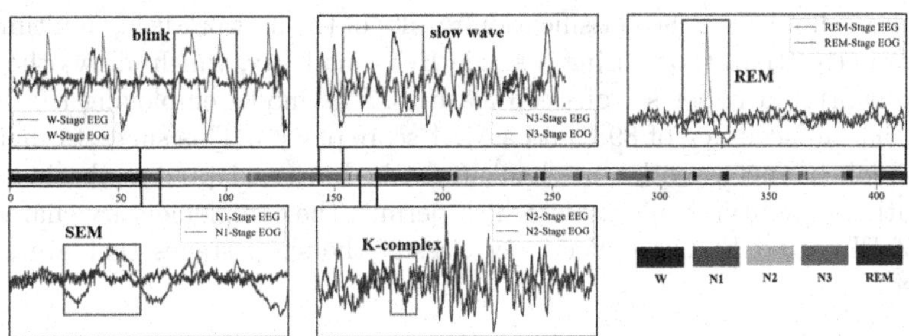

Fig. 4. The EEG (bule) and EOG (green) of 5 sleep stages extracted from subject SC4032E0 in the sleep-EDF dataset. (Color figure online)

waves that can be recorded on the EEG in both periods. However, there is little eye movement during these two periods and the recorded EOG is susceptible to fluctuations from the EEG during this time. Using the EOG alone as a training feature tends to reduce the accuracy of sleep staging, but using EEG in conjunction with EOG provides complementary patterning characteristics. Overall, the proposed model is effective in detecting complementary features in multimodal signals as well as noting the presence of conflicting features in the modalities.

3.5 Ablation Experiment

To validate the effectiveness of multimodal sleep signals and the multimodal channel attention mechanism in this model, we design the following experiments using different variant models:

- EOG: This model is a single stream hybrid network composed of one CNN branch and a solitary LSTM, which uses EOG signals only.
- EEG: This model is the same as the one mentioned above, and it uses EEG signals as input data.
- EEG+EOG: This model adds another CNN structure for EOG signals based on the previous EEG model. The modality fusion uses a simple concatenation operation.
- EEG+EOG+MCA: This model (MCASleepNet) with the addition of a multimodal channel attention module based on the last model for EEG and EOG.

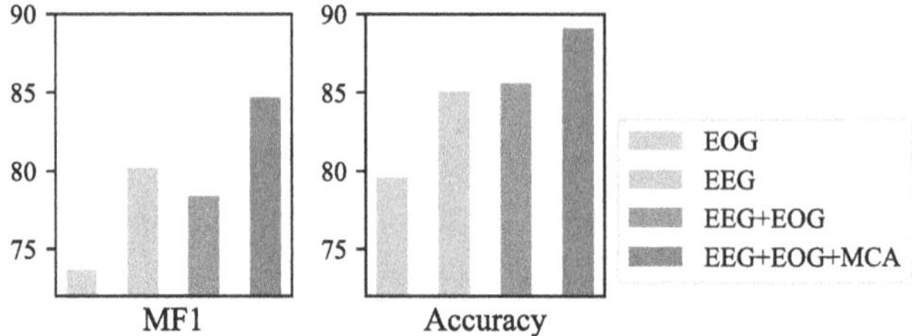

Fig. 5. The results of the ablation experiment.

Figure 5 shows that the classification results of the network using multimodal data are better than those using a single EEG modality, which allows the network to capture a richer set of sleep features. The model employing the MCA module has an accuracy of 89.1 and a MF1 score of 84.4. This suggests that the multimodal channel attention mechanism can be better adapted to obtain useful information in multimodal signals, which permits the complementary characteristics of EEG and EOG to effectively classify the sleep stages that are easily confused.

4 Conclusion

In this paper, we constructed a multimodal sleep stage detection network. The sleep staging network is the first attempt to apply a multimodal channel attention mechanism to a mixed deep neural network for sleep staging. MCASleepNet can effectively not only detect sleep patterns from different multimodal data for normal people but also learn the temporal relationships between sleep stages and detect transitions between them after modality fusion. The experimental results showed that MCASleepNet achieves better performance than the baseline methods and the significant improvement of using multimodal sleep signals together with the multimodal channel attention mechanism. The model has high accuracy and robustness in sleep stage classification and has the potential to help sleep specialists with manual sleep staging. In future studies, we will explore the potential of applying this sleep staging model to sleep stage classification for patients with disorders of consciousness through transfer learning and the implementation of a real-time sleep detection and assessment system.

Acknowledgement. This work was supported in part by the National Natural Science Foundation of China under grant 62076103 and the Special Innovation Project of Colleges and Universities in Guangdong Province under grant 2022KTSCX035.

References

1. Czeisler, C.A.: Duration, timing and quality of sleep are each vital for health, performance and safety. Sleep Health: J. Natl. Sleep Found. **1**(1), 5–8 (2015)

2. De Biase, S., et al.: The importance of polysomnography in the evaluation of prolonged disorders of consciousness: sleep recordings more adequately correlate than stimulus-related evoked potentials with patients' clinical status. Sleep Med. **15**(4), 393–400 (2014)
3. Eldele, E., et al.: An attention-based deep learning approach for sleep stage classification with single-channel EEG. IEEE Trans. Neural Syst. Rehabil. Eng. **29**, 809–818 (2021)
4. Feng, L.X., et al.: Automatic sleep staging algorithm based on time attention mechanism. Front. Hum. Neurosci. **15**, 692054 (2021)
5. Fraiwan, L., Lweesy, K., Khasawneh, N., Wenz, H., Dickhaus, H.: Automated sleep stage identification system based on time-frequency analysis of a single EEG channel and random forest classifier. Comput. Methods Prog. Biomed. **108**(1), 10–19 (2012)
6. Hassan, A.R., Bhuiyan, M.I.H.: A decision support system for automatic sleep staging from EEG signals using tunable q-factor wavelet transform and spectral features. J. Neurosci. Methods **271**, 107–118 (2016)
7. Iber, C., Ancoli-Isreal, S., Chesson, A.L., Quan, S.F.: The aasm manual for the scoring of sleep and associated events: rules, terminology, and techinical specifications (2007)
8. Jia, Z., Lin, Y., Wang, J., Wang, X., Xie, P., Zhang, Y.: Salientsleepnet: Multimodal salient wave detection network for sleep staging. arXiv preprint arXiv:2105.13864 (2021)
9. Kemp, B., Zwinderman, A.H., Tuk, B., Kamphuisen, H.A., Oberye, J.J.: Analysis of a sleep-dependent neuronal feedback loop: the slow-wave microcontinuity of the EEG. IEEE Trans. Biomed. Eng. **47**(9), 1185–1194 (2000)
10. Liu, C., Yin, Y., Sun, Y., Ersoy, O.K.: Multi-scale ResNet and BiGRU automatic sleep staging based on attention mechanism. PLoS ONE **17**(6), e0269500 (2022)
11. Mousavi, S., Afghah, F., Acharya, U.R.: SleepEEGNet: automated sleep stage scoring with sequence to sequence deep learning approach. PLoS ONE **14**(5), e0216456 (2019)
12. Ohayon, M.M.: Epidemiology of insomnia: what we know and what we still need to learn. Sleep Med. Rev. **6**(2), 97–111 (2002)
13. Phan, H., Andreotti, F., Cooray, N., Chén, O.Y., De Vos, M.: SeqSleepNet: end-to-end hierarchical recurrent neural network for sequence-to-sequence automatic sleep staging. IEEE Trans. Neural Syst. Rehabil. Eng. **27**(3), 400–410 (2019)
14. Phan, H., Chén, O.Y., Tran, M.C., Koch, P., Mertins, A., De Vos, M.: Xsleepnet: multi-view sequential model for automatic sleep staging. IEEE Trans. Pattern Anal. Mach. Intell. **44**(9), 5903–5915 (2021)
15. Rechtschaffen, A.: A manual of standardized terminology, techniques and scoring system for sleep of human subjects (1968)
16. Supratak, A., Dong, H., Wu, C., Guo, Y.: DeepSleepNet: a model for automatic sleep stage scoring based on raw single-channel EEG. IEEE Trans. Neural Syst. Rehabil. Eng. **25**(11), 1998–2008 (2017)
17. Supratak, A., Guo, Y.: TinySleepNet: an efficient deep learning model for sleep stage scoring based on raw single-channel EEG. In: 2020 42nd Annual International Conference of the IEEE Engineering in Medicine & Biology Society (EMBC), pp. 641–644. IEEE (2020)
18. Xu, Z., Yang, X., Sun, J., Liu, P., Qin, W.: Sleep stage classification using time-frequency spectra from consecutive multi-time points. Front. Neurosci. **14**, 14 (2020)

Multi-label Image Deep Hashing with Hybrid Loss of Global Center and Local Alignment

Ye Liu[1,3,4], Yan Pan[1,3], and Jian Yin[2,3](✉)

[1] School of Computer Science and Engineering, Sun Yat-sen University, Guangzhou, China
liuye7@mail2.sysu.edu.cn, panyan5@mail.sysu.edu.cn

[2] School of Artificial Intelligence, Sun Yat-sen University, Zhuhai, China
issjyin@mail.sysu.edu.cn

[3] Guangdong Key Laboratory of Big Data Analysis and Processing, Guangzhou, China

[4] Artificial Intelligence Department, Lizhi Inc., Beijing, China

Abstract. Deep hashing algorithms are widely used in large-scale image retrieval tasks. Based on deep neural network as the backbone, combined with the design of loss function, deep hashing can transform high-dimensional image inputs into binary hash codes, which better improves the efficiency of image retrieval and reduces the storage space. Most of the existing methods use image pairs or triplets for local similarity constraints, and recently hashing methods based on the global hash centers have been proposed. In this paper, we propose a novel deep hashing method that combines the global and local constraints in order to further improve the effect of deep hashing in image retrieval task. For multi-label images, we extend the global hash center generation method so that each image has multiple hash centers, represented by binary hash codes, with the same number of image categories. Then, multiple global hash central binary codes corresponding to the images are used as anchors, and dissimilar image pairs are selected to construct the triplet loss constraint linking global and local features. Moreover, we construct a partially similar loss function for the images where only part of the classification labels are similar, making more use of multiple labels. Furthermore, we combine the global and local loss functions and propose a novel hybrid loss function for multi-label image deep hashing. Extensive experiments on four multi-label image datasets for image retrieval demonstrate that the proposed method achieves substantial improvement over state-of-the-art hashing methods.

Keywords: Deep hashing · Multi-label image · Hybrid loss · Global center · Local alignment

L. Iliadis et al. (Eds.): ICANN 2023, LNCS 14263, pp. 320–332, 2023.
https://doi.org/10.1007/978-3-031-44204-9_27

1 Introduction

With the rapid development of the Internet, large-scale image retrieval technology has attracted much attention in recent years. Traditional image retrieval frameworks usually use manually designed image feature extraction methods, and the effect of such methods to obtain features is limited. Currently, in most scenarios, it has been replaced by image feature extraction algorithms based on deep neural networks [29]. In the classic image classification tasks, the original images and corresponding labels are used as input to the deep model through supervised learning [22]. Although the image feature representations obtained by the deep neural network pre-training model can better describe the image characteristics, there are still some improvements to be made in the face of large-scale image retrieval tasks. Through image hashing [30], the real number feature representations of high dimension can be mapped to the binary representations of low dimension, and the images can be transformed from original space to Hamming space [21] by designing transformation methods and corresponding loss functions [32]. Binary image hash coding in Hamming space can realize less storage space, and has obvious advantages in fast retrieval calculation.

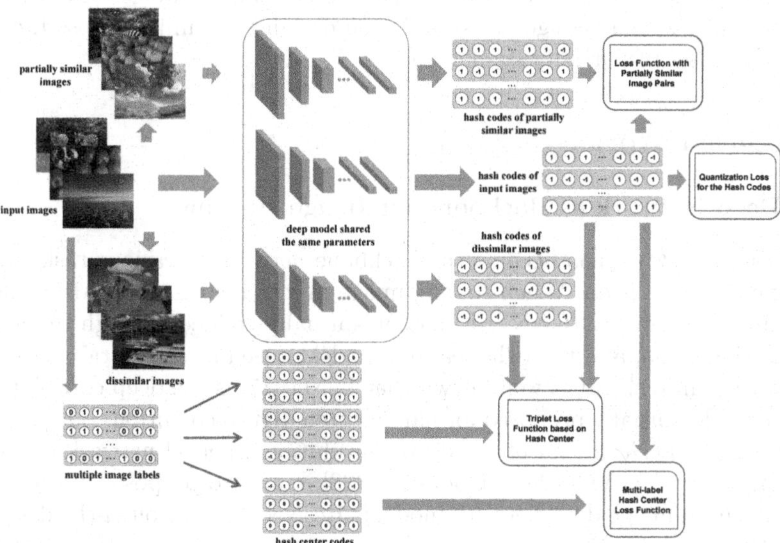

Fig. 1. Overview of the proposed deep hashing architecture for multi-label image with hybrid loss of global center and local alignment.

Due to the limitation of traditional image hashing algorithms (LSH [7], KSH [20], ITQ [9], SDH [26], etc.) in retrieval effect, deep hashing methods [5] are widely used as the current mainstream methods. Since the deep hashing framework CNNH [31] was first proposed, in terms of loss function design, it has been extended into deep hashing methods based on pairwise loss function or triplet loss function. These methods (DHN [35], HashNet [3], DCH [2], NINH [15]) are mainly based on the local relation between images to construct the loss functions. Recently, an important work on the design of deep hashing loss function is CSQ [33]. The core idea of the CSQ method is to construct the global hash centers and take the hash centers as the supervised tags for deep hashing network training. Meanwhile, these deep hashing methods usually construct similarity in a simple way when processing multi-label images, that is, when any pair of labels is similar, the corresponding original image pair is regarded as similar.

In order to improve the retrieval effect of multi-label image data through the deep hashing method, inspired by the above work, this paper designs a deep hashing framework for multi-label image data. Figure 1 shows our proposed framework for multi-label image deep hashing. The main contributions of this paper include several aspects: (1) A deep hashing framework is designed for multi-label image retrieval, in which the calculation method of hash center loss in previous work is replaced by a multi hash center loss function. (2) In each mini-batch training process, for each image and any one of its corresponding hash centers, select another image that is not similar, so that we put forward a novel way to construct the loss function of triples. (3) At the same time, we make better use of the image data with only part of the similar labels, construct the set of partially similar image pairs, and then design the similarity loss function based on the set of partially similar images.

2 Related Work

2.1 Deep Network as Backbone for Image Hashing

Deep neural network has become the backbone network of various tasks in the field of computer vision. When solving image processing tasks, the deep convolutional neural network (CNN [10]) model is usually trained through supervised classification tasks, and then the learned model is used as a pre-training model for downstream tasks. It is well known that LeNet [17] is the deep convolutional network model initially proposed for handwritten digit recognition. Based on the architecture of LeNet, a variety of deep convolutional neural network (AlexNet [14], ImageNet [24], VGG [27], GooLeNet [28], etc.) are proposed. Recently, a very influential image deep network model is ResNet [11]. Through the design of residual module, the deep network can become deeper, while significantly reducing the impact of the deep network on gradient back propagation, and achieving an effect close to that of human on the ImageNet dataset.

2.2 Deep Hashing for Multi-label Image Retrieval

Although in real world image data, an image usually corresponds to multiple semantic labels, most deep hashing methods simplify the construction of image similarity, ignoring the use of multiple labels for deep hashing. Deep hashing methods [19] have similar procedures for similarity comparison between local images [23]. If there are multiple labels in an image, the image pair is considered to be similar, only if one of the labels with the same category. In CSQ methods, when multiple labels exist in the image, simple embedding operation will be conducted on the hash codes of the corresponding hash center. For the multi-label images, these simplified calculation methods make the useful information lost in the process of training and learning. In the existing research work (e.g. [12,16,34]), for the multi-label image hashing task, more emphasis was focused on splitting or covering the images, so that the training process was separated with different labels corresponding to part of the whole image dataset, or label information was used as an indirect supplementary data to improve the hashing effect. Different from previous studies, multi-label information is directly fused into the end-to-end deep hashing training framework in the method proposed in this paper, so that it can be used for the deep hashing task of both single-label and multi-label images.

3 The Proposed Framework and Method

In general, the goal of deep image hashing is to learn a mapping function F, which takes the input image as features and converts it into binary Hamming codes, known as image hash codes. For the input image data, I is defined as the image dataset, then $I = \{I_x\}_{x=1,2,\ldots,N} \in \mathcal{I}$ is the input of function F, where $\mathcal{I}$ represents the space of the image set. And then the output of the deep hashing function F is defined as $H = \{H_x\}_{x=1,2,\ldots,N} \in \{-1,1\}^{N \times q}$, where q denotes the length of the hash code. For the deep hashing algorithm, the key problem is to maintain the similarity. The similar images in the original image space should still maintain close distance after being mapped to the binary hash space. When calculating the similarity of the original image, the classification label of the image is usually selected, so that two images are similar means that there is the same classification label.

As the basis for the deep hashing framework, we adopt ResNet as the backbone neural network since it achieves leading effect in the state-of-the-art work. The pre-trained parameters of ResNet are used for fine-tuning and learning to hash.

3.1 Image Multi Hash Centers Construction

The generation process of hash centers is proposed in CSQ [33], which gives the efficient construction of hash centers with Hadamard matrix and Bernoulli distribution. The semantic hash centers generated for single-label data are solid, however, calculating the centroid as the hash centers by voting at the same bit for multi-label image data may result in obtaining insufficient details. In our framework, we remove the procedure of calculating the centroid and extend the construction method of multi-label image hash centers, so that the hash centers of each image are directly integrated into the deep network training process, without the need for multiple training separately.

3.2 Loss Function Design

Multi-label Hash Center Loss Function. For image data with multiple classification labels, let N_{class} represent the number of total category labels, the hash centers can be denoted as $C = \{C_{x,y}\}_{x=1,2,...,N \text{ } and \text{ } y=1,2,...,N_{class}} \in \{-1,1\}^{N \times N_{class} \times q}$, then N_{class} hash centers can be generated according to the construction method of hash centers. For the convenience of following expression, let $H_{x,z}$ represent the z-th bit of the x-th image Hamming code, and $C_{x,y,z}$ is defined as the z-th bit of the y-th image hash center for the x-th image respectively.

Then, the multi-label hash center loss function L_{mc} is defined as below:

$$L_{mc} = \frac{1}{q} \sum_{x=1}^{N} \sum_{y=1}^{N_{class}} \sum_{z=1}^{q} \mathbb{I}(x,y) \frac{BCE(x,y,z)}{CNT(x)} \tag{1}$$

with the Indicator $\mathbb{I}(x,y)$ and the Binary Cross Entropy function $BCE(x,y,z)$:

$$\mathbb{I}(x,y) = \begin{cases} 0 & image\ x\ not\ belongs\ to\ category\ y \\ 1 & image\ x\ belongs\ to\ category\ y \end{cases} \tag{2}$$

$$\begin{aligned} BCE(x,y,z) &= 0.5 * (1 + C_{x,y,z}) \log 0.5 * (1 + H_{x,z}) \\ &+ [1 - 0.5 * (1 + C_{x,y,z})] \log [1 - 0.5 * (1 + H_{x,z})] \end{aligned} \tag{3}$$

where formula $CNT(x)$ is defined as the number of categories to which image x belongs:

$$CNT(x) = \sum_{y=1}^{N_{class}} \mathbb{I}(x,y) \tag{4}$$

Triplet Loss Function Based on Hash Center. Triplet loss function is generally used for the relationship among local images in deep hashing. In most of the deep hashing framework with triplet loss, for each image in the dataset, one similar image and another dissimilar image will be selected to form an image triplet. Different from the previous studies, this paper applies the construction of triplet between global hash center and local image pairs. At the same time, we combine the triplet constraint relation with multiple hash centers of multi-label image, and design the triplet loss function for multi-label image deep hashing.

Using the Indicator function $\mathbb{I}(x,y)$ and formula $CNT(x)$ defined above, the triplet loss function based on multi-label image hash center can be denoted as:

$$L_{tr} = \sum_{x=1}^{N} \sum_{y=1}^{N_{class}} \mathbb{I}(x,y) \frac{TRM(x,y)}{CNT(x)} \tag{5}$$

with the Triplet Margin Loss function first proposed in FaceNet [25], for the hash codes H_x of each image and any one of its hash center codes $C_{x,y}$, select the hash code $\hat{H}_x$ of the image that is not similar, and conduct distance constraint with the margin, then we get the equation of $TRM(x, y)$:

$$TRM(x,y) = \max(||C_{x,y} - H_x||_2^2 - ||C_{x,y} - \hat{H}_x||_2^2 + margin, 0) \quad (6)$$

where the formal definition of hash coding corresponding to dissimilar images is:

$$\hat{H}_x \subset H = \{H_z\}_{z=1,2,...,N} \in \{-1,1\}^{N \times q} \quad (7)$$

and the original images corresponding to H_x and $\hat{H}_x$ are completely different in any of the multi-label categories. The procedure of selecting $\hat{H}_x$ in each mini-batch is shown in Algorithm 1.

Algorithm 1. Procedure of Selecting $\hat{H}_x$ Dissimilar to H_x in Each Mini-batch

Input: a batch $I = \{I_x\}_{x=1,2,...,N_{batch}} \in \mathcal{I}$ of training images, the number of categories N_{class} in the image dataset, the category labels $G = \{G_x\}_{x=1,2,...,N_{batch}} \in \{0,1\}^{N_{batch} \times N_{class}}$ of the corresponding multi-label images, the number of bits q by hash coding, the threshold $\epsilon = 0$, maximum iterations N_{iter}.
Initialize: initialize all $\hat{H}_x = \mathbf{0}$.
for x=1 to N_{batch} **do**
  for t=1 to N_{iter} **do**
    Get index IND randomly sampled in the sequence $[1, ..., N_{batch}]$.
    if $IND = x$ **then continue.**
    Calculate the number of same categories $CLS = G_x \cdot G_{IND}^{\top}$.
    if $CLS = \epsilon$ **then** $\hat{H}_x = H_{IND}$ and **break.**
  end for
end for
Output: the hash codes of $\hat{H}_x$ dissimilar to H_x.

Loss Function with Partially Similar Image Pairs. In the similarity calculation of multi-label images, different from single-label images, there may be some image pairs with partial same category labels, rather than all the same or all different. In the practical application scenario of applying deep hashing to image retrieval, for a query image with multiple classification attributes, users not only expect to get images with the same category in all classifications, but also want to recall images with only part of the same category, so it is very meaningful to maintain the similarity of images with only part of the same category in the deep hashing. Based on this idea, we construct the loss function with partially similar image pairs to improve the effect of deep hashing in image retrieval task.

For any multi-label image, select another image where only part of the classification labels are the same, for constructing the loss function to constrain each bit of the learning procedure of hash codes, that is:

$$L_{ps} = \frac{1}{qN} \sum_{x=1}^{N} \sum_{z=1}^{q} SMT(H_{x,z}, H'_{x,z}) \quad (8)$$

with the Smooth $L1$ Loss proposed by Fast R-CNN [8], which synthesizes the advantages of $L1$ Loss and $L2$ Loss, to make the loss function more robust to outliers in terms of piecewise function:

$$SMT(H_{x,z}, H'_{x,z}) = \begin{cases} 0.5(H_{x,z} - H'_{x,z})^2 & if\ |H_{x,z} - H'_{x,z}| < 1 \\ |H_{x,z} - H'_{x,z}| - 0.5 & otherwise \end{cases} \tag{9}$$

where the description for hash codes of partially similar image is denoted as:

$$H'_x \subset H = \{H_z\}_{z=1,2,...,N} \in \{-1, 1\}^{N \times q} \tag{10}$$

and the original images corresponding to H_x and H'_x have some of the same category labels in multiple categories. The procedure of selecting H'_x in each mini-batch only needs to refer to Algorithm 1 for simple modifications.

Quantization Loss Function. After the image output coding obtained by the deep neural network and the *tanh* function calculation, the image coding obtained are continuous real numbers. Since the algorithm should actually obtain the hash hamming code composed of -1 and 1, the Quantization Loss function needs to be added in the output layer of encoding, so as to make the learned hash codes more accurate for image retrieval task.

Therefore, we also define the loss function to reduce the quantization error, as below:

$$L_{qe} = \frac{1}{q} \sum_{x=1}^{N} \sum_{y=1}^{q} (\|H_{x,y}\|_1 - 1)^2 \tag{11}$$

Hybrid Loss Function. The loss functions defined above are combined to form the hybrid loss function as the optimization objective for our proposed deep hashing framework.

Finally, we get the definition of the hybrid loss function:

$$L = L_{mc} + \lambda_1 L_{qe} + \lambda_2 L_{tr} + \lambda_3 L_{ps} \tag{12}$$

where λ_1, λ_2 and λ_3 are trade-off hyper-parameters for each part of the hybrid loss function.

4 Experiments

4.1 Datasets and Baselines

In the following experiments, we evaluate the proposed method on four benchmark datasets of multi-label images, including MS-COCO [18], VOC2012 [6], FLICKR-25K [13] and NUS-WIDE [4], and their statistics are summarized in Table 1.

Table 1. Metadata of Multi-label Image Datasets for Training and Retrieval.

	Multi-label Image Datasets			
	MS-COCO	VOC2012	FLICKR-25K	NUS-WIDE
#Train	10,000	4,000	4,000	10,000
#Test	5,000	1,000	1,000	5,000
#Retrieval	117,218	6,540	20,000	168,692
#Class	80	20	38	81

In the comparative experiment, we use mAP@5000 for the MS-COCO and NUS-WIDE dataset following the setting in [33], and we adopt mAP@ALL on the VOC2012 and FLICKR-25K image dateset.

In the experiment, we compare the method proposed in this paper with nine benchmark methods, including the traditional hashing methods (KSH [20], ITQ [9], SDH [26]) and the deep hashing methods (CNNH [31], NINH [15], NINH [15], DHN [35], HashNet [3], DCH [2], CSQ [33]) which recently obtained the most advanced results.

4.2 Evaluation Metric

To evaluate the performance, we adopt Mean Average Precision (mAP) [1] as metric for image retrieval performance. Specifically, the accuracy of the returned results is measured by mAP when the binary hash codes obtained by traditional hashing or deep hashing are evaluated in the image retrieval task.

Let $N_{database}$ denote the total number of images in the retrieval database, and N_x^{sim} denote the number of images in the database relevant to the x-th image query. Synchronously, we use the symbol $N_{x,k}^{sim}$ to represent the number of images with the similar category label of the x-th image query among the top-k images from the return image retrieval list. Then the average precision (AP) of the x-th image query AP_x can be defined as below:

$$AP_x = \frac{1}{N_x^{sim}} \sum_{k=1}^{N_{database}} \frac{N_{x,k}^{sim}}{k} REL(x,k) \tag{13}$$

with the Indicator function $REL(x,k)$:

$$REL(x,k) = \begin{cases} 0 & image\ x\ and\ k\ are\ dissimilar \\ 1 & image\ x\ and\ k\ are\ similar \end{cases} \tag{14}$$

For all image queries, mAP can be calculated by the formula based on the AP_x value of each image, so the mAP valuation is defined as:

$$mAP = \frac{1}{N_{query}} \sum_{x=1}^{N_{query}} AP_x \tag{15}$$

where N_{query} is used to define the total number of images in the query set.

4.3 Implementation Details

All experiments in this paper are based on the Pytorch framework, then the training and retrieval process of hashing algorithm experiments run on the server cluster with GeForce RTX series GPUs. The input training images are resized to 256×256 and cropped to 224×224 to fit the deep backbone network. In each deep hashing experiment, we set the initial learning rate for deep networks to 1×10^{-5}, and the number of images for each mini-batch is set to 64. We run the deep neural network model in 50 epochs on ResNet.

4.4 Analysis of Experimental Results

As shown in Table 2, on MS-COCO dataset, we compare the proposed method in this paper with nine traditional hash algorithms and deep hash algorithms. The comparative experimental results show that the proposed method achieves superior retrieval accuracies against the baseline methods on the mAP metric. The mAP evaluation metric results of the proposed method indicate an increase of 5.78%/1.53%/2.42% (1.13%/3.22%/3.02%) on MS-COCO dataset with 16/32/64 bits hash codes compared to the best contrast CSQ (CSQ*) method. In the comparison table of experimental results, CSQ* represents the results of the CSQ deep hashing algorithm in the original paper, and CSQ represents the results after our re-implementation based on the principle of the framework.

Table 2. MAP of Hamming ranking w.r.t different number of bits on MS-COCO dataset with ResNet as the backbone network.

Method	MS-COCO (mAP)		
	16 bits	32 bits	64 bits
KSH	0.523	0.535	0.536
ITQ-CCA	0.567	0.563	0.513
SDH	0.555	0.564	0.581
CNNH	0.601	0.619	0.622
NINH	0.645	0.653	0.648
DHN	0.721	0.732	0.745
HashNet	0.746	0.773	0.788
DCH	0.760	0.801	0.826
CSQ*	0.796	0.838	0.861
CSQ	0.761	0.852	0.866
Ours	**0.805**	**0.865**	**0.887**

In order to further verify the effectiveness of the proposed method, we selected the CSQ method with the best performance of all the contrast baselines, and continued the comparison experiments of retrieval effect on four multi-label image datasets. In horizontal comparison experiments with several image datasets, we validate synchronously the effectiveness of the hybrid loss function. Table 3 and Table 4 show the corresponding percentage increase of 1.53%~5.78%/10.31%~12.21%/8.47%~14.55%/3.86%~7.89% on MS-COCO/VOC2012/FLICKR-25K/NUS-WIDE, respectively. Ablation studies are conducted in the comparative experiments to verify the effectiveness of quantization loss function L_{qe}, triplet loss function based on hash center L_{tr} and loss function with partially similar image pairs in the hybrid loss function L_{ps}. For selecting the range of hyperparameters (λ_1, λ_2, λ_3), the coarse-to-fine method is adopted in the experimental design, which is combined with hyperparameter searching.

Table 3. MAP of Hamming ranking w.r.t different number of bits on MS-COCO and VOC2012 image datasets.

Method	MS-COCO (mAP)			VOC2012 (mAP)		
	16 bits	32 bits	64 bits	16 bits	32 bits	64 bits
CSQ	0.761	0.852	0.866	0.679	0.693	0.696
Ours ($\lambda_1 = 0$)	0.804	0.863	0.886	0.745	0.773	0.780
Ours ($\lambda_2 = 0, \lambda_3 = 0$)	0.795	0.861	0.885	0.734	0.744	0.752
Ours (*Best*)	**0.805**	**0.865**	**0.887**	**0.749**	**0.774**	**0.781**

Table 4. MAP of Hamming ranking w.r.t different number of bits on FLICKR-25K and NUS-WIDE image datasets.

Method	FLICKR-25K (mAP)			NUS-WIDE (mAP)		
	16 bits	32 bits	64 bits	16 bits	32 bits	64 bits
CSQ	0.685	0.693	0.694	0.725	0.745	0.748
Ours ($\lambda_1 = 0$)	0.740	0.772	0.793	0.746	0.782	0.805
Ours ($\lambda_2 = 0, \lambda_3 = 0$)	0.733	0.769	0.785	0.731	0.779	0.791
Ours (*Best*)	**0.743**	**0.775**	**0.795**	**0.753**	**0.785**	**0.807**

Furthermore, Fig. 2 shows the retrieval performance in precesion-recall curves, recall@top-N curves on four datasets with 64 bits hash codes. We set λ_2 and λ_3 of the hybrid loss function to zero as a simplified form of the proposed method to participate in the comparison with the full form of our proposed hybrid loss function, and the full form outperform the simple form and the best baseline of all the contrast methods.

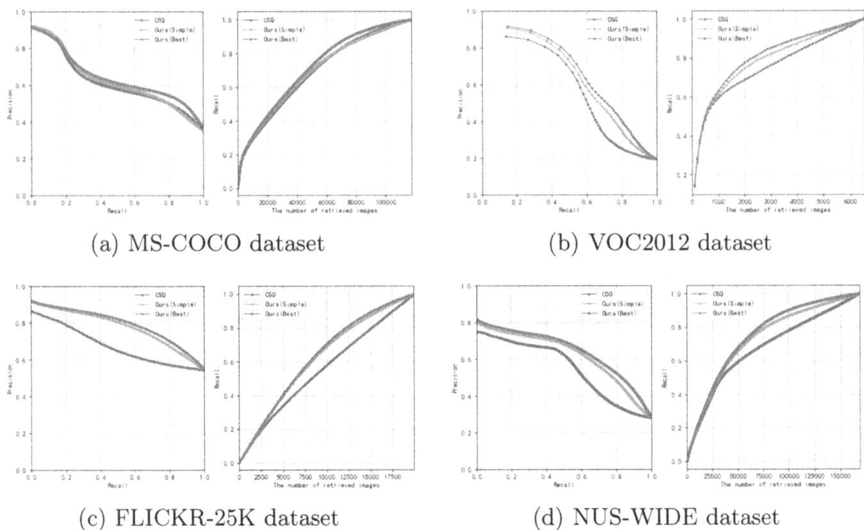

(a) MS-COCO dataset

(b) VOC2012 dataset

(c) FLICKR-25K dataset

(d) NUS-WIDE dataset

Fig. 2. Experimental results (Precesion-recall curves, Recall@top-Ncurves) with hash codes @64bits of our proposed method and CSQ method on four multi-label image datasets.

5 Conclusion

In this paper, we propose a novel deep hashing method for multi-label images by constructing the hybrid loss function with global center and local alignment. With the constraint of multi-label image hash centers and quantization error loss, the efficiency and effectiveness of the deep hashing model can be improved by global constraint. At the same time, the constraint of hash centers and dissimilar image pairs is established, and the global constraint and local constraint are combined to improve the effect of hash coding. In addition, the local feature constraint of some similar image pairs is added, and the coding efficiency is further improved based on the characteristic of multi-label image. Empirical evaluations show that our proposed deep hashing method for multi-label images yield state-of-the-art performance on multi-label image dataset.

In future work, we plan to try adding vision transformer to the algorithm framework of this paper and expand into the field of multi-modal hashing.

Acknowledgements. This work is supported by the National Natural Science Foundation of China (61772567, U1811262, U1911203, U2001211, U22B2060), Guangdong Basic and Applied Basic Research Foundation (2019B1515130001, 2021A1515012172, 2023A1515011400), Key-Area Research and Development Program of Guangdong Province (2020B0101100001).

References

1. Baeza-Yates, R., Ribeiro-Neto, B., et al.: Modern Information Retrieval, vol. 463. ACM press, New York (1999)
2. Cao, Y., Long, M., Liu, B., Wang, J.: Deep Cauchy hashing for hamming space retrieval. In: Proceedings of the IEEE Conference on Computer Vision and Pattern Recognition, pp. 1229–1237 (2018)
3. Cao, Z., Long, M., Wang, J., Yu, P.S.: Hashnet: deep learning to hash by continuation. In: Proceedings of the IEEE International Conference on Computer Vision, pp. 5608–5617 (2017)
4. Chua, T.S., Tang, J., Hong, R., Li, H., Luo, Z., Zheng, Y.: Nus-wide: a real-world web image database from national university of Singapore. In: Proceedings of the ACM International Conference on Image and Video Retrieval, pp. 1–9 (2009)
5. Dubey, S.R.: A decade survey of content based image retrieval using deep learning. IEEE Trans. Circ. Syst. Video Technol. **32**(5), 2687–2704 (2021)
6. Everingham, M., Winn, J.: The pascal visual object classes challenge 2012 (voc2012) development kit. Pattern Anal. Stat. Model. Comput. Learn., Tech. Rep 2007, 1–45 (2012)
7. Gionis, A., Indyk, P., Motwani, R., et al.: Similarity search in high dimensions via hashing. In: Vldb, vol. 99, pp. 518–529 (1999)
8. Girshick, R.: Fast R-CNN. In: Proceedings of the IEEE International Conference on Computer Vision, pp. 1440–1448 (2015)
9. Gong, Y., Lazebnik, S., Gordo, A., Perronnin, F.: Iterative quantization: a procrustean approach to learning binary codes for large-scale image retrieval. IEEE Trans. Pattern Anal. Mach. Intell. **35**(12), 2916–2929 (2012)
10. Gu, J., et al.: Recent advances in convolutional neural networks. Pattern Recognit. **77**, 354–377 (2018)
11. He, K., Zhang, X., Ren, S., Sun, J.: Deep residual learning for image recognition. In: Proceedings of the IEEE Conference on Computer Vision and Pattern Recognition, pp. 770–778 (2016)
12. Huang, C.Q., Yang, S.M., Pan, Y., Lai, H.J.: Object-location-aware hashing for multi-label image retrieval via automatic mask learning. IEEE Trans. Image Process. **27**(9), 4490–4502 (2018)
13. Huiskes, M.J., Lew, M.S.: The MIR Flickr retrieval evaluation. In: Proceedings of the 1st ACM International Conference on Multimedia Information Retrieval, pp. 39–43 (2008)
14. Krizhevsky, A., Sutskever, I., Hinton, G.E.: ImageNet classification with deep convolutional neural networks. Commun. ACM **60**(6), 84–90 (2017)
15. Lai, H., Pan, Y., Liu, Y., Yan, S.: Simultaneous feature learning and hash coding with deep neural networks. In: Proceedings of the IEEE Conference on Computer Vision and Pattern Recognition, pp. 3270–3278 (2015)
16. Lai, H., Yan, P., Shu, X., Wei, Y., Yan, S.: Instance-aware hashing for multi-label image retrieval. IEEE Trans. Image Processing **25**(6), 2469–2479 (2016)
17. LeCun, Y., Bottou, L., Bengio, Y., Haffner, P.: Gradient-based learning applied to document recognition. Proc. IEEE **86**(11), 2278–2324 (1998)
18. Lin, T.-Y., et al.: Microsoft COCO: common objects in context. In: Fleet, D., Pajdla, T., Schiele, B., Tuytelaars, T. (eds.) ECCV 2014. LNCS, vol. 8693, pp. 740–755. Springer, Cham (2014). https://doi.org/10.1007/978-3-319-10602-1_48
19. Liu, H., Wang, R., Shan, S., Chen, X.: Deep supervised hashing for fast image retrieval. In: Proceedings of the IEEE Conference on Computer Vision and Pattern Recognition, pp. 2064–2072 (2016)

20. Liu, W., Wang, J., Ji, R., Jiang, Y.G., Chang, S.F.: Supervised hashing with kernels. In: 2012 IEEE Conference on Computer Vision and Pattern Recognition, pp. 2074–2081. IEEE (2012)
21. Norouzi, M., Fleet, D.J., Salakhutdinov, R.R.: Hamming distance metric learning. In: Advances in Neural Information Processing Systems, vol. 25 (2012)
22. Rawat, W., Wang, Z.: Deep convolutional neural networks for image classification: a comprehensive review. Neural Comput. **29**(9), 2352–2449 (2017)
23. Rodrigues, J., Cristo, M., Colonna, J.G.: Deep hashing for multi-label image retrieval: a survey. Artif. Intell. Rev. **53**(7), 5261–5307 (2020)
24. Russakovsky, O., et al.: ImageNet large scale visual recognition challenge. Int. J. Comput. Vis. **115**(3), 211–252 (2015)
25. Schroff, F., Kalenichenko, D., Philbin, J.: FaceNet: a unified embedding for face recognition and clustering. In: Proceedings of the IEEE Conference on Computer Vision and Pattern Recognition, pp. 815–823 (2015)
26. Shen, F., Shen, C., Liu, W., Tao Shen, H.: Supervised discrete hashing. In: Proceedings of the IEEE Conference on Computer Vision and Pattern Recognition, pp. 37–45 (2015)
27. Simonyan, K., Zisserman, A.: Very deep convolutional networks for large-scale image recognition. arXiv preprint arXiv:1409.1556 (2014)
28. Szegedy, C., et al.: Going deeper with convolutions. In: Proceedings of the IEEE Conference on Computer Vision and Pattern Recognition, pp. 1–9 (2015)
29. Voulodimos, A., Doulamis, N., Doulamis, A., Protopapadakis, E.: Deep learning for computer vision: a brief review. Comput. Intell. Neurosci. 2018 (2018)
30. Wang, J., Zhang, T., Sebe, N., Shen, H.T., et al.: A survey on learning to hash. IEEE Trans. Pattern Anal. Mach. Intell. **40**(4), 769–790 (2017)
31. Xia, R., Pan, Y., Lai, H., Liu, C., Yan, S.: Supervised hashing for image retrieval via image representation learning. In: Twenty-eighth AAAI Conference on Artificial Intelligence (2014)
32. Xu, C., et al.: HHF: hashing-guided hinge function for deep hashing retrieval. IEEE Trans. Multimed. (2022)
33. Yuan, L., et al.: Central similarity quantization for efficient image and video retrieval. In: Proceedings of the IEEE/CVF Conference on Computer Vision and Pattern Recognition, pp. 3083–3092 (2020)
34. Zhang, Z., Zou, Q., Lin, Y., Chen, L., Wang, S.: Improved deep hashing with soft pairwise similarity for multi-label image retrieval. IEEE Trans. Multimed. **22**(2), 540–553 (2019)
35. Zhu, H., Long, M., Wang, J., Cao, Y.: Deep hashing network for efficient similarity retrieval. In: Proceedings of the AAAI Conference on Artificial Intelligence, vol. 30 (2016)

Multi-relation Representation Learning Based Deep Network for Patent Classification

Yuan Meng, Xuhao Pan, and Yue Wang(✉)

Shanghai University of International Business and Economics, Shanghai, China
nancymeng@suibe.edu.cn, wy416408@foxmail.com

Abstract. Our paper innovatively proposes a multi-relation representation learning framework for patent classification from the perspective of Entities Relation Representation and Citation Relation Representation. Based on this, an encode-decode framework is used to merge semantic information and relation representations. Experiments based on multi-field patents from Derwent Innovations Index (DII) show that classification performance can be effectively improved by the multi-relation representations. Our research not only demonstrates the effectiveness of using graph embedding model in learning representations among patent-related entity relationships, but also improves the classification accuracy of automatic patent classification in practical applications.

Keywords: Patent Classification · Patent Knowledge Graph · Patent Multi-relation Representations · Graph Embeddings

1 Introduction

Patent classification is the most important part of patent management and an important tool for patent search [1, 2]. However, the huge corpus, complex hierarchical structure and the size of the patent documents have brought some special challenges to this task [3]. For example, the International Patent Classification (IPC) includes 8 chapters, 128 categories, about 7200 major groups and about 72000 subgroups [4]. Due to the continuous growth of the number of patent applications and the emergence of new innovations, the scale is expected to grow further [5]. Therefore, it is particularly important to design effective patent classification methods.

Experts have done a lot of work in automatic patent classification task. Most of the researches regard it as a special text classification task [6–9]. They mainly focus on the patent text itself, such as title, abstract, claim or description, but ignore the possible relation information between patent-related entities, such as patent and its cited patents, assignee, patent application year, patent family countries, etc. However, patents owned by the same assignee are more likely to belong to the same class, and the same occurs between a patent and its referenced patents. Therefore, the relation information embeddings between patent-related entities may contribute to the accuracy of the patent classification task. In view of this, this study proposes a multi-relation representation learning framework (MR-Patent2Vec) based on patents text and patent-related entities

L. Iliadis et al. (Eds.): ICANN 2023, LNCS 14263, pp. 333–345, 2023.
https://doi.org/10.1007/978-3-031-44204-9_28

for multi-label patent classification task. Our main contributions are summarized as follows.

- We employ patent knowledge graph embedding model (TransD) to obtain Entities Relation Representation among patent-related entities.
- We apply an attention mechanism to obtain Citation Relation Representation between a given patent and its cited patents.
- We adopt an encode-decode framework to merge semantic representation and relation representations for patent classification task.

The remainder of this paper is structured as follows. Section 2 reviews the literature on automatic patent classification. Section 3 describes the way multi-relation representations are learned. Section 4 presents the experiment dataset and experimental results and Sect. 5 summarizes the whole paper.

2 Related Work

Early scholars mainly use word embedding techniques combining with deep learning models to learn semantic representations in patents for classification, such as word embedding combine with LSTM [7] or word embedding combine with CNN [10].

With the advent of pre-trained models with powerful semantic representation, patent classification tasks are also turning to pre-trained models. One of the most notable studies is the PatentBERT proposed by Lee et al. [11], who fine-tune the pre-training language model BERT on the large-scale patent classification dataset. Subsequently, a variety of large-scale language models have emerged in related studies. For example, Arousha et al. [8] fine-tune BERT, RoBERTA, XLNet, ELECTRA and other pre-training language models to conduct patent classification. Lee et al. [9] propose a new state-of-the-art method based on fine-tuning pre-training BERT model, and confirm that it is superior to DeepPatent.

To sum up, most relevant studies only consider obtaining patent representations from text, ignoring possible internal relationship information between patent-related entities. Considering that patent is a data object with many associated entities, we innovatively extract patent representations from patent-related entities, namely Entities Relation Representation and Citation Relation Representation. Besides, we explore patent classification performance under different combinations in order to provide reference for subsequent patent classification tasks.

3 Method

3.1 Overall Design

The overall design of this article is shown in Fig. 1. It is mainly composed of five parts: ① the generation of semantic representation, ② the generation of Entities Relation Representation, ③ the generation of Citation Relation Representation, ④ the encode-decode framework for patent classification, ⑤ evaluation and analysis.

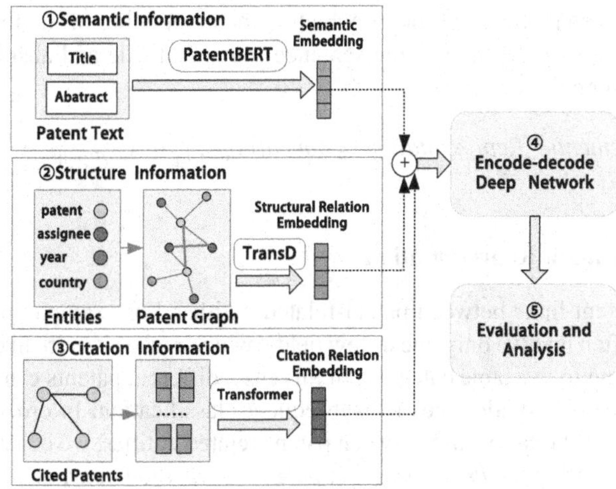

Fig. 1. Overall design.

3.2 Semantic Representation

In prior research, literature [8, 9, 11] has demonstrated that fine-tuning pre-trained language models for patent field data leads to improved performance in patent classification tasks. It has been observed that fine-tuned pre-trained language models are generally more adaptable to specific domains and exhibit better performance in tasks pertinent to those fields. Consequently, we employ the pre-trained language model bert-for-pants, released on Hugging Face (https://huggingface.co/anferico/bert-for-patents), to obtain PatentBERT embeddings for patent text and abstracts. Given the substantial number of parameters involved in the pre-trained language model, the fine-tuning process is time-consuming. Upon obtaining the PatentBERT embeddings, we opt not to fine-tune the PatentBERT model further and solely focus on fine-tuning other modules within the scope of this paper. The specific process is as follows:

First, calculate the embedding representation as Eq. 1:

$$output = nn.Embedding(text) + Position\_Embedding \tag{1}$$

where *output* represents the output of each layer, *text* refers to the title or abstract of each patent, *Position_Embedding* is designed to tell the PatentBERT the location information of each token in the text.

Then, calculate the output x of each layer for each block layer of PantentBERT(24 block layers in total) as Eq. 2 and Eq. 3:

$$attn = Norm(Multihead\_Attention(output) + output) \tag{2}$$

$$x = Norm(FFN(attn) + attn) \tag{3}$$

where *Multihead_Attention* represents the attention layer, the *FFN* represents the linear layers, and the *Norm* represents the layernorm.

Finally, concatenate the [cls] token (which is the embedding of the first token and it represents the whole meaning of the sentence) output of title and abstract to obtain Semantic Representation as Eq. 4:

$$Sementic\_Representation = concat(x_{title_{[cls]}} + x_{abstract_{[cls]}}) \tag{4}$$

3.3 Entities Relation Representation

There are important links between patent-related entities. For example, patents of the same assignee often involve only one or few fields, which makes it more likely that these patents will belong to the same category. In this case, different patents can be linked by the same assignee to provide clues for subsequent classification. In order to excavate the internal structural relationship between patent-related entities, we construct a Patent Graph from four entities: *patent*, *assignee*, *patent application year*, and *patent family countries*. Then, we extract five relations among these entities, namely *patent-patent, assignee-patent, patent-year, assignee-assignee, and patent-country*. The representation of each entity and relation is obtained using TransD [12].

TransD is an improvement of TransR/CTransR that takes into accounts not only the diversity of relationships but also entities. It has fewer parameters and no matrix vector multiplication operation, so it is more suitable for calculations of large-scale graphs. We apply TransD to extract the relationship between multiple entities of a patent.

Specifically, assume that there exist relations $r_0 \in R$ (set of relations) between entities $(h_0, t_0) \in E$ (set of entities), h, t, r denote the vectorized representations of h_0, t_0, r_0, respectively. TransD uses two vector representations for each named symbolic object (entity and relation). The first captures the meaning of the entities (relations) and the other is used to construct the mapping matrix. Given a triple (h, t, r), its vectors can be represented as $\boldsymbol{h}, \boldsymbol{h_p}, \boldsymbol{t}, \boldsymbol{t_p} \in R^n$and $\boldsymbol{r}, \boldsymbol{r_p} \in R^m$, where vectors with the suffix p p denote the mapping vectors. Thus, the definition of the mapping matrix $\boldsymbol{M_{rh}}, \boldsymbol{M_{rt}} \in \boldsymbol{R^{mxn}}$ is shown in Fig. 2.

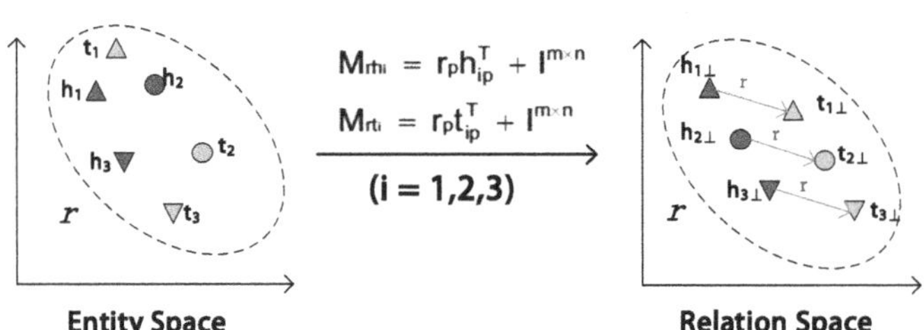

Fig. 2. TransD [12].

Where $\boldsymbol{I}^{m \times n}$ denotes the unit matrix. Use the scoring function Eq. (5) to measure the performance of the embedded triplet vector.

$$f_r(\boldsymbol{h}, \boldsymbol{t}) = \|\boldsymbol{h} + \boldsymbol{r} - \boldsymbol{t}\|_2^2 \tag{5}$$

Given the constraints $\|\boldsymbol{h}\|_2^2, \|\boldsymbol{r}\|_2^2, \|\boldsymbol{t}\|_2^2 \leq 1$, the loss function of the embedding training is Eq. (6).

$$L = \sum_{\sigma \in s} \sum_{\sigma' \in s'} \left[\gamma + f_r(\boldsymbol{h}, \boldsymbol{t}) - f_{r'}\left(\boldsymbol{h}', \boldsymbol{t}'\right)\right]_+ \tag{6}$$

where $[x]_+$ denotes $\max(0, x)$, γ denotes the hyperparameter of the edge distance, $\sigma \in s$ denotes the triplet (h, t, r) present in the patent graph, and $\sigma' \in s'$ denotes the negative samples generated by random sampling in the training triplet $\left(h', t', r'\right)$.

3.4 Citation Relation Representation

To highlight those more important cited patents in relation to the current patent, the representations of citation relation of patents are considered separately in this paper. We use the Encoder architecture of the Transformer model [13] to fuse the entities relation embeddings of those patents cited by the patents to be predicted (which can be obtained in Sect. 3.3) as the Citation Relation Representation of the patents. The generation process is shown in Fig. 3.

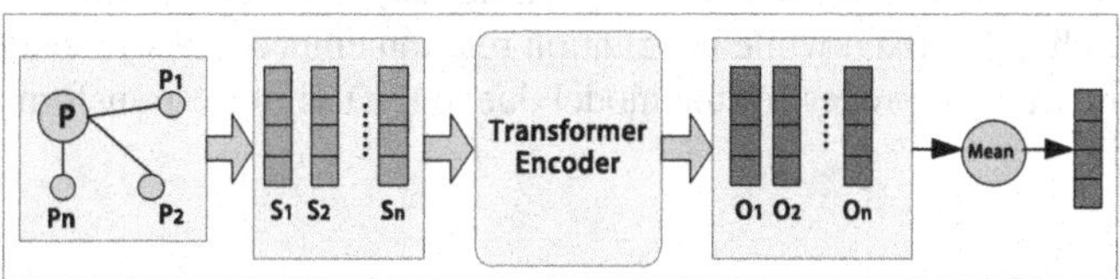

Fig. 3. Citation Relation Embeddings.

For a given patent $\boldsymbol{P}$, if it cites n patents, the Structure Relation Representations between $\boldsymbol{P}$ and each cited patent is denoted as $s_1, s_2 \ldots, s_n$ respectively. Input these representations into the Encoder part of the Transformer model, the corresponding outputs $s_1', s_2', \ldots s_n'$ can be obtained. Each output is the result of considering the other inputs through the self-attention process. Since the dimension of the Citation Relation Representation of each patents needs to be consistent in the subsequent deep learning model, we take the average of $s_1', s_2', \ldots s_n'$ as the Citation Relation Representation for patent $\boldsymbol{P}$. It is noted that the Transformer Encoder parameters will be continuously modified in the subsequent training of deep learning model.

3.5 Patent Classification Deep Network

An encode-decode framework is presented for patent classification as shown in Fig. 4.

It can be divided into two parts: Encoder part and Decoder part. The Encoder part fuses the semantic representation and relation representations while the Decoder part accepts two inputs, the encoded representations obtained by Encoder part and the classification category vector, respectively. If the number of labels in the dataset used is m, then there are m category vectors, so the input is a one-hot encoding of m categories.

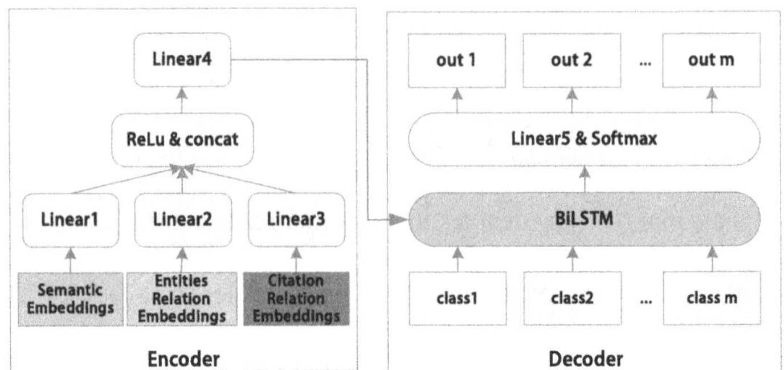

Fig. 4. Patent Classification Deep Network

After the input is transformed by the BiLSTM, linear layer and Softmax layer, a corresponding output is obtained for each classification category vector, ranging from 0 to 1. If the corresponding output of a category is greater than 0.5, the patent belongs to that category, otherwise the patent does not belong to that category. In this way, each output is a two-class problem, thereby enabling a multi-label classification task can.

It is worth noting that during model training, semantic embedding and entities-relation embedding are fixed while the citation relation embedding will change continuously with the training process of the model due to the use of the transformer encoder architecture.

4 Experiments

4.1 Dataset

The data used in this paper is from the Derwent Innovations Index (DII). We collected relevant data in the two different fields of graphene and silicon battery to form two data sets to verify the performance of the model proposed in this paper. The data set description is shown in Table 1 and Table 2. The size of each data set and the number of classes are different, which can more comprehensively and fully verify the effectiveness of the model in this paper. The average number of patent categories is greater than 1, indicating that some patents in each data set have more than one label, and the patent classification task is a multi-label classification task.

Table 1. Graphene

	Training data	Validate data
Patents Number	61518	6835
Average Categories Number	1.4137	1.3943
Class Number	8	8

Table 2. Silicon batter

	Training data	Validate data
Patents Number	31084	3453
Average Categories Number	1.2365	1.2369
Class Number	12	12

As described in the tables above, the two datasets differ in size and number of classes, thus allowing a more comprehensive and adequate validation of the validity of the model.

4.2 Evaluation Indicators

We choose three evaluation indicators that have been used in related studies for evaluating the performance of our multi-label patent classification model, namely label-based indicators, sample-based indicators, and ranking-based indicators.

Label-Based Indicators [14]. There are two average strategies for label-based indicators in our multi-label classification: macro average and micro average [16]. Yang et al. [17] point out that when the data is unbalanced, *Micro F1* is usually used to evaluate the performance. Therefore, this paper uses *Micro F1* evaluation metric. The calculation formula of *Micro F1* is shown in (7) ~ (10).

$$MicroF1 = \frac{2 \times MicroP \times MicroR}{MicroP + MicroR} \tag{7}$$

where

$$MicroP = \frac{TP}{TP + FP} \tag{8}$$

$$MicroR = \frac{TP}{TP + FN} \tag{9}$$

$$TP = \sum_{j=1}^{n} TP_j, FP = \sum_{j=1}^{n} FP_j, FN = \sum_{j=1}^{n} FN_j \tag{10}$$

Sample-Based Indicator [14]. Hamming loss is the most common sample-based indicator, which counts the proportion of labels that are misclassified. If there are *m* samples in the test dataset, the predicted label sequence of the *i* th sample is $pred_i$, and the actual label sequence is $true_i$, then Hamming Loss (recorded as H Loss) is calculated as follows.

$$Hamming\ Loss = \frac{1}{m} \sum_{i=1}^{m} \|pred_i! = true_i\| \tag{11}$$

where $\|pred_i! = true_i\|$ indicates the number of different values in the corresponding positions of two label sequences. The smaller the Hamming Loss value, the better the classification effect of the multi-label classification model.

Rank-based Indicator[15]. A@K(Accuracy @K) is used to calculate the proportion of correct labels in the first K results with the highest probability in the prediction results, which is calculated as follows.

$$Accuracy@k = \frac{TP@k+TN@k}{TP@k+FN@k+TN@k+FP@k} \quad (12)$$

In our paper, we set K = 1,3,5 respectively.

4.3 Experiment Environments

In the GPU training environment, the python version is 3.7.6, the torch version is 1.7.0, and the transformers version is 2.2.2. The output dimension of PatentBERT is 1024, after the linear layer the embedding dimension is set to 100, including 50 for the title and 50 for the abstract. The output dimension of TransD is also set to 100. Linear1 and Linear2 input and output dimensions are set to (100, 128), Linear3 input and output dimensions are set to (100, 100), and Linear4 input and output dimensions are set to ($128 \times 2 + 100$, 64). Last, BiLSTM input and hidden dimensions are set to (number of classification labels, 64), and Linear5 input and output dimensions are set to (64×2,2).

4.4 Experiment Results

Result Analysis. In the decoder part of our encoder-decoder architecture, the performance of BiLSTM module and RNN module are compared separately, and they are also compared with the model without the decoder part. Accordingly, three comparative models are established, which are respectively represented as **Model1**: MR-Patent2Vec(BiLSTM), **Model2**: MR-Patent2Vec(RNN), **Model3**: MR-Patent2Vec (noDecoder). The performance of the three models is shown in Table 3.

From the result, when the main body of the Decoder is set to the BiLSTM module, the performance of the model is the best. Taking the graphene dataset as an example, the *Micro F1* value of Model1 is 0.7677, A@5 Up to 0.9909. Model 2 takes the second place, and the results of each indicator are slightly worse than Model 1. By comparison, Model3 without Decoder module has poor performance, which validates the effectiveness of the Encoder-Decoder architecture proposed in this paper.

Considering the possible influence of parameters such as embedding dimension on the experimental results of the model, we test the effect of different embedding dimension and evaluate the experimental results with *Micro F1* values. With the change of embedding dimension, the classification effect of Model 1 demonstrates some changes, as shown in Fig. 5. As the embedding dimension increases, the classification results on both datasets show a trend of increasing and then decreasing, and the best value is achieved when the embedding dimension is set to 100. Therefore, the embedding dimension in our model is set to 100.

Ablation study. This paper proposes three different embedding representations: Semantic Representation, Entities Relation Representation, and Citation Relation Representation. In order to validate the effectiveness of these three representation, we conduct ablation experiments on the best model Model1: MR-Patent2Vec (BiLSTM). As shown in Table 4.

Table 3. Experimental Results.

Data	Indicator	Model1	Model2	Model3
Graphene	*Mic F1*	**0.7699**	0.7639	0.6306
	H loss	**0.0739**	0.0767	0.1078
	A@1	**0.8402**	0.8401	0.7135
	A@3	**0.9598**	0.9552	0.9012
	A@5	**0.9909**	0.9892	0.9685
Silicon battery	*Mic F1*	**0.7233**	0.6899	0.3387
	H loss	**0.0527**	0.0574	0.0859
	A@1	**0.7883**	0.7646	0.6429
	A@3	**0.9427**	0.9395	0.8717
	A@5	**0.9760**	0.9696	0.9418

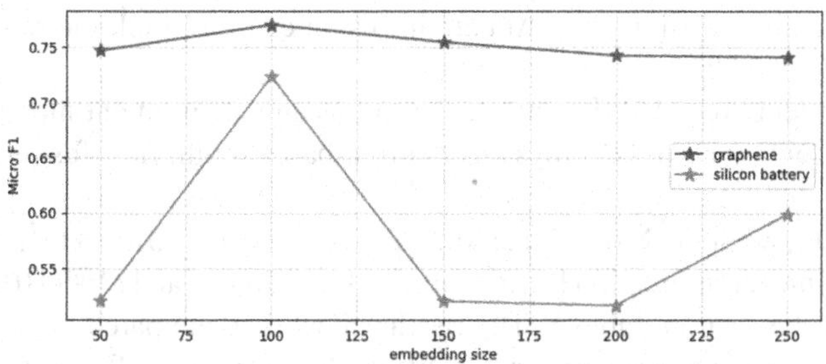

Fig. 5. Classification effect of the model with different embedding dimensions.

We remove each of these three representations and then rebuilt the model separately, named as Model4: MR-Patent2Vec (without Semantic Embedding), Model5: MR-Patent2Vec (without Entities Relation Embedding), and Model6: MR-Patent2Vec (without Citation Relation Embedding). After removing the corresponding representation, the effect of the model on most indicators has declined, and the Model1 can still achieve the best results, which confirms the effectiveness of each representation. In comparison, after deleting Semantic Representation, the performance of the model decreases the fastest, while after deleting the other two representation, the performance of the model decreases slightly.

Comparison with Baselines. We compare MR-Patent2Vec with some baseline models. The details of these baselines are illustrated as follows:

- Model7: FastText [18]. FastText is an efficient and competitive text classification method.
- Model8: PatentBert [11]. PatentBert is based on the pre-trained BERT model and fine-tunes it to implement patent classification.

Table 4. Ablation Study.

Data	Indicator	Model1	Model4	Model5	Model6
Graphene	*Mic F1*	**0.7699**	0.4016	0.7556	0.7649
	H loss	**0.0739**	0.1744	0.0759	0.0740
	A@1	**0.8402**	0.2433	0.8386	0.8328
	A@3	**0.9598**	0.5614	0.9405	0.9576
	A@5	**0.9909**	0.7754	0.9806	0.9803
Silicon battery	*Mic F1*	**0.7233**	0.4551	0.7142	0.7099
	H loss	**0.0527**	0.1031	0.0533	0.0533
	A@1	**0.7883**	0.1376	0.7800	0.7874
	A@3	**0.9427**	0.4855	0.9338	0.9350
	A@5	**0.9760**	0.6859	0.9645	0.9655

- Model9: Attention-Fusion [15]. Attention-Fusion can fuse multiple representations to a refined embedding.
- Model10: Patent2Vec [15]. Patent2Vec proposes an enhancement module to enrich single representations and deploys an attention-based multi-view fusion method.

Among them, we apply Model7 and Model8 to classify the abstract text of our patent data, and apply the representation learning methods of Model9 and Model10 on our data. The results can be seen in Table 5. The results show that compared with the baseline methods listed above, our method can achieve the best results in all indicators.

Table 5. Comparision with Baselines.

Data	Indicator	Model1	Mode7	Model8	Model9	Model10
Graphene	*Mic F1*	**0.7699**	0.7377	0.4465	0.4617	0.6495
	H loss	**0.0739**	0.1599	0.1316	0.1287	0.1042
	A@1	**0.8402**	0.5596	0.5639	0.5841	0.7390
	A@3	**0.9598**	0.8811	0.8474	0.8451	0.9094
	A@5	**0.9909**	0.9629	0.9583	0.9522	0.9751
Silicon battery	*Mic F1*	**0.7233**	0.6395	0.4138	0.4677	0.6729
	H loss	**0.0527**	0.1311	0.2033	0.1742	0.0851
	A@1	**0.7883**	0.5580	0.3333	0.2713	0.6073
	A@3	**0.9427**	0.8337	0.6632	0.6462	0.8839
	A@5	**0.9760**	0.9173	0.8329	0.7814	0.9508

Analysis of Representation Contribution. The t-SNE dimensionality reduction method is used to reduce the dimensionality of each embedding point, and the average distance between embeddings of the same category after the dimensionality reduction is used to measure the importance of each representation. The smaller the distance, the higher the importance. The boxplot of importance degree with the change of category and embedding is shown in Fig. 6. It can be observed that the degree of importance of embedding in each category is highest for semantic embedding, which aligns with the conclusion drawn from the ablation study. The difference of the three embeddings is not too great, which shows that the three embeddings reflect the category information to a certain extent, and have a positive effect on the performance of patent classification.

Such importance cannot well show the ability of each embedded feature, because in the comparison between model1 and model6 in Table 4, we can see that the *Mic F1* of the model does not decrease much without Citation Embedding. This is a problem.

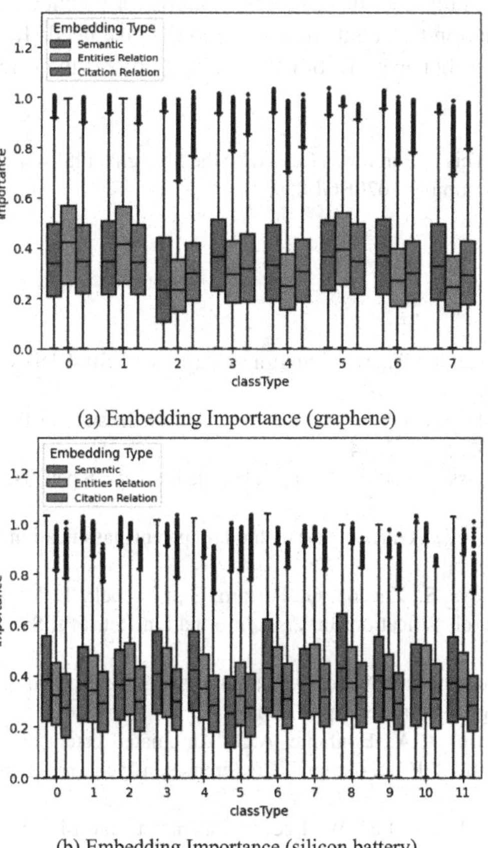

(a) Embedding Importance (graphene)

(b) Embedding Importance (silicon battery)

Fig. 6. Embedding Importance (a) Embedding Importance (graphene). (b) Embedding Importance (silicon battery).

We think that each different embeddings should have its own weight for better *Mic F1*, rather than simply adding or concatenation. This work we leave to the future.

5 Conclusions

This paper examines in detail the role of entities relation and citation relation information from patent-related entities for patent classification. Combined with the knowledge graph embedding model, we learn the efficient representations of the relation information between patents and their related entities. Further, using the attention mechanism of Transformer model, we additionally extract the citation relation information between a patent and its cited patents. The experimental results show that the performance of patent text classification can be significantly improved after considering the information from entities relation and citation relation. And we find that entity relation is more effective than citation relation, relatively.

This paper extracts three kinds of representations for patent classification. Whether there is other information that contribute more to the task needs further exploration. In the future, we will further explore other ways to improve the effectiveness of patent classification.

Acknowledgements. This research was funded by the Shanghai Philosophy and Social Sciences Planning Project, grant number 2020BGL009.

References

1. Zhang, L., Li, L., Li, T.: Patent mining: a survey. ACM SIGKDD Explorations Newslett. **16**(2), 1–19 (2015)
2. Abbas, A., Zhang, L., Khan, S.U.: A literature review on the state-of-the-art in patent analysis. World Patent Inf. **37**, 3–13 (2014)
3. Larkey, L.S.: Some issues in the automatic classification of US patents. In: AAAI-98 working notes (1998)
4. Chen, Y.L., Chang, Y.C.: A three-phase method for patent classification. Inf. Process. Manage. **48**, 1017–1030 (2012)
5. Seneviratne, D., Geva, S., Zuccon, G., Ferraro, G., Chappell, T., Meireles, M.: A signature approach to patent classification. In: Asia Information Retrieval Symposium, pp. 413–419 (2015)
6. Larkey, L.S.: A patent search and classification system. In: Proceedings of the Fourth ACM Conference on Digital Libraries, pp. 179–187
7. Grawe, M.F., Martins, C.A., Bonfante, A.G.: Automated patent classification using word embedding. In: 16th IEEE International Conference on Machine Learning and Applications (ICMLA)
8. Roudsari, A.H., Afshar, J., Lee, W., Lee, S.: PatentNet: multi-label classification of patent documents using deep learning based language understanding. Scientometrics **127**, 207–231 (2022)
9. Lee, J.-S., Hsiang, J.: Patent classification by fine-tuning BERT language model. World Patent Inf. (2020)

10. Li, S., Hu, J., Cui, Y., Hu, J.: DeepPatent: patent classification with convolutional neural networks and word embedding. Scientometrics **117**, 721–744 (2018)
11. Lee, J.S., Hsiang, J.: PatentBERT: patent classification with fine-tuning a pre-trained BERT Model. World Patent Inf. (2019)
12. Ji, G., He, S., Xu, L., et al.: Knowledge graph embedding via dynamic mapping matrix. In: Proceedings of the 53rd Annual Meeting of the Association for Computational Linguistics and the 7th International Joint Conference on Natural Language Processing, vol. 1, Long papers, pp. 687–696 (2015)
13. Vaswani, A., Shazeer, N., Parmar, N., et al.: Attention is all you need. arXiv (2017)
14. Tsoumakas, G., Katakis, I., Vlahavas, I.: Mining multi-label data. In: Maimon, O., Rokach, L. (eds.) Data Mining and Knowledge Discovery Handbook, pp. 667–685. Springer, Boston (2009)
15. Fang, L., Zhang, L., Wu, H., et al.: Patent2Vec: multi-view representation learning on patent-graphs for patent classification. World Wide Web **24**, 1791–1812 (2021). https://doi.org/10.1007/s11280-021-00885-4
16. Wu, X.Z., Zhou, Z.H.: A unified view of multi-label performance measures. In: International Conference on Machine Learning, PMLR, pp. 3780–3788 (2017)
17. Yang, B., Sun, J.T., Wang, T., Chen, Z.: Effective multi-label active learning for text classification. In: Proceedings of the 15th ACM SIGKDD International Conference on Knowledge Discovery and Data Mining, pp. 917–926 (2009)
18. Joulin, A., Grave, E., Bojanowski, P., Mikolov, T.: Bag of tricks for efficient text classification. arXiv preprint arXiv:1607.01759 (2016)

One Hip Wonder: 1D-CNNs Reduce Sensor Requirements for Everyday Gait Analysis

Jens Seemann[1(✉)], Tim Loris[1], Lukas Weber[1], Matthis Synofzik[2,3], Martin A. Giese[1], and Winfried Ilg[1,3]

[1] Section Computational Sensomotorics, Hertie Institute for Clinical Brain Research, Tübingen, Germany
jens.seemann@cin.uni-tuebingen.de
[2] Division of Translational Genomics of Neurodegenerative Diseases, Hertie Institute for Clinical Brain Research, Tübingen, Germany
[3] German Center for Neurodegenerative Diseases (DZNE), Tübingen, Germany

Abstract. Wearable inertial measurement units (IMU) enable large-scale multicenter studies of everyday gait analysis in patients with rare neurodegenerative diseases such as cerebellar ataxia. To date, the quantity of sensors used in such studies has involved a trade-off between data quality and clinical feasibility. Here, we apply machine learning techniques to potentially reduce the number of sensors required for real-life gait analysis from three sensors to a single sensor on the hip. We trained 1D-CNNs on constrained walking data from individuals with cerebellar ataxia and healthy controls to generate synthetic foot data and predict gait features from a single sensor and tested them in free walking conditions, including the everyday life of unseen subjects. We compare 14 stride-based gait features (e.g. stride length) with three sensors (two on the feet and one on the hip) with our approach estimating the same features based on raw IMU-data from a single sensor placed on the hip. Leveraging layer-wise relevance propagation (LRP) and transfer learning, we determine driving elements of the input signals to predict individuals' gait features. Our approach achieved a relative error ($< 5\%$) similar to the state of the art three-sensor approach. Thus, machine learning-assisted one-sensor systems can reduce the complexity and cost of gait analysis in upcoming clinical studies while maintaining clinical meaningful effect sizes.

Keywords: Clinical gait analysis · time-series · CNN · explainability · cerebellar ataxia

1 Introduction

In a wide variety of movement disorders, gait emerges as a cardinal symptom, which is often caused by progressive neurodegeneration. Accurate gait analysis

L. Iliadis et al. (Eds.): ICANN 2023, LNCS 14263, pp. 346–357, 2023.
https://doi.org/10.1007/978-3-031-44204-9_29

in real life is crucial for the evaluation of upcoming treatments in such disorders, extracting disease-specific gait features like highly variable stride lengths and increased upper body sway [3]. Gait analysis conducted via multiple IMU-sensors on different parts of the body accurately extracts sensitive gait features but lacks clinical feasibility as it is costly and inconvenient for patients to use on a daily basis. While one-sensor systems deliver reliable information for average values of gait speed or stride length, for measures of spatio-temporal variability they have been demonstrated to be less reliable and less sensitive than their three-sensor counterparts, including an additional sensor on each foot [5].

1.1 Motivation

Hereditary cerebellar ataxia is a neurodegenerative movement disorder that causes progressive difficulty with walking and balance, resulting in decreased quality of life [14]. Spatio-temporal gait features extracted from wearable IMU-sensors indicate higher effect sizes for disease severity of ataxic patients in real-life in comparison to constrained walking trials [12,23]. In particular, stride length variability has proved to be a strong indicator of whether and how fast the disease is progressing [11]. Gait features obtained with wearable IMU-sensors are thus promising response markers and can be used to validate future therapeutic approaches, as well as to enable online therapies [11]. Currently, no treatment for cerebellar ataxia exists, but gene therapies tested in mice are yielding promising results [6]. As cerebellar ataxia is a rare disease, validation of potential treatments often necessitates multicenter studies to ensure a sufficiently large number of subjects [22]. Reliable and feasible one-sensor systems are therefore particularly promising for upcoming therapy studies with real-life assessments, as these optimize patient convenience and reduce costs.

1.2 Objective

We hypothesize that machine learning can be used to predict various gait features represented only in hip data with high accuracy. Previous IMU-based machine learning approaches are limited to classification problems [13], are often based on constrained walking scenarios, [10] or clinically unfeasible sensor set-ups with 17 sensors [15]. Previously, 1D-CNNs have been used to predict five parameters simultaneously, based on a constrained walking dataset consisting of 1185 steps from 99 subjects, 54% of whom were diagnosed with a gait disorder or tendency to fall [8]. By contrast, we present an approach using 1D-CNN machine learning to reduce the number of sensors required for real-life gait analysis in cerebellar ataxia to one hip sensor only.

The aim of this study is to predict ataxic-sensitive gait features with small relative errors ($< 5\%$) using 1D-CNN-assisted one-sensor systems in everyday life. For an application in a clinical context it is crucial to find traceable mechanisms in gait feature prediction, which are revealed by explainability methods in the three- and one-sensor systems.

In this work, three approaches will be compared to investigate the impact of foot data on various stride-based gait features in subjects' everyday life:
(i) Using the complete set of three sensors (3S) resulting in 27 channels of IMU-data. (ii) Using the hip data and synthetic foot data (1S+2$\hat{S}$) resulting in 9 channels of orignal IMU-data + 18 channels of generated IMU-data. (iii) Only using the hip sensor (1S), resulting in 9 input channels of IMU-data. The different inputs are utilized in a 1D-CNN parameter prediction network (PN) of 14 stride-based gait features [2] (s. Fig. 1): 7 spatio-temporal features (stride length, gait speed, stride duration, circumduction, lateral deviation, foot elevation and double support fraction), 4 foot angles (pitch at heel strike/midswing/toe off and toe out) and 3 upper body sway measures (range of motion in sagittal, transverse and coronal plane). In approach (ii) a second encoder-decoder based network serves as a foot data generation network (FN), aiming to generate foot sensor data from hip sensor data, which can be used as additional input for PN in a one-sensor scenario. Finally, we investigate LRP-activation patterns for regression models [17] to identify the relevant input channels for each gait feature.

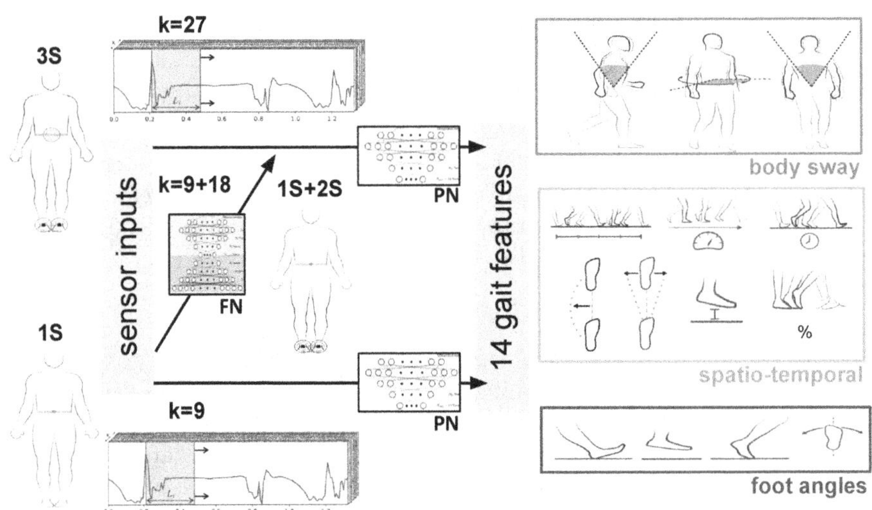

Fig. 1. Three approaches to predict 14 gait features from IMU-data using parameter prediction networks (PN) with different number of input channels k: Stride-based data from all three worn sensors (3S), one hip sensor (1S) and one hip sensor with synthetic foot data using a foot signal prediction network (FN) (1S+2$\hat{S}$). Gait features from: [2].

2 Methods

The dataset used here to train the two neural networks PN and FN is described in terms of data collection and clinically relevant details in [12] and [23].

2.1 Dataset

Gait data was collected from 47 healthy controls (HCs) and 59 patients with cerebellar ataxia (PATs) at a baseline, 1-year and eventually 2-years follow-up assessment by using three Opal sensors (APDM, v2), placed at the lumbar region and on both shoes. Each Opal sensor included triaxial accelerometers, gyroscopes and magnetometers with a fps = 128. Stride-based gait features were extracted from raw data using Mobility Lab (APDM, v2), validated in [20]. Each of the 106 subjects completed a constrained 50 m straight walk (NW). A subset of subjects (n = 87) participated in a 10 min observed free walk (OW) in- and outside the clinics including stairs and busy hallways. A subset of OW-subjects (n = 64) completed several hours of unsupervised home recordings reflecting individual daily living (DW). All sets contained an equal proportion of HCs and PATs.

Preprocessing of the raw data included segmenting the gait sequences into separate strides based on one-sided heel strike events (HS), removing exceptionally short or long strides, and inserting the IMU-data into channels with a fixed size of 170 data points (1.33 s). If a stride was shorter, it was inserted in the middle of the channel and filled up with original sensor data of the previous and next stride, resulting in a total of 10,715, 61,877, and 427,519 strides per gait task, respectively.

2.2 Network Architectures

Three PNs with different input channels k were trained to predict 14 gait features from different sensor-setups: using raw data from the hip sensor only (1S, k = 9), the hip plus FN-generated feet data (1S+2$\hat{S}$, k = 9+18) in comparison to the complete set of all three sensors (3S, k = 27). Using 1D convolutions layers, the shifting of the kernels is done on the time dimension with a step size of one. The PN consisted of three convolutional layers, with a max-pooling layer with a size of 2 following each layer and three fully connected layers (s. Fig. 2 (a)). The convolutional layers contained $N_1 = 32, N_2 = 64$ and $N_3 = 128$ kernels of size $L_1 = 30, L_2 = 15$ and $L_3 = 7$. The fully connected layer consisted of $N_4 = 4096, N_5 = 2048$ and $N_6 = 1024$ neurons and a corresponding number of bias values. The output layer of the network contained $N_{out} = 14$ neurons, corresponding to the 14 gait features. The FN was composed of an encoder and a decoder (s. Fig. 2 (b)). The encoder consisted of three convolutional layers, each followed by a max-pooling layer with window size two and four dense layers, resulting in $N_{encoded} = 750$. The decoder contained four dense layers. The neuron number of the readout layer N_{out} was $170 \cdot 9 \cdot 2 = 3060$ neurons and a matching number of bias values.

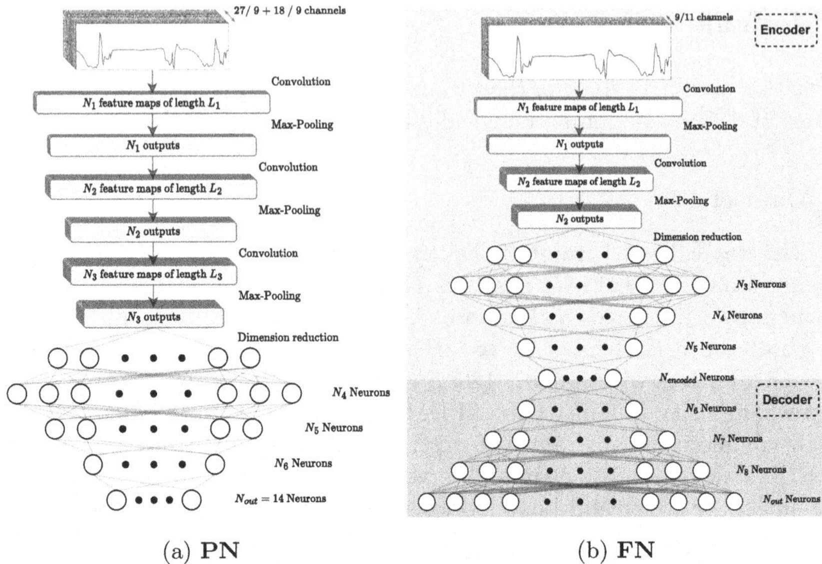

(a) **PN** (b) **FN**

Fig. 2. Architectures of the 1D-CNN networks for (a) parameter prediction (PN) and (b) foot signal prediction (FN), modified from [8].

2.3 Training

In the supervised training phase of all three PNs, we used 14 stride based gait features previously determined by a validated three-sensors algorithm as ground truth [20]. We selected a training scheme simulating a clinical trial: A base network was trained on a larger set of constrained walking data, and is then retrained with limited free walking data from new patients and tested on everyday data of the respective patients. Firstly, a 70:30 split of NW data set was done for training a base net for 1500 epochs. Next, the free walking data (OW) of unseen subjects was used as retraining data for 750 epochs. Finally, 1% of the DW data of the test subjects was utilized in a second retraining for 1500 epochs to explore further improvements.

For the PN network the learning rate α was $5 \cdot 10^{-6}$ with normal distribution ($\mu = 0,\ \sigma = 1$) as weight initialization. Adam optimization algorithm [16] was performed with $\beta_1 = 0.9$, $\beta_2 = 0.99$, and $\epsilon = 10^{-8}$ and a mini-batch size of 64. To prevent overfitting, the network was trained with a weight decay of 10^{-5}. To facilitate the training of the networks, all outputs were normalized between 0 and 1.

For the FN network the learning rate α was changed to $8 \cdot 10^{-7}$ with He initialization [9]. Additionally, gradient clipping was used with a value of 1 [21]. Soft-DTW from [4] and implementation of [18] was used as the loss function to quantify how similar the predicted foot data was to the original one [19].

2.4 Layerwise Relevance Propagation

For a deeper analysis of the networks of this work, LRP was utilized, which described on the basis of relevance scores what kind of influence the respective sensor input had on the prediction. LRP was implemented using the 'Epsilon-Plus' function of the zennit framework [1]. Thus, for convolutional layers the Alpha-Beta rule with $\alpha = 1$, $\beta = 0$, and for fully connected layer the Epsilon rule with $\epsilon = 1 * 10^{-6}$ was applied. To allow a specific interpretation of the inputs, the PNs were trained from scratch on only one gait features instead of all 14 for 500 epochs and were retrained for 150 epochs.

3 Results

In all approaches (1S), (1S+2$\hat{S}$), and (3S), we investigate whether transfer learning from an existing dataset of restricted walking trials (NW) to new patients based on a small set of recorded gait samples with 3 sensors in the clinics (OW) is beneficial to generalize to unseen real-life data (DW). First, the quality of the generated foot data is shown, then the predictions of the different gait features are compared, and finally a revealed mechanism for stride length is described as an example for LRP in gait analysis.

3.1 Generation of Foot Trajectories

Figure 3 visualizes the predictions of the networks that were trained on NW or OW data exclusively and those that were trained on NW and retrained with OW data. All networks were tested on the DW dataset. The foot data channels are estimated correctly on average, but the variance shows clear deviations: All trained networks overestimate the data of patients (s. Fig. 3, top). Especially, the variance in the predicted x-axis of the accelerometer indicates huge noise, that is not present in the original data. This is primarily during stance phase (0.3 s–0.75 s) where one foot is on the ground and thus not accelerating at all. Furthermore, the noise of the accelerometer is lower with HC compared to the patient group. Retraining on OW lower the standard deviations of the predicted DW curves and better fit the distribution of the data for HCs and PATs. The network trained on the OW data only shows the strongest fluctuations of all three networks for PATs. Since the network trained with the NW dataset and retrained with the OW dataset has the lowest error and makes the best predictions of the three networks on everyday data, this is further used to predict everyday foot data for the 1S+2$\hat{S}$ approach. The network trained on the OW data only shows the strongest fluctuations of all three networks for PATs. Since the network trained with the NW dataset and retrained with the OW dataset has the lowest error and makes the best predictions of the three networks on everyday data, this is further used to predict everyday foot data for the 1S+2$\hat{S}$ approach.

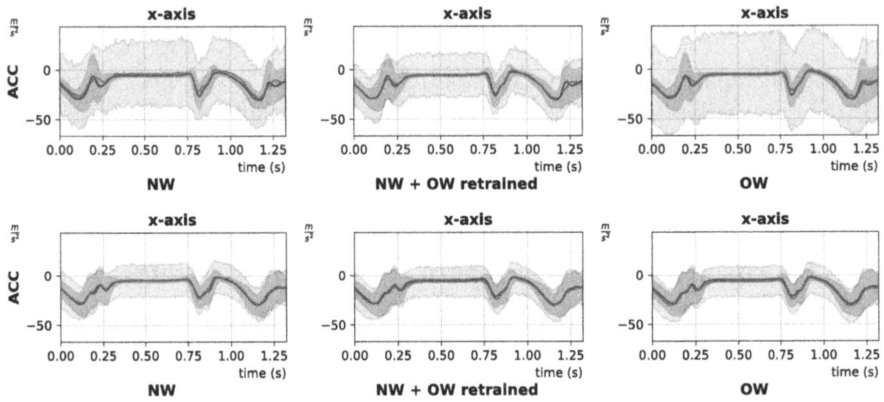

Fig. 3. Mean and standard deviation of original DW foot data (blue) and FN predictions (green) trained on NW data, and retrained on OW, and trained on OW exclusively for patients (top) and healthy controls (bottom). (Color figure online)

3.2 Prediction of Gait Features

First results deliver low (<5%) relative errors for stride duration, gait speed and stride length, using hip raw data only after retraining with OW-data (s. Table 1). For these gait features, using the complete set of sensor data shows similar results (e.g. stride duration rel. err: 0.72% (3S), 1.19% (1S)). All gait features benefit from an additional retraining on 1% of everyday data (e.g. stride length rel. err: 4.37% (1S, OW), 2.35% (1S, DW1%)).

The foot angles at TO and HS show small relative errors of 2.47% and 5.17% in the three-sensor approach, but can also be captured with medium deviations by the one-sensor approach (6.61% and 10.22% resp.). The relative error decreases to 3.16% resp. 6.90% when an additional 1% of the everyday data is used for retraining. For other foot related gait features like lateral deviation or toe-out angle, an accurate estimation seems to be difficult with all our approaches.

Predicting sway of the upper body reveals moderate relative errors (~10%) in both conditions (e.g. coronal sway rel. err.: 8.81% (1S), 11.1% (3S), transverse sway rel. err.: 10.02% (1S), 8.96% (3S)).

The estimation of almost all gait features is improved by generating foot trajectories from hip trajectories. Here, for example, the rel. error of the stride length decreases from 4.37% (1S) to 4.05%. Thus, using synthetic foot data can achieve mild improvements for gait feature predictions.

In terms of mean error and standard deviation per subject, it can be seen that for the stride length predominantly the outliers of the base nets lie closer to the straight lines after retraining and thus correspond better to the ground truth (s. Fig. 4). In general, subjects-wise stride length standard deviations lie mostly below the ground truth, so that the nets show a lower standard deviation per subject in their estimates.

Table 1. Relative errors of gait feature predictions for the sensor set-ups after retraining on OW and 1% of DW data set and tested on DW data set.

Rel. error	real feet (3S)		pred. feet(1S+$2\hat{S}$)		hip(1S)	
after retraining	OW	DW1%	OW	DW1%	OW	DW1%
stride duration [s]	0.72%	0.49%	1.39%	0.95%	1.19%	0.93%
gait speed [m/s]	2.53%	1.41%	3.82%	2.25%	4.13%	2.36%
stride length [m]	2.56%	1.49%	4.05%	2.18%	4.37%	2.35%
double support	3.26%	2.18%	7.70%	4.14%	7.74%	4.15%
circumduction [m]	17.31%	14.24%	35.81%	28.70%	38.23%	28.77%
foot elevation [m]	32.00%	22.83%	39.57%	30.20%	41.88%	31.91%
lateral dev. [m]	49.82%	37.19%	74.85%	64.39%	72.47%	62.49%
pitch at TO [°]	2.47%	1.52%	6.25%	3.16%	6.61%	3.16%
pitch at HS [°]	5.17%	3.50%	10.64%	7.00%	10.22%	6.90%
pitch at MS [°]	10.57%	8.17%	21.87%	15.53%	22.98%	15.18%
toe out[°]	34.77%	23.16%	84.41%	52.43%	85.43%	52.03%
transverse ROM [°]	8.96%	6.82%	11.35%	7.61%	10.20%	7.11%
coronal ROM [°]	11.11%	6.73%	9.88%	5.70%	8.81%	5.80%
sagittal ROM [°]	26.31%	19.21%	26.46%	18.06%	26.05%	18.86%

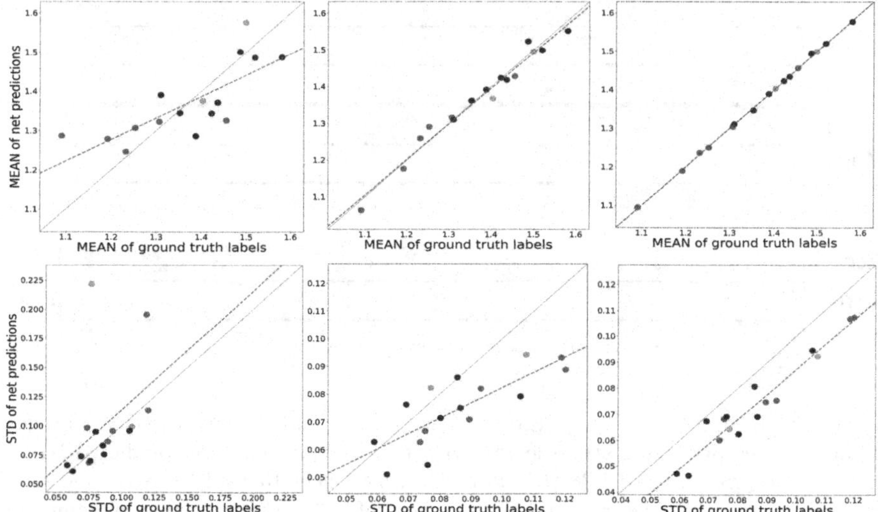

Fig. 4. Means (top) and standard deviations (bottom) of the 1S network and corresponding ground truth labels per subject for the stride length, comparing the base (left), OW-retrained (middle) and DW1%-retrained (right) networks. Blue: HCs, Red: PATs. (Color figure online)

However, foot-specific gait parameters not in gait direction such as lateral deviation, circumduction, toe out and foot elevation are inaccurately predicted with large relative errors in the single sensor condition (> 30%), but also while using all of the three sensors (> 15%) (s. Table 1).

3.3 Explainability

For stride length prediction in 3S, strongly positively relevant areas of the x and z axis of the accelerometer are specifically located in the swing phase (starting at 60% of the gait cycle) of the referenced foot (s. Fig. 5, top). The gyroscope does not appear to be used in any of the three sensor locations for stride length prediction. The magnetometer of the hip in x and z direction shows slight relevances during the whole swing phase.

If only the hip sensor (1S) is available, the positive relevances scatter in the whole range of the gait cycle, mainly occurring in the x and z channel of the accelerometer and magnetometer (s. Figure 5, bottom). The importance of the magnetometer is overall higher compared to 3S. The gyroscope is not relevant for stride length prediction in the 1S approach.

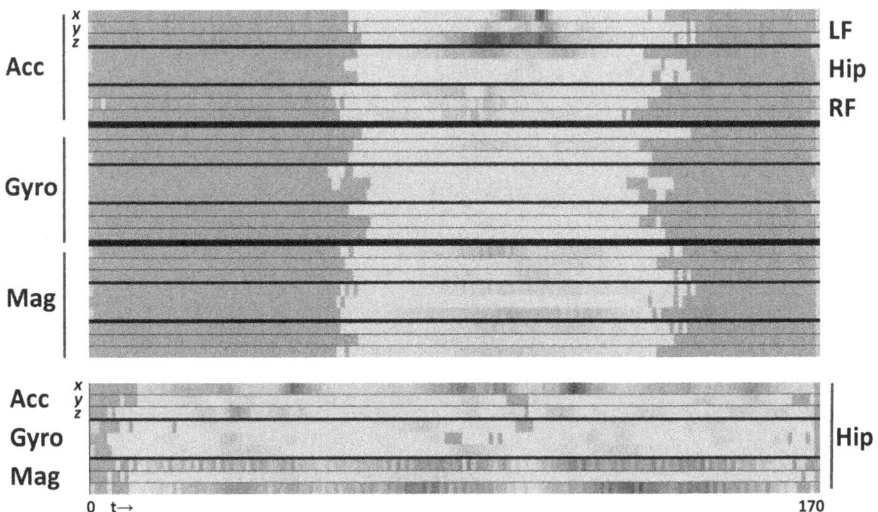

Fig. 5. Example stride with high (green), low (yellow) and slightly negative (orange) relevance scores predicting stride length with true label 1.31 m, and predicted stride length 1.32 m (3S, top) and 1.38 (1S, bottom), respectively. Rows: LRP extracted relevance scrores for IMU-sensor inputs with a length of 170 of the triaxial accelerometers (Acc), gyroscopes (Gyro) and magnetometers (Mag) of the OPAL-sensors placed on the left foot (LF), hip and right foot (RF). (Color figure online)

4 Discussion

Our key finding is that 1D-CNN based one-sensor systems are able to predict treatment responsive gait features with low relative error ($< 5\%$) in everyday life. Furthermore, LRP indicates that gait features are traceably represented in the hip when foot sensors are not available, facilitating assessment by clinicians.

For the analysis of everyday data, retraining with data previously recorded in the clinics is beneficial: key gait features responsive to ataxia, such as stride length, are predicted accurately with just one sensor on the hip. Since cerebellar ataxia is characterized by increased variability of gaits features, the variance of predicted values is highly relevant. Using retraining on individuals, both PN and FN networks are able to recognize individual peculiarities in real-life gait. This might be beneficial as different patients show individual gait patterns or compensation strategies. Additional retraining with a small portion of the everyday data was shown to be further beneficial. However, since this would require wearing three sensors to generate the ground truth in everyday life, this approach is not applicable in the clinics.

Unsurprisingly, accurate prediction of some foot-related features like the toe-out angle requires feet sensors due to insufficient representation of the degrees of freedom in the hip, knee and ankle joints, in the single hip sensor. Gait features such as lateral deviation that relate to changes between two strides are inadequately represented by single stride data. Implementing LSTMs or transformer models, future approaches should incorporate longer inputs with additional contextual information to improve the quality of predictions for lateral deviation.

Before gait parameters are estimated in $1S+2\hat{S}$, foot data is generated first, which show qualitative differences from the raw data. Before retraining the foot sensor predictions include significant noise on the x-axis of the ACC, in particular in the patient group. A possible reason for this could be highly altered gait patterns in the patient group with varying severities of ataxia. Improving the FN network can lead to using already existing three sensor based analysis pipelines with original hip data and synthetic foot data.

Analysing the 3S approach, LRP reveals acceleration in the direction of gait as highly relevant, which is initially read on the z axis due to the plantar flexion during early swing phase and primarily on the x axis during mid swing. This is an intuitively correct approach, because the stride length is defined as the distance covered by the referenced foot during the swing phase. The learnt mechanism of the 1S network to predict the stride length from the hip acceleration in vertical direction is consistent with conventional approaches using inverted pendulum models [7]. Biomechanically, larger strides tend to cause a larger displacement of the hip in the vertical direction during the gait cycle. In this respect, traceable areas of input are of great relevance in both the 1S and 3S approach.

For upcoming clinical trials, predicted gait features should be consistent with effect sizes from validated three sensor systems and surpass state of the art methods based on one sensor only, allowing everyday measurement of a larger number of patients for future therapy studies.

5 Conclusion

1D-CNN-assisted one-sensor systems are able to predict gait features from one hip raw data with low relative errors. For specific gait features, they do exhibit expected qualitative deficiencies compared to the use of three sensors, but these can be reduced by retraining on the individual patients. Explainability methods like LRP reveal meaningful mechanisms behind three- and one-sensor based gait feature predictions for clinicians and therapists. This work shows how established three-sensor based gait features from the laboratory can be transferred to everyday life by one sensor only, maximizing the clinical feasibility for future clinical studies.

Acknowledgments. The authors thank the International Max Planck Research School for Intelligent Systems (IMPRS-IS) for supporting Jens Seemann. This work was supported by Else Kröner-Fresenius-Stiftung: Project ClinbrAIn. Further support was received by the European Research Council ERC 2019-SYG under EU Horizon 2020 research and innovation programme (grant agreement No. 856495, RELEVANCE). ChatGPT generated the part of the title 'One Hip Wonder' given the abstract and the prompt to generate a fun title.

References

1. Anders, C.J., Neumann, D., Samek, W., Müller, K.R., Lapuschkin, S.: Software for dataset-wide xai: From local explanations to global insights with Zennit, CoRelAy, and ViRelAy. CoRR abs/2106.13200 (2021)
2. APDM: Mobility lab whitepaper (2015). https://apdm.wpengine.com/wp-content/uploads/2015/05/02-Mobility-Lab-Whitepaper.pdf
3. Buckley, E., Mazzà, C., McNeill, A.: A systematic review of the gait characteristics associated with cerebellar ataxia. Gait Posture **60**, 154–163 (2018)
4. Cuturi, M., Blondel, M.: Soft-DTW: a differentiable loss function for time-series. In: International Conference on Machine Learning (2017)
5. Czech, M., et al.: The impact of reducing the number of wearable devices on measuring gait in Parkinson disease: noninterventional exploratory study. JMIR Rehabil. Assist. Technol. **7**(2), e17986 (2020)
6. Ghanekar, S.D., Kuo, S.H., Staffetti, J.S., Zesiewicz, T.A.: Current and emerging treatment modalities for spinocerebellar ataxias. Expert Rev. Neurother. **22**(2), 101–114 (2022). pMID: 35081319
7. Goyal, P., Ribeiro, V.J., Saran, H., Kumar, A.: Strap-down pedestrian dead-reckoning system. In: International Conference on Indoor Positioning and Indoor Navigation (IPIN), 2011. pp. 1–7. IEEE/Institute of Electrical and Electronics Engineers Incorporated (2011)
8. Hannink, J., Kautz, T., Pasluosta, C.F., Gasmann, K.G., Klucken, J., Eskofier, B.M.: Sensor-based gait parameter extraction with deep convolutional neural networks. IEEE J. Biomed. Health Inf. **21**(1), 85–93 (2017)
9. He, K., Zhang, X., Ren, S., Sun, J.: Delving deep into rectifiers: surpassing human-level performance on ImageNet classification. In: 2015 IEEE International Conference on Computer Vision (ICCV), pp. 1026–1034 (2015)

10. Hossain, M.S.B., Dranetz, J., Choi, H., Guo, Z.: DeepBBWAE-Net: a CNN-RNN based deep superlearner for estimating lower extremity sagittal plane joint kinematics using shoe-mounted IMU sensors in daily living. IEEE J. Biomed. Health Inf. **26**(8), 3906–3917 (2022)
11. Ilg, W., et al.: the ESMI consortium: digital gait biomarkers allow to capture 1-year longitudinal change in spinocerebellar ataxia type 3. Mov. Disord. **37**(11), 2295–2301 (2022)
12. Ilg, W., et al.: Real-life gait assessment in degenerative cerebellar ataxia: toward ecologically valid biomarkers. Neurology **95**(9), e1199–e1210 (2020)
13. Jabri, S., Carender, W., Wiens, J., Sienko, K.H.: Automatic ML-based vestibular gait classification: examining the effects of IMU placement and gait task selection. J. Neuroeng. Rehabil. **19**(1), 132 (2022)
14. Joyce, M.R., et al.: Quality of life changes following the onset of cerebellar ataxia: symptoms and concerns self-reported by ataxia patients and informants. Cerebellum (London, England) **21**(4), 592–605 (2022)
15. Kadirvelu, B., et al.: A wearable motion capture suit and machine learning predict disease progression in Friedreich's ataxia. Nat. Med. **29**(1), 86–94 (2023)
16. Kingma, D.P., Ba, J.: Adam: A method for stochastic optimization. CoRR abs/1412.6980 (2014)
17. Letzgus, S., Wagner, P., Lederer, J., Samek, W., Müller, K.R., Montavon, G.: Toward explainable AI for regression models. IEEE Signal Process. Mag. **39**(4), 40–58 (2022). https://arxiv.org/pdf/2112.11407v2
18. Maghoumi, M., Taranta, E.M., LaViola, J.: DeepNAG: deep non-adversarial gesture generation. In: 26th International Conference on Intelligent User Interfaces, pp. 213–223 (2021)
19. Müller, M.: Dynamic Time Warping, pp. 69–84. Springer, Berlin (2007). https://doi.org/10.1007/978-3-540-74048-3_4
20. Morris, R., Stuart, S., McBarron, G., Fino, P.C., Mancini, M., Curtze, C.: Validity of mobility lab (version 2) for gait assessment in young adults, older adults and Parkinson's disease. Physiol. Meas. **40**(9), 095003 (2019)
21. Pascanu, R., Mikolov, T., Bengio, Y.: On the difficulty of training recurrent neural networks (2012)
22. Ruano, L., Melo, C., Silva, M.C., Coutinho, P.: The global epidemiology of hereditary ataxia and spastic paraplegia: a systematic review of prevalence studies. Neuroepidemiology **42**(3), 174–183 (2014)
23. Thierfelder, A., et al.: Real-life turning movements capture subtle longitudinal and preataxic changes in cerebellar ataxia. Mov. Disord.: Official J. Mov. Disord. Soc. **37**(5), 1047–1058 (2022)

Patches Channel Attention for Human Sitting Posture Recognition

Yongfang Ye, Shoudong Shi(✉), Tianxiang Zhao, Kedi Qiu, and Ting Lan

Ningbo University, Ningbo, ZheJiang, China
{2111082399,shishoudong}@nbu.edu.cn

Abstract. Individuals frequently maintain poor posture for extended periods while engrossed in their work, leading to potential health risks. Consequently, there is a pressing need for a robust sitting recognition system capable of reminding users to correct their posture. In this study, we propose a novel and efficient Patches Channel Attention (PatchesCA) module specifically designed for the sitting recognition task. The incorporation of PatchesCA guides the neural network's attention to focus on key areas, thereby improving the overall performance. As a plug-and-play module, PatchesCA can be inserted into MobileNetV3-large, resulting in a 42.59% parameter reduction and a 1.06% accuracy improvement. Furthermore, the lack of high-quality sitting posture datasets in the field of sitting recognition hampers the development and evaluation of sitting recognition algorithms. To address this issue, we have created a new dataset specifically designed for sitting posture recognition, offering a more comprehensive and diverse collection of human sitting posture samples. This new dataset will be an invaluable resource for advancing the field and improving the performance of sitting recognition algorithms.

Keywords: Sitting Posture Recognition · channel attention · Patches

1 Introduction

Human sitting posture recognition is a crucial technology for promoting a healthy lifestyle among sedentary individuals, such as the elderly, students and drivers. Prolonged improper sitting posture can result in chronic ailments such as obesity [2], cervical spondylosis [3], and scoliosis [5].

Sitting posture recognition methods can be divided into two main categories: contact [11–13] and contactless [4,14]. Contact sitting recognition methods usually rely on sensors, such as pressure sensors, accelerometers, gyroscopes, etc., which are mounted directly on the seat or worn on the human body. By analyzing the data collected by the sensors, the sitting posture of the user can be inferred. These methods have the following limitations: (1) real-time performance may be

Supported by China Innovation Challenge (Ningbo) Project (2022T001) and Zhejiang Provincial Public Welfare Technology Application Research Project (Grant No. LGF22F020029).

L. Iliadis et al. (Eds.): ICANN 2023, LNCS 14263, pp. 358–370, 2023.
https://doi.org/10.1007/978-3-031-44204-9_30

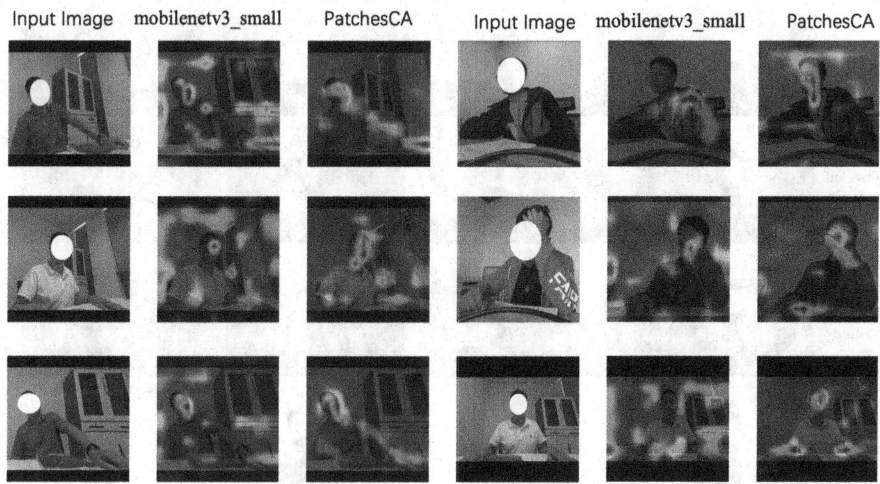

Fig. 1. Sample visualization on sitting posture dataset Val generated by GradCAM. All target layer selected is "layer 4.2". In order to protect the privacy of the participants, the faces of the individuals are masked.

limited by the speed of data acquisition and processing; (2) the layout and number of sensors can affect recognition performance; (3) they require user-specific hardware devices, which may lead to inconvenience and reduced comfort.

Contactless sitting recognition methods are usually based on visual information, such as RGB images, depth images or skeletal data. These methods mainly include traditional feature-based methods and modern deep learning-based methods. Feature-based methods usually require manual design of feature extractors and classifiers, while deep learning methods, such as convolutional neural networks (CNN) and human pose estimation networks (OpenPose [10], HRNet [15], etc.), can learn feature representations automatically. The advantage of contactless methods is that they do not require special hardware and can be implemented using ordinary cameras. However, these methods also have limitations. (1) Real-time performance is limited by convolutional neural network and hardware computing power; (2) A large amount of labeled data is required for training, especially for deep learning methods.

Building upon the discussion of the advantages and disadvantages of contact-based and non-contact methods. In this paper, we propose a novel non-contact approach to address some of the limitations and enhance the performance of posture recognition. Firstly, we introduce a novel Patches Channel Attention Module, named PatchesCA, which demonstrates superior performance in focusing on key regions of interest, as evidenced by the Grad-CAM visualization experiments in Fig. 1. While reducing the number of network parameters, the model achieves improved accuracy, making it suitable for resource-constrained platforms with real-time requirements. Secondly, to address the lack of high-quality datasets in the field of human posture recognition, we have created a compre-

Fig. 2. Dataset overview. The figure presents samples from our dataset, including front and left side views. "Raw" represents the original images captured by the camera, while "Corrected" refers to images that have been calibrated. "Sitting posture" denotes images with human bounding box and sitting posture category annotations, and "Matting" indicates annotations for human body segmentation. To protect the privacy of the participants, their faces have been masked.

hensive sitting posture dataset specifically designed for this task. It comprises over 3 million unlabeled human images, and after image rectification and manual marking, contains 23,997 high-quality images with class labels and human bounding box annotations, as well as foreground-background segmentation for human body extraction, as showing Fig. 2 In summary, this paper makes two main contributions. 1) We have developed an efficient and fast attention mechanism named PatchesCA, which is suitable for resource-constrained platforms. Compared to other methods, it achieves the best performance. 2) For the sitting posture recognition task, we have created a high-quality human sitting posture recognition dataset. These contributions enhance the understanding and advancement of sitting posture recognition and have the potential to improve overall workplace health.

2 Related Work

2.1 Sitting Posture Recognition

In this section, we discuss both contact-based and contactless methods.

Contact-Based Methods. Contact-based methods involve direct interaction with the user's body, typically through sensors placed on the chair or user's body. These sensors generate data related to acceleration or pressure, which is then analyzed to recognize sitting postures. Lin Feng et al. [1] employed RFID tags on the user's back, leveraging the correlation between RFID tag phase changes and sitting posture. They used machine learning algorithms for posture identification, demonstrating the effectiveness of contact-based approaches.

Contactless Methods. Contactless methods, predominantly rely on cameras to capture images of users and determine their sitting posture based on these images. Chen et al. [4] proposed a posture recognition approach grounded in human pose estimation. By processing RGB images through the OpenPose [10] network to obtain human skeletal features, the method achieves robust sitting posture recognition. This approach illustrates the potential of contactless methods in the field of sitting posture recognition.

2.2 Channel Attention Mechanisms

The attention mechanism is used to strength the allocation of the most informative feature expressions while suppressing the less useful ones, and thus makes the model attending to important regions within a context adaptively. Squeeze-and-Excitation Networks [6] (SE) learn to recalibrate channel-wise feature responses adaptively by explicitly modeling interdependencies between channels. The mechanism consists of a global average pooling operation followed by two fully connected layers, which provide a set of weights to emphasize informative channels selectively. Convolutional Block Attention Module [7] (CBAM) introduces an attention module that refines features adaptively in both the spatial and channel dimensions. By combining spatial and channel attention sequentially, CBAM effectively captures global context information and further enhances the discriminative ability of the features. Polarized Self-Attention [8] (PSA) focuses on high-quality pixel-wise mapping by employing polarized attention, which emphasizes the significance of local and global contextual information for each pixel. Spatial Group-wise Enhance [9] (SGE) is designed to enhance semantic feature learning by partitioning the spatial domain into several groups and applying channel-wise attention to each group.

3 Patches Channel Attention

3.1 Analysis on Squeeze and Excitation Operation

The Squeeze-and-Excitation (SE) operation in SE networks [6] adaptively recalibrates channel-wise feature responses by exploiting interdependencies between channels. Specifically, SE computes the attention weights through a two-layer MLP:

$$SE_{operate} = F_{ex}(F_{sq}(U)) \tag{1}$$

$$F_{sq}(U) = \frac{1}{W \times H} \sum_{i=1}^{W} \sum_{j=1}^{H} U(i,j) \tag{2}$$

$$F_{ex}(U_s, W) = \sigma(W_2 \delta(W_1 U_s)) \tag{3}$$

where F_{sq} and F_{ex} denote the squeeze and excitation functions, U is the input feature map, δ is the ReLU activation, σ is the sigmoid activation, and W_1, W_2 are the learnable weights.

The Squeeze-and-Excitation (SE) operation in SE networks mainly focuses on the channel-wise attention. However, due to the use of Global Average Pooling (GAP) in the squeeze operation, spatial location details are not preserved. Moreover, SE applies the same scaling factor to the entire spatial extent rather than on a per-pixel basis, which prevents the network from learning the importance of specific regions within the pixel space.

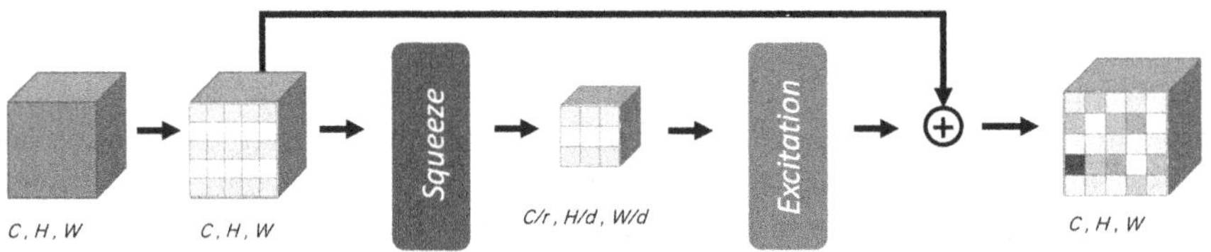

Fig. 3. Structure diagram of PatchesCA

After discussing the limitations of SE operation, it becomes apparent that there is a need for a more advanced approach that addresses these shortcomings. In this work, we introduce a pixel-wise attention mechanism within the channel attention framework by dividing the spatial dimensions of the feature maps into multiple non-overlapping regions, each associated with an importance mask. This innovative approach allows Patches Channel Attention Network to focus on key areas within the input image, effectively enhancing its ability to capture and emphasize critical information while maintaining a strong contextual understanding. The following sections will elaborate on the design and implementation of this Patches attention mechanism and demonstrate its efficacy in improving the performance of our proposed method.

3.2 Patches Channel Attention Module

The Patches Channel Attention (PatchesCA) is a lightweight computational module that processes an input $X \in R^{C \times H \times W}$, where C, H, and W denote the number of channels, spatial height, and width, respectively. PatchesCA transforms the input into a feature map output $U \in R^{C \times H \times W}$. We specifically employ the Patches Squeeze operation to produce $V_{C/G} \in R^{C/G \times H/D \times W/D}$, capturing spatial-wise statistics. Subsequently, the Excitation operation is utilized to restore the C, H, and W dimensions for $V_{C/G} \in R^{C/G \times H/D \times W/D}$, ensuring consistency with the input $X \in R^{C \times H \times W}$. The PatchesCA structure is illustrated in Fig. 3. The final formulations are as follows:

$$\begin{aligned} V_{C/G} &= \sigma(F_{ps}(X)) \\ U &= X + F_{ex}(V_{C/G}) \end{aligned} \tag{4}$$

Here, F_{ps} and F_{ex} denote the Patches Squeeze operation and Excitation operation, respectively. G and D refer to channel reduction ratio and spatial reduction ratio, respectively. σ represents the HardSigmoid activation function.

Patches Squeeze. Given an input $X \in R^{C \times H \times W}$, Patches Squeeze aggregates non-overlapping region features in the spatial dimensions. The computation can be expressed as:

$$\begin{aligned} V_{C/G} &= \sigma(F_{ps}(X)) \\ &= \sigma(DWConv(W_2, PWConv(W_1, X)) \end{aligned} \tag{5}$$

Here, σ represents the HardSigmoid activation function. $V_{C/G} = [v_1, v_2 .... v_{C/G}]$, where G is the channel reduction ratio. Additionally, $v_i \in R^{H/D \times W/D}$, and D is the spatial reduction ratio. Notably, D also denotes the patch size. $DWConv$ refers to the Depthwise Convolution operation [6], while $PWConv$ signifies the Pointwise Convolution operation [6]. For simplicity, bias terms are omitted in the notation.

Excitation. After the Patches Squeeze operation, the patch features of $X \in R^{C \times H \times W}$ are aggregated into $V_{C/G} \in R^{C/G \times H/D \times W/D}$. Each element in $V_{C/G}$ represents the information from $G \times D \times D$ patches in X.

The Excitation step aims to restore the shape of V from $C/G \times H/D \times W/D$ back to $C \times H \times W$, facilitating feature reconstruction. First, the channels are recovered using a Pointwise Convolution ($PWConv2d$). Subsequently, the width and height dimensions are restored through nearest neighbor interpolation. This computation can be expressed as follows:

$$\begin{aligned} U &= X + F_{ex}(V_{C/G}) \\ &= X + interpolate(PWConv2d(V_{C/G})) \end{aligned} \tag{6}$$

Here, *interpolate* denotes the nearest neighbor interpolation operation with a scaling factor of (D, D).

3.3 Sitting Posture Recognition Dataset

A major challenge in sitting posture recognition is the availability of high-quality sitting image datasets. While numerous high-quality human posture datasets exist, they often lack specific sitting posture labels and exhibit significant differences between various actions. To address this issue, we created three distinct indoor scenes and recruited 575 participants who each performed 42 different sitting postures under staff guidance.

Using dual fisheye cameras, we simultaneously captured 1,150 videos, each containing over 3,000 frames, resulting in a total of more than 3.45 million raw sitting images. After manual curation and annotation, we obtained a dataset consisting of 23,997 labeled sitting images with a resolution of 1280×720. The experiments presented in this paper were conducted on this dataset. Representative images from the dataset are shown in Fig. 2.

4 Experiments

4.1 Experiment Setup

All experiments were conducted using the same data augmentation strategy and hyperparameter settings to ensure consistency. Specifically, the input images were randomly cropped to a size of 224×224 and augmented using the TrivialAugmentWide [16] method. The spatial reduction rate D was set to 7, while the channel reduction rate G was set to 16 for both MobileNet-V3 [18] and EfficientNet [17]. The weight parameters (W_1, W_2) in F_{ps} and F_{ex} were initialized to 0, and the biases (b_1, b_2) were set to 1. All architectures were trained from scratch using stochastic gradient descent (SGD) with a weight decay of 1e−4, momentum of 0.9, and a mini-batch size of 96 (utilizing 1 RTX 3070 GPU) for 200 epochs. The initial learning rate was set to 1e−3 (with a linear warm-up of 10 epochs) and was gradually decreased using a cosine function until reaching 1e−5.

4.2 Comparison with Other Methods

In this section, we present a comparison of our proposed PatchesCA method with other state-of-the-art methods in terms of Top-1 Acc and the number of parameters (Param.). The results are shown in Table 1. For MobileNetV3-small, PatchesCA outperforms the competing methods, achieving a Top-1 Acc of 93.1564% with only 1.1M parameters, which is a significant improvement over PSA, SE, and CBAM. Similarly, with MobileNetV3-large, our PatchesCA method reaches the highest Top-1 Acc of 94.1620% using 3.1M parameters, surpassing PSA, SE, SGE, and CBAM. When applied to EfficientNet-b0, PatchesCA exhibits a Top-1 Acc of 94.0223% with 4.4M parameters, demonstrating a notable advantage over PSA, SE, and CBAM, albeit at a slightly higher parameter count. Finally, for ResNet-50, PatchesCA attains the best Top-1 Acc of 98.7878% using 29.5M parameters, outperforming Raw, SGE, SE, and CBAM methods.

Table 1. Comparative performance of various attention mechanisms with different backbones, including MobileNetV3-small, MobileNetV3-large, EfficientNet-b0, and ResNet-50. The table presents the Top-1 accuracy (%) and the number of parameters (Param., in millions) for each method. PatchesCA (ours) consistently achieves the highest Top-1 accuracy across all backbone architectures.

Methods	backbone	Top-1 Acc (%)	Param.(M)
PSA	MobileNetV3-small	88.4637	2.9
SE		92.0112	2.5
CBAM		92.8492	2.2
PatchesCA(ours)		**93.1564**	**1.1**
PSA	MobileNetV3-large	90.4469	8.7
SE		93.1006	5.4
SGE		93.2727	**2.7**
CBAM		93.5754	4.3
PatchesCA(ours)		**94.1620**	3.1
PSA	EfficicentNet-b0	91.7318	18.0
SE		93.7151	5.2
CBAM		93.9385	**3.9**
PatchesCA(ours)		**94.0223**	4.4
Raw	ResNet-50	97.1515	**23.5**
SGE		98.0303	23.6
SE		97.5757	33.6
CBAM		98.1212	33.6
PatchesCA(ours)		**98.7878**	29.5

These results highlight the superior performance of our PatchesCA method across various backbone architectures, emphasizing its effectiveness and efficiency in comparison to other state-of-the-art methods.

4.3 Ablation Experiments

Channel Down and Spatial Down. Due to the limited computational resources of low-cost devices, we chose MobileNetV3-small as the backbone for our ablation experiments. Firstly, we compared the performance of Channel Down, Spatial Down, and PatchesCA individually in the context of PatchesCA. The results are presented in Table 2. The data in the table shows that when only channel down is applied, the top-1 accuracy actually decreases. However, when spatial down is incorporated, the accuracy improves from 90.91% to 92.40%, providing strong evidence in support of our approach, which adds spatial attention to SE (without spatial attention). Ultimately, the top-1 accuracy in our work is enhanced from 90.91% to 93.15%.

Our interpretation for the observed results is that spatial down plays a more crucial role in capturing the local dependencies within the input features, while channel down focuses on global information across channels. Human sitting posture recognition at hand may inherently rely more on spatial dependencies and localized patterns, making spatial down more effective than channel down alone.

Up-Sampling Comparison. In the ablation study of our paper, we conducted experiments to investigate the performance of different upsampling techniques for sitting posture recognition. Specifically, we evaluated three commonly used upsampling methods, including nearest-neighbor interpolation, bilinear interpolation, and transposed convolution (also known as deconvolution). Our experimental results (shown in Table 3) demonstrated that the nearest-neighbor interpolation achieved the best performance among the three methods. This can be attributed to the simplicity and robustness of the nearest-neighbor interpolation. Unlike bilinear interpolation, which computes the output pixel value by taking a weighted average of the surrounding pixels, or transposed convolution, which involves learning parameters and could introduce artifacts or noise during the upsampling process, nearest-neighbor interpolation simply assigns the value of the nearest input pixel to the output pixel. This straightforward approach preserves the original spatial information and reduces the possibility of introducing unwanted artifacts or noise that may affect the performance of the posture recognition system. Furthermore, the nearest-neighbor interpolation is particularly well-suited for working in conjunction with non-overlapping downsampling methods, as it generates importance values for each image block. This compatibility enables a more coherent and consistent representation of the input image during the upsampling process, further enhancing the performance of our sitting posture recognition system.

Activation Function Comparison. Activation functions play a crucial role in transforming deep neural networks from linear to nonlinear systems, and the choice of an appropriate activation function can significantly enhance the network's accuracy. In this study, we investigated the impact of various activation functions on patch representation accuracy. Table 4 reveals that HardSigmoid

Table 2. Comparison of different attention modules for the backbone MobileNetV3-small. The table presents the Top-1 accuracy (%) and GFLOPs for each method, including the model with the SE module removed, the model with only Channel Down, the model with only Spatial Down, and the proposed PatchesCA method. The PatchesCA method achieves the highest Top-1 accuracy while maintaining a similar computational cost.

Method	backbone	Top-1 Acc (%)	GFLOPs
Removed SE module	MobileNetV3-small	90.91	0.1158
Only Channel Down		85.44	0.1508
only Spatial Down		92.40	0.1164
PatchesCA		**93.15**	0.1511

Table 3. Comparison of different upsampling methods for the backbone MobileNetV3-large. The table displays the Top-1 accuracy (%) for each method, highlighting the performance of nearest upsampling, bilinear upsampling, and convolutional upsampling. Nearest upsampling achieves the highest Top-1 accuracy.

Method	backbone	Top-1 Acc (%)
Bilinear upsampling	MobileNetV3-large	91.85
nerast upsampling		**94.16**
conv upsampling		92.93

Table 4. Comparison of different activation functions for the backbone networks MobileNetV3-small and EfficientNet-b0. The table presents the Top-1 accuracy (%) for each activation function, including GELU, Sigmoid, and HardSigmoid. For the MobileNetV3-small backbone, HardSigmoid achieves the highest Top-1 accuracy, while for the EfficientNet-b0 backbone, GELU performs best.

activate	backbone	Top-1 Acc (%)
GELU	MobileNetV3-small	92.4302
Sigmoid		92.7933
HardSigmoid		**93.1564**
HardSigmoid	EfficientNet-b0	94.0223
GELU		**94.2179**

achieves the best Top-1 Acc on MobileNetV3-small, surpassing GELU by approximately 0.72%. Conversely, GELU outperforms HardSigmoid by about 0.19% on EfficientNet-b0.

These performance differences between HardSigmoid and GELU can be attributed to the distinct architectural designs and capacities of MobileNetV3-small and EfficientNet-b0. Designed for lightweight efficiency, MobileNetV3-small has fewer parameters and layers than EfficientNet-b0. Consequently, the computationally inexpensive HardSigmoid activation function is more suitable for MobileNetV3-small, as it offers superior performance without substantially increasing network complexity.

In contrast, EfficientNet-b0 features a more intricate architecture, enabling it to learn richer features. In this scenario, the more expressive GELU activation function, characterized by its smooth, non-linear transition, can better capture the intricate relationships within the input data.

Considering that the primary application of this study is for low-cost embedded devices with limited computational power, we selected the slightly less accurate but faster HardSigmoid activation function.

Activation Function Position. The position of the activation function within the module influences the speed and accuracy of the neural network. We incorporated the activation function into three different positions within PatchesCA and

Table 5. Comparison of different activation function positions in the module for the MobileNetV3-small backbone. The table presents the Top-1 accuracy (%) for each activation position, including Pre-activation, Mid-activation, and Post-activation. Mid-activation achieves the highest Top-1 accuracy among the three positions.

Position	backbone	Top-1 Acc (%)
Pre-Activation	MobileNetV3-small	92.9274
Mid-Activation		**93.1564**
Post-Activation		92.7039

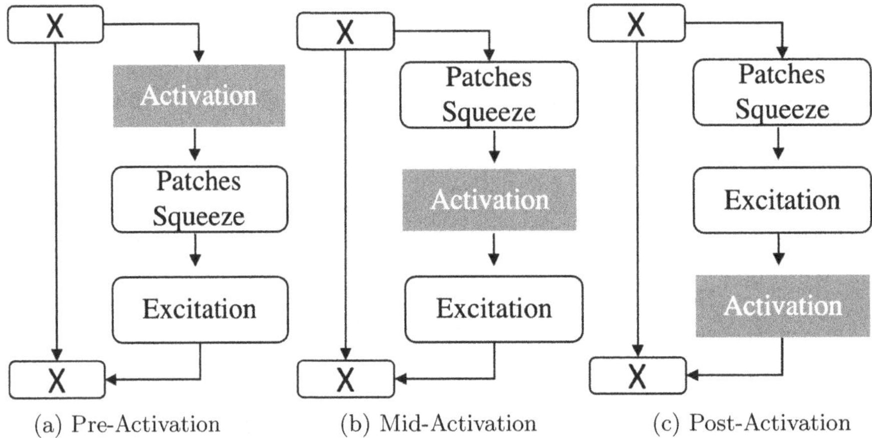

Fig. 4. Structure diagram of PatchesCA with three activation positions (i.e., (a) Pre-activation, (b) Mid-activation, (c) Post-activation).

designed experiments to assess its performance. The locations of the activation functions are illustrated in Fig. 4, and the corresponding experimental results are presented in Table 5. The placement of the activation function in the middle of the module likely provides the most optimal balance between non-linearity and information flow in the network. By positioning it in the middle, the activation function can efficiently introduce non-linearity to the network's computations, while still preserving essential spatial and channel-wise information. This balance results in improved accuracy and faster processing speeds compared to when the activation function is placed at the beginning or the end of the module.

5 Conclusion

In this work, we introduced a simple yet efficient channel attention module named PatchesCA for recognizing sitting postures. This module embeds spatial patches into channel attention and adjusts feature maps in patches to obtain richer spatial information while reducing the computational effort. We also created a new high-quality sitting posture dataset containing more than 23,997 sitting images and various sitting category labels. Compared to MobileNetV3-large, we have reduced the number of parameters by 42.59% and improved the accuracy by 1.06%.

In future work, we plan to investigate whether PatchesCA may be beneficial for other computer vision tasks (e.g., semantic segmentation), which we anticipate may also profit from the efficient use of spatial features. Moreover, we will gather more participants to expand the sitting posture dataset in indoor scenarios.

References

1. Feng, L., Li, Z., Liu, C., Chen, X., Yin, X., Fang, D.: SitR: sitting posture recognition using RF signals. IEEE Internet Things J. **7**, 11492–11504 (2020)
2. Church, T., Thomas, D., Tudor-Locke, C., Katzmarzyk, P., Bouchard, C.: Trends over 5 decades in U.S. occupation-related physical activity and their associations with obesity. PLoS One **6**, e19657 (2011)
3. Cagnie, B., Danneels, L., Tiggelen, D., Loose, V., Cambier, D.: Individual and work related risk factors for neck pain among office workers: a cross sectional study. Eur. Spine J. **16**, 679–686 (2007)
4. Chen, K.: Sitting posture recognition based on OpenPose. In: IOP Conference Series: Materials Science and Engineering, vol. 677, p. 032057 (2019)
5. Grivas, T., Vasiliadis, E., Mouzakis, V., Mihas, C., Koufopoulos, G.: Association between adolescent idiopathic scoliosis prevalence and age at menarche in different geographic latitudes. Scoliosis **1**, 9 (2006)
6. Jie, H., Li, S., Gang, S.: Squeeze-and-excitation networks. In: 2018 IEEE/CVF Conference on Computer Vision and Pattern Recognition (CVPR) (2018)
7. Woo, S., Park, J., Lee, J., Kweon, I.: CBAM: Convolutional Block Attention Module (2018)
8. Liu, H., Liu, F., Fan, X., Huang, D.: Polarized self-attention: towards high-quality pixel-wise mapping. Neurocomputing **506**, 158–167 (2022)
9. Li, X., Hu, X., Yang, J.: Spatial group-wise enhance: improving semantic feature learning in convolutional networks. arXiv abs/1905.09646 (2019)
10. Cao, Z., Hidalgo, G., Simon, T., Wei, S., Sheikh, Y.: OpenPose: realtime multi-person 2D pose estimation using part affinity fields. IEEE Trans. Pattern Anal. Mach. Intell. **43**, 172–186 (2021)
11. Yongxiang, J., et al.: Sitting posture recognition by body pressure distribution and airbag regulation strategy based on seat comfort evaluation. J. Eng. **2019** (2019)
12. Gelaw, T., Hagos, M.: Posture prediction for healthy sitting using a smart chair. arXiv E-prints (2022)
13. Fan, Z., Hu, X., Chen, W., Zhang, D., Ma, X.: A deep learning based 2-dimensional hip pressure signals analysis method for sitting posture recognition. Biomed. Signal Process. Control **73**, 103432 (2022)
14. Fang, Y., Shi, S., Fang, J., Yin, W.: SPRNet: sitting posture recognition using improved vision transformer. In: 2022 International Joint Conference on Neural Networks (IJCNN), pp. 1–6 (2022)
15. Sun, K., Xiao, B., Liu, D., Wang, J.: Deep high-resolution representation learning for human pose estimation. In: 2019 IEEE/CVF Conference on Computer Vision and Pattern Recognition (CVPR), pp. 5686–5696 (2019)

16. Müller, S., Hutter, F.: TrivialAugment: Tuning-free Yet State-of-the-Art Data Augmentation (2021)
17. Tan, M., Le, Q.: EfficientNet: rethinking model scaling for convolutional neural networks. arXiv abs/1905.11946 (2019)
18. Howard, A., et al.: Searching for MobileNetV3 (2019)

RA-Net: A Deep Learning Approach Based on Residual Structure and Attention Mechanism for Image Copy-Move Forgery Detection

Kaiqi Zhao[1], Xiaochen Yuan[2(✉)], Zhiyao Xie[2], Guoheng Huang[3], and Li Feng[1]

[1] School of Computer Science and Engineering, Macau University of Science and Technology, Macau SAR, China
2009853dii30002@student.must.edu.mo, lfeng@must.edu.mo

[2] Faculty of Applied Sciences, Macao Polytechnic University, Macau SAR, China
{xcyuan,p2215884}@mpu.edu.mo

[3] School of Computer Science and Technology, Guangdong University of Technology, Guangzhou, China
kevinwong@gdut.edu.cn

Abstract. To reduce the difficulty of image forensics on forgery images, in this paper, we present an efficient end-to-end deep learning approach using Residual Structure and Attention Mechanism (RA-Net) for image copy-move forgery detection (CMFD). The RA-Net can locate the forged areas and corresponding genuine areas, and it is composed of two modules, Residual Feature Extraction module (RFEM) and Feature Matching & Up-sampling module (FMUM). RFEM is designed to extract deep feature maps, which enriches the combination of gradient information and attention mechanism that focuses the attention of RA-Net to the forged areas. The FMUM assists RA-Net is used to detect copy-move forgery areas and return the previous output to the size of the input image for analysis and visualization of the results. Furthermore, we create a RANet-CMFD dataset for the training, the way to generate RA-Net-CMFD dataset could help solve the problem of not having enough dataset in some research areas. Otherwise, comparison results show that our model can achieve satisfied performance on CoMoFoD dataset at the pixel level, and performs superior than the compared methods.

Keywords: Copy-move Forgery Detection · Image Forensics · Residual Feature Extraction

This work was supported by the National Natural Science Foundation of China (Grant No. 61902448), the Science and Technology Development Fund of Macau SAR (Grant number 0045/2022/A), and the Research project of the Macao Polytechnic University (Project No. RP/FCA-12/2022).

L. Iliadis et al. (Eds.): ICANN 2023, LNCS 14263, pp. 371–381, 2023.
https://doi.org/10.1007/978-3-031-44204-9_31

1 Introduction

With the development of multimedia and computer technology, it is easier to forge images. Although this is certain to meet the needs of people, illegal image forgery has a problem with digital image information security. Especially, important image information forgery will increase the difficulty of image forensics. One type of image manipulation is copy-move forgery, which means copying a piece or several areas of an image and pasting the copied part to a certain location in this image. During the copy-move forgery, these areas may be deformed, scaled, rotated, etc. which makes the copy-move regions hard to find. The purpose of image copy-move detection (CMFD) is to detect the copy-move regions.

Various methods including traditional methods and deep learning methods have been presented for detecting copy-move forgery, and the main steps are basically feature extraction and feature matching. Traditional CMFD includes block-based approaches and keypoints-based approaches. The primary idea of block-based approaches is to divide an image into a number of patches, then compare them with each other to find the matched regions. The methods to extract the block features include Blur [1], Singular Value Decomposition (SVD) [6], Zernike [14], etc. And K-Dimensional tree (KD-Tree) [19] is often used to match features. The core of keypoints-based methods is to extract distinctive local features such as corners, blobs, and edges from the image. The feature extraction methods, such as Scale Invariant Feature Transform (SIFT) [5] and Speeded Up Robust Features (SURF)-based methods [11], extract the key points of copy-move areas. And nearest neighbor algorithm [5] checks out the similarity between points. Although a lot of block-based and keypoint-based approaches have been proposed for CMFD, there are several flaws exist. Block-based techniques are of high processing costs and undetectable large-scale distortion. Nevertheless, the performance of addressing smoothing forgery snip-pet is not really good with the keypoint-based techniques. Auxiliary deep learning methods have recently been proposed to help with various aspects of CMFD. [12] accelerates network convergence, however, it can only detect whether the image is tampered with, but not the localization of the tampered regions. [21] uses VGG16 for features extraction and self-correlation as a matching method, [8] also applies an encoder-to-decoder network and used a classification layer to get the copy-move area.

To optimize the repeated gradient information in the network, [18] proposes a Cross Stage Partial Network (CSPNet), which divides the feature maps into two parts and then fuses them through the proposed cross-stage hierarchical results. The main concept is to make the gradient flow propagate through different branches and prevent different layers from learning repeated gradient information. Otherwise, to pay more attention to the key information, [4] proposes the Squeeze and Excitation Net (SENet) which principle is to enhance the important features and weaken the unimportant features by controlling the weight, so as to make the extracted features more directivity.

We propose an efficient deep learning approach using Residual Structure and Attention Mechanism (RA-Net) for image CMFD. The proposed RA-Net can solve the shortcomings of the existing deep learning methods, e.g., [12] couldn't locate the copy-move area, [21] uses a pre-trained VGG16 model for feature extraction, which could ignore the copy-move areas with weak semantics. The contributions of RA-Net are: (1) we use the combination of Residual Structure and Attention Mechanism to reduce the repeated gradient information and pay more attention to the copy-move forgery areas. To the best of our knowledge, this structure has not been used in the existing CMFD methods; and (2) it is almost impossible to use the existing pre-trained models of image classification for CMFD, which aim to detect rich semantic information, such as VGG16. Therefore, we use no pre-trained model or weight for training RA-Net. There are not enough rich images in the public CMFD datasets, so we generate a RANet-CMFD dataset with original images from SUN [22] and COCO [10]. In this process, we not only select the objects but also the areas that contain less semantic information as copy-move regions.

The paper is organized as follows: Sect. 2 describes the proposed RA-Net for CMFD in detail, Sect. 3 shows the experimental results and discussion, which contains the comparisons between RA-Net and the state-of-the-art approaches. Finally, we give the conclusion and future work in Sect. 4.

2 Proposed RA-Net for CMFD

Figure 1 shows the architecture of the proposed RA-Net, which includes two modules: Residual Feature Extraction Module (RFEM), and Feature Matching & Up-sampling Module (FMUM). In the RFEM, the Pre-processing layer is mainly used to process the input image of any size into the fixed size of $256 \times 256 \times 3$ which is required by the network, and extract a rough feature map. And four Residual blocks follow the Pre-processing layer, Residual Block I, Residual Block II, Residual Block III, and Residual Block IV, each of them consists of two branch structures, a Bottleneck, and a convolution layer. In FMUM, a Deep Correlation layer is used to learn the correlation and calculate the similarity scores between each patch in the feature maps obtained with the RFEM, Sort & Select layer is used to sort these scores of each pixel in features from high to low and select the top scores for each pixel in features, finally, the Up-sampling layer resizes the image to its original size.

2.1 Residual Feature Extraction Module

In RFEM, before applying the Residual blocks, the Pre-processing layer as shown in Fig. 1-(a) should be applied to adjust the input image to the desired format required by the model. During the Pre-processing, we first adjust the shape of the input image to fit the shape of $256 \times 256 \times 3$ required by RA-Net, and then extract a rough feature map with the shape of $256 \times 256 \times 64$. The Residual blocks aim to obtain a feature map with rich gradient information, and each of the Residual Block which is shown as Fig. 1 includes dual Residual structures, in which, the Bottleneck is on the left branch and the layer of Conv_DWConv2D

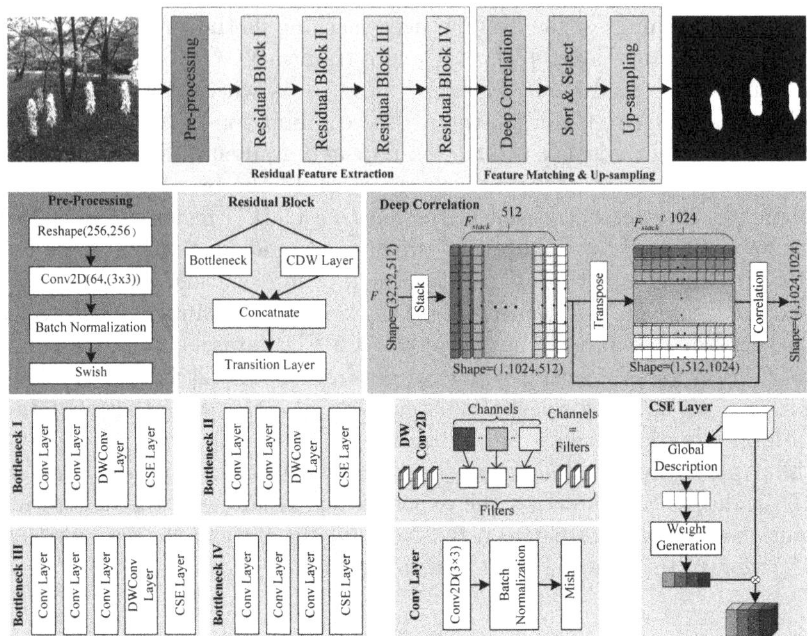

Fig. 1. Overview of the proposed RA-Net for CMFD.

(CDW) is on the right branch. A concatenate Layer combines the two branches in the end to merge the feature maps, and a traditional layer which contains a Convolution layer, BN and Mish is used to further extract features.

Specially, we use the structure of Residual Block I as an example. The $256 \times 256 \times 64$ feature map from the Pre-processing layer is split into two feature maps, the size of each is $256 \times 256 \times 32$. One feature map uses Bottleneck I while another takes CDW to extract interested features, which are then connected together by using concatenation. Using the split and merge strategy across stages can effectively reduce the possibility of duplication in the process of information integration, and greatly improve the learning ability of the network. One branch has a Bottleneck that contains multiple residual structures and convolution layers which refers to [16] and [2], Another branch CDW layer takes the standard 3×3 kernel convolution and Depth-wise Convolution (DWConv2D) with 1×1 kernel to improve the channels and reduce the size respectively. The output shape of each Bottleneck is $128 \times 128 \times 64$, $64 \times 64 \times 128$, $32 \times 32 \times 256$ and $32 \times 32 \times 256$ respectively in the subsequent four blocks and the same as the outputs of the CDW layer.

In Bottlenecks of Residual Blocks, the DWConv Layer consists of DWConv2D and BN-ReLU, where the 1×1 filter kernel is responsible for one channel, and is only convolved by one kernel, therefore the number of feature map channels generated in this process is exactly the same as the number of input channels. Moreover, we use the Channel Squeeze-and-Excitation (CSE) Layer to calculate the weights for each output, which is shown in Fig. 1. We assume the input of each CSE is x, so in the Weight Generation stage, the weight of x is calculated as Eq. (1).

$$W = Sigmoid(f_2(ReLU(f_1(g(x))))) \tag{1}$$

where $f_2(ReLU(f_1(g(x)))$ is the result of Global Description stage, g is a Global Pooling layer, f_1 is the first fully convolution layer, $ReLU$ is used to activate the first fully convolution layer, f_2 is the second fully convolution layer, and the $Sigmoid$ is to learn the activation values for each channel. Consequently, we consider the W is the importance of each channel of feature map after feature selection, then W is weighted to x channel by channel via multiplication to get the re-weighting feature map V, which is shown as Eq. (2).

$$V = W \otimes x \tag{2}$$

Moreover, in all CSE Layers in Bottleneck I-IV, the number of nodes in the first FC layer is $1/4$ of the characteristic matrix channels of the input layer, and the number of nodes in the second FC layer is the same as that of the characteristic matrix channels of the input layer. After a series of operations result of the residual branch is obtained with $128 \times 128 \times 64$.

2.2 Feature Matching and Up-Sampling Module

The FMUM which includes Deep Correlation, Sort & Select and Up-sampling layers is applied to match the characteristic representation, locate the tampered area by addressing the high-dimensional information and visualize the matching results. The input feature map F of FMUM with the shape of $32 \times 32 \times 512$. In the Deep Correlation layer, the correlation distance is an efficient indicator to identify the inherent connections between each patch, so we use Eq. (3) to calculate the correlation distance between each pair of patches.

$$d_{(i,j),(i',j')} = \hat{f}_{(i,j)} \left(\hat{f}_{(i',j')}\right)^T /512 \tag{3}$$

where (i, j) represents the a patch with 512 dimensions in F and (i', j') represents the other patch in F. $D_{(i,j)}$ denotes the correlation coefficient of $f_{(i,j)}$ with total calculate scores, $D_{(i,j)}$ denotes the correlation coefficient of $f_{(i,j)}$ with total calculate scores, and $D_{(i,j)} = \left\{d_{(i,j),(0,0)}, ..., d_{(i,j),(i',j')}, ..., d_{(i,j),(31,31)}\right\}$. The $f_{(i,j)}$ and $f_{(i',j')}$ are not a match when $d_{(i,j),(i',j')}$ is 0. Consequently, $\hat{f}_{(i,j)}$ and $\hat{f}_{(i',j')}$ are standard deviations of $f_{(i,j)}$ and $f_{(i',j')}$.

In order to better eliminate errors and over-fitting, we refine the output in the Sort & Select layer. Specifically, the final sequence of $d_{(i,j),(i',j')}$ is sorted from highest to lowest. Each patch generates a $d_{(i,j),(i',j')}$ tensor of $1 \times 1 \times 1024$ through the Deep Correlation layer. Therefore, the final algorithm results in a correlation coefficient matrix of $32 \times 32 \times 1024$. In other words, each patch selects the top K patches that most match it except itself. In RA-Net, we select $K = 128$, so we get a $32 \times 32 \times 128$ correlation coefficient tensor after the Sort & Select layer.

The previous steps are to analyze the local pixels of the image, so as to obtain the high-level feature information. For evaluating RA-Net and visualizing the result, we design an Up-sampling layer to get a matrix of $256 \times 256 \times 1$. Specially, we apply the transpose convolution in the Up-sampling layer. Transpose convolution can not only change the size and dimension of feature map, but also learn parameters just like convolution.

3 Experiments and Discussions

We implement the proposed RA-Net model in the Tensorflow platform with GPU of Tesla V100-SXM3-32GB. We set the initial learning rate to be 0.0001 at the beginning of training, for the purpose of obtaining a better solution quickly. Then, if the validation loss with the number of epochs reaches 20, the learning rate will be halved. In addition, The batch size is 16, and the maximum epoch is 500.

To evaluate the performance of the proposed RA-Net model, we calculate the metrics *Precision*, *Recall*, and *F1 score* respectively, and they are defined in Eq. (4), Eq. (5) and Eq. (6).

$$Precision = \frac{TP}{TP + FP} \tag{4}$$

$$Recall = \frac{TP}{TP + FN} \tag{5}$$

$$F1 = \frac{2 \times Precision \times Recall}{Precision + Recall} \tag{6}$$

where *TP* is *True Positives* that the numbers of predicting forged pixels as forged, *FP* is *False Positives* that the numbers of predicting genuine pixels as forged, and *FN* is *False Negatives* that the numbers of predicting forged pixels as genuine. And when the possibility is larger than 0.3, we denote the pixel is detected.

3.1 Datasets

Training Dataset. None of the existing dataset for CMFD provides enough images and corresponding ground truth masks for training. Since we do not use a pre-training model, we need lots of images containing copy-move forgery areas to train our proposed network. Therefore, in this paper, we build a RANet-CMFD dataset. With original images from SUN [22] and COCO [10], we select the source area by Labelme manually in each image. During the generation, we selected 550 images from SUN [22] and COCO [10], and applied attacks including rotation with rotation angles of 5°, 20°, 45°, 60°, 90°, 180°, and scaling with scaling degree of 30%, 50%, 100%, 110%, 120%, 150%, to the copied regions. In addition, different kinds of post-processing were applied after rotation and scaling, including Contrast adjustments (CA) with (0.01, 0.95), (0.01, 0.9), (0.01, 0.8), Image blurring (IB) with 3×3, 5×5, Gaussian noises addition (NA) with degree from 0.2 to 1, Brightness changing (BC) with factors of (0.01, 0.95), (0.01, 0.09), (0.01, 0.8). We select useful images about 50000 of them. In addition to the RANet-CMFD dataset, we use 50000 images from [21] and some other public copy-move datasets for training, including CMH [15], MICC-F220 [1], MICC-F600 [7], GRIP [3], Coverage [20], we also carry out post-processing for these datasets, except for [21].

Details of our training dataset are summarized in Table 1. In total, we collect 128,738 quality synthetic samples for copy-move detection, and 106,138 images are used for training, each with a corresponding binary mask distinguishing clone areas and general areas. The synthetic training data is split into training, validation and testing splits with an 8:1:1 ratio. Figure 2 shows the examples of forged images and corresponding ground truth from our training datasets.

Table 1. Details of our training datasets.

Dataset	Original numbers	Rotation & Scaling	Post-processing				Total numbers
			CA	IB	NA	BC	
RANet-CMFD	550	F	F	F	F	F	$550 \times 12 \times 11 = 72600$
[15]	108	–	F	F	F	F	$108 \times 11 = 1188$
[1]	110	–	F	F	F	F	$110 \times 11 = 1210$
[7]	160	–	F	F	F	F	$160 \times 11 = 1760$
[3]	80	–	F	F	F	F	$80 \times 11 = 880$
[20]	100	–	F	F	F	F	$100 \times 11 = 1100$
[21]	50000	–	–	–	–	–	50000

Testing Dataset. CoMoFoD [17] contains 200 basic images and 4800 copy-move forged images generated by applying various post-processing approaches: JPEG Compression, CA, NA, IB, BC, color reduction (CR), rotation and scaling.

3.2 Performance and Comparison on CoMoFoD Dataset

In addition to comparing RA-Net to other methods, we also compared it to Base-NR, which is its ablation framework, so as to prove the effectiveness of Residual structure in RFEM. To generate the Base-NR, instead of using the residual structure in RA-Net, we take the output of the previous layer completely into the next layer.

The comparison results are given in Table 2, where Proposed Base-NA is the ablation framework of RA-Net, [9,13] and [15] are traditional methods, [12] and [21] are DNN-based methods. It is worth mentioning that the DNN-based methods BusterNet [21] and the proposed RA-Net occupy the top two slots, and

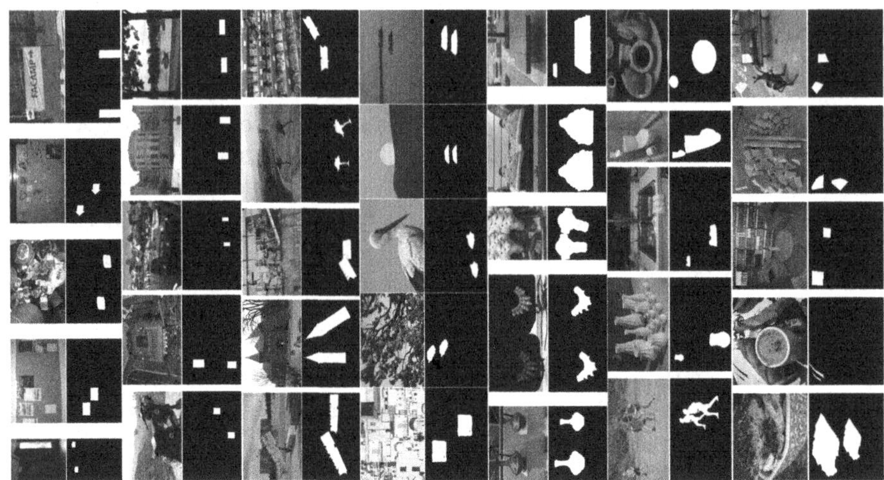

Fig. 2. Examples of forged images and corresponding ground truth from the training dataset. The seven groups in columns respectively show examples from CMH [15], MICC-F220 [1], MICC-F600 [7], GRIP [3], Coverage [20], BusterNet [21] and RANet-CMFD dataset.

our *F1* score is better. Nevertheless, the performance of traditional methods is not good, especially Deeper [15] which is aimed to solve the scaling copy move forgery areas rather than smooth areas. Figure 3 shows the visualization comparison between the state-of-the-art work BusterNet [21] and our proposed methods. Compared with BusterNet [21], RA-Net can detect more accurate copy-move areas, especially small regions. Base-NR always gets rougher results than RA-Net, because Base-NR can not extract the rich feature information from the copy-move images. In addition, without attention mechanism, BusterNet [21] and Base-NR cannot assign weights to features to focus more attention on copy-move areas accurately.

Table 2. Comparisons of the CMFD results on CoMoFoD dataset.

Metrics	[13]	[15]	[9]	[12]	[21]	Proposed Base-NR	Proposed RA-Net
Precision	0.336	0.067	0.089	0.316	0.404	0.391	0.413
Recall	0.325	0.066	0.088	0.216	0.333	0.305	0.360
F1	0.330	0.067	0.089	0.306	0.365	0.343	0.385

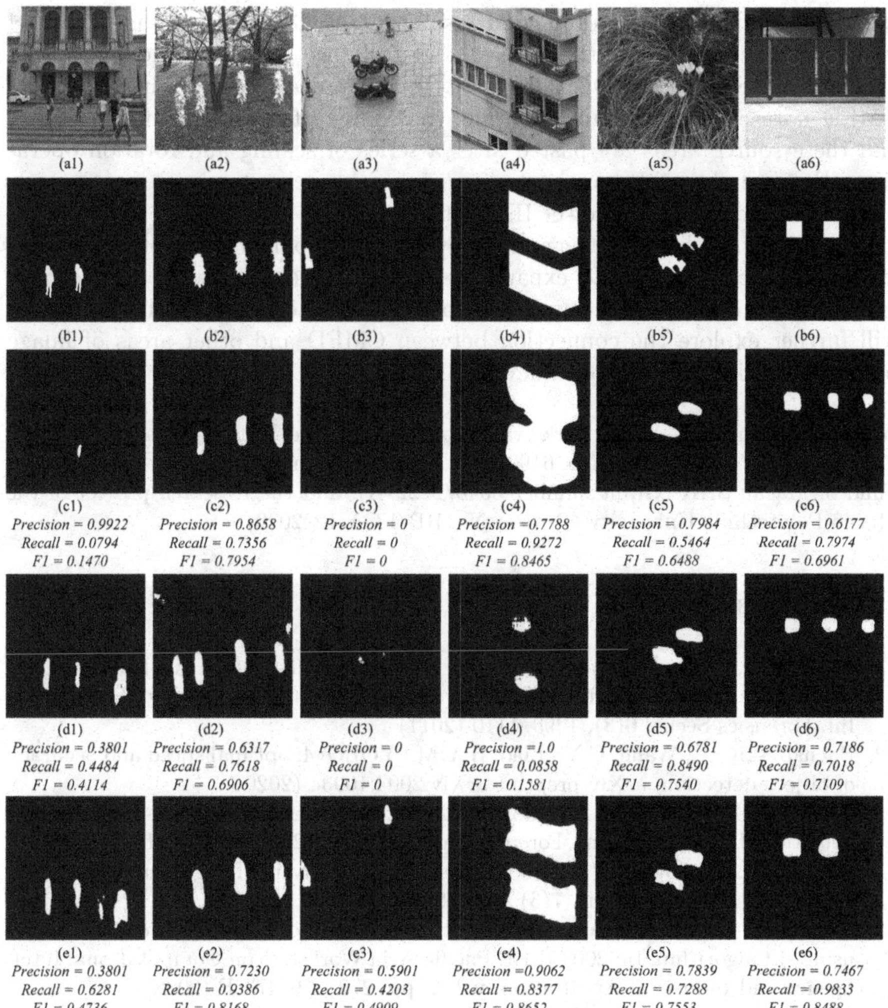

Fig. 3. The visualization comparison between the state-of-the-art work BusterNet [21] and our methods. The 1st and 2nd row shows the forgery images and the corresponding ground-truth. The 3rd, 4th and 5th rows show the detection results of BusterNet [21], Proposed Base-NR and RA-Net.

4 Conclusion

In this paper, we proposed an end-to-end neural network RA-Net for CMFD. We use the residual branches to reduce the repeated gradient information and achieve a richer combination of gradient information for extracting the feature maps, otherwise, we pay sufficient attention to the correlation between high-dimensional feature channels and use the corresponding enhanced Attention Mechanism to find the potential feature. Compared with other CMFD methods, the proposed RA-Net achieves good results in the CoMoFoD dataset in pixel level. Moreover, we create the RANet-CMFD dataset based on the benchmark images from SUN and COCO datasets. In the process of generating RANet-CMFD dataset, we manually pick out the source of copy-move forgery area, and these source areas are pasted after a series of scaling and rotation operations, then we also add some post-processing approaches to enrich our dataset. The method to create RANet-CMFD dataset can also be used to deal with other manipulations, such as splicing and removal, and be applied to the other research areas of image processing to expand the dataset for experiments. RA-Net also can be combined with any refine nets to get better accuracy. In the future, we will further explore the connection between CMFD and other areas of image processing to improve the accuracy of CMFD.

Acknowledgements. This work was supported by the National Natural Science Foundation of China (Grant No. 61902448), the Science and Technology Development Fund of Macau SAR (Grant number 0045/2022/A), and the Research project of the Macao Polytechnic University (Project No. RP/FCA-12/2022).

References

1. Amerini, I., Ballan, L., Caldelli, R., Del Bimbo, A., Serra, G.: A sift-based forensic method for copy-move attack detection and transformation recovery. IEEE Trans. Inf. Forensics Secur. **6**(3), 1099–1110 (2011)
2. Bochkovskiy, A., Wang, C.Y., Liao, H.Y.M.: YOLOv4: optimal speed and accuracy of object detection. arXiv preprint arXiv:2004.10934 (2020)
3. Cozzolino, D., Poggi, G., Verdoliva, L.: Efficient dense-field copy-move forgery detection. IEEE Trans. Inf. Forensics Secur. **10**(11), 2284–2297 (2015)
4. Fridrich, J., Kodovsky, J.: Rich models for steganalysis of digital images. IEEE Trans. Inf. Forensics Secur. **7**(3), 868–882 (2012)
5. Huang, H., Guo, W., Zhang, Y.: Detection of copy-move forgery in digital images using sift algorithm. In: 2008 IEEE Pacific-Asia Workshop on Computational Intelligence and Industrial Application, vol. 2, pp. 272–276. IEEE (2008)
6. Kakar, P., Sudha, N.: Exposing postprocessed copy-paste forgeries through transform-invariant features. IEEE Trans. Inf. Forensics Secur. **7**(3), 1018–1028 (2012)
7. Khotanzad, A., Hong, Y.H.: Invariant image recognition by Zernike moments. IEEE Trans. Pattern Anal. Mach. Intell. **12**(5), 489–497 (1990)
8. Koul, S., Kumar, M., Khurana, S.S., Mushtaq, F., Kumar, K.: An efficient approach for copy-move image forgery detection using convolution neural network. Multimed. Tools Appl. **81**(8), 11259–11277 (2022)
9. Li, J., Li, X., Yang, B., Sun, X.: Segmentation-based image copy-move forgery detection scheme. IEEE Trans. Inf. Forensics Secur. **10**(3), 507–518 (2014)
10. Lin, T.-Y., et al.: Microsoft COCO: common objects in context. In: Fleet, D., Pajdla, T., Schiele, B., Tuytelaars, T. (eds.) ECCV 2014. LNCS, vol. 8693, pp. 740–755. Springer, Cham (2014). https://doi.org/10.1007/978-3-319-10602-1_48
11. Mishra, P., Mishra, N., Sharma, S., Patel, R., et al.: Region duplication forgery detection technique based on surf and HAC. Sci. World J. **2013** (2013)

12. Rao, Y., Ni, J.: A deep learning approach to detection of splicing and copy-move forgeries in images. In: 2016 IEEE International Workshop on Information Forensics and Security (WIFS), pp. 1–6. IEEE (2016)
13. Ryu, S.J., Kirchner, M., Lee, M.J., Lee, H.K.: Rotation invariant localization of duplicated image regions based on Zernike moments. IEEE Trans. Inf. Forensics Secur. **8**(8), 1355–1370 (2013)
14. Ryu, S.-J., Lee, M.-J., Lee, H.-K.: Detection of copy-rotate-move forgery using Zernike moments. In: Böhme, R., Fong, P.W.L., Safavi-Naini, R. (eds.) IH 2010. LNCS, vol. 6387, pp. 51–65. Springer, Heidelberg (2010). https://doi.org/10.1007/978-3-642-16435-4_5
15. Silva, E., Carvalho, T., Ferreira, A., Rocha, A.: Going deeper into copy-move forgery detection: exploring image telltales via multi-scale analysis and voting processes. J. Vis. Commun. Image Represent. **29**, 16–32 (2015)
16. Simonyan, K., Zisserman, A.: Very deep convolutional networks for large-scale image recognition. arXiv preprint arXiv:1409.1556 (2014)
17. Tralic, D., Zupancic, I., Grgic, S., Grgic, M.: CoMoFoD-new database for copy-move forgery detection. In: Proceedings ELMAR-2013, pp. 49–54. IEEE (2013)
18. Wang, C.Y., Liao, H.Y.M., Wu, Y.H., Chen, P.Y., Hsieh, J.W., Yeh, I.H.: CSPNet: a new backbone that can enhance learning capability of CNN. In: Proceedings of the IEEE/CVF Conference on Computer Vision and Pattern Recognition Workshops, pp. 390–391 (2020)
19. Wang, J., Liu, G., Zhang, Z., Dai, Y., Wang, Z.: Fast and robust forensics for image region-duplication forgery. Acta Automatica Sinica **35**(12), 1488–1495 (2009)
20. Wen, B., Zhu, Y., Subramanian, R., Ng, T.T., Shen, X., Winkler, S.: Coverage-a novel database for copy-move forgery detection. In: 2016 IEEE International Conference on Image Processing (ICIP), pp. 161–165. IEEE (2016)
21. Wu, Y., Abd-Almageed, W., Natarajan, P.: BusterNet: detecting copy-move image forgery with source/target localization. In: Proceedings of the European Conference on Computer Vision (ECCV), pp. 168–184 (2018)
22. Xiao, J., Hays, J., Ehinger, K.A., Oliva, A., Torralba, A.: Sun database: large-scale scene recognition from abbey to zoo. In: 2010 IEEE Computer Society Conference on Computer Vision and Pattern Recognition, pp. 3485–3492. IEEE (2010)

Rethinking CNN Architectures in Transformer Detectors

Mengze Pan, Kai Tian, and Qingmin Liao(✉)

Tsinghua University, Hai Dian, Beijing, China
liaoqm@tsinghua.edu.cn

Abstract. Since the introduction of Transformer into the field of object detection, numerous researchers have endeavored to leverage its strong long-distance dependency modeling capabilities. However, huge computational cost and lack of prior knowledge are always the pain points. In this paper, we try to find an alternative method to improve DETR-like models by rethinking the possibility of CNN in DETR from different perspectives. We propose a novel multi-scale patch embedding module, a new DETR encoder module and an auxiliary assessment strategy, which bring prior knowledge into DETR to accelerate the convergence, and enhance the final performance.

Keywords: Transformer · CNN · DETR

1 Introduction

The object detection task is a fundamental problem in the field of computer vision, where researchers have developed a variety of algorithms based on different models. Convolutional Neural Network (CNN) has been a mainstream research hotspot for a long time. However, in recent years, the development of Transformer-based object detection methods have been gaining traction, with DETR [2] being one of the most prominent examples.

Since its inception, Convolutional Neural Networks (CNN) have demonstrated their efficacy in the field of Computer Vision due to their superior local feature extraction and expression capabilities. Subsequently, the Transformer model [21] was introduced to the field of Natural Language Processing (NLP) and, more recently, Computer Vision. The DETR series have further applied the Transformer model to the field of object detection. Theoretically, the Transformer model has better long-distance modeling capabilities than CNN, and it is expected that the Transformer model will leverage its advantages in object detection, particularly when dealing with targets in a complex environment. Ever since DETR [2] was proposed, several works, such as Deformable DETR [31] and SAM-DETR [25], have been proposed to improve the performance of the original

Supported by Tsinghua University.
The first two authors contribute equally to this paper.

L. Iliadis et al. (Eds.): ICANN 2023, LNCS 14263, pp. 382–393, 2023.
https://doi.org/10.1007/978-3-031-44204-9_32

Transformer detector, trying to address issues including difficulty in convergence and limited accuracy. However, even if numerous methods are adopted to boost the performance of DETR, the disadvantages of attention still exist, which are, a lack of necessary prior knowledge and neglect of local details. These defects often restrict Transformer's performances. However, these defects are also the strength of CNN. We consider that a combination of CNN-style design and Transformer's structure can make up for these drawbacks, achieving a better performance.

In this paper, we turn our attention to the CNN model, trying to combine the best knowledge from CNN with Transformer. We propose a new encoder unit and an additional flexible multi-scale patch embedding module, together with an auxiliary assessment strategy using an additional branch. Compared with previous DETR-like models, our model achieves a faster speed of convergence, as well as better performance on COCO.

2 Related Works

2.1 Object Detection

Traditional CNN detectors are commonly divided into two categories: one-stage detectors [13,15,27,30] and two-stage models [5,9,20,24]. The two-stage models like Faster-RCNN [9] have a process of selecting ROI region to balance the number of foreground and background candidate boxes, while one-stage detectors like RetinaNet [13] directly predict the results from feature maps. These two types of detectors usually generate a large number of prediction boxes, so complex pre-and post-processing operations, such as anchor or non-maximum suppression (NMS) are used to generate and de-duplicate candidate boxes. Such operations bring more hyperparameters, making the training process more complicated. In contrast, DETR [2] has been proposed in recent years, breaking the normal line of CNN. It is an end-to-end detection network, which transforms the classification and regression problems of object detection into a set matching problem via the Hungarian algorithm, getting rid of NMS. Nevertheless, its convergence and accuracy remain areas of focus for many researchers, with efforts being made to improve them.

2.2 Transformers in Computer Vision

In recent years, Transformer-based models [4,19] have been optimized in various fields, and have a considerable lead over the traditional CNN models. Swin [17] has been proven a remarkable backbone for downstream tasks, and PVT [22] uses pyramid architecture to make Transformer adaptable to large input sizes. Segformer [23] and other Transformer models also surpass traditional CNN in the field of semantic segmentation. Later, CNN models try to learn from Transformers, using large kernel size [3] or imitating the unique attention mechanism [10], which makes a good performance compared with previous Transformer models.

2.3 Variants of DETR

There have been many works on improving Transformer detectors since DETR was introduced. Some choose to find a better structure [1,6], the others choose to follow the pipeline of DETR and optimize the basic modules [8,14,18,25,26, 28,31]. Conditional-DETR [18] and Deformable DETR [31] are two representatives of them, using different strategies to accelerate the convergence of DETR. Conditional-DETR decouples the object query into content and position, which are independent when calculating cross-attention, significantly improving the convergence speed. The author of Deformable DETR astutely observed a considerable amount of sparsity in the core part of the DETR model's attention. Consequently, they proposed a localization concept: limiting the receptive field of the token to its immediate vicinity to expedite the convergence of attention. This ingenious idea has been proven successful.

Recently, the author of SAM-DETR [25] observed a semantic inconsistency between self-attention and cross-attention in the decoder stage of the DETR model, proposing that this inconsistency is a significant factor in the convergence of the DETR model. To address this issue, a key point alignment mechanism was introduced, which greatly accelerates the training process.

3 Our Methods

In this section, we introduce the architecture of our proposed Simple-DETR, which uses CNN's unique attributes to strengthen the prior information and local details of the detector from three different aspects. Our goal is to improve the DETR model using CNN's advantage mechanism and elaborate design. Specifically, we aim to achieve faster convergence speed while maintaining the highest possible accuracy in single-scale conditions. To this end, we suggest a multi-patch embedding module and a new encoder module that has not been widely explored. An auxiliary assessment strategy is also used to assess the quality of predicted bounding boxes. The overall structure is shown in Fig. 1.

3.1 Multi-patch Embedding

The DETR model utilizes the last layer's output of ResNet as its encoder's input, while Deformable DETR proposes a Multi-Scale method to enhance its adaptability to targets of different scales. All these methods have their drawbacks. On the one hand, Deformable DETR's multi-scale method allocates tokens' receptive fields from different scaled feature maps to achieve robustness in different scales, which is similar to the feature pyramid network [12]. This method is effective, yet its computational consumption and convergence difficulty cannot be underestimated. On the other hand, token partition operation in DETR is quite simple, position embedding or query embedding under such a small size lacks enough details, which means models commonly cannot gain enough position and content information from the last layer of the backbone. To enhance

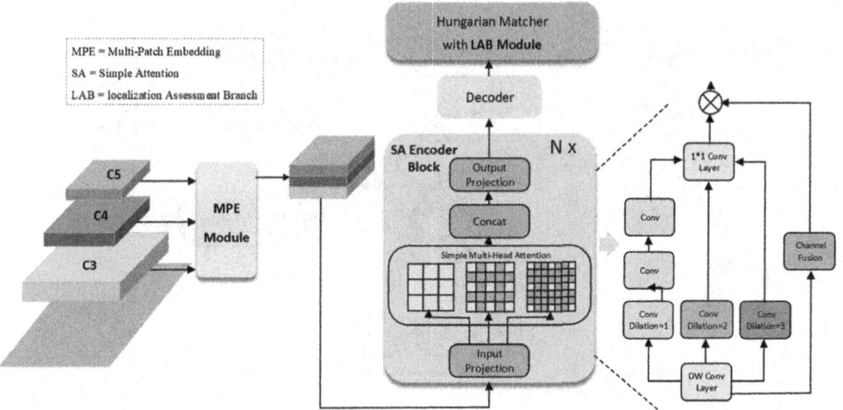

Fig. 1. The structure of our model, which has three key modules: MPE module, SA block and LAB module. The simple attention schematic is on the far right.

the robustness of the model to multi-scale features under the premise of single-scale, which means not always retaining multi-layer features in the reasoning process, we propose a multi-patch embedding module in the patch embedding stage of the encoder, the structure of this module is shown in Fig. 2. This module performs patch fusion on feature maps of different scales, and only retains the fused feature maps for subsequent processes. It differs from classic methods such as FPN and SSD, as we combine multi-scale fusion in Patch Embedding, which hardly brings any increase in the number of parameters or computation cost, but can significantly improve the accuracy of the model.

$$C_{in} = \{C_3, C_4, C_5\} \tag{1}$$

$$C_{out} = \sum P(C_i), i = 3, 4, 5 \tag{2}$$

$$P(C_i) = Merge(T(D(C_i))), i = 3, 4, 5 \tag{3}$$

$$Merge(x) = (Silu(Bn(Conv(x)))) \tag{4}$$

T means transferring information from the dimension of HW to the dimension of C, and D means divide feature maps into patches, and P(Ci) change the shape of Ci from $H_i * W_i * C_{in}$ to $H_i' * W_i' * C_{out}$. Specifically, our method will divide the feature maps of different scales into patches, and for many patches of each scale, select the important patches to merge and reorganize, transfer to the channel dimension, and patch with other scale feature maps. The embedding results are then merged, and only the final patch embedding results are retained. This patch screening and fusion process is realized by convolution.

As an example, utilizing ResNet50 as the backbone, we initially pass C3, C4, and C5 through linear projection in order to unify the channels of these feature maps into C_{out} (usually 128). Subsequently, patch embedding is performed on

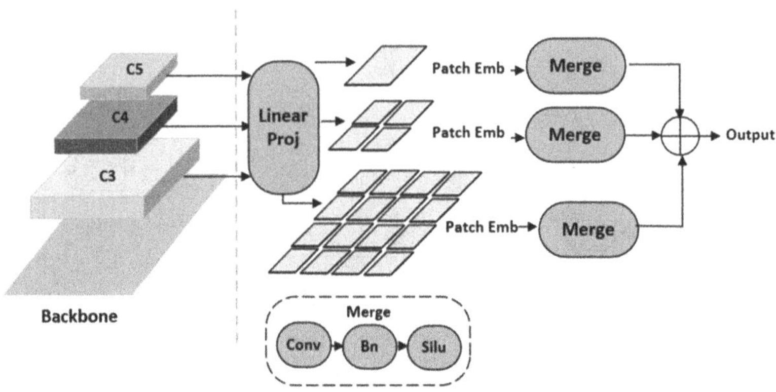

Fig. 2. The structure of multi patch emb.

new feature maps (C3′, C4′, C5′) with same channel numbers (C_{out}) mapping from C3, C4, C5.

For C3′ ($H * W * C_{out}$) with the largest size, the size of each patch is $4 * 4 * C_{out}$, the corresponding number of patches is $H * W/(4 * 4)$, and the feature size after transformation is $(H/4) * (W/4) * 16C_{out}$; for C4′ ($(H/2) * (W/2) * C_{out}$), the size of the patch is $2 * 2 * C_{out}$, and the output after reshaped is $(H/4) * (W/4) * 4C_{out}$, similarly for C5′ ($(H/4) * (W/4) * C_{out}$) then kept ($H/4 * W/4 * C_{out}$). It is observed that after this step, the spatial resolutions of the features of different layers became the same (H/4; W/4), yet the number of channels remained disparate.

Finally, the features of different levels are channel-aligned and fused. This process is realized through convolution. During the patch embedding process, the information contained in the feature map is generally transferred from the H and W dimensions to the channel dimension ($16C_{out}$;$4C_{out}$; C_{out}). Therefore, the merging in the subsequent process is essentially channel merging or channel selection. In this article, convolution, batch normalization, and SiLu are utilized to achieve this step.

3.2 Simple Attention

In the existing literature, few researchers have focused on the encoder stage of the DETR model, as most opinions suggest that the convergence difficulty of DETR is mainly in its decoder stage. However, encoder also plays an essential role. We argue that compared to the matching of object query and feature in the decoder stage, the encoder stage completes more screening and separation of features, which is not heavily dependent on long-distance modeling capabilities. At the feature level of encoder, CNN has the ability to extract global features similar to Transformer, and it can obtain more local details at the same time. Thus, we simplified and adjusted the attention of the encoder stage accordingly to make it more suitable for its function.

According to the above thinking, we designed the following attention mechanism in the encoder stage:

$$Attn_i = FE(F_{in}, d = i), i = 0, 1, 2...L \quad (5)$$

$$Attn = Concat(Attn_1, Attn_2, ..., Attn_L)) \quad (6)$$

$$C_{info} = CF(F_{in}) \quad (7)$$

$$F_{out} = MLP(norm(Attn * C_{info})) \quad (8)$$

FE represents the feature extraction layer corresponding to each scale level and CF represents the channel fusion operation. The key parts of the simple attention contain an attention weight calculation module and a channel fusion module. Dilated convolution is taken as our core component and different expansion coefficients can bring different sizes of receptive fields. We stack the expansion convolution horizontally and vertically, further compensate for the sparsity of the receptive field brought by large dilation coefficient, and enhance the range of receptive field brought by small dilation coefficient. This fusion method ensures that the overall module receptive field can cover different feature sizes and granularity.

The overall attention weight is calculated in three ways, and each branch is composed of several depth-wise dilated convolutions, which are designed to process features of different scales. Furthermore, additional channel information is introduced in the multi-patch embedding module beforehand. To guide its convergence, we added the calculation of channel interaction attention in the encoder's attention process, which is realized by the initial input tokens and multi-scaled adaptive attention fusion.

3.3 Location Assessment Branch

In this part, we focus on the weak prior knowledge of DETR and its mismatch between classification confidence and location quality. Several works [7,16] have explored enhancing the positioning ability of Transformers in the field of image classification. For the first time, we try to improve the location accuracy in DETR-based detectors. At present, the output of DETR is generally divided into two separate branches, the classification branch and the bounding box branch. Due to the lack of location prior information in Transformer, the classification confidence of DETR cannot represent the accuracy of predicted bounding boxes, which is harmful to performance. Based on this consideration, we propose an auxiliary branch to evaluate the quality of bounding boxes, which can effectively improve the accuracy with almost no extra computational cost. The method we propose is shown in Fig. 3 below. First, the output of the last decoder layer is fed into three embedding layers. The classification and box embedding are the same as in DETR. The location embedding layer consists of MLP layers along with a sigmoid operation, aiming to get the score of each predicted box. We follow the idea from Diou [29] to generate the ground-truth label of each assessment branch. Then, the final scores fed into the Hungarian matcher is obtained by multiplying the classification confidence and the location assessment score. During training, this branch is trained separately and a additional loss is added:

$$P_{label} = 1 - IOU(t*, t) + \rho^2(t*, t)/d^2 \tag{9}$$

$$L_{locconf} = |P_{out} - P_{label}| \tag{10}$$

t represents the output bounding box and $t*$ represents the corresponding label after matching. d represents the diagonal length of the smallest enclosing box covering two boxes, while $\rho(t*, t)$ represents the distance of central points of two boxes.

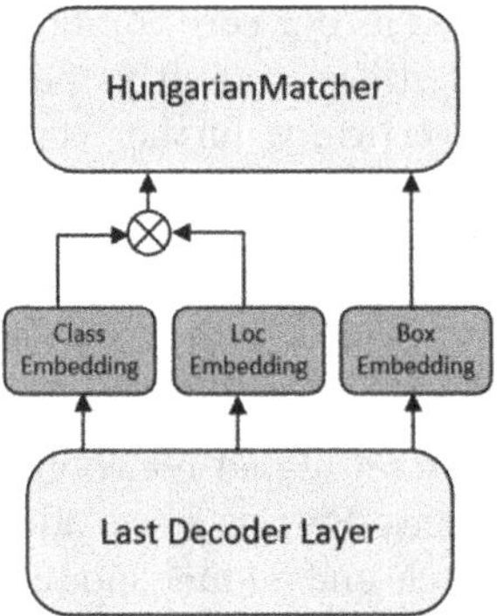

Fig. 3. The auxiliary assessment strategy

4 Experiments

In order to assess the effectiveness of the modules we designed, we conducted experiments on the overall network and ablation experiments on the modules, all of which are based on the COCO dataset. We compared our model with recent DETR-like models and Faster-RCNN together with its variants.

4.1 Dataset and Evaluation Metrics

The COCO 2017 dataset is utilized as the training and testing set, containing 117,000 training images and 5,000 testing images within 80 categories. The official evaluation metric for COCO is adopted, with particular attention paid to Average Precision (AP) and $AP_{0.5}$.

4.2 Implement Details

ResNet50 [11] pretrained on Imagenet is used as the backbone. With regard to the learning rate, we adopted the same settings as DETR. The initial learning rate is 1×10^{-4} for the encoder-decoder structure and 1×10^{-5} for the backbone, with a weight decay of 1×10^{-4}. The batch size is set to 16 in most of our experiments. When using ResNet50-DC5 as our backbone, the batch size is set to 8. We adopt the same data augmentation scheme as DETR, including horizontal flip, random crop and random resize. We adopt two training schemes for experiments, which include a 12-epoch scheme where the learning rate decays after 10 epochs, as well as a 50-epoch scheme where the learning rate decays after 40 epochs.

4.3 Experiment Results

Table 1 shows a comparison between our method and existing DETR-like object detection models and classic CNN-based object detectors on the MS COCO dataset. Under the scheme of 12 epochs, DETR is far from complete convergence, while Faster-RCNN still achieves a good performance. Most of the other DETR-like methods do make progress but still not enough to catch up with Faster-RCNN's performance. Our proposed Simple-DETR achieves a significant performance gain compared with the original DETR baseline (+14.3%AP). Simple DETR also outperforms Faster-RCNN by 0.9%AP and our baseline (SAM-DETR) by 3.2%AP. We also integrate our methods with other boosting methods (SMCA) for DETR to achieve better performance. With the combination of our model and SMCA, we achieve an improvement of 2.0%AP compared with our original simple DETR. The results under the scheme of 50 epochs also show our superiority over other boosting methods.

The comparison visualization results between our proposed method and other methods are shown in Fig. 4. Our model is able to find targets which are missed in SAM-DETR's results. (e.g., vehicles in a crowded scene, partially occluded athlete).

In conclusion, all these results demonstrate a performance improvement of Simple-DETR compared to the baseline, and it is competitive with the current mainstream object detection models. Additionally, we observed that our method has a slight reduction in the number of parameters and computational cost compared with our baseline SAM-DETR.

4.4 Ablation Study

In order to evaluate the effectiveness of our proposed methods, we conduct ablation experiments on the COCO dataset. We choose SAM-DETR as our baseline, which is an excellent recent boosting method for DETR. Experiments are performed with ResNet-50 under the 12-epoch training scheme.

Table 2 shows the results of the ablation study. Even only applying simple attention to the encoder, our model still outperforms baseline by 0.6%AP.

Table 1. Comparison between our model and the current mainstream model, including results in the early stage of training (12 epoch) and in the period of more complete convergence (50 epoch). The Table also contains results when combined with other methods (SMCA) or different backbones (DC5).

Method	Epochs	Params(M)	GFLOPs	AP	AP0.5	AP0.75	AP s	AP m	AP l
Faster-RCNN-R50-DC5	108	166	320	41.1	61.4	44.3	22.9	45.9	55.0
DETR-R50	500	41	86	42.0	62.4	44.2	20.5	45.8	61.1
DETR-R50-DC5	500	41	187	43.3	63.1	45.9	22.5	47.3	61.1
Faster-RCNN-R50	12	34	547	35.7	56.1	38.0	19.2	40.9	48.7
DETR-R50	12	41	86	22.3	39.5	22.2	6.6	22.8	36.6
Deformable-DETR-R50	12	34	78	31.8	51.4	33.5	15.0	35.7	44.7
Conditional-DETR-R50	12	44	90	32.2	52.1	33.4	13.9	34.5	48.7
SMCA-DETR-R50	12	42	86	31.6	51.7	33.1	14.1	34.4	46.5
SAM-DETR-R50	12	58	100	33.1	54.2	33.7	13.9	36.5	51.7
Simple-DETR-R50	12	56.8	94	**36.6**	56.0	38.8	17.5	40.9	54.2
Simple-DETR-R50 w/SMCA	12	56.8	94	**38.6**	59.6	39.9	18.7	42.2	55.6
Faster-RCNN-R50-DC5	12	166	320	37.3	58.8	39.7	20.1	41.7	50.0
DETR-R50-DC5	12	41	187	25.9	44.4	26.0	7.9	27.1	41.4
Deformable-DETR-R50-DC5	12	34	128	34.9	54.3	37.6	19.0	38.9	47.5
Conditional-DETR-R50-DC5	12	44	195	35.9	55.8	38.2	17.8	38.8	52.0
SMCA-DETR-R50-DC5	12	42	187	32.5	52.8	33.9	14.2	35.4	48.1
SAM-DETR-R50-DC5	12	58	210	38.3	59.1	40.1	21.0	41.8	55.2
Simple-DETR-R50-DC5	12	56.8	156	**41.1**	60.1	44.0	23.0	45.5	56.9
Simple-DETR-R50-DC5	50	56.8	156	**44.7**	64.0	48.1	27.5	49.0	59.5
Faster-RCNN-R50	36	34	547	38.4	58.7	41.3	20.7	42.7	53.1
DETR-R50	50	41	86	34.9	55.5	36.0	14.4	37.2	54.5
Deformable-DETR-R50	50	34	78	39.4	59.6	42.3	20.6	43.0	55.5
Conditional-DETR-R50	50	44	90	40.9	61.8	43.3	20.8	44.6	59.2
SMCA-DETR-R50	50	42	86	41.0	–	–	21.9	44.3	59.1
SAM-DETR-R50	50	58	100	39.8	61.8	41.6	20.5	43.4	59.6
Simple-DETR-R50	50	56.8	94	**42.6**	63.0	44.8	23.5	46.9	62.9

Fig. 4. The visual results of our methods and SAM-DETR.

Table 2. Results of Ablation experiment.SAM-DETR is chosen as our baseline. SA denotes the proposed simple attention, MPE denotes multi-patch embedding, and LAB denotes location assessment branch.

Method	epochs	SA	MPE	LAB	AP	$AP_{0.5}$
SAM-DETR	12				33.1	54.2
Ours	12	✓			33.7	54.5
Ours	12		✓		34.1	55.1
Ours	12			✓	34.8	55.0
Ours	12	✓	✓		35.1	55.9
Ours	12	✓	✓	✓	36.6	56.0

Multi-patch embedding improves the performance by 1.4%AP and location assessment branch improves the result by 1.5%AP. Each module makes a significant contribution to the performance of the model.

5 Conclusions

In this paper, we propose a novel encoder self-attention calculation mechanism, a multi patch embedding module and a location assessment branch to improve the accuracy and convergence of the DETR model. This model takes advantages of CNN architectures, enhancing the robustness of the DETR model while slightly reducing its parameter quantity and computing resource consumption. We believe that the DETR model has great potential, and its combination with CNN architectures can result in even greater performance improvements. We hope our proposed idea will be beneficial for subsequent research and application of DETR.

References

1. Beal, J., et al.: Toward transformer-based object detection. arXiv preprint arXiv:2012.09958 (2020)
2. Carion, N., Massa, F., Synnaeve, G., Usunier, N., Kirillov, A., Zagoruyko, S.: End-to-end object detection with transformers. In: Vedaldi, A., Bischof, H., Brox, T., Frahm, J.-M. (eds.) ECCV 2020. LNCS, vol. 12346, pp. 213–229. Springer, Cham (2020). https://doi.org/10.1007/978-3-030-58452-8_13
3. Ding, X., Zhang, X., Han, J., Ding, G.: Scaling up your kernels to 31×31: revisiting large kernel design in CNNs. In: Proceedings of the IEEE/CVF Conference on Computer Vision and Pattern Recognition, pp. 11963–11975 (2022)
4. Dosovitskiy, A., et al.: An image is worth 16 × 16 words: transformers for image recognition at scale. arXiv preprint arXiv:2010.11929 (2020)
5. Fan, Q., Zhuo, W., Tang, C.K., Tai, Y.W.: Few-shot object detection with attention-RPN and multi-relation detector. In: Proceedings of the IEEE/CVF Conference on Computer Vision and Pattern Recognition, pp. 4013–4022 (2020)

6. Fang, Y., et al.: You only look at one sequence: rethinking transformer in vision through object detection. In: Advances in Neural Information Processing Systems, vol. 34, pp. 26183–26197 (2021)
7. Gani, H., Naseer, M., Yaqub, M.: How to train vision transformer on small-scale datasets? arXiv preprint arXiv:2210.07240 (2022)
8. Gao, P., Zheng, M., Wang, X., Dai, J., Li, H.: Fast convergence of DETR with spatially modulated co-attention. In: Proceedings of the IEEE/CVF International Conference on Computer Vision, pp. 3621–3630 (2021)
9. Girshick, R.: Fast R-CNN. In: Proceedings of the IEEE International Conference on Computer Vision, pp. 1440–1448 (2015)
10. Guo, M.H., Lu, C.Z., Liu, Z.N., Cheng, M.M., Hu, S.M.: Visual attention network. arXiv preprint arXiv:2202.09741 (2022)
11. He, K., Zhang, X., Ren, S., Sun, J.: Deep residual learning for image recognition. In: Proceedings of the IEEE Conference on Computer Vision and Pattern Recognition, pp. 770–778 (2016)
12. Lin, T.Y., Dollár, P., Girshick, R., He, K., Hariharan, B., Belongie, S.: Feature pyramid networks for object detection. In: Proceedings of the IEEE Conference on Computer Vision and Pattern Recognition, pp. 2117–2125 (2017)
13. Lin, T.Y., Goyal, P., Girshick, R., He, K., Dollár, P.: Focal loss for dense object detection. In: Proceedings of the IEEE International Conference on Computer Vision, pp. 2980–2988 (2017)
14. Liu, S., et al.: Dab-DETR: dynamic anchor boxes are better queries for DETR. arXiv preprint arXiv:2201.12329 (2022)
15. Liu, S., Huang, D., et al.: Receptive field block net for accurate and fast object detection. In: Proceedings of the European Conference on Computer Vision (ECCV), pp. 385–400 (2018)
16. Liu, Y., Sangineto, E., Bi, W., Sebe, N., Lepri, B., De Nadai, M.: Efficient training of visual transformers with small-size datasets. arXiv preprint arXiv:2106.03746 (2021)
17. Liu, Z., et al.: Swin transformer: hierarchical vision transformer using shifted windows. In: Proceedings of the IEEE/CVF International Conference on Computer Vision, pp. 10012–10022 (2021)
18. Meng, D., et al.: Conditional DETR for fast training convergence. In: Proceedings of the IEEE/CVF International Conference on Computer Vision, pp. 3651–3660 (2021)
19. Touvron, H., Cord, M., Douze, M., Massa, F., Sablayrolles, A., Jégou, H.: Training data-efficient image transformers & distillation through attention. In: International Conference on Machine Learning, pp. 10347–10357. PMLR (2021)
20. Tychsen-Smith, L., Petersson, L.: Improving object localization with fitness NMS and bounded IoU loss. In: Proceedings of the IEEE Conference on Computer Vision and Pattern Recognition, pp. 6877–6885 (2018)
21. Vaswani, A., et al.: Attention is all you need. In: Advances in Neural Information Processing Systems, vol. 30 (2017)
22. Wang, W., et al.: Pyramid vision transformer: a versatile backbone for dense prediction without convolutions. In: Proceedings of the IEEE/CVF International Conference on Computer Vision, pp. 568–578 (2021)
23. Xie, E., Wang, W., Yu, Z., Anandkumar, A., Alvarez, J.M., Luo, P.: SegFormer: simple and efficient design for semantic segmentation with transformers. In: Advances in Neural Information Processing Systems, vol. 34, pp. 12077–12090 (2021)

24. Zhang, G., Lu, S., Zhang, W.: CAD-Net: a context-aware detection network for objects in remote sensing imagery. IEEE Trans. Geosci. Remote Sens. **57**(12), 10015–10024 (2019)
25. Zhang, G., Luo, Z., Yu, Y., Cui, K., Lu, S.: Accelerating DETR convergence via semantic-aligned matching. In: Proceedings of the IEEE/CVF Conference on Computer Vision and Pattern Recognition, pp. 949–958 (2022)
26. Zhang, H., et al.: Dino: DETR with improved denoising anchor boxes for end-to-end object detection. arXiv preprint arXiv:2203.03605 (2022)
27. Zhang, S., Wen, L., Bian, X., Lei, Z., Li, S.Z.: Single-shot refinement neural network for object detection. In: Proceedings of the IEEE Conference on Computer Vision and Pattern Recognition, pp. 4203–4212 (2018)
28. Zheng, M., et al.: End-to-end object detection with adaptive clustering transformer. arXiv preprint arXiv:2011.09315 (2020)
29. Zheng, Z., Wang, P., Liu, W., Li, J., Ye, R., Ren, D.: Distance-IoU loss: faster and better learning for bounding box regression. In: Proceedings of the AAAI Conference on Artificial Intelligence, vol. 34, pp. 12993–13000 (2020)
30. Zhou, X., Wang, D., Krähenbühl, P.: Objects as points. arXiv preprint arXiv:1904.07850 (2019)
31. Zhu, X., Su, W., Lu, L., Li, B., Wang, X., Dai, J.: Deformable DETR: deformable transformers for end-to-end object detection. arXiv preprint arXiv:2010.04159 (2020)

Robustness of Biologically-Inspired Filter-Based ConvNet to Signal Perturbation

Akhilesh Adithya[1], Basabdatta Sen Bhattacharya[1](✉), and Michael Hopkins[2]

[1] BITS Pilani, K K Birla Goa Campus, Goa, India
{f20190044,basabdattab}@goa.bits-pilani.ac.in
[2] University of Manchester, Manchester, UK
michael.hopkins@manchester.ac.uk
https://binnlabs-goa.in

Abstract. We have studied the effectiveness of a biologically-inspired filter in improving the performance of the VGG-16 ConvNet when presented with images perturbed by noise and distortion. Our work builds on the findings of Evans et al. (2021), who reported that biologically-inspired Gabor filter-based VGG-16 improved tolerance to perturbations. Previously, we have demonstrated that foveal filters perform better than Difference-of-Gaussian (DoG) filters, both of which are inspired by the primate retina, in terms of perceptual content retrieval from input images. Subsequently, we have observed that using foveal kernels improved the accuracy of a spiking ConvNet. In this work, we introduce the foveal filter-based VGG-16; our goal is to compare its robustness with other biologically-inspired filters, viz. DoG and Gabor, when presented with perturbed images. Our results showed that when tested with perturbed images, the foveal filter-based VGG-16 outperformed the standard, Gabor filter-based, and the DoG filter-based VGG-16. However, when tested with unperturbed images, the performances of all the biologically-inspired filter-based VGG-16 models were similar to, but not better than, those of the standard VGG-16. This implies that the biologically-inspired filters are particularly robust to noisy, distorted inputs; of these, the foveal filters are seen to be the most robust. To further test the foveal filters, we added perturbation to the training dataset and compared the standard and foveal filter-based VGG-16. The foveal filter-based VGG-16 once again outperformed the standard VGG-16, thus affirming its robustness to perturbation.

Keywords: biologically-inspired filters · foveal · DoG · perturbation · noise · distortion · image recognition · ConvNets · VGG-16 · CNN

This work was supported by the Science and Engineering Research Board (SERB), Govt. of India, Core Research Grant No. CRG/2019/003534. MH was supported by the European Union Flagship Human Brain Project Specific Grant Agreement 3 (H2020 945539).

L. Iliadis et al. (Eds.): ICANN 2023, LNCS 14263, pp. 394–406, 2023.
https://doi.org/10.1007/978-3-031-44204-9_33

1 Introduction

Deep convolutional neural networks (ConvNets) have revolutionized image recognition tasks in recent years, achieving high accuracy for applications such as object detection, face recognition, and scene understanding. These models are designed to automatically extract and classify relevant features from datasets. However, ConvNets can be sensitive and prone to overfitting, leading to poor performance on new or unseen data, or data with non-ideal properties compared to their training sets [12]. Such properties include perturbations that are unavoidable in real-life applications, and can include image noise, distortion, occlusion, lighting conditions, and variations in image orientation [5]. Regularization techniques such as dropout, early stopping, and weight decay have been developed to address this issue, but achieving robust and reliable models remains a challenge. Biological vision sets a high standard for image recognition, and current models are not yet able to match it in terms of processing distorted or noisy visual scenes [10]. Recently, a VGG-16 ConvNet [17] used with biologically-inspired filters was found to perform better than the standard VGG-16 ConvNet when tested with the CIFAR10 [9] dataset. We have been exploring the efficacy of biologically-inspired filters in encoding and retrieving perceptually important information from static grayscale images [16]. For this work, we have utilized four types of biologically-inspired filters (two from our previous works [15,16], two from [4]) with the VGG-16 architecture by replacing its first convolutional layer. With this set-up, we have conducted a comparative study of the biologically-inspired filters when tested with three open-source datasets: CIFAR-10 [9], MNIST [3], and EMNIST [1].

A set of Difference of Gaussian (DoG) kernels mimicking the spatial processing of static scenes in the retina was introduced by VanRullen and Thorpe to model the very fast early visual processing observed in experimental recordings from primates [19]. Subsequently, this model was implemented in [15] and was found to be successful in retrieving perceptually relevant information from static images at time scales that were in agreement with those reported in [19]. This research was further extended to incorporate increased biological plausibility by introducing foveal filter kernels [15,16]. The primate fovea is located in the central area of the retina, and is known to contain two cell types, viz. midget and parasol, each of which has corresponding on- and off-centre types, and varying spatial sizes [18]. Our research [16] demonstrated that the foveal kernels (which were fundamentally of the DoG type at different sizes/proportions) achieved superior performance compared to the DoG kernels implemented in [19]. Recently, we have also demonstrated the better performance of a foveal filter-based spiking ConvNet compared to its standard version [6]. Based on these previous researches, we have implemented the foveal filters in this work, as well as the DoG filters proposed in [19] referred to herewith as VRT-DoG to distinguish from the DoG filter specs defined in [4]. In addition to these three types, we have implemented the biologically-inspired Gabor filters as in [4].

We have trained and tested the biologically-inspired filter-based as well as the standard VGG-16 with both clean and perturbed images from the aforementioned three datasets. Our results show that the foveal filters outperform not only the standard but also other biologically-inspired filter-based VGG-16s in terms of accurate recognition of noisy unseen images. All biologically-inspired filters showed superior performance compared to the standard VGG-16 in the presence of all but one perturbations (Brightening, see Sect. 2.3). To further test this anomaly, we compared the foveal filter performance with the standard VGG-16 on a harder task (see Sect. 2.4); the standard VGG-16 continued to outperform the foveal filters for the same (Brightening) perturbation. This anomaly needs further investigation and will be taken up in a future work. However, we note that the foveal filter outperformed the other biologically-inspired filters for all types of perturbations. Overall, our study have confirmed earlier reports on biologically-inspired filter-based ConvNets as an effective approach to handle signal perturbations in image recognition and classification tasks. Our contribution is in introducing the biologically-inspired foveal filter that is shown to be a clear winner in terms of robustness to signal perturbation. Experimental methodology and results are presented in Sect. 2 and 3 respectively. We conclude the paper in Sect. 4.

2 Methods

2.1 Input Image Dataset

We have used three datasets in our study: First, the CIFAR-10 [9] dataset that contains 60,000 32×32 color images of 10 object classes. We converted the images to grayscale using the BT.601 luma transform conversion formula ($Y = 0.299 \cdot R + 0.587 \cdot G + 0.114 \cdot B$) based on the sensitivity of the human eye as in [4]; readers may note that we did not perform any other image scaling or transformation mentioned in [4] apart from the grayscale conversion. Second, the MNIST [3] dataset that contains 70,000 28×28 grayscale images of handwritten single digits. Finally, to test with a 'harder' input, we used the EMNIST [1] ByClass dataset that contains $814,255$ 28×28 grayscale images of alphanumeric (26 lowercase, 26 uppercase, and 10 digits) characters in 62 unbalanced classes. We mapped the pixel values of all images in the MNIST and EMNIST datasets to $[0, 1]$ to match the format of the CIFAR-10 dataset.

2.2 Biologically-Inspired Filters

The four types of biologically-inspired filters used in this work are shown in Fig. 1. All parameters used to generate the kernels are mentioned in Table 1.

Difference of Gaussian (DoG) Filters: The retinal ganglion cell receptive fields are of two types primarily viz. on-centre/off-surround and off-centre/on-surround, referred to herewith as on- and off-centre respectively. Rodieck [14] proposed that for "mathematical simplicity", a "convenient function to choose" for defining the centre-surround structure of the retinal ganglion cell receptive

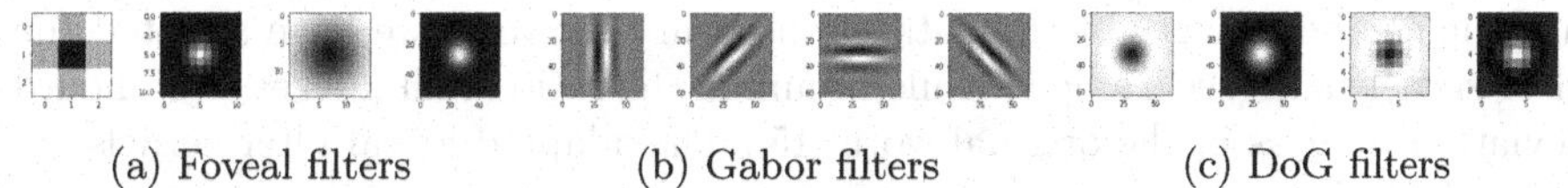

(a) Foveal filters (b) Gabor filters (c) DoG filters

Fig. 1. A few samples of the biologically-inspired filters that are used as the first layer of the VGG-16 ConvNet.

Table 1. Parameters for generating the biologically-inspired filter kernels.

DoG filters [4]	$\sigma = \{1, 2, 4, 8\}$, $\gamma = \{1.6, 1.8, 2.0, 2.2\}$, $\rho = \{+1, -1\}$, $n = 63$
VRT-DoG filters [15,19]	$s = [1, 8]$, $n = 3 \times 2^s - 1$, $\sigma = 0.5 \times 2^{s-1}$, $\gamma = 3$
Foveal filters [15,16]	Midget [off, on]: $n = [3, 11], \sigma = [0.8, 1.04], \gamma = 6.7$ Parasol [off, on]: $n = [15, 55], \sigma = [4, 5.2], \gamma = 4.8$
Gabor filters [4]	$\gamma = \{0.5\}$, $\sigma = \{8\}$, $b = \{1, 1.8, 2.6\}$, $\theta = \{0, \pi/4, 2\pi/4, 3\pi/4\}$, $\phi = \{\pi/2, 3\pi/2\}$

fields is the "sum of two Gaussian functions, a positive one and a wider negative one", as shown in Fig. 1(c), hence DoG, and is defined in Eq. (1):

$$\Phi(\mathbf{x}) = \frac{1}{2\pi\sigma_1^2} e^{\frac{-||x||_2}{2\sigma_1^2}} - \frac{1}{2\pi\sigma_2^2} e^{\frac{-||x||_2}{2\sigma_2^2}} \tag{1}$$

where $\mathbf{x} = (x, y)$ is a 2-dimensional (2-D) vector $\ni ||\mathbf{x}||_2 = x^2 + y^2$. The first term in Eq. (1) represents the centre of the DoG kernel with a standard deviation (s.d.) σ_1, while the second term represents the surround with opposite polarity and s.d. $\sigma_2 = \gamma\sigma_1$, where $\gamma > 1$.

VanRullen and Thorpe had implemented a spatial retina model using both on- and off-centre DoG, each of which were simulated at $n = 8$ scales; for each scale, the kernel sizes varied with the changing centre-surround widths (see Table 1). Subsequently, these filters were used in [15] for simulating fast information retrieval of visual information in primates. We refer to our DoG implementations as in these works as VanRullen-and-Thorpe-DoG (VRT-DoG) filters. In [4], similar DoG filters are used but with $n = 16$ scales and fixed kernel size 63×63 for all scales. We have used the DoG set up as in [4] after scaling down to a fixed kernel size of 9×9. This scaling down was needed as our dataset sizes were 28×28 for MNIST and EMNIST and 32×32 for CIFAR-10 (unlike in [4] where they use a scaled-up version of the CIFAR-10 dataset).

Foveal Filters: The foveal filters were proposed in [15] as a more biologically-plausible form compared to the VRT-DoG filters. The filter design was informed by physiological literature which identified four major varieties of ganglion cells in the primate retina foveal pit, viz. midget and parasol cells, each with an on- and off-centre variety. Furthermore, the on-centre widths were reported to be larger than those of the off-centres by 30% across the retina, even if the overall sizes of both types increased away from the foveal pit. The filter kernel sizes proposed in [15,16] were used with input image sizes of upto 256×256. To better suit the smaller images of the datasets used in this work, we have adapted the filter kernel sizes (see Table 1) while retaining the ratio of filter sizes to standard deviation $n : \sigma$ as in the original work [15]. The adapted foveal filter kernels are shown in Fig. 1(a).

Gabor Filters: The 1-D Gabor filters are about one hundred years old. Named after their proponent, Denise Gabor, they are used widely in their 2-D form for image signal processing. Previous studies have found that Gabor filters are a suitable model for replicating the Simple receptive fields of the visual cortex [8, 11]. Figure 1(b) illustrates the simulated Gabor filters in this work generated with the Scikit library [13] with the following parameters: wavelength of the sinusoidal carrier (λ), spatial aspect ratio of the Gaussian kernel (γ), standard deviation of the Gaussian envelope (σ), four orientations $(0, \pi/4, \pi/2, 3\pi/4)$ of the filters (θ), and phase offset used with the sinusoidal component (ϕ). All parameter values were adopted from [4] and are presented in Table 1. Additionally, after [4], a bandwidth parameter b is used to compute λ by applying the following equation: $\lambda = 42.71 \frac{(2^b+1)}{(2^b-1)}$.

2.3 Image Perturbation

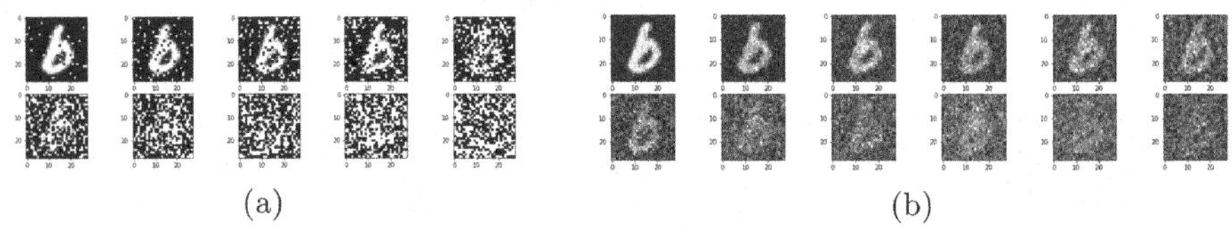

Fig. 2. Sample images of the MNIST dataset perturbed with (a) Salt and pepper noise with increasing $p \in \{0.1, 0.2, ..., 1\}$; (b) Gaussian noise with increasing $\sigma \in \{20, 40, ..., 240\}$.

Images of the dataset were perturbed by adding two types of noise, viz. Salt & pepper (Fig. 2(a)) and Gaussian (Fig. 2(b)). The pixels in the Salt and pepper noise were randomly set to either black or white with probability $p \in \{0.1, 0.2, ..., 1\}$, as done in [4]. The Gaussian noise was generated with mean

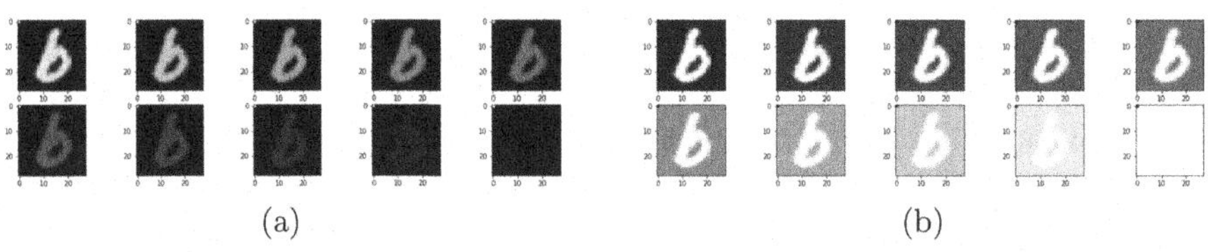

Fig. 3. Sample images of the MNIST dataset distorted by (a) Dimming and (b) Brightening with increasing values of $\alpha \in \{0.1, 0.2, ..., 1\}$.

$\mu = 0$ and the s.d. $\sigma \in \{20, 40, ..., 240\}$, when the image was scaled to the range of [0,255]. In addition, two distortions, Dimming and Brightening, were introduced into the datasets. For Dimming, the brightest pixel intensity (l_{max}) was decreased by a factor $\alpha \in \{0.1, 0.2, ..., 1\}$. This had the effect of decreasing the 'ceiling' of the image pixel intensity range to $l^d_{max} = (1-\alpha)l_{max}$. All other pixels were then mapped to this range [0, l^d_{max}]. For Brightening, the intensity of the darkest pixel (l_{min}) was increased by α. This increased the 'floor' of the image pixel intensity range to $l^b_{min} = (1-\alpha)l_{min} + \alpha$. All other pixels were then mapped in the range [0, l^b_{min}]. The effect of these distortions with different values of α can be seen in Figs. 3(a) and 3(b).

2.4 Simulation Set-Up and Methods

The Deep ConvNet: After [4], we have used the VGG-16 deep ConvNet architecture [17] comprising of 16 layers (13 convolutional + 3 dense), with the first convolutional layer replaced by one of four biologically-inspired filters described in Sect. 2.2. We trained five models on all the three datasets mentioned in Sect. 2.2: four models with the four biologically-inspired filters (see Table 1), the fifth being the standard VGG-16.

Training and Testing Methods: We employed the Adaptive Moment Estimation (Adam) optimiser instead of the Stochastic Gradient Descent (SGD) algorithm implemented in [4] to improve the generalisation speed of the network. To mitigate overfitting, Dropout and Batch Normalisation layers were inserted after each convolutional block. The learning rate was set to $1e-6$ and the cross-entropy loss function was utilised for training. For the MNIST dataset, 60,000 images were used for training and 10,000 for testing, equally split between 10 classes. Similarly for the CIFAR-10 dataset, 50,000 images were used for training, 10,000 for validation. The EMNIST dataset had 697,932 training images and 116,323 test images, split unequally between 62 classes. The class imbalance in EMNIST and its similar classes with overlapping features (e.g. '0', 'O' and 'o') make it harder to train than the 10 balanced classes in MNIST and CIFAR-10. Two training schemes were employed: the unperturbed datasets were used for training, and the model was tested with perturbed datasets; perturbed images from the 'difficult to train' EMNIST dataset were used for training two of the five models (standard and foveal filter-based VGG-16), and then tested with varying amounts of perturbation of the same type. The results from these two schemes are described in Sect. 3.1 and Sect. 3.2 respectively. Lastly, to provide a benchmark for the accuracy of the five model types on the three datasets and allow comparison with other works, a set of results was generated where both training and testing was done without perturbations. This set of results is mentioned in Table 2 and can also be inferred from Figs. 4 and 5.

Computational Methods: The models were trained using the open source Keras library on a server with three Nvidia GeForce RTX 2080 Ti GPUs and two 10-core Intel Xeon processors running on a Linux operating system. Readers may note that when noise is present, randomness is introduced into the results from both the stochastic nature of the noise and the model initialisation process, while the model initialisation is the only contribution when distortions are applied. To account for this randomness, the train-test cycle for each model and for each dataset was repeated five times. The final reported accuracies are averaged over these 5 repeated trials. The standard deviations are shown using error-bars in Figs. 4, 5, 6, 7 and 8. Below, we present our results. The code is available on Github (https://github.com/AkhileshAdithya/ICANN_2023_bio_inspired_filters).

3 Results

Table 2. Benchmark accuracy and training time for the various configurations described in Sect. 3 when trained and tested with unperturbed datasets.

Model	CIFAR-10		MNIST		EMNIST	
	Accuracy	*Training Time*	*Accuracy*	*Training Time*	*Accuracy*	*Training Time*
Base	84.12%	2 h	99.31%	35 min	86.12%	2 h
Foveal	81.61%	2 h	99.16%	50 min	85.51%	3 h
DoG	81.35%	2 h	99.27%	50 min	85.36%	3 h
Gabor	80.79%	2 h	99.12%	50 min	85.32%	3 h
VRT-DoG	74.26%	3 h	99.08%	55 min	85.05%	8 h

The results from training and testing with clean images from all three datasets are presented in Table 2 and serves as a benchmark. In particular, we note that the computation time of the foveal filter-based model and achieved accuracies are similar to those of the standard VGG-16. The VRT-DoG took the longest to execute, possibly because of its complex spatial scale structure.

3.1 Training with Unperturbed Datasets - Testing with Perturbed Datasets

Figures 4(a)–(d) show the performance of all the models trained with the MNIST (unperturbed) dataset and tested with perturbed images of the same dataset. For all perturbations except brightening, the foveal filters performed best among the biologically-inspired filters. In the case of brightening, the standard VGG-16 had the highest performance, although the foveal filter was still the best-performing of the biologically-inspired filters.

Comparable performance was observed for the models trained with the EMNIST (unperturbed) dataset and tested with perturbed images of the same dataset as shown in Figs. 5(a)–(d). Compared to Fig. 4, we observe a larger difference in performance across filters in Fig. 5. This may be due to the increased complexity of the EMNIST dataset. Also, we note that the VRT-DoG filters

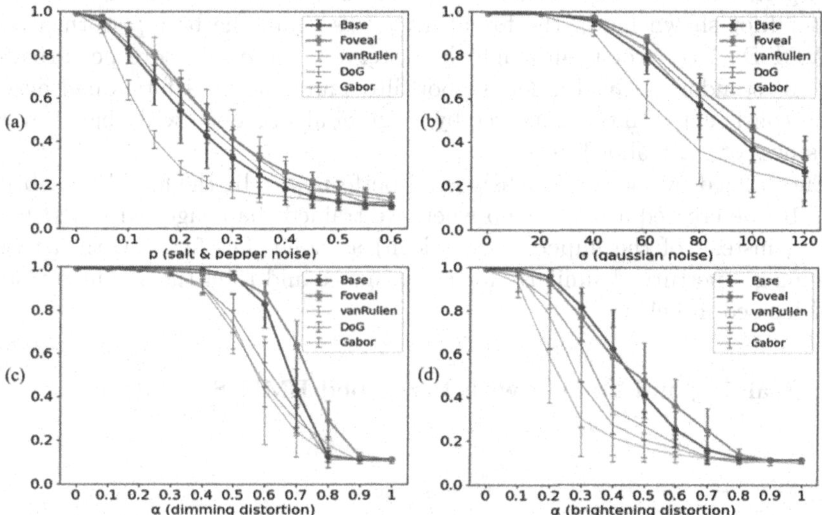

Fig. 4. A comparative study of the accuracies obtained with the five models, viz. the standard VGG-16 and the four biologically-inspired filter- (DoG, VRT-DoG, Foveal, Gabor) based VGG-16, when tested with perturbed MNIST dataset by adding (a) salt and pepper noise; (b) Gaussian noise; and then distorting the images by (c) dimming and (d) brightening the pixel intensities.

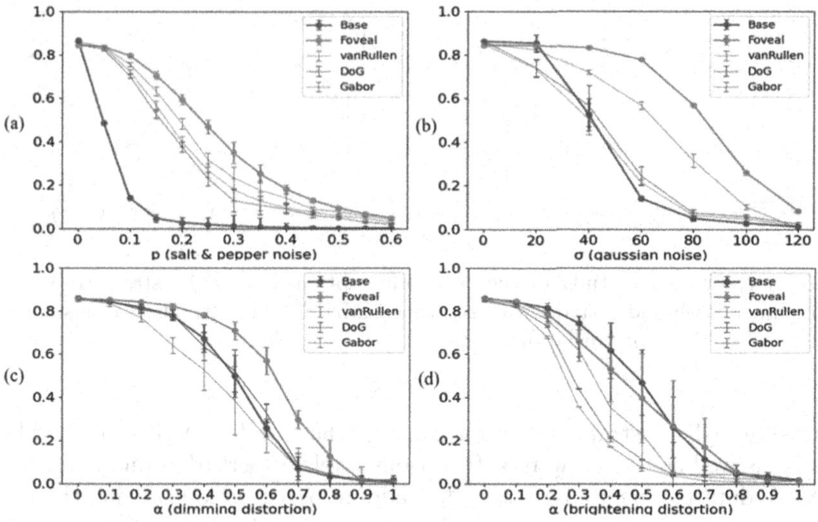

Fig. 5. A comparative study of the accuracies obtained when tested with perturbed EMNIST dataset with the various configurations of filters and perturbations as in Fig. 4.

again performed the worst of all biologically-inspired filters. For the CIFAR10 dataset (not shown here), the foveal filter was again the best performer, and the VRT-DoG the worst, although the latter was more robust to perturbation than the standard VGG-16. The Gabor filters and the DoG filters had performance consistent with that reported by Evans et al. [4], albeit with slightly worse robustness of the Gabor filters.

Encouraged by the continuously good performance by the foveal filter-based VGG-16, we created a new set-up where we trained the images with perturbed images, instead of the unperturbed (clean) as done thus far, and then tested with images perturbed similarly for performance and robustness. These results are discussed in below.

3.2 Training and Testing with Perturbed EMNIST Dataset

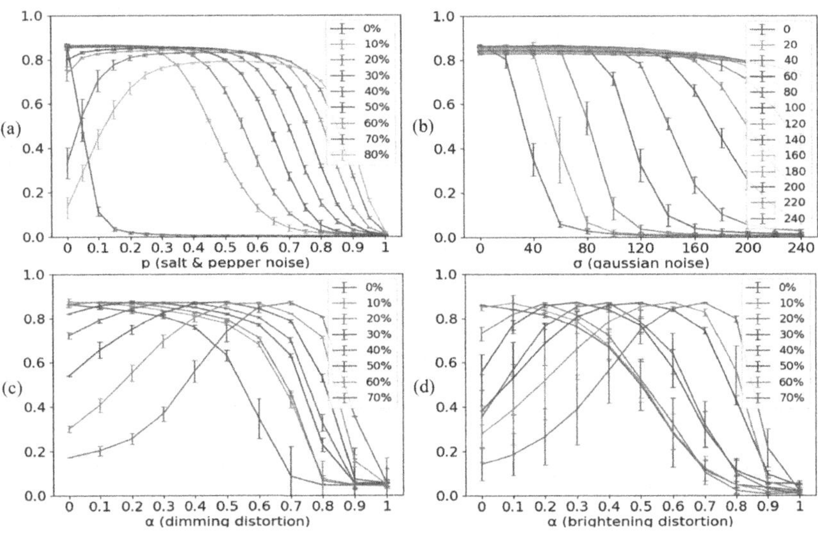

Fig. 6. A comparative study of the accuracies obtained with the standard VGG-16 when trained with and tested with perturbed EMNIST dataset. The various configurations of filters and perturbations in (a)–(d) are as in Fig. 4.

Figures 6(a)–(d) illustrate the performance of the standard VGG-16 when both training as well as testing were with various levels of perturbation added to the EMNIST dataset. It may be noted that adding perturbations during the training phase increases the robustness of the model for that type of perturbation. Figures 6(a), (c) and (d) suggest that the model is overfitting to a particular Signal to Noise Ratio (SNR) along with the features of the image, resulting in poor performance with clean or lightly perturbed images when trained on a dataset with high levels of perturbations, for all perturbations other than Gaussian noise. Similar trends, but with lesser intensities, have also been observed for other CNN architectures such as the LeNet and CapsNet in [7]. The model trained with Gaussian noise does not experience the same kind of overfitting, however the penalty for testing with high noise when trained with low noise is severe. Figures 7(a)–(d) show the performance of a foveal filter-based VGG-16 when trained on a perturbed version of the EMNIST dataset and tested on perturbed images of the same dataset. The results demonstrate that the foveal filter-based model is more resistant to overfitting to the SNR compared to the standard VGG-16. Additionally, the foveal filter does not experience the sharp decrease in accuracy of the Gaussian noise when the testing noise increases, as seen in Figs. 6(b) and 7(b), which further indicates improved robustness when compared to the standard VGG-16 model. We speculate that such robustness to noise in the foveal filter-based architecture is due to a balance between the efficient edge detection by the underlying DoG functions and the scales and sizes used in the filter design based on physiological literature.

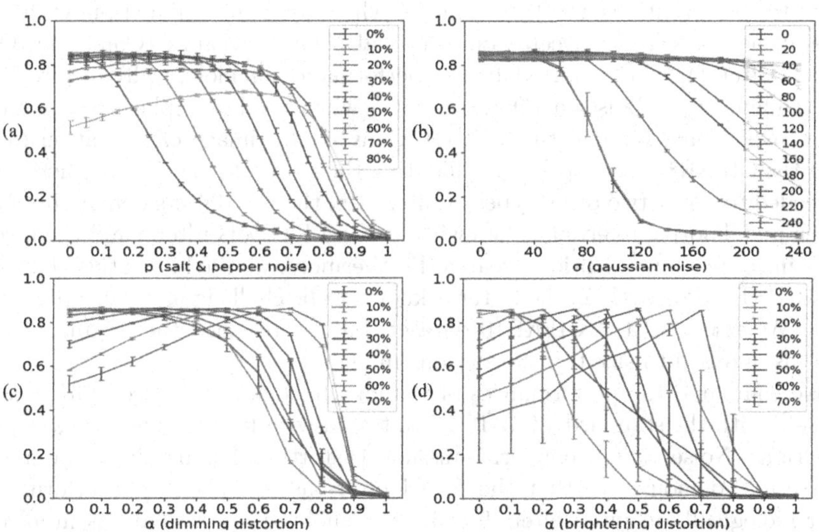

Fig. 7. A comparative study of the accuracies obtained with the foveal filter-based VGG-16 when trained and tested with perturbed EMNIST dataset by adding varying configurations of (a), (b), (c) and (d) as in Fig. 4.

Figures 8(a) and (b) compare the performances of a standard VGG-16 and a foveal filter-based VGG-16 for various types of noise and distortions. The addition of training noise improves the robustness of both models. Figure 8(b) shows that the foveal filter-based VGG-16 is less prone to overfitting to SNR and maintains a relatively high accuracy (51.89%) even when trained with substantial noise, whereas the standard VGG-16 fails to achieve high accuracy (17.34%) on clean images.

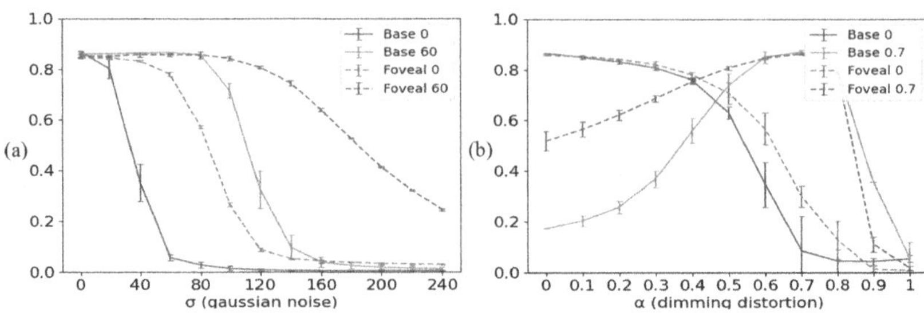

Fig. 8. A comparative study of the accuracies for the standard and foveal filter-based VGG-16, when trained with and without (a) Gaussian noise ($\sigma = 60$); (b) Dimming distortion ($\alpha = 0.7$) for various configuration of test noise on the EMNIST dataset.

4 Discussion and Conclusion

In this paper, we have demonstrated the suitability and robustness of the foveal filters to perturbations in static images when used in conjunction with the state-of-the-art VGG-16 Deep Convolutional Neural Network (ConvNet). Our work is after [4] who reported better performance of biologically-inspired filters (Difference-of-Gaussian (DoG), Gabor) when used as replacement for the first convolutional layer in the VGG-16 ConvNet for image classification tasks using the CIFAR10 dataset. Upon validating their work (not presented here), we proceeded to apply two other types of filters viz. the DoG filters defined by Van-Rullen and Thorpe, referred to herewith as the VRT-DoG filters, and the foveal filters introduced in our prior research. Furthermore, we used two other datasets viz. MNIST and EMNIST; the latter is known to be challenging for classification tasks. We also used the CIFAR10 dataset, but we retained the original image sizes (as opposed to size transformations in [4]).

We compared the performances of the four biologically-inspired filter-based VGG-16 with the standard VGG-16 when tested with four distinct types of perturbations (Noise: Salt & pepper, Gaussian; Distortion: Brightening, Dimming). Our results demonstrate that the foveal filter-based VGG-16 outperforms all other biologically-inspired filters for all the four image perturbations in all the three datasets. Furthermore, the foveal filter-based VGG-16 outperforms the standard VGG-16 against three (Salt & pepper, Gaussian, Dimming) of the four perturbations; there was diminished performance for one of the perturbations (Brightening) compared to the standard VGG-16 for distortions greater than 30–40%. The reason behind this drop in performance is a matter of current investigation and will be reported in a future work. In addition, we will test the Fashion-MNIST dataset on our proposed architecture. Readers may note that our approach has a similarity with [2] who proposed VOneNets where the front layers of CNNs were filters inspired by the primary visual cortex of primates. They too demonstrated better performance by their biologically-inspired CNN architecture. This work is distinct from VOneNets in that the DoG and foveal filters are inspired by the retina. While the Gabor filters are indeed a simulation of the receptive fields of visual cortical cells, this comparison is as in [4].

In summary, our study demonstrates that biologically-inspired filter-based standard ConvNets are better suited for recognition tasks in real world-like perturbed, unseen static scenes. In particular, the foveal filters are remarkably robust to input perturbations, and is a clear winner compared to other biologically-inspired filters.

References

1. Cohen, G., Afshar, S., Tapson, J., Van Schaik, A.: EMNIST: extending MNIST to handwritten letters. In: 2017 International Joint Conference on Neural Networks (IJCNN), pp. 2921–2926. IEEE (2017)
2. Dapello, J., Marques, T., Schrimpf, M., Geiger, F., Cox, D.D., DiCarlo, J.J.: Simulating a primary visual cortex at the front of CNNs improves robustness to image perturbations. In: Advances in Neural Information Processing Systems (NeurIPS) (2020)
3. Deng, L.: The MNIST database of handwritten digit images for machine learning research. IEEE Signal Process. Mag. **29**(6), 141–142 (2012)
4. Evans, B.D., Malhotra, G., Bowers, J.S.: Biological convolutions improve DNN robustness to noise and generalisation. Neural Netw. **148**, 96–110 (2022)
5. Geirhos, R., Janssen, D.H., Schütt, H.H., Rauber, J., Bethge, M., Wichmann, F.A.: Comparing deep neural networks against humans: object recognition when the signal gets weaker. arXiv preprint arXiv:1706.06969 (2017)
6. Gupta, S.T., Sen Bhattacharya, B.: Implementing a foveal-pit inspired filter in a spiking convolutional neural network: a preliminary study. In: International Joint Conference on Neural Networks (IJCNN), pp. 1–8. IEEE (2020)
7. Hopkins, M.W., Fil, J., Jones, E.G., Furber, S.B.: Bitbrain and Sparse Binary Coincidence (SBC) memories: fast, robust learning and inference for neuromorphic architectures. Front. Neuroinform. **17**, 24 (2023)
8. Jones, J.P., Palmer, L.A.: An evaluation of the two-dimensional Gabor filter model of simple receptive fields in cat striate cortex. J. Neurophysiol. **58**(6), 1233–1258 (1987)
9. Krizhevsky, A.: Learning multiple layers of features from tiny images. Master's thesis, University of Toronto (2012)
10. Malhotra, G., Evans, B., Bowers, J.: Adding biological constraints to CNNs makes image classification more human-like and robust. In: Conference on Cognitive Computational Neuroscience (2019)
11. Marĉelja, S.: Mathematical description of the responses of simple cortical cells. J. Opt. Soc. Am. **70**(11), 1297–1300 (1980)
12. Momeny, M., Latif, A.M., Sarram, M.A., Sheikhpour, R., Zhang, Y.D.: A noise robust convolutional neural network for image classification. Results Eng. **10**, 100225 (2021)
13. Pedregosa, F., et al.: Scikit-learn: machine learning in Python. J. Mach. Learn. Res. **12**, 2825–2830 (2011)
14. Rodieck, R.W.: Quantitative analysis of cat retinal ganglion cell response to visual stimuli. Vis. Res. **5**(12), 583–601 (1965)
15. Sen Bhattacharya, B.: Information recovery from rank-order encoded images. Ph.D. thesis, School of Computer Science, University of Manchester (2008)

16. Sen Bhattacharya, B., Furber, S.B.: Biologically inspired means for rank-order encoding images: a quantitative analysis. IEEE Trans. Neural Netw. **21**(7), 1087–1099 (2010)
17. Simonyan, K., Zisserman, A.: Very deep convolutional networks for large-scale image recognition. In: International Conference on Learning Representation (2015)
18. Soto, F., et al.: Efficient coding by midget and parasol ganglion cells in the human retina. Neuron **107**(4), 656–666 (2020)
19. VanRullen, R., Thorpe, S.: Rate coding versus temporal order coding: what the retinal ganglion cells tell the visual cortex. Neural Comput. **13**, 1255–1283 (2001)

Self-Supervised Graph Convolution for Video Moment Retrieval

Xiwen Hu[1], Guolong Wang[2], Shimin Shan[1](✉), Yu Liu[1], and Jiangquan Li[1]

[1] School of Software Technology, Dalian University of Technology, Dalian, China
huxw586@mail.dlut.edu.cn, {ssm,yuliu}@dlut.edu.cn

[2] School of Information Technology & Management, University of International Business and Economics, Beijing, China
wangguolong@uibe.edu.cn

Abstract. Video Moment Retrieval is a task locating a moment from an untrimmed video that are relevant to a given query. It is a highly challenging multi-modal task due to biased annotations and complex cross-model interaction. In this paper, we propose Self-Supervised Graph Convolution Network (SSGCN) for video moment retrieval. For biased annotations, we design a self-supervised auxiliary task to mine feature representation of inherit video and text information by randomly dropout moment-text relation. For complex cross-modal interaction, we use two Graph Convolutional Networks to obtain feature representations of both the video and text modalities. The feature representations of the two modalities are then used to acquire cross-modal information through cross-attention layers, which is treated as implicit graph matching edges to update the graph neural network. The effectiveness of the proposed model is validated through extensive experiments.

Keywords: Self-Supervised · GCN · Moment Retrieval · InfoNCE · Cross-Attention

1 Introduction

Video Moment Retrieval (VMR), also known as Natural Language Temporal Grounding or Temporal Sentence Grounding, has been brought to the fore by the heavy demand for multimedia retrieval. This task is to retrieve or locate video moments that are semantically related to a given query, which is particularly challenging because natural language descriptions of activity are flexible and complex. As shown in Fig. 1, given a query "Person opens a cabinet" and a corresponding video, the task is to locate the moment that best matches the query. The key to accurately locate the target moment is cross-modal reasoning. The recent methods have achieved high performance by learning multi-modal fusion with large-scale annotations [21,33]. However, its real application is hindered by biased annotations [1,27] and complex cross-modal relationship [29]. Therefore,

L. Iliadis et al. (Eds.): ICANN 2023, LNCS 14263, pp. 407–419, 2023.
https://doi.org/10.1007/978-3-031-44204-9_34

we propose a Self-Supervised Graph Convolution Network (SSGCN) by integrating a self-supervised objective into a graph matching framework between video and text.

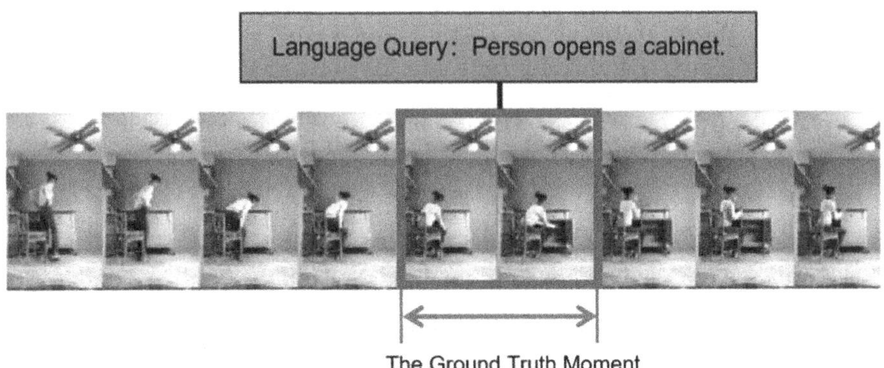

Fig. 1. An illustration of moment retrieval in an untrimmed video through a language query.

We utilize self-supervised contrastive learning to discover temporal relationship from data without annotations, aiming at solving biased annotations. Inspired by self-supervised methods [22] used in recommendation systems, we design a self-supervised auxiliary task to encourage our model to explore hard negative samples in multimodal interaction. Specifically, we randomly drop out the multimodal interaction information obtained by cross-attention, and then update the graph to obtain different views of the same video snippet or text token feature. We use InfoNCE to make the different views of the same snippet closer in the same subspace, while pushing different snippets' views further apart.

We adopt a proposal-based method using Graph Convolutional Networks (GCN) to obtain complex cross-modal relationship. Inspired by [17], we use GCN to capture high-order relationship among video moments and moment-query pairs. For video features, we extracted temporal and semantic information from video snippets to help the cross-modal model better understand the video context. For example, "first open a cabinet" and "second open a cabinet" have the same action but different temporal orders. For text features, we use a GCN to model the semantic relationships between words. After obtaining richer contextual information, we integrated the video and text features through cross-attention layers to obtain their interactive information. The interactive information can implicitly express the matching relationship between the video graph and the text graph, and thus update the GCN with this matching relationship. The overall contributions are as follows:

- We design a self-supervised task to make model learn from both annotations and data, in case they are biased by annotations.

- We adopt an implicit graph matching framework learning compound feature representation after cross-modal interaction and generate corresponding candidate proposals.
- Experiments validate the efficacy of our SSGCN on public datasets: Charades-STA [35] and ActivityNet-Captions [36].

2 Related Work

Video Moment Retrieval. Video Moment Retrieval can be categorized into three types according to the level of supervision: supervised, weakly supervised, and unsupervised [19]. The weakly supervised types can be further divided into three subtypes: multiple instance learning (MIL) [13,14,23], reconstruction [4,8,18], and reinforcement learning [2,9,23]. There are fewer related models of unsupervised type, so no universal classification has been produced. In this paper, we focus on supervised methods, which can be broadly classified into two types: proposal-based [3,25,26,34] and proposal-free [12,20,28,31,32]. Proposal-based methods generate multiple candidate proposals with different scales and rank them according to their matching scores with the ground-truth moment. Proposal-free methods directly predict the timestamps of the matching moment by cross-modal interaction of video and text features. Similar to these proposal-based method, our model SSGCN is also a proposal-based method.

Self-supervised Learning. Self-supervised learning aims to mine the intrinsic representation features of unlabeled data by designing auxiliary tasks as supervision signals, thereby enhancing the feature expression ability of the model. For example, BERT [6] enhances the ability of semantic understanding by masking some words and then predicting the masked part; in image processing, data augmentation methods such as cropping [7,16], changing color [30], rotating [11], etc. are often used to learn more rich knowledge. In videos, contrastive self-supervised learning [5,10] is commonly used, which is to construct representations by encoding the similarity or dissimilarity of two things, and to achieve self-supervised learning by constructing positive and negative samples and measuring the distance between them. We also apply data augmentation to video snippets and construct positive and negative examples to help SSGCN learn more semantic information.

GCN-Based Learning. GCN can capture the global information and the inter-node relationships of the graph, and enable information propagation across multiple domains through multi-layer graph convolution. Existing models [17,31,34] represent video frames and text queries as two graphs respectively, and then use GCN to learn the interactions between frames and queries, and finally use an attention mechanism to locate the moment in the video that corresponds to the query. Therefore, our SSGCN also leverages GCN to acquire more rich contextual knowledge, which facilitates the learning of multimodal feature representation.

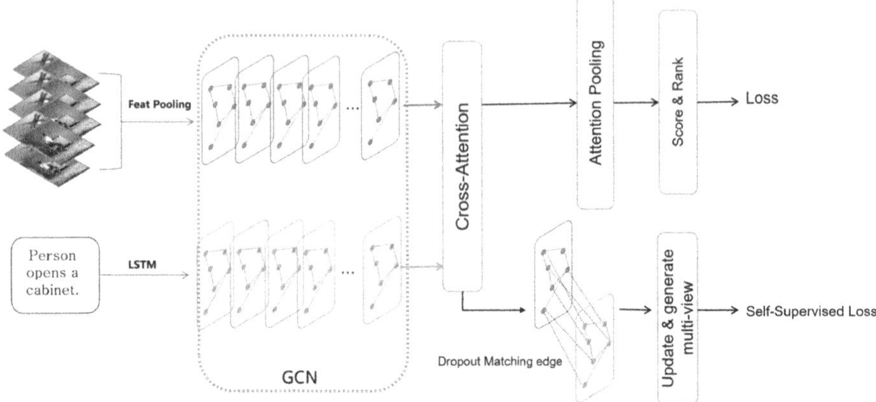

Fig. 2. Model Architecture. The inputs are token embeddings and snippet features. The video features are processed through feature pooling and graph convolution, while the text features are processed through LSTM and graph convolution. The cross-attention layer enables cross-modal interactions between graphs and updates the graph accordingly. We randomly dropout some implicit edges generated by cross-attention, thereby updating the graph and generating different views to construct the self-supervised loss InfoNCE. The retrieval loss is the same as previous work, relying on cross-modal interactive feature representation to generate candidate proposals and rank them.

3 Proposed Method

3.1 Problem Formulation

Our task aims to retrieval the best matching moment, given an untrimmed video $V = \{v_i\}_{i=1}^{n_v}$ and a language query $Q = \{q_i\}_{i=1}^{n_q}$, where v_i represents a video snippet, and q_i represent a token. As we adopt a proposal-based method, we generate m candidate moments, the i-th moment with its own start and end timestamps $t_{s,i}$, $t_{e,i}$, as well as the calculated matching score s_n.

3.2 Model Architecture

This section gives an overview of the whole model architecture, as illustrated in Fig. 2. Video features are enriched with semantic and temporal information through the feature pooling layer and GCN network, to enhance the overall visual representation. Text features are modeled with LSTM and SyntacGCN to capture temporal and semantic contextual knowledge based on the natural language syntax. After obtaining the feature representations of each modality, cross-attention layers are applied to obtain the cross-modal attention of text-to-video and video-to-text, which can be interpreted as implicitly modeling the matching edges between the video and text graphs and updating the original graph feature representations accordingly. We will introduce how to generate InfoNCE in detail in Sect. 2.4. The updated graph features are then used to generate n candidate proposals through attention pooling, and the proposals are finally scored with a multi-layer perceptron to predict the top-k moments.

3.3 Video Representation and Text Representation

Video Representation. To obtain temporal information from video features, we added positional encoding to the original C3D video features before feature pooling. As the features go through the GCN process, we explicitly encode both the temporal and semantic features of the video features, constructing both temporal and semantic edges. For temporal edges, we use multi-layer convolution to obtain temporal information. For semantic edges, we adopt k-nearest neighbor algorithm to obtain semantically related clusters and apply convolution to model the semantic information between moments based on the current moment.

$$V_{i+1} = (V_i + T_{i+1} + S_{i+1}), \tag{1}$$

In Eq. 1, V_{i+1}, T_{i+1} and S_{i+1} represents the result, the temporal information and semantic information after the i-th convolution, respectively. This information updated by modality interaction in turn update the features of the graph, thus dynamically modeling the temporal and semantic information, as modality interaction can change the original clustering. Eq. 2 and 3 are update functions for the graph, which consists of several convolutions. $A_{q2v,i}$ represents the attention of the textual query Q on the video V during the modality interaction. W_s and W_t respectively represent the weights for updating the semantic graph and the temporal graph.

$$S^v_{i+1} = update(V_i, A_{q2v,i}, W_s), \tag{2}$$

$$T^v_{i+1} = update(V_i, A_{q2v,i}, W_t), \tag{3}$$

Text Representation. The query features Q are captured by LSTM to obtain semantic and sequential information. Then, SyntacGCN is used to model the predefined syntax rules by Standford-NLP, which can effectively capture the grammatical relationships between words. By using the grammatical relationships between words, it is convenient to construct the adjacency matrix of the text graph. The process can be summarized as follows:

$$Q_{i+1} = SyntacGCN(Q_i, A_{v2q,i}). \tag{4}$$

SyntacGCN function is used to model the syntactic information of sentence tokens. The attention weight A_{v2q} (video feature to query feature) will modify the feature representation of Q, which is used for language graph updating.

3.4 Cross-Attention and Self-supervised

Cross-Attention. We use cross-attention to calculate the Query, Key, and Value of the video V and text query Q separately to better interact information between different modalities. We obtain similarity weight a_{v2q} by using $Query_v$ to calculate the similarity between Key_q (e.g., dot product) and normalization. a_{v2q} is used to weight the value, obtaining attention A_{v2q}. Similarly, we obtain A_{q2v}. Accordingly, we can pass back the updated graph structure to the graph neural network, as shown in Eqs. 2, 3, and 4.

We calculate cross-modal attention during the interaction between the video graph and the text graph. We regard the attention as implicit edges representing relationship between nodes. Therefore, we can use these implicit edges for data augmentation to generate multiple views. Specifically, we randomly dropout some edges on A_{v2q} and A_{q2v}, as shown below:

$$A^{'}_{v2q} = Randomdrop(A_{v2q} \odot M^{'}), \quad A^{''}_{v2q} = Randomdrop(A_{v2q} \odot M^{''}) \tag{5}$$

where $M^{'}$ and $M^{''}$ are two vectors used for attention masking. Since we consider attention as implicit edges, the semantic relationship between text and video nodes depends on the value of attention. Using the two newly generated $A^{'}_{v2q}$ and $A^{''}_{v2q}$ to update the graph can produce two different views. Combining these two views together can better capture local structural information of nodes. Similarly, the operation in Eq. 5. is also applied to A_{q2v}.

Self-supervised. After obtaining the two augmentable views of the text and video graph nodes, we consider them as positive pairs (i.e., $(V^{'}_i, V^{''}_i) \mid i \in n_v$) and different node views as negative pairs(i.e.,$(V^{'}_i, V^{''}_j) \mid i, j \in n_v$). To encourage consistency between different views of the same node and enhance the divergence between negative pairs, we can use InfoNCE to maximize the similarity of positive pairs and minimize the similarity of negative pairs:

$$\mathcal{L}_{ssl}^{video} = \sum_{u \in \mathcal{U}} -\log \frac{\exp\left(s\left(\mathbf{v}_i', \mathbf{v}_i''\right)/\tau\right)}{\sum_{v \in \mathcal{U}} \exp\left(s\left(\mathbf{v}_i', \mathbf{v}_j''\right)/\tau\right)}, \tag{6}$$

where $s(\cdot)$ represents the cosine similarity function used to calculate the similarity between two vectors, and τ is a hyperparameter representing the temperature parameter. Equation 6. can also be used to calculate the self-supervised contrastive loss for natural language queries $\mathcal{L}_{ssl}^{query}$. Combining the two losses, we obtain the objective loss function as $\mathcal{L}_{ssl} = \mathcal{L}_{ssl}^{video} + \mathcal{L}_{ssl}^{query}$ generated by the self-supervised process.

3.5 Loss Function

To improve the moment retrieval task, we adopt a multi-task training strategy to jointly optimize the traditional proposal-based task. Therefore, we need to obtain the IOU between the generated proposals and ground-truth to determine the retrieval effect. So we encode the generated candidate proposals through an additional mapping module, which encodes them into start and end timestamps $(t_{s,k}, t_{e,k} \mid k \in (0, m))$. We then calculate the IOU with the groundtruth using an MLP, which serves as an evaluation score (i.e., the i-th candidate proposals evaluation score is $score_i$). This allows us to easily supervise the score prediction process with a cross-entropy loss function:

$$\mathcal{L}_{main} = \frac{1}{m}\sum_{i=1}^{m} p_i \log(score_i) + (1 - p_i) \log(1 - score_i), \tag{7}$$

Where p_i is the label we assign to the i-th proposal, and let (b_1, b_2) be a threshold. If the $score_i$ is greater than b_2, then $p = 1$. If the score is less than b_1, then $p = 0$. If the $score_i$ is between b1 and b2, then $p = (score_i - b_1)/(b_2 - b_1)$. Thus, we obtain our total loss function by combining the self-supervised loss function and the localization loss function.

$$\mathcal{L} = \mathcal{L}_{main} + \lambda * \mathcal{L}_{ssl} \tag{8}$$

4 Experiment

4.1 Experiment Setting

Datasets. (1)ActivityNet-Caption is a dataset for dense captioning of video events. It is built on activitynet v1.3, which contains 20k untrimmed YouTube videos, each with 100k sentence descriptions with temporal boundaries. The videos are 120 s long on average. Most of the videos have over 3 annotated events with corresponding start/end time and human-written sentences, which have 13.5 words on average. (2)Charades-STA is a dataset for finding the part of a video that matches a sentence. It is based on Charades, which has videos of people doing daily activities. Charades-STA adds the start and end time of each sentence in the video. The dataset has 9848 videos and 16128 video-sentence pairs.

Implementation Details. We use StanfordNLP to extract the semantic relations of tokens in the text, and use the GloVe pre-trained model to obtain the feature representation of the text. For video features, we directly use the Charades-STA features pre-trained by C3D and the official ActivityNet features. All hidden dimensions of convolutional networks or pooling blocks in our experiments are set to 512. The settings of graph convolutional networks follow those of VLGNet [17]. We use the Adam optimizer and set the learning rate to 0.005. We set the number of snippets to 64 and produce 784 candidate proposals for each video based on this. The self-supervised loss function weights λ are set to 0.001 on Charades dataset and 0.01 on ActivityNet dataset. Our IOU threshold is set to $(0.5, 0.7)$. We run our experiments on a NVIDIA 3090.

Evaluation Metrics. We evaluate the model's performance using the metric $R\ n@m$, following [17]. This defines the predicted score as the percentage of top-n proposals with an IOU greater than m, and typically this percentage is multiplied by 100 for ease of viewing. Typically, we set n to (1, 5) and m to (0.5, 0.7).

4.2 Results and Discussion

Results on Charades-STA. As shown in Table 1, the table is divided into three parts. The first part is the proposal-free method, which does not need to generate intermediate proposals and directly predicts the timestamps. The second part is the proposal-based method, which needs to first generate candidate proposals, then rank them by matching scores and finally predict the results. Our model also belongs to the proposal-based category, as it also needs to generate proposals first. On the $R1@0.7$ metric, we outperform the state-of-the-art proposal-based methods, but slightly underperform the best proposal-free method. However, our model achieves the best results on $R5@0.5$ and $R5@0.7$. Our model demonstrates its effectiveness, especially on metric $R5$. We attribute this to the enhanced semantic learning from the modality interaction and the self-supervised clustering of positive examples, which widens the margin between positive and negative examples. As a result, our model achieves a larger improvement on top-5 and a smaller improvement on top-1.

Table 1. Moment Retrieval on Charades-STA.

Method	$R1@0.5$	$R1@0.7$	$R5@0.5$	$R5@0.7$
CBP [20]	36.80	18.87	70.94	50.19
2D-TAN [32]	39.81	**23.25**	79.33	**52.15**
MS-2D-TAN [31]	41.10	**23.25**	**81.53**	48.55
SV-VMR [24]	38.09	19.98	66.37	38.15
I2N [15]	**41.69**	22.88	75.73	46.85
QSPN [26]	35.60	15.80	79.40	45.40
SAP [3]	27.42	13.36	66.37	38.15
BPNet [25]	38.25	20.51	–	–
MIGCN [34]	**42.36**	**22.04**	–	–
SSGCN(ours.)	38.36	**22.74**	**82.20**	**59.20**

Results on ActivityNet. Table 2 follows the same structure as Table 1, dividing the models into proposal-free, proposal-based, and our own categories. It shows that our model achieves the best performance in $R1@0.7$ and $R5@0.7$, and outperforms the baseline model VLGNet in other metrics as well. Moreover, our model ranks second in $R1@0.5$ and $R5@0.5$. These results indicate that our model can effectively reduce the distance between positive pairs and increase the distance between negative pairs by using self-supervised methods.

The Effectiveness of Self-supervised Learning. This subsection focuses on the effect of self-supervised learning on the model. We compare models with

Table 2. Moment Retrieval on ActivityNet.

Method	$R1@0.5$	$R1@0.7$	$R5@0.5$	$R5@0.7$
CBP [20]	35.76	17.80	65.89	46.20
CMIN [34]	44.62	24.48	69.66	52.96
2D-TAN [32]	44.05	27.38	76.65	62.26
MS-2D-TAN [31]	46.16	29.21	**78.80**	60.85
DRN [28]	45.45	24.36	77.97	50.30
CSMGAN [12]	**49.11**	29.15	77.43	59.63
QSPN [26]	27.70	13.60	59.20	38.30
BPNet [25]	42.07	24.69	–	–
VLGNet [17]	46.32	**29.82**	**77.15**	**63.33**
SSGCN(ours.)	**47.01**	**30.73**	**78.49**	**65.26**

and without self-supervised structures. We examine how they differ on various metrics when they have the same initial parameters. We use data augmentation to create multiple views of the same snippets/words and apply the contrastive learning loss function InfoNCE to learn how to distinguish positive and negative samples. Since we do not introduce any new structures or parameters, it is fair to directly compare the model with its variants. Table 3 shows that the model with self-supervised learning performs better on ActivityNet, which means that self-supervised learning can help the model separate positive and negative samples better on the dataset. On Charades-STA, our model is slightly worse than w/o. self-attention on R1 metric, but much better on $R5$. We think that the videos on Charades-STA dataset are shorter than on ActivityNet dataset, so a snippet contains less information, which makes it harder for us to differentiate top-1 proposal from other positive examples.

Table 3. Explore the variants of our model and test them on Charades-STA and ActivityNet-Captions datasets with and without self-supervised learning.

	Charades-STA				ActivityNet-Captions			
Method	R1@0.5	R1@0.7	R5@0.5	R5@0.7	R1@0.5	R1@0.7	R5@0.5	R5@0.7
SSGCN w/o. ssl	39.01	**23.41**	80.00	57.34	46.35	29.59	77.26	64.04
SSGCN w/o. temp	**39.97**	22.47	79.41	55.35	44.76	28.51	74.90	59.97
SSGCN(ours.)	38.36	22.74	**82.20**	**59.20**	**47.01**	**30.73**	**78.49**	**65.26**

The Effectiveness of Model Temporal Feature. We discuss the role of explicitly modeling the temporal information of videos in two scenarios, as described in Sect. 3.3. First, we compare two groups of video features: one with temporal information of the modeled videos and one without it (SSGCN w/o. temp). Referring to Eq. 1, we remove the part of T_{i+1} so that the video feature representation is $V_{i+1} = (V_i + S_{i+1})$ to construct a video representation without temporal feature. As Table 3 shows, on Charades-STA, SSGCN w/o. temp performs worse than SSGCN w/o. ssl and the original model on all metrics except $R1@0.5$, suggesting that temporal information is beneficial for video understanding. Moreover, on Activitynet-caption, SSGCN w/o. temp performs worst on all metrics. Therefore, we conclude that SSGCN explicitly models time information to enhance the model's ability to capture contextual knowledge and improve feature representation.

Second, we selected natural query sentences from the original test dataset of Charades-STA that explicitly contain temporal order words to form a new test dataset. These words can help humans distinguish the same actions that occur at different times, such as "first", "second", "before", "after", "next", etc. Table 4 demonstrates that our model outperforms the baselines on $R1$, and also achieves a significant improvement on $R5$ where our iou is greater than 0.7. The 2D-TAN model dropped a lot on the $R1$ metric, but less on the $R5$ metric, which means that 2D-TAN can capture the semantic information between video snippets and query texts well. However, our SSGCN model achieved better results on $R1@0.7$ and $R5$ metrics, indicating that it can better distinguish temporal information compared to the previous model. It shows similar results to Table 3 on $R5@0.5$, our model only slightly worse on this metric. This also suggests that modeling the temporal feature in videos explicitly is beneficial for video understanding.

Table 4. We selected a new test dataset consisting of video-query pairs in which the query sentences clearly indicate the temporal order of words, and we tested our model on this dataset.

Method	$R1@0.5$	$R1@0.7$	$R5@0.5$	$R5@0.7$
2D-TAN [32]	19.44	8.33	**80.56**	38.89
SSGCN w/o. temp	**30.56**	13.89	72.22	55.56
SSGCN(ours.)	27.78	**16.67**	**80.56**	**63.89**

5 Conclusion

We propose Self-Supervised Graph Convolution for Moment Retrieval, which uses GCN to obtain richer feature representations of video and text. This enables us to acquire more abundant interactive information in modality interaction, which helps generate better candidate proposals. We then improve the feature representation of interactive information through self-supervised learning and contrastive learning. The experiments also demonstrate the positive effect of self-supervision on feature representation learning. Finally, we tune the model with a combination of localization loss and self-supervised loss, which leads our model to learn complex cross-modal relation while alleviating the biased annotations.

Acknowledgements. This work was supported by the Dalian Key Field Innovation Team Support Plan (Grant: 2020RT07).

References

1. Wang, G., Wu, X., Liu, Z., Qin, Z.: Reducing 0s bias in video moment retrieval with a circular competence-based captioner. Inf. Process. Manage. **60**(2), 103147 (2023)
2. Cao, D., Zeng, Y., Liu, M., He, X., Wang, M., Qin, Z.: Strong: spatio-temporal reinforcement learning for cross-modal video moment localization. In: Proceedings of the 28th ACM International Conference on Multimedia, pp. 4162–4170 (2020)
3. Chen, S., Jiang, Y.G.: Semantic proposal for activity localization in videos via sentence query. In: Proceedings of the AAAI Conference on Artificial Intelligence, vol. 33, pp. 8199–8206 (2019)
4. Chen, S., Jiang, Y.G.: Towards bridging event captioner and sentence localizer for weakly supervised dense event captioning. In: Proceedings of the IEEE/CVF Conference on Computer Vision and Pattern Recognition, pp. 8425–8435 (2021)
5. Chen, T., Kornblith, S., Norouzi, M., Hinton, G.: A simple framework for contrastive learning of visual representations. In: International Conference on Machine Learning, pp. 1597–1607. PMLR (2020)
6. Devlin, J., Chang, M.W., Lee, K., Toutanova, K.: BERT: pre-training of deep bidirectional transformers for language understanding. arXiv preprint arXiv:1810.04805 (2018)
7. Doersch, C., Gupta, A., Efros, A.A.: Unsupervised visual representation learning by context prediction. In: Proceedings of the IEEE International Conference on Computer Vision, pp. 1422–1430 (2015)
8. Duan, X., Huang, W., Gan, C., Wang, J., Zhu, W., Huang, J.: Weakly supervised dense event captioning in videos. In: Advances in Neural Information Processing Systems, vol. 31 (2018)
9. Hahn, M., Kadav, A., Rehg, J.M., Graf, H.P.: Tripping through time: efficient localization of activities in videos. arXiv preprint arXiv:1904.09936 (2019)
10. He, K., Fan, H., Wu, Y., Xie, S., Girshick, R.: Momentum contrast for unsupervised visual representation learning. In: Proceedings of the IEEE/CVF Conference on Computer Vision and Pattern Recognition, pp. 9729–9738 (2020)
11. Lee, H., Hwang, S.J., Shin, J.: Self-supervised label augmentation via input transformations. In: International Conference on Machine Learning, pp. 5714–5724. PMLR (2020)
12. Liu, D., Qu, X., Liu, X.Y., Dong, J., Zhou, P., Xu, Z.: Jointly cross-and self-modal graph attention network for query-based moment localization. In: Proceedings of the 28th ACM International Conference on Multimedia, pp. 4070–4078 (2020)
13. Ma, M., Yoon, S., Kim, J., Lee, Y., Kang, S., Yoo, C.D.: VLANet: video-language alignment network for weakly-supervised video moment retrieval. In: Vedaldi, A., Bischof, H., Brox, T., Frahm, J.-M. (eds.) ECCV 2020. LNCS, vol. 12373, pp. 156–171. Springer, Cham (2020). https://doi.org/10.1007/978-3-030-58604-1_10
14. Mithun, N.C., Paul, S., Roy-Chowdhury, A.K.: Weakly supervised video moment retrieval from text queries (2019)

15. Ning, K., Xie, L., Liu, J., Wu, F., Tian, Q.: Interaction-integrated network for natural language moment localization. IEEE Trans. Image Process. **30**, 2538–2548 (2021)
16. Noroozi, M., Favaro, P.: Unsupervised learning of visual representations by Solving Jigsaw puzzles. In: Leibe, B., Matas, J., Sebe, N., Welling, M. (eds.) ECCV 2016. LNCS, vol. 9910, pp. 69–84. Springer, Cham (2016). https://doi.org/10.1007/978-3-319-46466-4_5
17. Soldan, M., Xu, M., Qu, S., Tegner, J., Ghanem, B.: Vlg-net: video-language graph matching network for video grounding. In: Proceedings of the IEEE/CVF International Conference on Computer Vision, pp. 3224–3234 (2021)
18. Song, Y., Wang, J., Ma, L., Yu, Z., Yu, J.: Weakly-supervised multi-level attentional reconstruction network for grounding textual queries in videos. arXiv preprint arXiv:2003.07048 (2020)
19. Wang, G., Wu, X., Liu, Z., Yan, J.: Prompt-based zero-shot video moment retrieval. In: ACMMM, pp. 413–421 (2022)
20. Wang, J., Ma, L., Jiang, W.: Temporally grounding language queries in videos by contextual boundary-aware prediction. In: Proceedings of the AAAI Conference on Artificial Intelligence, vol. 34, pp. 12168–12175 (2020)
21. Wang, Y., Liu, M., Wei, Y., Cheng, Z., Wang, Y., Nie, L.: Siamese alignment network for weakly supervised video moment retrieval. IEEE Trans. Multimedia (2022)
22. Wu, J., et al.: Self-supervised graph learning for recommendation. In: Proceedings of the 44th International ACM SIGIR Conference on Research and Development in Information Retrieval, pp. 726–735 (2021)
23. Wu, J., Li, G., Han, X., Lin, L.: Reinforcement learning for weakly supervised temporal grounding of natural language in untrimmed videos. In: Proceedings of the 28th ACM International Conference on Multimedia, pp. 1283–1291 (2020)
24. Wu, Z., Gao, J., Huang, S., Xu, C.: Diving into the relations: leveraging semantic and visual structures for video moment retrieval. In: 2021 IEEE International Conference on Multimedia and Expo (ICME), pp. 1–6. IEEE (2021)
25. Xiao, S., et al.: Boundary proposal network for two-stage natural language video localization. In: Proceedings of the AAAI Conference on Artificial Intelligence, vol. 35, pp. 2986–2994 (2021)
26. Xu, H., He, K., Plummer, B.A., Sigal, L., Sclaroff, S., Saenko, K.: Multilevel language and vision integration for text-to-clip retrieval. In: Proceedings of the AAAI Conference on Artificial Intelligence, vol. 33, pp. 9062–9069 (2019)
27. Yuan, Y., Lan, X., Chen, L., Liu, W., Wang, X., Zhu, W.: A closer look at temporal sentence grounding in videos: dataset and metric. In: Proceedings of the 2nd International Workshop on Human-Centric Multimedia Analysis (2021)
28. Zeng, R., Xu, H., Huang, W., Chen, P., Tan, M., Gan, C.: Dense regression network for video grounding. In: Proceedings of the IEEE/CVF Conference on Computer Vision and Pattern Recognition, pp. 10287–10296 (2020)
29. Zeng, Y., Cao, D., Wei, X., Liu, M., Zhao, Z., Qin, Z.: Multi-modal relational graph for cross-modal video moment retrieval. In: Proceedings of the IEEE/CVF Conference on Computer Vision and Pattern Recognition, pp. 2215–2224 (2021)
30. Zhang, R., Isola, P., Efros, A.A.: Colorful image colorization. In: Leibe, B., Matas, J., Sebe, N., Welling, M. (eds.) ECCV 2016. LNCS, vol. 9907, pp. 649–666. Springer, Cham (2016). https://doi.org/10.1007/978-3-319-46487-9_40
31. Zhang, S., Peng, H., Fu, J., Lu, Y., Luo, J.: Multi-scale 2D temporal adjacency networks for moment localization with natural language. IEEE Trans. Pattern Anal. Mach. Intell. **44**(12), 9073–9087 (2021)

32. Zhang, S., Peng, H., Fu, J., Luo, J.: Learning 2D temporal adjacent networks for moment localization with natural language. In: Proceedings of the AAAI Conference on Artificial Intelligence, vol. 34, pp. 12870–12877 (2020)
33. Zhang, Y., Chen, X., Jia, J., Liu, S., Ding, K.: Text-visual prompting for efficient 2D temporal video grounding. In: Proceedings of the IEEE/CVF Conference on Computer Vision and Pattern Recognition (2023)
34. Zhang, Z., Lin, Z., Zhao, Z., Xiao, Z.: Cross-modal interaction networks for query-based moment retrieval in videos. In: Proceedings of the 42nd International ACM SIGIR Conference on Research and Development in Information Retrieval, pp. 655–664 (2019)
35. Sigurdsson, G.A., Varol, G., Wang, X., Farhadi, A., Laptev, I., Gupta, A.: Hollywood in homes: crowdsourcing data collection for activity understanding. In: Leibe, B., Matas, J., Sebe, N., Welling, M. (eds.) ECCV 2016. LNCS, vol. 9905, pp. 510–526. Springer, Cham (2016). https://doi.org/10.1007/978-3-319-46448-0_31
36. Krishna, R., Hata, K., Ren, F., Fei-Fei, L., Carlos Niebles, J.: Dense-captioning events in videos. In: Proceedings of the IEEE International Conference on Computer Vision, pp. 706–715 (2017)

Siamese Network Based on MLP and Multi-head Cross Attention for Visual Object Tracking

Piaoyang Li[1], Shiyong Lan[1(✉)], Shipeng Sun[1], Wenwu Wang[2], Yongyang Gao[1], Yongyu Yang[1], and Guangyu Yu[1]

[1] College of Computer Science, Sichuan University, Chengdu, China
lanshiyong@scu.edu.cn

[2] University of Surrey, Guildford GU2 7XH, UK

Abstract. Visual object tracking is an important prerequisite in many applications. However, the performance of the tracking system is often affected by the quality of the visual object's feature representation and whether it can identify the best match of the target template in the search area. To alleviate these challenges, we propose a new method based on Multi-Layer Perceptron (MLP) and multi-head cross attention. First, a new MLP-based module is designed to enhance the input features, by refining the internal association between the spatial and channel dimensions of these features. Second, an improved head network is constructed for predicting the location of the target, in which the multi-head cross attention mechanism is used to find the optimal matching between the template and the search area. Experiments on four datasets show that the proposed method offers competitive tracking performance as compared with several recent baseline methods. The codes will be available at https://github.com/SYLan2019/MLP-MHCA.

Keywords: Visual Object Tracking · Siamese Network · Attention

1 Introduction

Visual object tracking is an active field of research in computer vision. Traditional tracking algorithms are based on either generative or discriminative models. In generative algorithms [1], the target features are extracted for constructing an appearance model and then matched with those from the searching area. However, the performance of the generative models degrades in a complex environment, in the presence of illumination changes and occlusions. The discriminative models [4,5,9,17,30,31] convert the tracking problem into a classification and localization problem. To effectively identify the target in the search area, it is crucial to obtain robust and accurate feature representations for the targets.

This work was funded by 2035 Innovation Pilot Program of Sichuan University, China.

L. Iliadis et al. (Eds.): ICANN 2023, LNCS 14263, pp. 420–431, 2023.
https://doi.org/10.1007/978-3-031-44204-9_35

One of the most classic discriminative models is the Siam network [2], which simply translates the tracking problem into a problem of learning the matching between the target template and the search area. Siamese-based trackers usually consist of a backbone network and a head network, in which the backbone network is used to extract features, and the head network is used for target classification and localization. Existing Siamese-based trackers can be divided into convolutional neural networks (CNN)-based Siamese trackers [2,18] and Transformer-based Siamese trackers [5–7]. In CNN-based Siamese trackers [2], the target template is used to match with the search area through sliding convolution, and the area with the maximum response value is then obtained as the target position. However, during the correlation operation, CNN-based Siamese trackers tend to give locally optimal solutions, as the correlation operation itself is a local linear matching process [5]. In Transformer-based Siamese trackers [5,7], the correlation operation is replaced with Transformer, which can prevent the algorithm from converging to local minimum with the global information extracted from the image, but the entire transformer architecture leads to a high computational load.

Recently, several studies have been performed on replacing transformers with more efficient methods. For example, Tolstikhi et al [27] advocated that using only MLP can achieve the same performance as using transformers in visual classification tasks, but with significantly improved computational efficiency. Motivated by this work, we introduce MLPs in our tracking task to enhance feature representations, in order to improve the discrimination of the target in the search area for target localization. In addition, we design a simple cross attention module followed by another MLP for predicting the location of the target, rather than using a correlation operation between the template and the search area as used in previous work [2].

Our main contributions can be summarized as follows:

- We propose a new tracking framework based on MLPs and multi-head cross attention. In our proposed framework, a new MLP-based module is designed to enhance the feature representation by associating the channel and the spatial information within the input features. Our ablation experiments show the effectiveness of our modification.
- An improved head network is constructed with simple multi-head cross attention instead of using a conventional correlation filter for predicting the position of the target in a local search area.
- Extensive experiments on the OTB2015, UAV123, NFS, and VOT2020 datasets show that the proposed method outperforms the compared baselines.

2 Proposed Approach

2.1 Architecture

The architecture of the Siamese network that we propose for object tracking can be divided into three parts: backbone for feature extraction, neck network

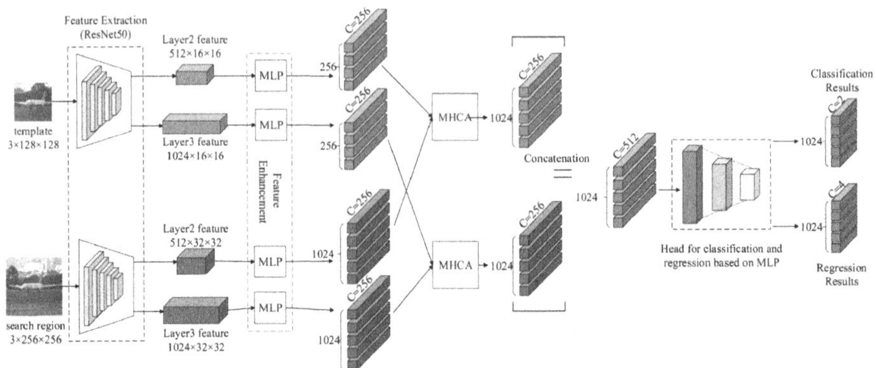

Fig. 1. The framework of the proposed Siamese network based on MLPs and multi head cross attention.

for feature enhancement, and head network for classification and regression, as shown in Fig. 1. Unlike TransT [5], our backbone Resnet50 extracts the features of different layers, including semantic information from deep layers and textural information from shallow layers, that are helpful for improving the performance of classification and regression [6]. In addition, we utilize a feature enhancement module based on MLPs to extract features at different scales and improve the ability of the network in feature representation. In the head network, we design an efficient multi-head cross attention to overcome local optimization problems of target localization in the search area.

2.2 Feature Enhancement Module Based on MLP

Convolution pays more attention to the spatial information on the feature map and ignores the information on the channel dimension. Here, we propose a feature enhancement network based on multi-layer perceptron to enhance the features. As shown in Fig. 2, the features extracted by the backbone are first passed through layer normalization, then they are reshaped and input into a multi-layer perception composed of two fully-connected layers and a GeLU [14] activation layer. Then, we reshape them and feed them into the next multilayer perceptron. That is, the spatial feature is extracted first, followed by the channel-wise feature. As shown in Fig. 1, we extract the features of the second and third layers in Resnet50, whose channel dimensions are 512 and 1024, respectively. To ensure that the feature dimensions from different layers are consistent to enable feature fusion, we chose to employ two fully-connected layers to lower the channel dimension. In this way, we can aggregate spatial features to achieve feature enhancement, in addition, we can reduce the computational cost to some extent.

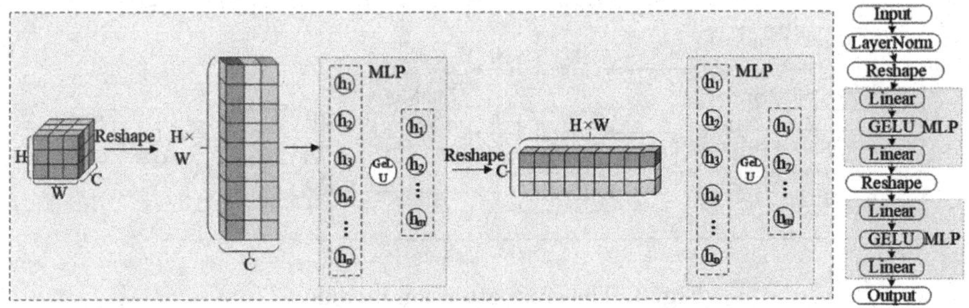

Fig. 2. Feature enhancement network based on MLP. The left figure shows the core idea, while the right shows the general process. The *linear* operation in the right figure corresponds to a full-connected layer in MLP. In addition, channel interaction is achieved in each Mixer operation by applying one-dimensional global average pooling and one-dimensional fully connected layers. The global average pooling captures global statistical information for each channel, while the fully connected layers in Mixer operation learn weights to model the relationships between channels.

2.3 Head Network Based on Multi-head Cross Attention (MHCA)

Existing Siamese network trackers use correlation operations [31] to find similarity between the template and the search area. However, the usual correlation operation itself is a local linear matching process [5], which is prone to taking the local optimal matching as the final result. To solve this problem, we introduce a multi-head cross attention module to identify the similarity between them and retains semantic features, as shown in Fig. 3. To determine the relationship between the features from the template and the features from the search region, we use the search region feature of dimension 1024×256 as K and V, and the template feature of dimension 256×256 as Q. Then, Q and K are passed through two different fully-connected layers, and then multiplied with each other. After that, the shape becomes 1024×256, then this result is mapped to the V vector (i.e., by multiplying the matrix with V). Finally, it is passed through the fully-connected layer to adjust the number of channels. In this way, we replace the correlation operations with the multi-head cross attention mechanism. The following is the initial cross-attention formula:

$$SelfAttention(Q, K, V) = softmax(\frac{QK^T}{\sqrt{d_k}})V \tag{1}$$

To construct the head networks, we use two cross-attention structures in our approach. The results are spliced through the channels to decrease the number of parameters. The formula is given as:

$$MultiHead(Q, K, V) = Linear(Concat(H_1, H_2)) \tag{2}$$

where $Concat(\cdot)$ means concatenate operation, H_1 and H_2 are the output of the MHCA module. The $Linear(\cdot)$ operation is achieved with a fully-connected layer that controls the number of channels.

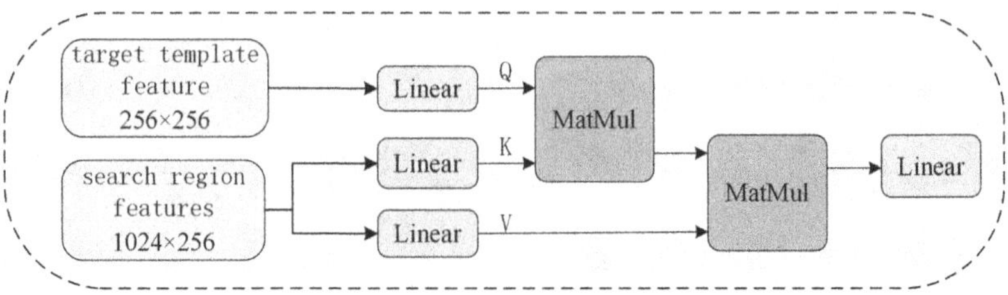

Fig. 3. The cross attention module.

2.4 Adaptive Multi-layer Feature Fusion

We extracted both shallow location information and deep semantic information for the tracking task in order to improve the performance of the model. The features from shallow layers contain detailed textural information which are suitable for localization, while the features from deep layers contain semantic information which are useful for classification [6,18]. As shown in Fig. 1, we extracted the layer2 and layer3 features from Resnet50. As a result, the features of the target template have a shape $512 \times 16 \times 16$ and $1024 \times 16 \times 16$. Both become $256 \times 16 \times 16$ after they are passed through the feature enhancing network. For the feature from the search region, its shape will eventually become $256 \times 32 \times 32$. In a typical feature fusion method, the shallow and deep features are concatenated before applying dimension reduction with convolution layers. Unlike this method, we treat them independently first, then splice them, as indicated in the formula:

$$\begin{aligned} &P^{cls}_{w\times h\times 2} \quad , \quad P^{reg}_{w\times h\times 4} \\ &= MLP([mHead_1(f_{t1}, f_{s1}), mHead_2(f_{t2}, f_{s2})]) \end{aligned} \tag{3}$$

The shallow and deep features of the target template are denoted by f_{t1} and f_{t2}, while the shallow and deep features of the search area are denoted by f_{s1} and f_{s2}, respectively. $mHead$ is a multi-head cross attention based head network proposed in this paper, and the symbol $[\cdot]$ denotes the channel splicing operation. P^{cls} and P^{reg} represent the prediction results of classification and regression, respectively.

3 Experiments

3.1 Experimental Setup

We train our model on four typical datasets including COCO [19], LaSOT [10], GOT-10K [15], and VOT2020 [16]. ImageNet [25] pretrained Resnet-50 [13] is used to initialize the parameters of the backbone, whereas Xavier init [12] is used to initialize the remaining parameters in our model. We employed two RTX3090 GPUs to train our model, with 10^{-5} as the learning rate for the backbone, and 10^{-4} for the others. The default batch size is 36, with each epoch having 1000 iterations and a total of 500 epochs. We use AdamW [20] as the optimizer. The

Table 1. Evaluation results on OTB2015, NFS and UAV123. Red and blue represent the top two track results, respectively. The symbol - is used to denote that the corresponding test results are not included in the official model.

Trackers	Years	OTB2015		UAV123			NFS
		AUC	Prec	AUC	P	NP	AUC
DaSiamRPN [31]	2018	0.650	0.880	0.568	0.796	–	–
SiamRPN++ [18]	2019	0.696	0.914	0.613	0.807	–	–
DiMP [3]	2019	0.688	0.900	0.597	0.152	0.441	0.620
SiamBAN [6]	2020	0.696	0.910	0.597	0.178	0.452	0.594
STARK [29]	2021	0.696	–	0.692	0.882	0.660	0.652
KeepKtack [22]	2021	0.709	–	0.697	–	–	0.664
TransT [5]	2021	0.696	–	0.691	0.876	0.694	0.657
RTS [24]	2022	–	–	0.676	0.894	0.816	0.654
ToMP [21]	2022	0.701	–	0.690	–	–	0.669
Mixformer [7]	2022	0.700	0.929	0.687	0.895	–	–
Ours	-	0.701	0.909	0.701	0.898	0.703	0.671

Table 2. Evaluation results on VOT2020. Red and blue represent the best two results respectively. The symbol - is used to denote that the corresponding test results are not included in the official model.

	Ours	Mixformer [7] 2022	ToMP [21] 2022	RTS [24] 2022	CSWinTT [26] 2022	TransT [5] 2021	STARK50 [29] 2021	D3S [16] 2020	ATOM [8] 2019	DiMP [3] 2019
EAO	0.509	0.527	0.297	0.506	0.304	0.293	0.308	0.439	0.271	0.274
Accuracy	0.723	0.746	0.453	0.710	0.480	0.477	0.478	0.699	0.462	0.457
Robustness	0.828	0.833	0.789	0.845	0.787	0.754	0.799	0.769	0.734	0.734
Δ EAO to ours	–	**↓0.018**	**↑0.212**	**↑0.003**	**↑0.205**	**↑0.216**	**↑0.201**	**↑0.07**	**↑0.238**	**↑0.235**

number of heads in multi-head cross attention is 8. The number of channels in the hidden layer was set to 2048.

3.2 Results and Analysis

We perform test of the model on several datasets, including OTB2015 [28], NFS [11], UAV123 [23] and VOT2020 [16]. Our model was trained on the LaSOT [10], GOT-10K [15] and COCO [19] datasets before the testing. We compare our method with state-of-the-art (SOTA) tracking algorithms qualitatively and quantitatively on OTB2015, NFS and UAV123 datasets. Table 1 shows AUC, Precision, Norm Precision results. It can be observed that our model outperforms all other methods on the UAV123 and NFS datasets while achieving competitive results on the OTB2015 dataset. Compared with TransT [5] and other SOTA methods, the AUC and precision scores in OTB2015 are both increased by 1.3% and 1.7%, respectively. On the NFS dataset, the AUC score is increased by 2.1%. On the UAV123 dataset, the precision score is increased by 2.5%. Furthermore, the NFS and UAV123 datasets involve more background clutter and camera viewpoint change. Our method achieves better performance on these two datasets than SOTA baselines. This demonstrates that the feature enhance module in our model can effectively improve the tracking robustness against the changes in visual attributes. In addition, the tracking speed of our model is about 40 FPS, which can meet the requirement of real-time tracking. These results show that the proposed method achieves competitive performance as compared with the SOTA baselines.

Figure 4 shows a comparison between our algorithm, SiamBan [6] and TransT [5] for helicopter tracking. The red, green, blue and cyan boxes represent the ground-truth position, and the position estimated by the proposed method, SiamBan and TransT, respectively. In total, eight frames are selected. The helicopter video sequence represents a challenging case with scale change of the target. It can be found that our algorithm can still accurately predict the location and size of the target when the target scale has changed.

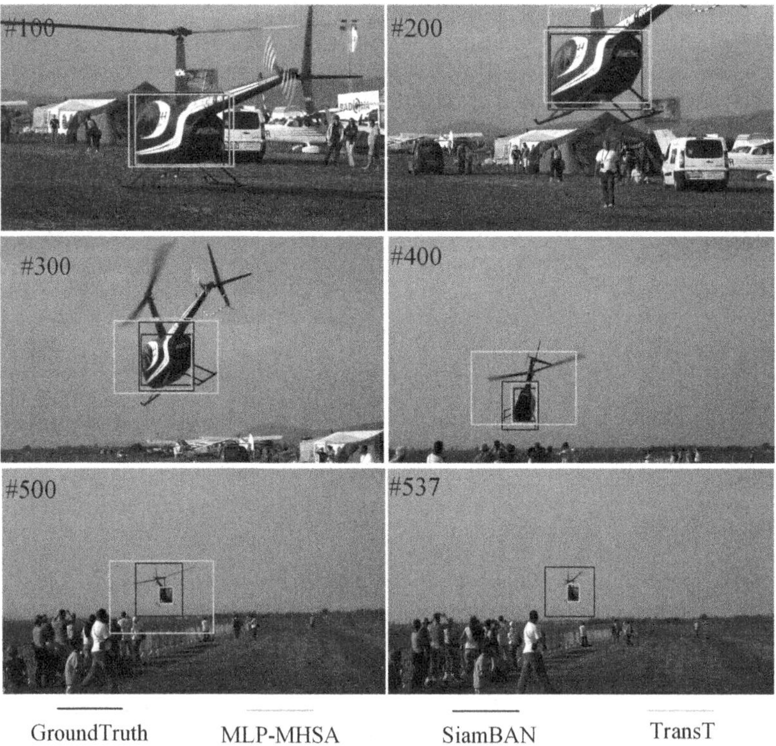

Fig. 4. The results of the methods in tracking the helicopter. The number in the upper left corner of each picture is the frame number in the helicopter video sequence.

We also evaluated our model on the VOT2020 [16] short-term tracking challenge, and compared it with recent trackers. The results are shown in Table 2, where EAO, A, R are classic tracking performance indicators used on this dataset, representing Expected Average Overlap, Accuracy and Robustness respectively. The proposed method offers a higher EAO score, as compared with RTS [24], CSwinTT [26] and ToMP [21], just a little less than Mixformer [7]. In addition, our method ranks second and third in terms of Accuracy and Robustness indicators, respectively. However, the proposed method gives a much higher EAO score than TransT [5], reaching 50.9%. All these experimental results demonstrate that our method can achieve competitive performance in short-term tracking challenge.

In addition, our proposed method can alleviate the computational limitations of the transformer module in object tracking to a certain extent. Table 3 shows that our method is more effective than TransT [5] and Mixformer [7]. Although MLP operations can also be computationally intensive, our approach employs a dimensionality reduction process in the MLP module, which enhances feature representation and reduces computation (as shown in Fig. 5, the computational cost is adjusted by controlling the scaling ratio of the output to the input in the FC layer). Therefore, our approach presents a promising alternative to the transformer module in terms of efficiency and effectiveness for object tracking.

Table 3. The comparison of the size of the three methods. "Linear" refers to the fully connected layer

method	TrasnT	Mixformer	MLP-MHCA
Number of parameters(MB)	23.0	35.1	20.0

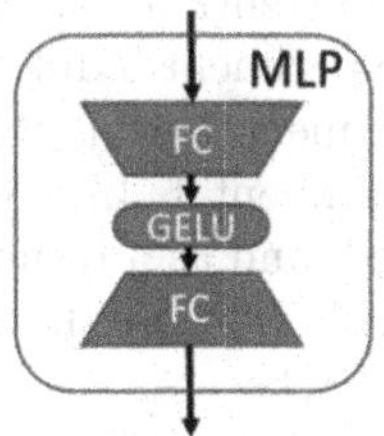

Fig. 5. The internal structure of an MLP.

3.3 Ablation Study

We carried out ablation experiments on the VOT2020 [16] dataset to demonstrate the effectiveness of various modules in the proposed model, including

Table 4. Ablation studies on the VOT2020 dataset. ✓ means the component is used, while × means that it is not used in the model.

number	Whether to use						VOT2020		
	mHead	Cor	Layer2	EN-MLP	Layer3	EN-MLP	A	R	EAO
1	✓	×	✓	✓	✓	✓	0.723	0.828	0.509
2	✓	×	✓	✓	×	✓	0.652	0.787	0.466
3	✓	×	×	✓	✓	✓	0.676	0.809	0.483
4	×	✓	✓	✓	✓	✓	0.563	0.749	0.448
5	✓	×	✓	×	✓	×	0.573	0.722	0.446
6	✓	×	×	×	✓	×	0.545	0.730	0.421

multi-head cross-attention, feature enhancement network based on multi-layer perceptron and multi-layer feature adaptive fusion. The ablation experiment results are shown in Table 4. Among them, mHead represents multi-head cross-attention, the correlation operation in Siamese network trackers is represented by Cor, layer2 represents the second layer feature of Resnet50, layer3 represents the third layer feature of Resnet50, and EN-MLP is the feature enhancement module based on multi-layer perceptron.

Experiment 1 represents our proposed method where the correlation operation is replaced with attention. Experiment 2 shows the outcomes of an experiment employing only the second layer of the Resnet50. The result of using only the third layer of Resnet50 is shown in experiment 3. Through the comparison of experiments 1, 2 and 3, it can be seen that the simultaneous selection of the second and third layers improves tracking performance. Experiment 4 shows the results of utilizing the traditional convolution operation rather than the attention mechanism. We can see that all the performance indexes decreased as compared with those in experiment 1, especially the Robustness and EAO, which showed that the multi-head cross-attention was helpful to improve the accuracy and robustness of the tracker. Experiment 5 did not use the MLP based feature enhancement module as in experiment 1, thus the performance scores obtained are also lower than those in experiment 1. In experiment 6, only the feature of the third layer of Resnet50 is used, and as a result, the accuracy and robustness scores are greatly reduced. This shows that the use of multi-layer features can improve the performance of the tracker.

Figure 6 visualises the feature map and response map in the ablation experiment. The red box in the search area surrounds the object *ant*. The features from both layer 2 and layer 3 show the contour of the object *ant* and the nearby *ant*. With the help of the MLP based feature enhancement module, the contour of the object becomes clearer with less clutter in surrounding area, which helps mitigate the impact of interference on the tracker. The response map of multi-head cross-attention has a dimension of 32×32. The region with a high response value still lies around the object in the response map of multi-head cross-attention (see Fig. 6 (e)) . However, as shown in Fig. 6 (f), the high response

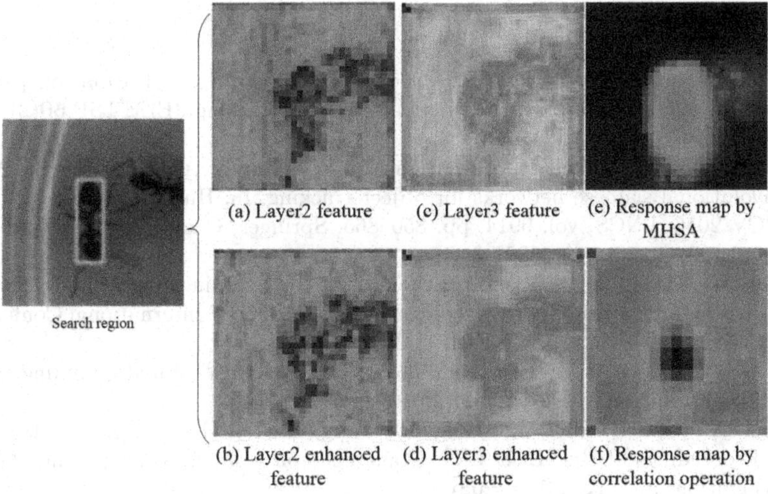

Fig. 6. Visualization results of feature map and response map. The two pictures in the first column show the features of Resnet Layer 2 that are not enhanced by MLP and the features of Resnet Layer 2 that are enhanced by MLP. The second column represents the performance results of Resnet Layer 3 features and MLP. The top of the third column represents the response map fused with the MHCA. The figure below represents feature map obtained by related operations.

value of correlation operation has deviated from the target location. Therefore, the experimental results demonstrate that the multi-head cross attention is more beneficial to improve the tracking accuracy and robustness over the correlation operation.

To sum up, the proposed multi-head cross-attention, feature enhancement module and multi-layer feature adaptive fusion indeed improve the performance of the tracker.

4 Conclusions

We have presented a Siamese network based on multi-layer perceptron and multi-head cross attention for visual tracking. We studied a new paradigm of MLP as feature enhancement, and the use of multi-head cross attention to replace the correlation operation in the Siamese network. This enables the extraction of shallow location information and deep semantic information simultaneously while utilizing multi-layer perceptron to enhance the features. The experiments on the OTB2015, VOT2020, NFS and UAV123 datasets show the effectiveness of our proposed method, as compared with several SOTA baseline methods. In the future, we will further study visual object tracking by taking the temporal information into account.

References

1. Arulampalam, M.S., Maskell, S., Gordon, N., Clapp, T.: A tutorial on particle filters for online nonlinear/non-Gaussian Bayesian tracking. IEEE TSP **50**(2), 174–188 (2002)
2. Bertinetto, L., Valmadre, J., Henriques, J.F., Vedaldi, A., Torr, P.H.S.: Fully-convolutional siamese networks for object tracking. In: Hua, G., Jégou, H. (eds.) ECCV 2016. LNCS, vol. 9914, pp. 850–865. Springer, Cham (2016). https://doi.org/10.1007/978-3-319-48881-3_56
3. Bhat, G., Danelljan, M., Gool, L., Timofte, R.: Learning discriminative model prediction for tracking. In: Proceedings of the IEEE/CVF International Conference on Computer Vision, pp. 6182–6191 (2019)
4. Chen, B., Tsotsos, J.K.: Fast visual object tracking with rotated bounding boxes. arXiv preprint arXiv:1907.03892 (2019)
5. Chen, X., Yan, B., Zhu, J., Wang, D., Yang, X., Lu, H.: Transformer tracking. In: Proceedings of the IEEE/CVF Conference on Computer Vision and Pattern Recognition, pp. 8126–8135 (2021)
6. Chen, Z., Zhong, B., Li, G., Zhang, S., Ji, R.: Siamese box adaptive network for visual tracking. In: Proceedings of the IEEE/CVF Conference on Computer Vision and Pattern Recognition, pp. 6668–6677 (2020)
7. Cui, Y., Jiang, C., Wang, L., Wu, G.: MixFormer: end-to-end tracking with iterative mixed attention. In: Proceedings of the IEEE/CVF Conference on Computer Vision and Pattern Recognition, pp. 13608–13618 (2022)
8. Danelljan, M., Bhat, G., Khan, F., Felsberg, M.: ATOM: accurate tracking by overlap maximization. In: Proceedings of the IEEE/CVF Conference on Computer Vision and Pattern Recognition, pp. 4660–4669 (2019)
9. Danelljan, M., Bhat, G., Khan, F.S., Felsberg, M.: ECO: efficient convolution operators for tracking. In: Proceedings of the IEEE Conference on Computer Vision and Pattern Recognition, pp. 6638–6646 (2017)
10. Fan, H., et al.: LaSOT: a high-quality benchmark for large-scale single object tracking. In: Proceedings of the IEEE/CVF Conference on Computer Vision and Pattern Recognition, pp. 5374–5383 (2019)
11. Galoogahi, H.K., Fagg, A., Huang, C., Ramanan, D., Lucey, S.: Need for speed: a benchmark for higher frame rate object tracking. In: Proceedings of the IEEE International Conference on Computer Vision, pp. 1125–1134 (2017)
12. Glorot, X., Bengio, Y.: Understanding the difficulty of training deep feedforward neural networks. In: Proceedings of the Thirteenth International Conference on Artificial Intelligence and Statistics, pp. 249–256 (2010)
13. He, K., Zhang, X., Ren, S., Sun, J.: Deep residual learning for image recognition. In: Proceedings of the IEEE Conference on Computer Vision and Pattern Recognition, pp. 770–778 (2016)
14. Hendrycks, D., Gimpel, K.: Bridging nonlinearities and stochastic regularizers with gaussian error linear units. arXiv1606.08415 (2016)
15. Huang, L., Zhao, X., Huang, K.: Got-10k: a large high-diversity benchmark for generic object tracking in the wild. IEEE Trans. Pattern Anal. Mach. Intell. **43**(5), 1562–1577 (2019)
16. Kristan, M., et al.: The eighth visual object tracking VOT2020 challenge results. In: Bartoli, A., Fusiello, A. (eds.) ECCV 2020. LNCS, vol. 12539, pp. 547–601. Springer, Cham (2020). https://doi.org/10.1007/978-3-030-68238-5_39

17. Lan, S., Li, J., Sun, S., Lai, X., Wang, W.: Robust visual object tracking with spatiotemporal regularisation and discriminative occlusion deformation. In: IEEE International Conference on Image Processing, pp. 1879–1883 (2021)
18. Li, B., Wu, W., Wang, Q., Zhang, F., Xing, J., Yan, J.: SiamRPN++: evolution of siamese visual tracking with very deep networks. In: Proceedings of the IEEE/CVF Conference on Computer Vision and Pattern Recognition, pp. 4282–4291 (2019)
19. Lin, T.-Y., et al.: Microsoft COCO: common objects in context. In: Fleet, D., Pajdla, T., Schiele, B., Tuytelaars, T. (eds.) ECCV 2014. LNCS, vol. 8693, pp. 740–755. Springer, Cham (2014). https://doi.org/10.1007/978-3-319-10602-1_48
20. Loshchilov, I., Hutter, F.: Decoupled weight decay regularization. arXiv preprint arXiv:1711.05101 (2017)
21. Mayer, C., et al.: Transforming model prediction for tracking. In: Proceedings of the IEEE/CVF Conference on Computer Vision and Pattern Recognition, pp. 8731–8740 (2022)
22. Mayer, C., Danelljan, M., Paudel, D., Gool, L.V.: Learning target candidate association to keep track of what not to track. In: Proceedings of the IEEE/CVF International Conference on Computer Vision, pp. 13444–13454 (2021)
23. Mueller, M., Smith, N., Ghanem, B.: A benchmark and simulator for UAV tracking. In: Leibe, B., Matas, J., Sebe, N., Welling, M. (eds.) ECCV 2016. LNCS, vol. 9905, pp. 445–461. Springer, Cham (2016). https://doi.org/10.1007/978-3-319-46448-0_27
24. Paul, M., Danelljan, M., Mayer, C., Van Gool, L.: Robust visual tracking by segmentation. In: Avidan, S., Brostow, G., Cissé, M., Farinella, G.M., Hassner, T. (eds.) ECCV 2022. LNCS, vol. 13682, pp. 571–588. Springer, Cham (2022). https://doi.org/10.1007/978-3-031-20047-2_33
25. Russakovsky, O., et al.: ImageNet large scale visual recognition challenge. Int. J. Comput. Vision **115**(3), 211–252 (2015)
26. Song, Z., Yu, J., Chen, Y., Yang, W.: Transformer tracking with cyclic shifting window attention. In: Proceedings of the IEEE/CVF Conference on Computer Vision and Pattern Recognition, pp. 8791–8800 (2022)
27. Tolstikhin, I., et al.: MLP-mixer: an all-MLP architecture for vision. In: Advances in Neural Information Processing Systems, vol. 34 (2021)
28. Wu, Y., Lim, J., Yang, M.: Online object tracking: a benchmark. In: Proceedings of the IEEE Conference on Computer Vision and Pattern Recognition, pp. 2411–2418 (2013)
29. Yan, B., Peng, H., Fu, J., Wang, D., Lu, H.: Learning spatio-temporal transformer for visual tracking. In: Proceedings of the IEEE/CVF International Conference on Computer Vision, pp. 10448–10457 (2021)
30. Yu, Y., Xiong, Y., Huang, W., Scott, M.: Deformable siamese attention networks for visual object tracking. In: Proceedings of the IEEE/CVF Conference on Computer Vision and Pattern Recognition, pp. 6728–6737 (2020)
31. Zhu, Z., Wang, Q., Li, B., Wu, W., Yan, J., Hu, W.: Distractor-aware siamese networks for visual object tracking. In: Proceedings of the European Conference on Computer Vision, pp. 101–117 (2018)

Taper Residual Dense Network for Audio Super-Resolution

Junmei Yang(✉), Haosen Lin, and Yiming Peng

South China University of Technology, Guangzhou, China
yjunmei@scut.edu.cn

Abstract. Audio Super-Resolution (Audio SR) aims to seek a mapping method from low-resolution audio to high-resolution audio, in which deep-learning-based approaches have achieved encouraging results in recent years. However, most Audio SR models do not break out of the limitations of the framework of UNet, which only have skip connections between the corresponding encoders and decoders. In this paper, we propose a taper residual dense network (TNet) for Audio SR. Specifically, 1) we introduce Residual Dense Block (RDB) and modify it to make it suitable for processing audio signals, which can fully utilize the features extracted by the network at different levels; 2) we design a taper network architecture that models and extracts features based on frequency-domain amplitude, frequency-domain phase as well as time-domain waveform in different lower branches, and then performs feature fusion in the upper branch. Experimental results show that our proposed TNet outperforms other baselines with fewer parameters.

Keywords: audio super resolution · deep learning · residual dense network

1 Introduction

With the advent of the era of intelligent information, voice, as an important way for humans to perceive the external world and communicate, plays an increasingly critical role in the field of human-computer interaction. Limited by the sampling rate, codec method of the voice acquisition device and transmission channel bandwidth, the frequency band and resolution of the audio will be compressed to varying degrees. Audio SR is a technique for reconstructing Super-Resolution (SR) audio according to Low-Resolution (LR) audio, also known as BandWidth Extension (BWE), which has important research significance and practical value.

Early research attempted to extend the bandwidth of audio by exploiting linear operations. At this stage, the speech bandwidth extension methods based on the source-filter model show good performance [12], the most important of which is the estimation of the high-frequency spectral envelope. Typical spectrum estimation methods include linear mapping [4,13], codebook mapping [16,21], Gaussian mixture model (GMM) [14,15] and Hidden Markov Model (HMM) [1,20].

L. Iliadis et al. (Eds.): ICANN 2023, LNCS 14263, pp. 432–443, 2023.
https://doi.org/10.1007/978-3-031-44204-9_36

In recent years, the research of deep learning has gradually expanded to the field of Audio SR, showing a strong ability of speech reconstruction. Among these deep-learning-based audio super-resolution studies, DNN-BWE [9], Audio-UNet [8] and TFNet [11] are some of the representative works, achieving audio reconstruction quality that exceeds traditional methods. Section 2 gives a more detailed summary of related research.

At present, the mainstream networks for Audio SR are mostly based on the UNet framework, which cannot make full use of the feature maps generated at each level due to the limitation of feature size. Besides, the research on modeling and feature extraction combining time-domain and frequency-domain information of audio signals has not received sufficient attention. In this paper, we propose a taper residual dense network for Audio SR. The main contributions are as follows: First, we introduce RDB [24] for audio super-resolution for the first time, and carry out the transformation adapted to one-dimensional audio signals, which can make full use of the features extracted by the network at different levels. Second, we design a taper architecture that can model and extract features according to Frequency-domain Amplitude (FA), Frequency-domain Phase (FP) as well as Time-domain Waveform (TW) in different lower feature Extraction and Fusion Branch (EFB), and perform feature fusion in Upper Fusion (UF) EFB. The taper architecture and the modified RDB together form a Taper residual dense Network (TNet), which outperforms the baseline methods in experiments with a lower amount of parameters. Figure 1 shows a simplified schematic diagram of the proposed TNet.

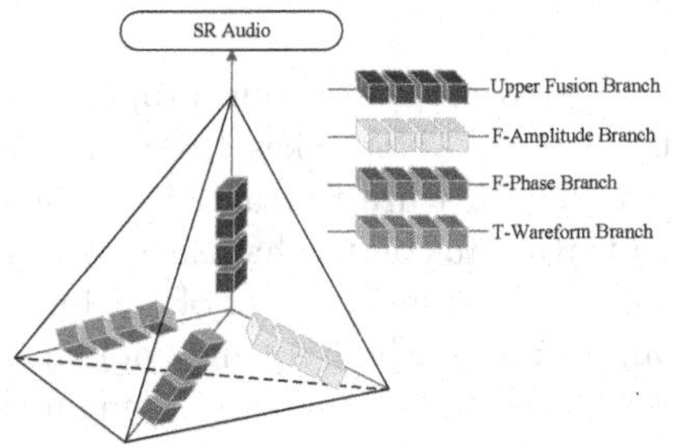

Fig. 1. Simplified schematic diagram of TNet.

The rest of the paper is organized as follows. In Sect. 2, we present the related research on Audio SR in categories and introduce RDB that perform well in the task of image super-resolution. In Sect. 3, we present our network design. Section 4 presents the experimental setup, results and comparisons. Finally, Sect. 5 concludes this paper.

2 Related Work

Frequency-Domain Approaches. Audio signal is transformed into frequency-domain through Fast Fourier Transform (FFT) or other time-frequency analysis methods, then a neural network is used to predict the missing high frequency components, and finally the frequency-domain information is restored to a time-domain waveform [3,7,9,10]. Although deep-learning-based frequency-domain approaches outperform traditional methods, their reconstruction quality is limited due to the lack of accurate phase estimates.

Time-Domain Approaches. Kuleshov et al. [8] introduced the Convolutional Neural Network (CNN) for Audio SR, and proposed a time-domain Audio SR network, Audio-UNet. Since then, on the basis of Audio-UNet, a series of time-domain approaches have been developed [2,17,23]. However, these time-domain approaches do not break through the limitations of the UNet framework, which only have residual connections between encoders and decoders with the same feature size, limiting the model's utilization of hierarchical features.

Time-Frequency Approaches. The above time-domain and frequency-domain approaches only focus on the single-domain information of the audio signals, while the TFNet proposed by Lim et al. [11] utilizes two UNets operating in the frequency and time domains respectively, which achieves better results than Audio-UNet. Such improvements inspired our work.

3 Proposed Model

Figure 2(a) shows the model overview of our proposed Taper residual dense Network (TNet). On the whole, TNet takes LR audio of length N as input, and passes it to the lower three feature Extraction and Fusion Branches (EFB) respectively. We design a feature fusion mechanism, which forces the three EFBs in the lower layer to focus on different features of LR for audio super-resolution modeling, namely, the amplitude in the frequency domain, the phase in the frequency domain, and the waveform in the time domain, thereby enabling the model to utilize both time and frequency domain information. In the following, we refer to the lower three EFBs as Frequency-domain Amplitude (FA) EFB, Frequency-domain Phase (FP) EFB and Time-domain Waveform (TW) EFB respectively. The three EFBs in the lower layer run in parallel, extract different features from the LR audio, and then the Upper Fusion (UF) EFB fuses the Feature Maps of various levels and types, and finally reconstructs the SR audio with a length of $N \times R$, where R is the upsampling ratio of audio signals. The remainder of this section further elaborates the details of our proposed TNet.

3.1 Residual Dense Block for Processing Audio Signals

In order to make full use of the hierarchical features of convolutional networks, we introduce the Residual Dense Block (RDB) for Audio SR, which is outstanding in

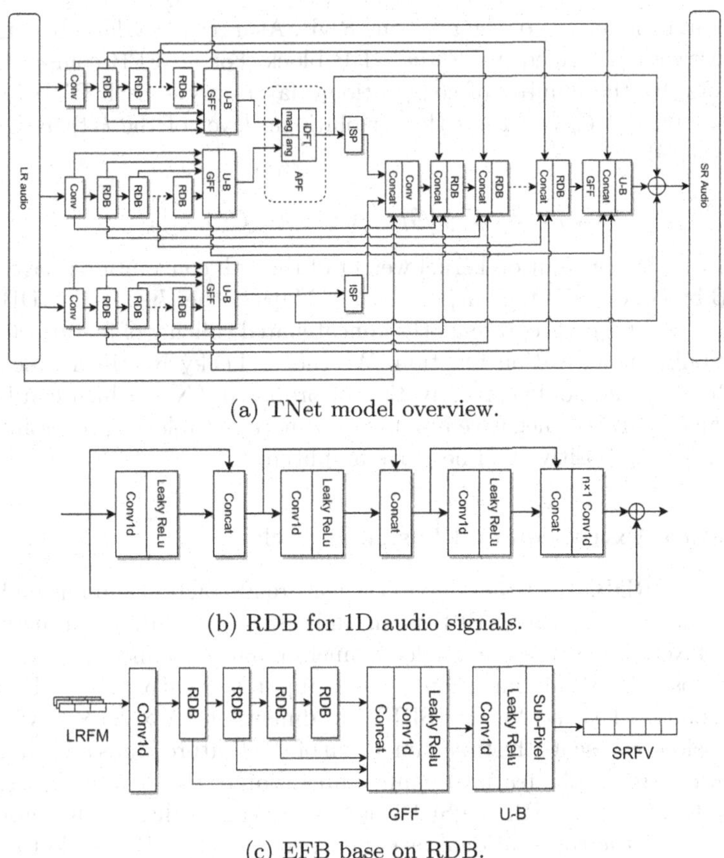

(a) TNet model overview.

(b) RDB for 1D audio signals.

(c) EFB base on RDB.

Fig. 2. Details of TNet for audio super-resolution. Figure 2(a) shows the model overview of TNet, which takes LR audio of length N as input and passes it to three feature Extraction and Fusion Branches (EFB) shown in Fig. 2(c) based on Residual Dense Block (RDB) shown in Fig. 2(b), respectively.

the image super-resolution task [24]. We make certain changes to RDB to make it suitable for processing one-dimensional (1D) audio signals, which is the first time RDB has been applied to Audio SR. In Fig. 2(b), we show the structural details of the RDB for audio signals, where Concat and Conv1d represent concatenating and 1D convolution operations, respectively.

The RDB is internally composed of convolutional layers, each consisting of multiple convolution kernels and a layer of nonlinear activation. The input of each convolutional layer is concatenated in series with the output and input of the previous convolutional layer in the feature channel dimension. At the same time, an additive skip connection is added between the input and output of the RDB to form residual learning. The core mechanism is that each convolutional layer of an RDB can obtain the output from the previous convolutional layers in this RDB and the output of the previous RDB. As a result, a densely connected residual network is formed inside the RDB block. For an EFB composed of K RDB blocks, let the number of convolutional layers inside each RDB block be T, then the output $C_{k,t}$ of the t-th convolutional layer of the k-th RDB block can be modeled as:

$$C_{k,t} = \sigma\left(W_{k,t}\left[G_{k-1}, C_{k,1}, \cdots, C_{k,t-1}\right]\right), \tag{1}$$

where $W_{k,t}$ is the convolution kernel weight of the t-th convolutional layer of the k-th RDB block; G_{k-1} is the output Feature Maps of the $(k-1)$-th RDB block; $[G_{k-1}, C_{k,1}, \cdots, C_{k,t-1}]$ represents the concatenated splicing of feature channels; σ is the nonlinear activation function. We choose Leaky Rectified Linear Unit (Leaky Relu) as the nonlinear activation of proposed TNet, which can be activated by any positive or negative input, and is more suitable for processing audio signals containing positive and negative amplitudes.

3.2 Feature Extraction and Fusion Branch

On the basis of RDB, we further design the feature Extraction and Fusion Branch (EFB) as shown in Fig. 2(c). EFB is an audio super-resolution sub-network of proposed TNet, which takes a single-channel or multi-channel Low-Resolution Feature Maps (LRFM) of dimension $N \times D$ as input, and outputs a single-channel Super-Resolution Feature Vector (SRFV) of dimension $(N \times R) \times 1$, where the first dimension represents the time dimension of the Feature Maps and the second dimension represents the feature channel dimension of the Feature Maps.

At the front of the EFB, the SRFV is first processed through K consecutive RDB blocks. As the convolutional layers deepen, the network is able to extract deeper features. Such a deep network structure also enables a small convolution kernel to obtain a large receptive field. After that, the outputs of each RDB block are concatenated in the dimension of the feature channel and output to the Global Feature Fusion (GFF) of the EFB through skip connections. As mentioned above, the concatenation operation will greatly increase the number of feature channels. The role of GFF is adaptive feature fusion and refinement, using a convolutional layer with a lower number of convolution kernels and convolution kernel size of 1.

The last block of the EFB is the Upsampling Block (U-B), which consists of a convolutional layer containing R kernels, nonlinear activation and Sub-Pixel (SP) layer [19]. The SP layer is essentially an Feature Maps shaping method that rearranges and integrates the elements of the feature channel dimension into the spatial dimension, which can realize the upsampling of the spatial dimension with a very low amount of computation. We implement SP and Inverse Sub-Pixel (ISP) for processing two-dimensional audio Feature Maps, which are applied to the various EFB of our proposed TNet.

3.3 Frequency-Domain Amplitude-Phase Fusion

Inspired by the Spectral Fusion method proposed by Lim et al. [11], we utilize a frequency-domain Amplitude-Phase Fusion (APF) layer to fuse the SRFV from the FA-EFB and the FP-EFB in the frequency domain, which prompts the EFBs to model audio signals from different angles. According to the Discrete Fourier Transform (DFT) of the finite-length sequence, a feasible method to reconstruct LR into SR is to establish a mapping from low-frequency amplitude and phase to high-frequency amplitude and phase, that is, restoring the amplitude and phase of the high frequency band. Starting from this, perform DFT on the SRFV output by FA-EFB, and take the DFT amplitude of each frequency point:

$$V_{FA} = \left| DFT\left(V_{FA-EFB}\right)\right| \tag{2}$$

Similarly, perform DFT on the SRFV output by FA-EFB, and take the DFT phase of each frequency point:

$$V_{FP} = \operatorname{atan2}\left(DFT\left(V_{FP-EFB}\right)\right) \tag{3}$$

Fusing feature vectors V_{FA} and V_{FP} with Euler's formula:

$$V_{fre} = V_{FA} e^{jV_{FP}} \tag{4}$$

Perform Inverse Discrete Fourier Transform (IDFT) on V_{fre} to recover the fused SRFV in the time domain:

$$X_{APF} = IDFT\left(V_{fre}\right) \tag{5}$$

APF forces the EFBs to model according to the frequency-domain amplitude and phase characteristics of audio signals. Selectively extracting Frequency-domain Amplitude and Frequency-domain Phase information from different EFBs can also make them focus on learning different types of latent features, instead of homogeneous or redundant ones, thereby enhancing the fitting ability of the overall network to the sample space.

3.4 Skip Connections Between the Upper and Lower EFBs

To further utilize the Feature Maps generated by the internal RDB of the lower EFBs, there are two parts of skip connections between the upper and lower EFB sub-networks in our proposed TNet.

On one hand, there are stacked skip connections between the RDBs of the same level of the three lower EFBs and the UF-EFB, where Feature Maps are concatenated on feature channels. It is worth emphasizing that there is no down-sampling operation such as Max Pooling in the convolutional layers of EFBs, and all convolution strides are 1, which maintains the consistency of the Feature Maps in the time dimension. In theory, TNet has more possible residual connection forms, which is more flexible than the UNet architecture that can only add residual connections in the convolutional layer of the symmetric layer. From this, the output of the t-th convolutional layer of the k-th RDB of UF-EFB can be modeled as:

$$C_{k,t}^{UF} = \sigma \left(W_{k,t}^{UF} \left[G_{k-1}^{FA}, G_{k-1}^{FP}, G_{k-1}^{TW}, G_{k-1}^{UF}, C_{k,1}^{UF}, \cdots, C_{k,t-1}^{UF} \right] \right), \tag{6}$$

where G_{k-1}^{FA}, G_{k-1}^{FP} and G_{k-1}^{TW} are the Feature Maps generated by the $(k-1)$-th RDB of the FA-EFB, FP-EFB and TW-EFB, respectively.

On the other hand, in order to enable UF-EFB to produce the same Feature Maps in time dimension as the three lower EFBs, we perform ISP operation on the output X_{TW} of the TW-EFB and the output X_{APF} of the APF respectively, remapping the two sets of SRFV to 2D Feature Maps of $N \times R$. After this, the two are concatenated with the original LR audio to get the input of the UF-EFB. Maintaining the consistency of the time dimension of the input, the four EFBs that are consistent in the network structure output SRFVs of the same size. Therefore, it is convenient to add additive skip connections between X_{TW} and X_{APF} to form residual learning between the upper and lower EFBs. To sum up, the audio signal finally reconstructed by TNet can be expressed as:

$$X_{SR} = X_{APF} + X_{TW} + X_{UF}, \tag{7}$$

where X_{UF} is the SRFV output by UF-EFB.

4 Experimental Setup and Results

4.1 Dataset and Baseline

We train and evaluate the models on the VCTK dataset [22], which contains recordings of 109 native English speakers with different accents. We first downsample the raw data to 16kHz as the target audio signals and then subsample the 16kHz-data at the desired scaling R as the LR audio signals with an order 8 Chebyshev type I low-pass filter. We train and test the model on both the single-speaker task $VCTK_S$ and the multi-speaker task $VCTK_M$. $VCTK_S$ takes the first 223 recordings of the speaker numbered p225 as the training set and uses the remaining 8 recordings of the p225 speaker for testing; $VCTK_M$ trains on the first 100 speakers and tests on the 9 remaining ones. To verify the effectiveness of our proposed model, we compare TNet with five different baselines, cubic spline interpolation, Audio-UNet [8], TFNet [11], TFiLM [2] and AFiLM [17], and refer to the network parameters and optimizers of the corresponding works for training.

4.2 Training Details

In the training stage, audio fragments with a frame length of 8192 (512 ms) are randomly selected from the training set as samples. Batch Size is set to 8, and training is performed for 100 epochs. The models are set to train 2500 steps in each epoch for $VCTK_M$, while the number of training steps is not limited for

$VCTK_S$, but the entire training set is fed to the models. For a fair comparison, all models are compared under the same training and testing conditions.

All convolution operations of our proposed TNet are 1D convolution, and the convolution stride is 1. Except that the convolution kernel size of the last layer of each RDB is 1, the convolution kernel size of other layers is set to 9. Except for GFF and U-B, the number of convolution kernels in all convolutional layers is set to 64. The number of convolution kernels of GFF and U-B is 32 and equal to R, respectively. The negative slope coefficient of Leaky Relu is set to 0.2. The combination of a convolutional layer and Leaky Relu is regarded as a Nonlinear Convolutional Layer (NCL), and each RDB contains 3 NCLs. At the same time, each EFB is composed of 4 RDBs, one GFF and one U-B. We train TNet using the Adam [6] optimizer. The learning rate is initially set to 0.0002, which decays by half after every 30 epochs. We train our network with a bitwise regression loss of the time-domain waveform, defined as the mean squared error (MSE) of the target audio signals and the reconstructed audio signals:

$$L(s, \hat{s}) = \frac{1}{N} \sum_{n=1}^{N} |s(n) - \hat{s}(n)|^2, \tag{8}$$

where s and $\hat{s}$ are the target audio signals and the reconstructed SR audio signals, respectively. N is the length of audio signals.

4.3 Evaluations

We select three objective indicators for evaluation, namely Signal-to-Noise Ratio (SNR), Scale-Invariant Signal-to-Distortion Ratio (SI-SDR) [18] and Log-Spectral Distance (LSD) [5].

- SNR measures the energy ratio of signal to noise from the perspective of the time domain, which is defined as follows:

$$SNR(\hat{s}, s) = 10\log_{10} \frac{\|s\|^2}{\|s - \hat{s}\|^2} \tag{9}$$

- SI-SDR is proposed on the basis of SNR, measures the per-sample fidelity up to a uniform scaling factor, which is defined as follows:

$$SI-SDR(\hat{s}, s) = 10\log_{10} \frac{\left\| \frac{\hat{s}^\top s}{\|s\|^2} s \right\|^2}{\left\| \frac{\hat{s}^\top s}{\|s\|^2} s - \hat{s} \right\|^2} \tag{10}$$

- LSD reflects the difference in the energy distribution of two signals in the frequency domain, which is defined as follows:

$$LSD\left(\hat{S}, S\right) = \frac{1}{L}\sum_{l=1}^{L}\sqrt{\frac{1}{M}\sum_{m=1}^{M}\left[\ln\left|S(l,m)\right|^2 - \ln\left|\hat{S}(l,m)\right|^2\right]^2}, \tag{11}$$

where $\hat{S}$ and S are the Short-Time Fourier Transform (STFT) coefficients of the reconstructed super-resolution audio signals and the target audio signals, respectively; l, m are the index of frames and frequencies, respectively; L and M are the size of the frame axis and the frequency axis, respectively. When performing STFT, we use a Hamming window of length 2048 and the frame shift step size is set to 512.

4.4 Results

Table 1. Experimental results of SR models at upscaling ratios $R = 2, 4$ and 8.

		$VCTK_S$					
R	Obj.	Spline	Audio-UNet	TFNet	TFiLM	AFiLM	TNet
2	SNR	18.97	19.50	19.53	19.48	19.24	**20.14**
	SI-SDR	18.92	19.47	19.55	19.39	19.20	**20.12**
	LSD	3.75	2.57	2.38	2.46	2.53	**2.15**
4	SNR	15.62	16.52	17.25	17.05	17.23	**17.41**
	SI-SDR	15.51	16.43	17.23	16.99	17.17	**17.36**
	LSD	6.06	3.70	3.07	3.56	3.36	**2.91**
8	SNR	6.84	11.13	10.83	10.88	**11.26**	10.95
	SI-SDR	6.35	10.78	10.65	10.52	**10.95**	10.57
	LSD	7.64	4.10	3.92	4.27	3.85	**3.57**
		$VCTK_M$					
R	Obj.	Spline	Audio-UNet	TFNet	TFiLM	AFiLM	TNet
2	SNR	17.67	18.50	19.28	18.77	18.76	**19.38**
	SI-SDR	17.57	18.41	19.19	18.68	18.64	**19.30**
	LSD	3.64	2.66	2.66	2.44	2.49	**2.43**
4	SNR	13.97	14.45	15.17	15.12	15.21	**15.29**
	SI-SDR	13.73	14.24	15.06	14.94	15.03	**15.12**
	LSD	5.96	3.83	3.47	4.11	3.47	**3.21**
8	SNR	6.49	8.47	9.73	9.97	9.46	**10.15**
	SI-SDR	5.82	7.78	9.22	9.47	8.78	**9.67**
	LSD	7.45	4.47	3.57	4.51	3.88	**3.43**

We compare our proposed TNet with five existing baselines at different upsampling ratios on the VCTK dataset. The experimental results are presented in Table 1. On the one hand, for SNR and SI-SDR, our proposed TNet outperforms the optimal baselines except when the upsampling ratios R = 8 in the $VCTK_S$ task. On the other hand, for LSD, our proposed TNet outperforms the baselines in various cases on the VCTK dataset.

Table 2. The number of trainable parameters and Floating-point Operations for the SR models.

Models	Audio-UNet	TFNet	TFiLM	AFiLM	TNet
Params	70.9M	35.5M	68.2M	134M	**5.49M**
FLOPs.	284M	142M	261M	384M	**11.6M**

Table 3. Ablation experiment results of TNet in the $VCTK_S$ task.

R	Obj.	TNet-T	TNet-F	TNet-AT	TNet
2	SNR	**20.16**	20.13	20.14	20.14
	SI-SDR	**20.16**	20.08	20.12	20.12
	LSD	2.31	2.17	2.16	**2.15**
4	SNR	17.33	17.32	17.30	**17.41**
	SI-SDR	17.29	17.29	17.24	**17.36**
	LSD	**2.80**	2.89	3.02	2.91
8	SNR	10.59	10.75	10.67	**10.95**
	SI-SDR	10.18	10.50	10.28	**10.57**
	LSD	3.73	3.62	3.76	**3.57**

Table 2 presents the number of trainable parameters and Floating-point Operations (FLOPs) of the SR models, showing that the number of trainable parameters and FLOPs of TNet are much lower than several other baseline models.

To further evaluate our proposed TNet, Table 3 presents ablation experiments with different EFB sub-networks removed from TNet. TNet-T means deleting FA-EFB and FP-EFB; TNet-F means deleting TW-EFB; TNet-AT means deleting APF, which is equivalent to the three EFBs in the lower layer are all TW-EFB. Overall, after TNet ablated a certain part of the structure, the SNR, SI-SDR and LSD shows different degrees of deterioration. Our proposed TNet exhibits the ability to balance time-domain metrics and frequency-domain metrics. Although TNet-AT has almost the same structure as TNet except without APF, the SNR, SI-SDR and LSD of TNet-AT are still inferior to TNet, especially when R is larger, the gap becomes more obvious. Ablation experiments show that forcing different EFBs to model SR from the perspective of time domain and frequency domain can enhance the representation ability and performance of the model.

5 Conclusion

We propose TNet for Audio SR, a deep learning model that combines frequency and time domains to reconstruct super-resolution audio signals. Our experimental results show that TNet outperforms other baselines in SNR, SI-SDR and LSD. Besides, our proposed TNet is more lightweight than other baselines in terms of parameters. What's more, since TNet is specially designed to not rely on the use of cubic spline interpolation to preprocess audio signals, we improve the speed of super-resolution reconstruction as well as training.

References

1. Bauer, P., Fingscheidt, T.: An HMM-based artificial bandwidth extension evaluated by cross-language training and test. In: 2008 IEEE International Conference on Acoustics, Speech and Signal Processing, pp. 4589–4592. IEEE (2008)
2. Birnbaum, S., Kuleshov, V., Enam, Z., Koh, P.W.W., Ermon, S.: Temporal FiLM: capturing long-range sequence dependencies with feature-wise modulations. In: Advances in Neural Information Processing Systems, vol. 32 (2019)
3. Botinhao, C.V., Carlos, B.S., Caloba, L.P., Petraglia, M.R.: Frequency extension of telephone narrowband speech signal using neural networks. In: The Proceedings of the Multiconference on "Computational Engineering in Systems Applications", vol. 2, pp. 1576–1579. IEEE (2006)
4. Chennoukh, S., Gerrits, A., Miet, G., Sluijter, R.: Speech enhancement via frequency bandwidth extension using line spectral frequencies. In: 2001 IEEE International Conference on Acoustics, Speech, and Signal Processing. Proceedings (Cat. No. 01CH37221), vol. 1, pp. 665–668. IEEE (2001)
5. Gray, A., Markel, J.: Distance measures for speech processing. IEEE Trans. Acoust. Speech Signal Process. **24**(5), 380–391 (1976)
6. Kingma, D.P., Ba, J.: Adam: a method for stochastic optimization. arXiv preprint arXiv:1412.6980 (2014)
7. Kontio, J., Laaksonen, L., Alku, P.: Neural network-based artificial bandwidth expansion of speech. IEEE Trans. Audio Speech Lang. Process. **15**(3), 873–881 (2007)
8. Kuleshov, V., Enam, S.Z., Ermon, S.: Audio super resolution using neural networks. arXiv preprint arXiv:1708.00853 (2017)
9. Li, K., Lee, C.H.: A deep neural network approach to speech bandwidth expansion. In: 2015 IEEE International Conference on Acoustics, Speech and Signal Processing (ICASSP), pp. 4395–4399. IEEE (2015)
10. Li, S., Villette, S., Ramadas, P., Sinder, D.J.: Speech bandwidth extension using generative adversarial networks. In: 2018 IEEE International Conference on Acoustics, Speech and Signal Processing (ICASSP), pp. 5029–5033. IEEE (2018)
11. Lim, T.Y., Yeh, R.A., Xu, Y., Do, M.N., Hasegawa-Johnson, M.: Time-frequency networks for audio super-resolution. In: 2018 IEEE International Conference on Acoustics, Speech and Signal Processing (ICASSP), pp. 646–650. IEEE (2018)
12. Makhoul, J., Berouti, M.: High-frequency regeneration in speech coding systems. In: ICASSP'79. IEEE International Conference on Acoustics, Speech, and Signal Processing, vol. 4, pp. 428–431. IEEE (1979)
13. Nakatoh, Y., Tsushima, M., Norimatsu, T.: Generation of broadband speech from narrowband speech using piecewise linear mapping. In: Fifth European Conference on Speech Communication and Technology (1997)
14. Nour-Eldin, A.H., Kabal, P.: Mel-frequency cepstral coefficient-based bandwidth extension of narrowband speech. In: Ninth Annual Conference of the International Speech Communication Association (2008)

15. Park, K.Y., Kim, H.S.: Narrowband to wideband conversion of speech using GMM based transformation. In: 2000 IEEE International Conference on Acoustics, Speech, and Signal Processing. Proceedings (Cat. No. 00CH37100), vol. 3, pp. 1843–1846. IEEE (2000)
16. Qian, Y., Kabal, P.: Wideband speech recovery from narrowband speech using classified codebook mapping. In: Australian International Conference on Speech Science, Technology, pp. 106–111 (2002)
17. Rakotonirina, N.C.: Self-attention for audio super-resolution. In: 2021 IEEE 31st International Workshop on Machine Learning for Signal Processing (MLSP), pp. 1–6. IEEE (2021)
18. Roux, J.L., Wisdom, S., Erdogan, H., Hershey, J.R.: SDR–half-baked or well done? In: ICASSP 2019–2019 IEEE International Conference on Acoustics, Speech and Signal Processing (ICASSP), pp. 626–630 (2019). https://doi.org/10.1109/ICASSP.2019.8683855
19. Shi, W., et al.: Real-time single image and video super-resolution using an efficient sub-pixel convolutional neural network. In: Proceedings of the IEEE Conference on Computer Vision and Pattern Recognition, pp. 1874–1883 (2016)
20. Song, G.B., Martynovich, P.: A study of hmm-based bandwidth extension of speech signals. Signal Process. **89**(10), 2036–2044 (2009)
21. Unno, T., McCree, A.: A robust narrowband to wideband extension system featuring enhanced codebook mapping. In: Proceedings. (ICASSP 2005). IEEE International Conference on Acoustics, Speech, and Signal Processing, 2005, vol. 1, pp. I-805. IEEE (2005)
22. Veaux, C., Yamagishi, J., MacDonald, K., et al.: CSTR VCTK corpus: English multi-speaker corpus for CSTR voice cloning toolkit. University of Edinburgh, The Centre for Speech Technology Research (CSTR) (2017)
23. Wang, H., Wang, D.: Time-frequency loss for CNN based speech super-resolution. In: ICASSP 2020–2020 IEEE International Conference on Acoustics, Speech and Signal Processing (ICASSP), pp. 861–865. IEEE (2020)
24. Zhang, Y., Tian, Y., Kong, Y., Zhong, B., Fu, Y.: Residual dense network for image super-resolution. In: Proceedings of the IEEE Conference on Computer Vision and Pattern Recognition, pp. 2472–2481 (2018)

VPNDroid: Malicious Android VPN Detection Using a CNN-RF Method

Nikolaos Polatidis[1], Elias Pimenidis[2](✉), Marcello Trovati[3], and Lazaros Iliadis[4]

[1] School of Architecture, Technology and Engineering, University of Brighton, BN2 4GJ Brighton, UK
N.Polatidis@Brighton.ac.uk

[2] School of Computing and Creative Technologies, University of the West of England, BS16 1QY Bristol, UK
Elias.Pimenidis@uwe.ac.uk

[3] Department of Computer Science, Edge Hill University, Ormskirk L39 4QP, UK
Marcello.Trovati@edgehill.ac.uk

[4] School of Engineering, Department of Civil Engineering, Democritus University of Thrace, Kimmeria, Xanthi, Greece
liliadis@civil.duth.gr

Abstract. Protecting online privacy using Virtual Private Networks (VPNs) is not as simple as it seems, since many well-known VPNs may not be secure. Despite appearing to be secure on the surface, VPNs can be a complete privacy and security disaster by stealing bandwidth, infecting devices with malware, installing tracking libraries, stealing personal data, and leaving data exposed to third parties. Therefore, Android users must exercise caution when downloading and installing VPN software on their devices. To this end, this paper proposes a neural network combined with a random forest that identifies malicious and malware-infected VPNs based on app permissions, along with a novel dataset of malicious and benign Android VPNs. The experimental results demonstrate that our classifier achieves high accuracy and outperforms other standard classifiers in terms of evaluation metrics such as accuracy, precision, and recall.

Keywords: Android · Permissions · Malware detection · VPN · Convolutional Neural Networks · Machine Learning

1 Introduction

The Android operating system, mainly used on mobile phones and tablets, has become widely popular due to its ease of installing applications from Google Play, third-party stores, or manual installation using an Android Package Kit (APK) file. However, this popularity has also made it a target for attackers utilizing various types of malwares. As a result, there has been significant effort put into detecting Android malware using a range of techniques, including static, dynamic, and hybrid approaches. Static approaches use static information such as permissions or signatures, while dynamic methods are based on information gathered during app execution. Hybrid approaches combine both static and dynamic methods [1].

L. Iliadis et al. (Eds.): ICANN 2023, LNCS 14263, pp. 444–453, 2023.
https://doi.org/10.1007/978-3-031-44204-9_37

A recent trend over the last few months in Android is the spreading of malicious VPNs which pretend to be legitimate VPN clients but are in fact malware such as Trojan and can be used to steal user information such as conversations and crypto currency data among other malicious activities. Furthermore, important legitimate VPN providers such as NordVPN have reached this conclusion as well [2–5].

In recent times, Machine Learning (ML) and particularly Deep Learning (DL) techniques are extensively utilized for malware detection. Various algorithms and datasets are available in the literature that offer highly precise results. The process of acquiring new data and creating a new algorithm is time-consuming. Additionally, recent studies have demonstrated that developing separate datasets and algorithms for different types of malwares is more computationally efficient and accurate such as Trojans, fake anti-malware, and more recently malicious VPNs [1, 6, 7]. Thus, it has become increasingly important to be able to detect such malware as accurate as possible.

To this end the following contributions are delivered:

- A Convolutional Neural Network combined with a random forest has been designed and developed to distinguish between benign and malicious VPN Android apps based on their app permissions.
- The suggested approach has undergone thorough evaluation and the results demonstrate its feasibility and efficiency. The detection accuracy is also found to be very high.

The rest of the paper is organized as follows: Sect. 2 presents the related work, Sect. 3 delivers the proposed methodology, Sect. 4 presents the experimental evaluation steps and results, and Sect. 5 contains the conclusion and future work.

2 Related Work

In the literature several works can be found in Android malware detection, which is still a field of constant research. In general, detection methods can be categorized in three broad categories: Static, Dynamic and Hybrid. Static methods examine an app by extracting their features such as permissions without executing the app while dynamic methods execute the app usually in a restricted environment to detect abnormalities. Finally, hybrid methods combine various characteristics of the two to detect malware.

The work in [1] is the most related work since it is the first one to deliver a malicious VPN dataset for the Android platform and uses a permission-based neural network to detect malicious VPNs with high accuracy. Furthermore, there are many more works that can be found which can be used to detect different types of malwares either using a static or a dynamic approach. The work in [6] delivers a dataset for Trojan detection based on app permissions as well and uses a convolutional neural network to detect such malicious app while the work in [7] uses a multi-Layer perceptron to detect malicious anti-malware and delivers a relevant dataset for this. The work in [8] is also a static based work that employs various methods to identify the important of Android app permissions and to identify possibly risky permissions. Then they use classical machine learning methods such as decision trees and random forest to detect malware. The work in [9] is yet another work that follows the static approach using Android app permissions to find malware.

To do this the authors use a signature database, a server that stores such information and an actual Android device. Another work in the static world is the one in [10]. The authors introduce a significant permission identification method based on permission usage and then they use typical machine learning methods such as decision trees and support vector machine to detect malware. The work in [11] uses a static approach for detection of malware as well based on a bag of words model. A more recent work that is based on static features which provides very high accuracy is the one in [12].

On the other hand, there are several works that use dynamic analysis as well. For example, the work in [13] uses sandbox detection methods to detect malware. The work in [14] uses an ensemble machine learning approach to detect malware based on dynamic feature behavior. The authors in [15] use a dynamic detection deep learning approach to detect persistent malware hiding inside other apps. The authors in [16] extracted 123 dynamic permissions from around 11000 apps and use various machine learning methods such as decision trees, random forests, and others to detect malware based on the permissions.

The work in [16] uses both static and dynamic features to detect malware using large datasets. Another hybrid approach is the one in [17]. The authors propose a tree augmented naïve bayes algorithm which provides better accuracy when both static and dynamic features are combined.

The closest work to the delivered work is the one in [1] which uses data preprocessing and a convolutional neural network to detect malicious VPNs. The current work further preprocesses the dataset by also removing the most used permissions and not only the least used and delivers a different convolutional neural network combined with a random forest which significantly increases the accuracy.

3 Proposed Method

The first steps of the proposed method are related to the preprocessing of the dataset. Initially, we use the dataset form [1] which is the only available dataset in the literature for malicious VPN detection based on permissions. The dataset contains 1179 non malicious apps and 121 malicious VPN apps, while the total number of permissions used is 184. However, we applied SMOTE to balance the dataset by oversampling the minority class resulting in 1179 non malicious apps and 1179 malicious VPNs. Subsequently, the first step is to reduce the permissions to find the most optimal number of permissions to use. To do this we applied Eqs. 1 and 2 to delete most unused permissions and Eqs. 3 and 4 to delete most used permissions and we identified 80% and 70% respectively provided the most accurate results.

Let D be a dataframe with n columns, indexed by j = 1, 2, …, n, and let C be the set of column indices C = {1, 2, …, n}. The set of columns to drop can be represented as:

$$S = \{j \in C | (D\_\{i, j\} = 0).mean() \geq 0.8\} \quad (1)$$

where D_{i,j} represents the (i,j)-th element of the dataframe D, and.mean() denotes the mean over all rows i. Then, the resulting dataframe D' can be obtained by dropping the columns in S:

$$D' = D.drop(columns = S) \quad (2)$$

where drop(columns = S) denotes the operation of dropping the columns in the set S from the dataframe D.

Let D be a dataframe with n columns, indexed by j = 1, 2, …, n, and let C be the set of column indices C = {1, 2, …, n}. The set of columns to drop can be represented as:

$$S = \{j \in C | (D\_\{i, j\} = 1).mean() \geq 0.7\} \quad (3)$$

where D_{i,j} represents the (i,j)-th element of the dataframe D, and.mean() denotes the mean over all rows i. Then, the resulting dataframe D' can be obtained by dropping the columns in S:

$$D' = D.drop(columns = S) \quad (4)$$

where drop(columns = S) denotes the operation of dropping the columns in the set S from the dataframe D.

By using Eqs. 1 and 2 171 permissions are dropped and by using Eqs. 3 and 4, further 4 permissions are dropped. Thus, the following 10 permissions are remaining in the dataset while the last column (the 11th) now represents malicious and non-malicious based on these permissions:

READ\nPHONE\nSTATE', 'WRITE\nEXTERNAL\nSTRORAGE', 'C2d\nMessage',

'ACCESS\nWIFI\nSTATE', 'FOREGROUND\nSERVICE',

'READ\nEXTERNAL\nSTORAGE', 'RECEIVE\nBOOT\nCOMPLETED', 'VIBRATE',

'BILLING', 'BIND GET\nINSTALL\nREFERRER\nSERVICE'

At the next step, a 1-dimensional CNN sequential architecture has been developed to classify botnets and the Python programming language with the Keras library. The architecture includes one 1D-CNN layer as shown with the convolution in Eq. 5. Where y is the output, n is the length of the convolution represented by x and the kernel represented by h. S is the number of positions the kernel shifts.

$$y(n) = \begin{cases} \sum_{id=0}^{k} x(n+i)h(i), & if\ n = 0 \\ \sum_{i=0}^{k} x(n+i+(s-1))h(i), & otherwise \end{cases} \quad (5)$$

The relu function as shown in Eq. 6 has been used where for the output y and the input x a value is returned from 0 to infinite.

$$y(x) = \max(0, x) \tag{6}$$

Then this layer is followed by a 1D MaxPooling layer and a Flatten layer follows which is then followed by 1 dense layer, 1 with 80 perceptrons and a dropout layer with a 20% dropping percentage. The dense layer is explained in Eq. 7 where Zm is the function output, f is the function name, followed by the function inputs and bias b.

$$Zm = f(x_n, w_{mn}) = b + \sum\nolimits_m x_n w_{mn} \tag{7}$$

The Specific settings used to train the neural network are as follows:

- The learning rate of 0.01 has been set using Adam.
- The number of epochs has been set to 50
- The batch size has been set to 16
- Bias has been set to false in the 1D CNN layer

Finally, a random forest classifier using 100 trees is trained from the inputs of the last dense layer as described in Eq. 7 above. Then, the random forest classifier is used for the final classification. The overall architecture is shown in Fig. 1.

4 Experimental Evaluation

For the experimental evaluation we have used the proposed method architecture described in Sect. 3 which has been developed using the Python programming language and Keras. 5-fold cross validation has been used for all experiments.

4.1 Evaluation Metrics

To evaluate we have used the Accuracy, Precision, Recall and F1 metrics which are described in Eqs. 8, 9, 10 and 11 respectively. TP represents true positives, TN represents true negatives, FP represents false positives and FN represents false negatives.

$$Accuracy = \frac{TP + TN}{TP + TN + FP + FN} \tag{8}$$

$$Precision = \frac{TP}{TP + FP} \tag{9}$$

$$Recall = \frac{TP}{TP + FN} \tag{10}$$

$$F1 = 2 * \frac{Precision * Recall}{Precision + Recall} \tag{11}$$

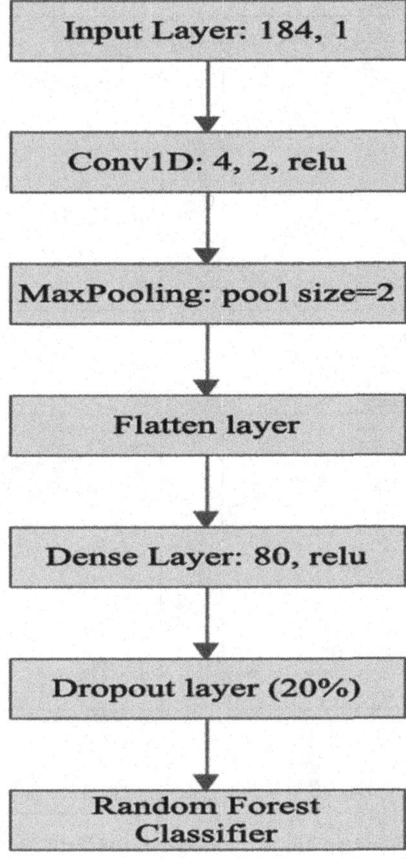

Fig. 1. Proposed method

4.2 Results

This section delivers the results of the experimental evaluation. Figure 2 presents the results of the proposed method architecture for both the train and test accuracy over 50 epochs. Figure 3 presents the loss results over 50 epochs.

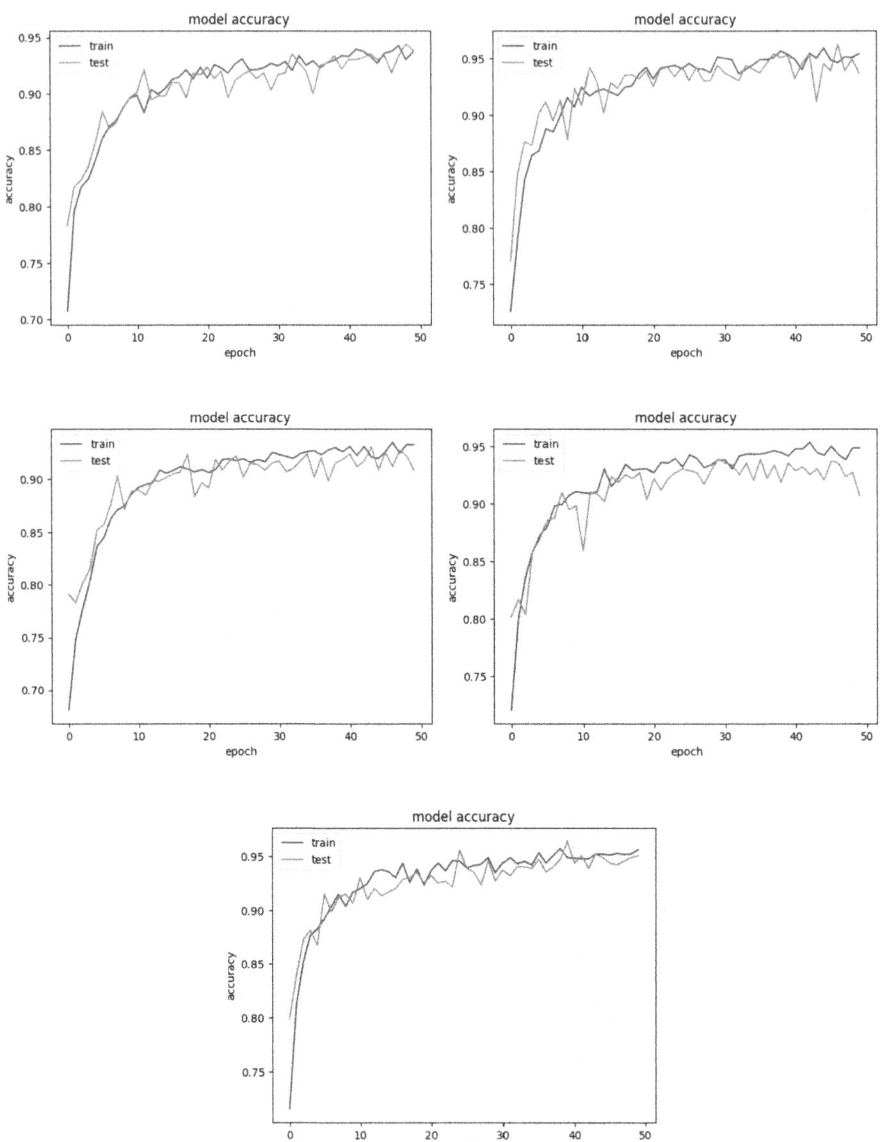

Fig. 2. Accuracy for each of the 5 folds

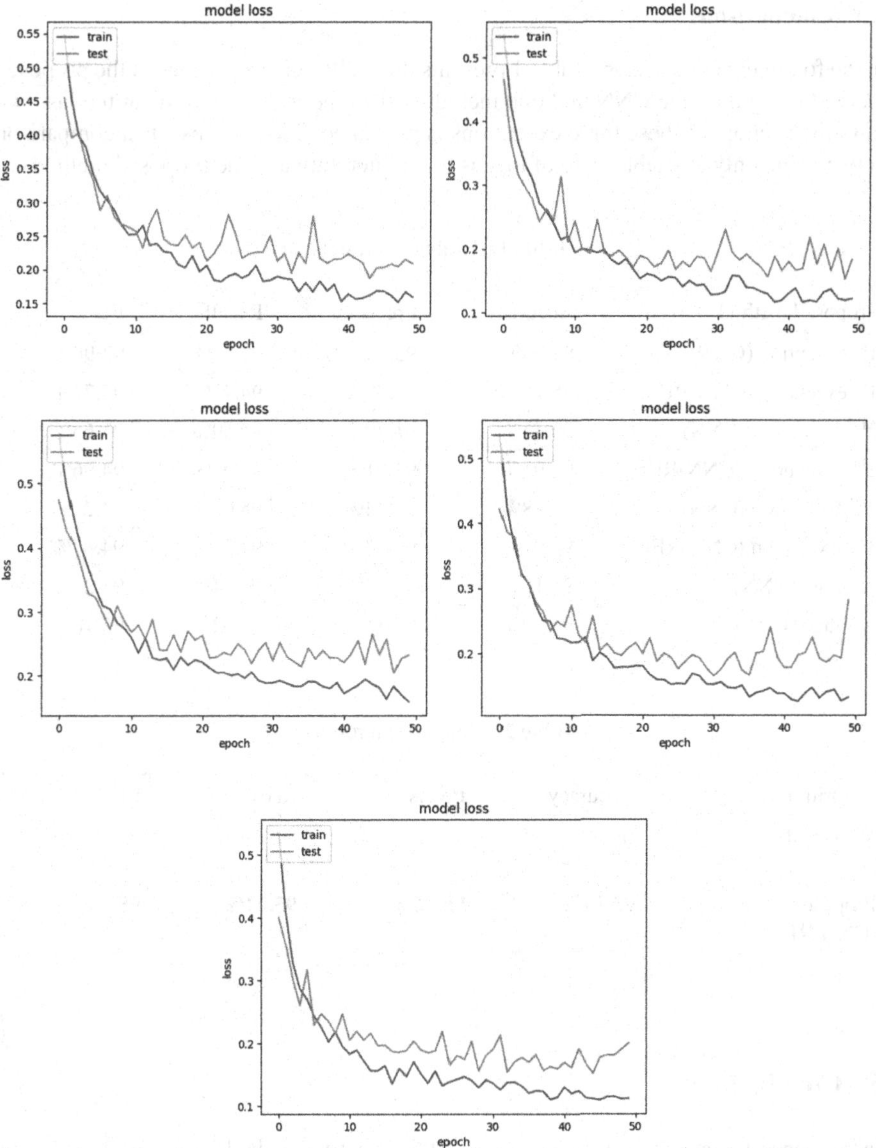

Fig. 3. Loss for each of the 5 folds

4.3 Comparisons

In the following comparisons Table 1 presents three different executions of the proposed method using only the CNN and one including the random forest while at the last two rows the average of these three executions is presented. Table 2 presents a comparison between the only available state of the art in the literature and the proposed method.

Table 1. Evaluation results

Proposed method	Accuracy	Precision	Recall	F1
1st execution (CNN)	92.85%	93.13%	92.68%	92.90%
1st execution (CNN-RF)	95.76%	96.55%	94.91%	95.72%
2nd execution (CNN)	93.46%	91.79%	95.59%	93.65%
2nd Execution (CNN-RF)	94.91%	94.01%	95.93%	94.96%
3rd Execution (CNN)	92.98%	91.44%	95.05%	93.21%
3rd Execution (CNN-RF)	94.91%	95.53%	94.23%	94.87%
Average (CNN)	93.10%	92.12%	94.44%	93.25%
Average (CNN-RF)	95.19%	95.36%	95.02%	95.18%

Table 2. Comparison results

Algorithm	Accuracy	Precision	Recall	F1
MVDroid [1]	%	%	%	%
Proposed method (CNN-RF)	**95.19%**	**95.36%**	**95.02%**	**95.18%**

5 Conclusions

In this paper we have delivered a malicious VPN detection method for Android platforms. We proposed a new method that identifies the most important permissions and then uses a CNN-RF approach to detect malicious VPNs with very high accuracy. The results indicate that by using the most important permissions of VPN apps, and genuine Android apps, malicious VPNS can be detected in a straightforward way which can be useful to beyond the research community.

In the future we plan to extend our proposed method to include the specific family that a malicious VPN belongs to and adjust it accordingly to detect the family as well. Moreover, we plan to investigate how to use permissions zero-day malicious VPNs.

References

1. Seraj, S., Khodambashi, S., Pavlidis, M., Polatidis, N.: MVDroid: an android malicious VPN detector using neural networks. Neural Comput. Appl. 1–11 (2023)
2. Bahar, Z.: Your free VPN app could be a trojan: How to spot fake vpns, NordVPN. Available at: https://nordvpn.com/blog/fake-vpn/ (2022). Accessed 22 Mar 2023
3. Glover, C.: Sandstrike fake VPN is latest in wave of new android malware, tech monitor. Available at: https://techmonitor.ai/technology/cybersecurity/android-malware-sandstrike-fake-vpn (2022). Accessed 22 Mar 2023
4. Editor. Eset Research: Bahamut Group targets android users with fake VPN apps; spyware steals users' conversations, ESET. Available at: https://www.eset.com/int/about/newsroom/press-releases/research/eset-research-bahamut-group-targets-android-users-with-fake-vpn-apps-spyware-steals-users-convers/ (2022). Accessed 22 Mar 2023
5. Crypto theft alert: New malware hijacks coins via phony VPN services. U.Today. https://u.today/crypto-theft-alert-new-malware-hijacks-coins-via-phony-vpn-services (2023). Accessed 8 Apr 2023
6. Seraj, S., Pavlidis, M., Polatidis, N.: TrojanDroid: android malware detection for Trojan discovery using convolutional neural networks. In: Engineering Applications of Neural Networks: 23rd International Conference, EAAAI/EANN 2022, Chersonissos, Crete, Greece, June 17–20, 2022, Proceedings, pp. 203-212. Springer International Publishing, Cham (2022)
7. Seraj, S., Khodambashi, S., Pavlidis, M., Polatidis, N.: HamDroid: permission-based harmful android anti-malware detection using neural networks. Neural Comput. Appl. **34**(18), 15165–15174 (2022)
8. Wang, W., Wang, X., Feng, D., Liu, J., Han, Z., Zhang, X.: Exploring permission-induced risk in android applications for malicious application detection. IEEE Trans. Inform. Forensics Security **9**(11), 1869–1882 (2014). https://doi.org/10.1109/TIFS.2014.2353996
9. Talha, K.A., Alper, D.I., Aydin, C.: APK auditor: permission-based android malware detection system. Digit. Investig. **13**, 1–14 (2015). https://doi.org/10.1016/j.diin.2015.01.001
10. Li, J., Sun, L., Yan, Q., Li, Z., Srisa-An, W., Ye, H.: Significant permission identification for machine-learning-based android malware detection. IEEE Trans. Indu. Inform. **14**(7), 3216–3225 (2018). https://doi.org/10.1109/TII.2017.2789219
11. Milosevic, N., Dehghantanha, A., Choo, K.K.R.: Machine learning aided android malware classification. Comput. Electr. Eng. Elsevier **61**, 266–274 (2017)
12. Sahin, D.O., Kural, O.E., Akleylek, S., et al.: A novel permission-based android malware detection system using feature selection based on linear regression. Neural Comput. Appl. **29**, 245–326 (2021)
13. Vidas, T., Christin, N.: Evading android runtime analysis via sandbox detection. In: Proceedings of the 9th ACM symposium on Information, computer and communications security, 447–458. (2014). https://doi.org/10.1145/2590296.2590325
14. Feng, P., Ma, J., Sun, C., Xu, X., Ma, Y.: A novel dynamic android malware detection system with ensemble learning. IEEE Access **6**, 30996–31011 (2018)
15. Haq, I.U., Khan, T.A., Akhunzada, A.: A dynamic robust DL-based model for android malware detection. IEEE Access **9**, 74510–74521 (2021)
16. Guerra-Manzanares, A., Bahsi, H., Nõmm, S.: KronoDroid: time-based hybrid-featured dataset for effective android malware detection and characterization. Comput. Secur. **110**, 102399 (2021)
17. Surendran, R., Thomas, T., Emmanuel, S.: A TAN based hybrid model for android malware detection. J. Inf. Secur. Appl. **54**, 102483 (2020)

Who Breaks Early, Looses: Goal Oriented Training of Deep Neural Networks Based on Port Hamiltonian Dynamics

Julian Burghoff[1], Marc Heinrich Monells[2], and Hanno Gottschalk[3](✉)

[1] Department of Mathematics & IZMD, University of Wuppertal, Wuppertal, Germany
burghoff@math.uni-wuppertal.de

[2] Department of Mathematics, University of Wuppertal, Wuppertal, Germany
marc.heinrich_monells@math.uni-wuppertal.de

[3] Institute of Mathematics, TU-Berlin, Berlin, Germany
gottschalk@math.tu-berlin.de

Abstract. The highly structured energy landscape of the loss as a function of parameters for deep neural networks makes it necessary to use sophisticated optimization strategies in order to discover (local) minima that guarantee reasonable performance. Overcoming less suitable local minima is an important prerequisite and often momentum methods are employed to achieve this. As in other non local optimization procedures, this however creates the necessity to balance between exploration and exploitation. In this work, we suggest an event based control mechanism for switching from exploration to exploitation based on reaching a predefined reduction of the loss function. As we give the momentum method a port Hamiltonian interpretation, we apply the 'heavy ball with friction' interpretation and trigger breaking (or friction) when achieving certain goals. We benchmark our method against standard stochastic gradient descent and provide experimental evidence for improved performance of deep neural networks when our strategy is applied.

Keywords: neural nets · momentum · goal oriented search · port Hamilton systems

1 Introduction

The success of deep neural networks (DNN) significantly depends on the cheap computation of gradients using back-propagation enabling gradient based minimization of the loss functions. As the parameter count of DNN ranges between several tens of thousand in small classification networks to several billion in large scale generative models, there seems to be no alternative to the use of gradients. However, gradient based optimization is beset with the problem of local minima, of which the energy landscape of DNN offers plenty. Exploitation of a local minimum with gradient descent comes with guarantees for progress relative to previous optimization steps, but does not guarantee a decent level

L. Iliadis et al. (Eds.): ICANN 2023, LNCS 14263, pp. 454–465, 2023.
https://doi.org/10.1007/978-3-031-44204-9_38

of performance. In order to go more global, momentum methods have therefore been introduced to overcome local minima.

As compared to gradient descent, momentum based methods have more parameters to adjust. Besides the strength of the inertial forces controlled by the 'mass' parameter, a 'friction' parameter has to be determined, which is responsible for slowing down the search motion and bringing it to rest, ultimately. Finally, the learning rate needs to be controlled throughout the progress of the optimization process, like in gradient descent.

The complexity in setting and controlling the aforementioned hyper-parameters can be alleviated by an interpretation of the optimization process in physical terms as already indicated by the physical connotations of 'mass' and 'friction'. It has been recently proposed to cast the optimization process in a port Hamiltonian framework, which makes the convergence of the optimization process to a stationary point transparent via energy based considerations, where loss is connected to potential and momentum to kinetic energy, whereas 'friction' accounts for energy dissipation and interdicts motion at high pace for unlimited time. It is clear that the friction/energy dissipation parameter is essential for the (non) locality of the optimization process: if high, friction essentially damps out all momentum and the procedure essentially 'just flows down the hill' as for gradient descent, resulting in low exploration and high exploitation. If low, the motion will go on essentially un-damped and not rest and thereby explore all of the accessible parameter space. Exploration is high, and exploitation is low in this setting.

Then, parameter settings can be modified over time or controlled adaptively as a part of the optimization algorithm is a familiar thought. The physics based intuition of port Hamiltonian systems can be helpful in the design of such adaptive strategies. Here we suggest a simple, event based adaptive parameter selection strategy that starts the optimization in an exploratory phase with low friction and turns over to exploitation by 'heavy breaking', once the potential energy (i.e. the loss function) is sufficiently reduced. Sufficiency is pre-defined as the minimum reduction goal of the optimization, which can be set, e.g., as the reduction of the loss obtained in previous trials.

In this paper, we show that the proposed strategy actually works for some classical examples in deep learning and improves the optimization loss and also the test accuracy for a standard, Le-Net-5 [1] based architectures on two well known academic classification tasks solved by deep learning, namely the CIFAR10 [2] and the FashionMNIST [3] data-sets.

In order to focus on the optimization only, we do not employ data augmentation, excessive hyperparameter adjustments, or pre-training and thereby do not achieve SOTA performance in our experiments. We however consistently achieve an advantage over the widely used stochastic gradient descent as a benchmark. We also observe consistent gains in performance after 'heavy breaking' is finally triggered.

Our paper is organized as follows: in Sect. 2 we give an overview over related work and in Sect. 3 we present the port Hamiltonian view on gradient based optimization with momentum and energy dissipation. Our experimental setup as well as our results are documented in Sect. 4. In the final Sect. 5 we present our conclusions and give an outlook to future research.

2 Related Work

The fact that neural networks with parameter counts ranging from some tenth of thousands to several hundreds of billions can actually be trained, largely depends on the cheap computation of gradients, see [1,4] for original work and [5] for a recent reference. Gradient based optimization itself has been studied since the days of Newton, see e.g. [6,7]. In the context of deep learning, the formation of randomly sub-sampled mini-batches is necessary as big data often exceeds the working memory available [8]. One has therefore to pass over to the stochastic gradient descent method (SGD) [9,10].

One of the problems in neural network training is the complex, non convex structure of the energy landscapes [11]. This makes it necessary to avoid local minima, which is mostly done by the momentum method [12–14]. From a theoretical side, momentum can be understood as a discretized version of a second order ordinary differential equation, which also provides theoretical insight to convergence to critical points [15–17], see also [18–20] for recent extensions.

The momentum method has recently be cast in a modern port Hamiltonian language [21–23]. Port Hamiltonian systems [24] are particularly suited to understand the long time behviour and hence convergence properties of momentum based methods.

For a long time, the control of hyperparemeters in the training of neural networks has been a topic of interest in the deep learning community [25]. While learning rate schedules [26,27] determine the setting for one specific parameter upfront, it has also been proposed to modify the dissipation parameter in momentum based optimization [16,28,29]. Other strategies, like the much used ADAM algorithm, rely on adaptive parameter control [30,31].

One specific adaptive strategy however much less considered is the goal oriented search, where one pre-defines the target value to achieve during optimization, see e.g. [32].

In our work, we thus make the following contributions:

- For the first time, we use the port Hamiltonian language in the training of reasonably *deep* neural networks in contrast to [21,22] where networks are shallow.
- We also introduce an adaptive, goal oriented strategy for the control of the friction constant, which goes in the opposite direction as [16,28,29] but is well-motivated in terms of combining exploration and exploitation in one algorithm.
- We show experimentally for standard deep learning problems in image recognition that this strategy consistently produces improvements over fixed-parameter strategies. We also provide a considerable amount of ablation studies related to our parameter settings.

3 The Goal Oriented PHS Method

The simple gradient descent algorithm to minimize a differentiable loss function $\mathscr{L}(\theta)$, namely $\theta_{k+1} = \theta_k - \alpha\nabla_\theta\mathscr{L}(\theta_k)$ can be seen as a first order Euler discretization of the gradient flow

$$\dot{\theta}(t) = -\nabla_\theta\mathscr{L}(\theta), \quad \theta(0) = \theta_0. \tag{1}$$

It is well known that under adequate conditions on $\mathscr{L}(\theta)$, the flow $\theta(t)$ converges for $t \to \infty$ to a critical point θ^* with $\nabla_\theta\mathscr{L}(\theta^*) = 0$, see e.g. [21,22]. Likewise, the gradient descent algorithm converges for $k \to \infty$ to a critical point, provided the step length α is suitably controlled, confer [15,16].

As mentioned in the introduction, the problem with gradient descent in the context of highly non-convex loss functions $\mathscr{L}(\theta)$, as especially in the context of the training of deep neural networks [5], lies in the fact that gradient flows and gradient descent algorithms get stuck in local minima.

To over come the strict locality of gradient flow and gradient descent, momentum based methods have been introduced. The update rule of gradient descent is changed to

$$\begin{aligned}\theta_{k+1} &= \theta_k + \alpha\frac{1}{m}p_k \\ p_{k+1} &= p_k - \alpha\frac{\gamma}{m}p_k - \alpha\nabla_\theta\mathscr{L}(\theta)\end{aligned} \tag{2}$$

where $m, \gamma > 0$ are parameters called mass and friction coefficient. p_k is the so-called momentum at iteration k. In fact, (2) can be understood as the discretized version of the following Hamiltonian set of equations

$$\begin{aligned}\dot{\theta}(t) &= \frac{1}{m}p(t) \\ \dot{p}(t) &= -\frac{\gamma}{m}p(t) - \nabla_\theta\mathscr{L}(\theta)\end{aligned} \tag{3}$$

with initial conditions $\theta(0) = \theta_0$ and $p(0) = p_0$.

To understand the global properties of the Hamiltonian dynamics, it is convenient to define a state variable $x(t) = \begin{pmatrix}\theta(t)\\p(t)\end{pmatrix}$ and the Hamiltonial function $H(x) = \frac{\|p\|^2}{2m} + \mathscr{L}(\theta)$ and a the symplectic matrix $J = \begin{pmatrix}0 & -1\\1 & 0\end{pmatrix}$ as well as a symmetric, positive resistive matrix $R = \begin{pmatrix}0 & 0\\0 & \frac{\gamma}{m}\end{pmatrix}$ so that we can rewrite (3) in the compact, port-Hamiltonian form

$$\dot{x}(t) = (J - R)\,\nabla_x H(x). \tag{4}$$

Using the chain-rule, (4) and $\nabla_x H(x(\tau))^\top J\nabla_x H(x(\tau)) = 0$ by the skew-symmetry of J, it is now easy to see that the following inequality holds for the dissipated total 'energy' measured by $H(x)$, where $\frac{\|p\|^2}{2m}$ takes the role of kinetic energy and the loss $\mathscr{L}(\theta)$ the role of potential energy

$$H(x(t)) - H(x(0)) = -\int_0^t \nabla_x H(x(\tau))^\top R \nabla_x H(x(\tau))\, \mathrm{d}\tau. \tag{5}$$

From this exposition it is intuitive, and in fact can be proven mathematically [15,16], that due to dissipation the state $x(t)$ ultimately has to come to a rest, if $\mathscr{L}(\theta)$ is bounded from below. Thus, if the stationary points x^* with $\nabla_x H(x^*) = 0$ of the system are isolated, $x(t)$ will asymptotically converge to a stationary point. Furthermore, for $x^* = \binom{\theta^*}{p^*}$, we find $p^* = 0$ and $\nabla_\theta \mathscr{L}(\theta^*) = 0$, hence the θ-component of stationary points are in one to one correspondence to the critical points of the original optimization problem.

Energy dissipation (5) thus is the key component that determines how fast $x(t)$ comes to rest, which conceptually is corresponding to convergence of the optimization algorithm. Apparently, the matrix R and thus the friction coefficient γ controls dissipation.

In fact, if $\gamma \approx 0$, essentially no energy is lost and the dynamics $x(t)$ will either move on for a very long time, or, in very rare cases, get to rest on a local maximum or saddle point. This perpetual motion through the accessible part of the 'phase space' can be seen as an exploitative strategy.

In contrast, if γ gets large, the friction essentially disperses energy and momentum and the motion of $x(t)$ behaves highly viscous, i.e. determined by the equality

$$-\frac{\gamma}{m} p(t) - \nabla_\theta \mathscr{L}(\theta) \approx 0 \quad \Leftrightarrow \quad \dot{\theta}(t) \approx -\frac{1}{\gamma} \nabla_\theta \mathscr{L}(\theta), \tag{6}$$

from which we see that in this high viscosity regime the port Hamiltonian flow essentially behaves like gradient descent (with a modified step length). Despite working with momentum, we are thus back in the exploitation phase of local minima.

The idea of this article is to use this physics based intuition to efficiently control the behavior of our port Hamiltonian optimization strategy in a goal oriented search. We thus propose to 'keep on moving' as long as we have not yet reached a predefined reduction of the initial loss function $\mathscr{L}(\theta_0)$. In many cases, it is known that $\mathscr{L}(\theta)$ is lower bounded by zero, and we can thus demand a 90%, 95% ... reduction in $\mathscr{L}(x(t))$, before we, upon reaching this target, instantaneously increase the value of γ in order to switch over from the low-viscous exploration phase to high-viscous exploitation. In this sense, our proposed optimization algorithm resembles the 'chicken game': who breaks too early, looses.

Before we come to the implementation and numerical tests of this strategy in deep learning, we discuss some peculiarities of the loss function in this case. We would like to learn a conditional probability density $p(y|x, \theta)$ from data independently sampled from the same distribution $\{(y_i, x_i)\}_{i=1}^n$, where x_i is some input and y_i takes values in some prescribed label space $\mathscr{C} = \{c_1, \ldots, c_q\}$. In applications in image recognition, $p(y|x,\theta)$ often consists of several stacked convolutional and fully connected layers and an ultimate softmax layer, cf. [5]. The 'cross entropy'/negative log likelihood loss is given by

$$\mathscr{L}(\theta) = -\frac{1}{n}\sum_{i=1}^{n}\log p(y_i|x_i,\theta). \tag{7}$$

The numerical problem to implement (7) directly lies in the memory constraints that do not permit to load the entire data set $\{(y_i,x_i)\}_{i=1}^{n}$ in the working memory. Therefore, mini batches B_j, i.e. small random subsets of $\{1,\dots,n\}$ are drawn and an update step of the parameters θ_k and the associated momentum is executed for a loss $\mathscr{L}_{B_j}(\theta)$ with the original data set replaced by $\{(y_i,x_i)\}_{i\in B_j}$. Nevertheless, as in image classification oftentimes the batch $|B_j|$ is quite large ($\gtrsim 10$), $\mathscr{L}_{B_j}(\theta)$ and $\mathscr{L}(\theta)$ tend do behave similar by the law of large numbers. In our numerical experiments, we therefore observe the behavior of the algorithm in accordance with intuition.

4 Experiments and Results

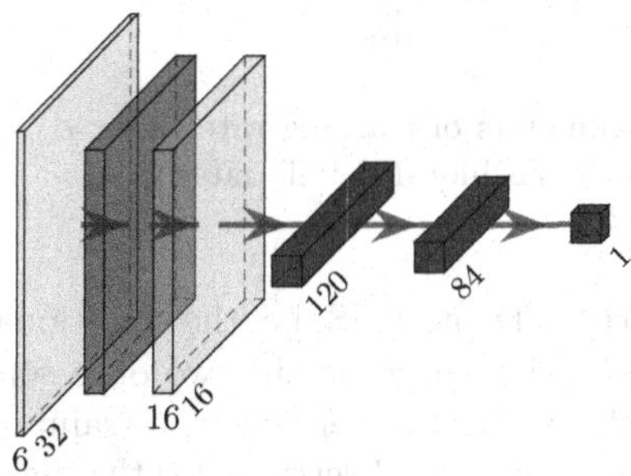

Fig. 1. Neural Net architecture which is similar to Le-Net-5. Orange are convolutional layers with a filter size of 5, red is the pooling layer and fully connected layers are violet. (Color figure online)

For our experiments, we use a Convolutional Neural Net (CNN) similar to the Le-Net-5 [1] which consists of two convolutional, one pooling and two fully connected layers as it is shown in Fig. 1 and has a total of 44,426 weights. For implementation we are using the PyTorch framework [33]. This network is chosen as it is a widely used standard architecture, although it is not eligible to compete with more sophisticated ResNet [34] or Transformer [35] architectures. Nevertheless, this architecture is still frequently used today (like in [36]) if the data allow compression to a small format or to get a first, quick feasibility study on whether a problem can be solved by machine learning. For this use case, this approach could be used as an alternative to the classic SGD optimisation algorithm. Furthermore, in order to focus on training exclusively, the networks are trained from scratch on the data sets and we use neither pre-training nor augmentation. The training is performed with respect to the usual cross-entropy loss without regularization.

On the hardware-side, we use a workstation with an Intel(R) Core(TM) i7-6850K 3.6GHz and two Nvidia TITAN Xp graphic units with 12GB VRAM each for our experiments.

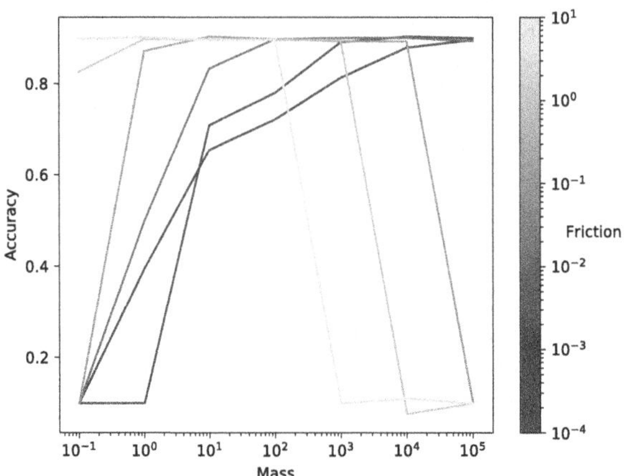

Fig. 2. Selecting hyperparameters of learning rate (here: $\alpha = 0.1$), mass and friction based on the accuracy on the Fashion-MNIST dataset

For a comparison with SGD and PHS, i.e. the traditional momentum method, we test our goal oriented PHS search on the two data sets CIFAR10 and FashionMNIST introduced above. We furthermore run trainings for a number of different learning rates α and for several settings for the mass and baseline friction parameter. To establish which parameter settings are rewarding, we consider the accuracies of the PHS for different learning rates ($0.0001 \leq \alpha \leq 0.1$), that can be achieved when mass and friction are included. This is shown in Fig. 2 for the example of $\alpha = 0.1$ on the Fashion-MNIST dataset. As one can already see, the trainings for many parameter settings work significantly worse or not at all. Therefore, only experiments that lie in a parameter range leading to reasonable results are included in our result tables. Concerning goal orientation, we aim at an reduction of the initial loss of 65% to 90% and then increase the friction significantly by a factor between 5 and 99. The results are given in Tables 1 for CIFAR10 and 2 for FashionMNIST.

As can be seen in Fig. 3a, the accuracy of the method is consistently improved by breaking after reaching the goal, and the subsequent occurrence of overfitting (as happens with the PHS) is avoided. The increase in test accuracy lies around and in many cases above 0.5% throughout parameter settings and the

Table 1. Comparison of training results with SGD, PHS and Goal-Oriented approaches for the CIFAR-10 dataset.

α	Optimizer	Fric	Mass	Acc
0.1	SGD	/	/	64.82%
0.1	PHS	0.1	100	66.45%
0.1	Goal-Oriented (breaking at 0.65 with factor 49)	0.1	100	**67.1%**
0.1	PHS	0.01	100	63.52%
0.1	Goal-Oriented (breaking at 0.9 with factor 99)	0.01	100	65.52%
0.01	SGD	/	/	63.53%
0.01	PHS	0.1	25	66.01%
0.01	Goal-Oriented (breaking at 0.7 with factor 10)	0.1	25	**66.49%**
0.01	PHS	0.01	25	62.98%
0.01	Goal-Oriented (breaking at 0.7 with factor 50)	0.01	25	63.44%
0.001	SGD	/	/	65.05 %
0.001	PHS	1	0.25	66.0 %
0.001	Goal-Oriented (breaking at 0.7 with factor 20)	1	0.25	**66.37%**
0.001	PHS	0.1	0.25	62.93%
0.001	Goal-Oriented (breaking at 0.85 with factor 50)	0.1	0.25	63.54%
0.0001	SGD	/	/	64.43%
0.0001	PHS	10	0.001	65.76%
0.0001	Goal-Oriented (breaking at 0.68 with factor 5)	10	0.001	**66.39%**
0.0001	PHS	1	0.001	62.24%
0.0001	Goal-Oriented (breaking at 0.8 with factor 100)	1	0.001	63.56%

two data sets employed, as documented in Table 1 for CIFAR10 and Table 2 for FashionMNIST.

The history of the test accuracy over the iteration count of the optimization procedure is shown in Fig. 3 for two example configurations of each dataset. As we observe, the sudden 'breaking' exploits a local minimum better and avoids overfitting (as it can be especially seen in Fig. 3a), i.e. the decrease of the ordinary PHS method in the further pursuit of the optimization. Interestingly, this hints that overfitting rather is a 'global' phenomenon associated with ongoing exploration, whereas exploitation of the local minimum seems less beset from overfitting issues. This is consistent with our observation that the training loss after 'breaking' quickly converges, whereas the training loss for SGD or PHS is further reduced. This suggest that the onset of overfitting could thus also be a useful triggering event for 'breaking' instead of goal orientation, as employed here.

Table 2. Comparison of training results with SGD, PHS and Goal-Oriented approaches for the FashionMNIST dataset.

α	Optimizer	Fric	Mass	Acc
0.1	SGD	/	/	90.04%
0.1	PHS	0.1	10	90.36%
0.1	Goal-Oriented (breaking at 0.15 with factor 50)	0.1	10	**91.02%**
0.1	PHS	0.01	10	83.31%
0.1	Goal-Oriented (breaking at 0.55 with factor 20)	0.01	10	87.19%
0.01	SGD	/	/	90.26%
0.01	PHS	1	0.1	90.49%
0.01	Goal-Oriented (breaking at 0.2 with factor 10)	1	0.1	**90.98%**
0.01	PHS	0.1	0.1	83.28%
0.01	Goal-Oriented (breaking at 0.5 with factor 5)	0.1	0.1	86.47%
0.001	SGD	/	/	89.61%
0.001	PHS	10	0.01	90.34%
0.001	Goal-Oriented (breaking at 0.15 with factor 5)	10	0.01	**90.8%**
0.001	PHS	1	0.01	90.13%
0.001	Goal-Oriented (breaking at 0.17 with factor 50)	1	0.01	90.77%
0.0001	SGD	/	/	88.86%
0.0001	PHS	10	0.001	90.17%
0.0001	Goal-Oriented (breaking at 0.2 with factor 100)	10	0.001	**90.54%**
0.0001	PHS	1	0.001	89.6%
0.0001	Goal-Oriented (breaking at 0.185 with factor 100)	1	0.001	90.12%

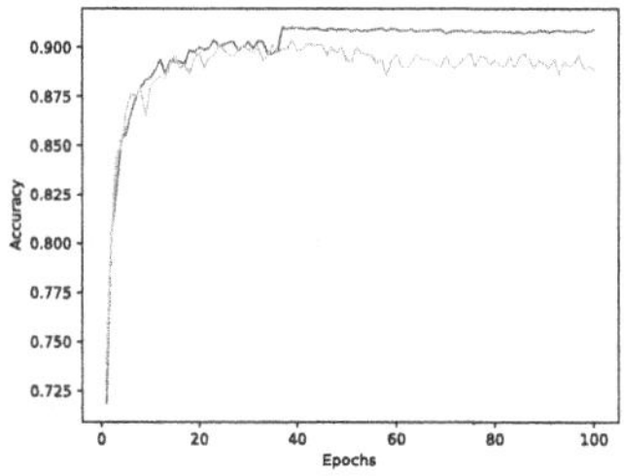

(a) $\alpha = 0.1$, friction $= 0.1$, mass $=$ 10 on Fashion-MNIST.

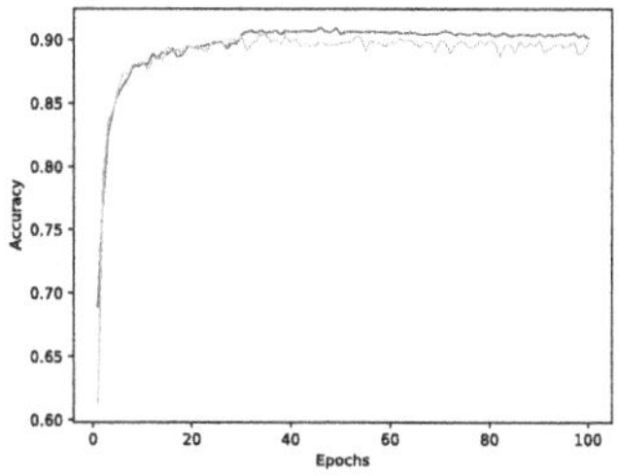

(b) $\alpha = 0.01$, friction $= 1$, mass $=$ 0.1 on Fashion-MNIST.

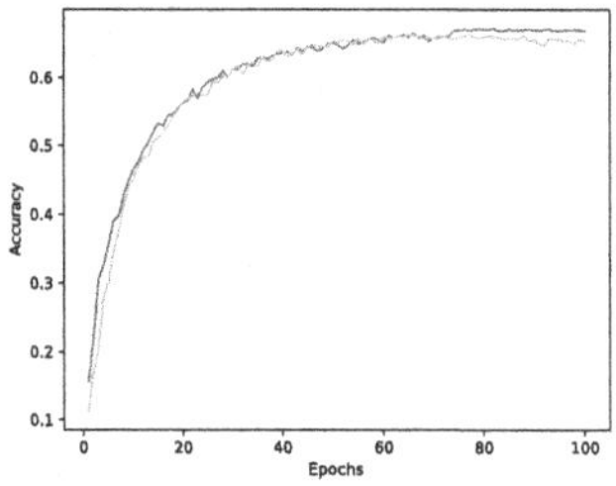

(c) $\alpha = 0.1$, friction $= 0.1$, mass $=$ 100 on CIFAR-10.

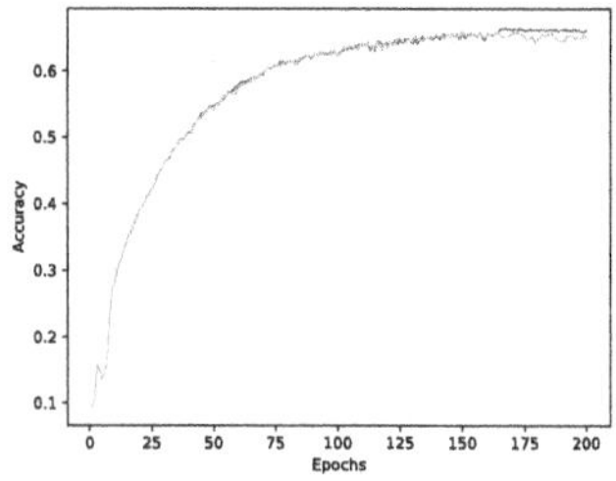

(d) $\alpha = 0.01$, friction $= 0.1$, mass $= 25$ on CIFAR-10.

Fig. 3. History of the accuracies over the epochs depending on the choosable hyperparameters learning rate α, friction and mass. PHS in orange, Goal-oriented approach in blue. (Color figure online)

5 Discussion and Outlook

In our paper, we have introduced a new goal oriented strategy for the training of deep neural networks. By the physics-motivated interpretation of momentum in a port Hamiltonian framework, we explained how different settings for the friction/dissipation correspond to an exploration or exploitation phase in the progress of optimization. By switching from exploration to exploitation when a certain minimal reduction of the loss function of a deep neural network is achieved, we obtain improved classification accuracy of image classification networks as compared with simple stochastic gradient descent or a momentum based optimization with fixed friction.

The outlined strategy can be extended in several ways. First, for the case where the minimal reduction is never achieved for a long time, the exploitation phase could be executed nevertheless starting from the best parameter setting found so far, or the target could be adjusted. This will robustify our algorithm. Second, after a first exploitation phase, a re-acceleration could be executed, e.g. by an external force or 'port', so that multiple promising local minima can be visited.

Acknowledgements. The authors thank Onur T. Doganay, Kathrin Klamroth, Matthias Rottmann and Claudia Totzeck for interesting discussions. This work is partially funded by the German Federal Ministry for Economic Affairs and Climate Action, within the project "KI Delta Learning", grant no. 19A19013Q.

References

1. LeCun, Y., Bottou, L., Bengio, Y., Haffner, P.: Gradient-based learning applied to document recognition. Proc. IEEE **86**(11), 2278–2324 (1998)
2. Krizhevsky, A., Hinton, G.: Learning multiple layers of features from tiny images (2009)
3. Xiao, H., Rasul, K., Vollgraf, R.: Fashion-MNIST: a novel image dataset for benchmarking machine learning algorithms. CoRR, vol. abs/1708.07747 (2017). arXiv: 1708.07747
4. Werbos, P.J.: Applications of advances in nonlinear sensitivity analysis. In: Drenick, R.F., Kozin, F. (eds.) System Modeling and Optimization. Lecture Notes in Control and Information Sciences, vol. 38, pp. 762–770. Springer, Heidelberg (2005). https://doi.org/10.1007/BFb0006203
5. Goodfellow, I., Bengio, Y., Courville, A.: Deep Learning. MIT Press, Cambridge (2016)
6. Bazaraa, M.S., Sherali, H.D., Shetty, C.M.: Nonlinear Programming - Theory and Algorithms, 3rd edn. Wiley, Hoboken (2006)
7. Wright, S., Nocedal, J., et al.: Numerical Optimization, vol. 35, no. 67–68, p. 7. Springer, New York (1999)
8. Li, M., Zhang, T., Chen, Y., Smola, A.J.: Efficient mini-batch training for stochastic optimization. In: Proceedings of the 20th ACM SIGKDD International Conference on Knowledge Discovery and Data Mining, pp. 661–670 (2014)
9. Saad, D.: Online algorithms and stochastic approximations. Online Learn. **5**(3), 6 (1998)

10. Shalev-Shwartz, S., Ben-David, S.: Understanding Machine Learning: From Theory to Algorithms. Cambridge University Press, Cambridge (2014)
11. Becker, S., Zhang, Y.: Geometry of energy landscapes and the optimizability of deep neural networks. Phys. Rev. Lett. **124**(10), 108301 (2020)
12. Nesterov, Y.: A method for unconstrained convex minimization problem with the rate of convergence o $(1/\hat{k}2)$. In: Doklady an USSR, vol. 269, pp. 543–547 (1983)
13. Goh, G.: Why momentum really works. Distill **2**(4), e6 (2017)
14. Qian, N.: On the momentum term in gradient descent learning algorithms. Neural Netw. **12**(1), 145–151 (1999)
15. Antipin, A.: Second order proximal differential systems with feedback control. Differ. Equ. **29**, 1597–1607 (1993)
16. Attouch, H., Chbani, Z., Peypouquet, J., Redont, P.: Fast convergence of inertial dynamics and algorithms with asymptotic vanishing viscosity. Math. Program. **168**, 123–175 (2018)
17. Polyack, B.: Some methods of speeding up the convergence of iterative methods. Z. Vylist Math. Fiz. **4**, 1–17 (1964)
18. Ochs, P., Chen, Y., Brox, T., Pock, T.: IPiano: inertial proximal algorithm for non-convex optimization. SIAM J. Imag. Sci. **7**, 1388–1419 (2014)
19. Ochs, P.: Local convergence of the heavy-ball method and iPiano for nonconvex optimization. J. Optim. Theory Appl. **177**, 153–180 (2018)
20. Ochs, P., Pock, T.: Adaptive FISTA for non-convex optimization. SIAM J. Optim. **29**, 2482–2503 (2019)
21. Massaroli, S., et al.: Port-Hamiltonian approach to neural network training. In: 2019 IEEE 58th Conference on Decision and Control (CDC), IEEE, pp. 6799–6806 (2019)
22. Poli, M., Massaroli, S., Yamashita, A., Asama, H., Park, J.: Port-Hamiltonian gradient flows. In: ICLR 2020 Workshop on Integration of Deep Neural Models and Differential Equations (2020)
23. Kovachki, N.B., Stuart, A.M.: Continuous time analysis of momentum methods. J. Mach. Learn. Res. **22**, 1–40 (2021)
24. Van Der Schaft, A., Jeltsema, D.: Port-Hamiltonian systems theory: an introductory overview. Found. Trends® Syst. Control **1**(2–3), 173–378 (2014)
25. Bengio, Y.: Practical recommendations for gradient-based training of deep architectures. In: Montavon, G., Orr, G.B., Müller, K.-R. (eds.) Neural Networks: Tricks of the Trade. LNCS, vol. 7700, pp. 437–478. Springer, Heidelberg (2012). https://doi.org/10.1007/978-3-642-35289-8_26
26. Darken, C., Moody, J.: Note on learning rate schedules for stochastic optimization. In: Advances in Neural Information Processing Systems, vol. 3 (1990)
27. Darken, C., Chang, J., Moody, J., et al.: Learning rate schedules for faster stochastic gradient search. In: Neural Networks for Signal Processing, vol. 2, pp. 3–12. Citeseer (1992)
28. Cabot, A., Engler, H., Gadta, S.: On the long time behavior of second order differential equations with asymptotically small dissipation. Trans. Am. Math. Soc. **361**, 5983–6017 (2009)
29. Chambolle, A., Dossal, C.: On the convergence of the iterates of the "fast iterative shrinkage/thresholding algorithm". J. Optim. Theory Appl. **166**, 968–982 (2015). https://doi.org/10.1007/s10957-015-0746-4
30. Kingma, D.P., Ba, J.: Adam: a method for stochastic optimization. arXiv preprint arXiv:1412.6980 (2014)
31. Bock, S., Weiß, M.: A proof of local convergence for the Adam optimizer. In: International Joint Conference on Neural Networks (IJCNN), pp. 1–8. IEEE (2019)

32. Forrester, A., Sobester, A., Keane, A.: Engineering Design Via Surrogate Modelling: A Practical Guide. Wiley, Hoboken (2008)
33. Paszke, A., et al.: PyTorch: an imperative style, high-performance deep learning library. In: Advances in Neural Information Processing Systems, vol. 32, pp. 8024–8035. Curran Associates Inc (2019). http://papers.neurips.cc/paper/9015-pytorch-an-imperative-style-high-performance-deeplearning-library.pdf
34. He, K., Zhang, X., Ren, S., Sun, J.: Deep residual learning for image recognition. In: Proceedings of the IEEE Conference on Computer Vision and Pattern Recognition, pp. 770–778 (2016)
35. Vaswani, A., et al.: Attention is all you need. In: Advances in Neural Information Processing Systems, vol. 30 (2017)
36. Islam, M.R., Matin, A.: Detection of COVID 19 from CT image by the novel LeNet-5 CNN architecture. In: 2020 23rd International Conference on Computer and Information Technology (ICCIT), IEEE, pp. 1–5 (2020)

BLR: A Multi-modal Sentiment Analysis Model

Yang Yang[1,2,3,4], Ye Zhonglin[1,2,3,4], Zhao Haixing[1,2,3,4](✉), Li Gege[1,2,3,4], and Cao Shujuan[1,2,3,4]

[1] College of Computer, Qinghai Normal University, Xining 810008, China
964520152@qq.com

[2] The State Key Laboratory of Tibetan Intelligent Information Processing and Application, Xining 810008, China

[3] Tibetan Information Processing and Machine Translation Key Laboratory of Qinghai Province, Xining 810008, China

[4] Key Laboratory of Tibetan Information Processing, Ministry of Education, Xining 810008, China

Abstract. In multi-modal sentiment analysis tasks, deep learning plays an important role due to its excellent performance. Compared with the traditional statistical approaches and machine learning approaches, deep learning methods have better performance and stability. However, there are still two problems in multi-modal sentiment analysis works, one is that the fused features lead to missing important information. Another is that the affiliation of each feature after fusion is not precisely defined and calculated. To deal with issues, we propose a BLR Multi-channel dual Fusion Model based on Bert,Lstm and ResNeST framework. Our model first ensures that the important features will not be lost after fusion to the maximum extent and then will be processed and optimized according to the contribution of each feature for the fusion. Finally, we conduct experiments on two datasets, the results show that the accuracy of our model gets 76.125% and 77.5%, growing 3.025% and 2.875% over the best baseline model, respectively. Thus, the proposed model BLR model, achieves better effectiveness in multi-modal sentiment analysis tasks.

Keywords: Transformer · Deep Learning · Multi-modal · Feature Fusion

1 Introduction

Sentiment analysis is the analysis of people's personal opinions and subjective feelings held about physical objects such as products and events. With the development of social networks, more social network users use a lot of text and pictures to record every day for their lives. Such as users sharing their food recommendations [1], reviews of movies [2–4], and opinions on certain hot events [5, 6]. This rich user sentiment has potential applications in stock movements [7, 8], movie box office prediction [9], and artificial intelligence. Compare to a single way of delivering information through text, using multiple media forms often provides more comprehensive sentiment information and helps models better understand human behavior and intentions. More and more

L. Iliadis et al. (Eds.): ICANN 2023, LNCS 14263, pp. 466–478, 2023.
https://doi.org/10.1007/978-3-031-44204-9_39

researchers have recognized the importance of analyzing multi-modal data and have proposed a range of approaches to improve the performance of multi-modal sentiment analysis [10, 11]. Multi-modal sentiment analysis refers to combining information from two or more modalities together for the prediction of sentiment categories, the features of each modality make the maximum contribution to the final result [12–14].

With the rise of deep learning and some fusion algorithms, multi-modal sentiment analysis techniques have been rapidly developed and the challenges have come with them. But there are several difficulties in multi-modal sentiment analysis tasks still. (1) Multi-modal sentiment analysis dataset. For multi-modal sentiment analysis, the dataset is small and mostly consists of three modalities that are visual, text, and speech, with fewer resources for body posture, brain waves, and other modalities. Therefore, high-quality and large-scale datasets are needed to improve the accuracy of sentiment analysis. (2) Algorithm complexity. The many modalities and complex algorithms will increase the complexity of the fusion algorithm when performing multi-modal sentiment analysis, and the few modalities will affect the accuracy of the results. Therefore, it is difficult to balance the complexity and accuracy. (3) Weighting problem of modalities during fusion. For modal fusion, the optimal weight assignment of different modalities in different environments is one of the important factors, which affect the results of sentiment analysis.

To challenge the above issues, we propose a novel fusion model-BLR model for sentiment analysis tasks.

2 Related Work

The most important and difficult point in multi-modal sentiment analysis is feature fusion, Huddar et al. [15] made a summary of the difficulty and importance of feature fusion in their literature. The multi-modal sentiment analysis task can be further divided into traditional methods, machine learning methods, and deep learning methods with the development of various new technologies, and Peng et al. [16] in this field have summarized the existing ideas and methods from different perspectives. Chen et al. [17] propose a Chinese microblog sentiment analysis model based on a multi-channel convolutional neural network, which can learn the connection between different input features through multifaceted information and mine more hidden feature information. Cao et al. [18] use a BGRU model for sentiment analysis of text modality, which analyzes the contextual extraction of textual information through BGRU, and it is shown through experiments that the inclusion of contextual information can effectively improve the accuracy. Wang et al. [19] propose a joint architecture of CNN and RNN, which uses coarse-grained local features generate by CNN as the input of RNN for sentiment analysis of short texts, so Liu et al. [20] propose a BERT-BILSTM model, which uses a BERT preprocessing model to improve the generalization ability of BLR on different datasets while ensuring high efficiency. For the visual feature extraction methods, Lu et al. [21] propose a CNN integration-based facial expression recognition method, which design three different structured sub-networks containing 3, 5, and 10 convolutional layers in a set of CNN networks. Deng et al. [22] propose a multi-modal neural network structure, this structure integrates temporally varying visual information with LSTM and combines it with audio and text information by feature-level fusion for sentiment analysis. Poria et al. [23] propose a convolutional recurrent multicore learning (CRMKL) model. Yu et al. [24] propose a deep CNN-based sentiment analysis method for microblogging visual and text, in which CNN and DNN are used to analyze the sentiment of textual and visual information, respectively. Poria et al. [25] propose a deep CNN-based feature extraction method using three modalities including text, video and audio for heterogeneous data.

3 Methodology

3.1 General Framework of BLR Model

In this paper, we propose a BLR model based on the existing model and its shortcomings, as shown in Fig. 1. The advantages of BLR model are as follows: (1) BLR retains all features extracted from both modal data as much as possible (2) weights are added to all features according to their contributions in the multi-modal sentiment analysis task to play their proper roles.

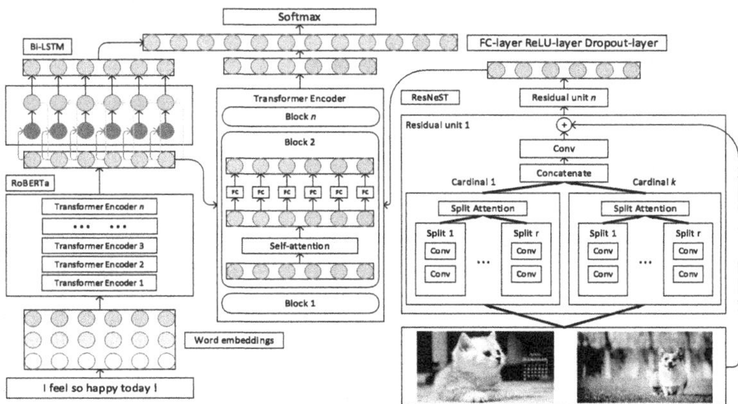

Fig. 1. BLR Multi-channel dual fusion model framework

In BLR model, visual features are first extracted using ResNeST [26] to obtain image features. Then the text information is feature extracted using the RoBERTa model to get text features, and then the extracted text features are processed twice by two channels. In the first channel, the text features are fuse with the visual features; in the second channel, the obtained text features are feature optimized by the Bi-LSTM model to obtain text optimized features containing temporal relationships. In the second channel, the text features are optimized by the Bi-LSTM model to obtain text-optimized features with temporal relationships, and the features are finally fuse with the Transformer Encoder layer and sent to the Softmax layer for classification. We do not add the Bi-LSTM layer before the feature fusion layer, because feature fusion should ensure the purity of the features before input as much as possible, and it should ensure that its dimensionality is not too much, otherwise the dimensionality of the fused features is too large, which will affect the accuracy of the final results, so BLR model uses the Bi-LSTM layer as the second channel of text feature processing, and proves that it improves the final results in the experiments.

This paper mainly uses a BLR model based on Transformer fusion method, as shown in Fig. 1, whose algorithmic framework consists of the following three modules.

Text Modeling: For text type data, BLR adopts an upgraded and optimized model of BERT model RoBERTa, which inherits the excellent performance of BERT model for the task of text-based natural language processing in addition to its robustness, model scale and arithmetic power than the original BERT model. Then the extracted text features are processed in two channels, in channel one, multi-modal feature fusion is performed with visual features, and in channel two, the extracted text features are sent into the Bi-LSTM model in this paper for processing again to obtain their temporal relationships, and text-optimized features containing temporal relationships are obtained.

Image Modeling: For visual type data, BLR uses a network of residual networks with the stacked Split-Attention Block, and the visual features input into each residual block are processed in separate channels, and in each channel, the features are grouped again, because the visual type data in multi-modal sentiment classification for the final result The contribution of visual type data to the final result is unstable, compared to text type data, image data has a lot of noise, so this paper divides the features in images into several groups of feature map bases to ensure maximum optimization of image features, and each group of features is continuously trained in 16 layers of residual blocks to derive the final result, and because an overly complex network model will have a negative impact on the final result, this paper uses a residual network to ensure good final results even in deeper and more complex networks.

Feature Fusion: The fusion method used in this paper is Transformer-based feature fusion model, considering that the fused features have the greatest influence in the results of multi-modal sentiment analysis, so this paper intends to ensure that the fused features can retain or even optimize the maximum information before fusion, so this paper uses Transformer encoding and decoding method to fuse the features, this Therefore, this paper uses Transformer encoding and decoding method to fuse the features, which can ensure that the extracted features retain the maximum features before fusion, and then fuse and encode the two modal features to output a segment of fused features after fusion. Feature classification: In multi-modal sentiment classification, the features of text modality are still the most important, so in this paper, after getting the fused features, we still choose to combine them with text-optimized features containing temporal relationships to make the model more accurate and stable, but considering the depth and complexity of the model, before the features are sent to the classifier, we do not use Transformer encoding and decoding to fuse the The FC-layer used is composed of two Dropout layers, two Linear layers and one ReLU activation layer, as shown in Fig. 2, and then the final obtained features are fed into the Softmax classifier to obtain their sentiment class labels (positive, neutral, negative).

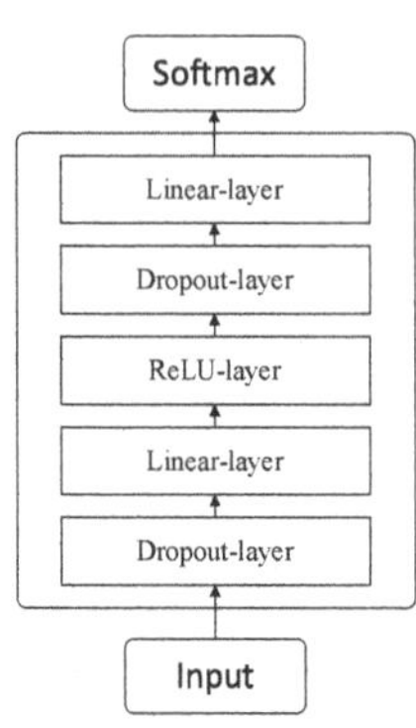

Fig. 2. FC-layer

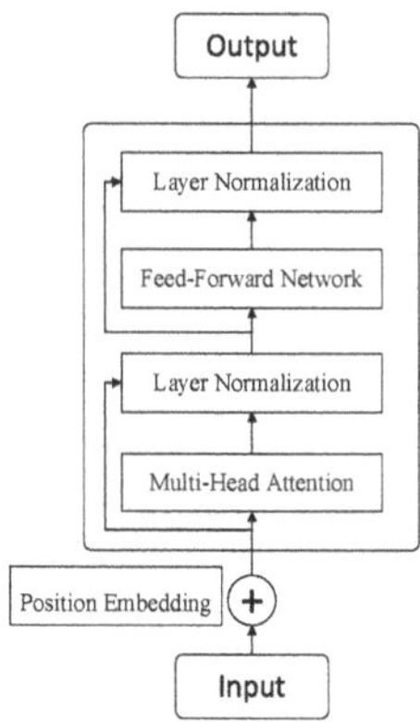

Fig. 3. Transformer Block

3.2 Text Modeling

(1) Brief Description of RoBERTa Model

The RoBERTa model framework consists of a word embedding layer, a feature processing layer, and an output. In the input side, the RoBERTa model uses three word embedding layers, as shown in Fig. 3, the Token Embeddings layer embeds a vector representation of the word itself; the Segment Embeddings layer embeds a vector representation that distinguishes two sentences; the Position Embedding layer encodes the position information of the word into a feature vector, solving the problem that the same word in different The Position Embedding layer encodes the position information of words into feature vectors, solving the problem that the same words in different positions are encoded into the same feature vectors. RoBERTa processing layer consists of a stack of 12 Transformer Encoder, which feeds the corresponding Token at the input side into RoBERTa processing, and each Transformer Encoder layer spits out the corresponding number of hidden vectors, passing on layer by layer until finally outputting the text features needed for the sentiment analysis task. (Transformer Encoder layer will be described in Sect. 3.4.)

(2) Brief Description of Bi-LSTM Model

The Bi-LSTM model consists of the input word of the moment, cell state, temporary cell state, hidden layer state, forgetting gate, memory gate, and output gate, and the computational process of LSTM can be summarized as follows: by forgetting the information in the cell state and remembering the new information, the information useful for the subsequent moment's computation is passed and the useless information is discarded, and the hidden layer state is output at each time step, where forgetting, memory and output are controlled by forgetting gates, memory gates, and output gates computed from the implicit state of the previous moment and the current input.

First, the text features X are fed into the Bi-LSTM model, with h_0 and C_0 defined by the model, to start calculating the value of the forgetting gate f_t, selecting the information to be forgotten.

$$f_t = \sigma(W_f \cdot [h_{t-1}, x_t] + b_f). \tag{1}$$

Calculate the memory gate i_t, select the information to be memorized, and obtain the temporary cell state $\tilde{C}_t$.

$$i_t = \sigma(W_i \cdot [h_{t-1}, x_t] + b_i), \tag{2}$$

$$\tilde{C}_t = \tanh(W_c \cdot [h_{t-1}, x_t] + b_C). \tag{3}$$

Calculate the cell state C_t at the current moment.

$$C_t = f_t * C_{t-1} + i_t * \tilde{C}_t. \tag{4}$$

Calculate the output gate o_t of the current moment cell state calculation and the current moment hidden layer state h_t.

$$o_t = \sigma(W_o[h_{t-1}, x_t] + b_o), \tag{5}$$

$$h_t = o_t * \tanh(C_t). \tag{6}$$

3.3 Image Modeling

In this BLR model, visual features are extracted using ResNeST, a residual network containing a Split-Attention Block (Distraction Block). The Split-Attention Block in this paper is a computational unit that consists of Feature-Map Group and Split-Attention operations. A residual unit of ResNeST is shown in Fig. 1. First, in this paper, the input image data are set with initial parameters (*C*, *H*, *W*), i.e., number of channels, length, and width. For the input data, this paper first performs one Conv (convolution processing), one BN (batch normalization), and one Relu (activation), and then feeds it into the Residual unit 1. In the ResNeST block, features can be divided into *C* groups by channel dimension, and the number of feature map groups is given by the cardinality hyperparameter *K*. In this paper, the obtained feature map groups are referred to as base groups. In this paper, a new base hyperparameter *R* is introduced, which indicates the number of further splits (secondary divisions) within the base group. Thus, the total number of feature groups is $G = KR$. A series of transformations $\{F1, F2, \ldots, FG\}$ can be applied to each individual split, and then the intermediate representation of each split is $U_i = F_i(X)$, since $i \in \{1,2,\ldots,G\}$. Because the results of ResNeST output can be formed into a combinatorial representation by fusing several basis arrays, i.e., summing by elements across multiple splits. The *k*th basis group representation is, $\hat{U}^k = \sum_{j=R(k-1)+1}^{Rk} U_j$ where $\hat{U}^k \in R^{H \times W \times C/K}$, $k \in 1,2,\ldots,K$, and *H*, *W*, *C* are the shapes of the block output feature maps. Global contextual information with embedded channel statistics can be assembled by global averaging pooling across spatial dimension $S^k \in R^{C/K}$. Here the cth component of the kth base array is calculated as follows:

$$s_c^k = \frac{1}{H \times W} \sum_{i=1}^{H} \sum_{j=1}^{W} \hat{U}{}_c^k(i, j). \tag{7}$$

The base array indicates that the weighted fusion of $V^k \in R^{H \times W \times C/K}$ is aggregated by soft attention by channel, where each feature map channel is generated using the weighted combination on splits. The cth channel is calculated as in Eq. 8.

$$V_c^k = \sum_{i=1}^{R} a_i^k(c) U_{R(k-1)+i}. \tag{8}$$

Here, $\alpha_i^k(c)$ denotes the assigned weight,

$$\alpha_i^k(c) = \begin{cases} \frac{exp(\mathcal{G}_i^c(s^k))}{\sum_{j=1}^{R} exp(\mathcal{G}_i^c(s^k))} & if\ R > 1, \\ \frac{1}{1+exp(-\mathcal{G}_i^c(s^k))} & if\ R = 1, \end{cases} \tag{9}$$

The mapping $\mathcal{G}_i^c$ determines the weight of each split of the cth channel based on the global context representation s^k.

The base array representation is then stitched together along the channel dimension as follows.$V = Concat\{V^1, V^2, ..., V^k\}$, Then the final output Y of Split-Attention Block is generated by the residual connection: $Y = V + X$, i.e., the visual features needed for the sentiment analysis task are obtained.

3.4 Feature Fusion

In this BLR model, we use the Transformer model to fuse the obtained text features with visual features. In this paper, the Transformer encoder is constructed as the core of the classifier. The Transformer encoder consists of a stack of N identical Transformer Blocks, as shown in Fig. 3, and the submodule contains two main parts, Multi-Head Attention and Feed-Forward Network, and introduces Residual Connection and Layer Normalization are introduced to prevent gradient degradation and accelerate the convergence of the algorithm.

First, the text features and visual features are stitched together and sent to the input of the Transformer model, where Position Embedding is used to describe the relative position relationship between the features and overlayed with the Embedding Layer. The position encoding in the Transformer model is calculated as in Eqs. 10 and 11.

$$PE(pos, 2i) = \sin(pos/10000^{2i/d_{model}}), \tag{10}$$

$$PE(pos, 2i + 1) = \cos(pos/10000^{2i/d_{model}}). \tag{11}$$

Here, pos represents the sequence length, i represents the dimensional subscript of the feature vector, and $d_{\text{mod}\,el}$ is the feature length. Because the sine and cosine functions are periodic, $PE(pos + k, n)$ can be expressed as a linear variation of $PE(pos, n)$ to identify the relative position relationship between features, which is processed and sent to the core unit of Transformer encoder, Multi-Head Attention, which can be considered as a combination of multiple attention mechanisms, and then n times attention calculation to derive the fused features.

The input matrix $X \in R^{s \times d_{\bmod el}}$ is obtained as the query matrix Q, the key matrix K and the value matrix V by three different linear transformations.

$$Q = W^Q X, \tag{12}$$

$$K = W^K X, \tag{13}$$

$$V = W^V X. \tag{14}$$

Here, $W^Q, W^K, W^V \in R^{d_{\bmod el} \times d_k}$, W^Q, W^K, W^V maps the embedding vector X from the $d_{\bmod el}$ dimension to the d_k dimensional space.

Multi-Head Attention is calculated as in Eqs. 15, 16, and 17.

$$Attention(Q, K, V) = soft\max(\frac{QK^T}{\sqrt{d_k}})V, \tag{15}$$

$$head_i = Attention(Q_i, K_i, V_i) \tag{16}$$

$$MultiHead(Q, K, V) = Concat(head_1, head_2, ..., head_i)W^o. \tag{17}$$

$\sqrt{d_k}$ is used to avoid the Softmax gradient being too low due to the large dot product. The attention distribution in multiple d_k dimensional spaces is spliced using Concat, and the final attention layer output is obtained after the weight matrix W^o transformation, and then enters the feedforward neural network layer, which consists of a two-layer fully connected network with each layer mapping linearly to the input vector, and the middle hidden layer is activated using the ReLu function, and the feedforward neural network is as in Eq. 18.

$$FFN(x) = \max(0, xW_1 + b_1)W_2 + b_2. \tag{18}$$

Here, x is the output vector after attention layer normalization, W is the weight vector, and b is the bias term, and finally the mean and variance are shared by each layer neuron in the layer normalization operation is used to normalize the layer input to a standard normal distribution and enhance the back propagation information mobility. As in Eqs. 19, 20 and 21.

$$\mu = \frac{1}{T}\sum_{i=1}^{T} X_i, \tag{19}$$

$$\sigma = \sqrt{\frac{1}{T}\sum_{i=1}^{T}(X_i - \mu)^2}, \tag{20}$$

$$LN(x) = \alpha \times \frac{x - \mu}{\sqrt{\sigma^2 + \varepsilon}} + \beta. \tag{21}$$

Here, T is the number of neurons in the layer, μ is the mean, σ is the standard deviation, X_i denotes the ith dimension of the feature vector X, α and β are the learnable model parameters, which are updated by backward transfer, and ε is the fractional number set to prevent the divisor from being 0.

The internal data of the Transformer Block connected by residuals are shown in Eqs. 22 and 23.

$$X' = LN(MultiHead(X)) + X, \tag{22}$$

$$X_{output} = LN(FFN(X')) + X'. \tag{23}$$

Here, X_{output} and X are the output and input matrices of Transformer Block, X' is the input matrix of feedforward network layer, LN is the layer normalization operation, and the output of multiple Transformer Blocks after superposition is the fused features in the sentiment analysis task.

4 Experiment

4.1 Baseline Model

The text uses five fusion models with different fusion methods as the baseline models in the experiments, namely the NaiveCat model, the NaiveCombine model, the Cross-ModalityAttentionCombine model, the HiddenStateTransformerEncoder model, and the OutputTransformerEncoder models, the five baseline models use the base BERT model for feature extraction in text modality and the ResNeT model for feature extraction of data in visual modality.

4.2 Datasets

The textual experiments used the baseline model dataset and the MVSA sub-dataset to validate the model accuracy.

4.3 Experimental Analysis

In this paper, multiple experiments are taken for each model, and the average accuracy is taken as the index of the experiments. Using the dataset described in 4.2, all five benchmark models are trained 10 times, and to demonstrate the stability of the BLR model proposed in this paper, 50 training sessions are conducted on BLR, and the average results are obtained, as shown in Table 1.

According to Table 1, the models using the Transformor fusion mechanism (HiddenStateTransformerEncoder, OutputTransformerEncoder, Our model) perform better than the base splicing as well as the decision-level fusion approach. The main reason

Table 1. Experimental results

DATA	Model	Aveacc	Maxacc	D-value
baseline dataset	NaiveCat	0.71	0.72125	0.01125
	NaiveCombine	0.72125	0.73175	0.0105
	CrossModalityAttentionCombine	0.66625	0.67125	0.005
	HiddenStateTransformerEncoder	0.72625	0.74125	0.015
	OutputTransformerEncoder	0.731	0.74875	0.01775
	Our model	0.76125	0.76625	0.005
MVSA sub-dataset	NaiveCat	0.721	0.73375	0.01275
	NaiveCombine	0.72625	0.731	0.00475
	CrossModalityAttentionCombine	0.713	0.72125	0.00825
	HiddenStateTransformerEncoder	0.74125	0.751	0.00975
	OutputTransformerEncoder	0.74625	0.75125	0.005
	Our model	0.775	0.77625	0.00125

why the CrossModalityAttentionCombine model is lower than the other models is that it splices the features that have gone through the attention mechanism with the original features. The attention mechanism is supposed to improve the efficiency of the model, but by splicing it with the original features, not only does it not play the effect of the attention mechanism, but also mixes in a large number of inefficient features, resulting in the model's effectiveness The HiddenStateTransformerEncoder model and the OutputTransformerEncoder model both use the Transformor fusion mechanism, and the HiddenStateTransformerEncoder model is more complex, but its effect is not as good as the OutputTransformerEncoder model. The reason is that the fused features are spliced with the directly extracted features before being fed into the final Softmax classifier, and the features are not spliced according to their contribution, resulting in too many invalid or inefficient features entering the final classifier, which makes the result inferior to that of a single Transformor fused feature.

The model in this paper builds on this by considering the completeness of the initially extracted features and by making these features as useful as possible according to their contribution to the sentiment analysis task. Comparing the baseline model, it can be seen that the model in this paper excels in the sentiment analysis task on the baseline dataset, achieving an accuracy of 0.76125, compared to the baseline model with the best results in the OutputTransformerEncoder model, which achieved an improvement of 3.025%, and also obtained an accuracy of 0.775 in the MVSA sub-dataset, which is 2.875% better than the OutputTransformerEncoder model, which has the highest accuracy in the baseline model, and can demonstrate that this paper's The fusion method used in this paper has better results in feature-level fusion, and also the model in this paper has the smallest average and the largest precision difference (D-value), which has the best stability.

In order to demonstrate the fusion effect of the model in this paper, the following ablation experiments are done in this paper, in which only the data of a single modality is input into the BLR model for training 10 times, and the average accuracy is taken to compare with the accuracy produced by multiple modalities to obtain the results. In order to demonstrate that the unimodal experiments do not suffer from missing features or contain a large number of invalid features, the ablation experiments in this paper use two extracted unimodal features directly fed into the Softmax classifier for sentiment classification, and the final results are obtained, as shown in Table 2.

Table 2. Results of ablation experiments

DATA	Model	Aveacc	Textacc	Imageacc
baseline dataset	Our model	0.76125	0.713	0.60125
MVSA sub-dataset	Our model	0.775	0.72125	0.631

According to the results of the ablation experiments in Table 2, in the baseline dataset, the fusion approach of this paper improves 3.825% compared to single-text modal sentiment analysis, and improves 16% accuracy compared to single-visual modal sentiment analysis, and in the MVSA sub-dataset, the fusion approach of this paper improves 5.375% compared to single-text modal sentiment analysis, and improves 14.4% accuracy compared to single-visual modal sentiment analysis. The accuracy of 14.4% proves that the fusion method proposed in BLR has a significant effect on the sentiment analysis task, and the same table shows that text features still provide the largest contribution in the sentiment analysis task.

5 Conclusion and Prospect

According to the experimental results, the BLR dual fusion model proposed in this paper achieves improvement over all five baseline models in the multimodal sentiment analysis task, and it is demonstrated through two data and multiple sets of experiments that the model proposed in this paper not only has improved accuracy but also stability, and it is also demonstrated that the feature fusion method used in this model is useful for the multimodal sentiment analysis task according to the ablation experiments proposed in this paper. The model1 proposed in this paper mainly solves the problem of

The model proposed in this paper mainly solves the problems of lack of large-scale datasets, overly complex models, and post-fusion weight assignment in multimodal sentiment analysis tasks, but there are still challenges in this task that need to be addressed in this paper. This paper summarizes some of the future work for this task:

(1) To address the problem of sparse multimodal datasets, unsupervised or semi-supervised approaches can also be taken to train models;
(2) Using a hypernetwork approach to establish relationships between multimodal data, feature tensor under complex relationships can be obtained;

(3) Most current methods consider only text, visual, and sound data, and sentiment analysis oriented to pose as well as ECG is extremely scarce, and cooperation with other fields should be strengthened to build more multimodal datasets in the future;
(4) Most current methods perform sentiment analysis on overall data, and in the future, sentiment analysis on entities in the data or sentiment analysis on aspect level can be considered.

Acknowledgement. This article is supported by the National Key Research and Development Program of China (No.2020YFC1523300), Innovation Platform Construction Project of Qinghai Province (2022-ZJ-T02).

References

1. Ji, S.P., Li, S.Y.: Food review mining based on emotional analysis. Comput. Knowl. Technol. **14**(29), 208–210 (2018)
2. Fan, Z., Guo, Y., Zhang, Z.H., et al.: Sentiment analysis of movie reviews based on dictionary and weak tagging information. J. Comput. Appl. **38**(11), 3084–3088 (2018)
3. Fen, S.: Research on emotional analysis of douban film review text – based on the crawler data of the 2017 film "Riding the wind and breaking the waves." China Stat. **427**(07), 30–33 (2017)
4. Huang, J.B., Chen, F.L., Ding, Y.D., et al.: Personalized movie recommendation based on sentiment analysis. Comput. Technol. Dev. **30**(09), 132–136 (2020)
5. Zhang, M.Y., Zhu, G.L., Zhang, S.X., et al.: Grouping microblog users of trending topics based on sentiment analysis. Data Anal. Knowl. Discov. **5**(2), 43–49 (2021)
6. Lou, Y., Yang, J.L., Huang, L.C., et al.: Analysis of public concerns and emotions of gerontechnology based on social Q&A community—taking "Zhihu" as an example. J. Intell. **39**(03), 115–122 (2020)
7. Liu, Y.L., Zhao, G.L., Zou, Z.R., et al.: Stock price prediction method based on sentiment analysis and generative adversarial network. J. Hunan Univ. (Nat. Sci.) **49**(10), 111–118 (2022)
8. Ran, Y.F., Jiang, H.X.: Stock prices prediction based on back propagation neural network and support vector regres-sion. J. Shanxi Universify **41**(01), 1–14 (2018)
9. Sun, C.H., Liu, Y.Z.: The impact of online release of movie trailers on box office: a text based emotional analysis approach. Chin. J. Manag. Sci. **25**(10), 151–161 (2017)
10. Bao, G.B., Li, G.L., Wang, G.W.: Bimodal interactive attention for multimodal sentiment analysis. J. Front. Comput. Sci. Technol. **16**(04), 910–916 (2022)
11. Wang, K.X., Xu, X.J., Liu, Y., et al.: Static multimodal sentiment analysis of online reviews. J. Appl. Sci. — Electron Inf. Eng. **1**(40), 25–35 (2022)
12. Liu, J.M., Zhang, P.X., Liu, Y., et al.: Summary of multi-modal sentiment analysis technology. J. Front. Com-put. Sci. Technol. **15**(07), 1165–1182 (2021)
13. Zhang, J.D., Zhang, H.D.: Multimodel user emotion analysis of emergencies based on attention mechanism. In-formation Stud.: Theory Appl. **45**(11), 170–177 (2022)
14. Yan, S.Y., Wang, J.Y., Liu, X.W., et al.: Zhang: microblog sentiment analysis with multihead self-attention pooling and multigranularity feature interaction fusion. Data Anal. Knowl. Discov. **7**(04), 32–45 (2023)
15. Huddar, M.G., Sannakki, S.S., Rajpurohit, V.S.: A survey of computational approaches and challenges in multimodal sentiment analysis. In-ternational J. Comput. Sci. Eng. **7**(1), 876–883 (2019)

16. Peng, X.J.: Multi-modal affective computing: a comprehensive survey. J. Hengyang Normal Univ. **39**(3), 31–36 (2018)
17. Chen, K., Liang, B., Ke, W.D., et al.: Chinese micro-blog sentiment analysis based on multi-channels convolutional neural net-works. J. Comput. Res. Dev. **55**(5), 945–957 (2018)
18. Cao, Y., Li, T.R., Jia, Z., et al.: BGRU: new method of Chinese text sentiment analysis. J. Front. Comput. Sci. Technol. **13**(6), 973–981 (2019)
19. Wang, X., Jiang, W., Luo, Z.Y.: Combination of convolutional and recurrent neural network for sentiment analysis of short texts. In: Proceedings of the 26th International Conference on Computational Linguistics, pp. 2428–2437. Osaka (2016)
20. Liu, J., Gu, F.Y.: Unbalanced text sentiment analysis of network public opinion based on BERT and BiLSTM hybrid method. J. Intelligence **41**(04), 104–110 (2022)
21. Lu, J.H., Zhang, S.M., Zhao, J.L.: Facial expression recognition based on CNN ensemble. J. Qingdao Univ. (Eng. Technol. Edition) **35**(2), 24–29 (2020)
22. Deng, D., Zhou, Y., Pi, J., et al.: Multimodal utterance-level affect analysis using visual, audio and text features. arXiv:1805.00625 (2018)
23. Poria, S., Chaturvedi, I., Cambria, E., et al.: Convolutional MKL based multimodal emotion recognition and sentiment analysis. In: Proceedings of the 16th International Confer-ence on Data Mining, pp. 439–448. Barcelona (2016)
24. Yu, Y., Lin, H., Meng, J., et al.: Visual and textual sentiment analysis of a microblog using deep convolutional neural networks. Algorithms **9**(2), 41 (2016)
25. Poria, S., Cambria, E., Gelbukh, A.: Deep convolutional neural network textual features and multiple kernel learning for utterance-level multimodal sentiment analysis. In: Proceedings of the 2015 Conference on Empirical Methods in Natural Language Processing, pp. 2539–2544. Lisbon (2015)
26. Zhang, H., Wu, C., Zhang, Z., et al.: ResNeSt: split-attention networks. In: CVPR2020 (IEEE Conference on Computer Vision and Pattern Recognition). Seattle (2020)

Detecting Negative Sentiment on Sarcastic Tweets for Sentiment Analysis

Qingyuan Li[1,2], Kai Zhang[3], Lin Sun[2], and Ruichen Xia[1,4](✉)

[1] College of Computer Science and Technology, Zhejiang University, Hangzhou, China
liqingyuan@mail.zju.edu.cn
[2] Department of Computer Science, Hangzhou City University, HangZhou, China
[3] Department of Computer Science and Engineering, Ohio State University, Columbus, USA
[4] Institute of Computer innovation, Zhejiang University, Hangzhou, China
rcxia@zjuici.com

Abstract. Sentiment Analysis (SA) is a fundamental and practical research problem in the field of natural language understanding(NLU). Meanwhile, sarcasm detection is a task to detect sarcasm in textual data. Previous works solve these two problems independently and neglect the fact that sarcasm is omnipresent and non-negligible during sentiment analysis. To explore this issue, in this paper, we formulate a general sentiment Analysis (GSA) problem where sarcastic data could be input and point out the limitations of current mainstream frameworks by systematic investigation. To address the GSA problem, we propose a sarcasm-perceivable SA (Sp-SA) training framework to train a model that is robust to sarcasm and able to achieve state-of-the-art performance. Extensive experiments and detailed analysis demonstrate our Sp-SA framework's effectiveness and interpretability. Code and dataset will be publicly available for future research.

Keywords: sentiment analysis · sarcasm detection · multi-task learning

1 Introduction

Sentiment analysis aims to identify the sentiment polarity (i.e., negative, neutral, or positive) of textual data, especially user-generated content like customer reviews [11] and tweets [10]. In recent years, with the power of pretrained language models (PLMs), sentiment analysis has achieved remarkable progress [7] and been widely applied in many domains including social media, finance, risk management, medicine, and politics, etc.

In social platforms like Twitter, sarcasm is an omnipresent form of human language expression [13] used to insult, mock, or amuse. As shown in Table 1,

L. Iliadis et al. (Eds.): ICANN 2023, LNCS 14263, pp. 479–491, 2023.
https://doi.org/10.1007/978-3-031-44204-9_40

Table 1. Sentiment analysis results identified by the SA model [19] on sarcastic tweets. P denotes positive (P) sentiment.

	Tweet	SA model
1	Really love being ignored at the party!	P
2	I'm so sore, work tomorrow is gonna be fun	P
3	Ah yes. Just what I wanted today-a pounding migraine.	P
4	This long drive home later in the snow is gonna be sweet.	P

there are tweets expressing negative emotion with many positive terms (e.g., love, fun, yes and sweet) on the surface, inherently leading to machines and even humans' misunderstanding [21]. Sarcasm on Twitter could account for 5% [23] to 23% [21] in different real-world datasets, or 6% to 20% in different events [25], especially scandal and economic events. A natural solution to avoid sarcasm is to detect (i.e., sarcasm detection) and filter them out, then perform SA on the remaining textual data. However, the performances of state-of-the-art sarcasm detection (SD) models are still far from perfect, specifically 78% in accuracy [5, 19]. Another series of research is to solve SA and SD tasks in a multi-task training framework and achieve performance gains on both tasks [18]. However, in our experiments, we find that the multi-task learning model still suffers from classifying sarcasm into incorrect sentiment polarity.

Therefore, this paper aims to expand the SA to a general and sarcasm-existed setting, namely **G**eneral **S**entiment **A**nalysis (GSA). This task assumes that the input might be in normal or sarcastic expressions and requires the model to identify the sarcasm as correct polarity, so users can obtain more comprehensive and unbiased analysis results. To construct a dataset to simulate the general situation, we combine sarcastic expressions [27] and tweets [22] with different ratios in a multi-task learning fashion [17]. Then we extensively review other training frameworks to demonstrate their limitations on this new benchmark. To address this issue, we propose a novel sarcasm-perceivable model-agnostic training framework to enhance the robustness of models. Detailed experimental results demonstrate that our training framework enables the model to generalize significantly better on sarcastic tweets while maintaining comparable performance on normal data. To sum up, the contributions of our work are: **(1)** We formulate a general SA setting where sarcasm exists, systematically investigate mainstream training frameworks of sentiment analysis, and point out their vulnerabilities in this setting; **(2)** We propose a sarcasm-perceivable SA framework to effectively train a state-of-the-art SA model with robustness and generalization; **(3)** The performance results, cases and detailed analysis demonstrate our framework's effectiveness and interpretability.

2 Related Work

Our work focuses on sentence-level sentiment polarity classification and sarcasm detection on the data from the most popular social media, Twitter.

Twitter Sentiment Polarity Classification. Sentence-level sentiment analysis is the basic task of natural language understanding (NLU) [16,24,29–31] which aims to extract and analyze people's sentiments or attitudes toward various entities including products, services, and topics in a given text. In recent years, sentence-level SA task has been well-explored as the deep models develop from recursive nets [26], convolutional nets [12] to PLMs [7].

Despite the success of SA in formal genres like online reviews and news articles, SA in Twitter [8] is still a challenging task because of tweets' informal and creative text genre including misspellings, slang, and new words. Bermingham et al. [2] investigated the differences in SA between microblogs and micro-reviews, demonstrating the difficulty of correctly identifying the sentiment in microblogs. Kouloumpis et al. [15] proved that automated part-of-speech (POS) and n-gram features may not be useful on tweets as formal texts. Researchers achieved performance gain by incorporating hashtags and smileys [6], word lengthening [3], POS-specified prior polarity features [1], contextual information [28], and ensemble learning [4].

Sarcasm in Sentiment Analysis. Conducting SA without considering sarcasm could lead to incorrect results and over-confident conclusion [14]. Rosenthal et al. [23] discovered approximately 5% sarcasm in all tweets. Van Hee et al. [27] demonstrated that the SA model performed poorly on sarcastic data. Hashtag supervision is a frequent way to annotate sarcasm datasets [20,21]. However, according to a qualitative analysis [25], hashtag-supervised sarcasm datasets may result in a high proportion of noisy data. So automated systems could not filter sarcasm out via hashtags and machine learning models trained on them are likely to be impacted by these wrong annotations.

In a word, making data both in training and real-world streaming sarcasm-free is an essential step for better models and more accurate conclusions. That being said, current SA and SD methods can only be used to solve two tasks separately. Meanwhile, because current SD methods perform unsatisfactorily, filtering out sarcasm by SD is not a feasible way to help sentiment analysis.

3 Problem Definition and Solution

In this section, we formally define our new task in Sect. 3.1 and illustrate the pipelines. Then we systematically review the current training frameworks in Sect. 3.2. Finally we introduce Sp-SA model in Sect. 3.3.

3.1 GSA Definition

Traditional SA task ignores the existence of sarcasm and in effect adversely influence the correctness of the downstream analysis. Formally, traditional SA models categorizes the emotional samples $\mathcal{D}_e$, a sarcasm-free scenario.

To deal with sarcasm, one option is the SD-SA pipeline in Fig. 1 (a) that combines these two separate tasks. This pipeline first performs SD on all data, then filter out sarcasm data, and finally conducts SA on the remaining NS data.

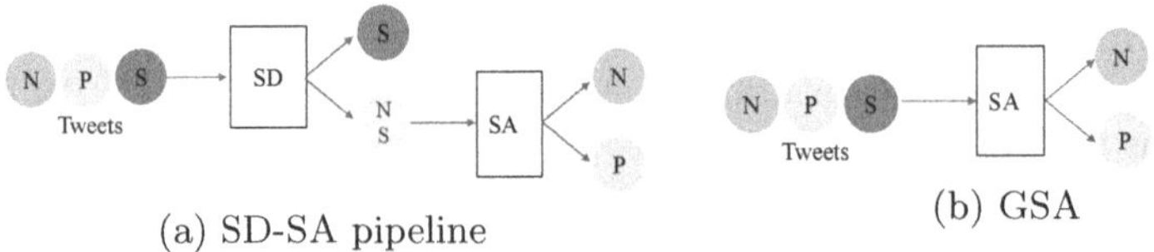

(a) SD-SA pipeline (b) GSA

Fig. 1. Illustration of two frameworks concerning sarcastic tweets. P, N, S, and NS denote positive, negative, sarcasm, and non-sarcasm categories, respectively.

However, our later experiments in Table 6 show that the sarcasm detection model will wrongly identify 21% positive and 48% neutral sentimental data as sarcasm. Filtering out such a considerable amount of useful sentiment examples will lead to data waste and less comprehensive analysis.

In contrast, GSA in Fig. 1 (b) aims to solve the SA problem in a real-world setting where models are required to identify the sentiments of a huge amount of user-generated texts including normal and sarcastic expressions. Here, the GSA task refers to a sentence-level binary- or multi-class sentiment classification task except including a proportion of sarcastic tweets. Aside from classifying normal input as sentiment polarities like the SA task, *the GSA also aims to identify sarcastic tweets as negative sentiment*

Formally speaking, given a data set $\mathcal{D}$ including sarcastic data $\mathcal{D}_s$ and common emotional data $\mathcal{D}_e$, models are required to categorize the emotional samples $\mathcal{D}_e$ into pre-defined C-class sentiment types and meanwhile identify the negative sentiment of sarcastic samples $\mathcal{D}_s$.

3.2 Common Framework Review

We comprehensively review several widely used SA training frameworks as baselines. As Fig. 2 demonstrated, the backbones of all frameworks are BERTweet [19], a language model pretrained on Twitter data. The classifiers are one fully connected (FC) layer on the [CLS] token representation and the loss function is cross-entropy loss. The differences between models only lie in the design of training strategies and the use of sarcastic data. Details are described below

SA Model. In Fig. 2 (a), the most common SA solution is trained on the sentiment analysis dataset consisting of positive (P) and negative (N) sentiments, where $\{P, N\} \in \mathcal{D}_e$. We refer to the model as the SA model.

SA-S Model. A way of identifying the negative emotion of sarcastic utterances is to directly add the sarcastic tweets (S) into the negatives (N) of the training set in the SA model [9], where $S \in \mathcal{D}_e$. We refer to the model in Fig. 2 (b) as SA-S.

SA+SD MTL Model. Figure 2 (c) is the multi-task learning (MTL) framework, which is a practical way of using sarcasm data to enhance model. We

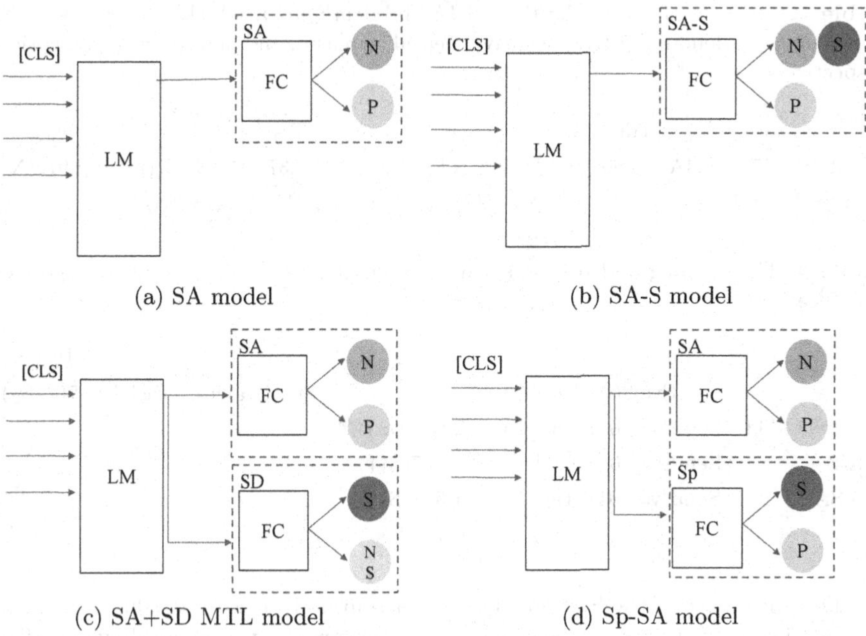

Fig. 2. Illustration of the common SA frameworks.

denote this model as SA+SD MTL. There are two training sets: sentiment analysis for SA task where {P, N} $\in \mathcal{D}_e$ and sarcasm detection for SD task where {S, NS} $\in \mathcal{D}_s$. The loss function for training is defined as follows:

$$\mathcal{L} = \mathcal{L}_{\mathtt{SD}} + \mathcal{L}_{\mathtt{SA}} \quad (1)$$

where $\mathcal{L}_{\mathtt{SD}}$ and $\mathcal{L}_{\mathtt{SA}}$ are cross-entropy functions for SD and SA tasks, respectively.

Both SA-S and SA+SD MTL models use SD-SA paradigm in Fig. 1 (a) to identify the sentiment polarity of sarcastic tweets. In the next section, we introduce a novel SA model for GSA paradigm Fig. 1 (b).

3.3 Sp-SA Model

Can we utilize simply a unified SA model to identify the sentiment polarity of sarcasm as well as do standard sentiment classification on normal textual data? To solve this problem, we propose a novel training framework for GSA, namely Sarcasm-perceivable SA (Sp-SA), as shown in Fig. 2 (d). In the training stage, more than the traditional SA task, we design a novel auxiliary classification task, namely Sp, for differentiating the positive data and sarcasm. The training procedure is sentiment analysis for SA task (i.e., P and N) and the positive data and sarcasm for Sp task (i.e., P and S) with a loss weight α and total optimization function is $\mathcal{L} = \alpha \cdot \mathcal{L}_{\mathtt{Sp}} + \mathcal{L}_{\mathtt{SA}}$. In the testing stage, our model is required to perform under the GSA framework using only the SA classifier.

Table 2. Statistics of SemEval2017-Task4A and SemEval2018-Task3A datasets. P, N, NT, S, and NS denote positive, negative, neural, sarcasm, and non-sarcasm categories, respectively.

	Train	Test
SemEval2017-Task4A	19,902(P)+22,591(NT)+7,840(N)	2,375(P)+5,937(NT)+3,972(N)
SemEval2018-Task3A	1,911(S)+1,925(NS)	311(S)+473(NS)

Table 3. The training and testing settings for sentiment (positive/neutral/negative) classification.

	Train	Test_{ST}	Test_{SC}
SA	SemEval2017-Task4A	SemEval2017-Task4A	705(S_2)
SA+SD MTL	SemEval2017-Task4A + 2018-Task3A		
SA-S	SemEval2017-Task4A + 1,517(S_1)		
Sp-SA	SemEval2017-Task4A + 1,517(S_1)		

The advantage of the Sp task is that it attempts to resolve the hard problem of classification between positive sentiment and sarcasm that could have positive words. The advantage of the Sp-SA model over the SA-S model is that the separate task Sp can learn to classify the sarcasm and positive sentiments without hurting the capability of modeling negative sentiment. Note that our solution is a general and model-agnostic framework, so the base model could be any future strong models and it could be combined with any more linguistic features and external knowledge.

4 Experimental Settings

4.1 GSA Benchmarks

To evaluate the effects of sarcasm sentiment on sentiment analysis, we build a group of data settings on the existing sentiment analysis and sarcasm detection datasets as shown in Table 2.

SemEval2017-Task4A [22]. This dataset is used for sentiment analysis. It has over 50,000 sentiment polarity instances in the train set and more than 10,000 examples in the test set.

SemEval2018-Task3A [27]. This dataset is used for sarcasm detection. It contains approximately 4,000 data samples for training and 700 data for test. We use 2,222 sarcasm samples which are divided into a new split of 1,517 and 705 to train and test SA-S and Sp-SA models, as shown in Table 2.

We set 2-class and 3-class sentiment classification benchmarks for baseline models respectively. The 3-class sentiment classification benchmarks is shown in Table 3, which list two testing sets, Test_{ST} and Test_{SC}. Test_{ST} is used to evaluate performance on the sentiment analysis dataset. Test_{SC} is used to evaluate how many sarcastic tweets are recognized as negative sentiment. The combination set $\text{Test}_{\text{ST}} \cup \text{Test}_{\text{SC}}$ denotes more general tweet datasets with sarcastic tweets for GSA evaluation, the percentage of which are 10% and 5.2% in the 2-class and 3-class sentiment classification benchmarks, respectively. And in the 2-class sentiment classification setting, neutral sentiment samples are removed from the SemEval2017-Task4A dataset.

4.2 Metrics

We use macro-F1 and Accuracy metrics to measure the SA performances on the Test_{ST} and $\text{Test}_{\text{ST}} \cup \text{Test}_{\text{SC}}$ sets. "S→N" denotes the percentage of sarcastic tweets that can be recognized as negatives on the Test_{SC} set.

4.3 Implementation Details

We use Adam with a learning rate of 1e−5 to fine-tune the BERTweet and FC classifier. The batch size to 32 and weight α in the Sp task is set to 0.4. In the training of the Sp task in the Sp-SA model, the size of positive and sarcasm samples are significantly imbalanced, i.e., 19,902 positives and 1,911 sarcasm. Therefore, we under-sample 3,822 positive samples to maintain a ratio of 2:1 for the sizes of P and S in each training epoch. For 3-class sentiment, in the Sp task, we combine the neutral and positive sentiment training sets $P \cup NT$ to replace P, and also under-sample 3,822 samples from $P \cup NT$ for each training epoch.

5 Results

We perform all models fine-tuned with the training strategies aforementioned on GSA benchmarks, note that we only use the SA part of SA+SD MTL to do the GSA task because SD can not identify the sentiment polarity of sarcasm. Table 4 and Table 5 show the performances of models on 2-class and 3-class sentiment benchmarks, respectively. We separate GSA data (i.e., $\text{Test}_{\text{ST}} \cup \text{Test}_{\text{SC}}$) into sentiment data part Test_{ST} and sarcasm data part Test_{SC} for more detailed analysis. Following observations can be obtained through these two tables:
(1) Our Sp-SA model achieves best GSA performance on $\text{Test}_{\text{ST}} \cup \text{Test}_{\text{SC}}$. Specifically, it can perform competitively with the SA model on Test_{ST} sentiment data part, showing that the Sp-SA model can handle standard SA tasks. More importantly, compared to original SA model, the Sp-SA model can achieve much better performance on Test_{SC} sarcasm data part (55.8% -> 75.3% on 2-class sentiment and 40.4% -> 55.1% on 3-class sentiment). These improvements show that our Sp-SA training strategy can successfully increase models' capabilities of identifying sarcasm as negative polarity.
(2) Introducing sarcasm in training can lead all four models' performances to drop on Test_{ST} sentiment data part, especially the SA-S which drops more than 4% absolute F1 score on two benchmarks. In contrast, MTL and Sp-SA remain

Table 4. Performance of 2-class sentiment classification (%). The results are the averages over 8 runs.

	$Test_{ST}$				$Test_{SC}$	$Test_{ST} \cup Test_{SC}$			
	$F1^P$	$F1^N$	macro-F1	Acc	S→N	$F1^P$	$F1^N$	macro-F1	Acc
SA	**93.4**	**96.1**	**94.7**	**95.1**	55.8	87.7	93.1	90.4	91.2
SA+SD MTL	92.4	95.4	93.9	94.2	41.9	85.1	91.2	88.1	89.0
SA-S	86.4	92.9	89.6	90.6	**87.3**	84.7	92.8	88.8	90.3
Sp-SA	91.9	95.3	93.6	94.0	75.3	**88.6**	**94.1**	**91.3**	**92.2**

Table 5. Performance of 3-class sentiment classification (%). The results are the averages over 8 runs.

	$Test_{ST}$					$Test_{SC}$	$Test_{ST} \cup Test_{SC}$				
	$F1^P$	$F1^N$	$F1^{NT}$	macro-F1	Acc	S→N	$F1^P$	$F1^N$	$F1^{NT}$	macro-F1	Acc
SA	**72.1**	75.0	**71.6**	**72.8**	**72.9**	40.4	68.7	73.1	**70.5**	70.8	71.1
SA+SD MTL	70.6	74.1	71.5	72.0	72.2	24.1	66.2	70.6	70.2	69.0	69.6
SA-S	66.7	69.5	63.8	66.7	66.7	**82.9**	65.7	71.9	63.5	67.1	67.5
Sp-SA	**72.1**	**75.1**	70.4	72.4	72.5	55.1	**69.0**	**74.3**	69.7	**71.1**	**71.4**

most of the SA performance with only less than 1% drop on two benchmarks. We believe the reason is that MTL and Sp-SA introduce sarcasm in a different optimization objective that is separate from SA training, while SA-S directly mixtures sarcasm data during the SA training.
(3) Despite good performance on the $Test_{ST}$ sentiment data part, MTL performs unfavorably on $Test_{SC}$ sarcasm data part, even surprisingly worse than the original SA model. This proves the way of introducing sarcasm can not increase its capability of casting sarcasm as negative polarity.
(4) SA-S can achieve best performance on $Test_{SC}$ sarcasm data part among all models. However, the significant performance drop of $Test_{ST}$ sentiment data part leads to inferior overall GSA performance on $Test_{ST} \cup Test_{SC}$.

6 Discussion and Analysis

6.1 SD-SA Pipeline Results

A standard pipeline system filters sarcasm and conducts sentiment analysis. We use the SD part in the SA+SD MTL model to conduct the SD task on the $Test_{ST}$ sentiment data part. The SD part of MTL can achieve 78% accuracy, a comparable performance with the state-of-the-art model [19] on the widely-used SD benchmark SemEval2018-Task3A. Table 6 shows the results of sarcasm detection. In the 2-class sentiment benchmark, 21.8% of positive examples are identified as sarcasm while in the 3-class sentiment benchmark, 21.4% of positive and 48.1% of neutral examples are filtered out regrading the sarcasm detection results.

Table 6. Proportion of sarcasm identification results on the positive and neutral sentiment data detected by SD (%).

	2-class sentiment	3-class sentiment	
	P→S	P→S	NT→S
SD	21.8	21.4	48.1

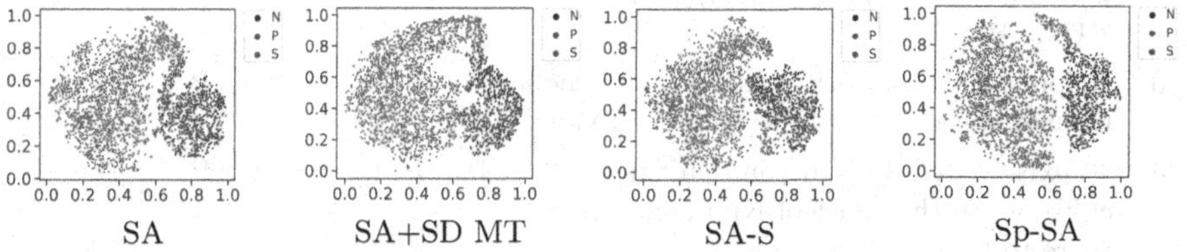

SA SA+SD MT SA-S Sp-SA

Fig. 3. 2D visualization of BERTweet embeddings for positive, negative, and sarcasm sentiment samples on 10% of the training set from SemEval2017Task4A w/o NT and 2018Task3A w/o NS.

Discarding so much valuable sentimental information will lead to very biased analysis results and highly possible wrong conclusions, which is not acceptable in real-world sentiment analysis applications. Therefore, we believe it's better to use our Sp-SA model to obtain a more comprehensive sentiment analysis.

6.2 Encoding Feature Visualization

We utilize the sentence embeddings of BERTweet to visualize the representations of 10% textual data from the train set of GSA benchmark. Both in Fig. 3, without learning to deal with sarcasm, the SA model mix the sarcasm with positive and negative samples, randomly distributing the sarcastic examples in the semantic space. This observation well illustrates the unsatisfactory performance of SA in classifying sarcasm as negative polarity. Similarly, the SA+SD MTL model is inclined to categorize sarcasm as positive or neutral sentiment. In contrast, the training frameworks of Sp-SA and SA-S can better distinguish sarcasm from common sentiment types. From the above observations, the illustration of sentence embeddings for GSA clearly shows the superiority and interpretability of our Sp-SA model.

6.3 Case Study

Table 7 demonstrates some results of the models on SemEval2018-Task3A and SemEval2017-Task4A. Cases 1–9 come from SemEval2017-Task4A. The top 5 of them are politician-included tweets, including Trump, Farage, Obama, and Kim Jong Un. Twitter users like to use sarcasm to express their feelings or just make jokes about politics or politicians. Meanwhile, their's opinions about politicians or governments are very important to social analysis like election prediction and

Table 7. Example comparison of different SA models. Correct predictions are in bold.

		SA	SA+SD MTL	SA-S	Sp-SA
1	first date dream: take me to an anti-trump protest	P	P	P	**N**
2	In Scotland, Trump Built a Wall. Then He Sent Residents the Bill. #StrongerTogether #StillWithHer #UniteBlue"	P	P	P	**N**
3	Helping Melania work on her next Michelle Obama speech. #KeepsTrumpUpAtNight	P	P	P	**N**
4	@FoxNewsSydMUN16 you don't need coffee when the spirit of Kim Jong-un is there to keep you awake	P	P	P	**N**
5	"Dear NO voters, are you celebrating your victory? So are Nigel Farage and Marine Le Pen. Enjoy the lovely company. #ItalyReferendum"	P	P	P	**N**
6	@AliVelshi Forget the pipeline. There is endless sunshine and plentiful wind to provide us with power. Why fossil fuels? That's crazy!	P	P	P	**N**
7	"*Friday Night*Me: Siri, we're friends, right?Siri: Uh...Who is Siri? I am a Galaxy Note 7. *Catches Fire*Me: Huh. Third one this month..."	P	P	P	**N**
8	"Nice! Have fun! #SMITHRADIO @FallonTonight @user #GilmoreGirls #GilmoreGirlsRevival...	**P**	**P**	N	**P**
9	#hatchimals #BlackFriday My daughter would love this	**P**	**P**	N	**P**
10	".@JaniceDean, Michael Bloomberg will be wearing his speedo for the #GlobalWarming with his bodyguards. @FoxNews"	P	P	P	**N**
11	"Time to free ourselves of the Tyranny of the USA and lean towards more tolerant societies, like those of Russia and China."	P	P	P	**N**
12	Perfect time to get really sick	**N**	**N**	**N**	**N**

issuance of a policy. So our Sp-SA model is more likely to get a precise result for important political events.

Cases 6–7 show that our Sp-SA model can work more generally not only in political tweets. Cases 8–9 show the Sp-SA training can keep the model's capability of positive sentiment identification. Cases 10–12 come from SemEval2018-

Task3. Cases 10–11 show that our Sp-SA model can successfully categorize sarcasm into negative polarity while results of other models can be wrong results because of the positive words like "love", "free", and so on. Case 12 show that our Sp-SPC model can the performance categorize sarcasm into negative polarity. We find that SA and MTL models only categorize sarcasm when these examples have obviously negative words on the surface like "no", "sick", and so on.

7 Conclusion

In this paper, we analyze several mainstream sentiment polarity classification models and pipelines, demonstrating their vulnerabilities in real-world sentiment analysis situations where sarcasm exists. To solve this general setting of sentiment classification, we formulate a general sentiment polarity classification task and propose a Sp-SA framework to initially settle this new problem. Extensive experiments show that our Sp-SA framework could achieve comparable performance as well as much more robustness to the state-of-the-art models. In the future, more sarcasm-tolerating strategies and a strong text encoder could be applied to enhance the overall performance to increase the effectiveness of general sentiment polarity classification.

References

1. Agarwal, A., Xie, B., Vovsha, I., Rambow, O., Passonneau, R.J.: Sentiment analysis of twitter data. In: Proceedings of the Workshop on Language in Social Media (LSM 2011), pp. 30–38 (2011)
2. Bermingham, A., Smeaton, A.F.: Classifying sentiment in microblogs: is brevity an advantage? In: Proceedings of the 19th ACM International Conference on Information and Knowledge Management, pp. 1833–1836 (2010)
3. Brody, S., Diakopoulos, N.: Cooooooooooooooollllllllllllll!!!!!!!!!!!!!! using word lengthening to detect sentiment in microblogs. In: Proceedings of the 2011 Conference on Empirical Methods in Natural Language Processing, pp. 562–570 (2011)
4. Da Silva, N.F., Hruschka, E.R., Hruschka, E.R., Jr.: Tweet sentiment analysis with classifier ensembles. Decis. Support Syst. **66**, 170–179 (2014)
5. Dadu, T., Pant, K.: Sarcasm detection using context separators in online discourse. In: Proceedings of the Second Workshop on Figurative Language Processing, pp. 51–55. Association for Computational Linguistics, Online (2020)
6. Davidov, D., Tsur, O., Rappoport, A.: Enhanced sentiment learning using Twitter hashtags and smileys. In: Coling 2010: Posters, pp. 241–249. Coling 2010 Organizing Committee, Beijing, China (2010)
7. Devlin, J., Chang, M.W., Lee, K., Toutanova, K.: BERT: pre-training of deep bidirectional transformers for language understanding. In: Proceedings of the 2019 Conference of the North American Chapter of the Association for Computational Linguistics: Human Language Technologies, vol. 1 (Long and Short Papers), pp. 4171–4186. Association for Computational Linguistics (2019)
8. Giachanou, A., Crestani, F.: Like it or not: a survey of twitter sentiment analysis methods. ACM Comput. Surv. **49**(2), 1–41 (2016)

9. González-Ibáñez, R., Muresan, S., Wacholder, N.: Identifying sarcasm in Twitter: a closer look. In: Proceedings of the 49th Annual Meeting of the Association for Computational Linguistics: Human Language Technologies, pp. 581–586. Association for Computational Linguistics, Portland, Oregon, USA (2011)
10. Gyanendro Singh, L., Mitra, A., Ranbir Singh, S.: Sentiment analysis of tweets using heterogeneous multi-layer network representation and embedding. In: Proceedings of the 2020 Conference on Empirical Methods in Natural Language Processing, pp. 8932–8946. Association for Computational Linguistics, Online (2020)
11. Hu, M., Liu, B.: Mining and summarizing customer reviews. In: Proceedings of the Tenth ACM SIGKDD International Conference on Knowledge Discovery and Data Mining, pp. 168–177. KDD 2004, Association for Computing Machinery, New York, NY, USA (2004)
12. Hu, Z., Ma, X., Liu, Z., Hovy, E., Xing, E.: Harnessing deep neural networks with logic rules. In: Proceedings of the 54th Annual Meeting of the Association for Computational Linguistics (Volume 1: Long Papers), pp. 2410–2420. Association for Computational Linguistics, Berlin, Germany (2016)
13. Joshi, A., Bhattacharyya, P., Carman, M.J.: Automatic sarcasm detection: a survey. ACM Comput. Surv. **50**(5), 1–22 (2017)
14. Khare, A., Gangwar, A., Singh, S., Prakash, S.: Sentiment analysis and sarcasm detection of indian general election tweets. arXiv preprint arXiv:2201.02127 (2022)
15. Kouloumpis, E., Wilson, T., Moore, J.: Twitter sentiment analysis: the good the bad and the omg! In: Proceedings of the International AAAI Conference on Web and Social Media, vol. 5, pp. 538–541 (2011)
16. Liu, B., Zhang, L.: A survey of opinion mining and sentiment analysis. In: Aggarwal, C., Zhai, C. (eds.) Mining Text Data, pp. 415–463. Springer, Boston (2012). https://doi.org/10.1007/978-1-4614-3223-4_13
17. Ma, W., Lou, R., Zhang, K., Wang, L., Vosoughi, S.: GradTS: a gradient-based automatic auxiliary task selection method based on transformer networks. In: Proceedings of EMNLP 2021, pp. 5621–5632. Association for Computational Linguistics, Online and Punta Cana, Dominican Republic (2021)
18. Majumder, N., Poria, S., Peng, H., Chhaya, N., Cambria, E., Gelbukh, A.: Sentiment and sarcasm classification with multitask learning. IEEE Intell. Syst. **34**(03), 38–43 (2019)
19. Nguyen, D.Q., Vu, T., Nguyen, A.T.: BERTweet: a pre-trained language model for English Tweets (2020)
20. Rajadesingan, A., Zafarani, R., Liu, H.: Sarcasm detection on twitter: A behavioral modeling approach. In: Proceedings of the Eighth ACM International Conference on Web Search and Data Mining. pp. 97–106. WSDM 2015, Association for Computing Machinery, New York, NY, USA (2015)
21. Riloff, E., Qadir, A., Surve, P., De Silva, L., Gilbert, N., Huang, R.: Sarcasm as contrast between a positive sentiment and negative situation. In: Proceedings of the 2013 Conference on Empirical Methods in Natural Language Processing, pp. 704–714 (2013)
22. Rosenthal, S., Farra, N., Nakov, P.: SemEval-2017 task 4: sentiment analysis in twitter. In: Proceedings of the 11th International Workshop on Semantic Evaluation (SemEval-2017), pp. 502–518 (2017)
23. Rosenthal, S., Ritter, A., Nakov, P., Stoyanov, V.: SemEval-2014 task 9: sentiment analysis in Twitter. In: Proceedings of the 8th International Workshop on Semantic Evaluation (SemEval 2014), pp. 73–80. Association for Computational Linguistics, Dublin, Ireland (2014)

24. Sun, L., Zhang, K., Ji, F., Yang, Z.: TOI-CNN: a solution of information extraction on Chinese insurance policy. In: Proceedings of the NAACL-HLT 2019, pp. 174–181. Association for Computational Linguistics, Minneapolis, Minnesota (2019)
25. Sykora, M., Elayan, S., Jackson, T.W.: A qualitative analysis of sarcasm, irony and related# hashtags on twitter. Big Data Soc. **7**(2), 2053951720972735 (2020)
26. Tai, K.S., Socher, R., Manning, C.D.: Improved semantic representations from tree-structured long short-term memory networks. In: Proceedings of the 53rd Annual Meeting of the Association for Computational Linguistics and the 7th International Joint Conference on Natural Language Processing (Volume 1: Long Papers), pp. 1556–1566. Association for Computational Linguistics, Beijing, China (2015)
27. Van Hee, C., Lefever, E., Hoste, V.: Semeval-2018 task 3: Irony detection in English tweets. In: Proceedings of The 12th International Workshop on Semantic Evaluation, pp. 39–50 (2018)
28. Vosoughi, S., Zhou, H., Roy, D.: Enhanced Twitter sentiment classification using contextual information. In: Proceedings of the 6th Workshop on Computational Approaches to Subjectivity, Sentiment and Social Media Analysis, pp. 16–24. Association for Computational Linguistics, Lisboa, Portugal (Sep 2015)
29. Zhang, K., Gutiérrez, B.J., Su, Y.: Aligning instruction tasks unlocks large language models as zero-shot relation extractors. In: Findings of ACL 2023 (2023)
30. Zhang, K., Sun, L., Ji, F.: A TOI based CNN with location regression for insurance contract analysis. In: 2019 International Joint Conference on Neural Networks (IJCNN), pp. 1–8 (2019)
31. Zhang, K., et al.: Open hierarchical relation extraction. In: Proceedings of NAACL 2021 (2021)

Local or Global: The Variation in the Encoding of Style Across Sentiment and Formality

Somayeh Jafaritazehjani[1,3](✉), Gwénolé Lecorvé[2], Damien Lolive[3], and John D. Kelleher[4]

[1] ADAPT Centre, Technological University Dublin, Dublin, Ireland
somayeh.x.jafaritazehjani@mytudublin.ie
[2] Orange, Lannion, France
[3] Univ Rennes, CNRS, IRISA, Lannion, France
[4] ADAPT Research Centre, Maynooth University, Kildare, Ireland
John.Kelleher@mu.ie

Abstract. Research on textual style transfer has observed that the concept of style can vary across domains. This research examines the encoding of style across the sentiment and formality domains and observes that formality appears to be more globally encoded, and sentiment more locally encoded. The work also shows how the encoding of a style can inform the appropriate choice of method to compute content preservation during textual style transfer.

Keywords: Sentiment · Formality · Style · Local · Global

1 Introduction

Textual Style Transfer (TST) attempts to generate text in a given style from a input text in a different style while preserving as much information from the input as possible. Even though style is a key element in this field, there is yet no consensus and clear definition for it. Previous work has identified that the concept of style varies across different domains [10]. However, this prior research does not explain how the encoding of style differs across these domains. This is the question that this paper addresses. By the encoding of style we mean the distribution of the components of a text that carry stylistic information. If a style is locally encoded this implies that frequently only a relatively small number of local changes are necessary to transfer the style (such as changing a few keywords), whereas if a style is globally encoded then typically a general reworking of a text is required in order to transfer the style.

We focus on sentiment and formality (two commonly used styles in *TST* research) and examine the differences in the style encoding when it is equated with sentiment polarity versus formal register of a text. Based on observations

L. Iliadis et al. (Eds.): ICANN 2023, LNCS 14263, pp. 492–504, 2023.
https://doi.org/10.1007/978-3-031-44204-9_41

from a number of experiments, we argue that style varies in terms of its local versus global encoding. In particular, we find that transforming formality requires a more global adaptation of a text as compared to sentiment-transfer.

The paper begins by proposing a refinement to training regime of a state-of-the-art transformer-based (T-based) TST model [4] which reduces the computational cost[1] The paper then reports a set of probing experiments that examine the entanglement of style across the layers of a transformer architecture in both the sentiment and formality domains. Building on these results it presents a unigram based analysis of the overlap between original and human style adapted paraphrases of a text in both domains. The probing experiments and unigram overlap results indicate that the encoding of formality is more global (requiring extra layers of processing to encode, and resulting in lower unigram overlap) as compared to the encoding of sentiment. Finally, informed by the distinctions between the encoding of these style domains we reflect on the standard metrics used to assess content preservation (CPP) within TST research, and show that contextual embeddings [25] are more accurate for computing semantic similarity between source and paraphrased texts in the formality domain, whereas, GloVe embeddings [21] result in more accurate CPP scores in sentiment domain.

2 Literature Review

Most TST approaches use end2end strategies to learn a latent representation of the input [13] and condition the generation of style-shifted text on this representation. In the case of using parallel data to train models, TST is similar to a supervised NMT problem [18]. However, the majority of previous TST research has addressed the task in an unsupervised framing and compensate for the lack of parallel labelled data using adversarial techniques to guide the training towards generating text in a desired style.

The majority of TST networks have employed standard seq2seq RNN-based models [1,29] with some integrating variational encoders, multi-encoder, or multi-decoder [4,7–10,12,26–28]. Some previous TST work has analysed the role of different subnetworks of end2end RNN-based models as well as investigating the intermediate representations created by them [6,9,10,15].

Recently, [4] proposed a transformer-based (T-based) TST model. In a pilot experiment on our datasets we found that this model outperformed state-of-the-art RNN-based models (Table 1, see rows 1, 2, 3). Consequently, we the decided to use this model for our experimental work. However, this T-based model took a significant amount of time to converge, and so we adapted the training regime in order to reduce the computational cost.

3 Transformer-Based (T-Based) TST Model

In this section, we describe the architecture and the adapted training regime of our T-based TST model consisting of: (i) a generator and (ii) a discriminator.

[1] The code is released: https://github.com/somayeJ/Transformer-based-style-transfer.

Table 1. Higher CPP and SSP show better performance, but lower values of $PPLX$ reflect better fluency. α and β (Eq. 3) of T-based models are 0.25 & 0.5.

Dataset	Yelp			GYAFC		
Model/Evaluation metrcis	CPP	PPLX	SSP	CPP	PPLX	SSP
RNN-based model [27]	0.9261	**37.98**	81.8%	0.9088	26.81	**65.11%**
Multi-E RNN-based model [10]	0.9289	41.37	79.8%	0.911	**28.84**	58.82%
T-based model [4]	0.9717	106.07	78.50%	0.9516	289.20	28.99%
Our T-based model	**0.9718**	126.12	**83.00 %**	**0.9741**	141.44	47.19%

Generator (***Gen***) is a seq2seq pipeline where the encoder (***E***) and decoder (***D***) are transformers [30]. ***E*** consists of a sequence of 4 stacks, each including a fully connected self-attention, fully connected point-wise feed-forward, and normalization layers. ***E*** takes a text x (of length T and original style s_1) and a desired style s_2 as the input. The processing within ***E*** projects the input tokens through layers where the model learns the contextual and positional information of the tokens.

The final layer of ***E*** creates a sequence of latent token representations: $z = (z_0, z_1, ..., z_T)$ where z_0 is the dense vector of the desired style. ***D*** is similar to ***E***, but also contains an attention layer where z is fed from ***E***. ***D*** also has a projection layer which takes the output of ***D*** and generates tokens.

Reconstruction Loss. The reconstruction loss is designed to encourage the model to retain relevant content. We use two types of reconstruction loss during training, the self-reconstruction and cycle loss. During training (Fig. 1), ***Gen*** generates two text for each input $\mathbf{x}$ it receives, i.e. given $\mathbf{x}$, ***Gen*** creates its reconstructed version $\widetilde{\mathbf{x}}^{rec}$ as well as its style-shifted version $\widetilde{\mathbf{x}}^{trf}$. $\widetilde{\mathbf{x}}^{rec}$ is used to compute the self-reconstruction loss as follows. During training the negative log probability of x and $\widetilde{x}^{rec}$ is minimized.

$$\mathcal{L}_{self_{rec}} = -\log \Pr(\widetilde{x}^{rec} = x|x, s) \tag{1}$$

Using the self-reconstruction loss, ***Gen*** is trained to reconstruct text where the style of the input and the desired target style of the output text are the same. Here, the model functions as an auto-encoder (AE).

The style-shifted text, on the other hand, is used as an intermediate representation for the cycle loss which is calculated in Eq. 2.

$$\mathcal{L}_{cycle_{rec}} = -\log \Pr(\widetilde{\widetilde{x}}^{rec} = x|\widetilde{x}^{trf}, s) \tag{2}$$

$L_{cycle_{rec}}$ is designed to encourage the model to preserve the non-stylistic information of the input. To do so, the model is trained to generate $\widetilde{\widetilde{x}}^{rec}$ (a reconstructed version the input x) given $\widetilde{x}^{trf}$ (style-shifted version of x) by following these cycle of generation steps where $s_1 \neq s_2$:

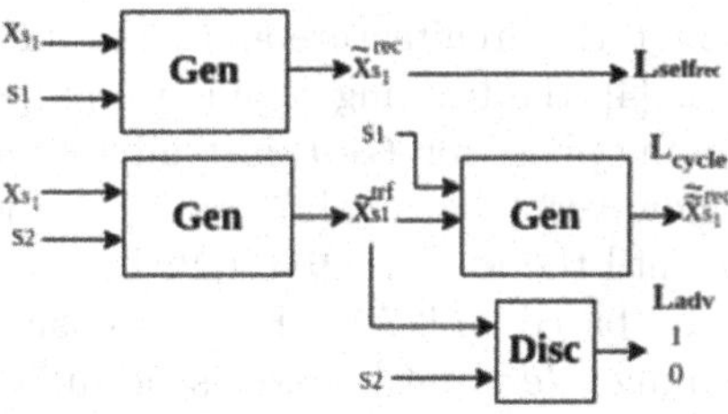

Fig. 1. For input x_{s_1}, ***Gen*** creates $\widetilde{\mathbf{x}}_{s_1}^{rec}$ & $\widetilde{\mathbf{x}}_{s_2}^{trf}$, also re-creates $\approx{\mathbf{x}}_{s_1}^{rec}$. ***Disc*** gets $\widetilde{\mathbf{x}}_{s_1}^{trf}$ & its desired style s_2, and labels it as style-shifted (0) or reconstructed (1).

- Generating $\widetilde{x}^{trf}$ by feeding ***Gen*** with x and the desired style s_2.
- Generating $\approx{x}^{rec}$ by feeding ***Gen*** with $\widetilde{x}^{trf}$ and the desired style s_1.

While training, Eq. 2 is used to minimize the negative log probability of each input x and its reconstructed text $\approx{x}^{rec}$.

The reconstruction loss is then computed using the Eq. 3 as the weighted summation of a self-reconstruction and a cycle-reconstruction loss.

$$\mathcal{L}_{rec} = \alpha\mathcal{L}_{self_{rec}} + \beta\mathcal{L}_{cycle_{rec}} \tag{3}$$

Discriminator (***Disc***) consists of a sequence of a transformer (with the same architecture as the transformer E) , and a classifier (a feed-forward network with a single hidden layer and a softmax output layer), similar to the discriminator used in [23] and [5]. It takes as input a text and a style and attempts to learn whether or not the style matches the original style of the given text. Specifically, it is trained to label pairs where the style matches the original style of the text as positive and pairs where the style is not the original style of the text as negative, i.e. it learns to return true for ($\mathbf{x}_{s_1}$, s_1) and ($\widetilde{\mathbf{x}}_{s_1}^{rec}$, s_1) and false for ($\widetilde{\mathbf{x}}_{s_1}^{trf}$, s_2) and ($\mathbf{x}_{s_1}$, s_2). This is done by minimizing the Eq. 4, the binary cross-entropy over the two classes where $s_1 \neq s_2$. ***Disc*** is trained in parallel with ***Gen***.

$$\mathcal{L}_{Disc} = -\log(Disc(\widetilde{\mathbf{x}}_{s_1}^{rec}, s_1)) - \log(1 - Disc(\widetilde{\mathbf{x}}_{s}^{trf}, s_2)) \tag{4}$$

Adversarial Loss. A key component of the adversarial training is ***Disc*** which is in competition with ***Gen***: ***Gen*** attempts to generate style-shifted text that ***Disc*** will categorize as original text, and ***Disc*** is attempting to detect style-shifted sequences. To encourage ***Gen*** to generate style-shifted text that can convince ***Disc*** that the style-shifted text is actually original text, an adversarial loss is defined in Eq. 5 ($\overline{s}$ is the source and s is the desired style of text) and is minimized during the training together with the total loss ($\mathcal{L}_{rec} + \mathcal{L}_{adv}$).

$$\mathcal{L}_{adv} = -\log(Disc(\widetilde{\mathbf{x}}_{\overline{s}}^{trf}, s)) \tag{5}$$

Training Regime. Although the architecture and loss functions we use (Sects. 3, 3, and 3) are the same as [4], the training regime we propose is different. First, we do not use a pre-training phase for ***Gen***, instead ***Gen*** and ***Disc*** are trained in parallel throughout. However, following [27], we do not use the adversarial loss in the training of ***Gen*** until the loss of ***Disc*** falls below a pre-set threshold (a hyper-parameter set to 1.2 based on [27]). This is to ensure that the adversarial loss is not used in training ***Gen*** until ***Disc*** is of sufficient quality that the adversarial loss it returns is informative. Also, when updating ***Gen*** weights, we only do a single backpropogation+weight update pass, using the summation of the losses, as compared to [4] that uses two backpropogation+weight update passes, first, the self reconstruction, the summation of the adversarial and cycle loss. Our training regime is as follows where given a corpus, X_{s_1} and X_{s_2} are portions of this corpus containing styles s_1 and s_2.

Step 1: Sample two different-styled mini-batches of size k (k indicates batch-size and is set to 1 here for simplicity): $\{x_{s_1}\} \in X_{s_1}$, and $\{x_{s_2}\} \in X_{s_2}$.
Step 2: Generates a reconstructed and a style-shifted text for each sequence:
$\widetilde{\mathbf{x}}_{s_1}^{rec} = Gen(x_{s_1}, s_1)$, $\widetilde{\mathbf{x}}_{s_2}^{trf} = Gen(x_{s_1}, s_2)$
$\widetilde{\mathbf{x}}_{s_2}^{rec} = Gen(x_{s_2}, s_2)$, $\widetilde{\mathbf{x}}_{s_1}^{trf} = Gen(x_{s_2}, s_1)$
Step 3: Compute $L_{self_{rec}}$ using the Eq. 1.
Step 4: Compute L_{Disc} using the Eq. 4 and update θ_{Disc}.
Step 5: If $L_{Disc} < 1.2$, compute $L_{cycle_{rec}}$ and L_{adv} and update θ_{Gen} using the total loss. Otherwise, perform update θ_{Gen} using the Eq. 1.
Step 6: For batches of one epoch, repeat steps 1–5.
Step 7: Use the model with lowest total loss (best model) as the initial model in the next epoch. Stop after 20 epochs.

4 Data, Experimental Set up and Evaluation Methodology

Data. Yelp and GYAFC datasets are used throughout the experiments of this paper. Yelp is a restaurant review dataset where the positive or negative label of each review is considered as its style. For our experiments, we use the dataset provided and preprocessed by [17].

GYAFC (Grammarly's Yahoo Answers Formality Corpus) [24] is a parallel dataset which is used in a non-parallel mode in our experiments. It contains text from the domains of Entertainment & Music and Family & Relationships. We compose and shuffle the data from these domains and do the following preprocessing steps (around 2% of the data is removed in the resulting dataset).

First, we make the tokens more consistent by: 1. Lower casing the tokens. 2. Replacing the numbers, website addresses, email addresses and emojis with special tokens. 3. Inserting space between token and punctuation as well as punctuation and punctuation. 4. In informal data, for the tokens with high frequency such as *oh* converting all non-standard forms, such as *ohhhh* or *oooohhhhh* into one non-standard form *ohh* to reduce the size of vocabulary and also the number of unknown tokens (`<unk>`). 5. Filtering the non-English sequences. To do so, we manually filter the list of sequences marked as non-English by the python language detector library. This is to reduce the possibility of removing the English sequences which are detected as non-English specifically due to the characteristics of informal data which contains many non-standard variations of the tokens. 6. Considering a box plot of the sentence length distribution and filtering all sequences whose lengths were outside the whiskers of the plot.

Experimental Set Up. While building the vocab, the tokens with frequency lower than 5 were considered as <unk>. Each stack of $\boldsymbol{E}$ and $\boldsymbol{D}$ of out T-based model has 4 attention heads. The size of token embeddings, positional embeddings, style vectors and the hidden size of the model are 256[2] (Table 2).

Table 2. Data distribution of the datasets, (l:length).

Data	Yelp		GYAFC	
Style	Positive	Negative	Formal	Informal
Train	267314	176787	102502	104044
Dev	2000	2000	5064	5111
Test	500	500	2076	2739
Avg-l	8.45	9.66	12.4	12
Vocab-size	9352		11409	

Evaluation Methodology. We use three evaluation metrics designed to çover the multiple objectives of TST: style-shift, content maintenance and fluency [11].

Style-shif power (SSP) determines the power of a TST model in shifting the style, prior work has trained separate classifiers for each domain to measure the presence of a desired style in the style-shifted text [7,8,12,16,17,22,27,28]. Accordingly, we train two separate binary classifier using GYAFC and Yelp data using the TextCNN model proposed by [14]. Style shift power SSP metric is the score returned by this classifier for the target style of style-shifted text.

To compute Content Preservation Power (CPP), we use an embedding-based approach to measure the similarity between an input x and style-shifted text $\widetilde{x}^{trf}$. First, the tokens of x and $\widetilde{x}^{trf}$ are mapped into an embedding space using a pretrained model. Vector representations of x and $\widetilde{x}^{trf}$ are then created by taking the average of their token embeddings. Finally, these vector pairs are compared with cosine similarity [7]. In our experiments, we use both a 100-dimensional GloVe model [21] and a 768-dimensional SBERT model[3] [25] as pre-trained embeddings models. To improve the interpretability of CPP scores, we compute the semantic similarity between randomly selected sequences as

[2] Other hyperparameters adapted from (http://github.com/fastnlp/style-transformer).

[3] http://huggingface.co/cross-encoder/stsb-TinyBERT-L-4.

the CPP lower bound (LB) scores. The respective GloVe- and SBERT-based LB scores for the sentiment domain are 0.86 and 0.09387 and for the formality domain are 0.87 and 0.0672.

To evaluate the fluency of the generated texts we follow previous research [12,31] and train separate language models for each domain. These LMs are single-layer RNN with GRU cells [2]. We then use the average perplexity scores of these models on the style-shifted texts of a TST model as its PPLX. Lower PPLX indicates the TST model generates more fluent text.

5 Experiments

To investigate the variations in sentiment and formality encoding, an interesting experiment is re-weighting the TST model so that it performs more similar to an AE (Sect. 5). The idea being that the more a TST model is weighted towards acting as an AE the less likely it is to perform global rewrites and so this change is likely to be reflected in changes of the SSP of the system in domains where style is globally encoded. Also, we study how sentiment and formality are encoded by different layers of the T-based encoder of our TST model (Sect. 4) and compare it with the variations observed by studying the human-generated data across these style domains (Sect. 4).

Reconstruction Versus Adversarial Balance. Table 1 lists the results generated using the training regime from [4] (row 3) and our adapted training regime (row 4). The results reveal a slight improvement with the new training regime with improvements in CPP and SSP on Yelp and a larger improvement in CPP for GYAFC with a drop in SSP. However, these results are recorded from single runs of the model and so we do not claim a statistical difference here. More importantly, however, the adapted training regime required much less training time to achieve these results[4].

Neither the total loss nor the reconstruction loss (Eq. 3) normalize the contribution of the losses. Therefore, α and β summing to less and more than 1 indirectly puts greater emphasis during training on the adversarial loss and reconstruction loss, respectively. T-models listed in Table 1, use a total weight of 0.75 ($\alpha = 0.25$ and $\beta = 0.5$) to reconstruction and 1 to adversarial loss.

We investigate the effect of increasing the weight of reconstruction loss by doubling the summation of α and β and training two new models: T_1; $\alpha = 1$, $\beta = 0.5$, and T_2; $\alpha = 0.5$, $\beta = 1$. Comparing the results of T_1 and T_2 in Table 3 with the scores of our T-based model (Table 1) shows that in Yelp, T_1 performs better than the T-based model in every evaluation aspect and T_2 also has a better CPP and fluency. In GYAFC, however, this weight modification does not appear to be as beneficial overall, although, in T_1, it results in an improvement in CPP and fluency, the SSP drops by a large amount. The fact that increasing the weighting of the reconstruction loss relative to the adversarial loss encourages

[4] Training of our T-based model on Yelp took around 36 h using single Quadro RTX 8000 ss GPU, compared to 75 h while applying the training regime from [4].

a model to act more like an AE, and that this is beneficial for both CPP and SSP in the sentiment domain but results in much lower SSP in the formality domain, suggests that shifting sentiment requires fewer text changes compared to the formality (i.e., sentiment is more locally encoded compared to formality).

Table 3. α and β (Eq. 3) of T_1: $\alpha = 1$, $\beta = 0.5$, and T_2: $\alpha = 0.5$, $\beta = 1$.

	Datasets		Yelp		GYAFC	
	Models		T1	T2	T1	T2
Automatic Evaluation	SSP		83.8%	70.9%	32.71%	41.52%
	PPLX		107.07	99.88	101.57	154.35
	CPP	GloVe	0.9732	0.9767	0.9743	0.9714
		SBERT	0.5869	0.6177	0.8595	0.8108
Layer-wise probing of Transformer encoder	GloVe-baseline		85.80%		71.01%	
	Embedding layer		89.9%	87.4%	75.74%	78.69%
	Stack1		100%	90.5%	74.18%	80.48%
	Stack2		100%	100%	99.63%	88.2%
	Stack3		100%	100%	100%	100%
	Stack4		100%	100%	100%	100%

Layer-Wise Probing of Transformer $\boldsymbol{E}$. An interesting aspects of transformer models is that they include multiple self-attention layers. Indeed, researchers interested in understanding how transformers encode linguistic information have probed how the encoding of this information varies across the layers of transformers trained for different text NLP-related problems [19,20]. However, to the best of our knowledge the encoding of style across the layers of a TST transformer has not yet been examined. Inspired by previous work on probing [3,9,10] we designed a classification experiment to examine the extent to which style is encoded at each layer of the transformer $\boldsymbol{E}$ for formality and sentiment domains.

We train 5 separate probes, one for each of the layers of $\boldsymbol{E}$: the embedding layer, and each of the 4 stacks of $\boldsymbol{E}$. Each probe, a feed-forward network with a single hidden layer and a sigmoid output layer, is trained to detect the source style of an input text from the embedding of the text generated by that probe's corresponding layer in the transformer. The higher the accuracy of a probe is, the more source-stylistic features are present in the text embedding. The text embedding for a layer is the average of the embeddings of the text tokens generated by that layer.

As a baseline for this task, for each dataset we train a probe on GloVe-based embeddings to identify the style of a text sequence. The GloVe-based embedding for a given sequence is computed by mapping its tokens to their pre-trained GloVe embeddings and then taking the average of these token embeddings. The accuracy of the source style identification probes trained on GloVe-based embeddings of Yelp and GYAFC test sequences (i.e., original text sequences that have not been style-shifted) are 85.80% and 71.01%, respectively. GloVe token embeddings are trained on the nonzero elements in a word-word co-occurrence matrix [21], and we generated the GloVe-based sequence embeddings by averaging GloVe token embeddings. Consequently, it is likely that our GloVe-based sequence embeddings primarily encode word co-occurrence information and neglect word order, essentially functioning as a bag-of-words. Given this, the higher score on identifying source style in the sentiment domain using GloVe embeddings compared to the formality domain suggests that a bag-of-word representation is better at identifying sentiment compared to formality. This also suggests that sentiment is more locally encoded as compared to formality (sentiment being more readily identifiable based on the presence/absence of particular words, whereas the identification of formality may require more structural information).

Table 3 lists the results from the layer-wise probing of transformer embeddings. The attention mechanism within each layer of $\boldsymbol{E}$ allows the embeddings for a word to be fine-tuned to its context of use by integrating information from across the input sequence. Consequently, as we move up through the layers of the network it is to be expected that the embeddings at each subsequent layer encode a more global perspective on the meaning of a sequence, as more and more information from across the sequence is integrated into each of the token embeddings. As a result, comparing the performance of a probe within a style domain across the layers of a transformer architecture can provide insight into sensitivity of that style to global structure of the sequence. Given this, it is interesting that in the sentiment domain the probe achieves 100% performance at an earlier layer as compared with the formality domain, suggesting that in general the encoding of formality requires more information from across a sequence to be integrated into the embeddings of each of the tokens in the sequence.

Taken together, these probing results suggest that sentiment is encoded in a more local (e.g., keywords are very informative) manner as compared with formality. Based on this observation, we hypothesise that in general formality transfer requires more global changes to a text as compared with sentiment shift, that may be achieved in some instances by just swapping a single word.

Unigram Based Analysis. To further test our hypothesis, sentiment is encoded more locally compared to formality, we run a word overlap (WO) analysis. The intuition being that if sentiment is more local in its encoding relative to formality, a higher WO between style-shifted texts and inputs are expected in this domain compared to the formality. To do this analysis, we use the gold style-shifted text for the test sets of Yelp and GYAFC . In GYAFC, there are 4 human gold sets for each domain and style. We use all these files for analysis and the results reported are the average of the scores computed for each files.

To compute WO, following [12] given x and $\widetilde{x}^{trf}$, we first filter stop words, then compute the score as $\frac{count(x \cap \widetilde{x}^{trf})}{count(x \cup \widetilde{x}^{trf})}$. We augment our analysis of the WO of manually style-shifted texts with an analysis of how successfully the human 'style translators' were at the task. To do this, we use accuracy of the *SSP* classifiers (introduced in Sect. 2) in detecting the desired style of human-generated files across the two domains. The intuition being that if a human style translator has successfully shifted the style of the text into the desired style the *SSP* classifier should recognise this desired style with high confidence.

The results of our WO analysis show slightly higher WO between source and gold style-shifted text in sentiment 0.4253 as compared to the formality 0.4057 (LB of WO is 0.0035). This together with higher accuracy of classifiers in labeling sentiment 77.2% compared to 70.45% in formality illustrates that even though more unigrams are swapped in formality transfer, we still observe lower *SSP* in the style-shifted files which supports our hypothesis.

6 The Interaction of Style Characteristics and *CPP*

The experiment presented here investigates the performance of GloVe- and SBERT-based *CPP* metrics for the sentiment- and formality-transfer tasks. For each style domain, we randomly selected 200 samples from the test set of that domain as the source texts. For each of these source sequences we composed a target set containing its corresponding gold style-shifted text and 499 other randomly selected texts. Then, we computed the *CPP* scores between each source sequence and each of the sequences in its target set using both GloVe- and SBERT-based embeddings. We expect that given a source text a good *CPP* metric assigns a higher value to the pair <source text, gold style-shifted text> rather than to the pairs of <source text, random text 1>, ..., <source text, random text 499>.

The SBERT-based CPP metric assigns the highest value to the <source text, gold style-shifted text> pair in 95.5% of cases in the formality domain and 75.5% in sentiment domain. The GloVe-based CPP metric assigns the highest value to <source text, gold style-shifted text> pair in 71% cases in the formality domain and in 84% in sentiment domain. These results indicate that for formality the SBERT-based *CPP* metric works better than the GloVe-based metric (95.5% > 71%), whereas the GloVe-based *CPP* outperforms SBERT-based *CPP* for sentiment (84% > 75.5%). The variation in the relative performance of SBERT and GloVe across the two domains is inline with the hypothesis that formality is relatively globally encoded (SBERT is better) whereas sentiment is locally encoded. Indeed, texts having different sentiments seem to be very close in the GloVe embedding space as compared to the SBERT embedding space. Computing the similarity of the text while ignoring their sentiment variations makes GloVe-based *CPP* metrics more suitable for the sentiment domain.

7 Conclusion

Throughout our experiments we observed that sentiment is more locally encoded whereas formality is more globally encoded. In brief, this observation indicates that sentiment TST can often be achieved by changing a small number of keywords in a text, whereas formality TST frequently required more global reworking of a text. This clarification can improve TST research in a number of ways. First, we observed that SBERT-based *CPP* metric works better for formality, whereas, GloVe-based metric computes more accurate scores in sentiment domain. This is inline with the insight that formality is encoded as a global property of a text (beyond the representational capacity of a bag-or-words) compared to the encoding of the sentiment which is more token-based. Clarifying the encoding of style in different domains can also inform the appropriate use of TST modelling approaches. Some approaches that attempt to directly filter markers of style in the input, assume that stylistic features are detectable and separable from the content [16,17]. However, other approaches consider each style to be a separate language and adapt methods inspired by Neural Machine Translation to the TST problem [4,7,8,12,18,26–28]. This distinction between approaches may be inline with the observed global versus local style encoding distinction.

References

1. Bahdanau, D., Cho, K.H., Bengio, Y.: Neural machine translation by jointly learning to align and translate. In: 3rd International Conference on Learning Representations, ICLR 2015 (2015)
2. Chung, J., Gulcehre, C., Cho, K., Bengio, Y.: Empirical evaluation of gated recurrent neural networks on sequence modeling. In: Proceedings of the 28th Neural Information Processing Systems (NIPS), Workshop on Deep Learning (2014)
3. Conneau, A., Kruszewski, G., Lample, G., Barrault, L., Baroni, M.: What you can cram into a single vector: probing sentence embeddings for linguistic properties. In: Proceedings of the 56th Annual Meeting of the Association for Computational Linguistics (ACL), vol. 1: Long Papers, pp. 2126–2136 (2018)
4. Dai, N., Liang, J., Qiu, X., Huang, X.: Style transformer: unpaired text style transfer without disentangled latent representation. CoRR abs/1905.05621 (2019). http://arxiv.org/abs/1905.05621
5. Devlin, J., Chang, M.W., Lee, K., Toutanova, K.: BERT: pre-training of deep bidirectional transformers for language understanding. arXiv preprint arXiv:1810.04805 (2018)
6. Elazar, Y., Goldberg, Y.: Adversarial removal of demographic attributes from text data. In: Proceedings of the 2018 Conference on Empirical Methods in Natural Language Processing, pp. 11–21. Association for Computational Linguistics, Brussels, Belgium (2018). https://doi.org/10.18653/v1/D18-1002. https://aclanthology.org/D18-1002
7. Fu, Z., Tan, X., Peng, N., Zhao, D., Yan, R.: Style transfer in text: exploration and evaluation. In: Proceedings of the AAAI Conference on Artificial Intelligence, vol. 32 (2018)
8. Hu, Z., Yang, Z., Liang, X., Salakhutdinov, R., Xing, E.P.: Controllable text generation. CoRR abs/1703.00955 (2017). http://arxiv.org/abs/1703.00955
9. Jafaritazehjani, S., Lecorvé, G., Lolive, D., Kelleher, J.: Style versus content: a distinction without a (learnable) difference? In: Proceedings of the 28th International Conference on Computational Linguistics, pp. 2169–2180. International Committee on Computational Linguistics, Barcelona, Spain (2020). https://doi.org/10.18653/v1/2020.coling-main.197, https://aclanthology.org/2020.coling-main.197

10. Jafaritazehjani, S., Lecorvé, G., Lolive, D., Kelleher, J.D.: Style as sentiment versus style as formality: the same or different? In: ICANN (2021)
11. Jin, D., Jin, Z., Hu, Z., Vechtomova, O., Mihalcea, R.: Deep learning for text style transfer: a survey. Comput. Linguist. **48**(1), 155–205 (2022). https://doi.org/10.1162/coli_a_00426
12. John, V., Mou, L., Bahuleyan, H., Vechtomova, O.: Disentangled representation learning for non-parallel text style transfer. In: Proceedings of the 57th Annual Meeting of the Association for Computational Linguistics, pp. 424–434 (2019)
13. Kelleher, J.D.: Deep Learning. MIT Press, Cambridge (2019)
14. Kim, Y.: Convolutional neural networks for sentence classification. In: Proceedings of the Conference on Empirical Methods in Natural Language Processing (EMNLP), pp. 1746–1751 (2014)
15. Lample, G., Subramanian, S., Smith, E., Denoyer, L., Ranzato, M., Boureau, Y.L.: Multiple-attribute text rewriting. In: International Conference on Learning Representations (2019). https://openreview.net/forum?id=H1g2NhC5KQ
16. Leeftink, W., Spanakis, G.: Towards controlled transformation of sentiment in sentences. In: Proceedings of the 11th International Conference on Agents and Artificial Intelligence, vol. 2: ICAART, pp. 809–816. SCITEPRESS (2019)
17. Li, J., Jia, R., He, H., Liang, P.: Delete, retrieve, generate: a simple approach to sentiment and style transfer. In: Proceedings of the 16th Conference of the North American Chapter of the Association for Computational Linguistics: Human Language Technologies (NAACL-HLT), vol. 1 (Long Papers), pp. 1865–1874 (2018)
18. Ma, S., Sun, X.: A semantic relevance based neural network for text summarization and text simplification. Comput. Linguist. **1**(1) (2017)
19. Nedumpozhimana, V., Kelleher, J.: Finding BERT's idiomatic key. In: Proceedings of the 17th Workshop on Multiword Expressions (MWE 2021), pp. 57–62. Association for Computational Linguistics (2021). https://doi.org/10.18653/v1/2021.mwe-1.7, https://aclanthology.org/2021.mwe-1.7
20. Nedumpozhimana, V., Klubička, F., Kelleher, J.D.: Shapley idioms: analysing BERT sentence embeddings for general idiom token identification. Front. Artif. Intell. **5**, 813967 (2022). https://doi.org/10.3389/frai.2022.813967, https://www.frontiersin.org/article/10.3389/frai.2022.813967
21. Pennington, J., Socher, R., Manning, C.: GloVe: global vectors for word representation. In: Proceedings of the 2014 Conference on Empirical Methods in Natural Language Processing (EMNLP), pp. 1532–1543 (2014)
22. Prabhumoye, S., Tsvetkov, Y., Salakhutdinov, R., Black, A.W.: Style transfer through back-translation. In: Proceedings of the 56th Annual Meeting of the Association for Computational Linguistics (ACL), Volume 1: Long Papers, pp. 866–876. Association for Computational Linguistics (2018). http://aclweb.org/anthology/P18-1080
23. Radford, A., Narasimhan, K., Salimans, T., Sutskever, I.: Improving language understanding by generative pre-training (2018)
24. Rao, S., Tetreault, J.R.: Dear sir or madam, may i introduce the GYAFC dataset: corpus, benchmarks and metrics for formality style transfer. In: NAACL-HLT (2018)
25. Reimers, N., Gurevych, I.: Sentence-BERT: sentence embeddings using siamese BERT-networks. In: Proceedings of the 2019 Conference on Empirical Methods in Natural Language Processing. Association for Computational Linguistics (2019). https://arxiv.org/abs/1908.10084

26. Romanov, A., Rumshisky, A., Rogers, A., Donahue, D.: Adversarial decomposition of text representation. In: Proceedings of the 2019 Conference of the North American Chapter of the Association for Computational Linguistics: Human Language Technologies (NAACL-HLT), vol. 1 (Long and Short Papers), pp. 815–825 (2019)
27. Shen, T., Lei, T., Barzilay, R., Jaakkola, T.: Style transfer from non-parallel text by cross-alignment. In: Guyon, I., et al. (eds.) Proceedings of the Conference in Neural Information Processing Systems, vol. 30 (NIPS), pp. 6830–6841. Curran Associates, Inc. (2017). http://papers.nips.cc/paper/7259-style-transfer-from-non-parallel-text-by-cross-alignment.pdf
28. Singh, A., Palod, R.: Sentiment transfer using seq2seq adversarial autoencoders. CoRR abs/1804.04003 (2018). http://arxiv.org/abs/1804.04003
29. Sutskever, I., Vinyals, O., Le, Q.V.: Sequence to sequence learning with neural networks. In: Proceedings of the Conference in Neural Information Processing Systems (NIPS), pp. 3104–3112 (2014)
30. Vaswani, A., et al.: Attention is all you need. In: Advances in Neural Information Processing Systems, vol. 30 (2017)
31. Zhao, J., Kim, Y., Zhang, K., Rush, A., LeCun, Y.: Adversarially regularized autoencoders. In: Dy, J., Krause, A. (eds.) Proceedings of the 35th International Conference on Machine Learning. Proceedings of Machine Learning Research, vol. 80, pp. 5902–5911. PMLR, Stockholm (2018). http://proceedings.mlr.press/v80/zhao18b.html

Prompt-Oriented Fine-Tuning Dual Bert for Aspect-Based Sentiment Analysis

Wen Yin[1,2], Yi Xu[1,2](✉), Cencen Liu[1,2], Dezhang Zheng[1,2], Qi Wang[3], and Chuanjie Liu[3]

[1] School of Information and Software Engineering, University of Electronic Science and Technology of China, Chengdu 610054, China
yinwenok@std.uestc.edu.cn, xuyi0421@uestc.edu.cn

[2] Trusted Cloud Computing and Big Data Key Laboratory of Sichuan Province, Chengdu 611731, China

[3] Chengdu Jiuzhou Electronic Information System Co., Ltd., Chengdu, China

Abstract. Aspect-Based Sentiment Analysis (ABSA) is a fine-grained sentiment analysis task that aims to predict sentiment polarity towards a specific aspect occurring in the given sentence. Recently, pre-trained language models such as BERT have shown great progress in this regard. However, due to the mismatch between pre-training and fine-tuning, dealing with informal expressions and complex sentences is facing challenges and it is worthwhile devoting much effort to this. To tackle this, in this paper, we propose a **P**rompt-oriented **F**ine-tuning **D**ual **BERT** (**PFDualBERT**) model that considers the complex semantic relevance and the scarce data samples simultaneously. To reduce the impact of such mismatches, we design a ProBERT influenced by the idea of prompt Learning. Specifically, we design a SemBERT module to capture semantic correlations. We refit SemBERT with aspect-based self-attention. The experimental results on three datasets certify that our PFDualBERT model outperforms state-of-the-art methods, and our further analysis substantiates that our model can exhibit stable performance in low-resource environments.

Keywords: ABSA · BERT · Prompt learning

1 Introduction

Aspect-based sentiment analysis(ABSA) is a branch of sentiment analysis, which aims to extract all the aspects and their corresponding sentiments within the sentence simultaneously [1]. Recent ABSA studies concentrated on three subtasks, i.e., Aspect Sentiment Classification(ASC) [2], Aspect Term Extraction (ATE) [12], Aspect Sentiment Triplet Extraction (ASTE) [3]. ASC determines the sentiment polarity of given aspects in a sentence. For example, given the sentence "The food in this restaurant is very good, but the service is bad". This sentence mentions two aspects: Food and service, and for the ASC task, the purpose is to give the sentiment polarity of the two aspects "food" and "service" as positive and negative, respectively.

L. Iliadis et al. (Eds.): ICANN 2023, LNCS 14263, pp. 505–517, 2023.
https://doi.org/10.1007/978-3-031-44204-9_42

Recently, The emergence of large-scale pre-trained language models, such as Bidirectional Encoder Representations from Transformers (BERT) [4], has ushered natural language processing into a new era. Through training on a large corpus of Wikipedia documents and books, BERT acquires a nuanced understanding of language, syntax, and semantics through contextual analysis. In ABSA, recent work [10,11,15,21] achieved appealing results based on pre-training models with BERT. Although great success has been achieved by the above studies, some critical problems remain when directly applying attention mechanisms or fine-tuning the pre-trained BERT in the task of ABSA.

Specifically, when BERT is used for downstream task fine-tuning, the [MASK] token does not appear, it only appears in the pre-training task. This creates a mismatch between pretraining and fine-tuning. Without the [MASK] token for fine-tuning, the model seems to have no starting point and no idea where to start. Meanwhile, simply initializing the encoder with a pre-trained BERT does not effectively handle informal expressions and complexity in ABSA as we expected. Thus, to better solve the above two types of problems, we propose a novel model, Prompt-oriented Fine-tuning Dual-BERT.

For the first challenge, we construct a Prompt-based BERT (ProBERT) by using sentence pair input with aspect words and a MASK token, which is used to indicate the emotional polarity of aspect words. This method is inspired by the idea of prompt learning because prompt-based fine-tuning with the objective of language modeling enables models to achieve significantly better performance on in-distribution cases than PLMs [19]. For the second, we construct a semantic aspect-based BERT (SemBERT) by utilizing a new attention mechanism, which combines the self-attention mechanism with the aspect-attention mechanism [23]. we expect that SemBERT could learn semantic representations different from syntactic representations. Our model concatenates the above two modules for emotional polarity classification and obtained good results on public datasets.

Our main contributions are as follows:

(1) To the best of my knowledge, this is the first work to apply the idea of cue learning to ABSA. Moreover, it shows superiority in low-resource environments and Few-Shot Learning.
(2) We propose a framework, Prompt-oriented Fine-tuning Dual-BERT, to improve the mismatch between pre-training and fine-tuning and the difficulty in analyzing the complex semantics of whole sentences and the syntactic semantics of aspects, respectively.
(3) We conduct extensive experiments on three widely-used datasets, and the results demonstrate the effectiveness, rationality, and interpretability of the proposed model. Additionally, the source code and preprocessed datasets used in our work are provided on GitHub[1].

[1] https://github.com/yinwen2019/DualBERT_ABSA.

2 Related Work

2.1 ABSA

Aspect-based sentiment analysis (ABSA) is a task in sentiment analysis that aims to determine the sentiment polarity of a sentence in one or more specific aspects. ABSA allows for a deeper understanding of the sentiment expressed in a sentence by identifying the specific aspects that are being evaluated.

In recent years, graph neural networks have achieved widespread success on ABSA tasks, and graph neural networks are favored for their ability to better handle tree structures and resolve long-distance dependencies. [18] defined a new dependency tree structure based on the target aspect so that it is rooted in the target aspect and only the edges that have direct dependencies with the aspect are retained. To consider the type of dependency, [16] proposed a method based on a graph convolutional network that can use an attention mechanism to distinguish the importance of different edges, and proposes an attentive layer ensemble to learn from different levels of models. Although graph neural networks have shown certain advantages in ABSA tasks, there are still some drawbacks and limitations. Models based on graph structures are limited by the size of the graph, and their scalability is relatively poor.

The advent of pre-trained language models has significantly improved the accuracy and efficiency of aspect-based sentiment analysis. For instance, [20] proposed a model BERT4GCN, which integrates grammatical sequential features from BERT and syntactic structure information from the dependency graph to improve sentiment analysis tasks. Another study by [11] proposes two modules, parallel aggregation, and hierarchical aggregation, which improve the performance of BERT in extracting aspects and predicting the sentiment associated. To address the challenges caused by adding dynamic semantic changes to the ABSA task, [22] proposed a dynamic re-weighting BERT model (DR-BERT), which adds aspect-aware dynamic semantics to the learning framework of the pre-trained model. How to effectively leverage semantic understanding from BERT models remains a major challenge in current ABSA tasks.

2.2 Prompt Learning

A major existing problem in NLP is the need for task-specific supervised data, however, for many tasks, there are gaps in the amount of supervised data available. Prompt-based NLP learning methods try to solve this problem by learning a language model that is usually pre-trained first, to reduce or avoid the need for the number of supervised datasets. Most PLMS are pre-trained with modeling language objectives, whereas downstream tasks have very different objectives. To overcome the gap between pretraining and downstream tasks, some scholars [9,13] have proposed to introduce prompt-tuning.

In the prompt-tuning paradigm, the downstream task is formalized as a language modeling problem by inserting a prompt template, and the results of language modeling can correspond to the solutions of downstream tasks. According to [13], a prompt function consists of two parts: 1)Design a template with two slots: one slot [input] for inputting text x and another slot [MASK] for an intermediate generated answer text mask, which will be mapped to output y. 2)Fill the slot [input] with the input text x.

In general, for tasks related to generation, or solved using the standard autoregressive language model, prefix prompts tend to be more conducive to solving because they are well integrated with the left-to-right nature of the model. [9] proposed a prompt-based sentence embedding method, which enables BERT to achieve sentence embedding better. [8] pre-trained the prompt by adding soft prompts in the pre-training for the few-shot learning, to obtain better initialization. [5] proposed a modular framework called OpenPrompt, whose composability allows the freedom to combine different PLM, task formats, and prompt modules within a uniform paradigm. However, we find it a challenge to apply the generative hinting paradigm to ABSA in a high-quality way. Thus, our model utilizes prompt learning as an aspect of emotional representation and is the first to apply the prompts method to this problem.

3 Methodology

In this section, we will introduce the technical details of PFDualBERT. Specifically, we will begin with the problem definition, and then present an overview of the PFDualBERT architecture, which is illustrated by Fig. 1.

3.1 Overview

Problem Statement. For Aspect Sentiment Classification (ASC), a sentence and a predefined aspect set (**S**, **A**) is given. In this paper, we let $\mathbf{S} = \{w_1, w_2, ...w_n\}$ and $\mathbf{A} = \{a_1, a_2, ...a_n\}$ represent a sentence and a predefined aspect set, where n and m are the numbers of words in **S** and the number of aspects in **A**, respectively. For each **S**, $\mathbf{A_s} = \{a_i | a_i \in A, a_i \in \mathbf{S}\}$ denotes the aspects contained in **S**. We treat each multiple-word aspect as a single word for simplicity, so a_i also means the i-th word of **S**. The goal of ASC is to predict the sentiment polarity $y_i \in \{\text{positive}, \text{negative}, \text{neutral}\}$ of the given aspect $a_i \in \mathbf{A_s}$ in the input sentence.

Overall Architecture. As shown in Fig. 1, our proposed PFDualBERT takes the sentence and one of the aspects that appear in the text as the input and outputs the sentiment predictions of the aspects. It consists of two modules (i.e., Prompt-based BERT and Semantic aspect-based BERT), which share the same embedding input. 1) The Prompt-based BERT learns the word embedding output of the [MASK] token and fine-tunes the model using the Masked Language Model loss. 2)The Semantic-based BERT learns output representations associated with aspectual words through self-attention and aspect-aware attention mechanisms. 3)The sentiment classifier takes output representations of the above two modules to make predictions.

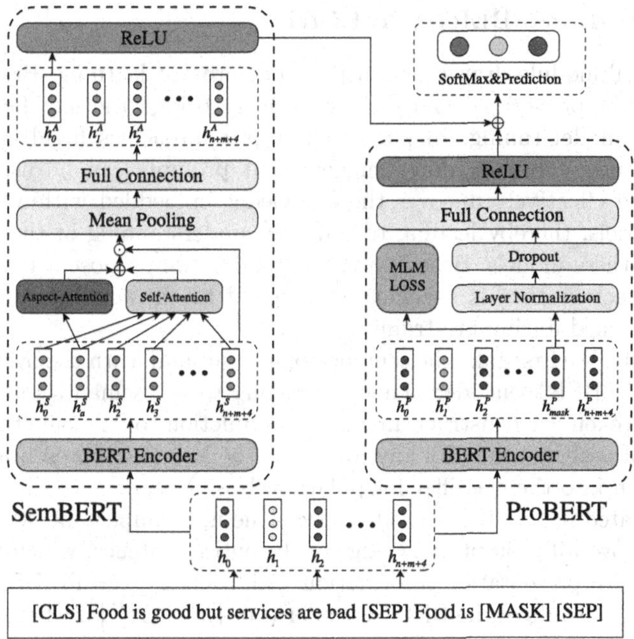

Fig. 1. Overall architecture of PFDualBERT

3.2 Context Encoder

To better represent the semantic information of aspect words and context words, we begin by mapping each word into a low-dimensional vector. For the input sequence, we construct an original sentence pair input, inspired by the idea of prompt learning. Specifically, the sentence pair for sequence input consists of the following:

$$\text{[CLS]}\ \ \textit{sentence}\ \ \text{[SEP]}\ \ \textit{aspect}\ \text{is}\ \ \text{[MASK]}\ \ \text{[SEP]} \tag{1}$$

where *sentence* and *aspect* represent whole-sentence input $\mathbf{S}$ and a single aspect input $a_i \in \mathbf{A_s}$, respectively, [MASK] token represents the masked label in the BERT model. We use BERT to get our sentence embedding $H = \{h_1, h_2, ...h_{n+m+4}\}$.

In this paper, we leverage BERT [4] as a context encoder to extract hidden contextual representations. We get the output hidden states of the BERT encoder layer $H^S = \{h_1^S, h_2^S, ...h_{n+m+4}^S\}$ and $H^P = \{h_1^P, h_2^P, ...h_{n+m+4}^P\}$, which are input into the ProBERT and SemBERT modules respectively. Notably, the size of the embedded layer generated by the encoder used by the two modules is different. Specifically, the size of the hidden layer of the former is set to the BERT vocabulary size, which is used to prompt knowledge learning. In contrast, the size of the hidden layer of the latter is set as described in [4]. In the following section, we provide detailed information about our proposed PFDualBERT model.

3.3 Prompt-Based BERT (ProBERT)

The ProBERT module draws inspiration from prompt learning. Prior research has shown that prompt learning can effectively bridge the gap between pre-training and model tuning. In particular, this approach is highly effective in low-data regimes. These findings suggest that prompts can be used to more efficiently and effectively uncover the knowledge embedded within pre-trained language models, thereby leading to a deeper understanding of the underlying principles of these models. Based on these insights, we propose a Prompt-based BERT architecture that is specifically designed to extract important prompt knowledge learned during pre-training.

Specifically, We first take the sentence pair input and learn the overall semantics by the ProBERT encoder. Then, according to the semantics suggested by the [MASK] token, we construct an extra loss function to fine-tune the semantic association of aspect words. Finally, we input the learning representation of the [MASK] token into the classifier for polarity classification.

As illustrated in Fig. 1, our model selects the most important [MASK] token based on the overall prompt knowledge of the entire sentence, which then serves as the operative presentation information. Additionally, the ProBERT module takes the final outputs of the BERT encoder (i.e. $\{h_i^P \in H^P\}$), where the hidden size is equal to the vocabulary size) as inputs. Then, we select the word representation embedding of the [MASK] token (i.e. h_{mask}, where $mask$ represents the index of the [MASK] token in the sentence) as the next layer input, which represents the predicted information for the masked words.

After extracting the [MASK] token representation in the auxiliary clause of each sentence, we feed it into a Multilayer Perceptron (MLP) and map it to lower dimensions via a ReLU layer:

$$\begin{aligned} h_{mask}^{*} &= \text{LayerNorm}\left(h_{mask}^{P}\right) \\ d_{mask} &= \text{Dropout}\left(h_{mask}^{*}\right) \\ R_{mask} &= \text{Relu}\left(\mathrm{W_p} d_{mask} + \mathrm{b_p}\right) \end{aligned} \tag{2}$$

where W_p, b_p are learned parameters, while h_{mask} represents the MASK token representation selected from H^P.

Masked Language Model Loss. Furthermore, we utilize a special mask language model loss (MLM Loss) to optimize this module. Before doing so, we refactor the ground-truth label that is used to calculate our MLM Loss. Specifically, we assign three sentiment polarity words (i.e., *Positive*, *Negative*, and *Neutral*) based on the ground-truth label, which serves as the ground truth of prompt knowledge. Subsequently, we select the corresponding indices of sentiment words in the vocabulary and generate one-hot vectors, which serve as the ground truth word distribution for the [MASK] token prompt knowledge. Finally, we calculate the cross-entropy loss between the word distribution vector and the embedding of the [MASK] token in the final output of ProBERT, which serves as the ultimate MLM loss:

$$\mathcal{L}_{mask} = - \sum_{(s,a)\in\mathcal{D}} \sum_{c\in\mathcal{V}} \log p\left(a\right) \tag{3}$$

where $\mathcal{V}$ represents the set of all words in the vocabulary table and. But we're really only looking at labels that relate to emotional polarity. In other words, the loss function is calculated by the distribution probability of the corresponding words determined according to the polarity of the target. We believe that this loss function can effectively optimize the intermediate layers of ProBERT.

3.4 Semantic-Based BERT (SemBERT)

In contrast to ProBERT, SemBERT does not utilize [MASK] prompt knowledge. Instead, SemBERT obtains an aspect-based attention matrix in the form of an adjacency matrix through a self-attention and aspect-aware mechanism. The attention mechanism is a commonly used method for capturing interactions between aspect and context words [7]. To enhance the semantic features, we adopt the aspect-attention and self-attention mechanism as proposed in [23]. Specifically, we learn the attention scores from the output of the SemBERT Encoder. Next, we will provide a detailed introduction to these two mechanisms.

Self-Attention. Self-attention [17] is a technique that calculates the attention score of each pair of elements in parallel, allowing for the capture of interactions between any two words within a sentence. This involves computing a query and a key, which are then used to determine the attention score.

$$A_{self} = \frac{QW^Q \times \left(KW^K\right)^T}{\sqrt{d}} \tag{4}$$

where matrices Q and K are both equal to the word representations of the last layer of our SemBERT encoder H^S, while $W^Q \in \mathbb{R}^{n\times n}$ and $W^K \in \mathbb{R}^{n\times n}$ are both learnable weights. In addition, d is the dimensionality of the input node feature.

Aspect-Attention. ABSA task requires modeling the specific semantic correlation between the aspect term and its context sentence, which is different for each aspect term. To capture this correlation, we compute an additional attention score matrix A_{aspect} using aspect-attention [23]. The aspect-attention mechanism allows the model to attend more to the words that are related to the aspect term and ignore the irrelevant words in the sentence. This attention score matrix is computed by considering the aspect term as a query and the contextual words as keys, and it is used to weight the contextual word representations in the final classification layer.

$$A_{aspect} = \tanh\left(Q_a W^a \times \left(KW^K\right)^T + b\right) \tag{5}$$

where matrices K is equal to H^S produced by SemBERT encoder. $W^a \in \mathbb{R}^{n\times n}$ and $W^K \in \mathbb{R}^{n\times n}$ are both learnable weights. We compute aspect representation by applying mean pooling on h_a and copying it n times to obtain $Q_a \in \mathbb{R}^{n\times n}$. Then, we integrate the aspect-attention score with the self-attention score:

$$A = A_{self} + A_{aspect} \tag{6}$$

After obtaining the attention score matrix, we multiply it with the original word representation to obtain sentiment knowledge. Then, we use polarity classifiers to predict the sentiment of the aspect term in the given context sentence.

$$\begin{aligned} H^A &= A \times H \\ E_{cls} &= \text{Relu}\left(W_c\left(h_{cls}^A\right) + b_c\right) \end{aligned} \tag{7}$$

where W_c, b_c are learnable parameters, while h_{cls}^A represents the first token representation selected from H^A.

3.5 Model Training

After passing through ProBERT and SemBERT, the original word embeddings (H) are respectively transformed into feature representations R and E. Finally, we utilize the Softmax function for sentiment polarity classification:

$$\hat{y} = \text{Softmax}\left(W_{sem}E_{cls} + W_{pro}R_{mask} + b\right) \tag{8}$$

where W_{sem}, W_{sem}, b are learnable parameters and bias, while $\hat{y}$ is the predicted sentiment polarity distribution.

Finally, we apply the cross-entropy loss function for model training:

$$\mathcal{L} = -\sum_{(s,a)\in\mathcal{D}}\sum_{c\in C}\log p\left(a\right) \tag{9}$$

where $\mathcal{D}$ contains all the sentence-aspect pairs and a represents the aspect appearing in sentence s. θ represents all the trainable parameters and C is the collection of sentiment polarities.

Finally, we add the model loss and the MLM loss mentioned above to obtain the total loss. Our training goal is to minimize the following total objective function:

$$\mathcal{L}_{total} = \lambda_1\mathcal{L} + \lambda_2\mathcal{L}_{mask} + \beta\|\theta\|_2^2 \tag{10}$$

where λ_1, λ_2 and β are regularization coefficients and θ represents all trainable model parameters.

4 Experiment

4.1 Datasets

The experiments were conducted on three benchmark ABSA datasets: SemEval 2014 Task 4 Restaurant and Laptop reviews [14], and Twitter posts [6]. Each data item was labeled with one of the three sentiment polarities: positive, negative, or neutral. The statistical information of the dataset is shown in Table 1.

Table 1. Statistics for the three experimental datasets.

Dataset	#positive		#negative		#neutral	
	Train	Test	Train	Test	Train	Test
Restaurant	2164	727	807	196	637	196
Laptop	976	337	851	128	455	167
Twitter	1507	172	1528	169	3016	336

4.2 Implementation Details

For our experiments, we initialize word embeddings with the official bert-large-uncased[2] models provided by [4] (n_{layers}=24, n_{heads}=16, n_{hidden}=1024). The learning rate is set as 2e-5 and the dropout rate is set as 0.3. The batch size is manually tested in [16]. The hyper-parameter λ_1, λ_2 and β have been carefully adjusted, and final values are set to 0.5, 0.5, and 100 respectively. The model is trained using the Adam optimizer and evaluated by two widely used metrics. We run our model three times with different seeds and report the average performance.

4.3 Baselines

To comprehensively evaluate the performance of our model, we compare it with state-of-the-art baselines:

a)BERT-PT [21] explore a novel post-training approach on BERT to enhance the performance. b)BERT-SPC [15] feeds sequence "[CLS] + context + [SEP] + target + [SEP]" into the basic BERT model for sentence pair classification task. c)AEN-BERT [15] proposes an Attentional Encoder Network. d)BERT-AT [10] proposes a novel architecture called BERT Adversarial Training to utilize adversarial training. e)R-GAT+BERT [18] proposes a relational graph attention network. f)BERT4GCN [20] integrates the grammatical sequential features from BERT and the syntactic knowledge from dependency graphs. g)TGCN-BERT [16] uses an attentive layer ensemble to learn the contextual information from different GCN layers. h)SSEGCN-BERT [23] proposes a novel Syntactic and Semantic Enhanced Graph Convolutional Network. i)DR-BERT [22] proposes a novel method designed to learn dynamic aspect-oriented semantics.

4.4 Main Results

To demonstrate the effectiveness of PFDualBERT, we compared our model with previous works using accuracy and F1-score as evaluation metrics. The results, as shown in Table 2, indicates that our PFDualBERT model outperforms all previous works on the three datasets. Our comparison of non-specific BERT models (i.e., BERT and BERT-PT) with task-specific models (e.g., DGEDT-BERT and

[2] https://github.com/huggingface/transformers.

Table 2. Experimental results comparison on three publicly available datasets.

Models	Restarant		Laptop		Twitter	
	Acc	F1	Acc	F1	Acc	F1
BERT-PT [21]	84.95	76.96	78.07	75.06	–	–
BERT-SPC [15]	84.46	76.98	78.99	75.03	74.13	72.73
AEN-BERT [15]	83.12	73.76	79.93	76.31	74.71	73.13
BERT-AT [10]	86.03	79.24	79.35	76.50	–	–
RGAT-BERT [18]	86.60	81.35	78.21	74.70	76.15	74.88
BERT4GCN [20]	84.75	77.11	77.49	73.01	74.73	73.76
TGCN+BERT [16]	86.61	79.95	80.88	77.03	76.45	75.25
SSEGCN+BERT [23]	87.31	81.09	81.01	77.96	77.40	76.02
DR-BRET [22]	87.72	82.31	81.45	78.16	77.24	76.10
Our PFDualBERT	**88.11**	**82.62**	**83.07**	**80.03**	**77.84**	**76.73**

TGCN+BERT) for ABSA, revealed that task-specific BERT models perform better than non-specific models. Furthermore, we observed a performance trend where DR-BERT > SSEGCN+BERT > T-GCN > RGAT-BERT > AEN-BERT > BERT-PT. It can be inferred from this trend that aspect-related information is a critical factor influencing the performance of ABSA models. Despite the outstanding performance of previous models, ourPFDualBERT still outperforms the most advanced baseline (i.e., DR-BERT or SSEGCN-BERT) no matter in terms of Accuracy or F1-score. The results indicate that our strategy based on prompt knowledge and aspect attention is effective. At the same time, this also suggests that our proposed integration of two BERT together can better capture the deep semantics of sentences.

Table 3. Experimental results comparison on three publicly available datasets

Models	Restarant		Laptop		Twitter	
	Acc	F1	Acc	F1	Acc	F1
Our PFDualBERT	**88.11**	**82.62**	**83.07**	**80.03**	**77.84**	**76.73**
w/o self-attention	84.93	79.17	79.29	76.36	75.02	74.17
w/o aspect-attention	86.29	80.96	81.13	78.06	76.18	74.27
w/o mask language model loss	87.36	81.08	81.99	79.03	77.03	73.43

4.5 Ablation Study

As shown in Table 3, we conducted an ablation study to examine the effectiveness of different modules in PFDualBERT. We considered the basic PFDualBERT as the baseline model. The results reveal that removing the self-attention module significantly degrades the performance, confirming the necessity of the global semantics of the sentence for ABSA. We also observed that removing the aspect-attention module resulted in unsatisfactory performance, indicating that capturing aspect-related semantics is crucial, leading to a 1.82%, 1.94%, and 1.66% reduction in accuracy on the three datasets, respectively. This highlights the importance of aspect-attention in capturing correlated semantic information between aspects and contextual words. Additionally, removing the masked language loss module resulted in a performance drop of 0.75%, 1.08%, and 0.81% in accuracy on three datasets, respectively, indicating that the masked language model can assist in better learning prompt knowledge in the original encoder. Finally, removing masked language loss and aspect-attention led to a drop in performance, further emphasizing their crucial roles in PFDualBERT for ABSA. In conclusion, the ablation experimental results demonstrate that each component contributes significantly to the effectiveness of our entire model.

Table 4. Experimental results comparison on Laptop datasets by sampling datasets of various proportions.

Dataset	Train Size	25% Data		50% Data		75% Data		100% Data	
	Model	Acc	F1	Acc	F1	Acc	F1	Acc	F1
Laptop	SSEGCN+BERT	76.18	72.55	78.32	74.06	79.91	75.65	81.01	77.96
	PFDualBERT	79.59	76.46	81.65	78.39	82.14	78.18	83.07	80.06
	vs.	+3.41	+3.91	+3.33	+3.79	+2.23	+2.53	+2.06	+2.10

4.6 Few-Shot Study

In order to investigate the effectiveness of PFDualBERT in low-resource settings, we conducted a few-shot study using various scaled versions of the Laptop dataset, with proportions of 25%, 50%, and 75%. SSEGCN [23] was used as the baseline model for comparison. As depicted in Fig. 4, the results show that PFDualBERT outperforms SSEGCN in terms of accuracy and F1-score. Moreover, as the size of the dataset decreases, both the accuracy and recall of the model decrease. However, PFDualBERT exhibits better performance than SSEGCN-BERT with smaller datasets, resulting in accuracy increases of 2.23%, 3.33%, and 3.41% for the 25%, 50%, and 75% proportions, respectively. These results suggest that PFDualBERT is more effective at handling sentiment information with limited training data in aspect-based sentiment analysis.

5 Conclusions

In this paper, we propose PFDualBERT, a novel model that integrates prompt knowledge and semantic correlations into aspect-based sentiment analysis. Our approach employs a unique sentence pair input that is based on prompts, which enhances the sentence encoding process. We evaluate PFDualBERT on three public datasets, and our experimental results demonstrate its effectiveness, especially in low-resource environments. Moreover, we plan to further optimize the number of model parameters and investigate other potential uses of our approach.

Acknowledgement. This research work was supported by the National Natural Science Foundation of China (NSFC) (U19A2059).

References

1. Chen, W., Du, J., Zhang, Z., Zhuang, F., He, Z.: A hierarchical interactive network for joint span-based aspect-sentiment analysis. In: Proceedings of COLING 2022, pp. 7013–7019 (2022). https://aclanthology.org/2022.coling-1.611
2. Chen, X., et al.: Aspect sentiment classification with document-level sentiment preference modeling. In: Proceedings of ACL 2020, pp. 3667–3677 (2020)
3. Chen, Y., Chen, K., Sun, X., Zhang, Z.: A span-level bidirectional network for aspect sentiment triplet extraction. In: Proceedings of EMNLP 2022, pp. 4300–4309 (2022). https://aclanthology.org/2022.emnlp-main.289
4. Devlin, J., Chang, M., Lee, K., Toutanova, K.: BERT: pre-training of deep bidirectional transformers for language understanding. In: Proceedings of NAACL-HLT 2019, pp. 4171–4186 (2019)
5. Ding, N., et al.: Openprompt: an open-source framework for prompt-learning. In: Proceedings of ACL 2022–System Demonstrations, pp. 105–113 (2022)
6. Dong, L., Wei, F., Tan, C., Tang, D., Zhou, M., Xu, K.: Adaptive recursive neural network for target-dependent twitter sentiment classification. In: Proceedings of ACL 2014, pp. 49–54 (2014)
7. Fan, F., Feng, Y., Zhao, D.: Multi-grained attention network for aspect-level sentiment classification. In: Riloff, E., Chiang, D., Hockenmaier, J., Tsujii, J. (eds.) Proceedings of the 2018 Conference on Empirical Methods in Natural Language Processing, pp. 3433–3442 (2018)
8. Gu, Y., Han, X., Liu, Z., Huang, M.: PPT: pre-trained prompt tuning for few-shot learning. In: Proceedings of ACL 2022, pp. 8410–8423 (2022)
9. Jiang, T., et al.: Promptbert: improving BERT sentence embeddings with prompts. In: Proceedings of EMNLP 2022, pp. 8826–8837 (2022). https://aclanthology.org/2022.emnlp-main.603
10. Karimi, A., Rossi, L., Prati, A.: Adversarial training for aspect-based sentiment analysis with BERT. In: ICPR 2020, pp. 8797–8803 (2020)
11. Karimi, A., Rossi, L., Prati, A.: Improving BERT performance for aspect-based sentiment analysis. In: 4th International Conference on Natural Language and Speech Processing, Trento, Italy, 12–13 November 2021, pp. 196–203 (2021)
12. Kumar, A., Srikanth, V.A., Narapareddy, V.T., Aruru, V., Neti, L.B.M., Malapati, A.: Aspect term extraction for opinion mining using a hierarchical self-attention network. Neurocomputing **465**, 195–204 (2021)

13. Liu, P., Yuan, W., Fu, J., Jiang, Z., Hayashi, H., Neubig, G.: Pre-train, prompt, and predict: a systematic survey of prompting methods in natural language processing. ACM Comput. Surv. **55**(9), 195:1–195:35 (2023)
14. Pontiki, M., Galanis, D., Pavlopoulos, J., Papageorgiou, H., Androutsopoulos, I., Manandhar, S.: Semeval-2014 task 4: aspect based sentiment analysis. In: Proceedings of SemEval@COLING 2014, pp. 27–35 (2014)
15. Song, Y., Wang, J., Jiang, T., Liu, Z., Rao, Y.: Attentional encoder network for targeted sentiment classification. CoRR abs/1902.09314 (2019). http://arxiv.org/abs/1902.09314
16. Tian, Y., Chen, G., Song, Y.: Aspect-based sentiment analysis with type-aware graph convolutional networks and layer ensemble. In: Proceedings of NAACL-HLT 2021, pp. 2910–2922 (2021)
17. Vaswani, A., et al.: Attention is all you need. In: Advances in Annual Conference on Neural Information Processing Systems 2017, pp. 5998–6008 (2017). https://proceedings.neurips.cc/paper/2017/hash/3f5ee243547dee91fbd053c1c4a845aa-Abstract.html
18. Wang, K., Shen, W., Yang, Y., Quan, X., Wang, R.: Relational graph attention network for aspect-based sentiment analysis. In: Proceedings of ACL 2020, pp. 3229–3238 (2020)
19. Wang, L., Lepage, Y.: Masked prompt learning for formal analogies beyond words. In: Proceedings of (IJAI-ECAI 2022)). CEUR Workshop Proceedings, vol. 3174, pp. 1–14 (2022). http://ceur-ws.org/Vol-3174/paper1.pdf
20. Xiao, Z., Wu, J., Chen, Q., Deng, C.: BERT4GCN: using BERT intermediate layers to augment GCN for aspect-based sentiment classification. In: Proceedings of EMNLP 2021, pp. 9193–9200 (2021)
21. Xu, H., Liu, B., Shu, L., Yu, P.S.: BERT post-training for review reading comprehension and aspect-based sentiment analysis. In: Proceedings of NAACL-HLT 2019, pp. 2324–2335 (2019)
22. Zhang, K., et al.: Incorporating dynamic semantics into pre-trained language model for aspect-based sentiment analysis. In: Findings of ACL 2022, pp. 3599–3610 (2022)
23. Zhang, Z., Zhou, Z., Wang, Y.: SSEGCN: syntactic and semantic enhanced graph convolutional network for aspect-based sentiment analysis. In: Proceedings of NAACL 2022, pp. 4916–4925 (2022)

Towards Energy-Efficient Sentiment Classification with Spiking Neural Networks

Junhao Chen[1,2], Xiaojun Ye[1,2], Jingbo Sun[1,2], and Chao Li[1,2](✉)

[1] College of Computer Science and Technology, Harbin Engineering University, Harbin, China
lichao006@hrbeu.edu.cn

[2] Modeling and Emulation in E-Government National Engineering Laboratory, Harbin, China

Abstract. Artificial Neural Networks (ANNs) have recently shown surprising results in Natural Language Processing (NLP) tasks. However, high energy consumption has become a major drawback of ANNs in NLP applications, which is contrary to the goal of sustainable and efficient computation. In this paper, we propose a novel energy-efficient sentiment classification model based on Spiking Neural Networks (SNNs), which achieves high energy efficiency by exploiting the sparsity of neural activity and using spikes to encode and transmit information. Unlike conventional neural networks that perform continuous and intensive computation, SNNs only fire spikes when they receive sufficient input stimuli, thereby reducing memory and computational overhead. We evaluate our model on the IMDB movie review dataset for sentiment classification tasks. The experimental results show that compared with the current state-of-the-art Transformer model, the energy consumption of the spike encoder model is reduced to 1.36% of the former, which is a 64.93-fold improvement in energy efficiency ratio. Furthermore, our model maintains an acceptable performance variance of 2%. Our research advances the field of "high-performance NLP models" and promotes further exploration of "low-energy NLP models".

Keywords: Spiking Neural Networks · Sentiment Classification · Energy-Efficient Models

1 Introduction

In recent years, deep neural networks have achieved excellent performance in a variety of natural language processing (NLP) tasks [1]. Automated sentiment analysis can solve the problem of classifying the sentiment of user comments and opinions in a big data model and has a high commercial value [2]. Transformer architecture-based models such as ELECTRA and GPT-3 have performed well in sentiment classification tasks, but because traditional ANNs use continuous

L. Iliadis et al. (Eds.): ICANN 2023, LNCS 14263, pp. 518–529, 2023.
https://doi.org/10.1007/978-3-031-44204-9_43

numerical computation to simulate neuronal activity, they require a lot of arithmetic power to perform matrix multiplication operations [3], which This leads to problems such as excessive energy consumption and high computational costs. With the introduction of GPT-4, this energy consumption bottleneck has highlighted the need for energy-efficient NLP models.

Existing research has focused on reducing the parameter size of models through techniques such as knowledge distillation or channel pruning [4], rather than addressing the underlying problem that requires a lot of arithmetic power: a lot of matrix multiplication.

SNNs use discrete impulse signals to process information, mimicking the mechanisms of the human brain, using sparse matrices and impulse coding to reduce matrix multiplication operations, and have been shown to have higher energy efficiency and more biologically sound computational potential, while still performing competitively in a variety of tasks, offering a promising alternative to traditional neural models. While SNNs have been successfully applied to computer vision tasks, their application to natural language processing, particularly for sentiment analysis, is still limited.

Inspired by biological neurons in the brain [5], we propose a model for energy-efficient emotion classification based on SNNs. Our spiking encoder consists of multiple bidirectional SNN layers that encode the input text as a representation, using discrete activations derived from trainable parameters. We also explore various gradient substitution methods to achieve back-propagation of the impulse process and find a more suitable differentiable function for gradient substitution. We evaluate the effectiveness of our model on sentiment classification tasks in terms of accuracy and energy consumption, and compare it with traditional models such as Transformer, Recurrent Neural Network(RNN), Text Convolutional Neural Networks(TextCNN), Long Short-Term Memory Networks(LSTM), Gate Recurrent Unit(GRU), Robustly Optimized BERT Pretraining Approach(RoBERTa) and GPT-3.

2 Related Work

In this section, we review the development of ANN-based models for sentiment analysis tasks and the progress of SNN models for natural language processing. We discuss the advancements and limitations of these models to provide context for our novel SNN-based sentiment analysis model.

Aytuğ Onan et al. propose a bidirectional convolutional recurrent neural network architecture that uses two independent bidirectional LSTM and GRU layers, and uses a grouping enhancement mechanism for the features extracted from the bidirectional layers, dividing the features into multiple categories, enhancing the important features in each group while weakening the less important features [6]. Chi Sun et al. used BERT for aspect-level sentiment analysis. However, their extensive use of matrix multiplications contributes to considerable energy costs [7].

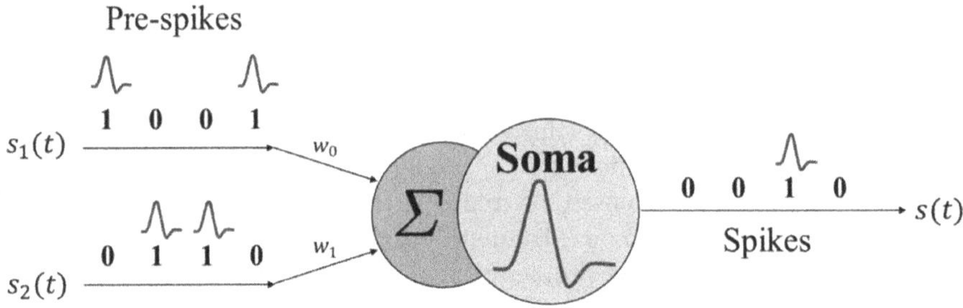

Fig. 1. SNN signal processing illustration and SNN cell computation paradigm

Song Han et al. proposed a method to jointly train weights and connections to improve the efficiency of neural networks [8]. By pruning and quantization techniques, the number of parameters and the computational effort of the network were significantly reduced; Chenquan Gan et al. proposed a sparse attention-based separable dilated convolutional neural network (SA-SDCCN), which used a sparse attention mechanism to simplify the parameters and computational effort [9]; it can be seen that currently people still mainly reduce the computational effort by reducing hidden layers and optimising pruning operations.

Rong Xiao et al. [10] proposed a bi-directional SNN and tested it using machine translation and sentiment classification datasets, achieving a significant reduction in the required computational energy to 0.82%. Tavanaei et al. [11] proposed a bioheuristic impulse neural network for unsupervised learning of temporal features in speech signals, demonstrating the potential of SNNs for processing natural language tasks [12].

Figure 1 shows a typical single SNN neuron, which has a similar structure to an ANN neuron, but behaves differently. The impulse neurons communicate with each other through binary events, rather than continuous activation values.

The output spike $s(t)$ is determined by the following conditions:

$$s\left(t\right) = \begin{cases} 1, if \ u\left(t\right) \geq u_{th} \\ 0, if \ u\left(t\right) < u_{th} \end{cases} \tag{1}$$

When the membrane voltage $u(t)$ reaches or exceeds the threshold voltage u_{th}, the neuron generates an output spike, and its membrane voltage is reset to u_{r_2}. Otherwise, the output spike remains at 0 [13]. As shown in Fig. 2. When the membrane potential reaches a certain threshold, it triggers a spike and resets the membrane potential. The reset voltage remains in a refractory period for a short period of time, which is considered to account for an absolute refractory period.

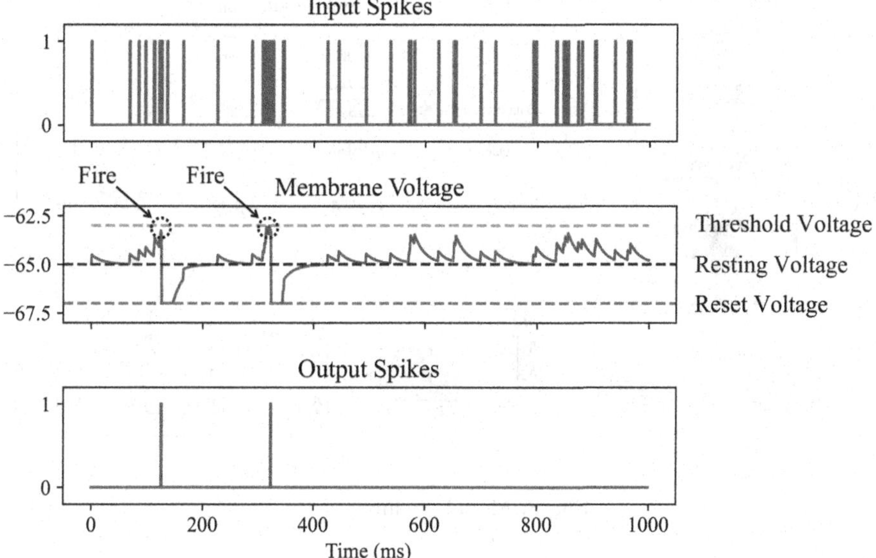

Fig. 2. The process of pulse signal processing in SNN involves accumulating pulse sequences as inputs, and the model integrates them into a membrane potential [14].

3 Methods

3.1 Architecture

The high-level architecture of the model is shown in Fig. 3. For our sentiment classification task on the IMDB dataset, we propose a spiking neural network architecture that incorporates the attention mechanism and sentiment lexicon, as discussed in the previous sections. The architecture is inspired by the Transformer model [15]. We adapt the Transformer model to the spiking domain to leverage the advantages of SNNs, such as energy efficiency and event-driven processing.

3.2 Attention-Based Spike Encoding

Word Embeddings. Utilizing the pre-trained Word2Vec model [16], we represent input text words as continuous-valued vectors, enabling efficient SNN processing and learning.

Token Shift. The token shifting operator [17] combines global context with the original token, enhancing contextual information and strengthening relationships between tokens, thereby improving the model's context awareness.

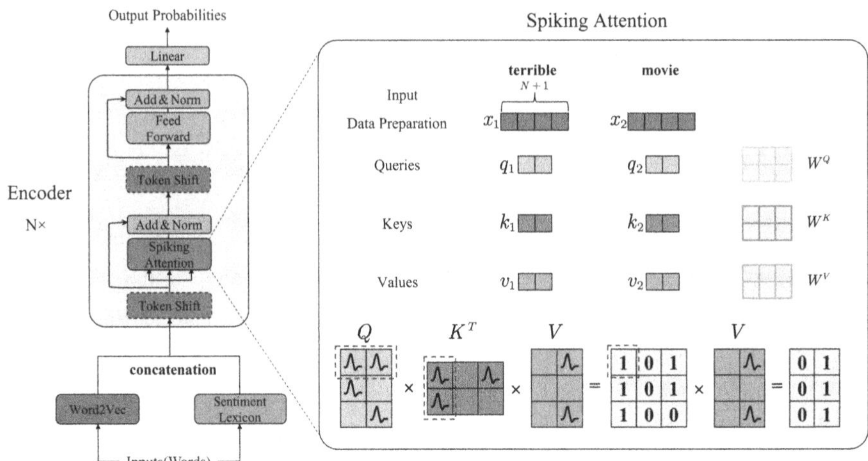

Fig. 3. Model Architecture

Sentiment Lexicon. We utilize the Valence Aware Dictionary and sEntiment Reasoner (VADER) [18] sentiment lexicon to assign sentiment scores to words in the input text. The VADER lexicon provides a polarity score for each word, indicating its positive, negative, or neutral sentiment, along with an intensity score.

Let s_i denote the sentiment score of the ith word in the input text, where a higher score indicates a stronger sentiment polarity. The sentiment scores for all words in the input text are combined into a sentiment score vector S, where $S = [s_1, s_2, ..., s_n]$ and n is the total number of words in the input text.

Custom Attention Mechanism. We design a custom attention mechanism sensitive to sentiment and transition words by incorporating sentiment scores into attention score computation.

Given input word embeddings $X = x_1, x_2, \ldots, x_n$ and sentiment scores $S = s_1, s_2, \ldots, s_n$, attention scores $A = a_1, a_2, \ldots, a_n$ are computed as:

$$a_i = f(x_i) + \alpha \cdot |s_i| \tag{2}$$

Here, $f(x_i)$ is the original attention score function, α is a hyperparameter, and s_i is the ith word's sentiment score. We take the absolute value of s_i to focus on sentiment polarity magnitude.

Attention probabilities $P = p_1, p_2, \ldots, p_n$ are calculated using the softmax function:

$$p_i = \frac{\exp(a_i)}{\sum_{j=1}^{n} \exp(a_j)} \tag{3}$$

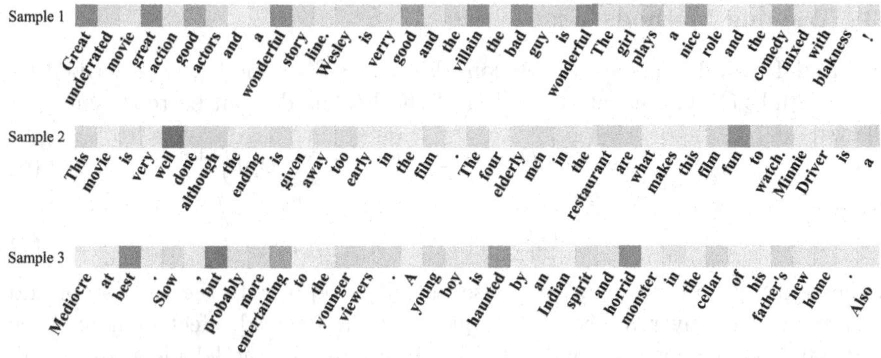

Fig. 4. Visualisation of attentional weights. Darker colours represent higher sensitivity to emotive and transitional words.

Weighted embeddings $Y = y_1, y_2, \ldots, y_n$ are obtained by multiplying input word embeddings by attention probabilities:

$$y_i = p_i \cdot x_i \tag{4}$$

Our model thus becomes more sensitive to sentiment and transition words, better capturing sentiment information in the input text. As shown in Fig. 4.

Spike Encoding. In SNN, input data is represented as spike streams, calculated using spike-timing-based learning rules. The leaky integrate-and-fire (LIF) model accumulates spikes as membrane potential, firing a spike to the next neuron when the voltage reaches a certain threshold. As shown in Fig. 5.

To encode text sequence information into spike trains efficiently, we use a rate-based encoding method. This approach retains as much information as possible from the original sequence while facilitating efficient SNN processing. The method calculates neuron firing rates proportional to input feature values and converts these rates into spike trains by thresholding the input features based on a specific quantile. The threshold is determined by calculating the input features' specified quantile, and any input feature above this threshold generates a spike in the corresponding spike train.

$$S_{ij} = \begin{cases} 1, if\ F_{ij} > T \\ 0, otherwise \end{cases} \tag{5}$$

where S_{ij} is the spike train for neuron i at time step j, F_{ij} is the input feature value for neuron i at time step j, and T is the threshold calculated based on the specified quantile. Using the rate-based encoding method, we generate spike trains that preserve essential temporal information from the original text sequence while ensuring sparsity and efficient processing in the spiking neural network.

3.3 Training Methods

Forward Pass. In this study, we consider a LIF SNN model, as described by Eqs. (6) and (7). The iterative version of the LIF model can be represented as follows:

$$u_i^{t+1,n+1} = e^{-\frac{dt}{\tau}} u_i^{t,n+1}(1 - o_i^{t,n+1}) + \sum_j w_{ij}^n o_j^{t+1,n} \tag{6}$$

$$o_i^{t+1,n+1} = f(u_i^{t+1,n+1} - u_{th}) \tag{7}$$

In the equation, o represents the pulse output, t represents the time step, and n represents the layer index. $e^{-\frac{dt}{\tau}}$ represents the delayed effect of membrane potential. $f(\cdot)$ is the step function. This iterative LIF model incorporates all the behaviors of the original neuron model, including integration, firing, and resetting.

Gradient Approximation Functions. In SNNs, the relationship between the membrane potential u and the output o is described by a step function that is non-differentiable (Fig. 5). To overcome the problem of non-differentiability in the step function, various gradient approximation functions were used (Fig. 6), including rectangular, triangular, sigmoid, Gaussian and Fourier series functions. The expressions for these functions are as follows :

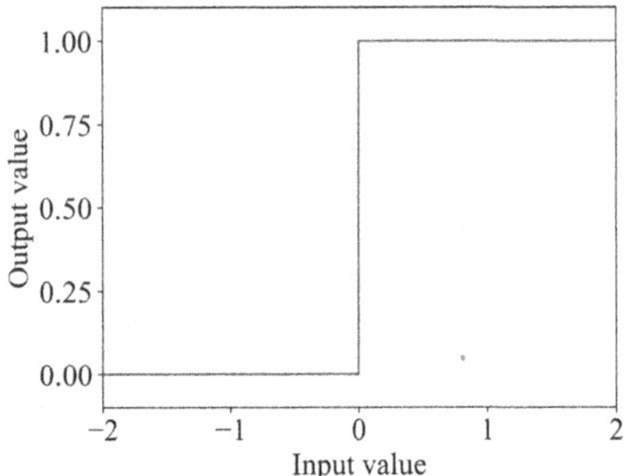

Fig. 5. Pulse signal processing in the SNN. In this case, we determine the activity threshold as 0.

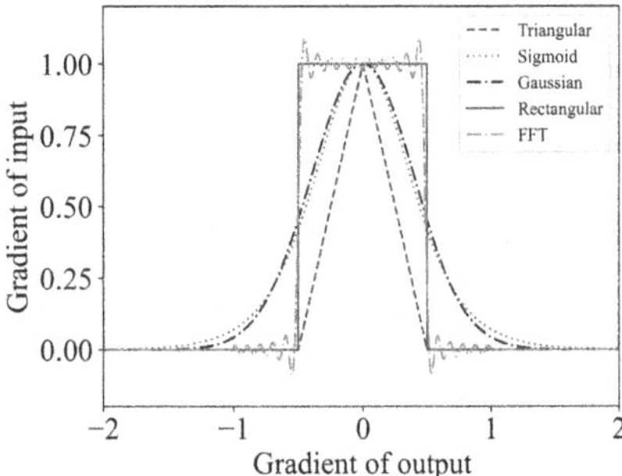

Fig. 6. Use different functions for gradient substitution.

We used different gradient approximation methods in the SNN training method. These methods have different characteristics. Rectangular and trigonometric functions are easy to compute, but may lead to large gradient errors. sigmoid and Gaussian functions can approximate the gradient more smoothly, but with higher computational complexity. Fourier series, on the other hand, allow us to flexibly approximate complex impulse signal shapes, but the computational complexity increases with the number of terms in the series. We discuss the impact of different alternative functions on the correctness and computational cost in Sect. 5.2.

Backpropagation. In the experimental section, we discuss a comparison of different gradient alternatives and finally choose the Gaussian distribution function as a replacement.

The gradient from the membrane potential u to the output o is a step function, which is non-conducting. To solve this problem, the following auxiliary function calculates the value of the derivative of output o to the membrane potential u:

$$\frac{\partial o}{\partial u} = \frac{1}{\sqrt{2\pi\sigma^2}} e^{-\frac{(u-u_{th})^2}{2\sigma^2}} \tag{8}$$

where σ is the standard deviation and determines the width of the Gaussian distribution. We use a Gaussian distribution function to replace the original auxiliary function.

4 Experiment

4.1 Experimental Dataset

We use the IMDB [19] Large Movie Review dataset for our experiments. This dataset consists of 50,000 movie reviews, with an equal number of positive and negative reviews. The dataset is split into 25,000 training samples and 25,000 testing samples, with an even distribution of positive and negative samples in both sets. Each movie review is labeled with a sentiment polarity: positive (1) or negative (0).

4.2 Baseline Models

To demonstrate the effectiveness of our proposed SNN-based sentiment classification method, we compared its performance with several state-of-the-art NLP models on sentiment classification tasks, including LSTM, GRU, Transforer, TextCNN, RoBERTa, and GPT-3.

4.3 Evaluation Metrics

Accuracy. Accuracy measures the model's ability to distinguish between positive and negative sentiments. It is calculated as the ratio of correctly classified instances to the total number of instances.

Energy Consumption. Energy consumption is crucial for evaluating a model's energy efficiency. We measure it during training and inference phases using:

$$\text{EC} = N_{add}C_{add} + N_{mul}C_{mul} \tag{9}$$

where C_{add} and C_{mul} are energy consumption for addition and multiplication, and N_{add} and N_{mul} are their respective operation counts.

Energy Efficiency Ratio. This ratio assesses the trade-off between performance and energy savings, defined as accuracy to energy consumption. Higher values indicate lower energy consumption with maintained accuracy.

$$\text{EER} = \frac{\text{Accuracy}}{\text{EC}} \tag{10}$$

Storage. Storage is a fundamental metric for assessing the complexity and memory requirements of a model. We use memory monitoring techniques to measure the storage requirements of our models during training and inference.

4.4 Experimental Parameters

For a fair comparison, we set the same network structure and word embedding dimension for all baseline implementations and our proposed models. In all models, we initialized the word embeddings using pre-trained Word2Vec word vectors with a word embedding dimension of 300, a learning rate of 0.001, and a loss rate of 0.001. For the SNN, we set the decay factor to 0.35, the neuron threshold to 0.00, and the time step to 0.001. The results for each experiment represent the mean and variance of the prediction accuracy of 10 independent experiments.

5 Results and Analysis

5.1 The Impact of Hyperparameters in SNN

Time Step. Smaller time steps provide higher temporal resolution, enabling the capture of fast changes and high-frequency information in input data. However, this increases the computation and memory requirements of the network, reducing efficiency. Large time steps cause information loss and reduced accuracy. We choose dt=0.001 to balance correctness and computational cost (Fig. 7).

Neuron Threshold. The neuron threshold determines when a neuron emits impulses. High thresholds make activation difficult, potentially causing insensitivity to input responses. Low thresholds facilitate activation, possibly leading to overresponse and overfitting (Fig. 8).

5.2 The Impact of Different Gradient Substitution Methods

The experimental results are shown in Table 1 and show that the Gaussian method has the highest accuracy while maintaining low energy consumption; the Triangular method, although avoiding a large number of operations, has a large loss in accuracy. The Fourier series method has a serious disadvantage in terms of energy consumption. The example above uses a Fourier series of $N = 30$.

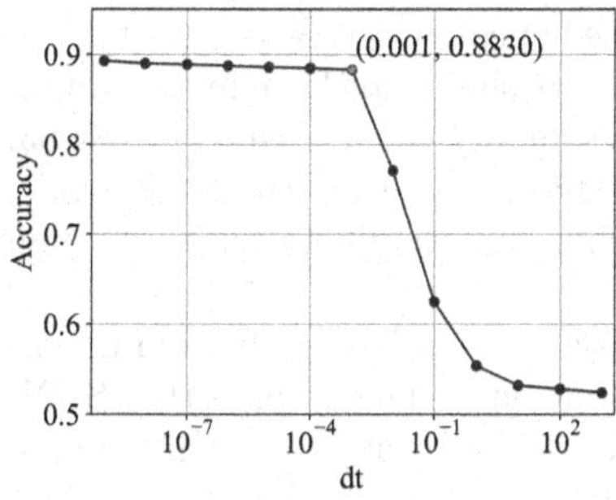

Fig. 7. Comparison of the correctness of SNN models regarding IMDB tasks at different time steps dt.

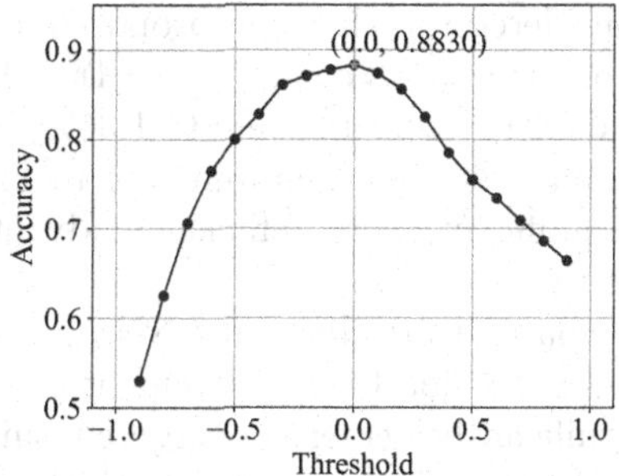

Fig. 8. Comparison of the correct rate of the SNN model regarding the IMDB task under different pulse excitation thresholds.

Table 1. Performance of SNN models with different gradient substitution methods on IMDB dataset.

Gradient substitution method	Accuracy(%)	Compute Cost(Flops)
Triangular	81.22	1
Sigmoid	86.93	4
Gaussian	88.30	7
Fourier series approximation	87.13	N*6

Table 2. The classification accuracy, energy consumption, and energy efficiency ratio of the IMDB task models. GPT-3 is tested using openai's interface, so memory detection is N/A.

Model	Parameters	Accuracy (%)	Energy Consumption (%)	Energy Efficiency Ratio	Memory Cost (%)
Transformer	1.62 M	90.06±0.45	100.00	0.90	100.00
TextCNN	0.27 M	89.42±0.53	97.81	0.91	17.16
LSTM	2.16 M	88.42±0.38	251.36	0.35	133.76
GRU	1.62 M	88.17±0.48	193.43	0.46	98.02
SNN-based	1.78 M	**88.30±0.46**	**1.36**	**64.93**	**2.47**
RoBERTa	125 M	92.43±0.37	1920.0	0.048	1189.0
GPT-3	175 B	95.21±0.86	23040	0.004	N/A

5.3 Energy Consumption

The energy consumption analysis table for each model is presented below in Table 2. The energy consumption of addition and multiplication operations are 1 and 10, respectively ($C_{add} = 1$ and $C_{mul} = 10$).

Considered together, our proposed SNN-based encoder decreases about 2% in terms of correctness compared to Transformer, but significantly reduces computational energy consumption to 1.36%, improves energy efficiency ratio to 64.93, and reduces storage requirements to 2.47%. This shows that the SNN model has a significant energy efficiency advantage while maintaining a relatively high correct rate.

Compared to traditional ANNs, SNNs exhibit only a slight reduction in correctness but a notable improvement in energy efficiency. This implies that SNNs can significantly decrease energy consumption and hardware costs while maintaining high performance in practical applications.

Although SNNs have a slight correctness disadvantage compared to large models such as RoBERTa and GPT-3, their significant improvement in energy efficiency ratio and reduced energy consumption and storage requirements make them highly valuable, especially in environments with strict energy and storage constraints.

6 Conclusion

In this paper, we propose an energy-efficient sentiment classification model based on spiking neural networks (SNN), aiming to reduce energy consumption while maintaining a high accuracy rate. We present the basic principles of SNN in detail and compare it with existing baseline models (including LSTM, GRU, TextCNN, Transformer, RoBERTa, and GPT-3) on a large IMDB movie review dataset.

The experimental results show that although the proposed SNN model has a slight decrease in correctness (about 2%), its energy consumption and memory usage are substantially lower, at 1.36% and 2.47% of Transformer's, respectively. This indicates that the SNN model has a significant energy consumption advantage while maintaining a relatively high accuracy rate. In addition, we also provide a detailed analysis of the hyperparameters in SNN, offering useful guidance for practical applications.

In conclusion, our proposed SNN-based energy-efficient sentiment classification model provides an effective energy-efficiency solution for the field of sentiment analysis. Future work will explore how to further improve the accuracy of the SNN model and apply the approach to other natural language processing tasks.

References

1. Singh, A., Pathak, K.: Sentiment analysis through Fourier transform techniques in NLP. In: Kumar, S., Sharma, H., Balachandran, K., Kim, J.H., Bansal, J.C. (eds.) Third Congress on Intelligent Systems. CIS 2022. LNNS, vol. 608, pp, 505–514. Springer, Singapore (2023). https://doi.org/10.1007/978-981-19-9225-4_37
2. Trisna, K.W., Jie, H.J.: Deep learning approach for aspect-based sentiment classification: a comparative review. Appl. Artif. Intell. **36**(1), 2014186 (2022)

3. Pfeiffer, M., Pfeil, T.: Deep learning with spiking neurons: opportunities and challenges. Front. Neurosci. **12**, 774 (2018)
4. Jin, X., et al.: RC-Darts: resource constrained differentiable architecture search. arXiv preprint arXiv:1912.12814 (2019)
5. Rueckauer, B., Lungu, I.-A., Yuhuang, H., Pfeiffer, M., Liu, S.-C.: Conversion of continuous-valued deep networks to efficient event-driven networks for image classification. Front. Neurosci. **11**, 682 (2017)
6. Onan, A.: Bidirectional convolutional recurrent neural network architecture with group-wise enhancement mechanism for text sentiment classification. J. King Saud Univ.-Comput. Inf. Sci. **34**(5), 2098–2117 (2022)
7. Sun, C., Huang, L., Qiu, X.: Utilizig bert for aspect-based sentiment analysis via constructing auxiliary sentence. arXiv preprint arXiv:1903.09588 (2019)
8. Han, S., Pool, J., Tran, J., Dally, W.J.: Learning both weights and connections for efficient neural networks. In: Proceedings of the 28th Advances in Neural Information Processing Systems (NeurIPS), pp. 1135–1143 (2015)
9. Chenquan Gan, L., Wang, Z.Z., Wang, Z.: Sparse attention based separable dilated convolutional neural network for targeted sentiment analysis. Knowl.-Based Syst. **188**, 104827 (2020)
10. Xiao, R., et al.: Towards energy-preserving natural language understanding with spiking neural networks. IEEE/ACM Trans. Audio Speech Lang. Process. 1–9 (2022)
11. Tavanaei, A., Ghodrati, M., Kheradpisheh, S.R., Masquelier, T., Maida, A.: Deep learning in spiking neural networks. Neural Netw. **111**, 47–63 (2019)
12. Tavanaei, A., Maida, A.: Bio-inspired multi-layer spiking neural network extracts discriminative features from speech signals. In: Liu, D., Xie, S., Li, Y., Zhao, D., El-Alfy, E.S. (eds.) Neural Information Processing. ICONIP 2017. LNCS, vol. 10639, pp. 899–908. Springer, Cham (2017). https://doi.org/10.1007/978-3-319-70136-3_95
13. Tavanaei, A., Maida, A.S.: Bio-inspired spiking convolutional neural network using layer-wise sparse coding and STDP learning. arXiv preprint arXiv:1611.03000 (2016)
14. Xie, X., Sun, F., Lin, J., Wang, Z.: Fast-ABC: a fast architecture for bottleneck-like based convolutional neural networks. In: 2019 IEEE Computer Society Annual Symposium on VLSI (ISVLSI), pp. 1–6. IEEE (2019)
15. Vaswani, A., et al.: Attention is all you need. In: Advances in Neural Information Processing Systems, pp. 5998–6008 (2017)
16. Tang, D., Wei, F., Yang, N., Zhou, M., Liu, T., Qin, B., et al.: Learning sentiment-specific word embedding for twitter sentiment classification. In: ACL, vol. 1, pp. 1555–1565 (2014)
17. Zhu, R.J., Zhao, Q., Eshraghian, J.K.: Spikegpt: generative pre-trained language model with spiking neural networks. arXiv preprint arXiv:2302.13939 (2023)
18. Hutto, C., Gilbert, E.: Vader: a parsimonious rule-based model for sentiment analysis of social media text. In: Proceedings of the International AAAI Conference on Web and Social Media, vol. 8, pp. 216–225 (2014)
19. Maas, A., Daly, R.E., Pham, P.T., Huang, D., Ng, A.Y., Potts, C.: Learning word vectors for sentiment analysis. In: Proceedings of the 49th Annual Meeting of the Association for Computational Linguistics: Human Language Technologies, pp. 142–150 (2011)

Using Masked Language Modeling to Enhance BERT-Based Aspect-Based Sentiment Analysis for Affective Token Prediction

Weiqiang Jin, Biao Zhao(✉), Chenxing Liu, Heng Zhang, and Mengying Jiang

School of Information and Communications Engineering, Xi'an Jiaotong University, Xi'an, Shaanxi, China
{weiqiangjin,lcx459455791,ZhangHENGHENG,myjiang}@stu.xjtu.edu.cn, biaozhao@xjtu.edu.cn

Abstract. Aspect-based sentiment analysis is a challenging yet critical task for recognizing emotions in text, with various applications in social media, commodity reviews, and movie comments. Many researchers are working on developing more powerful sentiment analysis models. Most existing models use the pre-trained language models based fine-tuning paradigm, which only utilizes the encoder parameters of pre-trained language models. However, this approach fails to effectively leverage the prior knowledge revealed in pre-trained language models. To address these issues, we propose a novel approach, Target Word Transferred Language Model for aspect-based sentiment analysis (WordTrans-ABSA), which investigates the potential of the pre-training scheme of pre-trained language models. WordTransABSA is an encoder-decoder architecture built on top of the Masked Language Model of Bidirectional Encoder Representation from Transformers. During the training procedure, we reformulate the previous generic fine-tuning models as a "Masked Language Model" task, which follows the original BERT pre-training paradigm. WordTransABSA takes full advantage of the versatile linguistic knowledge of Pre-trained Language Model, resulting in competitive accuracy compared with recent baselines, especially in data-insufficient scenarios. We have made our code publicly available on GitHub (https://github.com/albert-jin/WordTransABSA).

Keywords: Natural language processing · Aspect-based sentiment analysis · Masked language model · Few-shot supervised learning

1 Introduction

Aspect-based Sentiment Analysis (ABSA) is a challenging task in the field of Natural Language Processing (NLP) and has gained increasing attention in artificial intelligence. ABSA involves fine-grained textual emotional recognition that aims to identify human attitudes and sentiment polarities towards an aspect term

L. Iliadis et al. (Eds.): ICANN 2023, LNCS 14263, pp. 530–542, 2023.
https://doi.org/10.1007/978-3-031-44204-9_44

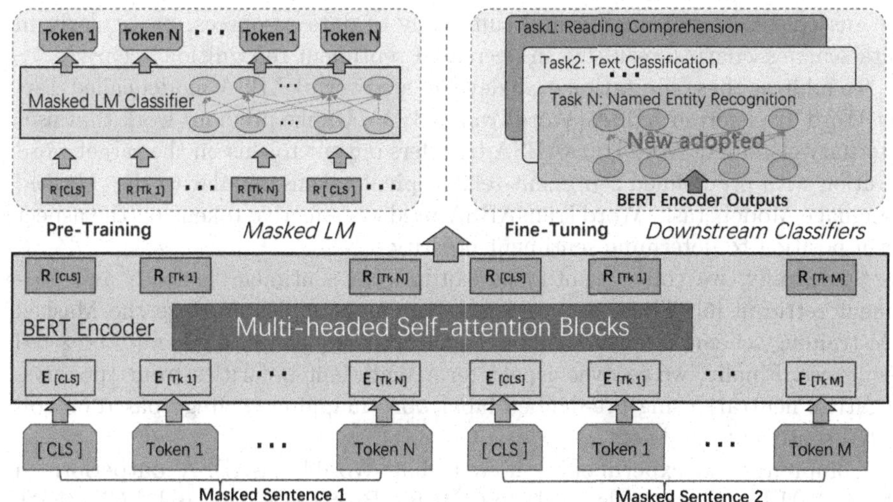

Fig. 1. The concept-level visualizations of pre-training and fine-tuning stages in most PLMs (such as Transformer BERT) are shown in the top-left and top-right positions, respectively.

in unstructured opinionated texts [16]. ABSA has numerous applications in various communities, such as e-commerce and internet forums [3,24,28]. Accurately recognizing these emotional associations with aspect topics can provide valuable insights, enabling operations supervisors to make strategic decisions.

Recently, deep learning methods based on pre-trained language models (PLMs) for ABSA have gained immense popularity [7,12,27], as they leverage the powerful semantic representations of PLM encoders, including BERT, BART, and T5 [1,10,18]. By utilizing the encoder of pre-trained language models, these models use downstream classifiers to predict sentiment polarity, leading to state-of-the-art performance. To stay competitive in the field, researchers are working to develop better sentiment classifiers that can effectively utilize the semantic representations generated by the PLM encoders.

Due to the generic nature of fine-tuning paradigms, the existing PLM-based ABSA methods discard the decoder part of the pre-trained language model's encoder, resulting in the prior knowledge of PLMs not being effectively utilized. As shown in Fig. 1, a representative Transformer BERT, the downstream decoding layers of the fine-tuning paradigm adopt a newly-introduced fine-tunable adaption module with external parameters, whereas the pre-training "Masked Language Model" task drops the decoder part of Transformer. Due to the parameters distribution discrepancy between pre-training and fine-tuning stages, the optimal fine-tuned ABSA model requires good optimizations of PLM parameters, leading to a time-consuming and unstable training procedure. Moreover, due to the characteristics of the general fine-tuning paradigm, these methods are susceptible to the quality and sufficiency of data resources, particularly in data-scarce scenarios, resulting in decreased sentiment recognition accuracy.

To address these limitations, we develop a powerful ABSA model called Target Word Transferred ABSA (WordTransABSA). Unlike previous work that uses a ternary classifier, WordTransABSA transfers output tokens on the target word position with pre-defined sentiment-related pivot tokens, similar to the "Masked Language Model" task. WordTransABSA predicts affective tokens on the aspect term position to determine sentiment polarity.

Specifically, we collect sentiment words from sentiment lexicons and document retrieval [6]. Then, we construct training samples and use the Masked LM training scheme to encode and decode input sequences to generate targeted sequences. Finally, we recover aspect term sentiment polarities from {positive, negative, neutral} using pre-defined label word mapping strategy based on collected sentiment word sets.

Comprehensive experiments showed that WordTransABSA outperformed other PLM-based methods, including BERT-BiLSTM-CRF, and LCF-BERT [13,26]. WordTransABSA also demonstrated overwhelming superiority and superior low-resource convergence capability under different few-shot settings, a fundamental characteristic given the current lack of corpus resources.

Our contributions in this paper can be summarized as follows:

- We propose WordTransABSA, which subverts the conventional criterion of Transformer-based fine-tuning methods by utilizing the entire parameters in Transformer, to fully exploit the prior knowledge.
- We explore different measures to search for high-quality sentiment-related pivot tokens and try additional transferred word optimization strategies to stimulate the semantic understanding potential of PLMs.
- The experiments under both data-sufficient and few-shot scenarios validate the superiority of WordTransABSA, suggesting that regressing to the Transformer pre-training paradigm is a better solution for ABSA.
- We have publicly released the implementation of WordTransABSA on Github[1] to encourage further research in this area and ensure reproducibility.

2 Related Works

2.1 Pre-trained Language Models

Pre-trained language models have achieved remarkable results in ABSA by leveraging vast amounts of unsupervised data through self-supervised learning [5]. These models are based on the Transformer architecture, consisting of multiple identical multi-head self-attention blocks. Each block in Transformer is composed of multi-head self-attention and position-wise feed-forward layers [5].

[1] https://github.com/albert-jin/WordTransABSA.

BERT [1] uses a bidirectional deep Transformer as the main structure and applies auto-encoding language modeling. RoBERTa [29] improved BERT by removing the "NSP" pre-training task and optimizing other training rules. SpanBERT [8] better represents and predicts text spans by masking contiguous spans rather than individual tokens. ALBERT [9] is a lightweight BERT that reduces parameters by adopting factorized embedding parametrization and cross-layer parameter sharing. T5 [18] converts all language tasks into a unified text-to-text format, while BART [10] simultaneously generalizes the bidirectional encoding scheme of BERT and the left-to-right decoding scheme of GPT.

Among them, BERT is widely used in ABSA fine-tuning studies. For fair comparison, we use BERT-base as the backbone for WordTransABSA throughout the experiments.

2.2 Fine-Tuned PLM Methods for ABSA

In recent years, traditional machine learning (ML)-based solutions for ABSA have been replaced by PLM-based fine-tuning approaches, which continuously achieve state-of-the-art results [16,28].

Several PLM-based ABSA models have been proposed with different downstream classifier architectures, pre-trained language model backbones, and model augmentation strategies. Li *et al.* [11] use PLMs such as BERT and RoBERTa as embedding backbones and combined them with several downstream classifier network layers. Xu *et al.* [25] introduce a BERT Post-Training method (BERT-PT) for ABSA. Zeng *et al.* [26] developed LCF-BERT, a Local Context Focus mechanism for ABSA. Jin *et al.* [7] propose DictABSA, which injects external knowledge to enhance the sentiment prediction ability. Sun *et al.* [23] propose CAS-(T)ABSA, which converts ABSA to a sentence-pair classification task.

PLM-based approaches are superior due to their prior knowledge learned from large-scale data, making it crucial to discover and leverage this internal knowledge for ABSA. To this end, this paper proposes WordTransABSA, which simulates PLM's pre-training paradigm to tackle ABSA, offering a novel ABSA solution different from previous fine-tuning methods.

3 WordTransABSA

WordTransABSA is a novel ABSA approach that leverages pre-defined sentiment-related pivot tokens to determine the final sentiment polarities of aspect terms. It involves two main research aspects: pivot token engineering and WordTrans LM fine tuning:

- **Sentiment pivot token engineering**: Discovering sentiment-related words that can effectively adapt to the adopted Transformer;
- **WordTrans language model fine-tuning**: Developing specific practices for transferring the "Masked LM" pre-training paradigm to a new training model.

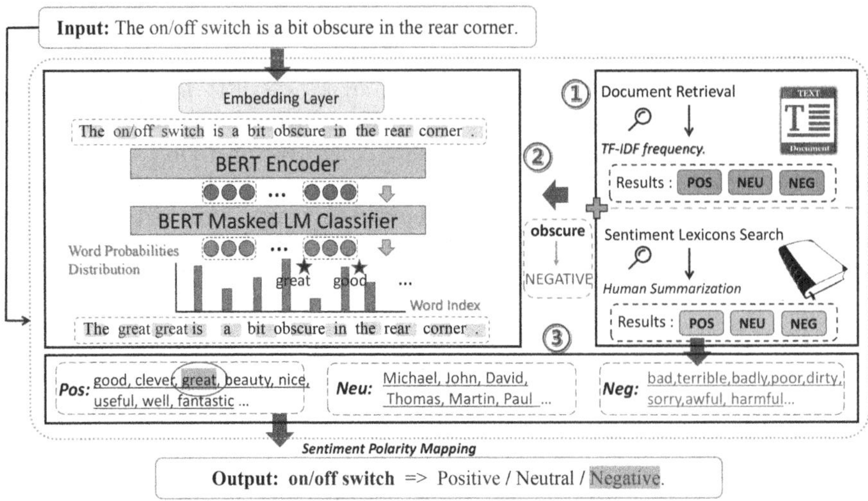

Fig. 2. The proposed WordTransABSA can be divided into three main parts. (1) involves searching for sentiment-related pivot tokens, including *Document Retrieval* and *Sentiment Lexicons Search*; (2) is responsible for generating probabilities of the sentiment-related pivot tokens using the Transformer BERT; (3) implements a sentiment word mapping strategy to predict the final label.

Figure 2 provides a comprehensive visualization of the proposed framework, showing the procedures for pivot token engineering, WordTrans LM fine tuning, and the selected sentiment-related pivot tokens.

3.1 Sentiment Pivot Token Engineering

Word Transferred Language Model (WordTrans LM) is crucial in WordTrans-ABSA. We believe the contextual consistency theory of linguistic corpora, which suggests that phrases or words with positive sentiment are often found in a semantic-positive context [4]. Thus, finding pivot words for word substitution is necessary to build its core module. However, this process requires domain expertise and appropriate selection strategy. To maintain a comprehensive search scope, we use the following detection processes:

1. Document Retrieval. To collect sentiment-rich pivot words, automatic retrieval from large-scale corpora is practical. Three channels of interest are user comments on social platforms, service evaluations on online shopping platforms, and user expressions from ABSA datasets.

Specifically, we download user comments from Twitter[2] related to COVID-19, use the well-organized *Amazon Review Data* corpus with 60 million reviews[3], and leverage the training and validation sets of adopted ABSA datasets.

[2] https://developer.twitter.com/en.

[3] https://nijianmo.github.io/amazon/index.html.

The collected data is processed through high-quality justifications and is then filtered using the term frequency-inverse document frequency (TF-IDF) weighting technique for information retrieval and text mining [6]. After calculating the TF-IDF of each word, we perform data normalization operations to obtain the topic word ranking results for each predefined topic. Then, we filter non-adjective parts-of-speech and cross-topic word conflicts through manual post-processing based on affective expertise knowledge. Finally, we retain the highly-ranked words as sentiment-related pivot words for each predefined topic.

2. Sentiment Lexicons Search. Furthermore, another practical way to acquire sentiment-related pivot words is searching sentiment lexicons, such as the **NRC** Word-Emotion Association Lexicon [15] and OpenHowNet[4].

The NRC lexicon[5] includes manually annotated English words and their associations with coarse-grained emotions and fine-grained sentiments. However, the OpenHowNet sentiment lexicon provides well-organized sentiment words but includes too many noise words. We used it as a filtering requirement for the NRC lexicon output, resulting in hundreds of candidate sentiment pivot words for positive and negative sentiments.

Following the sentiment lexicon search, we identified hundreds of candidate sentiment pivot words related to positive and negative sentiments.

3. Affective Words Integration. Finally, we integrate these discovered sentiment pivot words through weight-based operations.

For positive and negative categories, we select the intersection words in document retrieval and lexicon search results. For neutral pivot words, we use words discovered in document retrieval and select the name of a person token due to its representation universality.

Moreover, we validate all selected words through manual inspection, ensuring their comprehensiveness and quality.

As the filtered affective words are numerous, they cannot be directly used in WordTransLM. Therefore, we integrate them as unique label tokens to denote sentiment polarities. Specifically, we construct sentiment-related pivot tokens $T_{pos}, T_{neu}, T_{neg}$ based on affective word sets $[\{w_i\}_{i=1}^{o}; \{w_j\}_{j=1}^{p}; \{w_k\}_{k=1}^{q}]$, appending them to BERT's vocabulary. Then, we obtain initial vector representations $E(w_i)$ for each affective word through BERT's embedding layer, and use the average pooling strategy to obtain representations of the sentiment-related pivot tokens $E(T)$. For instance, to obtain the positive sentiment-related pivot token $E(T_j)$, we perform a bit-wise average vector operation on positive affective words $\{E(w_i)\}_{i=1}^{M_{pos}}$:

$$E(T_j) = Average(\{E(w_i)\}_{i=1}^{M_j}), \quad j \in \{pos, neu, neg\}. \tag{1}$$

where $E(\cdot)$ represents the embedding operation by BERT's embedding layer, and M_j denotes the number of affective words for the j-th sentiment polarity (i.e., pos, neu, and neg).

[4] https://openhownet.thunlp.org/about_hownet.

[5] https://www.saifmohammad.com/WebPages/NRC-Emotion-Lexicon.htm.

3.2 WordTrans LM Fine-Tuning

After acquired sentiment-related pivot tokens, we focus on modeling the affective word transferred fine-tuning Language Model (WordTrans LM).

WordTrans LM uses a unified architecture with the Transformer BERT as its backbone and downstream sentiment recognizer. The Masked LM decoder of BERT predicts substituted affective words (i.e. sentiment-related pivot tokens) for specific aspect terms at corresponding positions. Thus, it preserves the PLM's original pre-training characteristics during the model predicting procedure without adding extra parameters or reformulating loss objectives.

We divide the WordTransABSA architecture into the following two modules:

1. WordTransLM Optimization Objective. The module fine-tunes BERT 's internal parameters to generate an ideal decoded sequence based on the original sequence input. Concretely, to obtain the transferred sequence $S_{[Trans]}$, we replace all aspect terms in a given original sentence S with the sentiment-related pivot tokens.

In Fig. 2, aspect terms in sentences are replaced with sentiment-related pivot tokens. For example, if "great" is the pivot token used, we replace "on/off switch" with "great great".

We use a mapping function $\mathcal{M}$: $\mathcal{X}$ (original words of aspect terms) $\rightarrow$ $\mathcal{T}$ (sentiment pivot token of aspect terms) to replace aspect terms with sentiment pivot tokens, and the Word Transferred LM predicts the transferred sequence $S_{[Trans]} = \{x_1, ..., \mathcal{M}(x_k), ..., x_n\}$ based on the input sentence $S = \{x_1, ..., x_k, ..., x_n\}$. The model's feature forward processes are similar to the Masked LM task, including the BERT encoder, decoder, and probability distribution prediction. The final optimization strategy uses the cross-entropy loss function between the output sequence and the gold-transferred sequence on top of the downstream classifier.

The objective function of Word Transferred LM is formulated as follows:

$$\mathcal{L}_{WordTransLM} = -\sum_{i=1}^{n} \log P\left(o_i = x_i^{Trans} \mid S\right) \tag{2}$$

where o_i is the output sequence's i-th word, x_i^{Trans} is the transferred sequence's i-th word, and S is the original input sentence. We calculate $P(o_i = x_i^{Trans} \mid S) = SoftMax(W_{ph} \cdot H_d^S + b_{ph})$, where H_d^S is the encoded internal representation of S.

2. Affective Words Mapping Strategy. The mapping strategy from Transformer BERT outputs to fine-grained sentiment polarity is a crucial issue. The BERT decoder outputs logits values, indicating word probability distributions, which are not directly applicable for determining the final sentiment polarity. Therefore, it is necessary to devise an effective mapping strategy for emotional recognition.

To effectively determine the sentiment polarity, we use a vertical detection strategy based on the training mechanism of the Word Transferred LM: 1). We

Table 1. The statistics of several ABSA benchmarks adopted in our experiments.

Dataset	Train	Dev	Test	Total
Twitter	1687 (72%)	422 (18.1%)	233 (9.9%)	2342
SemEval	1796 (69.7%)	181 (7%)	601 (23.3%)	2578
ACLShortData	5623 (81%)	625 (9%)	692 (10%)	6940

first choose the predicted word with the highest probability at the starting position of the aspect term. 2). If this does not determine the sentiment polarity, we focus on the internal sorting outcome of the start position and select the sentiment-related pivot token with the highest ranking probability as an indication of the sentiment polarity.

Once again, WordTransABSA breaks the traditional fine-tuning method for Transformers, where the training process retains all the sub-modules used in the pre-training stage. Instead, WordTransABSA employs all the parameters of the original Transformer to fully utilize the versatile linguistic knowledge in the pre-trained language models.

4 Experiments

4.1 Metric, Dataset and Settings

Metric. This study uses accuracy as the performance evaluation metric for ABSA, which is widely adopted in previous research, instead of precision/recall/F1 [28]. Accuracy is a standard metric for evaluating label classification tasks and a higher accuracy indicates better performance of the ABSA approach.

Dataset. We use three real-world benchmarks annotated with aspect categories, aspect terms, and sentiment polarities for experimental evaluation:

- SemEval [17]: A restaurant domain for ABSA provided at the SemEval-2014 competition.
- Twitter [14]: A dataset collected from Twitter social platform, and we use the latest edition rearranged by Li et al. [11].
- ACLShortData [2]: A review dataset introduced in ACL'14 and is annotated through Amazon's Mechanical Turk.

More statistical details about these benchmarks are provided in Table 1.

Experimental Settings. The Transformer BERT used is the standard HuggingFace BERT (Bert-Base-Uncased)[6], with 12 transformer blocks, 768 hidden dimensions, and 12 multi-head self-attentions. To ensure accurate performance comparisons, we strictly control the hyperparameters during training WordTransABSA. This includes setting a fixed random seed, a dropout rate of 0.00001,

[6] https://huggingface.co/bert-base-uncased.

using the AdamW optimizer with decoupled weight decay regularization, a batch size of 16, and a maximum sentence length following BERT's configurations. Following previous related literature [20,21], the models are trained for a fixed of 20 epochs with early stopping applied on the development sets to prevent overfitting.

4.2 Baselines

We compare WordTransABSA with the following several state-of-the-art models:

- **BERT-SPC** [22]**:** uses BERT for sentence pair classification, constructed as "[CLS]" + global context + "[SEP]" + an additional sentence + "[SEP]".
- **BERT-BiLSTM-CRF** [13]**:** utilizes BERT for character-level word representations instead of pre-trained word embeddings.
- **BERT-PT** [25]**:** applies a post-training technique to BERT to enhance fine-tuning performance for RRC tasks.
- **LCF-BERTC** [26]**:** bases on BERT with a local context focus mechanism to capture extended relationships of sentence contexts and aspect terms.
- **BERT-ADAC** [19]**:** integrates text from additional sources and examines cross-domain training methods for various fine-tuning approaches.

4.3 Results Analysis

Model Comparisons. Table 2 statistics the performance comparisons of WordTransABSA with state-of-the-art baselines. Notably, the results of baselines marked with an asterisk (*), BERT-PT, LCF-BERT, and BERT-ADA, are taken directly from their original papers [19,26] instead of reproduced experiments.

Table 2 presents a comparison of different models in terms of accuracy on three benchmarks. The results show that WordTransABSA achieves the highest accuracy on the AclShortData benchmark (73.4%) and competitive performance on the Twitter benchmark (77.4%), with an absolute accuracy gain of approximately 1.4% over the second-best model (LCF-BERT).

However, on the SemEval benchmark, WordTransABSA's performance is not as high as some other models, such as BERT-ADA and BERT-BiLSTM-CRF. As shown in the second column of Table 2, WordTransABSA achieves an accuracy of 87.3% on the SemEval benchmark, which is slightly lower than the performance of some other models such as BERT-ADA (87.7%) and BERT-BiLSTM-CRF (87.3%). This could be due to the quality of the SemEval dataset itself, which is known to be challenging and prone to inconsistencies in annotations. For example, some annotations may not be clear or consistent, making it difficult for models to learn accurate and reliable sentiment analysis.

Despite this limitation, WordTransABSA demonstrates its superior performance compared to other state-of-the-art ABSA models. It is competitive with the current ABSA baselines, thanks to its word transferred language model strategy that captures diverse knowledge. The approach allows WordTransABSA to retain all the parameters from Transformer and fully utilize the versatile linguistic knowledge stored in the PLMs, suggesting that this approach is a better solution than traditional fine-tuning.

Table 2. The experimental performance comparisons (% Accuracy) between WordTransABSA and baselines.

Models	SemEval %acc	Twitter %acc	AclShortData %acc
BERT-PT*	85.0	–	–
BERT-SPC	86.0	76.0	70.3
BERT-BiLSTM-CRF	<u>87.3</u>	76.4	70.9
LCF-BERT*	87.1	<u>76.6</u>	<u>72.7</u>
BERT-ADA*	**87.7**	75.8	71.6
WordTransABSA	<u>87.3</u>	**77.4**	**73.4**

Few-Shot Experiments. Inspired by the success of prompt-tuning in data-scarce scenarios, we investigated whether WordTransABSA can perform well under few-shot learning settings. By training it on a limited amount of labeled data, demonstrate the model's ability in real-world data-scarce scenarios.

Due to experimental constraints, we couldn't consider multiple baselines including BERT-PT, LCF-BERT, and BERT-ADA [19,25,26]. Instead, we used BERT-BiLSTM-CRF and BERT-SPC [13,22] as few-shot comparison baselines. This decision was a trade-off between demonstration quality and experimental capacity constraints.

Table 3 presents the performance comparisons of these models under different few-shot settings, corresponding to 5-shots, 20-shots, and 50-shots, respectively. Results are based on 10 runs for experimental authenticity. Based on the provided table, we can conduct an academic analysis of the superiority of WordTransABSA compared to other models and highlight how the performance gap between the models narrows as the number of shots increases from 5 to 50.

Table 3. The averaged % Accuracy over 10 runs of WordTransABSA and baselines in different few-shot settings (5-/20-/50-shots).

Few-shot Settings	Models	SemEval	Twitter	ACLShortData
5	BERT-SPC	0.542	0.547	<u>0.498</u>
–	BERT-BiLSTM-CRF	<u>0.575</u>	<u>0.562</u>	0.474
shots	WordTransABSA	**0.625**	**0.653**	**0.571**
20	BERT-SPC	0.602	<u>0.624</u>	<u>0.668</u>
–	BERT-BiLSTM-CRF	<u>0.640</u>	0.605	0.662
shots	WordTransABSA	**0.647**	**0.638**	**0.695**
50	BERT-SPC	<u>0.729</u>	<u>0.722</u>	<u>0.691</u>
–	BERT-BiLSTM-CRF	0.723	0.715	0.677
shots	WordTransABSA	**0.745**	**0.774**	**0.758**

From Table 3, it is evident that WordTransABSA consistently outperforms both BERT-SPC and BERT-BiLSTM-CRF in all tasks and few-shot settings. WordTransABSA outperforms all baselines over all the benchmarks by obtaining absolute accuracy gains of 2% to 6%. This demonstrates the superiority of our proposed method over the other models. Furthermore, as the number of shots increases from 5 to 50, the performance gap between the models narrows, suggesting that our model is particularly advantageous when fewer samples are available. For instance, in the 5-shot setting, WordTransABSA outperforms the second-best model (BERT-BiLSTM-CRF) in the SemEval task by 5.0%, while in the 50-shot setting, the gap narrows to 2.2%. This pattern is consistent across all tasks, emphasizing the strengths of this approach in low-resource scenarios.

5 Conclusion

The current approaches to ABSA mainly focus on developing downstream classification networks, which do not fully exploit the rich knowledge learned from large unlabeled corpora in PLMs. To address these limitations, we propose a novel PLM-based fine-tuning method for ABSA called Target Word Transferred ABSA (WordTransABSA). It introduces a novel modeling approach, the word transferred language model strategy, which is a disruptive training design that differs from existing PLM-based fine-tuning solutions. WordTransABSA achieves significant improvement over state-of-the-art ABSA baselines in the regular training. Furthermore, extensive few-shot comparison experiments demonstrate the effectiveness of our method for handling data-insufficient scenarios, which is particularly important for real-world practical deployments. In the future, we plan to apply this technique to other tasks like named entity recognition, document reading comprehension, and relation extraction. Furthermore, we plan to combine ChatGPT with WordTransABSA to fully utilize the potential of ChatGPT with the WordTrans LM strategy.

Acknowledgements. This work was funded by the Natural Science Basis Research Plan in Shaanxi Province of China (Project Code: 2021JQ-061). This work was conducted by the first two authors, Weiqiang Jin and Biao Zhao, during their research at Xi'an Jiaotong University. The corresponding author is Biao Zhao. Thanks to the action editors and anonymous reviewers for improving the paper with their comments, and recommendations.

References

1. Devlin, J., Chang, M.W., Lee, K., Toutanova, K.: BERT: pre-training of deep bidirectional transformers for language understanding. In: Proceedings of the 2019 Conference of the North American Association for Computational Linguistics, pp. 4171–4186. ACL, Minneapolis, Minnesota, June 2019. https://doi.org/10.18653/v1/N19-1423
2. Dong, L., Wei, F., Tan, C., Tang, D., Zhou, M., Xu, K.: Adaptive recursive neural network for target-dependent Twitter sentiment classification. In: Proceedings of the 52nd Annual Meeting of the Association, pp. 49–54. ACL, Baltimore, Maryland, June 2014. https://doi.org/10.3115/v1/P14-2009

3. Gao, J., Yu, H., Zhang, S.: Joint event causality extraction using dual-channel enhanced neural network. Knowl.-Based Syst. **258**, 109935 (2022). https://doi.org/10.1016/j.knosys.2022.109935
4. Gao, T., Fisch, A., Chen, D.: Making pre-trained language models better few-shot learners. In: Proceedings of the 59th Association for Computational Linguistics, pp. 3816–3830. ACL, Online, August 2021
5. Han, X., Zhang, Z., Ding, N., Gu, Y., Liu, X., Huo, Y.E.A.: Pre-trained models: past, present and future. AI Open **2**, 225–250 (2021). https://doi.org/10.1016/j.aiopen.2021.08.002
6. Jin, W., Zhao, B., Liu, C.: Fintech key-phrase: a new Chinese financial high-tech dataset accelerating expression-level information retrieval. In: Wang, X., et al. (eds.) Database Systems for Advanced Applications. DASFAA 2023. LNCS, vol. 13945, pp. 425–440. Springer, Cham (2023). https://doi.org/10.1007/978-3-031-30675-4_31
7. Jin, W., Zhao, B., Zhang, L., Liu, C., Yu, H.: Back to common sense: oxford dictionary descriptive knowledge augmentation for aspect-based sentiment analysis. Inf. Process. Manag. **60**(3), 103260 (2023). https://doi.org/10.1016/j.ipm.2022.103260
8. Joshi, M., Chen, D., Liu, Y., Weld, D.S., Zettlemoyer, L., Levy, O.: SpanBERT: improving pre-training by representing and predicting spans. Trans. Assoc. Comput. Linguist. **8**, 64–77 (2020). https://doi.org/10.1162/tacl_a_00300
9. Lan, Z., Chen, M., Goodman, S., Gimpel, K., Sharma, P., Soricut, R.: Albert: a lite bert for self-supervised learning of language representations. In: International Conference on Learning Representations (2020). https://openreview.net/forum?id=H1eA7AEtvS
10. Lewis, M., et al.: BART: denoising sequence-to-sequence pre-training for natural language generation, translation, and comprehension. In: Proceedings of the 58th Association for Computational Linguistics, pp. 7871–7880. ACL, Online, July 2020. https://doi.org/10.18653/v1/2020.acl-main.703
11. Li, X., Bing, L., Zhang, W., Lam, W.: Exploiting BERT for end-to-end aspect-based sentiment analysis. In: Proceedings of the 5th Workshop on Noisy User-generated Text (W-NUT 2019), pp. 34–41. ACL, Hong Kong, China, November 2019. https://doi.org/10.18653/v1/D19-5505
12. Liu, H., Wang, N., Li, X., Xu, C., Li, Y.: BFF R-CNN: balanced feature fusion for object detection. IEICE Trans. Inf. Syst. **105**(8), 1472–1480 (2022)
13. Liu, L., et al.: Empower sequence labeling with task-aware neural language model. In: Proceedings of the Thirty-Second AAAI Conference. AAAI'18/IAAI'18/EAAI'18, AAAI Press, New Orleans, Louisiana, USA (2018)
14. Mitchell, M., Aguilar, J., Wilson, T., Van Durme, B.: Open domain targeted sentiment. In: Proceedings of the 2013 Conference on Empirical Methods in Natural Language Processing, pp. 1643–1654. ACL, Seattle, Washington, USA, October 2013. https://aclanthology.org/D13-1171
15. Mohammad, S.M., Turney, P.D.: Crowdsourcing a word-emotion association lexicon. Comput. Intell. **29**(3), 436–465 (2013). https://doi.org/10.1111/j.1467-8640.2012.00460.x
16. Nazir, A., Rao, Y., Wu, L., Sun, L.: IAF-LG: an interactive attention fusion network with local and global perspective for aspect-based sentiment analysis. IEEE Trans. Affect. Comput. **13**(4), 1730–1742 (2022). https://doi.org/10.1109/TAFFC.2022.3208216

17. Pontiki, M., Galanis, D., Pavlopoulos, J., Papageorgiou, H., Androutsopoulos, I., Manandhar, S.: SemEval-2014 task 4: aspect based sentiment analysis. In: Proceedings of the 8th International Workshop on Semantic Evaluation (SemEval 2014), pp. 27–35. ACL, Dublin, Ireland, August 2014. https://doi.org/10.3115/v1/S14-2004
18. Raffel, C., et al.: Exploring the limits of transfer learning with a unified text-to-text transformer. J. Mach. Learn. Res. **21**(1) (2020)
19. Rietzler, A., Stabinger, S., Opitz, P., Engl, S.: Adapt or get left behind: domain adaptation through BERT language model finetuning for aspect-target sentiment classification. In: Proceedings of the Twelfth Language Resources and Evaluation Conference, pp. 4933–4941. European Language Resources Association, Marseille, France, May 2020. https://aclanthology.org/2020.lrec-1.607
20. Shen, Y., Ma, X., Tan, Z., Zhang, S., Wang, W., Lu, W.: Locate and label: a two-stage identifier for nested named entity recognition, pp. 2782–2794. ACL, Online, August 2021. https://doi.org/10.18653/v1/2021.acl-long.216
21. Shen, Y., et al.: Parallel instance query network for named entity recognition, pp. 947–961. ACL, Dublin, Ireland, May 2022. https://doi.org/10.18653/v1/2022.acl-long.67
22. Song, Y., Wang, J., Jiang, T., Liu, Z., Rao, Y.: Targeted sentiment classification with attentional encoder network. In: Tetko, I.V., Kůrková, V., Karpov, P., Theis, F. (eds.) ICANN 2019. LNCS, vol. 11730, pp. 93–103. Springer, Cham (2019). https://doi.org/10.1007/978-3-030-30490-4_9
23. Sun, C., Huang, L., Qiu, X.: Utilizing BERT for aspect-based sentiment analysis via constructing auxiliary sentence. In: Proceedings of the 2019 Conference of the North American Association for Computational Linguistics, pp. 380–385. ACL, Minneapolis, Minnesota, June 2019. https://doi.org/10.18653/v1/N19-1035
24. Xia, N., Yu, H., Wang, Y., Xuan, J., Luo, X.: DAFS: a domain aware few shot generative model for event detection. Mach. Learn. **112**(3), 1011–1031 (2023). https://doi.org/10.1007/s10994-022-06198-5
25. Xu, H., Liu, B., Shu, L., Yu, P.: BERT post-training for review reading comprehension and aspect-based sentiment analysis. In: Proceedings of the 2019 Conference of the North American Association for Computational Linguistics, pp. 2324–2335. ACL, Minneapolis, Minnesota, June 2019. https://doi.org/10.18653/v1/N19-1242
26. Zeng, B., Yang, H., Xu, R., Zhou, W., Han, X.: LCF: a local context focus mechanism for aspect-based sentiment classification. Appl. Sci. **9**(16) (2019). https://doi.org/10.3390/app9163389
27. Zhao, B., Jin, W., Ser, J.D., Yang, G.: Chatagri: exploring potentials of chatgpt on cross-linguistic agricultural text classification (2023)
28. Zhou, J., Huang, J.X., Chen, Q., Hu, Q.V., Wang, T., He, L.: Deep learning for aspect-level sentiment classification: survey, vision, and challenges. IEEE Access **7**, 78454–78483 (2019). https://doi.org/10.1109/ACCESS.2019.2920075
29. Zhuang, L., Wayne, L., Ya, S., Jun, Z.: A robustly optimized BERT pre-training approach with post-training. In: Proceedings of the 20th Chinese National Conference on Computational Linguistics, pp. 1218–1227. Chinese Information Processing Society of China, Huhhot, China, August 2021. https://aclanthology.org/2021.ccl-1.108

Author Index

L. Iliadis et al. (Eds.): ICANN 2023, LNCS 14263, pp. 543–545, 2023.
https://doi.org/10.1007/978-3-031-44204-9

Printed in the United States
by Baker & Taylor Publisher Services

Printed in the United States
by Baker & Taylor Publisher Services